Bhutan

Bhutan

New Pathways to Growth

Edited by

SABYASACHI MITRA
and
HOE YUN JEONG

Co-publication of the Asian Development Bank
and Oxford University Press India

OXFORD
UNIVERSITY PRESS

Oxford University Press is a department of the University of Oxford. It furthers the University's objective of excellence in research, scholarship, and education by publishing worldwide. Oxford is a registered trademark of Oxford University Press in the UK and in certain other countries.

Published in India by
Oxford University Press
YMCA Library Building, 1 Jai Singh Road, New Delhi 110 001, India

6 ADB Avenue, Mandaluyong City
1550 Metro Manila, Philippines
Tel +63 2 632 4444
Fax +63 2 636 2444
www.adb.org

First Edition published in 2017

ISBN-13: 978-0-19-947401-1
ISBN-10: 0-19-947401-X

Typeset in Dante MT Std 10.5/13
by Tranistics Data Technologies, New Delhi 110 044
Printed in India by Replika Press Pvt. Ltd

Notes: In this publication, '$' refers to US dollar, unless stated otherwise. ADB recognizes 'China' as the People's Republic of China, 'Korea' as the Republic of Korea, 'USA' as the United States, and 'Vietnam' as Viet Nam.

Contents

Tables, Figures, and Boxes

Tables

Figures

Boxes

Foreword

Located in the eastern Himalayas, north of India and south of the People's Republic of China, the Kingdom of Bhutan is a landlocked and mountainous country in Asia. It is a country with a strong, ancient Buddhist culture that was almost completely cut off from foreign influences for centuries. It is unique, both culturally and environmentally. As the world's sole Buddhist kingdom, it is home to the development philosophy of Gross National Happiness (GNH) in which development is measured using a holistic approach of well-being, rather than being based solely on the conventional measure of gross domestic product (GDP).

Bhutan's rapid development under unique circumstances is impressive. Its economic expansion in recent decades is among the most rapid of any economy at a similar stage of development. Despite its locational challenges and limited access to global markets, Bhutan unlocked its growth potential by tapping its huge hydropower reserves. In 1961, Bhutan's GPD per capita was estimated at only $51, then the lowest in the world. By 2015, GDP per capita had risen to approximately $2,611. Furthermore, annual growth in real GDP averaged 8 per cent during 1981–2014 and per capita income rose at an average of 6 per cent annually over the same period. This phenomenal growth allowed Bhutan to significantly reduce poverty and raise living standards through investment in services and physical and social infrastructure.

As a small, landlocked, rugged, mountainous, and remotely located country, Bhutan faces unique geographic hurdles in its development. This inherent vulnerability creates a number of challenges for achieving sustained, inclusive, socio-economic green growth. Foremost among these is the country's narrow economic base and small population size.

Dependence on hydropower sector has exerted macroeconomic challenges to the country. Hydropower-related investments have propelled the country's economic growth. However, the dominance of the hydropower industry comes at a price, with about one-third of the economy dependent on this capital-intensive industry. Such a heavy reliance on hydropower has bound the country's growth to a sector that provides only limited employment opportunities.

The Asian Development Bank (ADB) has supported Bhutan's development through various programmes in the energy, transport, finance, and urban infrastructure services. Since 1982, ADB has provided Bhutan with loans, grants, and technical assistance amounting to nearly $764 million. ADB's lending operations continue to support these priority sectors as well as initiatives in the key areas of private sector development, governance, and capacity development.

This book is an outcome of knowledge collaboration and technical assistance in support of the development of a macroeconomic monitoring framework for Bhutan. ADB is closely coordinating with the government agencies tasked with economic management functions, such as Ministry of Finance, Ministry of Economic Affairs, and Royal Monetary Authority of Bhutan. ADB also mobilized nine international experts to guide this effort. The quality and significance of the work completed will make an immense contribution to developing the macroeconomic monitoring and management framework in the country.

While this book endeavours to address the issues and challenges faced by Bhutan today, it also undertakes to guide policymakers in unlocking Bhutan's substantial economic potential by navigating through the risks and vulnerabilities of the economy, reducing inequality and making growth inclusive, developing the financial sector and monetary framework; and steering the economy towards a GNH–compatible trade policy, as well as a host of other essential policy outcomes.

This book represents a unique and rare Bhutanese literature as it is the first academic publication that analyses the country's economic potential. With contributions coming from well-respected international experts, this book stands as an elite knowledge product detailing the development path undertaken by the Royal Government.

I extend my sincere appreciation to the contributors and editors, Sabyasachi Mitra and Hoe Yun Jeong; ADB Bhutan Resident Mission;

and South Asia Department staff and consultants for adding to our knowledge and understanding of Bhutan's socio-economic development.

I hope readers will immerse themselves in the technical details and rich insights presented in this book. There is so much to take from Bhutan's experience. The immediate impact of the book will be better-informed and developed policies for economic management and risk mitigation. Its longer-term outcomes will include the region's policy-makers having access to timely and rigorous analysis of macroeconomic data and economic studies, as well as a deeper understanding of many development issues based on the experiences of Bhutan. This book will ultimately promote better economic management in developing countries under both normal and trying conditions.

Dasho Tshering Tobgay
Prime Minister
Royal Government of Bhutan

Acknowledgements

This book is an output of Asian Development Bank (ADB) knowledge collaboration and technical assistance to strengthen Bhutan's macroeconomic surveillance and design a revised roadmap for developing an integrated macroeconomic framework. These initiatives were closely coordinated with Bhutan's Ministry of Finance and other agencies tasked with economic management functions, and have produced a large body of work on the development of a comprehensive macroeconomic framework for Bhutan.

ADB's significant investments in Bhutan have given it singular insight into the country's development progress and challenges, putting it in a position to chronicle Bhutan's distinct development journey and vision for the future. Accordingly, ADB has obtained the support of Oxford University Press (India) to produce a book detailing the unique development path taken by Bhutan.

This publication was prepared under the guidance of Hun Kim, Director General, South Asia Department (SARD), ADB. Ronald Antonio Butiong, Director, Regional Cooperation and Operations Coordination Division (SARC), SARD, encouraged the creation of this knowledge output with strong support. Sabyasachi Mitra, Deputy Representative, European Representative Office, and Hoe Yun Jeong, Senior Economist, SARC, led efforts on strengthening the macroeconomic monitoring framework and edited and supervised the production of this volume. Noel Reyes, Project Coordinator, made important contributions to the completion of the book and ensured quality control. Lani Garnace, Associate Economics Officer, and consultants Leilanie Basilio, Macrina Mallari, Ivan Cesar Magadia, and Kevin Donahue also provided important contributions to the publication of this book. We also wish to acknowledge the invaluable assistance provided by Tshewang Norbu, Resident Representative, and Thinley Om, former Senior Operations Assistant at ADB's Bhutan Resident Mission.

We further acknowledge the support and assistance provided by the leadership and staff of the Ministry of Finance, Ministry of Economic Affairs, and Royal Monetary Authority of Bhutan (RMA). In particular, we thank Lam Dorji, former Secretary, and Choiten Wangchuk, former Director General, Department of Public Accounts, Ministry of Finance, for their significant support. We would like to extend our gratitude to the peer reviewers who critiqued each of the book's chapters and suggested valuable alternative viewpoints. These experts include Chandan Sapkota, Utsav Kumar, Takaaki Nomoto, Thiam Hee Ng, Cigdem Akin, and Yoko Niimi. Staff from the RMA and ADB's South Asia Energy Division also provided invaluable comments and suggestions.

Finally, we would like to take this opportunity to thank those who contributed their ideas, time, and efforts to this endeavour, including Joshua E. Greene, Patrick Guillaumont, Karma Ura, Sarah Carrington, Anthony Baluga, Hwee Kwan Chow, Elbe Aguba, Inkyo Cheong, Taeho Bark, Hooi Hooi Lean, Russell Smyth, and Rebel A. Cole.

The views expressed in this publication are solely those of the authors and do not necessarily reflect the views or policies of ADB, its Board of Directors or member country governments, or any particular institution or set of institutions.

Abbreviations

ADB	Asian Development Bank
ADF	Augmented Dickey–Fuller
ATM	Automated Teller Machine
BDFCL	Bhutan Development Finance Corporation Limited
BIL	Bhutan Insurance Limited
BNBL	Bhutan National Bank Limited
BOB	Bank of Bhutan
BoP	Balance of Payments
CAR	Capital Adequacy Ratio
CBS	Centre for Bhutan Studies
CCCB	Countercyclical Capital Buffer
CDP	Committee for Development Policy
CIB	Credit Information Bureau
CIFP	Country Indicators for Foreign Policy
CPI	Consumer Price Index
CPIA	Country Policy and Institutional Assessment
CSO	Civil Society Organization
DLZ	Dry Land Zone
ECT	Error-correction Term
EVI	Economic Vulnerability Index
FDI	Foreign Direct Investment
FSI	Fragile States Index
FSI	Financial Stability Indicator
FY	Fiscal Year
GDP	Gross Domestic Product
GNH	Gross National Happiness
GNHC	Gross National Happiness Commission

GNI	Gross National Income
GNIpc	Gross National Income per capita
HAI	Human Assets Index
ICIMOD	International Centre for Integrated Mountain Development
IMF	International Monetary Fund
LDC	Least Developed Country
LECZ	Low Elevation Coastal Zones
MOEA	Ministry of Economic Affairs
NFA	Net Foreign Assets
NPL	Non-performing Loan
NPPF	National Pension and Provident Fund
Nu	ngultrum
PBA	Performance-based Allocation
PNB	Punjab National Bank
PPP	Purchasing Power Parity
PRC	People's Republic of China
PSAV	Political Stability and Absence of Violence
PVCCI	Physical Vulnerability to Climate Change Index
RGOB	Royal Government of Bhutan
RICBL	Royal Insurance Corporation of Bhutan Limited
RMA	Royal Monetary Authority of Bhutan
Rs	Indian National Rupees
SBI	State Bank of India
SCR	Sectoral Capital Requirement
SHI	Structural Handicap Index
SIC	Schwarz Information Criterion
SLR	Statutory Liquidity Ratio
SOE	State-owned Enterprise
STLAW	Short-Term Liquidity Adjustment Window
SWB	subjective well-being
TYDL	Toda and Yamamoto and Dolado and Lutkepohl
UN	United Nations
UNCTAD	United Nations Conference on Trade and Development
UNDP	United Nations Development Programme
UTB	Unit Trust of Bhutan
WDI	World Development Indicators
WPI	Wholesale Price Index

Introduction

SABYASACHI MITRA AND HOE YUN JEONG

The tiny Kingdom of Bhutan—nestled in the rugged Himalayan peaks and straddled by two neighbouring giants, India and the People's Republic of China—has undergone a significant structural transformation over the past five decades. Jigme Dorji Wangchuck, the third King of Bhutan, opened the doors of the Himalayan kingdom to the world in 1958 and set the landlocked country on its unique path of political and economic development (Figures I.1 and I.2).[1] That same year, the Government of Bhutan adopted its First Five Year Plan. Until now, the government has formulated 11 Five-Year Plans, each of which has set out clear goals and strategic priorities to address the country's evolving development challenges.

A decade later, his successor, King Jigme Singye Wangchuck, unveiled the concept of Gross National Happiness (GNH), an inimitable development policy that has since intrigued and inspired practitioners of development economics, policymakers, and scholars. GNH takes a holistic approach towards notions of progress and gives equal importance to non-economic aspects of well-being. Bhutan's development journey has been guided by its philosophy of GNH as the country continues to delicately balance economic progress with spiritual advancement and total well-being. The collective pursuit of GNH and economic

[1] Jawaharlal Nehru, India's first Prime Minister, was the first foreign leader to visit Bhutan in 1958. He undertook a gruelling, week-long journey travelling by horse and yak through the rugged terrain to establish bilateral relations between the two neighbours and introduce Bhutan to the rest of the world.

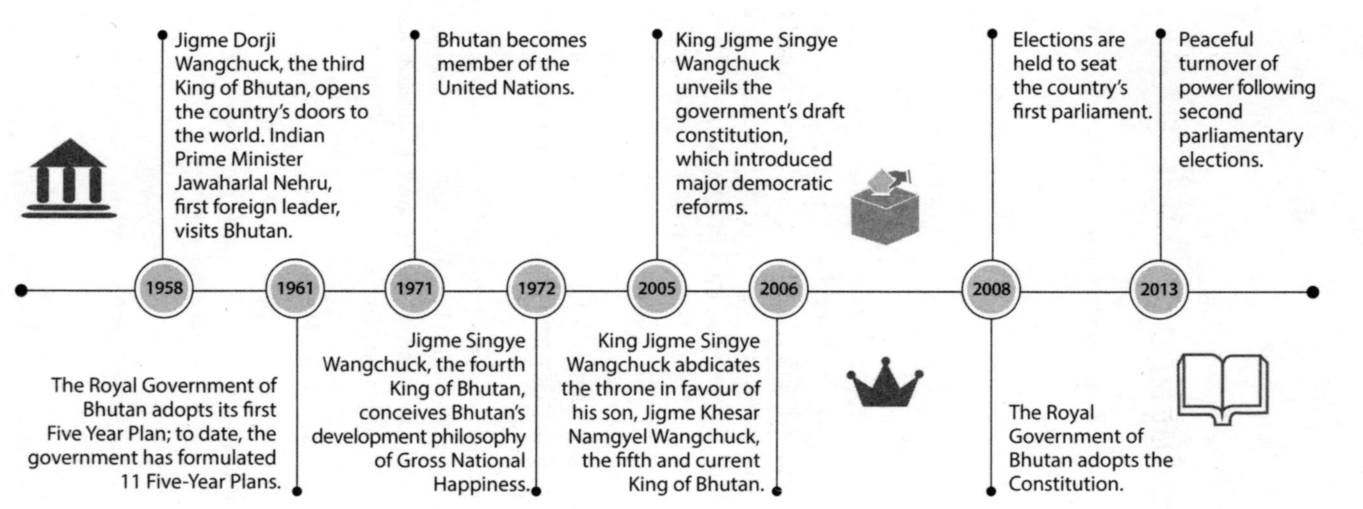

FIGURE I.1 Timeline of Key Milestones in Bhutan's Political Development

Source: Compiled by authors based on various official government sources and ADB publications.

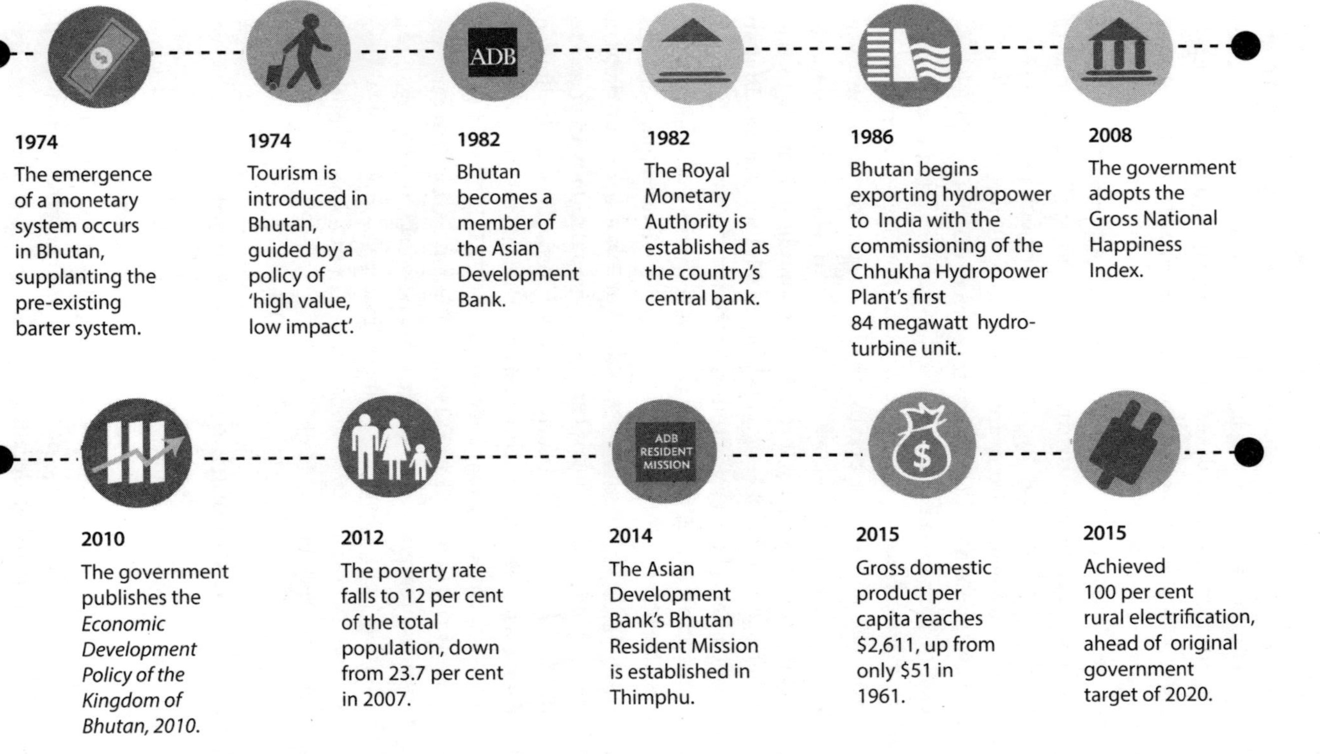

FIGURE I.2 Timeline of Key Milestones in Bhutan's Economic Development

Source: Compiled by authors based on various official government sources and ADB publications.

transformation has resulted in significant progress in economic and social development within a relatively short span of time. Bhutan's development plans have catalysed its modernization without compromising the rich cultural heritage and abundant natural resources of the country.

Until the 1960s, Bhutan remained isolated and depended heavily on subsistence agriculture to sustain its economy. The absence of infrastructure facilities and the inadequacy of social services, such as education and healthcare, were conspicuous. Before the advent of planned development in the country, there were no motorized vehicles, electricity, or paved roads. Bhutan also lacked postal and telecommunication systems prior to the 1960s and did not have any air links to connect its people with the outside world. Access to the country was difficult as the northern route was inaccessible in winter and the southern route required a journey through dense and hostile jungle terrain in the Indian states of West Bengal and Assam. Not surprisingly, Bhutan did not welcome its first foreign tourists until 1974. Nine years later, the first commercial flight departed for Kolkata from the Paro valley.

The modernization of Bhutanese society occurred rapidly following its opening up to the outside world. From having no electricity in the 1960s and only about 20 per cent of the population with access to electricity in 2003, there is nearly universal electrification in Bhutan today. Along with significant reductions in maternal, infant, and underfive mortality rates, the average life expectancy has increased to more than 69 years from only 37 years in 1960. As Bhutan took its first cautious steps towards integration with the rest of the world, it also began the transformation from a barter to a monetized economy in 1974. Less than a decade later, the Royal Monetary Authority was established in 1982 as the country's central bank.

Economic Transformation: 1961 to Present

Bhutan's economy has steadily progressed from a traditional stage of economic development, with limited production almost wholly rooted in the primary sector, to achieving the preconditions for an economic take off. Bhutan has undergone exceptional structural change in the past three decades since it first partnered with the Asian Development Bank (ADB) in 1982 (ADB 2014). The economic

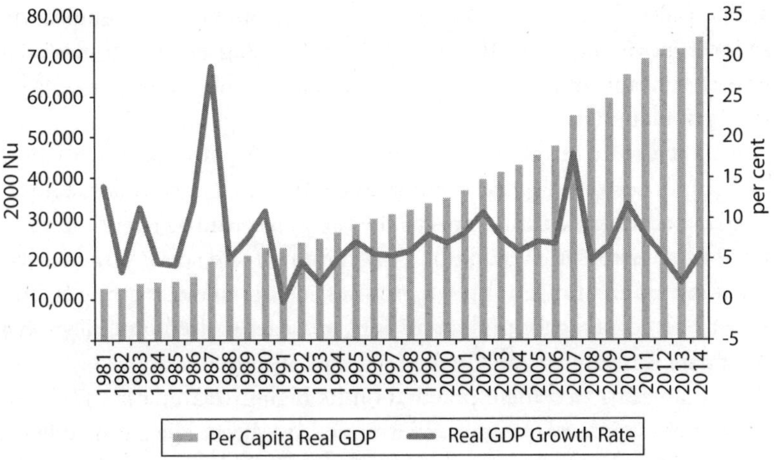

FIGURE I.3 Bhutan's Per Capita Real GDP and Real GDP Growth Rate, 1981–2014

Note: GDP = gross domestic product; Nu = Ngultrum.

Source: National Statistics Bureau (n.d.).

expansion it has experienced is one of the most rapid among economies at a similar stage of development.

Despite its geographical challenges and limited linkages to global markets, Bhutan managed to generate and sustain high economic growth by unlocking its massive hydropower potential. In 1961, Bhutan's gross domestic product (GDP) per capita was estimated at only $51, then the lowest in the world. By 2015, it had risen to approximately $2,611. The real GDP annual growth rates averaged 8 per cent during 1981–2014 and per capita income rose on an average of 6 per cent annually (Figure I.3).[2] This phenomenal growth has allowed Bhutan to significantly reduce poverty and raise living standards through investment in physical

[2] The biggest impetus to economic growth has been provided by foreign aid and large-scale hydropower projects. Real GDP growth increased to 18 per cent in 2007 from 6.9 per cent in 2006 mainly on account of the commissioning of the Tala hydroelectric project. The small base of the national economy makes it possible for a single large industrial activity to boost growth substantially. Of an annual growth rate of 12.6 per cent in 2007, the electricity subsector accounted for 18.4 per cent of GDP.

and social infrastructure. At the same time, Bhutan has significantly reduced poverty (proportion of population living below the national poverty line) from about 23 per cent in 2007 to about 12 per cent of total population in 2012.

The structure of the economy has also undergone a transformation in terms of sector-wise contribution to GDP. The changes reflect a modernizing economy as the shares of the secondary and tertiary sectors in GDP have increased. In addition to community and social services, the top contributors to GDP by sector now include: (i) electricity, gas, and water; (ii) construction; (iii) transport, storage, and communications; (iv) finance, insurance, and real estate; and (v) agriculture.

Bhutan aims to remain perched on its high-growth path and accelerate inclusive development underpinned by the guiding principle of GNH. This goal is enunciated in the *Economic Development Policy of the Kingdom of Bhutan, 2010* (Royal Government of Bhutan 2010), which seeks to 'promote a green and self-reliant economy sustained by an IT-enabled knowledge society guided by the philosophy of GNH'. The policy's stated objectives are to achieve economic self-reliance by the year 2020 and to sustain full employment.[3]

Development Constraints and Hurdles

The road ahead for Bhutan is full of challenges. Its economy remains based largely on hydropower, agriculture, and forestry, which provide the primary livelihoods for more than half of the population. Because rugged mountains dominate the terrain and make the building of roads and other infrastructure difficult and expensive, industrial production is primarily of the cottage industry type. The economy is closely aligned with India's through strong trade and monetary links, and Bhutan is dependent on India for financial assistance and migrant labourers for development projects (for example, road construction).

[3] The *Economic Development Policy of the Kingdom of Bhutan, 2010* seeks to attain economic self-reliance and full employment by: (i) diversifying the economic base with a minimal ecological footprint; (ii) harnessing and adding value to natural resources in a sustainable manner; (iii) increasing and diversifying exports; (iv) promoting Bhutan as an organic brand; (v) promoting industries that build the Brand Bhutan image; and (vi) reducing dependency on fossil fuel, especially with respect to transportation.

Complicated controls and uncertain policies in areas such as industrial licencing, trade, labour, and finance continue to hamper foreign investment. The high volume of imported materials needed to build hydropower plants has increased Bhutan's trade and current account deficits. As economic growth has been largely financed by external aid and (increasingly) external investment, the Government of Bhutan's fiscal deficit has widened and overall external debt levels are high. Rising capital expenditures reflect ongoing hydropower construction and an increasing civil service wage bill.

Climate change is also a serious concern for Bhutan. According to a recent Japan International Cooperation Agency report, Bhutan is experiencing an increase in the number of disasters related to hydrometeorological hazards, such as flash floods and cyclones, resulting from climate change. This poses urgent environmental and economic challenges for Bhutan.

Future Prospects

The economic prospects for Bhutan remain bright. It has thus far harnessed only 6 per cent of its 23,730 megawatt hydropower capacity. However, dependence on hydropower comes at a price, with about one-third of the economy dependent on this capital-intensive industry. Such a heavy reliance on hydropower has bound the country's growth to a sector that provides only limited employment opportunities. Furthermore, volatility in hydropower investment inflows from India and cyclicality in production, depending on hydrologic conditions, have often led to external imbalances and shortage of Indian rupees. Most non-natural resources based sectors of the economy remain largely underdeveloped. A narrow economic base, limited private sector development, and an underdeveloped financial sector have led to inadequate income opportunities and inequality.

Bhutan's Eleventh Five Year Plan sets out its current development priorities, which is guided by the visioning pronouncements of Jigme Khesar Namgyel Wangchuck, the fifth King of Bhutan.[4] The plan sets out an ambitious development agenda to fulfil the government's pledge

[4] In December 2006, the fourth king abdicated the throne in favour of his son, Jigme Khesar Namgyel Wangchuck.

of *Wangtse Chhirpel* or ensuring prosperity for all through effective empowerment of the people.[5]

While aggregate poverty reduction has been impressive, Bhutan's poverty and inequality indicators remain high, especially in the rural and remote areas. In 2012, about 97 per cent of the poor resided in rural areas where there is a lack of opportunities for employment outside agriculture. The delivery of crucial social services to isolated areas is costly and such capacities are limited, adding to the problem of inequality.

For Bhutan to achieve stronger and more stable growth that is inclusive, the underlying economic imbalances need to be addressed through structural reforms. The economy needs to be broad-based, with multiple, diverse sectors driving economic growth and providing more employment opportunities. To achieve this, Bhutan has to tackle critical constraints to growth and welfare improvement, including: (i) inadequate infrastructure, particularly with regard to transport and connectivity; (ii) narrow fiscal space; (iii) lack of access to finance by small enterprises; (iv) market failures that limit product diversification and competition; and (v) limited and unequal access to quality education, and labour market mismatches (ADB 2013).

This book is an attempt to chronicle Bhutan's remarkable economic journey and the challenges confronting its future, including vulnerabilities and potential risks. The discussion will cover a range of policies that can unlock the country's economic potential and overcome its limitations. This book consolidates a body of knowledge accumulated by ADB while working with the Government of Bhutan on monitoring and strengthening its macroeconomic management framework, and through support to development activities throughout the country.

Organization of the Book

The book comprises 10 main chapters. Chapter 1 deals with 'Bhutan's Macroeconomic Challenges' that have arisen in recent decades amid

[5] The King's development guidance can be summarized as: (i) ensuring the peace and well-being of the people and the sovereignty and security of the country; (ii) ensuring the security that comes when people are united in their love for their country and in their efforts to further secure, consolidate, and pass on an even stronger nation to their children; (iii) building a vibrant democracy; (iv) achieving self-reliance; and (v) realizing the development philosophy of GNH.

rapid growth and development. It describes how Bhutan's remarkable growth, in the face of limited domestic resources, has led to rising incomes. At the same time, given the lack of domestic production of consumer goods, such growth has also resulted in a large import bill and a steady deterioration of the current account balance. This chapter explores the viability of ongoing balance of payments deficits and identifies the lack of production diversification as a key source of this imbalance. In Chapter 2, 'Vulnerability and Resilience: A Conceptual Framework for Bhutan', the focus shifts to construction of a conceptual framework for measuring vulnerability and improving resilience of developing countries, with particular application to Bhutan's case. The discussion looks at whether Bhutan's inherent vulnerability of its exposure to macroeconomic shocks will increase and what it can do to build resilience to such shocks.

Chapter 3, 'The Experience of Gross National Happiness as a Development Framework', expounds on the country's unique institutional development framework. It explains the GNH principles that affect the way Bhutanese society and the state interact, and reviews GNH principles in practice by assessing policy intentions versus policy outcomes and declarations. It concludes that Bhutan's experiment with GNH remains dynamic and evolving, and suggests that this policy process might also be of interest to the international community and those intrigued by the original idea of GNH.

Chapter 4, 'Unlocking Bhutan's Potential: Measuring Potential Output for the Nation', develops the first macroeconomic model for Bhutan's potential output and analyses the impact of several policy options on potential growth for Bhutan over the period 2014–30. The results show that, given Bhutan's current physical as well as human capital stock distribution, investment in the quality of factors of production (for example, education and support for the broader diffusion of technology) will yield much higher potential output growth path than a narrower focus on further hydropower plant investment. Given the cumulative nature of growth rates on the level of output over time, higher potential growth rates today can have a significant impact on output levels in the future, suggesting that dual focus on human and physical capital investment would optimize Bhutan's standard of living over time.

Chapter 5, 'Bhutan's Rupee Crisis: Macroeconomic Causes and Cures' discusses the rupee crisis. With over 74 per cent of Bhutan's trade taking place with India, ample holdings of Indian rupee reserves are critical for trade, much of which includes importing essential food items from India. This chapter analyses the causes of and cures for the Indian rupee crisis and finds that excessive monetary growth, inflation differentials between India and Bhutan, and terms of trade imbalances are key factors in the Bhutanese liquidity crisis.

The discussion of the crisis is then followed by two related chapters. Chapter 6, 'Monetary Policy Framework for the Royal Government of Bhutan' explores various models for forecasting monetary aggregates that are relevant for guiding the monetary and economic authorities in the annual planning process. The models generate one-step ahead (static) as well as one-year ahead (dynamic) forecasts of monetary aggregates. Pure time series models using only the past values of monetary aggregates and an error correction model including seasonal dummies are examined.

The dynamics of price transmission from external markets are explained in Chapter 7, 'Bhutan's Consumer Price Inflation and Price Transmission from India', which includes an examination of Bhutan's heavy reliance on food imports from its larger neighbour, India. With the currency pegged to the Indian rupee, Bhutan is vulnerable to price shocks from India, particularly with regard to imported food, which is given significant weight in the consumption basket.

Chapter 8, 'A Framework of Trade Policy for Bhutan Compatible with the Gross National Happiness', discusses the relationship among GNH, industrial policies, and trade policies; and analyses trade policy issues that are relevant for Bhutan. It also points out that the structure of the Bhutanese government is less oriented to trade policy than neighbouring governments, and suggests a new organization for promoting a more active trade policy.

Chapter 9, 'Electricity Consumption, Output, and Trade in Bhutan', examines the relationship between electricity consumption, international trade, and economic growth within an augmented production function framework. The findings suggest that given Bhutan economy's energy dependence, any increase in electricity consumption and trade would have a positive effect on economic growth in the long run.

The final chapter, Chapter 10, 'Banking in Bhutan: An Assessment of Financial Sector Development', presents the results of an investigation into the performance and stability of Bhutan's banking system. The study found that economic growth has fuelled high demand for household credit in recent years; banks have responded by substantially increasing their loan portfolios. The chapter discusses policy recommendations to strengthen and improve the banking sector, including fostering banking sector competition, improving regulatory practices with regard to both monitoring and the enforcement, and enhancing risk diversification and liquidity management practices.

An earlier versions of some of the chapters were published as South Asia Working Papers (SAWP): Chapter 3 (SAWP 42), Chapter 4 (SAWP 32), Chapter 5 (SAWP 40), Chapter 8 (SAWP 39), Chapter 9 (SAWP 34), and Chapter 10 (SAWP 44). In addition, Chapter 2 was published by Fondation pour es Études et Recherches sur le Développement International.

References

Asian Development Bank (ADB). 2013. *Bhutan: Making Progress on the Path to Prosperity Development Effectiveness Brief.* ADB: Manila.

______. 2014. *Three Decades of Development Partnership: Royal Government of Bhutan and Asian Development Bank*. ADB: Manila.

National Statistics Bureau. n.d. National Accounts Report. Available at http://www.nsb.gov.bt/nsbweb/publication/publications.php?id=4 (last accessed on 5 May 2015).

Royal Government of Bhutan. 2010. *Economic Development Policy of the Kingdom of Bhutan, 2010*. Thimphu.

Royal Government of Bhutan, Gross National Happiness Commission. 2013. *Eleventh Five-Year Plan—Main Document Volume I*. Thimphu.

1

JOSHUA E. GREENE

Bhutan's Macroeconomic Challenges

Bhutan—a small, landlocked country of about 750,000 inhabitants located along India's northeastern border—has been among the fastest-growing economies in South Asia since 2000. During the 11-year period from fiscal year (FY) 2001 through FY2011, real gross domestic product (GDP) growth averaged 8.7 per cent per year (Table 1.1).[1] Growth slowed to 6.5 per cent in FY2012 and declined further to 3.2 per cent in FY2013. Bhutan's rapid growth allowed real per capita income to more than double in local currency terms between FY2001 and FY2012, reaching nearly Nu72,400 in constant 2000 prices by the end of the review period. Using the Atlas method, the World Bank estimated gross national income (GNI) per capita to be $2,420 in 2012, which is comparable to the GNI per capita of $2,439 for FY2012 shown in Table 1.1. Measured in constant 2005 US dollars at purchasing power parity, GNI approximately doubled between FY2000 and FY2012 to reach $5,246, which was well above the average for South Asia (World Bank 2014). During this period, life expectancy

[1] The fiscal year (FY) of the government ends on 30 June. FY before a calendar year denotes the year in which the fiscal year ends; that is FY2001 ends on 30 June 2001.

TABLE 1.1 Bhutan: Real Growth and Per Capita Gross National Income

	FY2001	FY2002	FY2003	FY2004	FY2005	FY2006	FY2007	FY2008	FY2009	FY2010	FY2011	FY2012	FY2013
							(in Nu million)						
GDP at constant 2000 prices	20,545.4	22,500.6	24,552.0	26,329.9	28,030.9	29,858.7	33,623.1	37,256.5	39,392.9	43,046.9	47,375.3	50,457.7	52,054.8[a]
							(in per cent)						
Real GDP growth	7.6	9.5	9.1	6.7	6.5	7.0	12.6	10.8	5.7	9.3	10.1	6.5	3.2
							(in $)						
Gross National Income per capita	–	–	–	1,032.7	1,177.8	1,315.0	1,533.7	1,884.8	1,721.2	1,976.6	2,357.7	2,439.1	2,513.2

Notes: 1. GDP = gross domestic product.

2. [a]GDP at constant 2000 prices for FY2013 has been calculated from data for calendar years 2012 and 2013.

Sources: ADB (2014); RMA (2013).

rose about 10 per cent to 67.6 years. However, a low level of educational attainment—less than three years on average according to data from the United Nations Development Programme (UNDP)—has kept Bhutan's Human Development Index at only 0.538, which ranked 140th out of 187 countries in 2013 (UNDP 2013).

While Bhutan exports some minerals, its scenic, mountainous terrain and considerable rainfall have provided opportunities to earn additional income from both tourism and hydropower development. Through careful planning, Bhutan has worked to develop high-end ecotourism, limiting the number of tourists from countries other than India in order to preserve the natural environment while at the same time generating relatively high receipts per tourist. In addition, Bhutan has embarked on a major programme of building 16 hydropower projects to provide electricity to the domestic and Indian markets. As of 2013, four projects were already producing electricity and work had started on another four. In 2014, a fifth project (Dagachu) was expected to start generating electricity, with work planned to begin on five more projects. Electricity sales of Nu48.2 billion are forecast for FY2026 when all 16 projects are projected to have reached their full capacity, nearly seven times the estimated sales of Nu7.1 billion in FY2013. With domestic sales of Nu6.6 billion, exports could reach Nu41.6 billion, according to government estimates.[2]

Bhutan's economic growth and development projects, while raising incomes and living standards, have also created macroeconomic challenges. Similar to many other developing countries, Bhutan's balance of payments (BoP) is typically in deficit. It is financed by a mix of grants for capital projects, external loans, and some foreign direct investment (FDI). Bhutan's current account deficit is unusually large. Except for the period FY2006–FY2009, the current account deficit has exceeded 15 per cent of GDP every year since FY2002. Since FY2010, the current account deficit has exceeded 20 per cent of GDP (Table 1.2). In most years, grants, borrowing, and FDI have more than offset these deficits, allowing the gross reserves of the Royal Monetary Authority of Bhutan (RMA) and commercial banks to triple to $916.9 million

[2] Figures reflect projections made in November 2013 by the Ministry of Economic Affairs, Department of Hydropower and Power System.

TABLE 1.2 Bhutan: Summary Balance of Payments

Category	FY2008	FY2009	FY2010	FY2011	FY2012	FY2013
						Prel.
			(in Nu million)			
Current Account	**–4,486.7**	**–3,631.2**	**–14,863.5**	**–23,621.4**	**–19,774.3**	**–25,769.3**
with India	–3,498.8	–3,554.4	–9,211.2	–18,171.5	–15,685.8	–26,625.8
Trade Balance	–1,836.4	–3,529.0	–12,568.3	–20,835.3	–19,880.6	–20,708.5
with India	–27.8	–593.2	–5,855.3	–15,160.0	–12,795.1	–17,468.8
Exports	24,170.8	24,343.0	24,480.1	30,160.1	30,997.4	29,931.5
with India	21,721.8	22,936.0	22,461.9	25,460.6	27,546.8	27,559.3
Imports	26,007.2	27,872.0	37,048.4	50,995.4	50,878.1	50,640.0
with India	21,749.7	23,529.2	28,317.2	40,620.6	40,342.0	45,028.1
Services	–2,655.4	–2,018.0	–3,315.8	–4,283.1	–4,749.9	–2,972.6
Credit	2,205.8	2,700.0	3,210.0	3,703.8	5,146.0	6,764.6
Debit	4,861.2	4,718.0	6,525.8	7,986.9	9,896.0	9,737.3
Primary Income	–1,399.3	–1,560.4	–3,335.7	–4,709.7	–5,922.4	–9,085.7
Credit	1,397.6	1,012.6	762.4	753.6	875.1	965.9
Debit	2,796.9	2,573.0	4,098.1	5,463.3	6,797.5	10,051.6
Secondary Income (Current Transfers)	1,404.5	3,476.3	4,356.2	6,206.7	10,778.7	6,997.5
Credit	3,456.4	5,181.9	6,435.0	8,562.2	12,907.3	8,684.7
Of which: Budgetary Grants	2,574.8	4,001.7	4,669.7	6,540.0	9,020.7	4,716.2
Debit	2,051.8	1,705.6	2,078.8	2,355.5	2,128.6	1,687.1

Capital and Financial Account	**4,297.8**	**7,883.2**	**15,918.5**	**26,240.7**	**19,978.4**	**33,902.4**
Capital Account	3,360.6	3,269.2	6,985.6	7,609.7	4,755.1	14,459.0
Of which: Budgetary grants for investment	3,360.6	2,510.6	3,920.6	3,957.7	3,436.5	4,698.6
Of which: Grants for hydro-power development	0.0	758.7	3,065.0	3,652.0	1,318.6	9,760.4
Financial Account	936.8	4,613.5	8,933.9	18,632.7	15,222.1	19,443.4
Foreign direct investment	125.0	865.8	3,468.6	1,408.8	1,209.7	2,707.8[a]
Of which: Equity Capital	29.9	349.1	753.3	770.5	589.3	2,619.1
Portfolio Investment	0.0	0.0	0.0	0.0	0.0	0.0
Other Investment (net chg. In assets less net chg. In liabil.)[a]	811.8	3,747.7	5,465.3	17,223.9	14,012.4	16,082.6
Net acquisition of financial assets	512.6	–396.4	57.9	–147.6	–63.4	956.5
Net acquisition of financial liabilities	1,324.4	3,351.4	5,523.2	17,076.3	13,949.0	17,692.2
o/w RGOB loans	–638.8	1,318.1	4,359.0	11,974.7	11,435.1	–
o/w Other loans	2,150.0	1,988.3	444.0	4,618.7	2,950.8	–
Net Errors and Omissions	877.9	2,321.1	3,354.0	–1,823.4	–9,271.4	1,079.1
Overall Balance	**688.6**	**6,572.6**	**4,410.0**	**797.5**	**–9,068.4**	**9,212.2**
Gross International Reserves in Banking System (at end of Fiscal Year)						
Rupee reserves (Rs million)	858.2	628.1	1,378.6	774.6	1,516.3	11,352.2
Of which: Royal Monetary Authority	135.1	118.4	137.3	91.2	229.9	10,706.4

(Cont'd)

Table 1.2 (*Cont'd*)

Category	FY2008	FY2009	FY2010	FY2011	FY2012	FY2013
						Prel.
Convertible currency reserves ($ million)	527.2	662.2	729.8	778.9	647.4	726.7
Of which: Royal Monetary Authority	503.9	637.5	698.5	731.8	623.6	692.7
Total reserves ($ million)	547.1	675.2	759.4	796.2	674.3	916.9
Of which: Royal Monetary Authority	507.0	640.0	701.4	733.8	627.7	872.1
Total reserves in months of imports (from BoP in $)	10.2	13.9	11.5	8.5	8.0	13.0
Memo: Net Rupee Reserves (in Rs million): Total Res. Less BoP Fin'g	23,497.9	29,754.0	32,388.0	27,691.3	26,813.8	36,039.3
Memo: Outstanding Debt for BoP Financing	0.0	3,000.0	3,000.0	7,914.8	11,156.0	18,699.6
i. Overdraft from SBI and PNB	–	–	–	4,914.8	5,156.0	3,289.7
ii. GOI Line of Credit		3,000.0	3,000.0	3,000.0	6,000.0	10,000.0
iii. RBI Swap	–	–	–	0.0	0.0	5,409.9
Exchange rate, end of period (FY, June): Nu per $	42.82	47.77	46.56	44.59998	55.6	59.53
Exchange rate used to convert rupee reserves into $	42.95	48.51	46.6	44.72	56.31	59.70
Exchange rate, average (FY, June)	40.37	47.78	46.65	45.33	50.27	54.86

Nominal GDP at market prices (FY)[b]	52,084.8	57,968.2	66,860.1	78,723.3	91,201.5	101,415.7
Data for Flow of Funds						
Net exports of goods and services	–4,491.9	–5,547.0	–15,884.0	–25,118.5	–24,630.6	–23,681.1
Goods (Trade balance)	–1,836.4	–3,529.0	–12,568.3	–20,835.3	–19,880.6	–20,708.5
Services (Net services)	–2,655.4	–2,018.0	–3,315.8	–4,283.1	–4,749.9	–2,972.6
Net primary income	–1,399.3	–1,560.4	–3,335.7	–4,709.7	–5,922.4	–9,085.7
Net secondary income (current transfers)	1,404.5	3,476.3	4,356.2	6,206.7	10,778.7	6,997.5
Current account balance from above	–4,486.7	–3,631.2	–14,863.5	–23,621.4	–19,774.3	–25,769.3
Current account as reported	–4,486.7	–3,631.2	–14,863.5	–23,621.4	–19,774.3	–25,769.3
Discrepancy: Current account reported less sum of elements	0.0	0.0	0.0	0.0	0.0	0.0
			(in per cent of GDP)			
Total External Debt	**65.2**	**65.8**	**61.8**	**74.8**	**84.5**	**96.5**
Debt in Indian Rupees	36.4	37.1	35.0	45.1	53.0	63.8
Debt in Convertible Currencies	28.8	28.6	26.8	29.7	31.5	32.7
Memo: Hydropower debt	33.2	30.2	27.3	31.1	35.1	42.1
Current Account Balance	**–8.6**	**–6.3**	**–22.2**	**–30.0**	**–21.7**	**–25.4**

Notes: 1. BoP = balance of payments; RGOB = Royal Government of Bhutan.

2. [a]Net incurrence of liabilities for direct investment in Bhutan.

3. [b]For FY2011 through FY2013: calculated from calendar year data for 2010 through 2014.

Sources: ADB (2014); RMA (2013).

between the end of both FY2001 and FY2013. Relative to imports, however, gross reserves declined from the equivalent of more than 15 months of imports at the end of FY2001 to the equivalent of 13 months at the end of FY2013. In addition, nominal external debt rose five-fold over this period to more than $1.6 billion at the end of FY2013 from less than $300 million at the end of FY2001. Over the same period, external debt as a share of GDP increased from about 57 per cent to more than 98 per cent.

Bhutan's large current account deficit has made its economy heavily dependent on foreign financing. Major difficulties can arise when financing proves inadequate, including periodic shortages of Indian rupees given that nearly 80 per cent of all imports come from India. In both December 2011 and February 2012, commercial banks found themselves unable to meet customer demand for rupees. In December 2011, the RMA converted about $200 million of its non-rupee reserves to rupees to meet the demand of commercial banks (Rashid 2013). In February 2012, the RMA stopped satisfying bank requests for rupees and instituted several administrative measures to curb rupee payments, including blocking payments for imports of automobiles and construction materials for private projects, prohibiting local currency bank accounts for foreigners not holding work permits, having all rupee payments settled through the banking system, and requiring that all rupee export earnings be repatriated through the banking system within 91 days. In addition, credit and debit card payments in rupees were limited and cash withdrawals in rupees were capped before subsequently being temporarily suspended.

In March 2012, the Ministry of Economic Affairs announced that import licences would be issued for only about 50 items classified as essential. More than 5,000 items were deemed non-essential (Economist Intelligence Unit 2012a). The RMA agreed to provide rupees for those imports deemed essential. In April 2012, the RMA reduced the cash reserve requirement from 17 per cent to 10 per cent to allow banks to access more of their funds, especially as the closing of foreign bank accounts drained more than Nu1.3 billion from the banking system (Economist Intelligence Unit 2012b). The RMA also established a policy rate at 6 per cent and minimum lending rates of 10.4 per cent to 12.7 per cent for banks and 13 per cent for non-bank financial institutions (ADB 2013).

Despite these measures, the BoP recorded a sharp deficit in FY2012 and gross international reserves in the banking system fell more than $120 million to $674 million at the end of FY2012. However, the BoP improved considerably during FY2013 as the continuation of import restrictions slowed credit growth and curbed import of vehicles and construction equipment. Measured in US dollars, the trade deficit narrowed as imports fell by 6.5 per cent, although a decrease in water flowing through dams contributed to a small decline in export earnings derived from hydropower generation. While a worsening of the income balance and current transfers caused the current account deficit to expand, a sharp rise in capital transfers and loan proceeds caused net capital and financial inflows to soar, leading to a large BoP surplus and a rise in gross international reserves to $916.9 million at the end of FY2013. However, growth in private sector credit plummeted to 6.8 per cent in FY2013 from 29.9 per cent in FY2012, and economic growth slowed to 5.2 per cent from 6.5 per cent over the same period (ADB 2014). Furthermore, there was a smaller-than-expected fiscal deficit of 0.9 per cent of GDP as grants increased substantially and tax revenue exceeded expectations. These monetary trends continued during the first half of FY2014 as gross international reserves in the banking system rose an additional $17.6 million to $934.5 million and domestic credit fell 8.4 per cent amid a sizable decline in net credit to the government that more than offset a rise in private credit.[3]

Sources of the Balance of Payments Problem

Despite the apparent success of the import and payments restrictions during FY2013, their long-term viability can be questioned. Three days before the end of FY2013, the RMA converted another $200 million of convertible currency to Indian rupees, ostensibly to have a larger supply to meet potential demand in the coming months. Export surrender requirements and limits on cash withdrawals along with restrictions on importing vehicles, construction materials for private

[3] See Table 2 (Monetary Survey) and Table 14 (Gross International Reserves) in RMA (2014).

projects, and other non-essential items would seem inconsistent with establishing a liberal market economy and providing incentives for growth. Thus, it is worth analysing Bhutan's macroeconomic situation further to understand the sources of its BoP difficulties and see whether more market-friendly strategies are available to generate a more sustainable BoP.

Hydropower Is Not the Source of the Problem

The massive undertaking associated with Bhutan's power projects necessitates asking if the electricity sector is responsible for the country's BoP difficulties. The data suggest otherwise. Table 1.3 provides a summary of the BoP for the hydropower sector, identifying export earnings, associated imports, interest payments, grants, and loan proceeds related to the various power projects using data assembled by the Ministry of Economic Affairs. Although the current account for the hydropower sector's BoP has recorded a deficit every fiscal year since FY2011—resulting from rising project-related imports and service payments (for example, imported labour and professional services)—project grants (capital account) and net loan disbursements (financial account) substantially outweigh the current account deficit in each of these fiscal years. Thus, the sector is contributing a net surplus to the BoP, making the projects a net source of foreign exchange, although the earnings may not be fully available to fund other imports or debt service as a portion is used by Bhutanese firms and workers engaged in the projects. Projections from the Ministry of Economic Affairs show a large surplus continuing through FY2018, although the overall balance in the BoP is expected to shrink substantially in FY2019 when large loan repayments for the two Punachu projects and the Mangdachu project begin as these projects reach full production capacity. A smaller surplus is projected to continue at least through FY2023 as rising export sales and declining imports of machinery and equipment offset declining grants and rising debt service payments on project loans. In addition, hydropower debt, which was equivalent to 45.5 per cent of GDP at the end of FY2013, represented less than half of all external debt (Table 1.4). By comparison, the non-hydropower sector has consistently recorded large payment imbalances (Table 1.5).

TABLE 1.3 Bhutan: Balance of Payments for Hydropower Sector

Category	FY2008	FY2009	FY2010	FY2011	FY2012	FY2013	FY2014	FY2015
						Prel.	Proj.	Proj.
				(in Nu million)				
Current Account	**3,856.0**	**6,873.0**	**1,871.1**	**–3,880.5**	**–2,211.7**	**–11,878.3**	**–24,303.4**	**–31,412.8**
Trade Balance	5,609.0	9,121.6	5,609.2	1,608.7	2,629.2	–3,633.6	–14,034.5	–18,660.3
Exports	6,049.0	10,641.8	10,413.7	10,275.9	9,865.6	9,842.0	5,282.3	5,538.7
Imports	440.0	1,520.2	4,804.5	8,667.2	7,236.4	13,475.6	19,316.8	24,199.0
Services	–200.0	–691.0	–2,183.9	–3,939.6	–3,289.3	–6,125.3	–8,780.3	–10,999.5
Income	–1,553.0	–1,557.6	–1,554.2	–1,549.6	–1,551.7	–2,119.4	–1,488.5	–1,753.0
Capital and Financial Account	**–875.4**	**264.1**	**5,862.5**	**12,378.6**	**10,354.0**	**22,475.5**	**32,646.4**	**40,785.8**
Capital Account: Grants for Hydropower	320	758.7	3,065.0	3,652.0	1,318.6	9,760.4	11,961.4	13,786.1
Financial Account	–1,195.4	–494.6	2,797.5	8,726.6	9,035.4	12,715.2	20,685.0	26,999.6
Loan Disbursements	480	1,146.0	4,497.0	10,488.6	10,822.4	15,136.6	22,460.6	28,982.2
Loan Repayments	1,675.4	1,640.6	1,699.4	1,762.0	1,787.0	2,421.4	1,775.6	1,982.6
Hydropower BoP	**2,980.6**	**7,137.0**	**7,733.7**	**8,498.1**	**8,142.3**	**10,597.2**	**8,343.0**	**9,373.0**

(Cont'd)

TABLE 1.3 (*Cont'd*)

Category	FY2016	FY2017	FY2018	FY2019	FY2020	FY2021	FY2022	FY2023
	Proj.	Proj.	Proj.	Proj.	Proj.	Proj.	Proj.	Proj.
	(in Nu million)							
Current Account	**–35,971.4**	**–41,130.4**	**–39,474.4**	**–42,082.0**	**–45,588.8**	**–42,282.0**	**–32,059.1**	**–12,474.2**
Trade Balance	–21,829.0	–25,576.6	–22,609.2	–15,473.6	–18,017.6	–14,917.8	–6,267.2	11,118.7
Exports	5,436.3	5,262.3	11,147.9	17,381.7	18,321.6	20,160.5	23,186.7	27,763.0
Imports	27,265.3	30,838.9	33,757.1	32,855.3	36,339.3	35,078.3	29,453.9	16,644.3
Services	–12,393.3	–14,017.7	–15,344.1	–14,934.2	–16,517.9	–15,944.7	–13,388.1	–7,565.6
Income	–1,749.1	–1,536.1	–1,521.1	–11,674.2	–11,053.3	–11,419.6	–12,403.8	–16,027.3
Capital and Financial Account	**45,522.6**	**50,369.0**	**54,331.4**	**43,554.2**	**51,393.7**	**52,157.5**	**37,024.8**	**13,610.3**
Capital Account: Grants for Hydropower	14,682.4	14,432.3	14,400.8	13,737.5	16,164.2	17,326.5	13,354.7	8,086.0
Financial Account	30,840.2	35,936.7	39,930.6	29,816.8	35,229.5	34,831.0	23,670.0	5,524.3
Loan Disbursements	33,023.2	38,009.3	42,085.8	41,451.6	46,250.0	46,206.9	36,017.3	20,649.1
Loan Repayments	2,183.0	2,072.6	2,155.1	11,634.8	11,020.4	11,375.9	12,347.2	15,124.8
Hydropower BoP	**9,551.2**	**9,238.5**	**14,857.0**	**1,472.2**	**5,805.0**	**9,875.5**	**4,965.6**	**1,136.0**

Notes: BoP = Balance of Payments; FY = fiscal year.

Source: Data provided by the Ministry of Economic Affairs, Department of Hydropower and Power Systems, Bhutan.

Table 1.4 Bhutan: External Debt

Category	FY2008	FY2009	FY2010	FY2011	FY2012	FY2013
	Gross debt stock at end of period (in Nu million)					
Total External Debt	**33,970.6**	**38,124.8**	**41,350.3**	**59,228.2**	**78,338.8**	**95,926.6**
Debt (in Rs)	18,966.5	21,529.5	23,406.1	35,697.3	49,165.5	61,341.7
Hydropower Debt	17,320.2	17,483.4	18,277.6	24,647.5	32,546.3	44,369.0
Chhuka (repaid by end-2007/08)	0.0	0.0	0.0	0.0	0.0	0.0
Kurichhu	1,493.3	1,306.7	1,120.0	933.3	46.7	560.0
Tala	15,346.9	13,951.7	12,556.6	11,161.4	9,766.2	7,384.3
Punatsangchhu I	480.0	2,225.0	4,601.0	10,169.5	15,260.5	21,596.6
Punatsangchhu II	0.0	0.0	0.0	1,638.0	4,113.0	9,353.4
Mangdechhu	0.0	0.0	0.0	745.3	2,659.9	5,474.7
Accrued interest on hydro debt	18.1	129.1	628.2	1,635.0	3,614.7	6,590.4
Non-hydropower debt	1,628.1	3,917.3	4,500.3	9,414.8	13,004.6	16,269.2
Govt. of India Line of Credit	0.0	3,000.0	3,000.0	3,000.0	6,000.0	10,000.0
Overdraft Facility	1,628.1	917.3	500.0	4,914.8	5,156.0	0.0
RBI Swap Facility	0.0	0.0	0.0	0.0	0.0	5,409.9
Dungsam Cement Corp (Private)	0.0	0.0	0.0	1,500.0	1,848.6	859.3
Debt in Convertible Currencies	15,004.1	16,595.3	17,944.2	23,530.9	29,173.3	34,584.9
(in $ million)	350.4	347.4	385.4	527.6	524.7	579.3
	(in per cent of GDP)					
Total external debt	65.2	65.8	61.8	74.8	84.5	98.4
Debt (in Rs)	36.4	37.1	35.0	45.1	53.0	62.9
Debt in Convertible Currencies	28.8	28.6	26.8	29.7	31.5	35.5
Memo: Hydropower debt	33.2	30.2	27.3	31.1	35.1	45.5

Note: GDP = gross domestic product.

Source: Author's calculations based on RMA (2013).

TABLE 1.5 Balance of Payments for Non-Hydropower Sector

Category	FY2008	FY2009	FY2010	FY2011	FY2012	FY2013
						Prel.
			(in Nu million)			
Current Account	**–8,342.7**	**–10,504.1**	**–16,734.7**	**–19,741.0**	**–17,562.5**	**–15,580.7**
Trade Balance	–7,445.4	–12,650.6	–18,177.5	–22,444.0	–22,509.8	–18,374.8
Exports	18,121.8	13,701.1	14,066.4	19,884.2	21,131.8	20,089.5
Imports	25,567.2	26,351.7	32,243.9	42,328.3	43,641.7	38,464.3
Services, Net	–2,455.4	–1,327.0	–1,131.9	–343.5	–1,460.7	2,809.7
Income, Net	153.7	–2.8	–1,781.5	–3,160.1	–4,370.7	–7,146.9
Current Transfers	1,404.5	3,476.3	4,356.2	6,206.7	10,778.7	7,131.3
Credit	3,456.4	5,181.9	6,435.0	8,562.2	12,907.3	8,417.7
Of which: Budgetary Grants	2,574.8	4,001.7	4,669.7	6,540.0	9,020.7	4,716.2
Debit	2,051.8	1,705.6	2,078.8	2,355.5	2,128.6	1,286.4
Capital and Financial Account	**5,492.7**	**7,618.7**	**10,056.9**	**13,863.8**	**9,623.2**	**9,232.9**
Capital Account: Budgetary Grants for Invest.	3,360.6	2,510.6	3,920.6	3,957.7	3,436.5	4,698.6
Financial Account	2,132.1	5,108.1	6,136.4	9,906.1	6,186.6	4,534.2
Foreign direct investment	125.0	865.8	3,468.6	1,408.8	1,209.7	1,166.8
Of which: Equity capital	29.9	349.1	753.3	770.5	589.3	1,111.3
Portfolio Investment	0.0	0.0	0.0	0.0	0.0	0.0
Other investment (net chg. in assets less net chg. in liabil.) 1/	2,007.1	4,242.3	2,667.8	8,497.3	4,976.9	3,367.5
Net acquisition of financial assets	512.6	–396.4	57.9	–147.6	–63.4	934.4

Net acquisition of financial liabilities	2,519.8	3,846.0	2,725.7	8,349.7	4,913.6	4,301.9
o/w RGOB loans excl. hydropower	556.6	1,812.7	1,561.4	3,248.1	2,399.7	5,739.5
o/w Other loans	2,150.0	1,988.3	444.0	4,618.7	2,950.8	–512.9
Net Errors and Omissions	557.9	2,321.1	3,354.0	–1,823.4	–9,271.4	4,962.8
Overall Balance for Non-Hydropower Activities	**–2,292.0**	**–564.4**	**–3,323.7**	**–7,700.6**	**–17,210.7**	**–1,385.0**
Overall balance excluding errors and omissions	–2,849.9	–2,885.5	–6,677.7	–5,877.2	–7,939.4	–6,347.8
Memo: Overall Balance, hydro plus non-hydro sectors	**688.6**	**6,572.6**	**4,410.0**	**797.5**	**–9,068.4**	**9,212.2**

Note: RGOB = Royal Government of Bhutan.

Source: RMA (2013).

The Central Government Budget Is Not a Major Source of the Problem (at least not directly)

Karma Ura, President of the Centre for Bhutan Studies and GNH Research, has argued that the government has contributed to the BoP problem by boosting civil service employment, which attracts workers from and drives up wages in the private sector, thereby encouraging private firms to use less expensive imported workers on construction projects (Ura 2013). While these secondary effects may be relevant and will be discussed later, the direct impact of on-budget fiscal policy outside the hydropower sector on the BoP appears to be modest.

Macroeconomic theory holds that a country's savings-minus-investment balance—the difference between gross national savings and total investment—equals (and is, in fact, identical to) the current account balance (CAB) in the BoP. In mathematical terms, this can be expressed as

$$S - I = CAB \tag{1}$$

where S is gross national savings (gross national disposable income less total consumption) and I is total investment. When the current account records a deficit, total investment exceeds gross national savings and foreign financing (FDI, grants for investment, and net borrowing) is needed to fund the shortfall.

The economy's savings-minus-investment balance can be decomposed into separate balances for the public and private (government and non-government) sectors. Thus, equation (1) can be rewritten as:

$$(S - I)_g + (S - I)_{ng} = CAB \tag{2}$$

where $(S - I)_g$ represents the savings-minus-investment balance for the government sector and $(S - I)_{ng}$ is the balance for the non-government sector. The government's savings-minus-investment balance turns out to be equal to the overall budget balance, excluding net lending. Thus, the government's contribution to the economy-wide CAB can be determined by examining the overall fiscal balance, ideally excluding net lending. If net lending is included and represents a net outflow from the government budget, any deficit in the overall fiscal balance arguably exceeds the government's contribution to the external current account deficit.

Table 1.6 presents a summary of the central government budget—the main element comprising the government sector—as a percentage of GDP, along with the external CAB for FY2001–FY2013.[4] The table shows that the budget deficit has not been a major contributor to the CAB since FY2006, when the budget deficit fell below 3 per cent of GDP. Between FY2007 and FY2010, the government recorded budget surpluses. Although deficits re-emerged between FY2011 and FY2013, official data show that these deficits never exceeded 2.1 per cent of GDP except FY2013 and represented less than 10 per cent of the overall current account deficit, which itself equalled 20 per cent or more of GDP. Off-budget and unrecorded government activity may play a role in Bhutan's BoP difficulties. However, it appears unlikely that the central government's budget has been a major contributor to the current account deficit since FY2008.

Other Factors

Since neither the hydropower sector nor the central government budget is a major source of the current account deficit, something else must be. The answer can be found in the non-government sector: specifically, the demand for import of goods and services arising from firms, households, and state-owned enterprises (SOEs). Although SOEs represent an important part of Bhutan's economy, the private sector (households and private firms) appears to be the significant contributor to the problem, partly as a result of the buoyant credit conditions that led private sector credit to grow by nearly 32 per cent in FY2011 and almost 30 per cent in FY2012.

How can the private sector be the main source of the current account deficit? The answer lies in the nature of Bhutan's economy. Apart from tourism, electricity generation, trade, and mineral production, Bhutan's economy produces few goods and services. Because tourism and the hydropower sector employ relatively few people, most of the adult population is engaged in subsistence agriculture. As noted earlier, average educational attainment is low, while those who complete secondary or higher education have few opportunities to apply their skills outside

[4] The International Monetary Fund (2011: 20–1) shows higher budget deficits through 2011, but the deficits were still only a small fraction of the current account deficit.

Table 1.6 Bhutan: Summary Government Budget

	FY2001	FY2002	FY2003	FY2004	FY2005	FY2006	FY2007	FY2008	FY2009	FY2010	FY2011	FY2012	FY2013
	(in per cent of GDP)												
Revenues and Grants	41.2	36.3	25.6	36.5	30.9	35.0	35.7	35.2	40.4	46.4	35.8	35.8	30.2
Expenditure and Net Lending	53.0	41.4	36.1	34.6	37.9	35.9	35.1	34.4	38.5	44.7	37.9	36.9	34.4
Overall Balance	−11.8	−5.0	−10.5	1.9	−7.0	−0.8	0.6	0.8	1.9	1.6	−2.1	−1.1	−4.2
GDP at current market prices[a]	21,107.6	24,292.7	27,540.0	30,409.8	33,978.8	38,392.8	45,065.1	52,100.4	57,982.4	66,858.6	78,723.3	91,201.5	101,415.7
Memo: Current account balance	−9.2	−15.8	−24.2	−18.5	−30.9	−4.4	8.2	−8.6	−6.3	−22.2	−30.0	−21.7	−25.4

Notes: 1. GDP = gross domestic product.

2. [a]For FY2011 through FY 2013: calculated from calendar year data for 2010 through 2014.

Sources: Data provided by the Royal Government of Bhutan; ADB (2014).

of the government. Though Ura (2013) views government as competing with the private sector, the private sector can employ only a small percentage of graduates. Moreover, the virtual absence of industry means that almost all consumption and investment goods must be imported. Earned income therefore generates demand for imports; various observers have commented that the import propensity of income in Bhutan is high.[5] Relatively high per capita incomes in a region where per capita incomes are typically far lower aggravate the problem by making domestic agricultural production expensive, thereby creating demand for imported fruits and vegetables and encouraging local builders to hire foreign labourers who will accept lower wages (Ura 2013: 8).

However, the basic problem is that Bhutan produces little those citizens earning an income want to buy. Unless competitive domestic industries develop to reduce the demand for imports—or earnings from tourism and hydropower grow exponentially to exceed the cost of imports, services, and debt service payments—it is hard to see how the BoP problem can be resolved without restraining private sector imports either through controls or more market-oriented measures. Devaluing the ngultrum, which is currently pegged at one-to-one to the Indian rupee, would cause sharp increases in debt service payments and possibly trigger serious inflation since most goods are imported from India, thereby cutting or even eliminating the gains in competitiveness from the exchange rate adjustment. If devaluation is to be avoided, what else can be done to reduce private demand for imports? Alternatively, how can foreign earnings from exports of goods and services increase sufficiently to meet private demand, particularly for consumer goods and services?

Policy Options

Boosting Exports of Goods and Services

1. *Increasing tourism.* One option to address the BoP problem is to boost earnings from tourism. Although the government has been reluctant to allow a massive increase in the number of tourists, it has

[5] Ura (2013: 8) finds that the marginal propensity to import is 0.63. Rashid (2013: 4) contends that the elasticity of imports to real economic growth exceeded 2.0 during 2010 and 2011.

allowed growth in high-end tourism. Tourist arrivals rose 41.4 per cent to about 42,000 and tourist earnings increased 48.4 per cent to $55.8 million in FY2012. Arrivals rose an additional 6 per cent and earnings 13.8 per cent in FY2013. However, arrivals and earnings appear to have declined slightly during the first half of FY2014 compared with the same period in FY2013.[6] Presumably, these figures could rise again in future years, with the government aiming to increase average receipts per tourist.

2. *Promoting exports of agricultural products.* Another way to boost exports would be to promote the production and sale of agricultural products. Bhutan's large herds and temperate climate give it a natural advantage in the production of dairy products including yogurt and cheese, and processed fruits and vegetables. Its location on India's border provides a ready market for such products. Thus, it would be worthwhile to explore expanding Bhutan's existing manufacturing facilities for milk, juice, produce, and related products. In addition, steps could be taken to expand Bhutan's private sector, which currently accounts for only about 8 per cent of GDP. Although Bhutan receives some FDI, the investment climate could be stronger. Bhutan ranked 141st out of 189 economies in the World Bank's Doing Business survey in 2014, with especially low scores in getting construction permits (132), protecting investors (147), trading across borders (172), and resolving insolvency (189) (World Bank 2013). Reforms are under way in other areas covered by the Doing Business survey, including ease of starting a business (Bhutan is currently ranked 89th), and getting credit (Bhutan is currently ranked 109th). Bhutan's Parliament is also considering reforms to allow the registration of partnerships and sole proprietorships, remove the requirement for separate operating licences, allow online company registration, and eliminate the need for company seals (World Bank 2014).
3. *Boosting education to promote employment, including overseas workers and migrant remittances.* While Bhutan spent 7.3 per cent of GDP and nearly 17 per cent of government outlays on education in FY2012, public schooling is assured only through grade 10 and educational attainment in Bhutan lags behind that of its per capita level income peers.[7]

[6] See Table 17 in RMA (2014).

[7] See Table 17 in RMA (2014).

Helping reach children in poor areas and areas where attendance falls short of full enrolment and strengthening education through grade 12 and at the college level could prove a good investment, particularly since Bhutanese students have already developed a strong facility in English. Although some graduates could fill existing vacancies in the private sector and SOEs, particularly in the construction sector, well-designed programmes to promote the placement of Bhutanese graduates abroad—as India and the Philippines have done—could generate increased worker remittances as one means of improving the BoP. Such a programme would be especially useful in light of Bhutan's youthful population and the limited job opportunities for highly educated workers.

4. *Raising revenue from electricity.* A fourth option could be to revisit the terms of Bhutan's existing arrangements with India and raise prices for electricity exports. This approach may be difficult because Bhutan relies heavily on budgetary grants and loans from India. Any effort to adjust electricity tariffs could lead to offsetting reductions in such assistance. Thus, the other options discussed might be preferable.

Curbing Private Sector Imports

1. *Developing competitive, import-substituting consumer industries* (for example, food production). One way to reduce private sector imports would be to develop competitive, import-substituting consumer industries. The food industry would seem a prime candidate for this initiative. Ura (2013) notes that relatively low productivity and rising labour costs have encouraged imports of fruits and vegetables despite Bhutan's natural advantages in production. By tailoring education to support agriculture and investing in appropriate infrastructure, Bhutan could help restore the attractiveness of domestically produced fruits and vegetables. In addition, investments in food processing could promote the development of competitive, domestically produced substitutes for imported processed foods. With the Dungsam Cement Company beginning production, Bhutan should also be able to increase cement production and reduce imports of construction materials. This could extend to other products if Bhutan can develop

competitive ways to make higher-value-added products from its existing mineral resources.

2. *Using monetary policy to curb consumer lending, especially for cars and construction materials.* Since March 2012, Bhutan has used monetary and regulatory policies to discourage consumer lending as a way of curbing imports. As noted earlier, lending rates were raised for all financial institutions. In addition, the RMA still maintains a ban on lending for private vehicles and housing. While these restrictions severely limit consumer choice, they have helped restrain imports and reorient borrowing towards business activities. If the BoP improves over time, replacing these outright bans with limits on the ratio of loan to asset value—for example, limiting loans to 50 per cent of a vehicle or property's value—would be more in line with regulatory policies in other market economies.
3. *Replacing import bans with excise taxes.* Another market-oriented approach to curb consumer imports would be to replace existing bans with excise taxes, which are special levies that raise the price of an item. Because vehicles are imported, an excise tax could be imposed on vehicles at the border in a manner similar to customs duties. This would, however, avoid the need to impose formal customs duties, which might contravene existing trade agreements with India. Excise taxes related to private construction might involve excises on imported construction equipment and materials not going towards hydropower or business projects. Another option would be to impose fees on newly constructed buildings when issuing occupancy permits.

Excise taxes have the advantage of letting private demand determine who imports vehicles and construction equipment and in what quantity. In addition, these measures would raise government revenue, providing additional funding for education and business development programmes. However, replacing import bans with heavy excises could also open the door for smuggling. Despite Bhutan's reputation for transparency and good governance, private contractors might have an incentive in some cases to bribe customs officials for a certification exempting imported construction equipment and materials from excise taxes.

Given the limited number and modest incomes of customs officers, it might be simpler to maintain the existing bans until such time as they can be lifted, at which point general excise taxes applicable to all vehicle and construction-related imports could be imposed.

★★★

Bhutan's rapid growth and limited domestic resources have produced a fragile BoP situation that is likely to persist for a decade or more, or at least until planned hydropower projects are fully operational in FY2026. With little domestic industry to expand, rising incomes will likely mean rising imports and a steadily deteriorating external CAB unless other measures are taken. The measures implemented thus far, which include blocking certain imports and banning lending for private vehicles and housing, represent a severe constraint on private sector development. Thus, other policies are worth exploring as alternatives. For example, promoting growth in high-end ecotourism is one option to address the BoP problem while also preserving the environment. Progress being made towards boosting average receipts per tourist, rather than focusing on increasing the number of tourist arrivals, is evidenced in the growth in Bhutan's tourist earnings outpacing growth in tourist arrivals in FY2012 and FY2013.

Improving the business climate to facilitate both domestic investment and FDI, particularly in agricultural and mineral products; expanding measures to boost education and promote foreign employment opportunities for Bhutanese graduates, thereby generating increased remittances; establishing relatively low loan-to-value ceilings for loans on private vehicles and construction materials; and instituting sizable excise taxes on vehicles and private housing units may offer more market-friendly alternatives to the current bans on private imports and lending for vehicles and housing. Until more domestic industries are developed, however, some measures will be needed to keep private imports from exacerbating the BoP problem.

References

Asian Development Bank (ADB). 2013. *Asian Development Outlook 2013*. Manila.

______. 2014. *Asian Development Outlook 2014*. Manila.

Economist Intelligence Unit. 2012a. *The Authorities Move to Curb Foreign Outflows*. 3 May, available at http://country.eiu.com/article.aspx?articleid=46901183

1&Country=Bhutan&topic=Economy&subtopic=Current+policy&oid=47781589&aid=1 (last accessed on 23 April 2014).

______. 2012b. *The RMA Cuts the Cash Reserve Ratio*. 3 May, available at http://country.eiu.com/article.aspx?articleid=469011831&Country=Bhutan&topic=Economy&subtopic=Current+policy&oid=47781589&aid=1 (last accessed on 23 April 2014).

International Monetary Fund. 2011. *Bhutan: 2011 Article IV Consultation—Staff Report*. Washington, DC, available at http://www.imf.org/external/pubs/ft/scr/2011/cr11123.pdf (last accessed on 23 April 2014).

Rashid, H. 2013. *Understanding the Causes of the Rupee Shortfall*. New York: United Nations Department of Social Affairs, available at http://www.un.org/en/development/desa/policy/capacity/country_documents/Understanding%20the%20Rupee%20Shorfall.pdf (last accessed on 23 April 2014).

Royal Monetary Authority of Bhutan (RMA). 2013. *Annual Report 2012/13*. Thimphu.

______. 2014. *Monthly Statistical Bulletin*. March. Thimphu.

United Nations Development Programme (UNDP). 2013. *Human Development Report 2013*. New York.

Ura, K. 2013. 'The Rupee Crisis: Macroeconomic Causes and Cures', *The Bhutanese*, 4 October, available at http://www.thebhutanese.bt/the-rupee-crisis-macroeconomic-causes-and-cures-2/ (last accessed on 23 April 2014).

World Bank. 2013. *Ease of Doing Business in Bhutan*, available at http://www.doingbusiness.org/data/exploreeconomies/bhutan (last accessed on 23 April 2014).

______. 2014. *Bhutan Country Snapshot*. March, available at http://www.worldbank.org/content/dam/Worldbank/document/SAR/bhutan-country-snapshot-spring-2014.pdf (last accessed on 23 April 2014).

2

PATRICK GUILLAUMONT*

Vulnerability and Resilience

A Conceptual Framework for Bhutan

The last three decades of economic development have presented the world's economies with avenues for economic growth and development based on global integration and cooperation. Many Asian economies have leveraged the opportunity provided by an accommodating economic environment to obtain levels of growth thought to be inaccessible by preceding generations. However, these opportunities do not come without risks. As many Asian economies realized in the late 1990s, these risks can materialize in the form of economic crises. Indeed, the recurrence of crises, shocks, and spillovers from within Asia and through interregional contagion over the past two decades has demonstrated to developing Asian economies that they need to be alert to the dangers of economic shocks in such an open environment. To economies that have made such hard-won gains, the importance of identifying their exposure to adverse economic shocks early on and building resilience to their vulnerabilities is recognized.

* The bulk of the statistical work has been done at Ferdi, France, by Sosso Feindouno. Sylviane Guillaumont Jeanneney reviewed several versions of the study. Sarah Carrington contributed to a preliminary version of this chapter. Their contributions are all strongly acknowledged.

Vulnerability does remain an issue that needs to be addressed. Both cross-country econometric studies and case studies have documented the impact of external, climatic, and political shocks on growth, development, and poverty reduction in various parts of the world. Although some progress has been made in addressing economic vulnerability, it remains limited. Moreover, the scope of vulnerability itself has been changing with the emergence of new social and environmental dimensions. In the present chapter, Bhutan and its vulnerability have been briefly introduced.

What Is Vulnerability? And Why Should It Be Measured?

Addressing vulnerability requires an identification of the sources and determinants of vulnerability, including a conceptual clarification with respect to its broadening scope. Since a country's vulnerability is the risk of being affected by exogenous events, it can be evidenced by an impact on economic variables (either related to welfare or to development), sociopolitical variables, or environmental variables. At first glance, it seems reasonable to identify three main areas of macro-vulnerability: economic, social, and environmental. These three areas of vulnerability correspond to the three dimensions generally referred to in the presentation of the agenda of sustainable development. In these three areas, vulnerability appears as the opposite of sustainability (Guillaumont 2013); it is a threat to sustainability.

Another distinction made in each of these three areas is between structural vulnerability, which depends on long-lasting or structural factors beyond the immediate control of a country, and general vulnerability, which depends both on the structural factors and a country's policies. The next section of this chapter proposes a conceptual framework in which structural economic vulnerability is distinguished from general economic vulnerability. Several vulnerability indices will be discussed as well.

There are three main reasons why the measurement of vulnerability, in particular structural vulnerability, is needed. One is the use of vulnerability indicators as a tool for monitoring the impact of policies on reducing vulnerability. Another reason, related to structural vulnerability only, is that structural vulnerability indices, which are used for the identification of least developed countries (LDCs), can also be used as criteria for the international allocation of concessional resources dedicated to development or to adaptation to climate change.

Indices of structural vulnerability provide a useful tool for the international allocation of resources in support of policies aimed at structural transformation and sustainable development. Structural vulnerability is exogenous to current policy and if adequately measured, may be a relevant criterion for the international allocation of concessional resources. A third reason, related to general vulnerability only, is the need to have indicators of the risk of occurrence of a crisis or a growth collapse.

Need for Indices Within a Conceptual Framework

Indices should be used comparatively, either over time or between countries. To be used over time and to assess changes in vulnerability, in order to compare levels of vulnerability between countries, indices should be designed and calculated in the same way and use equally reliable data. Comparisons of vulnerability indices are generally made between countries. Comparisons over time (for example, has vulnerability decreased or increased?) are less frequent.

Various vulnerability indices have been proposed reflecting economic, social, and environmental aspects of vulnerability, without a clear distinction between what is exogenous and what depends on the country policy, and without an agreed conceptual framework combining the various kinds of vulnerability. In this chapter, not only do we compare our proposed indices with those that already exist, but we also try to combine them in an integrated framework.

The main features and the evolution of vulnerability are analysed for Bhutan and compared to several groups of developing countries. Despite being on the cusp of graduation, Bhutan remains an LDC for the time being. LDCs are designated by the United Nations (UN) as poor countries suffering from structural handicaps to (sustainable) development. They are identified using three criteria: (i) low level of income per capita, (ii) low level of human capital, and (iii) high structural economic vulnerability as measured by the Economic Vulnerability Index (EVI). At the same time, the EVI should be supplemented by other indices that reflect the various dimensions of vulnerability.

If vulnerability indices are designed specifically for each possible dimension of vulnerability, there may be some overlap in the measurement of the various dimensions of vulnerability. This increases the need for an integrated framework of vulnerability analysis, encompassing indices designed specifically for each dimension. Within this framework, it should also be possible to examine the interactions among economic, social, and environmental vulnerabilities, and between structural and policy-based vulnerabilities. In particular, the link between state fragility and various kinds of structural vulnerabilities will have to be explored.

While the larger and more established market economies may have the resources and capacity to develop defences against future economic shocks, in Asia, as elsewhere, it is the small and/or remotely located economies that remain highly vulnerable to external shocks and often lack the wherewithal to protect themselves from the development reversals that usually accompany such shocks. Bhutan deserves special attention in this respect.

The Himalayan Kingdom of Bhutan, located between the People's Republic of China (PRC) and India, was considered a low-income country for a long time. Today, Bhutan is a middle-income country, committed to preserve its environment, culture, and religious values.

Bhutan's recent growth performance has been nothing less than astonishing. Its economy expanded at an average rate of 7.9 per cent during 1980–2012 and tripled its gross domestic product (GDP) per capita during 2000–12 (World Bank 2013)—all of this has been achieved against the odds. Bhutan is a remote, landlocked nation with a small population of around 766,000 inhabitants that is largely dispersed across some of the most rugged terrains in the world. In Bhutan, natural disasters such as landslides and flooding are not uncommon, and they are likely to become more common as the threat of global warming increases the likelihood of floods resulting from retreating glaciers. Geopolitically, Bhutan has a long history of tensions with the neighbouring countries and has become quite dependent on India. Its large neighbour has become Bhutan's dominant trading partner in recent years and now accounts for nearly three-quarters of Bhutan's total trade. Economically, Bhutan remains dependent on hydropower production, its one truly flourishing industry, with a gradual structural transition under way from small-scale agriculture to the barely evident manufacturing and service sectors. The large majority of employment is confined to low-productive activities in the agriculture sector. Finally, the economy's prevalence of low-skilled and vulnerable citizens makes it particularly exposed to exogenous economic shocks: literate Bhutanese make up less than 53 per cent of the adult population and about 53.1 per cent of the labour force falls into the vulnerable employment category (World Bank 2014).

While average GDP growth in Bhutan was very high during 2000–13, the growth pattern was remarkably volatile with the standard deviation of the growth rate reaching 5.3 percentage points (from mean growth of 7.9 per cent) over this period. Such volatile growth rates over such a long period (32 years) are a strong indicator of the susceptibility of output to economic disturbances. Although some of this vulnerability may be due to choices and policies made by economic managers, given Bhutan's distinct characteristics described above, it is probable that much of the observed output fluctuations are inherent in the structure and nature of the economic, geographic, and political characteristics of the country. Indeed, it is likely that this inherent vulnerability has played a key role in restraining Bhutan's development and its ability to deal with development challenges over time, instigating a vicious circle. Certainly, there is much evidence that economic volatility has the potential to cause severe negative impacts on development prospects, particularly impacting the most vulnerable.

Bhutan has been a recipient of large sums of development assistance from multilateral institutions and bilateral aid agreements for more than three decades. Hence, the growth volatility could have been much worse. The assistance is likely to have masked the underlying vulnerability by providing a buffer, without which Bhutan may have experienced large economic downturns. Consequently, while growth instability has not historically led to significant contractions in GDP, the questions of whether Bhutan's exposure to macroeconomic shocks will increase and what it can do to counter them has become important, as Bhutan consolidates its middle-income status and the development assistance subsides. With this in mind, the increasing share of national income generated by tourism is a growth driver as well as a source of vulnerability.

Will Bhutan's exposure to macroeconomic shocks increases as aid assistance reduces? And if so, to what extent it is within Bhutan's power to voluntarily reduce this exposure? Essentially, the answers and their implications depend on the nature of vulnerability in each country. Whether some countries are innately more vulnerable to unstable growth than others is an area of research that has been gaining increasing attention in both the academic and policy-focused literature.[1]

[1] Much attention has been given both to small island developing states and LDCs. As part of this, measures of a country's level of vulnerability have been developed (see, for example, Guillaumont 2009a).

Our chapter investigates the extent to which Bhutan's exposure to economic shocks is inherent (structural) (Guillaumont 2009b, 2013), and to what extent it is brought about by actions taken by the economic managers (policy-induced).

Further, while such economic vulnerability is inherent in Bhutan, it can also build resilience by fostering economic adaptability in the face of exogenous shocks. Given that the resilience of the country will impact the net vulnerability, the degree to which the countries remain resilient in the face of adverse shocks is also examined. The generation of an early warning system that forewarns of increased vulnerability is of potential interest as it can mitigate the development of policy-induced vulnerability. Such an early warning system is designed to indicate when an economy is accumulating imbalances in a way that makes it susceptible to the adverse effects of an economic shock. Correspondingly, this chapter establishes a set of customized measures that form a benchmark against which structural features and policies can be assessed to achieve a flexible and resilient economy.

A Conceptual Framework for the Measurement of Vulnerability and Resilience

The international community seems to be increasingly aware that vulnerability matters and it has various dimensions. But, paradoxically, the more it is seen as being important, the more it becomes elusive and the more a general conceptual framework is needed. As the international community has modified its understanding of the role that vulnerability plays in development over time, so have the measures that are used to capture the concept of vulnerability evolved. Economic vulnerability can itself be assessed as a short-term conjunctural feature, or as a long-term structural one.

Conjunctural Approaches to the Measurement of Economic Vulnerability and Their Limitations

Existing measures of vulnerability are targeted to capture the circumstances under which countries are prone to crisis episodes (Dabla–Norris and Gündüz 2014). This vulnerability refers to the risk of occurrences of growth collapses or balance of payments crises triggered by exogenous shocks that only occur due to underlying economic imbalances.

In the aftermath of the 1997/98 Asian financial crisis, international institutions such as the International Monetary Fund (IMF) and the World Bank started to measure variables that were associated with financial crises and denote threshold levels of these variables as indicative of vulnerability. The risk of occurrence of a crisis is estimated on a large set of countries by panel econometric (probit) models with various kinds of explanatory variables, including (i) size of and exposure to the shocks, (ii) rate of exchange (mis)alignment, (iii) stock of external reserves, (iv) debt-to-GDP ratios, and (v) growth patterns and previous occurrence of crises. The level of crisis probability is then taken as a vulnerability index or an 'early warning system' (Dabla–Norris and Gündüz 2014). When economic imbalances exist in key sectors of the economy, the economy becomes more susceptible to growth collapses or financial crises that arise from an exogenous shock.

While the probability of a crisis reflects the current or conjunctural vulnerability of a country, it does not reflect structural economic vulnerability, which is less transitory and does not depend on present policy stances. Similarly, approaches for determining vulnerable economies primarily that consider growth volatility—an indicator widely used on account of its apparent simplicity and alleged impact on average growth (Ramey and Ramey 1995)—also miss the mark. The standard deviation of the annual growth rate of GDP per capita over a given number of years (for example, 9–10 years) is generally a proxy for growth volatility (World Bank 2014). However, this approach is not appropriate for the measurement of structural economic vulnerability for several reasons. The main reason is that growth rate instability may result not just from structural factors, but also from transitory and reversible ones. It may then reflect changes in domestic policy. Finally, the measurement of growth rate instability is highly sensitive to the length of the period covered. It should cover a minimum number of years to reflect a structural feature; but the longer the period, the higher the risk that the standard deviation simply reflects a trend change.

If the aim of measuring vulnerability is to capture the extent to which countries are intrinsically vulnerable, regardless of their policy choices, then a measure that captures structural economic vulnerability is needed. This objective is shared by multilateral donors, for example, when they use a vulnerability measure as an input to aid allocation decisions; a structurally vulnerable country is likely to be allocated a larger amount of grants or concessional loans.

Structural Economic Vulnerability and Its Components

To effectively present the concept of structural economic vulnerability, we must use wording similar to that used in the previous publications, in particular Guillaumont (2014), which applies the same concept to African countries instead of Asian countries. Vulnerability, at both the macro and micro level, is the risk of being hampered by exogenous shocks, whether natural (for example, droughts) or external (for example, fall in terms of trade). Structural vulnerability includes factors that do not depend on a country's current policies and is entirely determined by exogenous and persistent factors; general vulnerability also includes the effect of current and future policies, and therefore changes more rapidly (Guillaumont 1999, 2006). Accordingly, the index that we propose captures only the factors that make a country structurally vulnerable. A country's structural economic vulnerability should also be understood as the risk for a country of having its economic growth, and more generally its development rate, slowed by exogenous shocks occurring independently of its own policy choices. It is not only a risk of static loss of welfare. The factors to be taken into account in the design and measurement of structural economic vulnerability should be the ones that likely to lower the rate of economic growth. An even broader meaning of structural economic vulnerability would include the risk of country's development becoming unsustainable, again because of shocks and factors independent of its will (Guillaumont 2014).

Further, the proposed conceptual framework distinguishes between vulnerability and lack of resilience. Resilience refers to the capacity to cope with exogenous shocks using decisive measures to become more adaptable. In this sense, there are two main dimensions of country vulnerability—intensity of shocks and the economy's sensitivity to these shocks—and one dimension of resilience, which encompasses the measures taken to improve the country's mitigation capacity when shocks hit. Thus, the essential elements to capture for each shock type are:

- size of exogenous shocks;
- country's exposure to those shocks (for example, a small population size); and
- country's resilience or capacity to cope with or adapt to them.

Structural vulnerability thus results from the sum of the expected impacts from shocks over a given period, which is based on the size of the shocks and the country's exposure to them. General vulnerability also depends on the resilience of the country to the shock, as it relates more to the current policy and less to the structural factors. There are indeed structural factors that determine the resilience of a country, such as its level of human capital and, more generally, its level of development or income per capita. Most often, however, income per capita or level of human capital are not taken into account in the measurement of structural economic vulnerability since these factors are used together with EVI as complementary criteria for the identification of LDCs. In our framework, however, we will be considering these factors since we are proposing a measure that aims at incorporating all information that indicates the level of structural vulnerability. For instance, the EVI does not include income per capita and level of human capital since their values are used separately as LDC identification criteria. However, in our framework for measuring vulnerability, we will be considering these structural factors in the assessment of vulnerability as we are not using them for separate functions. The ways by which these factors will be included are discussed in the third section.

Towards an Economic Vulnerability Index: Origin, Revisions, and Remaining Gaps

With the objective of quantifying innate macroeconomic vulnerability, the UN's Committee for Development Policy (CDP) in 2000 began to design a composite measure which reflects the intensity of recurrent shocks to economies, both natural and external. The present structure of this index was designed in 2005 (Guillaumont 2009a, 2009b; United Nations 2008). It was used for the triennial reviews of the list of LDCs in 2006, 2009, and 2012 (Guillaumont 2013). Its principle is to combine with equal weights a group of three subindices that reflect the intensity of recurrent shocks, natural and external, and a group of four or five subindices reflecting exposure to those shocks.[2] The structure of the index is shown in Figure 2.1 in its 2006, 2009, and 2012 (revised) versions.

[2] The weights have been arbitrarily assigned by the UN's CDP with the aim of setting a balance between exposure and shocks components.

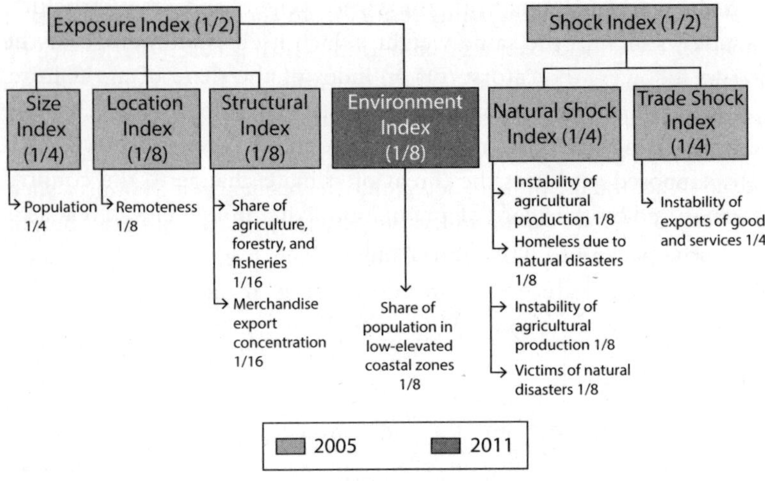

FIGURE 2.1 Economic Vulnerability Index, 2005–9 and 2011–12
Source: Designed from United Nations (2005, 2011).

The main change in the 2012 revised version was the addition of an environmental component measuring the share of population living in low coastal areas (located less than 5 metre above sea level), which was compensated for by reducing the weight of another component (small population size).

The structure and components of the EVI are presented in Figure 2.2 (for more details, see Cariolle and Goujon 2013; Guillaumont 2009b, 2015; United Nations 2008):

1. As for the intensity of recurrent shocks, two indices are retained with equal weight: (a) one reflecting the trade shocks, measured by the intensity of the exports of goods and services; and (b) the other reflecting the natural shocks, measured by the average of two indices: one being the instability of agricultural production and the other an index of the number of victims of natural disasters (which replaced in 2012 an index of the homeless population due to natural disasters).
2. As for the exposure to these shocks, the index combines five (four prior to 2012) indicators: (a) an index of smallness of population size, with one-fourth of the exposure index, that is, one-eighth of the EVI (previously one-half of the exposure index, that is, one-fourth of the EVI); (b) an index of location that measures the remoteness from the

main world markets with the same weight; and (c) a structural index, still with the same weight, which itself is an average of the two following indicators: (c1) an index of the share of agriculture, forestry, and fisheries in GDP, and (c2) an index of merchandise export concentration; and (d) an environment index (since 2012) that is supposed to reflect the threat of climate change to the country, measured by the share of population living in low elevated coastal areas (less than 5 metre above sea level).

Although the EVI set up by the CDP seems to be the best index of structural economic vulnerability presently used, and the only one officially endorsed by the UN for the identification of the LDCs and as an aid allocation criterion for smoothing their graduation, it is not a perfect index. While the EVI has maintained a focus on structural characteristics to measure vulnerability, it has extended itself to allow for environmental sources of vulnerability, but has not done so comprehensively. As such, several key measures of vulnerability—even those that fall on the same spectrum—are missing from the framework.

The new environmental component encompasses exposure to flooding from rising sea levels but does not combine this with a comparable indicator that would reflect the exposure to aridity in those countries with a large share of dry land, which is prone to droughts and threatened by water scarcity. Correcting much of this bias (for the use of the index) is relatively straightforward. It requires balancing the low elevation coastal zones (LECZ) component with a dry land zones (DLZ) component. This could be the share of arid (but not desert) lands in the total non-desert area of the country, or the share of the population living in dry land (and possibly in desert areas). Such an index can be calculated using the definitions of arid and desert areas provided by the United Nations Environment Programme as has been done by La Fondation pour les Études et Recherches sur le Développement International (Ferdi) (Guillaumont 2014). This DLZ index can be included either as averaged with the LECZ index, or by taking the maximum of the two indices (LECZ and DLZ).

Second, another default of the new LECZ component is that it only captures the risk of flooding due to the impact of global warming on sea level. However, the risk of flooding as a consequence of global warming is related not only to the rise in sea level, but also to the melting of lake glaciers, which is particularly relevant for Bhutan.

Another feature of the EVI is that it recognizes the exposure associated with having a high concentration of exports (the index of which is produced by United Nations Conference on Trade and Development [UNCTAD]), but only accounts for exports of merchandise and not of services. The concentration of exports of services may be a source of vulnerability, in particular for tourism sector. In Bhutan, the export of services through tourism represents a significant (although changing) part of the total export of goods and services. According to World Development Indicators (WDI), the figures for 2011 and 2012 are 10.2 per cent and 13.5 per cent respectively, in Bhutan (World Bank 2014). However, even without a conceivable synthetic index of the concentration of goods and services, vulnerability due to service exports is captured through the instability of exports of goods and services as a shock index rather than as an exposure index.

Not included (or only partially included) in the services are the remittances, which in the case of Bhutan represent only 2.7 per cent of the total export of goods, services, and remittances, or the equivalent of 0.9 per cent of the GDP (World Bank 2014).

A related factor that impacts vulnerability, and one that is likely to be specific to small countries such as Bhutan, is having a very concentrated mix of output and exports. In Bhutan's case, the hydropower sector comprised 9.8 per cent of GDP and 31.2 per cent of all exports in fiscal year (FY) 2014 (RMA 2014), a proportion that indeed affects the export concentration coefficient of Bhutan. However, as we shall see, the level of this coefficient is not so high compared with those of other LDCs. It might be due to a rather diversified structure of exports other than hydropower (RMA various years). For Bhutan, the dominant hydropower sector is the key driver of the economy, and anything that hurts or hinders its output, trade, or revenue also puts the entire economy at risk. With regard to the risks faced by the country, it also appears that the exposure components do not include any indicator of the geographical concentration of exports, which can be high in a country like Bhutan, as we would see in the third section.

Thus, the EVI, as it is presently designed or might be revised, can only give a partial assessment of structural economic vulnerability, since it does not take into account the structural components of resilience, which are numerous and depend on the overall level of development.

Social factors of a structural nature include variables such as the level of human capital and its distribution throughout the economy, as well as the median or the average level of income. Further, a higher incidence of absolute poverty is likely to result in a reduced capacity to cope with adverse shocks.

To sum up, the present EVI may lack a few components which could have been included in what we can call an 'augmented EVI'. These components include the risk of ice melting as an indicator of shock, the geographical concentration of exports, and the share of the population living in arid or desert areas.

Structural Resilience within a Broader Index of Structural Economic Vulnerability

The economy's structural characteristics that create a lack of resilience are also essentially sources of structural vulnerability as well as those that linked to the overall level of development. Measures that give information about the level of human capital (such as health and education, and variables that influence the ability of countries to respond to shocks), as well as overall level of income per capita (a variable which tells us how well the inhabitants of a country are able to face weather shocks on average) are critical characteristics impacting on structural vulnerability. Specifically, where human capital and income levels are particularly low, economies do not have the flexibility or resources to respond adaptively to shocks. Further, as such countries are prone to being hit harder by shocks, they fall into a 'trap' or a vicious circle where, because they are underdeveloped, they bear more costs as the result of a shock, which further lowers their human capital and income levels over time, leaving them even more vulnerable in the future (Guillaumont 2009a). In essence, the risk of getting trapped, results from the conjunction of structural economic vulnerability and low human capital in countries with low income per capita. This is the reason why a low level of income per capita, a high EVI, and a low level of human capital are considered complementary criteria for the identification of the LDCs.

In this chapter, we propose a measure that aims at incorporating all the information that indicates the level of structural vulnerability of Bhutan. The measure that is accepted as one encompassing human components of structural resilience is that of the Human Assets Index (HAI). This is a composite index of health and education indicators. It is conceivable to aggregate the EVI and the low level of HAI in a composite Structural Handicap Index (SHI), which is a measure of structural economic vulnerability in a broad sense, allowing for a limited substitutability between EVI and HAI to remain consistent with the initial hypothesis of complementarity between these two handicaps.

Is Resilience Measurable?

Resilience depends on so many factors that, in the end, it is difficult to measure. However, a proxy indicator could be estimated through a regression of growth volatility on EVI, run on a large sample of countries (as suggested in Guillaumont 2009b). The residual, that is, the part of growth volatility not explained by structural economic vulnerability, would be a proxy of economic resilience. If EVI only is considered as an explanatory variable, the proxy includes the impact of the structural factors of resilience, such as the level of human capital and income per capita. If these last two factors are added into the regression as well as EVI, the residual would only be a proxy of the nonstructural resilience.

There are several limitations to this tentative measurement of resilience. Some are related to the estimation method, in particular the measurement of growth volatility itself and the possible omission of structural factors of volatility.

More importantly, resilience may also operate through a weak transmission of growth volatility to the average growth rate. Then a supplementary proxy of resilience would be given by the residual of an estimation of the average growth rate as a function of growth volatility (and other structural factors). A proxy of total resilience in terms of growth would be given by the residual of an estimation of the average growth rate as a function of EVI: with other structural factors of growth included in the regression, in particular HAI and gross national income per capita (GNIpc), the residual would become a proxy of nonstructural resilience.

Resilience may also operate through a weak transmission of exogenous shocks and income volatility to the social dimensions of development. For instance, as far as it is now well-established on a cross-country basis that exogenous shocks and income volatility have detrimental consequences on variables such as poverty, crime, and corruption (Cariolle 2016; Guillaumont 2009a), so a lower than expected reaction of these variables to shocks and volatility reveals the resilience of a country. In Bhutan, where the concept of gross national happiness is intended to replace the gross national income, resilience could be assessed as a weak reaction of gross national happiness to exogenous shocks.

Vulnerability to Climate Change: Physical versus General Vulnerability

The conceptual definitions given in the introduction of this section are those we previously used in other works applied to another set of countries (see, for instance, Guillaumont 2015).

Since the meaning of sustainability, as reflected in the Sustainable Development Goals of the UN's post-2015 development agenda, now covers several dimensions—economic, environmental, and sociopolitical—the vulnerability to climate change should deserve special attention. Indeed, some climatic factors of economic vulnerability are already taken into account in the design of the EVI, in particular through the components of the index of natural shocks (the instability of agricultural production and the percentage of the population affected by natural disasters) or through some of the components of exposure, in particular the share of agriculture, forestry, and fisheries in the GDP and the new indicator of population living in low elevated coastal areas. But these indicators are related to permanent geoeconomic features and to any kind of shocks, but not to climate change per se. Vulnerability to climate change, which is a vulnerability to a specific kind of shock, stems from a risk of long-term change in geophysical conditions rather than from a growth handicap in the medium term. In other words, it is more physical than economic, and has a longer time horizon. As with structural economic vulnerability, and in fact more so, the physical vulnerability to climate change is designed to be independent of present (and future) country policy. For this reason, its measurement should be based only on physical characteristics and trends, as is the case in the

Physical Vulnerability to Climate Change Index (PVCCI)[3] established by Ferdi (see Guillaumont and Simonet 2011a), which is a distinctive feature of this index compared to other assessments of the vulnerability to climate change.

Physical vulnerability to climate change, like structural economic vulnerability, should reflect two main kinds of components: shock intensity due to climate change (for example, the sea level rise) and the exposure to this shock (for example, the share of areas likely to be flooded). The lack of socio-economic components in the design of a PVCCI is all the more legitimate given that any assessment of future adaptation capacity is highly uncertain. Because it is controversial to forecast the likely socio-economic consequences of climate change, there is a rationale for setting up an index of vulnerability which relies solely on physical components. Further, blending the measurement of structural economic vulnerability and physical vulnerability to climate change is conceivable, but it would risk blurring information about the type of vulnerability a given country is facing. The weight that would then be given to each of the two indices depends on the country's time preference (see Guillaumont 2013).

The proposed index of vulnerability to climate change— PVCCI—is summarized in Figure 2.2.

This chapter proposes the use of PVCCI, as designed in Guillaumont and Simonet (2011a) and Guillaumont (2015). As shown in Figure 2.2, this index combines the physical impact of two kinds of shocks: (a) the progressive shocks, namely flooding due to global warming, most often caused by rising sea levels (but also through other specific channels) and the aridification (two trends), and (b) the intensification of recurrent shocks in temperature and rainfall (captured by the trends in the size of the shocks) (see details in Guillaumont 2015; Guillaumont and Simonet 2011a). For these kinds of shocks, we combine an indicator of shock with an indicator of the country's exposure to the shock. Moreover, to better capture the vulnerability to any

[3] The PVCCI has been augmented from the time this chapter was written until it has been published. To find out more about the new version of the index and data, refer to Guillamumont, Simonet, Closset, and Feindouno (2016). Some information on the new index can also be found in Guillaumont (2015).

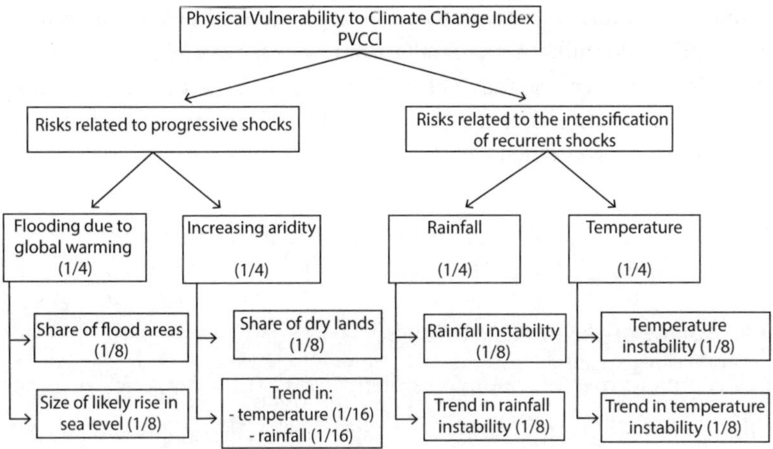

FIGURE 2.2 The Physical Vulnerability to Climate Change Index
Source: Guillaumont and Simonet (2011a).

kind of shock linked to climate change, we use a quadratic average of the main components instead of an arithmetic one.[4]

In the same way as with EVI, some important measures of vulnerability (for example, climate change) may be missing in the PVCCI, as it is presently built. For instance, in the case of the risk of flooding, it is related only to the sea level rise in the PVCCI, but not to ice melting, which may be important in countries such as Bhutan and Nepal. An augmented PVCCI should replace the risk of flooding related only to sea level rise by the risk due to any reason. Also, the risks related to the intensification of recurrent shocks, presently limited to rainfall and temperature shocks, should be extended to violent winds and cyclones.

Since this index relies on physical components, it does not take into account the resilience to climate change, neither the structural resilience nor the resilience dependent on policy (like the EVI). The structural

[4] A quadratic average is used to aggregate the various kinds of risks, those related to progressive shocks and to the intensification of progressive shocks, then for the two components of these two kinds of shocks, while each of the four components of exposure and shocks is averaged. A new version of the index in preparation will also use a quadratic average to combine shock and exposure indices.

resilience to climate change depends on the same kinds of factors for economic vulnerability, essentially the level of income per capita and the level of human capital. The policy resilience (or the lack of it), as for economic vulnerability, depends on a set of factors closely linked to sociopolitical vulnerability.

Resilience, Possibly Undermined by Sociopolitical Vulnerability and State Fragility

The Essence of the Resilience Concept

Conceptually, macroeconomic resilience comprises the policy or other transitory economic, environmental, and social factors that allow a country to be more adaptive and less exposed to an exogenous shock. One can compare two countries which are equally structurally vulnerable, but are differently abled to the weather shocks due to their levels of resilience. The more resilient economy will be one that is less exposed due to policy implementation. Policies that would fall into this category are those that (a) discourage the accumulation of large external financial imbalances (unless they are being used for productive investment that can finance the repayment of debt over time), (b) promote financial market stability and prudential behaviour by financial entities, (c) foster depth of and access to the financial system including insurance, (d) encourage responsible fiscal expenditure and adequate revenue collection, (e) facilitate a social welfare safety net to assist those who are hit adversely by exogenous shocks, (f) enable a flexible but fair labour market that allows for easy job transfer while minimizing exploitation, and (g) enable appropriate checks and balances with respect to the political and judicial systems such that accountability of decision-makers is ensured.

Lack of Resilience and State Fragility

There are also sociopolitical factors that can play an important role in the resilience of a country. State fragility—a condition where the sociopolitical structure of the country is fragile—is often presented as close to structural vulnerability, although it is conceptually quite different. State fragility is designed and identified from present policy and institutional factors (lack of state capacity, political will, and political legitimacy); it is not independent of policy actions and outcomes (Guillaumont and Guillaumont Jeanneney 2009). Accordingly, this concept is best accounted for within the (low) resilience dimension of vulnerability.[5]

Definitions of state fragility have most often come from an assessment of policies and institutions through the World Bank's Country Policy and Institutional Assessment (CPIA).[6] Countries with a low CPIA rating and/or civil conflict are often found to have weak resilience to external or natural exogenous shocks. Accordingly, countries with weak institutional and state capacity can find themselves in a 'fragility trap' (Andrimihaja, Cinyabuguma, and Devarajan 2011); countries are more fragile because they lack resilience in the face of exogenous shocks, which, in turn, weaken the resources and capacity of the state to build resilience and reduce their exposure to shocks. Those that are more innately vulnerable due to structural and physical characteristics are even more at the mercy of this vicious circle. Thus, in the framework of this chapter, state fragility is a concept related to a lack of resilience that can be partly addressed through voluntary actions over time.

Definition and Measurement of State Fragility

There are various (and often changing) definitions of 'fragile states' and measurements of 'state fragility' (see Guillaumont and Guillaumont Jeanneney 2009). Besides the lists and indices produced by private institutions or universities, lists have been set up by international organizations either for (i) operational purposes (mainly aid allocation as explained below), in particular by the multilateral banks; or (ii) simply for statistical

[5] It is important to understand that while state fragility is a measure of a lack of resilience, structural economic vulnerability significantly influences state fragility. Consequently, there are structural determinants of resilience. It has been found that the level of the country policy and institutional assessment (CPIA) is significantly and negatively influenced by the level of EVI, and among the components of the CPIA particularly by the level of export instability. The impact is all the more important when the level of CPIA is lower (see Guillaumont, McGillivray, and Wagner 2013). Other works also show evidence of the impact of the various exogenous sources of instability on the risk of civil conflict (see for instance for price and/or export instability Chauvet and Guillaumont 2007, and for droughts see Brückner and Ciccone 2010; Miguel, Satyanath, and Sergenti 2004).

[6] The CPIA includes 16 criteria grouped in four clusters (see Annexure 2B).

information and monitoring, in particular by the Organisation for Economic Co-operation and Development (OECD).

After using separate (and sometimes diverging) lists, the multilateral development banks now produce a 'harmonized list' of fragile states or countries in fragile situation: in these countries, the CPIA (not higher than 3.2, on a scale of 1 to 6),[7] or UN and/or regional peacekeeping missions or political and peacebuilding missions are present. The reference to the CPIA, which is a subjective assessment of policies, shows the contrast between state fragility and structural economic vulnerability as measured by EVI, and thus between the concepts of fragile states and LDCs.

As for the list of fragile states (revised annually) used at the OECD, 'it is assembled by combining the latest harmonized list of fragile situations of the World Bank, African Development Bank, Asian Development Bank with those countries that have a ranking above 90 on the Failed States Index developed by the Fund for Peace' (OECD 2014). For 2012, this OECD list included 47 countries, 27 of which were African countries, all south of the Sahara, all but four of which were LDCs. It is worth noting that at that time, it did not include Mali, Burkina Faso, Libya, and Egypt, showing how volatile and little informative it could be in terms of the real political risks faced by the countries. It seems more a tool for designing curative measures than for preventing the occurrence of failing states. The reason why Mali was not considered a fragile state until recently was due to previous policy improvement—Mali having a CPIA above 3.2, although it was highly vulnerable.[8]

The instability of the OECD's list of fragile states is illustrated by the changes from 47 to 51 countries during 2012–14 (OECD 2012, 2014). There were eight new countries considered fragile (three low income: Burkina Faso, Madagascar, and Mali; and five middle income: Egypt, Libya, Mauritania, Syria, and Tuvalu). Four countries were no longer

[7] This is using a harmonized average of the CPIA scores of the World Bank and the Asian Development Bank or the Africa Development Bank.

[8] This is based on the recent information note of the World Bank's Harmonized List of Fragile Situations on the CPIA, revising the threshold score for fragile states, that is, only country with overall CPIA score of 3.2 or lower is included in the fragile state list. More information on CPIA can be found at the World Bank Group. Country Policy and Institutional Assessment Database, available at http://www.worldbank.org/ida (last accessed on 10 December 2015).

considered fragile (Georgia, Iran, the Kyrgyz Republic, and Rwanda). The latest OECD publication in 2015 maintains the same number of 51 fragile states; however, Rwanda is back in the list, while Burkina Faso is not but would probably go back in the list next year due to recent events. The (shorter) harmonized list of the multilateral banks relying on the CPIAs of the World Bank, the African Development Bank, and the Asian Development Bank (ADB) has also changed between FY2013 and FY2014 with the inclusion of Madagascar, Malawi, and Mali, and with the exclusion of Angola and Guinea (the list increasing from 35 to 36 countries or territories).

The category of fragile state was introduced to solve the problem of the multilateral development banks in the performance-based allocation (PBA) of their aid. The strict application of the PBA appeared to require an exception for the states considered fragile; below a given CPIA threshold, an exception to the strict PBA rule was applied. Without discussing the consistency of the rule and its exceptions (see Guillaumont 2013; Guillaumont and Guillaumont Jeanneney 2000), it should be noted that from a methodological viewpoint, there is a built-in weakness in the category of fragile states. State fragility is indeed a big issue, but it requires a qualitative (rather than quantitative) assessment, allowing observers and donors to adapt their diagnostic and support (Collier 2009). On the contrary, structural economic vulnerability, as well as physical vulnerability to climate change, can be roughly evaluated and legitimately used for international allocation of resources (Guillaumont and Guillaumont Jeanneney 2000).

Despite its widespread use and high visibility, the identification of the fragile states does not offer a great help for the assessment of the sociopolitical vulnerability of countries. As we will see when considering the case of Bhutan, clearer information seems to emerge by using more specific and outcome-based indicators, such as those related to conflict and crime. Some components or subcomponents of the fragile states index (FSI), political stability and absence of violence (PSAV), and/or the Country Indicators for Foreign Policy (CIFP) may also offer clearer information than the composite indices in which they are included.

Violent Events as Alternative Approach to Fragility

In the previous definitions, the state fragility is identified using indicators involving a subjective assessment of policies and institutions. An alternative or complementary approach would be to assess fragility from internal violent events which by their frequency or depth reveal state fragility. It would be an outcome-based fragility.

The majority of conflicts and crimes happen in the developing countries, hindering their chances of development. A poor country is correlated with most forms of violence (United Nations Development Programme 2008). Violence is a complex and multi-faceted phenomenon, indicators of which are sometimes based on experts' judgements. Ferdi is working to propose an internal violence index (IVI) built from actual quantitative data to capture the internal violence events for 132 developing countries on an outcome basis.[9] The IVI is a weighted mean of the level of internal violence for each country during 2008–12, giving greater weight to the most recent years. Based on further analysis of the existing data, nine variables pertaining to the internal violence have been selected and divided into four clusters: internal conflicts,[10] criminality, terrorism, and political violence. Equal weight (25 per cent) is assigned to each cluster of the index. The scores of the IVI are ranked from the least violent country (0) to the most violent country (100). The average value of the index stands at 20.6. The three most violent countries are Pakistan (63), Colombia (59.90), and Syria (59.40); and the three least violent countries are Tuvalu (1.20), Singapore (0.95), and Brunei Darussalam (0.50).

A Spearman's rank correlation analysis between IVI and other fragility indices such as FSI, CPIA, and PSAV has been performed for a large sample of developing countries including small island developing states (SIDS). The results are recorded in Table 2.1. Clearly, the correlation between IVI and CPIA is low for the 70 Internal Development Association (IDA) eligible countries. Reflecting the aspects of state fragility, the components of the two indices are completely different. Nevertheless, the correlation between IVI and PSAV is relatively high for a sample of 132 countries, demonstrating that several components or variables (internal conflicts, terrorism, riots, etc.) appear in the two indices. In addition, for these common components or variables, the sources of data are the same most of time. Finally, IVI is moderately

[9] The authors try standing out against other indices often rooted in subjective judgments or experts' opinions (Feindouno, Goujon, and Wagner 2016).

[10] We exclude all external conflicts.

TABLE 2.1 Correlation between the Internal or Domestic Violence Index and Other Indices

	Spearman's Rank Correlations		
Indicators	Mixed-Sample	SIDS	Non-SIDS
IVI/CPIA*	0.19	–0.25	0.22
	(70)	(17)	(53)
IVI/PSAV*	0.69	0.35	0.67
	(132)	(30)	(102)
IVI/FSI*	0.51	0.11	0.53
	(132)	(30)	(102)

Notes: 1. CPIA = Country Policy and Institutional Assessment; FSI = Failed States Index; IVI = Internal Violence Index; PSAV = Political Stability and Absence of Violence Index; SIDS = small island developing states.
2. The sample size is given in brackets.
3. CPIA* = 100 – Rescaled CPIA
4. FSI* = Rescaled FSI
5. PSAV* = 100 – PSAV
6. The indicator for IVI is proposed by FERDI.
Sources: Fund for Peace, Country Profiles, available at www.statesindex.org (last accessed on 12 November 2015); World Bank, Country Policy and Institutional Assessment Database, available at http://www.worldbank.org/ida (last accessed on 12 November 2015); World Bank, Worldwide Governance Indicators Database, available at http://info.worldbank.org/governance/wgi/index.aspx#home (last accessed on 12 November 2015).

correlated with FSI which is composed of several social, economic, political, and military indicators grouped in 12 clusters. We emphasize that correlation between IVI and CPIA, PSAV, or FSI is very low for SIDS compared with non-SIDS developing countries, and even negative if we consider the correlation with CPIA.

Figure 2.3 gives a summary of the conceptual framework outlined in the previous paragraphs.

The three main dimensions of vulnerability (economic, environmental, and sociopolitical), corresponding to the three main dimensions of sustainable development, are presented in three vertical blocks or columns.

For each column, two horizontal parts are distinguished: (i) one corresponding to the *structural vulnerability*, EVI for the structural

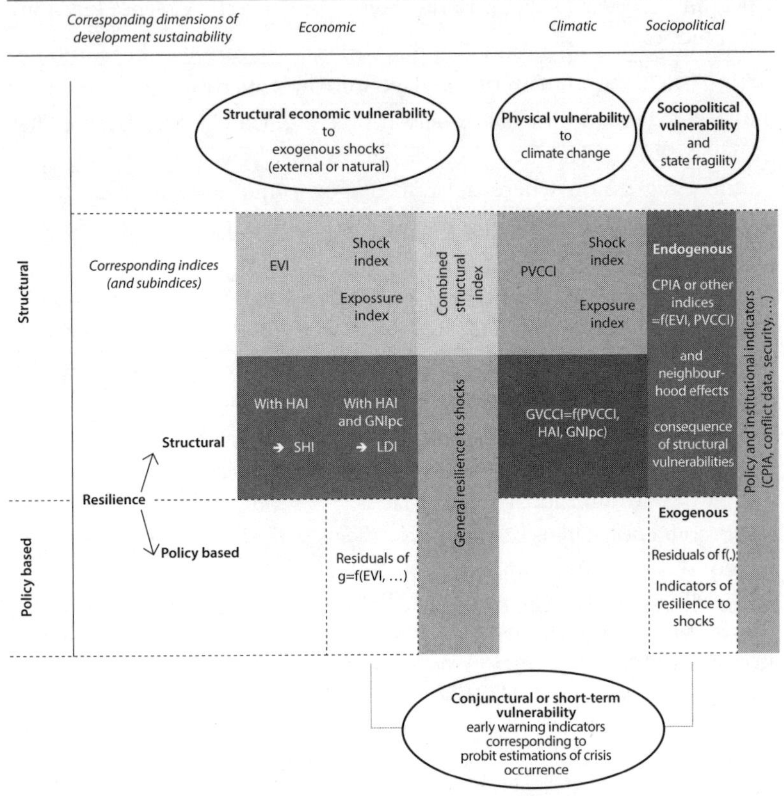

FIGURE 2.3 Conceptual Framework for Vulnerability Assessment

Notes: EVI=economic vulnerability index; HAI= human assets index; SHI= structural handicap index; GNIpc= gross national income per capita; PVCCI= physical vulnerability to climate change index.

Source: Fondation pour les Études et Recherches sur le Développement International.

economic vulnerability, PVCCI for the vulnerability to climate change, both with their respective shock index and exposure index (and a possible combined structural index); and (ii) the other one corresponding to the *policy-based vulnerability*. Resilience overlaps these two parts of vulnerability, since it is structural for one part, captured by the HAI and GNIpc indices, and it is related to policy for the other part. The structural part can be combined with EVI in broader indices of vulnerability, through the SHI combining EVI and HAI or the least development index (LDI) combining EVI, HAI, and GNIpc. Similarly, it can also be combined with PVCCI, through an index of general or structural vulnerability to climate change, which is a function of PVCCI, HAI, and GNIpc. The policy-based resilience can be assessed ex post by the residual of cross-country regression where the rate of economic growth or any other indicator of progress is a function of the various structural components of shocks and vulnerability.

The third column, related to the sociopolitical vulnerability and state fragility and assessed by indicators such as the CPIA (although entirely related to policy), is itself the addition of two parts: (i) one which is 'endogenous', corresponding to the impact of structural vulnerabilities (EVI, PVCCI, HAI, GNIpc) as well as of neighbouring country situation on the policy indicators; and (ii) one which is 'exogenous', corresponding to the autonomous policy, that is, the policy not determined by structural factors. This second part reflects well the factors of resilience linked to the present and autonomous will of the country.

Finally, at the bottom of the graph is the conjunctural or short-term vulnerability, that is, the present risk of a growth collapse or of a balance of payments crisis. It is not a structural feature or a structural vulnerability, but it can get influenced not only by the macroeconomic variables likely to change in the short run, but also by the three kinds of vulnerability, including their structural components. It is this conceptual framework that we try to apply.

Following the conceptual framework presented above, we can successively consider the main kinds of possible vulnerability, with a special focus on structural vulnerability, then examine to what extent Bhutan may be considered resilient to exogenous shocks, and whether the application of macroeconomic early warning systems is relevant for the country.

In each case, we will compare Bhutan data or indices to those of comparable sets of countries, in particular the LDCs, and other landlocked developing countries.

Economic Vulnerability: Structural versus Conjunctural

In this section, we consider the economic vulnerability of Bhutan, distinguishing between structural vulnerability (beyond the present will or policy of the countries and moving slowly) and conjunctural vulnerability (influenced by the present policy and moving fast). We then focus on structural economic vulnerability, examined mainly through the EVI, and consider some adjustments likely to be made to this index due to the limitations of its application.

First Approach: Income Growth and Volatility

A usual first approach to vulnerability is to consider the volatility of income growth. As growth volatility over a given period cannot be assessed without considering the average growth rate over the same period, we consider both of them.

Since 1993, Bhutan has registered a high growth rate of GDP per capita, transforming this former low-income country into a middle-income one and probably making it eligible for graduation for the first time from the LDC category in 2015. Eligibility is assessed every three years at the UN triennial review of the list by the CDP which may recommend graduation by the UN General Assembly only after having found the country eligible at two successive reviews. The graduation becomes effective only three years after the decision of the UN General Assembly. It means that Bhutan may no longer be a LDC in 2021 (see Drabo and Guillaumont (2014) for the graduation process and prospects, and Marshall (2013) for an examination of the case of Bhutan).

Figure 2.4a evidences a high and moderately stable growth rate during 1992–2006. Growth became more unstable, although remained high, beginning in 2000 with GDP growth rates of about 4 per cent in 2000, 15 per cent in 2007, 3 per cent in 2008, 7 per cent in 2010, and 3 per cent in 2012 (World Bank 2014). These recent developments of Bhutan's economy illustrate some specific aspects of its vulnerability. For purposes of comparison with other remote, developing economies, the Maldives and Nepal are included in Figures 2.4a–2.4c as well as Table 2.2.

First, although the average growth rate is high, compared with the average of LDCs or landlocked developing countries, its instability is also high and has been higher for the last 10 years. It may be supposed that the social consequences of a given growth volatility (as measured by the standard deviation of the growth rate) are smaller when the average growth rate is high, and never become negative (hence being less likely to generate poverty traps).

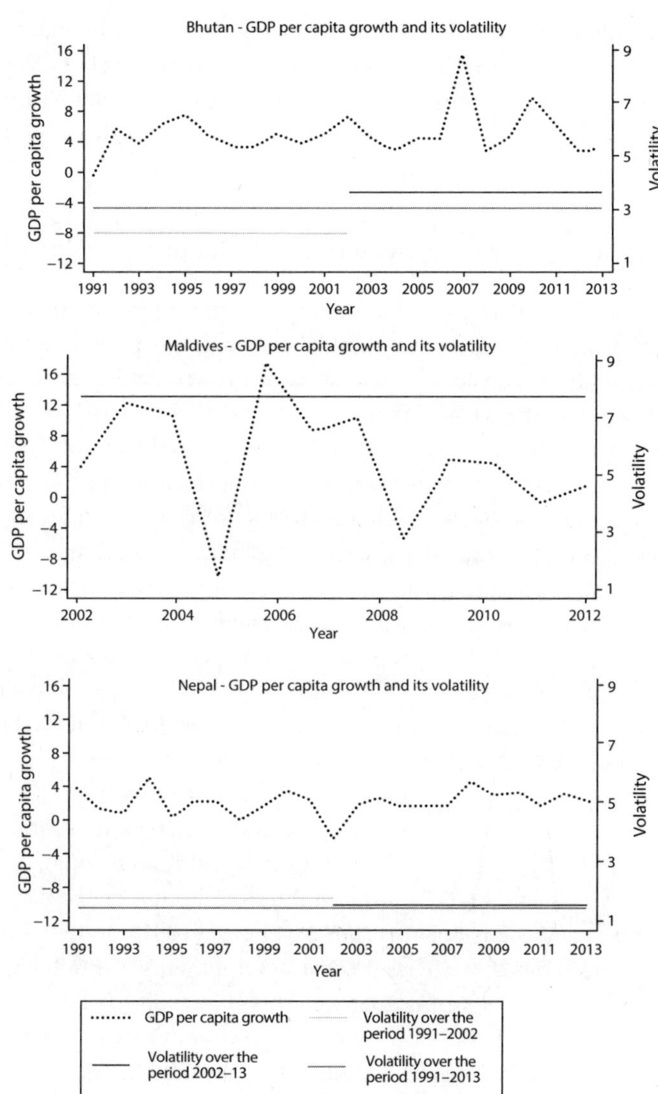

FIGURE 2.4A Gross Domestic Product Per Capita Growth Rate and Its Volatility in Bhutan, the Maldives, and Nepal, 1991–2013

Note: GDP = gross domestic product.

Source: Author's calculation using World Bank, *World Development Indicators* (2013).

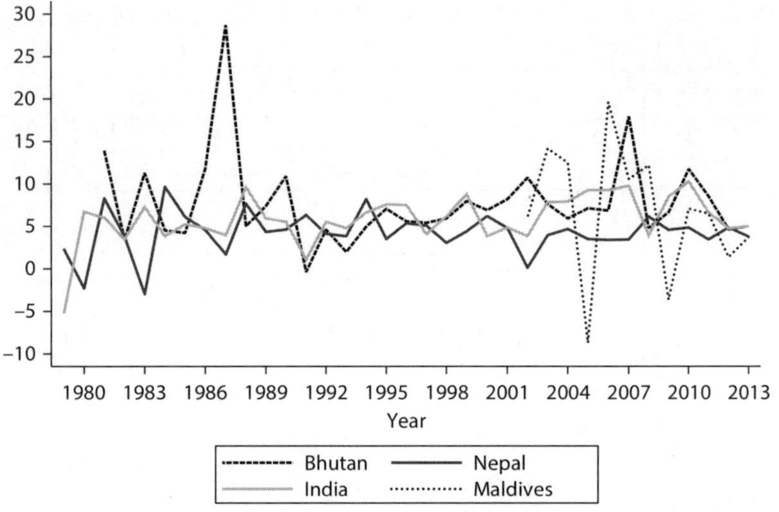

FIGURE 2.4B Annual Growth Rate of Gross Domestic Product: Bhutan, India, the Maldives, and Nepal (%)
Source: World Bank, *World Development Indicators* (2013).

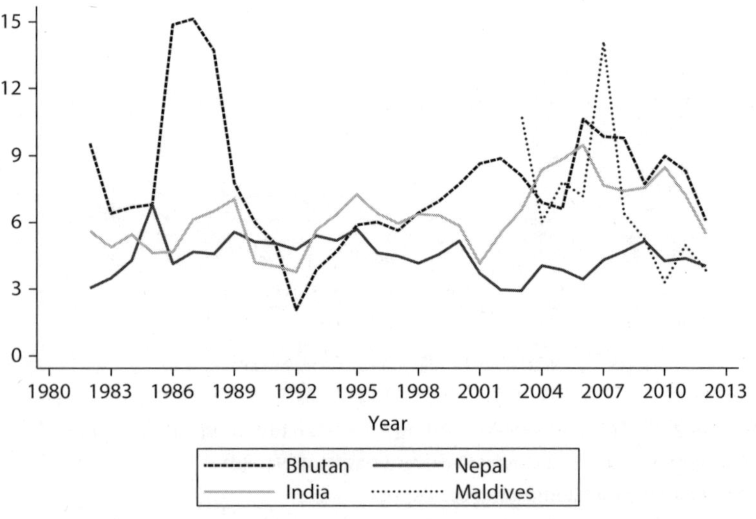

FIGURE 2.4C Growth Rate of Gross Domestic Product (3-Year Moving Average): Bhutan, India, the Maldives, and Nepal
Source: World Bank, *World Development Indicators* (2013).

TABLE 2.2 Average Growth Rates and Volatility in Bhutan, the Maldives, Nepal, and Other Groups of Countries

Country (Country Category)	GDP growth per capita		Volatility of GDP growth per capita	
	1991–2002	2002–13	1990–2001	2002–13
Bhutan	5.00	6.11	2.13	3.72
Maldives		4.58		7.76
Nepal	2.17	2.96	1.86	1.60
Developing Countries (132)	1.45	2.92	3.38	2.89
ADB Developing Countries (30)	2.76	3.39	3.53	2.29
ADB–Asia Developing Countries (21)	3.28	4.77	2.21	2.06
ADB–Pacific Developing Countries (9)	1.93	1.02	4.38	2.97
LDCs (48)	0.99	2.86	4.02	3.15
ADB LDCs (13)	2.83	4.96	3.84	3.24
Developing Landlocked (29)	1.35	3.08	3.6	2.72
ADB Landlocked (5)	3.13	6.12	1.99	3.72
Fragile States (40)	0.77	2.86	4.3	3.35
ADB Fragile States (13)	2.83	3.96	2.94	2.06
SIDS (34)	2.10	1.68	3.70	3.23
ADB SIDS (11)	2.23	1.76	4.28	3.26

Notes: ADB = Asian Development Bank; GDP = gross domestic product; LDCs = least developed countries; SIDS = small island developing states.
Source: Calculated using World Bank, *World Development Indicators* (2013).

Second, the recent growth volatility in Bhutan is linked to few specific factors. Indeed, Bhutan was indirectly affected by the world financial crisis of 2007–8, but the main driver of volatility has been the hydropower activity—its timing, its building, and the electricity generation from the big new project—leading to a growth peak. Another source of volatility results from climatic conditions, which may affect both agricultural production and hydropower activity.

Third, an overwhelming and specific factor of Bhutan's vulnerability comes from its dependency on India, whose population is 200 times larger and with whom Bhutan relies on for more than three-quarters of its trade. Furthermore, the local currency (ngultrum) is pegged to the Indian rupee at a 1:1 ratio. We will have to test the relevance of the conceptual framework in the case of Bhutan, and examine whether it needs some adaptations. Figures 2.4b and 2.4c show the evolution of the annual growth rates in Bhutan and in India, with a 3-year moving average: the relation is strong and increasing, but leaves room for Bhutan-specific variations. It means that the income volatility of Bhutan is driven not only by Indian developments, but also by Bhutan-specific factors.

Structural Economic Vulnerability of Bhutan: What the Economic Vulnerability Index Tells Us

Given the choice to examine structural economic vulnerability and physical vulnerability to climate change separately, the 2006–9 definition of EVI—all of whose components can be considered potential contributors to slower growth—is preferred to the revised EVI calculated in 2011. For that, we refer to the new calculations of the EVI made at Ferdi (Guillaumont, Cariolle, and Goujon 2014) on the basis of the 2006–9 UN definition of the EVI (Table 2.3). In the same way, the EVI's evolution using a constant definition (from 2006 and 2009, rather than 2012) is considered (Cariolle 2011; Cariolle and Goujon 2013; Cariolle and Guillaumont 2011).[11]

From the EVI scores presented in Table 2.3, it is clear that Bhutan with an EVI of 49.6 (using the 2006–9 definition) has a significantly higher index than most of other groups of developing countries: LDCs, landlocked developing countries (LLDCs), all developing countries, and ADB Asian developing countries (Asia only, not including Pacific countries). The high level of EVI for Bhutan is due both to the shock and the exposure components of the index.

It should be noted that the results obtained with the 2011 definition, used for the 2012 review of the list of LDCs, differ significantly, particularly in the case of Bhutan. This evidences a lower EVI than the average of the LDCs, both for the exposure component (due to the zero value of the LECZ component) and the shock component (as a

[11] Several other improvements could be brought to the measurement of the EVI, in particular, in the way by which the components are averaged (presently an arithmetic average) (see Guillaumont 2009a, 2009b).

result of the shift from homeless due to natural disasters to victims of natural disasters).

Indeed there are large differences between the relative levels of the EVI's components of Bhutan, the Maldives, and Nepal, reflecting the heterogeneity of sources of structural vulnerability among countries (see Table 2.3 and Annexure 2A).

As for the *shock index components*, the relative levels of the three component subindices appear to differ strongly among the three countries and within each of them. The *instability of exports* (of goods and services) is higher in the Maldives (24.9) than in Bhutan (16.76) and Nepal (9.2), and higher than the average of all developing countries and all ADB developing countries, but lower than the average of all LDCs and LLDCs (see Table 2.4). The instability of exports, as measured in the EVI, is an index calculated from a sample with upper and lower bounds, not the gross measure of instability. Moreover, since the population size on which the export to GDP ratio depends is taken into account separately in the EVI, the instability is not weighted by this ratio, although its impact is a function of this ratio.

The index of the number of *victims of disasters* is moderately high in Bhutan and Nepal, but lower than the average level of LDCs or LLDCs, and curiously low in the Maldives, although severely affected by the 2004 tsunami. A quite different picture was given by the previous index of the number of the homeless: low for Bhutan (lower than any comparator group), very high in Nepal (higher than any comparator group), and low in the Maldives (see Table 2.8).

The *instability of agricultural production* for Bhutan (index of 40.9) and the Maldives (index of 41.2) is clearly higher than the average level of any other group of developing countries (index of 24.3 for LDCs and 27.1 for LLDCs), but it is particularly and curiously low in Nepal (index of 2.6), where the share of the value added is the highest (see Table 2.8). Figure 2.A1 in the Annexure shows the evolution of the agricultural production in the three countries.

As for the exposure components, it is clear that the component pulling up the level of the Maldives's exposure (with the 2006–9 definition of EVI) and that of Bhutan is population size, which is quite small in both the Maldives (300,000) and Bhutan (700,000). Smallness of the population is indeed a major structural factor of vulnerability. With the 2011 definition of EVI, where the weight given to this component is

TABLE 2.3 Bhutan's Economic Vulnerability Index Compared to Other Countries and Groups of Countries

Country (Country Category)	Components of EVI 2011 definition		Components of EVI 2006–9 definition		EVI 2011 (2011 definition)	EVI 2011 (2006–9 definition)	EVI 2011–EVI 2000 (2006–9 definition)
	Exposure	Shock	Exposure	Shock			
Bhutan	40.4	44.5	56.5	42.7	42.4	49.6	4.5
Maldives	69.3	35.0	66.0	32.8	52.1	49.4	5.4
Nepal	26.8	27.4	32.4	25.3	27.1	28.8	–8.5
Developing Countries (130)	37.2	36.3	43.5	30.8	36.7	37.2	–3.8
ADB Developing Countries (30)	41.0	35.7	42.2	32.3	38.3	37.3	–4.6
ADB–Asia Developing Countries (21)	31.7	32.2	29.6	29.1	31.9	29.34	–4.8
ADB–Pacific Developing Countries (9)	62.7	43.8	71.7	39.7	53.3	55.7	–4.0
LDCs (48)	42.1	47.0	48.9	38.4	44.5	43.6	–4.5
ADB LDCs (13)	49.3	44.3	53.2	39.3	46.8	46.2	–6.1
Developing Landlocked (22)	37.9	44.5	47.7	32.8	41.2	40.2	–2.2
ADB Landlocked(5)	32.9	46.5	41.9	33.3	39.7	37.6	–8.7
Fragile States (37)	36.6	47.5	41.8	37.3	42.0	39.5	–6.5
ADB Fragile States (9)	39.6	42.4	39.7	40.8	41.0	40.3	–1.9
SIDS (34)	51.8	37.3	62.2	32.2	44.6	47.2	–6.4
ADB SIDS (11)	60.9	41.3	68.1	39.9	51.1	54.0	–2.5

Notes: ADB = Asian Development Bank; EVI = Economic Vulnerability Index; LDCs = least developed countries; SIDs = small island developing states.

Source: Calculated using World Bank, *World Development Indicators* (2013).

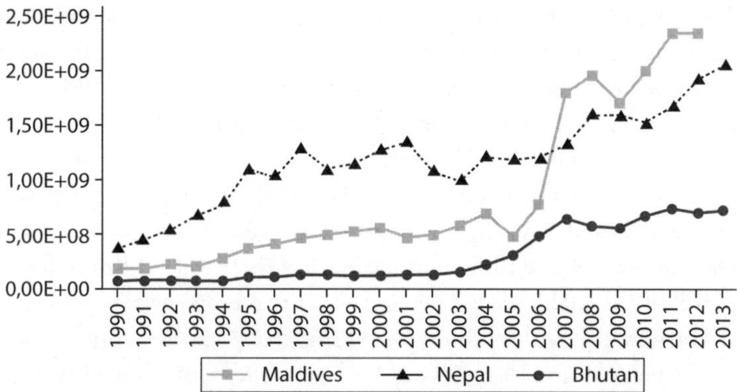

FIGURE 2.5 Evolution of the Exports of Goods and Services in Bhutan, the Maldives, and Nepal
Source: World Bank, *World Development Indicators* (2013).

reduced by half to allow the addition of the new LECZ component, the exposure index of the Maldives has increased (LECZ being at its maximum level), while the index of Bhutan has reduced (instead of being higher than the average of the LDCs). Due to its much higher population size (28 million, that is, around 100 times bigger than the Maldives and 40 times bigger than Bhutan), and due to its low export concentration index (linked to its size) and to its zero level of LECZ with the 2011 definition, Nepal seems to be clearly less exposed to exogenous shocks than Bhutan and the Maldives (see Table 2.8).[12]

What the EVI Does Not Tell Us, but Could Do

These measures should be taken as proxies of structural economic vulnerability for international comparison purposes. Their design and calculation could, of course, be discussed and improved. To better capture the vulnerability of a country such as Bhutan, several adaptations should be applied.

As for the *exposure* components, a first needed adaptation is related to the *concentration of exports* (besides what is discussed in the general

[12] The remoteness index is similar in the three countries and similar to the average of developing countries, a result of the expansion of Asian markets.

framework about the inclusion of services). The present coefficient captures the concentration byproduct, which is already high in Bhutan due to hydropower exports to India, and therefore a factor of vulnerability that it is associated with a concentration by destination.

An index of geographical concentration of exports is calculated according to the same method as for the coefficient of concentration by product calculated by UNCTAD (normalized Herfindahl index). As it appears in Tables 2.4 and 2.5, the Bhutan index reaches three to four times the average level of the Maldives and nearly twice the average level of LLDCs.

To assess the vulnerability resulting from export concentration, it might be relevant to replace the present index of concentration by product by an average (arithmetic or preferably quadratic) of this index and the index of concentration by destination. It would give a ranking where the combined index is the highest for Bhutan, lower for the Maldives, and lower still for Nepal (Table 2.5).

Another index which could be debated is that of remoteness. This index has now a relatively low level in Bhutan due to the growth of the Chinese market, without taking into account the high geographical barriers between Bhutan and the People's Republic of China (though it already takes into account being landlocked). In another context (the assessment of the need for regional integration), we have proposed a new measure of the remoteness of foreign markets, combining the traditional (geographical distance) not only with being landlocked (already taken into account in EVI), but also with the level of infrastructure (on which the impact of being landlocked depends) (Guillaumont and Guillaumont Jeanneney 2009). This index has only been calculated for African countries.

The way by which the share of agriculture, fishery, and forestry is calculated might be debated; and the percentage of value added could be replaced by the percentage of population working in this sector, quite higher in Bhutan than in other countries with similar level of income, and even in other LDCs. The share of agriculture in employment in 2013 was 62 per cent for Bhutan and 75 per cent for Nepal, but only 11 per cent for the Maldives; while the share of the value added by agriculture was 17 per cent for Bhutan, 35 per cent for Nepal, and 4 per cent for the Maldives (Table 2.7). For comparison, the average percentage for the LDCs is 29 for the share of the value added and almost 57 for the share of the agriculture employment.

Table 2.4 Instability of Exports and Remittances in Bhutan, the Maldives, Nepal, and Other Groups of Countries, 1999–2013

Country (Country category)	Instability						
	Exports of goods and services [A]	Remittances [B]	Exports of goods and services weighted by the share of exports in GDP [C]	Remittances weighted by the share of remittances in GDP [D]	Exports of goods and services + Remittances [E]	Exports of goods and services + Remittances weighted by the share of exports of goods and services + Remittances in GDP [F]	Sum of weighted instabilities of exports of goods and services and remittances [G]= [C]+[D]
Bhutan	16.76 (12.49)	–	6.06 (4.51)	–	–	–	–
Maldives	24.90 (24.90)	44.94 (37.70)	20.64 (20.64)	0.16 (0.14)	24.74 (24.74)	20.60 (20.60)	20.80 (20.78)
Nepal	9.15 (7.85)	45.68 (27.28)	1.51 (1.29)	5.19 (3.10)	5.97 (5.79)	1.69 (1.64)	6.70 (4.39)
Developing Countries	13.16 (11.86)	28.28 (22.96)	4.77 (4.35)	0.78 (0.61)	10.58 (9.58)	4.18 (3.79)	5,55 (4.96)
ADB Developing Countries	10.96 (10.18)	24.78 (21.02)	5.12 (4.85)	0.84 (0.68)	9.58 (9.06)	4.70 (4.52)	5.96 (5.53)
ADB–Asia Developing Countries	10.53 (9.71)	22.71 (18.77)	5.52 (5.21)	0.66 (0.48)	9.50 (8.90)	4.67 (4.46)	6.18 (5.69)
ADB–Pacific Developing Countries	12.32 (11.68)	31.41 (27.76)	3.85 (3.71)	1.38 (1.29)	9.87 (9.67)	4.82 (4.73)	5.23 (5.00)

(Cont'd)

Table 2.4 *(Cont'd)*

Country (Country category)	Instability						
	Exports of goods and services [A]	Remittances [B]	Exports of goods and services weighted by the share of exports in GDP [C]	Remittances weighted by the share of remittances in GDP [D]	Exports of goods and services + Remittances [E]	Exports of goods and services + Remittances weighted by the share of exports of goods and services + Remittances in GDP [F]	Sum of weighted instabilities of exports of goods and services and remittances [G]= [C]+[D]
LDCs	16.08	32.59	4.38	1.33	11.00	3.23	5.71
	(14.25)	(28.20)	(3.88)	(1.03)	(10.14)	(2.92)	(4.91)
ADB LDCs	11.15	30.92	3.39	1.78	8.57	3.40	5.17
	(10.06)	(26.30)	(3.09)	(1.40)	(8.39)	(3.33)	(4.49)
Developing Landlocked	14.60	31.64	4.30	1.46	11.71	4.93	5.76
	(12.61)	(27.93)	(3.65)	(1.07)	(10.70)	(4.31)	(4.72)
ADB Landlocked	12.54	42.60	4.40	2.22	9.76	4.20	6.62
	(11.00)	(35.98)	(3.89)	(1.50)	(9.27)	(3.94)	(5.39)
Fragile States	17.58	35.84	4.16	1.14	11.52	2.74	5.30
	(15.51)	(29.93)	(3.70)	(0.84)	(10.73)	(2.58)	(4.54)
ADB Fragile States	10.72	22.43	2.52	1.43	7.18	2.27	3.95
	(9.80)	(14.90)	(2.36)	(0.95)	(6.70)	(2.13)	(3.31)

SIDS	11.29	35.25	5.48	0.90	9.56	5.29	6.38
	(10.42)	(29.32)	(5.15)	(0.77)	(9.03)	(5.02)	(5.92)
ADB SIDS	13.50	33.67	7.66	1.18	12.84	7.98	8.84
	(12.96)	(29.42)	(7.45)	(1.10)	(12.68)	(7.90)	(8.55)

Notes: 1. ADB = Asian Development Bank; GDP = gross domestic product; LDCs = least developed countries; SIDS = small island developing states.

2. In brackets, the value of instability is calculated from the best model's forecast accuracy among five models (revised method). Unlike instability calculated in the EVI, the values are not standardized here. The ratio of exports to GDP used for weighting is the ratio of the sum of exports to the sum of GDP over the period.

Source: Calculated from World Bank, *World Development Indicators* (2013).

TABLE 2.5 Geographic and Merchandise Export Concentration for Bhutan (2012), the Maldives (2013), and Nepal (2013)

Country	Geographical concentration of exports	Merchandise Export concentration	Arithmetic mean	Quadratic mean
Bhutan	0.78	0.34	0.56	0.60
Maldives	0.27	0.70	0.48	0.53
Nepal	0.60	0.14	0.37	0.43

Source: Author's calculations based on data from World Bank, *World Integrated Trade Solution* (n.d.).

TABLE 2.6 Evolution of the Geographical Concentration of the Exports of Goods

Country (Country Category)	2009	2010	2011	2012
Bhutan	0.78	0.67	0.61	0.78
Maldives	0.16	0.23	0.17	0.19
Nepal	0.56	0.58	0.60	0.61
Developing Countries	0.31	0.32	0.30	0.31
	(104)	(104)	(98)	(92)
ADB Developing Countries	0.27	0.28	0.27	0.28
	(23)	(24)	(24)	(23)
LDCs	0.33	0.34	0.33	0.35
	(32)	(31)	(30)	(25)
Developing Landlocked	0.37	0.36	0.37	0.42
	(17)	(17)	(17)	(15)
Fragile States	0.30	0.31	0.30	0.35
	(22)	(24)	(21)	(18)
SIDS	0.33	0.35	0.36	0.33
	(25)	(24)	(23)	(21)

Notes: 1. ADB = Asian Development Bank; LDCs = least developed countries; SIDS = small island developing states.
2. figures in brackets = the effective sample size used for computation.
Source: Author's calculations based on data from World Bank, *World Integrated Trade Solution* (n.d.).

TABLE 2.7 Comparison of the Relative Share of Agriculture in Gross Domestic Product and in Employment

Country (Country Category)	Value added by agriculture (% of GDP)	Employment in agriculture (% of total employment)
Bhutan	17.07	62.20
Maldives	4.20	11
Nepal	35.09	75
Developing Countries	16.01 (110)	30.24 (100)
ADB Developing Countries	16.21 (25)	36.25 (24)
ADB–Asia Developing Countries	15.26 (20)	34.01 (18)
ADB–Pacific Developing Countries	19.99 (5)	42.98 (6)
LDCs	29.32 (37)	56.89 (25)
ADB LDCs	24.55 (9)	47.6 (8)
Developing Landlocked	26.02 (22)	58.43 (14)
ADB Landlocked	23.82 (5)	53.50 (3)
Fragile States	30.28 (27)	49.77 (20)
ADB Fragile States	21.60 (6)	41.71 (6)
SIDS	11.48 (28)	18.92 (25)
ADB SIDS	14.88 (7)	33.81 (8)

Notes: 1. ADB = Asian Development Bank; GDP = gross domestic product; LDCs = least developed countries; SIDS = small island developing states.
2. figure in brackets = the effective sample size used for computation.
Source: World Bank, *World Development Indicators* (2013).

TABLE 2.8 Components of the Economic Vulnerability Index in Bhutan, the Maldives, Nepal, and Various Country Groupings, 2011

Country (Country Category)	Components of EVI 2011								
	Exposure Index					Shock Index			
	Population	Remoteness	Export concent	Share of Agric	Share of LECZ	Instab of Agric	Instab of Export	Victims of disasters	Homeless
Bhutan	75.7	55.6	31.2	29.2	0	40.9	36.7	63.7	36.8
	(79.6)	(70.2)	(32.7)	(48.4)	(0)	(22.6)	(32.9)	(63.8)	
Maldives	87.8	56.2	61.4	4.7	100	41.2	24.0	50.7	43.4
	(90.8)	(62.8)	(24.8)	(7.5)	(100)	(34.0)	(5.1)	(5.3)	
Nepal	20.0	55.8	4.8	57.9	0	2.6	20.8	65.6	73.2
	(22.5)	(69.2)	(25.5)	(62.1)	(0)	(16.6)	(27.2)	(60.1)	
All Developing Countries (130)	42.8	55.9	33.7	27.3	19.5	24.1	30.1	60.8	54.3
ADB Developing Countries (30)	42.8	60.5	28.6	28.9	32.0	21.2	27.3	67.0	67.1
ADB–Asia Developing Countries (21)	25.4	49.2	20.8	27.8	27.9	20.9	20.2	67.5	66.1
Pacific Developing Countries (9)	83.7	86.8	46.7	31.4	41.4	21.7	43.8	65.7	69.4
LDCs (48)	43.4	60.9	42.8	48.2	18.6	24.3	47.4	68.8	55.3
ADB LDCs (13)	56.6	67.0	40.4	40.0	33.3	21.2	43.5	69.3	66.5
Developing Landlocked (22)	37.3	73.7	37.1	43.7	0.0	27.1	37.0	76.7	48.5
ADB Landlocked (5)	42.4	55.6	24.0	43.3	0.0	29.4	40.0	76.4	50.3
Fragile States (37)	31.1	55.3	44.4	49.8	12.7	20.9	50.2	69.0	54.6

ADB Fragile States (9)	35.9	57.9	33.1	38.9	28.5	14.7	41.7	71.8	68.7
SIDS (34)	78.9	63.7	37.8	19.5	35.9	31.0	29.9	58.5	57.3
ADB SIDS (11)	80.6	81.2	45.5	26.1	45.9	30.0	38.4	58.4	68.8

Notes: 1. ADB = Asian Development Bank; LDCs = least developed countries; LECZ = low elevation costal zones; SIDS = small island developing states.
2. The values of the corresponding component for 2000 are given in brackets. For comparison, the last column gives the values of the 'homeless' (due to natural disasters), which was replaced in 2012 by 'victims of disasters'. These figures are calculated by the Secretariat of the United Nations Committee for Development Policy as indices from gross figures with lower and upper bounds (to make the components comparable), not the gross figures themselves. Therefore, they may differ from the corresponding gross figures given in other tables.
Source: Cariolle and Goujon (2013).

And if we refer to the new definition, including LECZ, it would be useful to supplement this index by the consideration of the share of the population living in areas likely to be affected by ice melting.

Has Structural Economic Vulnerability (According to Economic Vulnerability Index Components) Decreased during the 2000s?

The evolution of the official EVI—as calculated for each triennial review of the list of LDCs—does not give information about the change in structural vulnerability, because the design of the official index (its composition and/or the calculation of the components) has changed from one review to another. To overcome this difficulty, the evolution in structural vulnerability has been assessed at Ferdi according to two retrospective series of the EVI, based on constant definitions, those used respectively for the 2006 and 2012 reviews of the list of LDCs. The real change in structural economic vulnerability is thus isolated from the impact of the change in the design of the index (components, weighting, methods of calculation, as well as data updating) (see Cariolle, Goujon, and Guillaumont 2014). For the reasons given above and for the consistency of our conceptual framework, the series using the 2006 definition of EVI are preferred here.

According to these series, from 1990 to 2011 the structural economic vulnerability has evidenced a late and slight fall for the average of LDCs.[13] The retrospective series with the 2006–9 design, however, shows more variability over time than that with the 2012 design, due to the way some exposure components are now calculated (3-year averaged export concentration and agriculture share indices and the remoteness index). The slightly declining trend of EVI recorded for the average of LDCs is less than for the other developing countries and results more from the trend in the exposure subindex than in the shock subindex. It should be noted that the exposure trend is highly influenced by population growth, a factor which does not really reflect a relevant structural change.

[13] The evolution of EVI is not significantly different between LDCs and non-LDCs.

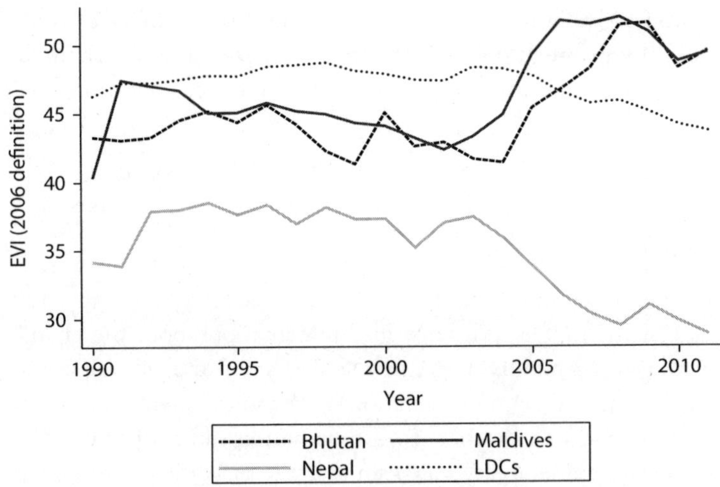

FIGURE 2.6 Evolution of the Economic Vulnerability Index (2006–9 definition) in Bhutan, the Maldives, and Nepal compared to the LDC average, 1990–2011

Note: EVI= Economic Vulnerability Index; LDCs = least developed countries.
Source: Cariolle and Goujon (2013).

Did the structural economic vulnerability, assessed through an EVI calculated according to a constant definition, increase or decrease in Bhutan, Nepal, and the Maldives during 2000–11? While it declined for the average of ADB Asian countries (–4.8) and the average of developing countries (–3.8) or African countries (–2.6), it increased in Bhutan (+4.5) and the Maldives (+5.4). Thus, during 2000–11 as measured by EVI, the difference in structural economic vulnerability between either Bhutan or the Maldives and the average LDC or LLDC appears to have increased (Table 2.3).

In Bhutan, where remoteness decreased, and where the share of agriculture, forestry, and fishery dramatically decreased (index value of 29.2 instead of 48.4), the increase in the retrospective EVI was mainly due to the increase in agricultural instability (index value of 40.9 instead of 22.6), and in export instability (36.7 instead of 32.9) (Table 2.8). Looking only at the exposure subindex, which may better reflect a structural change, the picture appears similar for Bhutan (–7.2) and Nepal (–7.1)

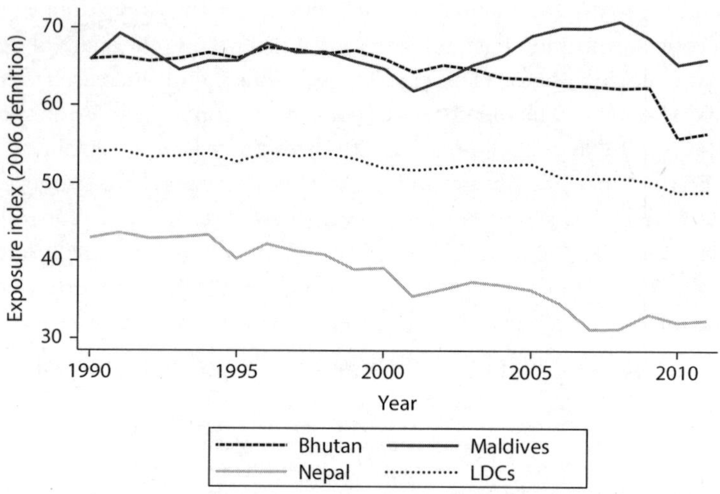

FIGURE 2.7 Evolution of the Exposure Index (2006–9 definition) in Bhutan, the Maldives, and Nepal Compared to the LDC average, 1990–2011
Note: LDCs = least developed countries.
Source: Cariolle and Goujon (2013).

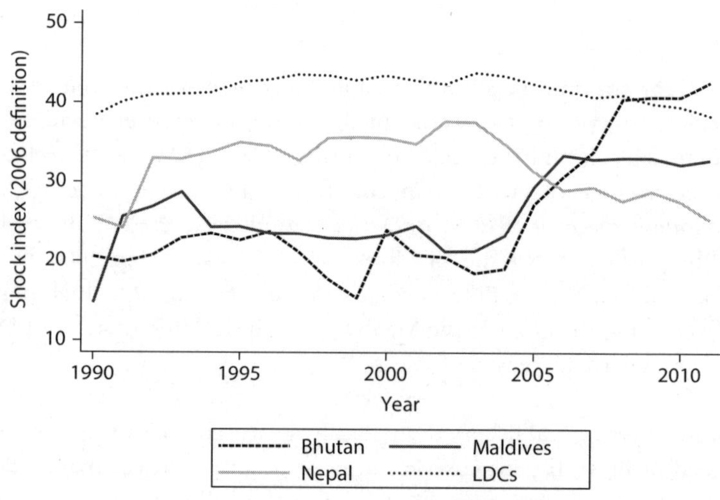

FIGURE 2.8 Evolution of the Shock Index (2006–9 definition) in Bhutan, the Maldives, and Nepal Compared to the Average of LDCs, 1990–2011
Note: LDCs = least developed countries.
Source: Cariolle and Goujon (2013).

according to the 2011 definition (see Table 2.A2 in the Annexure I),[14] the export concentration having fallen more in Nepal and the share of agriculture more in Bhutan. This exposure subindex slightly increased for the Maldives (+1.8). The picture is of course more contrasted for the shock index (see Table 2.A2 in the Annexure I), for the reasons given above.

To sum up, while Bhutan and the Maldives have registered important structural changes in recent years, their structural economic vulnerability assessed through the EVI does not seem to have decreased significantly. An additional indicator, not included in the EVI, underlines the remaining vulnerability of Bhutan: the high concentration of exports to its main partner—India, and this has been reinforced by the implementation of the new hydropower projects.[15] It may not be a factor slowing down the growth rate in the long run. As for Nepal, the weakness and decrease of its structural economic vulnerability are probably overestimated, mainly because the share of remittances in current external resources has not been taken into account in EVI, nor its rapid increase in the 'retrospective EVI'.

However, if we consider the structural economic vulnerability through a broader index taking into account the 'structural resilience' resulting from the level of human capital, the picture looks differently. The structural handicap index (SHI) measured by an average of the EVI and the (low) human assets index (HAI) indices, either arithmetic (SHI1) or quadratic (SHI2), has dramatically decreased in Bhutan and Nepal from 1989 to 2011, more than the average for LDCs or LLDCs;[16]

[14] According to the 2006–9 definition, the figures are –9.6 for Bhutan, –6.7 for Nepal, and +1.2 for the Maldives.

[15] As noted above, I have calculated an index of geographical concentration of exports comparable to other countries by the same way that the coefficient of concentration of exports by product (Herfindahl index). The evolution of this index is shown in Figure 2.7. Moreover, an increasing trend of export concentration by product was recently noted by the IMF, which highlighted the decreasing diversification into an extensive margin (number of active export lines) using the method employed by Cadot, Carrère, and Strauss-Kahn (2013).

[16] The respective levels of SHI1 and SHI2 in 2011 were 38.2 and 37.9 for Bhutan, 46.7 and 45.2 for the average of LDCs, 43.8 and 42.4 for the average of LLDCs, 31.1 and 27.7 for the average of all developing countries (Closset, Feindouno, and Goujon 2014).

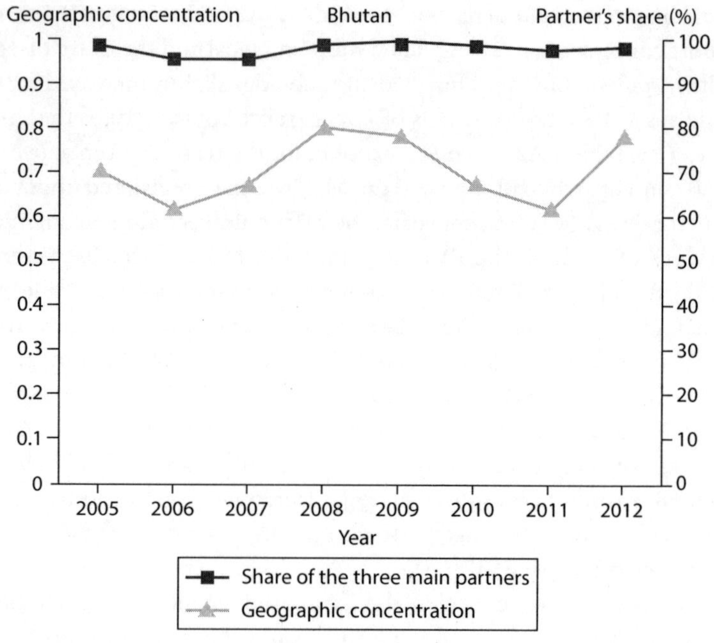
Geographic concentration
Bhutan
Partner's share (%)
Year
Share of the three main partners
Geographic concentration

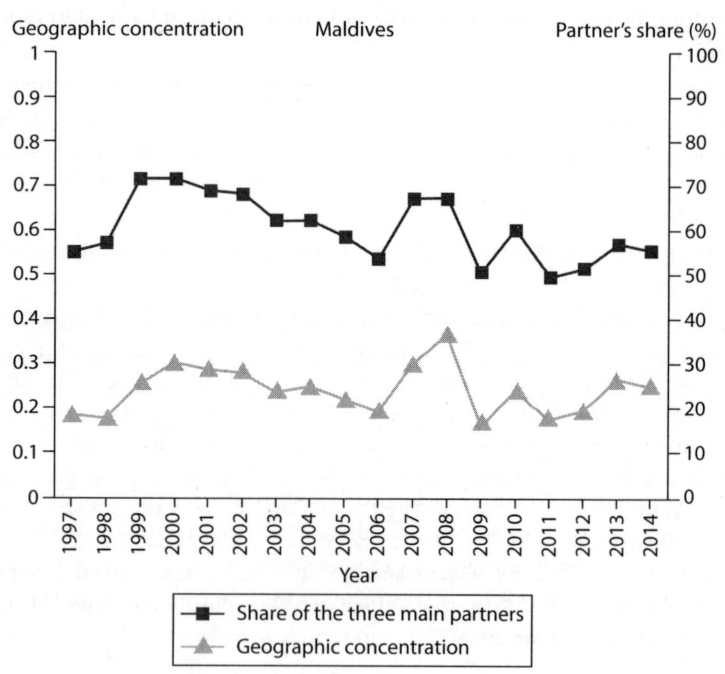
Geographic concentration
Maldives
Partner's share (%)
Year
Share of the three main partners
Geographic concentration

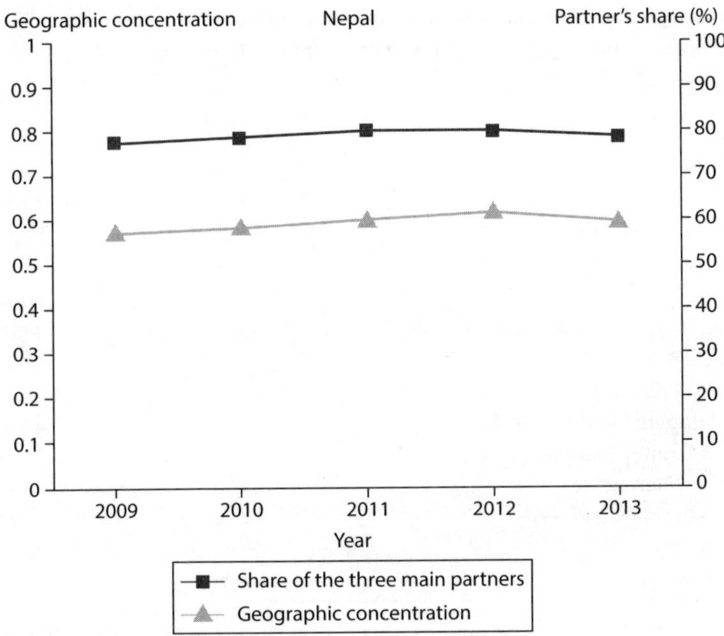

FIGURE 2.9 Geographic Concentration and Partner's Share of Exports for Bhutan, the Maldives, and Nepal, 2005–14

Notes: For the analysed periods, India is the main destination for exports of goods and services from Bhutan. The second most popular destination was either Hong Kong, China (2005–2007, 2010–2011), or Bangladesh (2008, 2009, 2012). The third fluctuated between Bangladesh (2005, 2010, 2011); Hong Kong, China (2009); Singapore (2006); Thailand (2007); Nepal (2008); and Italy (2012).

Source: Author's calculations from World Integrated Trade Solution Data on Exports.

and it decreased even more for the Maldives from 1989 to 2003, but without any clear trend after 2004, due to the evolution of the shock index after the tsunami. The future evolution of the index in Nepal is likely to evidence a similar shape (increase and stagnation or slow decline). In the three countries, the decline was due to the rapid improvement of the level of health and education (Figure 2.10).

Unlike for Bhutan and Nepal whose three main partner shares were stable, there is wide variability in the top three partners of the Maldives. In 1998–2004, the US was the primary destination for exports from the Maldives, but since 2005 Thailand has held this position. Sri Lanka

TABLE 2.9 Level of the Structural Handicap Index in 2011 for Bhutan, the Maldives, Nepal, and Various Country Groupings

Country (Country Category)	SHI1	SHI2
Bhutan	38.17	37.93
Maldives	28.61	16.31
Nepal	33.12	32.57
Developing Countries (117)	31.14	27.72
ADB Developing Countries (27)	29.30	25.27
ADB–Asia Developing Countries (20)	27.08	24.36
ADB–Pacific Developing Countries (7)	35.66	27.88
LDCs (43)	46.73	45.21
ADB LDCs (12)	38.30	35.49
Developing Landlocked (20)	43.80	42.38
ADB Landlocked (5)	37.69	35.98
Fragile States (33)	45.36	43.74
ADB Fragile States (9)	37.29	34.62
SIDS (29)	29.00	21.78
ADB SIDS (8)	34.78	26.44

Notes: 1. ADB = Asian Development Bank; EVI = Economic Vulnerability Index; HAI = Human Assets Index; LDCs = least developed countries; SHI = Structural Handicap Index, SIDS = small island developing states.
2. $\text{SHI1} = 0.5 \star \left[(100 - HAI) + EVI\right]$ Arithmetic SHI.
3. $\text{SHI2} = \sqrt{(100 - HAI) \star EVI}$ Geometric SHI.
Sources: Author's calculations from Feindouno and Goujon (2016) and Closset, Feindouno, and Goujon (2014).

habitually was the second most popular destination. However, since 2011 this position has been held by France. The third most popular trade partner varies greatly from year to year.

Vulnerability to Climate Change: Physical versus General

Vulnerability to climate change, as designed in the conceptual framework, is here understood as a vulnerability to a specific global and progressive shock, likely to translate into country-specific shocks through various events.

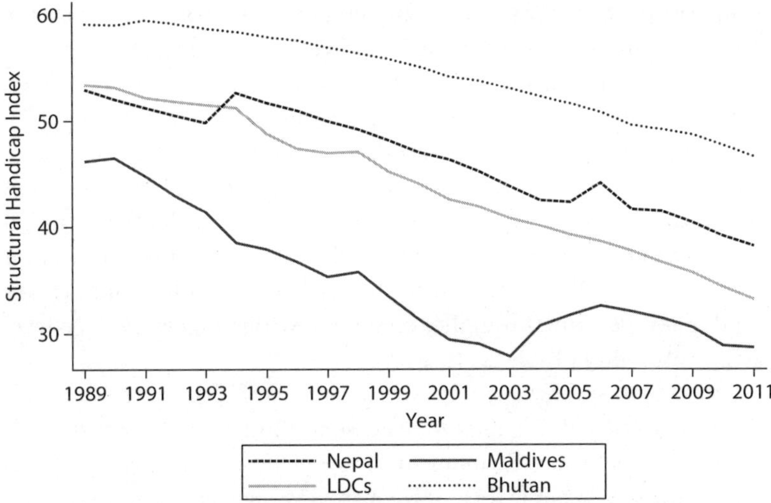

FIGURE 2.10 Evolution of the Structural Handicap Index in Bhutan, the Maldives, Nepal and Various Groupings of Countries, 1989–2011

Notes: LDCs = least developed countries; SHI = Structural Handicap Index.

Sources: Author's calculations from Feindouno and Goujon (2016) and Closset, Feindouno, and Goujon (2014).

Vulnerability to Climate Change in Bhutan, the Maldives, and Nepal According to the Level of the Physical Vulnerability to Climate Change Index and Its Components

According to the PVCCI, calculated through an arithmetic or a quadratic average, the physical vulnerability to climate change in Bhutan may seem moderate. With an arithmetic or quadratic average, the index is 26/34 for Bhutan, compared to an average of 37/44 for LDCs and 39/47 for LLDCs. The moderate or low level of PVCCI in Bhutan is due mainly to the subindex of progressive shocks, and to a quite lesser extent to the subindex of intensification of recurrent shocks for Bhutan (Table 2.10).

As for the intensification of recurrent shocks, while the level of Bhutan (46.1) is lower than the average of LDCs or of ADB Asian developing countries (Table 2.10). This is due to a significantly lower intensification of rainfall shocks (20.8). Meanwhile, for purposes of comparison, the intensification of temperature shocks is nearly the same in Bhutan (61.8) as in the Maldives (63.9) and higher than in Nepal (55.3). The sources of this discrepancy remain to be elucidated, since the value of each index is the product of a 'shock index' (the trend in the rainfall or temperature instability), and of an 'exposure index' (the average level of this rainfall or temperature instability). Bhutan shows both a lower trend and a lower level of rainfall shocks than the other two countries, while its index of intensification of temperature shocks, similar to that of Nepal, results from a lower trend in temperature instability combined with a higher average level of this instability (Table 2.11).

Due to this difference between the rainfall and temperature components of vulnerability in the case of Bhutan, it is not surprising that the gap between the index of intensification of recurrent shocks in Bhutan and Nepal is lower when the average of the temperature and rainfall subcomponents is quadratic rather than arithmetic (Table 2.10).

Besides or Inside the Physical Vulnerability to Climate Change Index: The Risk of Flooding Due to Ice Melting

The PVCCI is a tentative index set up to show that a cross-country comparison of the exogenous vulnerability to climate change is possible, and could be used for policy purposes, in particular for the allocation of concessional resources for adaptation (Guillaumont 2015). We have already noted some improvements which can be brought to the index, in particular the increase in the risk of storms or hurricanes, the recurrence of which is poorly reflected in the intensification of the instability of rainfall and temperature.

A quite specific vulnerability to climate change concerns Bhutan. Due to global warming, some highly elevated ice lakes may burst out, their disruption being likely to destroy and flood low-lying areas, with disastrous immediate impact on people and crops, and longer term impact on material capital and fertility in this area. A side effect is indeed the lower fertility of areas flooded by water from the melting ice and all that it carries with it. While this risk is well identified by Bhutan's authorities and by the International Centre for Integrated Mountain Development (ICIMOD) in Kathmandu, it is difficult to assess the extent of arable

Table 2.10 Physical Vulnerability to Climate Change Index in Bhutan, the Maldives, Nepal, and Various Country Groupings

Country Category	Arithmetic			Quadratic		
	Progressive Shocks	Recurrent Shocks	PVCCI	Progressive Shocks	Recurrent Shocks	PVCCI
Bhutan	10.7	41.3	26.0	15.2	46.1	34.3
Maldives	60.7	57.3	59.0	72.3	57.6	65.4
Nepal	9.3	59.5	34.4	13.2	59.6	43.2
Developing Countries (132)	25.4	47.5	36.4	33.5	48.4	42.8
ADB Developing Countries (41)	26.6	46.9	36.8	33.3	48.0	42.9
ADB-Asia Developing Countries (28)	24.0	49.7	36.9	32.6	50.8	44.4
ADB-Pacific Developing Countries (13)	32.2	40.8	36.5	35.0	41.7	39.6
LDCs (48)	23.8	50.6	37.2	31.8	51.6	44.0
ADB LDCs (13)	21.9	47.8	34.8	26.2	49.0	40.9
Developing Landlocked (29)	27.7	50.5	39.1	39.1	51.8	47.2
ADB Landlocked (12)	31.1	48.6	39.9	44.0	50.2	48.9
Fragile States (40)	25.7	49.1	37.4	34.3	50.2	44.1
ADB Fragile States (13)	27.7	46.2	36.9	34.3	47.0	43.0
SIDS (29)	24.9	43.5	34.2	27.8	44.4	37.8
ADB SIDS (10)	30.9	41.5	36.2	34.5	42.6	39.8

Notes: ADB = Asian Development Bank; LDCs = least developed countries; PVCCI = Physical Vulnerability to Climate Change Index; SIDS = small island developing states.

Source: Cariolle and Goujon (2013).

TABLE 2.11 Main Components of the Physical Vulnerability to Climate Change Index for Bhutan, the Maldives, Nepal, and Various Country Groupings

Country (Country Category)	PVCCI			
	Progressive shocks		Recurrent shocks	
	Sea level Rise	Increasing of aridity	Rainfall	Temperature
Bhutan	0	21.4	20.8	61.8
Maldives	100	21.5	50.6	63.9
Nepal	0	18.6	63.6	55.3
Developing Countries (132)	6.6	44.2	41.8	53.2
ADB Developing Countries (41)	15.2	38.0	40.3	53.5
ADB–Asia Developing Countries (28)	5.0	43.0	43.0	56.5
ADB–Pacific Developing Countries (13)	37.2	27.1	34.5	47.1
LDCs (48)	5.2	42.4	45.7	55.5
ADB LDCs (13)	15.4	28.3	42.5	53.0
Developing Landlocked (29)	0	55.4	43.2	57.8
ADB Landlocked (12)	0	62.2	39.7	57.6
Fragile States (40)	6.6	44.8	43.0	55.2
ADB Fragile States (13)	18.3	37.1	41.9	50.4
SIDS (29)	20.8	28.9	38.2	48.8
ADB SIDS (10)	35.3	26.6	34.3	48.7

Notes: ADB = Asian Development Bank; LDCs = least developed countries; PVCCI = Physical Vulnerability to Climate Change Index; SIDS = small island developing states.
Source: Cariolle and Goujon (2013).

areas likely to be flooded (or the size of the population to be affected by such flooding) in a way which could allow the aggregation of this figure in the PVCCI with the percentage of population likely to be flooded by the rising sea levels.[17]

[17] Ferdi is pursuing a dialogue with the Royal Government of Bhutan and ICIMOD in order to develop a proxy evaluation that will then be immediately incorporated in the PVCCI.

TABLE 2.12 Components of the Physical Vulnerability to Climate Change Index for Bhutan, the Maldives, Nepal, and Various Country Groupings

Country Category	PVCCI							
	Progressive shocks				Intensification of recurrent shocks			
	Flood risk due to sea level rise	Temperature trend	Rainfall trend	Dry land	Rainfall shocks level	Temp. shocks level	Trend of rainfall shocks	Trend of temperature shocks
Bhutan	0	10.2	75.5	0	31.3	69.6	10.4	54.0
Maldives	100	19.6	66.4	0	68.8	73.9	32.4	54.0
Nepal	0	8.1	66.4	0	100	47.8	27.2	62.8
Developing Countries (132)	6.6	34.0	72.5	35.2	48.7	49.2	35.0	57.1
ADB Developing Countries (41)	15.2	31.1	74.2	23.4	46.5	50.9	34.1	56.1
ADB–Asia Developing Countries (28)	5.0	34.1	69.6	34.2	51.9	57.1	34.2	55.8
ADB–Pacific Developing Countries (13)	37.2	24.7	83.9	0	34.9	37.5	34.1	56.8
LDCs (48)	5.2	32.9	75.4	30.7	54.8	51.6	36.7	59.4
ADB LDCs (13)	15.4	20.4	78.9	7.0	52.4	49.8	32.6	56.2
Developing Landlocked (29)	0	44.4	69.5	53.8	53.1	58.2	33.4	57.5
ADB Landlocked (12)	0	53.5	68.4	63.4	49.7	58.0	29.7	57.2
Fragile States (40)	6.6	35.0	74.5	34.8	49.9	50.1	36.0	60.3
ADB Fragile States (13)	18.3	28.9	76.9	21.2	48.6	44.5	35.3	56.4
SIDS (29)	20.8	30.3	78.1	3.7	43.0	39.4	33.4	58.1
ADB SIDS (10)	35.3	21.1	85.1	0	36.3	40.9	32.4	56.5

Notes: ADB = Asian Development Bank; LDCs = least developed countries; PVCCI = Physical Vulnerability to Climate Change Index; SIDS = small island developing states.

Source: Cariolle and Goujon (2013).

Mixing Physical Vulnerability to Climate Change Index with Economic Vulnerability Index: Relevance and Results

It would be possible to combine the PCCVI with the EVI (taking its 2005–9 definition) to avoid partial overlap through the share of population living in low coastal zones (the new EVI component introduced in 2001). Due to different time horizons of the EVI and the PVCCI, the weight given to each of them would reflect a time preference. If the EVI and the PVCCI were given equal weights, Sudan, Gambia, and Eritrea would obtain the highest average values. Without calculating such a heterogeneous average, a picture of the two vulnerabilities can be given by representing the two indices on the same graph, as shown in Figure 2.11 for Asian and Pacific countries, where the horizontal and vertical lines correspond to the medians of the two indices. Above the oblique line are the 40 per cent of countries which have the highest average combined index.

We can locate Bhutan on this graph according to the present—and to some extent debatable for reasons given above—values of the two indices, Bhutan has a high EVI and a rather low but underestimated PVCCI. As in Nepal, the PVCCI for Bhutan is itself underestimated due to the risk of the glacial lake outburst flood. The likely underestimation is approximately represented in Figure 2.11 by an arrow for each of the two countries.

When mixing the two indices, it would be useful to check their mutual consistency and to refine each of them accordingly, taking into account the suggestions above.

Sociopolitical Vulnerability and Resilience

State fragility is a sociopolitical dimension of vulnerability. It is not structural like the EVI and PVCCI. Does Bhutan suffer from state fragility based on current assessments? And to what extent does it result from structural vulnerability?

Sociopolitical Vulnerability and State Fragility in Bhutan

Bhutan is not considered a fragile state today even though it has been in the past. In 2013, Bhutan was above the Country Policy and Institutional Assessment (CPIA) threshold of 3.2 with a score of 3.68. Its CPIA score

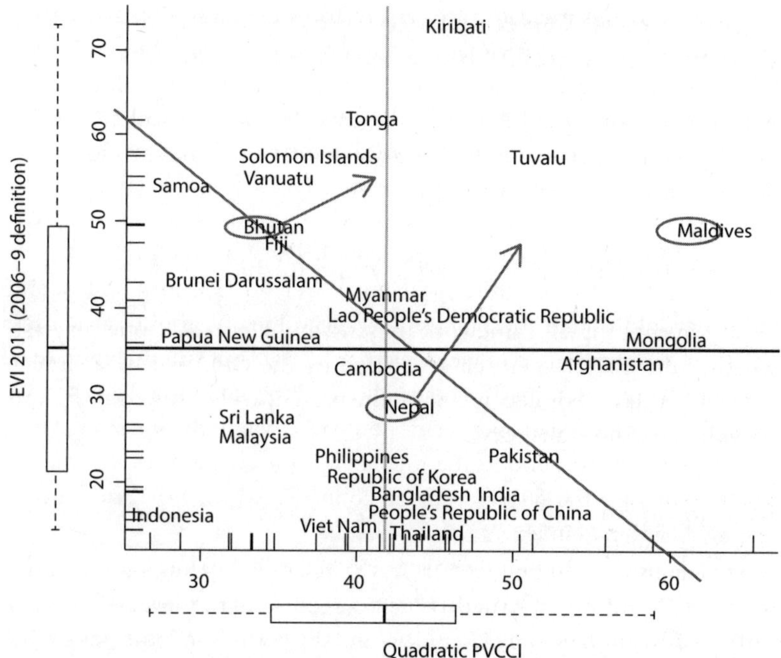

FIGURE 2.11 Combined Economic Vulnerability Index and Physical Vulnerability to Climate Change Index for Selected Asian countries
Notes: EVI = economic vulnerability index; PVCCI = physical vulnerability to climate change index.
Source: Cariolle and Goujon (2013).

decreased in 2011 and 2012 and remained flat in 2013, generating a global ranking of 73 in 2011, 61 in 2012, and 65 in 2013 in terms of the world's most fragile country.

Lessons from an Internal Violence Indicator

The state fragility here is approached through violent events, divided into four clusters: internal conflicts,[18] criminality, terrorism, and political violence, with equal weight (25 per cent) assigned to each cluster.

[18] All external conflicts are excluded.

The scores of this indicator are ranked from the least violent country (score of 0) to the most violent country (score of 100). Bhutan is well below the LDC average in terms of violence and ranks 30th overall out of 132 countries. Table 2.13 presents the internal violence index for Bhutan in comparison with the Maldives, Nepal, and groupings of developing, landlocked, and fragile states.

Structural Vulnerability, Fragility, and Resilience

To fit the conceptual framework presented in Figure 2.1, one may ask whether the state fragility as measured by the CPIA (or by a similar index) is structural or dependent on the present will of the country, and so 'voluntary' or 'transitory'.

Resilience as Residual

A partial answer can be given from the relationship linking the CPIA to the EVI and other structural factors, such as the level of human capital (measured by the HAI index) and the level of income per capita (Guillaumont, McGillivray, and Wagner 2013). The expected value of the CPIA is a proxy of the structural fragility, while the residual of the regression may reflect the fragility which is more linked to the current policy. From a regression estimated on 55 IDA–eligible countries and during 1996–2007—while for this period the level of the World Bank CPIA was on average similar for Bhutan and the Maldives and significantly higher than for Nepal—the structural component of the CPIA was the highest for the Maldives, followed by Nepal, then Bhutan. By difference, it follows that the residual, that is, the 'voluntary' component, that may be seen as an indicator of resilience, was significantly higher in Bhutan than in the Maldives, and even more than in Nepal, underlining the differences in the quality of policy and the 'autonomous resilience'. According to this test, Bhutan was even found to have the highest residual out of the 55 IDA–eligible countries.[19]

[19] For this period, the level of the CPIA in Bhutan was 3.91 (ranked 2nd), its expected or structural value was 3.15 (ranked 28th), and its residual value 0.77 (ranked 1st).

TABLE 2.13 Internal Violence Index: Bhutan, the Maldives, Nepal, and Various Country Groups

Country (Country Category)	Internal Conflict	Criminality	Terrorism	Political Violence	IVI
Bhutan	0.0	1.1	0.3	36.1	9.4
Maldives	0.0	4.4	0.0	23.7	7.0
Nepal	0.4	3.4	32.6	61.6	24.5
Developing countries (132)	7.7	14.0	12.9	47.7	20.5
LDCs (49)	9.8	10.8	11.6	47.6	19.9
Developing Landlocked (22)	9.6	13.8	11.5	48.3	20.8
Fragile States (38)	15.6	10.4	23.7	62.5	28.0

Notes: IVI = Internal Violence Index; LDCs = least developed countries.
Source: Fondation pour les Études et Recherches sur le Développement International (2015b).

It should be remembered that the validity of this test of 'autonomous resilience' depends both on the quality of the explained variable (the CPIA) as a proxy for resilience, and on the quality of the structural explanatory variables, in particular the EVI, the limitations of which have been underlined above.

Summary and Concluding Remarks

This chapter presents a conceptual framework for the study of the vulnerability in Bhutan—with a particular focus on the structural vulnerability. Three kinds of vulnerability have been considered: economic, climatic, and political. Political vulnerability is considered through the debated notion of state fragility. The identification of structural vulnerability is indeed more relevant for the economic and climatic vulnerabilities than for state fragility. For a comparative assessment of countries, the examination has to rely on available and comparable indicators, such as the EVI and PVCCI. Although the measurement and the comparison of state fragility indicators remain debatable, a tentative index of internal violence has been proposed as an outcome-based index of fragility, for it is less subjective and more parsimonious than other indices of state fragility.

Comparison: Bhutan, the Maldives, and Nepal

Taking the indicators as they are, it is possible to summarize and compare the profile of vulnerability of Bhutan, the Maldives, and Nepal.

Figures 2.12 and 2.13 show the level of the main indicators considered for each kind of vulnerability and for the three countries. In order to make them comparable, these indicators have been put on the same scale.

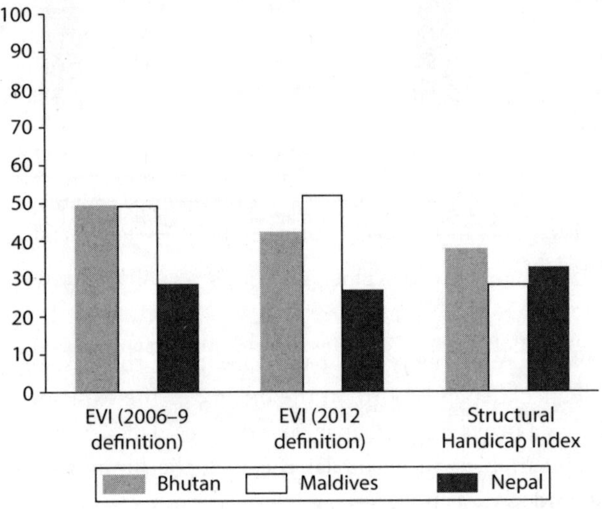

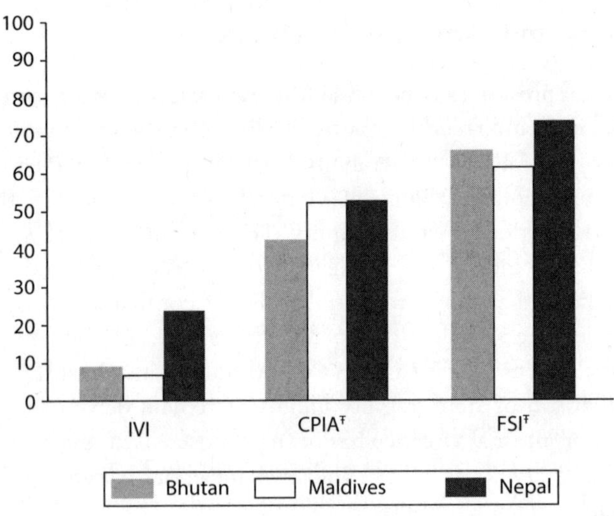

(*Cont'd*)

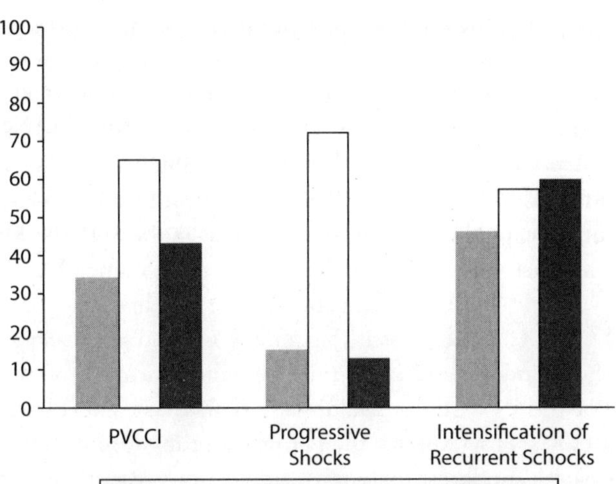

FIGURE 2.12 Comparison of Vulnerability Indices in Bhutan, the Maldives, and Nepal

Notes: 1. CPIA = Country Policy and Institutional Assessment; EVI = Economic Vulnerability Index; FSI = Failed States Index; IVI = Internal Violence Index; PVCCI = Physical Vulnerability to Climate Change Index.

2. All indicators have been normalized to 100 using the procedure min–max.

3. Since the CPIA is an indicator of low fragility (a high score of the CPIA means that country is less fragile), we compute CPIA* as follows: CPIA* = 100 – normalized CPIA. CPIA* may therefore be considered as an indicator of fragility, moving in the same direction as the CIFP and the FSI.

Sources: Fondation pour les Études et Recherches sur le Développement International (2013, 2014, 2015a, 2015b) ; Country Profiles, available at www.statesindex.org (last accessed on 4 November 2015); World Bank, Country Policy and Institutional Assessment Database, available at http://www.worldbank.org/ida (last accessed on 4 November 2015); World Bank, Worldwide Governance Indicators Database, available at http://info.worldbank.org/governance/wgi/index.aspx#home (last accessed on 4 November 2015).

Figure 2.12 (histogram) compares three indicators in each of the three dimensions (that is, indicators for each country): (i) EVI using two definitions and SHI for the economic vulnerability; (ii) PVCCI and its two main components (progressive shocks and intensification of recurrent shocks) for the vulnerability to climate change; and (iii) low CPIA, FSI, PSAV, CIPF, and IVI for the state fragility. In Figure 2.13

(cobweb diagram), the comparison is limited to six indicators: the two main components of EVI (shock and exposure), the two main components of PVCCI (progressive shocks and intensification of recurrent shocks), and the two main indices of state fragility (CPIA and FSI).

As for structural economic vulnerability, Bhutan has the highest level with the 2006–9 definition. If the structural resilience due to the level of human capital is taken into account, as in the SHI, the Maldives becomes the least vulnerable and Bhutan the most vulnerable.

As for vulnerability to climate change, the Maldives has the highest level of the PVCCI because of its bigger exposure to sea level rise ('progressive shock index') and high index of 'intensification of recurrent shocks'. For the PVCCI, the Maldives is ranked 1st, and Bhutan 46th among 51 LDCs. However, for the Himalayan Kingdom of Bhutan, the PVCCI is clearly underestimated, as it does not presently capture the risk of flooding due to ice melting.

Bhutan is the least fragile among the three South Asian countries with regard to CPIA. The internal violence index also shows Bhutan as the least fragile of the three.

Linking the Indicators: Vulnerability Profile Rather than Aggregate Index

Since it is difficult to merge all the components of vulnerability in a single index, even only those of structural vulnerability, it appears more relevant to design a vulnerability profile like the one represented in Figure 2.11. The point is that the aggregation of too many heterogeneous indices in a composite index, although it is a popular exercise, blurs the meaning of the index. It is better to handle a small set of well-specified indices, each of which relies on a small number of relevant and well-identified components. A 'vulnerability profile',[20] which gathers

[20] The usefulness of a 'vulnerability profile' was recognized in 1999 by the expert group of the CDP which adopted the principle of using an EVI as a criterion for the identification of the LDCs. Vulnerability profiles are now regularly produced by UNCTAD during the process of identification of the LDCs eligible for graduation (more detail in Guillaumont 2009). Such profiles give information supplementing the measurement and ranking of EVI, for that specific purpose, which is different from the broader present framework.

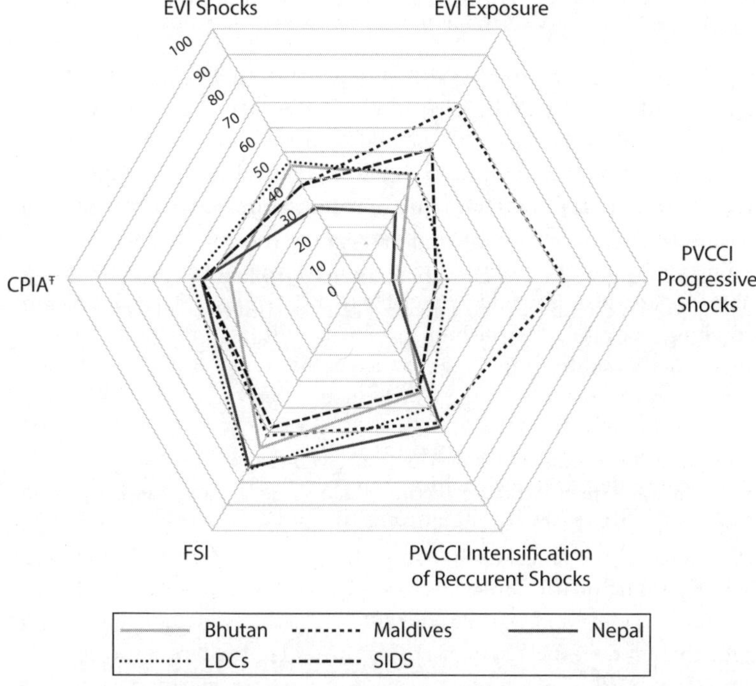

FIGURE **2.13** Components of Vulnerability Indices for Bhutan Compared to the Averages for Least Developed Countries and Landlocked Developing Countries

Notes: 1. CPIA= Country Policy and Institutional Assessment; EVI = Economic Vulnerability Index; FSI = Failed States Index; LDCs = least developed countries; PVCCI = Physical Vulnerability to Climate Change Index; SIDS = small island developing states.

2. CPIA*=100 – Rescaled CPIA.

Sources: Fondation pour les Études et Recherches sur le Développement International (2013, 2015a); Fund for Peace, Country Profiles, available at www.statesindex.org (last accessed on 27 October 2015); World Bank, Country Policy and Institutional Assessment Database, available at http://www.worldbank.org/ida (last accessed on 27 October 2015).

such indices in a consistent framework and possibly supplements them by more qualitative information, is preferable to very broad and elusive composite indices. However, the use of separate indices may be required to assess the eligibility of Bhutan to the graduation from the category of the least developed countries (see Box 2.1).

Box 2.1 From Vulnerability Assessment to Graduation Prospects

The three indicators: structural economic vulnerability, physical vulnerability, and lower state fragility, have been presented separately in the previous section. However, at the end of the second section, the possibilities and difficulties of mixing the Economic Vulnerability Index (EVI) and the Physical Vulnerability to Climate Change Index (PVCCI) were examined. Any other mix of the various components of the structural vulnerability in its economic, climatic, and political dimensions is conceivable. In particular, it would be possible to include the structural resilience resulting from the levels of human capital, with the Structural Handicap Index (SHI), and from the level of income per capita in an even broader index. For instance, combining EVI, Human Assets Index (HAI), and Gross National Income Per Capita (GNIpc) in a synthetic measure, reflecting the structural likelihood of growth over a given future period, or what we call 'natural expected future income', allows us to rank the least developed countries (LDCs) according to their prospects of graduation from the category. We find that Bhutan is the 5th or 7th out of 46 LDCs for which graduation has not yet been decided by the United Nations General Assembly (Drabo and Guillaumont 2014). And the estimation did not take into account the expected impact of last hydroelectric power project. This mixed index still has a limited scope as it does not include components reflecting the physical vulnerability to climate change. As for structural components of state fragility, they would not add anything since they correspond to structural factors of resilience, which could already be taken into account through SHI.

Source: Author.

From Figure 2.13, it appears that Bhutan exhibits a lower general vulnerability than the Maldives, and lower than Nepal with respect to the CPIA, FSI, and PVCCI, but higher than Nepal with respect to the EVI as calculated by the UN. The graph also allows comparison of the vulnerability profile of each of the three countries with the average vulnerability profiles of the LDCs and the SIDS. For instance, Bhutan has

1. a structural economic vulnerability, close to the average of LDCs and LLDCs, both for the exposure and the size of the shocks (although with some high values for several components);

2. a physical vulnerability to climate change lower than the average of these two groups, in particular for the vulnerability to progressive shocks, but with the omission of some specific possible factors of vulnerability, such as ice melting; and
3. a lower state fragility, reflected both by the CPIA and the FSI and corresponding to a part of Bhutan's resilience to exogenous shocks.

Improving Current Vulnerability Indices

The previous analyses relied on three main kinds of indices that are unequally recognized in the international community. Their application to Bhutan, the Maldives, and Nepal has revealed some drawbacks in their design, and the need for revising or refining their content, if they are to be used in the formulation of international policies. It is particularly the case for the UN–EVI used for the identification of the LDCs and proposed as an aid allocation criterion. We briefly recall here the main adjustments proposed for this index:

1. taking the relative share of the world population rather than the absolute number;
2. using an ad hoc export concentration index, including the exports of goods and services, instead of only the exports of goods and taking into account the geographical composition of exports;
3. adding the share of population threatened by flooding due to ice melting to share of the population living in low-lying coastal areas;
4. replacing the share of the population living in low-elevated coastal areas by the average of this share and the share of the dryland areas in the total of non-desert areas (Guillaumont 2014); and
5. calculating the instability of exported goods and services over a 15-year period and from a trend estimated and time squared in order to take into account the non-linearity.

As for the PVCCI, its present formulation and calculation should also be improved by a better measurement of the intensification of storms and typhoons, as well as by an assessment of the impact of ice melting.

Early Warning Systems: When Are They Relevant?

At the beginning and end of our conceptual framework, we have noted the attempts to set up early warning systems to predict and possibly avoid growth collapses or external payments crises. Most recent articles (see, for example, Dabla–Norris and Gündüz 2014) use two approaches: (i) a multivariate probit model, where the dependent variable is the occurrence of the shock event and the explanatory variables are the various likely factors (policy, institutions, and size of the exogenous shocks); and (ii) a calculation of a vulnerability index from bivariate probit regressions, the results of which are used as weights for the index. In this approach, three groups of factors are examined: (i) overall economy and institutions (for example, CPIA), (ii) external sector (for example, reserve coverage and lagged export growth), and (iii) fiscal sector (for example, government budget balance and public debt). In both cases, the estimations are made from pooled data covering a large set of years and countries. 'The results show that country fundamentals, exchange rate regimes, institutional quality, and the size of shocks are important determinants of growth crises in low income countries' (Dabla–Norris and Gündüz 2014).

These models offer useful general lessons, but their results do not seem very informative when applied to the three countries. For instance, Bhutan does not suffer from a 'growth crisis' as defined by the authors, and the 'overall vulnerability index' drawn from the second approach barely deviates from the minimum level. This does not mean that Bhutan is not vulnerable, even in the short term, but its vulnerability results from structural and specific factors, as explained in this report.

On the macro side, an indicator of macroeconomic vulnerability may be the risk of an appreciation of the real exchange rate leading to a loss of competitiveness after a surge in domestic demand (see Box 2.2 on the risk of a 'Dutch disease' in Bhutan). Another indicator frequently used is the ratio of foreign reserves to imports, but its relevance is ambiguous in Bhutan due to institutional specificity (see Box 2.2). It does not mean that the early warning is useless to reduce vulnerability, but its most useful application is related to to geo-climatic events. As well documented by the work of the ICIMOD, very useful early warning systems can be implemented to

Box 2.2 Is There a Risk of Dutch Disease in Bhutan?

Bhutan may also face macroeconomic shocks. Some risks are linked to hydropower production, being dependent on the Indian demand (which however could be considered as unlimited). Moreover, the emerging activities of tourism and manufacturing are also dependent on India's activity, as well as the world demand and the real rate of exchange. In the case of Bhutan, whose currency (ngultrum) is pegged to the Indian rupee, one might wonder whether there is a risk of an overvaluation. The risk could either come (i) from an overvaluation of the Indian rupee itself, again underlining the dependence on the Indian economy, but with limited impact on Bhutan exports due to the high concentration of trade with India; or (ii) from an overvaluation with regard to the Indian rupee, which has a moderate probability due to the high correlation observed in the past between price movements in Bhutan and India. But if there is a rise in domestic demand based on hydropower investment and production, there might be a risk of an increase of the price of domestic ('not tradable') goods, a so-called Dutch disease, as if Bhutan were an oil exporter. A risk is not a curse, and an overvaluation can be avoided by an appropriate use of additional resources to increase the supply of domestic goods. The risk depends on the quality of governance, which in Bhutan is assumed to be high.

Source: Author.

learn about the proximity of river floods in countries such as Nepal and Bhutan.

Final Remarks

The purpose of this chapter was to design a conceptual framework of the various kinds of vulnerability, mainly the structural ones, which are likely to affect LDCs, particularly in Asia, and applicable to Bhutan. Two difficulties have been met.

One difficulty is both to have a conceptual framework general enough to make comparisons between countries, mainly LDCs, and to capture specific country features of vulnerability. In order to design a general framework acceptable for international comparisons, we have started from agreed measures of the various kinds of vulnerability and tried to combine them consistently. But the application to the three countries has led to consideration of some possible improvements or component additions to the usual measures, such as the UN–EVI. Case studies lead to improvements in general concepts and measures.

A second difficulty is to establish a link between the assessment of the structural vulnerabilities that concern a long period or are likely to affect long-term growth, and the estimation of the risk of occurrence of a growth collapse or a payments crisis in the short term. Short-term risks depend not only on the structural vulnerabilities, but also on specific dated exogenous events and current macroeconomic situation, the latter being linked to the current policy rather than to structural features. Attempts to predict a short-term risk through early warning systems neglect structural vulnerability. Structural vulnerability analyses fail to be used as early warning of specific events. For each country, only an exchange with local authorities permits casting light on the link between specific structural vulnerabilities and current economic policy. Let us flag major vulnerabilities as they appear.

For now, it seems that the main structural vulnerability of Bhutan, linked to its small population size and its geographical location, is the persistently strong concentration of its exports on hydropower and to India. To some extent, it makes the vulnerability of Bhutan determined by India. Another vulnerability, which is difficult to assess and common to Bhutan and Nepal, is that resulting from the impact of global warming on ice melting.

Annexure 2A. Supplementary Tables

TABLE 2A.1 Economic Vulnerability Index (2012 definition) for Present and Former LDCs, 2011

Country	EVI 2011 (2012 definition)								
	Exposure Index		Shock Index		EVI 2011		Change in exposure index (Exposure index 2011–Exposure index 2000)	Change in Shock index (Shock index 2011–Shock index 2000)	Change in EVI (EVI 2011–EVI 2000)
	Value	Rank	Value	Rank	Value	Rank			
Afghanistan	26.04	1	48.93	33	37.48	17	–11.07	14.10	1.52
Angola	38.06	21	61.34	42	49.70	35	0.32	–3.26	–1.47
Bangladesh	34.40	13	28.51	6	31.46	6	–5.11	–0.90	–3.00
Benin	37.85	20	31.70	10	34.78	8	–6.95	–13.30	–10.13
Bhutan	**40.37**	**26**	**44.50**	**28**	**42.43**	**24**	**–7.23**	**6.45**	**–0.39**
Botswana	*47.12*	*39*	*34.54*	*14*	*40.83*	*21*	*2.63*	*–11.27*	*–4.32*
Burkina Faso	34.99	15	38.85	19	36.92	16	–2.70	–12.11	–7.40
Burundi	42.18	31	65.64	45	53.91	43	–6.02	10.59	2.28
Cambodia	41.91	29	58.76	40	50.34	37	–5.51	–23.25	–14.38
Cape–Verde	*43.10*	*33*	*27.16*	*4*	*35.13*	*9*	*–1.29*	*–5.03*	*–3.16*
Central African Republic	43.43	35	19.11	1	31.27	4	–5.04	2.17	–1.43
Chad	37.68	19	74.33	47	56.01	46	–4.24	35.96	15.86
Comoros	57.32	44	38.45	18	47.89	33	–0.98	–14.53	–7.75
Democratic Republic of the Congo	29.68	8	45.72	30	37.70	18	–5.59	1.66	–1.97
Djibouti	48.09	40	44.13	27	46.11	31	1.65	–24.24	–11.29

(*Cont'd*)

Table 2A.1 *(Cont'd)*

Country	EVI 2011 (2012 definition)								
	Exposure Index		Shock Index		EVI 2011		Change in exposure index (Exposure index 2011–Exposure index 2000)	Change in Shock index (Shock index 2011–Shock index 2000)	Change in EVI (EVI 2011–EVI 2000)
	Value	Rank	Value	Rank	Value	Rank			
Equatorial Guinea	43.13	34	41.12	24	42.12	22	–4.08	–14.65	–9.37
Eritrea	29.27	6	88.70	51	58.99	47	–0.72	–	–
Ethiopia	30.13	9	32.63	13	31.38	5	–5.81	–	–
Gambia	49.78	42	84.90	50	67.34	50	–2.28	37.08	17.40
Guinea	34.59	14	20.27	2	27.43	3	–1.34	3.31	0.98
Guinea-Bissau	58.02	45	61.64	43	59.83	48	1.41	–4.92	–1.76
Haiti	35.14	16	54.17	38	44.65	26	2.95	–0.01	1.47
Kiribati	85.50	51	78.75	49	82.13	51	2.36	–7.65	–2.65
Lao People's Democratic Republic	35.38	17	36.03	16	35.71	12	–7.58	–28.72	–18.15
Lesotho	44.56	38	39.82	21	42.19	23	–0.88	–3.35	–2.11
Liberia	49.30	41	53.60	37	51.45	40	–2.16	–22.93	–12.54
Madagascar	33.56	10	40.10	22	36.83	15	–1.59	14.04	6.22
Malawi	41.55	28	54.51	39	48.03	34	–3.30	–4.72	–4.01
Maldives	***69.26***	***49***	***34.96***	***15***	***52.11***	***41***	***1.81***	***22.58***	***12.19***
Mali	38.14	22	32.47	12	35.31	10	–1.57	4.10	1.27
Mauritania	43.56	36	47.79	32	45.67	30	–4.65	22.38	8.87
Mozambique	39.62	25	51.13	34	45.37	29	0.96	–4.88	–1.96
Myanmar	34.24	12	46.00	31	40.12	20	–6.74	11.50	2.38

Nepal	**26.80**	**2**	**27.44**	**5**	**27.12**	**2**	**–7.06**	**–5.34**	**–6.20**
Niger	34.09	11	41.68	25	37.89	19	–1.94	–7.97	–4.95
Rwanda	38.76	24	51.16	35	44.96	27	–3.98	–4.75	–4.37
Samoa	*68.97*	*48*	*32.06*	*11*	*50.51*	*38*	*–0.93*	*–13.41*	*–7.17*
Sao Tome and Principe	55.84	43	29.96	8	42.90	25	–2.53	–24.78	–13.65
Senegal	35.79	18	37.03	17	36.41	14	–1.32	–4.32	–2.82
Sierra Leone	41.01	27	59.11	41	50.06	36	–3.65	4.70	0.53
Solomon Islands	61.95	47	39.80	20	50.88	39	–1.10	–5.51	–3.31
Somalia	42.83	32	51.17	36	47.00	32	–3.25	–25.34	–14.30
Sudan	29.52	7	75.24	48	52.38	42	2.63	–1.96	0.34
Timor-Leste	43.65	37	64.18	44	53.91	44	–7.01		
Togo	38.34	23	28.76	7	33.55	7	–0.97	–9.93	–5.45
Tuvalu	81.29	50	40.90	23	61.10	49	2.99	–22.64	–9.83
Uganda	28.60	5	42.79	26	35.69	11	–8.17	–16.16	–12.16
United Republic of Tanzania	26.81	3	26.90	3	26.86	1	–2.86	–2.78	–2.82
Vanuatu	59.97	46	30.54	9	45.25	28	0.28	–20.37	–10.04
Yemen	27.11	4	44.72	29	35.92	13	–5.17	–17.63	–11.40
Zambia	41.96	30	67.25	46	54.60	45	1.66	17.05	9.36

Notes: 1. EVI = Economic Vulnerability Index.

2. Bhutan, the Maldives, and Nepal in bold; former least developed countries in italics.

Source: Fondation pour les Études et Recherches sur le Développement International.

TABLE 2A.2 Economic Vulnerability Index (2006 Definition) for Present and Former Least Developed Countries, 2011

Country	EVI 2011 (2006–2009 definition)								
	Exposure Index		Shock Index		EVI 2011		Change in exposure index (Exposure index 2011–Exposure index 2000)	Change in Shock index (Shock index 2011–Shock index 2000)	Change in EVI (EVI 2011–EVI 2000)
	Value	Rank	Value	Rank	Value	Rank			
Afghanistan	28.74	3	40.41	34	34.57	9	–16.25	9.32	–3.47
Angola	44.28	21	40.44	35	42.36	28	–1.82	–19.71	–10.76
Bangladesh	14.80	1	22.61	7	18.70	1	–6.10	–1.53	–3.82
Benin	41.35	16	31.30	19	36.32	13	–5.02	–6.57	–5.80
Bhutan	**56.50**	**37**	**42.62**	**37**	**49.56**	**38**	**–9.57**	**18.66**	**4.55**
Botswana	*65.59*	*43*	*32.40*	*24*	*49.00*	*34*	*–0.03*	*1.77*	*0.87*
Burkina Faso	44.23	20	39.77	33	42.00	26	0.68	7.14	3.91
Burundi	52.26	32	53.70	44	52.98	39	–5.94	15.61	4.83
Cambodia	34.77	11	30.99	16	32.88	8	–6.18	–43.31	–24.75
Cape-Verde	*57.84*	*40*	*21.77*	*6*	*39.81*	*19*	*–6.66*	*–5.85*	*–6.25*
Central African Republic	57.59	39	25.56	10	41.58	24	–3.03	3.42	0.20
Chad	47.92	24	67.65	48	57.79	46	–6.64	34.59	13.98
Comoros	72.76	46	34.70	27	53.73	41	–6.75	–9.77	–8.26
Democratic Republic of the Congo	34.06	8	49.87	43	41.96	25	–2.39	3.97	0.79
Djibouti	52.31	33	32.00	23	42.16	27	–0.01	–32.63	–16.32
Equatorial Guinea	61.91	42	31.77	22	46.84	32	–5.77	–23.40	–14.59

Eritrea	49.03	28	76.62	50	62.83	49	7.93	–	–
Ethiopia	31.94	5	15.20	2	23.57	3	–5.77	–	–
Gambia	53.79	34	85.30	51	69.54	50	–1.24	36.76	17.76
Guinea	40.60	15	9.36	1	24.98	4	–3.89	1.28	–1.30
Guinea-Bissau	61.85	41	46.53	41	54.19	43	–4.15	–16.53	–10.34
Haiti	39.76	14	33.39	26	36.57	14	–1.72	–26.55	–14.14
Kiribati	84.68	51	60.95	46	72.82	51	8.03	–0.98	3.52
Lao People's Democratic Republic	42.58	18	35.74	28	39.16	16	–8.91	–25.80	–17.36
Lesotho	56.95	38	21.31	5	40.62	21	–1.56	2.34	–0.10
Liberia	56.33	36	26.28	12	41.31	23	–2.23	–46.49	–24.36
Madagascar	39.06	13	40.47	36	39.77	18	–3.71	17.58	6.94
Malawi	48.51	26	38.92	31	43.72	29	–6.46	–15.98	–11.22
Maldives	***66.01***	***44***	***32.78***	***25***	***49.40***	***36***	***1.24***	***9.48***	***5.36***
Mali	47.74	23	31.61	21	39.67	17	–1.10	5.85	2.37
Mauritania	47.96	25	44.20	39	46.08	31	–3.59	25.80	11.10
Mozambique	41.76	17	31.54	20	36.65	15	–1.16	–10.63	–5.90
Myanmar	25.85	2	55.94	45	40.89	22	–6.10	9.87	1.89
Nepal	**32.42**	**6**	**25.26**	**9**	**28.84**	**5**	**–6.69**	**–10.24**	**–8.47**
Niger	43.54	19	20.72	4	32.13	7	–2.00	–6.72	–4.36
Rwanda	48.61	27	31.06	18	39.84	20	–3.46	–8.73	–6.09
Samoa	*80.27*	*49*	*28.10*	*14*	*54.18*	*42*	*2.82*	*–13.42*	*–5.30*
Sao Tome and Principe	73.17	47	25.75	11	49.46	37	–1.70	–2.69	–2.19

(*Cont'd*)

TABLE 2A.2 (*Cont'd*)

Country	EVI 2011 (2006–2009 definition)								
	Exposure Index		Shock Index		EVI 2011		Change in exposure index (Exposure index 2011–Exposure index 2000)	Change in Shock index (Shock index 2011–Shock index 2000)	Change in EVI (EVI 2011–EVI 2000)
	Value	Rank	Value	Rank	Value	Rank			
Senegal	34.25	9	36.83	29	35.54	10	–1.48	7.95	3.23
Sierra Leone	49.85	29	38.47	30	44.16	30	–5.38	–13.45	–9.41
Solomon Islands	72.56	45	43.06	38	57.81	47	0.26	4.20	2.23
Somalia	52.09	31	45.93	40	49.01	35	–5.16	–31.73	–18.44
Sudan	35.27	12	71.65	49	53.46	40	1.33	–1.21	0.06
Timor-Leste	54.66	35	62.67	47	58.67	48	–8.18	–	–
Togo	47.18	22	24.51	8	35.85	12	–1.60	–9.55	–5.57
Tuvalu	84.26	50	30.89	15	57.57	45	13.13	–44.30	–15.59
Uganda	34.33	10	27.03	13	30.68	6	–6.69	–17.19	–11.94
United Republic of Tanzania	30.51	4	16.56	3	23.54	2	–4.41	–4.26	–4.34
Vanuatu	79.33	48	30.99	17	55.16	44	2.30	–15.22	–6.46
Yemen	32.61	7	38.96	32	35.79	11	–6.82	–33.36	–20.09
Zambia	49.86	30	47.58	42	48.72	33	–0.85	20.84	9.99

Notes: 1. EVI = Economic Vulnerability Index.

2. Bhutan, the Maldives, and Nepal in bold; former least developed countries in italics.

Source: Fondation pour les Études et Recherches sur le Développement International.

Table 2A.3 Impact of the Change in the Environment Component of the Economic Vulnerability Index for Present and Former Least Developed Countries

Country	EVI 2012 (according to Official definition)		EVI (using maximum of LECZ/Dry land)		Difference in Ranking (2)=[C]-[A]	EVI (using mean of LECZ/Dry land)		Difference in Ranking (3)=[D]-[A]
	Value	Rank [A]	Value	Rank [C]		Value	Rank [D]	
Afghanistan	37.5	17	48.8	29	12	43.1	22	5
Angola	49.7	35	52	37	2	50.9	40	5
Bangladesh	31.5	6	31.5	4	–2	27.2	3	–3
Benin	34.8	8	34.8	7	–1	34.2	7	–1
Bhutan	**42.4**	**24**	**42.4**	**16**	**–8**	**42.4**	**21**	**–3**
Botswana	*40.8*	*21*	*53.3*	*40*	*19*	*47.1*	*31*	*10*
Burkina Faso	36.9	16	47.7	25	9	42.3	20	4
Burundi	53.9	43	53.9	41	–2	53.9	43	0
Cambodia	50.3	37	50.3	31	–6	47.5	32	–5
Cape-Verde	*35.1*	*9*	*45.4*	*21*	*12*	*40.3*	*15*	*6*
Central African Republic	31.3	4	31.9	5	1	31.6	5	1
Chad	56	46	67.5	48	2	61.8	48	2
Comoros	47.9	33	47.9	26	–7	46.6	30	–3
Democratic Republic of the Congo	46.1	31	51.4	35	4	48.7	35	4
Djibouti	37.7	18	37.7	11	–7	37.7	12	–6
Equatorial Guinea	42.1	22	42.1	15	–7	41.5	18	–4
Eritrea	59	47	71.1	50	3	65	49	2

(Cont'd)

Table 2A.3 (*Cont'd*)

Country	EVI 2012 (according to Official definition)		EVI (using maximum of LECZ/Dry land)		Difference in Ranking (2)=[C]-[A]	EVI (using mean of LECZ/Dry land)		Difference in Ranking (3)=[D]-[A]
	Value	Rank [A]	Value	Rank [C]		Value	Rank [D]	
Ethiopia	31.4	5	38.3	12	7	34.8	8	3
Gambia	67.3	50	71	49	–1	69.2	50	0
Guinea	27.4	3	27.4	2	–1	26.7	1	–2
Guinea-Bissau	59.8	48	59.8	45	–3	57.4	46	–2
Haiti	44.7	26	44.7	18	–8	44.4	25	–1
Kiribati	82.1	51	82.1	51	0	75.9	51	0
Lao People's Democratic Republic	35.7	12	35.7	8	–4	35.7	9	–3
Lesotho	42.2	23	45.5	22	–1	43.8	23	0
Liberia	51.5	40	51.5	36	–4	50.1	39	–1
Madagascar	36.8	15	37.6	10	–5	37.2	11	–4
Malawi	48	34	48.4	28	–6	48.2	34	0
Maldives	***52.1***	***41***	***52.1***	***38***	***–3***	***45.9***	***29***	***–12***
Mali	35.3	10	46.5	24	14	40.9	17	7
Mauritania	45.7	30	52.8	39	9	49.3	37	7
Mozambique	45.4	29	45.9	23	–6	45.6	28	–1
Myanmar	40.1	20	40.1	13	–7	37.8	13	–7
Nepal	**27.1**	**2**	**27.1**	**1**	**–1**	**27.1**	**2**	**0**
Niger	37.9	19	50.4	32	13	44.1	24	5

Rwanda	45	27	45	19	–8	45	27	0
Samoa	*50.5*	*38*	*50.5*	*33*	*–5*	*47.6*	*33*	*–5*
Sao Tome and Principe	42.9	25	42.9	17	–8	40.6	16	–9
Senegal	36.4	14	41.3	14	0	38.8	14	0
Sierra Leone	50.1	36	50.1	30	–6	49.2	36	0
Solomon Islands	50.9	39	50.9	34	–5	49.4	38	–1
Somalia	47	32	58.6	44	12	52.8	41	9
Sudan	52.4	42	64.7	47	5	58.6	47	5
Timor-Leste	53.9	44	53.9	42	–2	53.6	42	–2
Togo	33.5	7	33.5	6	–1	32.5	6	–1
Tuvalu	61.1	49	61.1	46	–3	54.8	44	–5
Uganda	35.7	11	37.3	9	–2	36.5	10	–1
United Republic of Tanzania	26.9	1	31	3	2	28.9	4	3
Vanuatu	45.3	28	45.3	20	–8	44.8	26	–2
Yemen	35.9	13	48	27	14	42	19	6
Zambia	54.6	45	57.3	43	–2	55.9	45	0

Notes: 1. EVI= Economic Vulnerability Index.

2. Bhutan, the Maldives, and Nepal in bold; former least developed countries in italics.

Source: Fondation pour les Études et Recherches sur le Développement International.

TABLE 2A.4 Ranking Differences Between Present and Former Least Developed Countries for Two Substitute Indicators: Homeless and Victims of Disasters, 2011

Country	Victims		Homeless		Difference in Ranking [A]-[B]
	Value	Rank [A][1]	Value	Rank [B][2]	
Afghanistan	73.16	27	50.77	21	+6
Angola	55.93	13	51.53	22	–9
Bangladesh	93.31	46	75.27	42	+4
Benin	72.3	25	73.63	39	–14
Bhutan	**63.7**	**16**	**36.8**	**13**	**+3**
Botswana	*65.78*	*19*	*63.45*	*31*	*–12*
Burkina Faso	52.71	10	0.00	1	+9
Burundi	85.39	38	53.71	24	+14
Cambodia	95.25	48	64.48	32	+16
Cape-Verde	*67.33*	*23*	*57.97*	*27*	*–4*
Central African Republic	36.89	6	66.08	35	–29
Chad	81.4	32	55.68	25	+7
Comoros	80.59	31	79.63	46	–15
Democratic Republic of the Congo	37.83	7	47.5	19	–12
Djibouti	96.00	49	72.29	36	+13
Equatorial Guinea	6.42	3	31.52	8	–5
Eritrea	96.2	50	43.71	17	+33
Ethiopia	81.42	33	41.74	14	+19
Gambia	55.62	12	52.37	23	–11
Guinea	49.38	8	5.33	3	+5
Guinea-Bissau	71.16	24	46.81	18	+6
Haiti	88.68	40	81.97	47	–7
Kiribati	91.11	44	31.83	9	+35
Lao People's Democratic Republic	85.3	37	90.72	51	–14
Lesotho	85.69	39	18.83	4	+35
Liberia	65.79	21	33.00	11	+10
Madagascar	78.62	30	76.35	44	–14
Malawi	96.58	51	60.88	29	+22
Maldives	***50.66***	***9***	***43.37***	***16***	*–7*
Mali	66.88	22	65.42	33	–11
Mauritania	88.93	42	73.7	40	+2
Mozambique	90.3	43	60.08	28	+15

(Cont'd)

TABLE 2A.4 *(Cont'd)*

Country	Victims		Homeless		Difference in Ranking [A]-[B]
	Value	Rank [A][(1)]	Value	Rank [B][(2)]	
Myanmar	57.99	14	88.56	50	–36
Nepal	**65.63**	**18**	**73.18**	**38**	**–20**
Niger	92.56	45	32.36	10	+35
Rwanda	72.66	26	35.03	12	+14
Samoa	*83.08*	*35*	*86.32*	*49*	*–14*
Sao Tome and Principe	0.00	1	0.00	1	0
Senegal	63.8	17	50.19	20	–3
Sierra Leone	53.42	11	26.2	5	+6
Solomon Islands	75.66	29	83.64	48	–19
Somalia	93.78	47	74.57	41	+6
Sudan	83.26	36	72.38	37	–1
Timor-Leste	34.46	5	28.71	6	–1
Togo	60.82	15	61.24	30	–15
Tuvalu	0.00	1	75.94	43	–42
Uganda	65.79	20	56.8	26	–6
United Republic of Tanzania	74.66	28	42.1	15	+13
Vanuatu	81.7	34	77.65	45	–11
Yemen	31.66	4	65.63	34	–30
Zambia	88.83	41	31.34	7	+34

Notes: 1. Bhutan, the Maldives, and Nepal in bold; former least developed countries in italics.
2. [(1)]Ranking made from the country with the fewest number of victims to the country with the highest number of victims.
3. [(2)]Ranking made from the country with the fewest number of the homeless to the country with the highest number of the homeless.
Source: Fondation pour les Études et Recherches sur le Développement International.

TABLE 2A.5 Physical Vulnerability to Climate Change Index and Its Two Main Components for Present and Former Least Developed Countries, 2012

Country	Progressive Shocks		Intensification of recurrent shocks		PVCCI	
	Value	Rank	Value	Rank	Value	Rank
Afghanistan	56.91	47	54.97	32	55.95	+46
Angola	28.21	30	60.29	44	47.07	+33
Bangladesh	13.00	2	60.67	45	43.87	+27
Benin	24.88	25	47.99	18	38.22	+14
Bhutan	**15.17**	**5**	**46.10**	**12**	**34.31**	**+6**
Botswana	*60.87*	*50*	*50.29*	*23*	*55.83*	*+45*
Burkina Faso	50.71	36	56.48	36	53.67	+41
Burundi	23.33	23	71.97	51	53.50	+40
Cambodia	19.00	13	56.90	37	42.42	+24
Cape Verde	*50.59*	*35*	*50.21*	*22*	*50.40*	*+35*
Central African Republic	14.87	4	44.06	7	32.88	+4
Chad	52.39	38	53.35	28	52.87	+39
Comoros	29.43	32	28.96	1	29.19	+3
Democratic Republic of the Congo	18.21	11	43.54	6	33.37	+5
Djibouti	53.50	42	38.86	5	46.76	+31
Equatorial Guinea	18.06	9	47.10	15	35.67	+9
Eritrea	50.15	34	46.43	14	48.33	+34
Ethiopia	35.41	33	45.53	10	40.79	+20
Gambia	51.79	37	58.03	41	55.00	+43
Guinea	20.87	14	53.01	27	40.28	+18
Guinea-Bissau	22.28	20	62.39	47	46.84	+32
Haiti	25.19	26	50.33	24	39.80	+16
Kiribati	54.99	43	34.64	3	45.96	+30
Lao People's Democratic Republic	11.74	1	63.52	48	45.68	+28
Lesotho	22.02	19	49.60	21	38.37	+15
Liberia	18.96	12	47.16	16	35.94	+10
Madagascar	22.76	22	53.77	29	41.29	+21
Malawi	25.59	27	51.37	26	40.58	+19
Maldives	***72.33***	***51***	***57.64***	***40***	***65.40***	***+51***
Mali	52.59	39	51.06	25	51.83	+37
Mauritania	56.01	44	57.28	38	56.65	+48
Mozambique	26.91	28	55.25	33	43.46	+26

(*Cont'd*)

TABLE 2A.5 (*Cont'd*)

Country	Progressive Shocks		Intensification of recurrent shocks		PVCCI	
	Value	Rank	Value	Rank	Value	Rank
Myanmar	16.37	6	56.47	35	41.57	+22
Nepal	**13.17**	**3**	**59.60**	**43**	**43.16**	**+25**
Niger	56.88	46	55.49	34	56.19	+47
Rwanda	21.99	18	54.63	31	41.64	+23
Samoa	*21.16*	*15*	*34.64*	*3*	*28.71*	+2
Sao Tome and Principe	18.18	10	71.29	50	52.02	+38
Senegal	53.29	40	54.22	30	53.76	+42
Sierra Leone	24.65	24	46.11	13	36.97	+11
Solomon Islands	22.60	21	47.86	17	37.43	+12
Somalia	53.32	41	57.44	39	55.42	+44
Sudan	58.24	49	62.09	46	60.20	+49
Timor-Leste	18.03	8	33.24	2	26.74	+1
Togo	17.93	7	46.06	11	34.95	+8
Tuvalu	57.36	48	44.34	9	51.27	+36
Uganda	21.92	17	48.89	20	37.88	+13
United Republic of Tanzania	28.81	31	48.45	19	39.86	+17
Vanuatu	21.67	16	44.14	8	34.77	+7
Yemen	56.25	45	66.47	49	61.57	+50
Zambia	28.207319	29	58.45	42	45.89	+29

Notes: 1. PVCCI = Physical Vulnerability to Climate Change Index.
2. Ranking from less vulnerable to more vulnerable country. Bhutan, the Maldives, and Nepal in bold; former least developed countries in italics.
Source: Fondation pour les Études et Recherches sur le Développement International.

TABLE 2A.6 Physical Vulnerability to Climate Change Index in Bhutan, the Maldives, and Nepal: Value and Rank for Each Component and Subcomponent

Indices	Bhutan		Maldives		Nepal	
	Value	Rank	Value	Rank	Value	Rank
PVCCI	34.3	6	65.4	51	43.2	25
Progressive shocks	15.2	5	72.3	51	13.2	3
Intensification of recurrent shocks	46.1	12	57.6	40	59.6	43
Flooding due to SLR	0	1*	100	51	0	1*
Increasing aridity	21.5	5	21.5	6	18.6	3
Rainfall	20.8	3	63.9	30	63.6	47
Temperature	61.8	40	50.6	42	55.3	29
Share of drylands	0	1*	0	1*	0	1*
Rainfall instability	31.3	9*	68.8	35	100	51
Temperature instability	69.6	41*	73.9	44*	47.8	21
Trend in temperature	10.2	8	19.6	15	8.1	7
Trend in rainfall	75.5	37	66.4	1*	66.4	1*
Trend in rainfall instability	10.4	2	32.4	6*	27.2	5
Trend in temperature instability	54.0	4*	54.0	4*	62.8	41

Notes: 1. PVCCI = Physical Vulnerability to Climate Change Index.
2. An * denotes a country that has the same rank as at least one another country.
Source: Fondation pour les Études et Recherches sur le Développement International. Physical Vulnerability to Climate Change.

TABLE 2A.7 Composite Indicators of State Fragility in Former and Present Least Developed Countries

Country	Composite indicators of state fragility																
	CPIA index Score 2011 [A]		CPIA index Score 2012 [B]		CPIA index Score 2013 [C]		FSI 2013 [D]		IVI [E]		CIFP fragility score 2012 [F]		CIFP security and crime component 2012 [G]		Difference in Ranking: Rank[C]-Rank[A]	Difference in Ranking: Rank[C]-Rank[B]	Difference in Ranking: Rank[C]-Rank[D]	Difference in Ranking: Rank[E]-Rank[G]
	Value	Rank	Value	Rank	Value	Rank	Value	Rank	Value	Rank	Value	Rank	Value	Rank				
Afghanistan	2.68	41	2.68	42	2.65	43	106.7	43	52.7	50	7.05	47	8.77	49	+2	+1	0	+1
Angola	2.69	40	2.67	43	2.67	42	87.1	20	17.7	32	5.67	15	3.35	27	+2	–1	+22	+5
Bangladesh	3.28	22	3.28	20	3.27	21	92.5	31	26.5	39	5.53	13	4.9	37	–1	+1	–10	+2
Benin	3.47	11	3.47	12	3.51	10	77.9	6	12.3	21	5.77	19	2.46	6	–1	–2	+4	+15
Bhutan	**3.85**	**3**	**3.68**	**9**	**3.68**	**8**	**81.8**	**10**	**9.4**	**13**	**5.2**	**8**	**2.22**	**4**	**+5**	**–1**	**–2**	**+9**
Botswana	–	–	–	–	–	–	*64.0*	*1*	*10.0*	*15*	*4.46*	*2*	*2.32*	*5*	–	–	–	*+10*
Burkina Faso	3.77	6	3.77	5	3.77	5	90.2	26	11.2	18	5.71	17	3.21	24	–1	0	–21	–6
Burundi	3.11	28	3.24	24	3.24	24	97.6	36	29.3	42	6.67	42	5.74	40	–4	0	–12	+2
Cambodia	3.41	17	3.45	14	3.43	15	88.0	22	15.3	25	5.4	11	3.15	21	–2	+1	–7	+4
Cape Verde	*4.01*	*2*	*3.92*	*2*	*3.94*	*2*	*73.7*	*3*	*5.5*	*9*	*4.9*	*5*	*3.82*	*32*	*0*	*0*	*–1*	*–23*
Central African Republic	2.76	39	2.71	40	2.50	46	105.3	41	41.1	45	7.17	49	7.95	45	+7	+6	+5	0
Chad	2.43	44	2.51	45	2.60	44	109.0	45	19.2	34	6.58	41	3.16	22	0	–1	–1	+12
Comoros	2.65	43	2.78	38	2.76	41	84.0	15	3.7	6	5.94	24	3	18	–2	+3	+26	–12
Djibouti	3.18	27	3.09	27	3.09	27	85.5	17	12.0	19	5.92	22	2.71	12	0	0	+10	+7

(Cont'd)

TABLE 2A.7 (*Cont'd*)

Country	Composite indicators of state fragility																	
	CPIA index Score 2011 [A]		CPIA index Score 2012 [B]		CPIA index Score 2013 [C]		FSI 2013 [D]		IVI [E]		CIFP fragility score 2012 [F]		CIFP security and crime component 2012 [G]		Difference in Ranking: Rank[C]-Rank[A]	Difference in Ranking: Rank[C]-Rank[B]	Difference in Ranking: Rank[C]-Rank[D]	Difference in Ranking: Rank[E]-Rank[G]
	Value	Rank	Value	Rank	Value	Rank	Value	Rank	Value	Rank	Value	Rank	Value	Rank				
Democratic Republic of the Congo	2.67	42	2.71	40	2.88	38	111.9	47	52.2	49	7.09	48	8.1	46	–4	–2	–9	+3
Equatorial Guinea	–	–	–	–	–	–	86.1	18	19.8	37	6.1	30	2.09	3	–	–	–	+34
Eritrea	2.16	46	2.08	47	1.99	48	95.0	33	27.0	41	6.34	37	3.2	23	+2	+1	+15	+18
Ethiopia	3.46	13	3.44	15	3.44	13	98.9	37	33.2	43	6.52	39	7.14	42	0	–2	–24	+1
Gambia	3.47	11	3.35	19	3.27	21	81.8	11	16.3	30	6.28	35	2.61	9	+10	+2	+10	+21
Guinea	2.86	37	2.97	33	2.97	33	101.3	40	16.3	29	6.52	39	3.11	19	–4	0	–7	+10
Guinea-Bissau	2.83	38	2.62	44	2.53	45	101.1	39	9.3	12	6.92	45	5.17	38	+7	+1	+6	–26
Haiti	2.90	36	2.90	36	2.83	39	105.8	42	12.0	20	6.07	28	3.33	26	+3	+3	–3	–6
Kiribati	3.03	30	2.88	37	2.91	37	–	–	2.5	4	4.68	4	1.16	2	+7	0	–	+2
Lao People's Democratic Republic	3.36	19	3.40	17	3.36	19	83.7	14	9.4	14	5.74	18	3.23	25	0	+2	+5	–11
Lesotho	3.43	16	3.48	11	3.47	11	79.4	7	16.2	28	5.3	9	2.91	17	–5	0	+4	+11
Liberia	3.03	30	3.06	28	3.13	26	95.1	34	11.0	16	6.31	36	3.64	30	–4	–2	–8	–14

Madagascar	3.23	25	3.04	30	3.02	31	82.7	12	19.4	35	6.08	29	3.5	29	+6	+1	+19	+6
Malawi	3.27	24	3.16	26	3.07	28	89.2	23	11.1	17	5.82	20	2.83	16	+4	+2	+5	+1
Maldives	***3.33***	***20***	***3.28***	***20***	***3.23***	***25***	***75.4***	***5***	***7.0***	***11***	***5.16***	***7***	***2.47***	***7***	***+5***	***+5***	***+20***	***+4***
Mali	3.64	10	3.38	18	3.38	17	89.3	25	19.7	36	6.81	43	7.32	43	+7	–1	–8	–7
Mauritania	3.20	26	3.23	25	3.29	20	91.7	29	17.3	31	6.16	33	3.11	19	–6	–5	–9	+12
Mozambique	3.68	9	3.73	7	3.62	9	82.8	13	13.3	23	5.96	25	3.89	33	0	+2	–4	–10
Myanmar	–	–	–	–	2.95	35	94.6	32	41.2	46	6.4	38	7.61	44	–	–	+3	+2
Nepal	**3.28**	**23**	**3.27**	**22**	**3.38**	**18**	**91.8**	**30**	**24.5**	**38**	**5.69**	**16**	**5.47**	**39**	**–5**	**–4**	**–12**	**–1**
Niger	3.40	18	3.48	10	3.46	12	99.0	38	12.5	22	6.17	34	4.67	36	–6	+2	–26	–14
Rwanda	3.82	4	3.84	3	3.93	3	89.3	24	37.3	44	6.12	32	6.73	41	–1	0	–21	+3
Samoa	*4.10*	*1*	*4.06*	*1*	*4.00*	*1*	*68.7*	*2*	*3.4*	*5*	*4.63*	*3*	*2.62*	*10*	*0*	*0*	*–1*	*–5*
Sao Tome and Principe	3.05	29	3.05	29	3.05	30	74.6	4	1.3	3	6.01	27	4.06	34	+1	+1	+26	–31
Senegal	3.78	5	3.82	4	3.82	4	81.4	9	18.4	33	5.6	14	4.63	35	–1	0	–5	–2
Sierra Leone	3.31	21	3.27	22	3.27	21	91.2	27	7.0	10	6.11	31	2.56	8	0	–1	–6	+2
Solomon Islands	2.93	35	2.96	35	2.93	36	85.2	16	1.2	2	2.04	1	2.74	14	+1	+1	+20	–12
Somalia	–	–	–	–	–	–	113.9	48	57.4	51	7.81	50	8.8	50	–	–	–	+1
Sudan	2.36	45	2.32	46	2.36	47	111.0	46	52.2	48	7.01	46	8.55	47	+2	+1	+1	+1
United Republic of Tanzania	3.70	8	3.75	6	3.76	6	81.1	8	15.4	26	5.51	12	2.75	15	–2	0	–2	+11
Timor-Leste	3.02	32	3.02	31	3.06	29	91.5	28	4.2	8	5.92	22	3.68	31	–3	–2	+1	–23
Togo	2.99	33	2.97	33	2.97	33	87.8	21	14.0	24	5.98	26	2.66	11	0	0	+12	+13
Tuvalu	–	–	2.77	39	2.77	40	–	–	1.2	1	–	–	–	–	–	+1	–	–

(*Cont'd*)

Table 2A.7 (*Cont'd*)

Country	Composite indicators of state fragility																	
	CPIA index Score 2011 [A]		CPIA index Score 2012 [B]		CPIA index Score 2013 [C]		FSI 2013 [D]		IVI [E]		CIFP fragility score 2012 [F]		CIFP security and crime component 2012 [G]		Difference in Ranking: Rank[C]-Rank[A]	Difference in Ranking: Rank[C]-Rank[B]	Difference in Ranking: Rank[C]-Rank[D]	Difference in Ranking: Rank[E]-Rank[G]
	Value	Rank	Value	Rank	Value	Rank	Value	Rank	Value	Rank	Value	Rank	Value	Rank				
Uganda	3.77	6	3.72	8	3.72	7	96.6	35	26.6	40	5.91	21	3.39	28	+1	−1	−28	+12
Vanuatu	3.43	15	3.44	15	3.44	13	–	–	3.8	7	4.98	6	1.14	1	−2	−2	–	+6
Yemen	2.98	34	2.99	32	2.99	32	107.0	44	51.8	47	6.83	44	8.59	48	−2	0	−12	−1
Zambia	3.46	13	3.46	13	3.42	16	86.6	19	15.7	27	5.36	10	2.72	13	+3	+3	−3	+14

Notes: 1. CPIA = Country Policy and Institutional Assessment; IVI = Internal Violence Index; CIFP = Country Indicators for Foreign Policy; FSI = Failed States Index.

2. Bhutan, the Maldives, and Nepal in bold; former least developed countries in italics.

3. The ranking is from less fragile to more fragile country.

a. Rank [A] excludes Botswana, Equatorial Guinea, Myanmar, Somalia, and Tuvalu.

b. Rank [B] excludes Botswana, Equatorial Guinea, Myanmar, and Somalia.

c. Rank [C] excludes Botswana, Equatorial Guinea, and Somalia.

d. Rank [D] excludes Kiribati, Tuvalu, and Vanuatu.

e. Rank [F] and Rank [G] exclude Tuvalu.

Sources: Fund for Peace, Country Profiles, available at www.statesindex.org (last accessed on 9 October 2015); World Bank Group, Country Policy and Institutional Assessment Database, available at http://www.worldbank.org/ida (last accessed on 9 October 2015); Fondation pour les Études et Recherches sur le Développement International; Carleton University, Country Indicators for Foreign Policy, available at http://www4.carleton.ca/cifp/ (last accessed on 9 October 2015).

Annexure 2B. Composite Indicators of Policy and State Fragility Used in the Fourth Section

The Failed States Index Developed by the Fund for Peace

The Fragile States Index is based on the proprietary Conflict Assessment System Tool analytical platform of the Fund for Peace. Using comprehensive social science methodology, data from three primary sources are triangulated and subjected to critical review to obtain final scores for the Failed States Index. The following 12 primary social, economic, and political indicators of the Conflict Assessment System Tool methodology, developed by the Fund for Peace, are used:

1. Social Indicators
   a. demographic pressures
   b. refugees and internally displaced persons
   c. group grievance
   d. human flight and brain drain
2. Economic Indicators
   a. uneven economic development
   b. poverty and economic decline
3. Political and Military Indicators
   a. state legitimacy
   b. public services
   c. human rights and rule of law
   d. security apparatus
   e. factionalized elites
   f. external intervention

The rank order of the states is based on the total scores of the 12 indicators. For each indicator, the ratings are placed on a scale of 0 to 10, with 0 being the lowest intensity (most stable) and 10 being the highest intensity (least stable). The total score is the sum of the 12 indicators and is on a scale of 0–120.

Country Policy and Institutional Assessment

The overall country score of the country policy and institutional assessment, as developed by the World Bank, is obtained from a set of 16 criteria grouped in four equally weighted clusters:

1. Economic Management
   a. Monetary and exchange rate policies
   b. fiscal policy
   c. debt policy and management
2. Structural Policies
   a. trade
   b. financial sector
   c. business regulatory environment
3. Policies for Social Inclusion and Equity
   a. gender equality
   b. equity of public resource use
   c. building human resources
   d. social protection and labour
   e. policies and institutions for environmental sustainability
4. Public Sector Management and Institutions
   a. property right and rule-based governance
   b. quality of budgetary and financial management
   c. efficiency of revenue mobilization
   d. quality of public administration
   e. transparency, accountability, and corruption in the public sector

For each of the 16 criteria, countries are rated on a scale of 1 (low) to 6 (high). The scores depend on the level of performance in a given year assessed against the criteria, rather than on changes in performance compared to the previous year. The ratings depend on actual policies and performance, rather than on promises or intentions.

For further information on the criteria, go to this page: http://www.worldbank.org/ida/IRAI/2011/webFAQ11.pdf

Country Indicators for Foreign Policy

Country Indicators for Foreign Policy's fragile states index, developed by Carleton University, is obtained by grouping structural indicators into six clusters, capturing different facets of state fragility and robustness: governance, economics, security and crime, human development, demography, and environment. Global scores are distributed across a nine-point index. The best performing state receives a score of one, the worst a score of nine. The rest are continuously distributed between these two extremes based on relative performance.

To know more about the six clusters used for the computation of the global score, visit this page: http://www4.carleton.ca/cifp/ffs_indicator_descriptions.htm

Political Stability and Absence of Violence Measured by the Worldwide Governance Indicators

Political stability and absence of violence, as measured by the Worldwide Governance Indicators, is one of the six broad dimensions of governance. It captures perceptions of the likelihood that the government will be destabilized or overthrown by unconstitutional or violent means, including political violence and terrorism.

For further information about the variables used to construct the indices, see http://info.worldbank.org/governance/wgi/pdf/pv.pdf

References

Andrimihaja, N.A., M. Cinyabuguma, and S. Devarajan. 2011. 'Avoiding the Fragility Trap in Africa', World Bank Policy Research Working Paper. No. 5884. Washington, DC: World Bank.

Brückner, M. and A. Ciccone. 2010. 'International Commodity Prices, Growth, and the Outbreak of Civil War in Sub-Saharan Africa', *The Economic Journal*, 120(544): 519–34.

Cariolle, J. 2011. 'The Economic Vulnerability Index: 2010 Update'. Ferdi Working Paper Innovative Indicators Series. No. 117.

______. 2016. 'The Voracity and the Scarcity Effects of Exports Booms and Busts on Bribery', Working Paper no. 146, Fondation pour les Études et Recherches sur le Developpement International, ClermontFerrand.

Cariolle, J. and M. Goujon. 2013. 'A Retrospective Economic Vulnerability Index, 1990–2011: Using the 2012 UN-CDP definitions, Ferdi Working Paper Innovative Indicators Series No. I17. Paris: La Fondation pour les Études et Recherches sur le Développement International.

Cariolle, J. and P. Guillaumont. 2011. 'A Retrospective Economic Vulnerability Index: 2010 update', Ferdi Policy Brief No. 17. Paris: La Fondation pour les Études et Recherches sur le Développement International.

Cariolle, J., M. Goujon, and P. Guillaumont. 2014. *Has Structural Economic Vulnerability Decreased in Least Developed Countries? Lessons Drawn from Retrospective Indices*. Paris: La Fondation pour les Études et Recherches sur le Développement International.

Closset M., S. Feindouno, and M. Goujon. 2014. 'Human Assets Index Retrospective Series: 2013 Update', Working Paper no. 110, Fondation pour les Études et Recherches sur le Developpement International, Clermont-Ferrand.

Collier, P. 2009. *The Political Economy of Fragile States and Implications for European Development Policy.* Oxford: Oxford University Press.

Dabla–Norris E. and Y.B. Gündüz. 2014. 'Exogenous Shocks and Growth Crises in Low-Income Countries: A Vulnerability Index', *World Development,* 59: 360–78.

Drabo, A. and P. Guillaumont. 2014. 'Assessing the Prospects of Accelerated Graduation of the Least Developed Countries', *Istanbul Programme of Action for the LDCs (2011–2020): Monitoring Deliverables, Tracking Progress—Analytical Perspectives*. pp. 71–103. London, United Kingdom: Commonwealth Secretariat, Marlborough House.

Fondation pour les Études et Recherches sur le Développement International. 2013. *Retrospective Economic Vulnerability Index Database.* Paris: La Fondation pour les Études et Recherches sur le Développement International.

______. 2014. *Retrospective Human Assets Index Database.* Paris: La Fondation pour les Études et Recherches sur le Développement International.

______. 2015a. *Physical Vulnerability to Climate Change Index Database.* Paris: La Fondation pour les Études et Recherches sur le Développement International.

______. 2015b. *Internal Violence Index Database.* Paris: La Fondation pour les Études et Recherches sur le Développement International.

Feindouno S. and M. Goujon M. 2016. 'The Retrospective Economic Vulnerability Index, 2015 Update', Working Paper P147, Fondation pour les Études et Recherches sur le Developpement International, Clermont-Ferrand.

Feindouno, S., M. Goujon, and L. Wagner. 2016. *Internal Violence Index: A Composite and Quantitative Measure of Internal Violence and Crime In Developing Countries*. Ferdi.

Fund for Peace. 2013. *Failed States Index*, available at http://library.fundforpeace.org/fsi13 (last accessed on 25 November 2016).

Guillaumont, P. 1999. 'On the Economic Vulnerability of Low Income Countries'. *FERDI Études et Documents.* Paris: La Fondation pour les Études et Recherches sur le Développement International.

______. 2006. 'Macro Vulnerability in Low-Income Countries and Aid Responses', in F. Bourguignon, B. Pleskovic, and J. van der Gaag (eds), *Securing Development in an Unstable Word: Annual World Bank Conference on Development Europe*, pp. 65–108. Washington, DC: Word Bank.

______. 2009a. *Caught in a Trap: Identifying the Least Developed Countries*. Paris: Economica.

______. 2009b. 'An Economic Vulnerability Index: Its Design and Use for International Development Policy', *Oxford Development Studies*, 37(3): 193–228.

______. 2010a. 'Assessing the Economic Vulnerability of Small Island Developing States and the Least Developed Countries', *Journal of Development Studies*, 46(5): 828–54.

______. 2013. 'Measuring Structural Vulnerability to Allocate Development Assistance and Adaptation Resources' *Ferdi Working Paper.* No. 68. Paris: La Fondation pour les Études et Recherches sur le Développement International.

______. 2014. 'A necessary small revision to the EVI to make it more balanced and equitable'. *Ferdi Policy Brief.* No. 98. Paris: La Fondation pour les Études et Recherches sur le Développement International.

______. 2015. 'Measuring Structural Economic Vulnerability in Africa', in J. Yifu Lin and C. Monga (eds), *The Oxford Handbook of Africa and Economics, Volume I: Context and Concepts*, pp. 407–26. Oxford, UK: Oxford University Press.

Guillaumont, P. 2015. 'Measuring Vulnerability to Climate Change for Allocating Funds to Adaptation' in S. Barrett, C. Carraro, and J. de Melo (eds), *Towards a Workable and Effective Climate Regime*, pp. 515–33. CEPR and Ferdi.

Guillamumont, P., C. Simonet, M. Closset, and S. Feindouno. 2016. 'A Physical Vulnerability to Climate Change Index: Which are the Most Vulnerable developing Countries?', Ferdi Working Paper.

Guillaumont, P. and L. Chauvet. 2007. *Aid, Volatility and Growth Again When Aid Volatility Matters and When it Does Not,* CERDI Working Papers 200707. Paris: La Fondation pour les Études et Recherches sur le Développement International.

Guillaumont, P. and S. Guillaumont Jeanneney. 2000. Options for Exchange Rate Policy in Selected Least Developed Countries (Bangladesh, Bhutan, Cambodia, Lao PDR, and Nepal). *Options for Exchange Rate Policies: Least Developed Countries Series No 3*. Bangkok: United Nations Economic and Social Commission for Asia and Pacific.

Guillaumont, P. and S. Guillaumont Jeanneney. 2009. 'State Fragility and Economic Vulnerability: What is Measured and Why?' Paper prepared for the European Report of Development, Barcelona, 7–8 May.

Guillaumont, P., M. McGillivray, and L. Wagner. 2013. 'Performance Assessment: How it Depends on Structural Economic Vulnerability and Human Capital. Implications for the Allocation of Aid', Ferdi Working Paper No. 71. Paris: La Fondation pour les Études et Recherches sur le Développement International.

Guillaumont, P. and C. Simonet. 2011a. 'Designing an Index of Structural Vulnerability to Climate Change', FERDI Policy Brief No. 18. Paris: La Fondation pour les Études et Recherches sur le Développement International.

International Centre for Integrated Mountain Development. 2011. *Glacial Lakes and Glacial Lake Outburst Floods in Nepal*. Kathmandu: ICIMOD.

Marshall, R. 2013. 'Graduation from the Group of Least Developed Countries: Prospects and Challenges for Bhutan', 12th Round Table Meeting, 11–12 December, Thimphu.

Miguel E., S. Satyanath, and E. Sergenti. 2004. 'Economic Shocks and Civil Conflict: An Instrumental Variables Approach', *Journal of Political Economy*, 112(4): 725–53.

Organisation for Economic Co-operation and Development (OECD). 2010. *Resource Flows to Fragile and Conflict-Affected States*. Paris: OECD Publishing.

______. 2012. *Fragile States 2013: Resource Flows and Trends in a Shifting World*. Paris: DAC International Network on Conflict and Fragility.

______. 2014. *Fragile States 2014: Domestic Revenue Mobilisation in Fragile States*. Paris.

Ramey, G. and V.A. Ramey. 1995. 'Cross-Country Evidence on the Link between Volatility and Growth', *The American Economic Review*, 85(5): 1138–51.

Rice, Susan E. and Stewart Patrick. 2008. *Index of State Weakness in the Developing World*, Brookings Institution, available at http://www.brookings.edu/research/reports/2008/02/weak-states-index (last accessed on 13 September 2016).

Royal Monetary Authority of Bhutan (RMA). various years. *Annual Reports*. Thimphu: RMA.

United Nations. 2005. *Development Challenges in Sub-Saharan Africa and Post-conflict Countries, United Nations, 2005*. Report on the seventh session, Economic and Social Council Official Records.

______. 2008. *Handbook on the Least Development Country Category: Inclusion, Graduation and Special Support Measures*. New York: Committee for Development Policy and UN Department of Economic and Social Affairs.

______. 2011. 'Committee for Development Policy', Report on the thirteenth session, Economic and Social Council Official Records.

United Nations Development Programme. 2008. *Post-Conflict Economic Recovery: Enabling Local Ingenuity*. New York.

World Bank. 2013. *World Development Indicators 2013*. Washington, DC: World Bank.

______. 2014. *World Development Report 2014: Risk and Opportunity—Managing Risk for Development*. Washington, DC: World Bank.

World Bank. 2016. *FY 2016 Information Note: The World Bank Group's Harmonized List of Fragile Situations.* Washington, DC: World Bank.

______. n.d. *World Integrated Trade Solution*, available at http://wits.worldbank.org/ (last accessed on 10 November 2015).

3

KARMA URA

The Experience of Gross National Happiness as a Development Framework*

In 1972, His Majesty King Jigme Singye Wangchuck first introduced the gross national happiness (GNH) concept by stating that gross domestic product (GDP) was less important than GNH because GDP alone could not deliver happiness and well-being. The last 40 years have shown that many societies are interested in not only GDP but also something more. Oswald (2010: 10) said, 'GDP is a gravely dated pursuit.' The GDP-based system preceded any knowledge of climate change or the finite limits of the earth's resources. GDP is an accounts system that measures external conditions of human existence, as far as they can be measured, through prices. One of the reasons why monetary measures of economic performance have come to play such an important role is that the monetary valuation of goods and services makes it easy to add up quantities of

* I am most grateful to Sabina Alkire, Director of the Oxford Poverty and Human Development Initiative at the University of Oxford for her detailed comments on the draft. I am equally thankful to Hoe Yun Jeong, Senior Economist at the South Asia Department, Asian Development Bank for his guidance and comments. Two anonymous referees also provided very helpful feedback.

very different natures (Stiglitz, Sen, and Fittoussi 2010). However, things are more complicated than this in practice. Prices may not exist for some goods and services. Moreover, even if prices do exist, they may deviate from a society's underlying valuation. According to Van den Bergh (2009: 120), 'GDP information influences all agents in the economy: consumers, savers, investors, banks, stock and option markets, private companies, the government, central banks, and international organizations. Because of the misleading nature of GDP information, economic agents take wrong decisions from the perspective of social welfare.' Van den Bergh has pointed out that GDP does not clearly differentiate between costs and benefits, or stocks and flows, and, therefore, violates the two fundamental principles of good bookkeeping.

The limitations of GDP as a measure of progress are that it does not (i) make any distinction between GDP from good development and GDP from bad development, (ii) adequately value natural human and social capital, (iii) value free time and leisure, (iv) value unpaid work, and (v) explicitly provide for equity. GNH attempts to correct those shortcomings with proxy measures for social welfare. In the same vein, the present King, His Majesty Jigme Khesar Namgyel Wangchuck, has said that GNH measures the quality of a country in a more holistic way and believes that the beneficial development of human society takes place when material and spiritual development occur side by side as complements reinforcing each other. Article 9 of the Constitution of the Kingdom of Bhutan emphasizes that 'the State shall strive to promote those conditions that will enable the pursuit of GNH'. GDP does not receive specific mention in the constitution as GNH does, although phrases such as 'economic self-reliance', 'open and progressive economy', and 'fair market competition' are mentioned. Furthermore, even in Bhutan, the government has increasingly begun to use GDP-related indicators—which can be misleading, as van den Bergh contended, with respect to social welfare—while dualistically striving towards maximizing GNH. Balancing between GNH and GDP poses an ever-greater challenge to governance.

This chapter explores GNH as a framework for socio-economic development in Bhutan by elucidating GNH principles that affect the way Bhutanese society and the government interact. This chapter explores how Bhutan is developing, in practice, by assessing policy intentions versus policy outcomes and declarations.

An ideal society, according to the GNH vision as expressed in the Constitution, is presented in this chapter. The discussion of the conceptual structure of GNH is not just an expression of idealism. This section includes self-reported causes of happiness found in the national GNH Survey and the findings inform the conceptual structure of GNH. Next is a discussion of the three key concepts of happiness: (i) subjective well-being (SWB); (ii) Buddhist happiness; and (iii) GNH. How a GNH vision of a happy society is structured around the nine domains of GNH is then explained.

A short account of the rationale for GNH indicators is given before the hierarchy of indicators is presented. The methodology behind the construction of GNH indicators based on datasets collected from a series of nationwide surveys is then explained.

The most distinctive findings from GNH surveys and their implications for development policies are discussed further. Not surprisingly, analysis of the data shows that equality, family integrity, health, gender equity, and job satisfaction were among the perceived drivers of happiness. There are many other less emphasized aspects that play a critical role in happiness such as emotional robustness, meditation, age, supportive relationships, and community vitality. The GNH surveys confirm the importance of these intangible and relational factors that governance should address.

In the section 'Multidimensional Framework: State and Non-official Institutions and Actors', a multidimensional framework for governance and the actors and institutions responsible for increasing GNH are assessed. These institutions include the commanding heights of decision-making such as the Cabinet, central ministries, and central autonomous agencies. The roles of administrative and legislative personnel at the district and *gewog* (county) levels and how they are accountable to multiple authorities for programme implementation are also presented. Recent political dynamics among state and non-official actors are discussed to assess the GNH framework's emerging impacts. Non-official actors such as donors, civil society organizations (CSOs), and business corporations—with their distinctive interests and preferences—add complexity to implementation of the GNH framework.

The section 'Using the Gross National Happiness Policy-screening Tool in Decision-making' presents the GNH decision-making and monitoring tools that are used in policymaking and their limitations, including Five-Year Plans. This section also discusses political and economic pressures that can potentially override or subvert GNH.

The section 'Gross National Happiness Socio-economic Impacts and Policy Outcomes' provides concrete examples of how government policies related to tourism, the media, and wildlife have sought to reflect GNH, and highlights various points of contention. The dynamics of outcomes by testing for GNH on the ground are shown through a summary of case studies (Ritu and Ura forthcoming) and a PhD thesis by Schroeder (2014).

The section 'Gross National Happiness Outreach' describes how the concept of GNH is shared with the citizenry, for example, via the dissemination activities of the Centre for Bhutan Studies and through a revised, more holistic educational curriculum. It discusses the outreach efforts that aim to broaden and deepen GNH in the minds and hearts of Bhutanese through the media, primary and secondary schools, and universities (both in and outside the country). It also assesses the progress made so far in the domestic and international spheres.

The section 'Future Outlook' concludes with the assertion that Bhutan's experiment with GNH remains dynamic and evolving, and suggests that the policy process surrounding it may be of interest to those in the international community who have been intrigued by the idea of GNH. This concluding section also provides an outlook on whether GNH offers a realistic alternative towards attaining higher SWB and reducing unsustainable development in Bhutan.

Visions of the Individual, Society, and Governing Systems

A person envisioned in the GNH framework is embedded in the values of a fulfilled society. GNH envisions a person to be bonded deeply to his or her safe and supportive community in which the trustworthiness of people is high and fear of victimization by other human beings is ideally non-existent. A community envisioned in the GNH framework is set deeply in a nurturing ecology just as an individual is deeply bonded to a community.

A person's psychological attributes begin with freeing his or her basic good nature of kindness, generosity, forgiveness, contentment, and compassion from repression by blinding negative emotions like anger, jealousy, and selfishness. This inner view of a person is the subject of the psychological domain of GNH.

The domains of good governance, living standards, health, and education in GNH articulate familiar developmental perspectives. In the health domain, a person envisioned in the GNH framework should experience more than 26 healthy days a month, have a high level of self-reported health, and must not suffer serious deprivations from disability. In the education domain, GNH indicators are broadened to cultivate values against self-destructive and other destructive actions in mind, body, and speech. Certain alternative knowledge that is transmitted outside formal institutions is included in the education indicators. Knowledge transmission takes place everywhere.

These familiar domains are complemented by the domains of environmental diversity, community vitality, cultural diversity, and time use. By including time as an independent element in GNH, a person as envisioned in a GNH-based society should not suffer from a poverty of available time. He/she should experience joy of slowness and the daily right of ample time for socializing, active leisure, and wholesome sleep (Kundera 1996).

In order to realize this vision of society, the role of the ideal government, as identified in 1729 in the legal code of Bhutan and described by the eighteenth-century *Je Khenpo* (Chief Abbot of the Central Monastic Body of Bhutan) Tenzin Chogyal is as follows: 'The purpose of the government is to provide happiness to its people. If it cannot provide happiness, there is no reason for the government to exist.' The government's aim should be to provide enabling conditions for happiness as it cannot directly provide happiness. Alongside the objectives and values of GNH that shape agencies, the actors and institutions of the state and society should manifest GNH in practice. Achieving coherence in practice in both the state and society is a challenge because of diverse interests and motivations.

Conceptual Structure of Subjective Well-being, Buddhist Happiness, and Gross National Happiness

There are three broad concepts of happiness relevant to the discussion in this chapter. Happiness, defined as subjective well-being (SWB), is argued to be the sole relevant moral consideration by Layard (2005).

In addition, Buddhists see happiness as a universal goal of all sentient beings and, therefore, the basis of ethics. It is relevant to introduce the Buddhist concept of happiness since Buddhism influences Bhutan and much of the Himalayas. GNH, which is a melding of both objective and subjective elements, is the third concept of happiness.

Subjective Well-being

SWB is measured either as a short-term emotional experience or a long-term judgement of life as a whole, usually measured on a self-reported scale of 0–10.[1] As a short-term emotional experience, questions posed consist of variations of how happy a person is either currently or the day before. Psychologists call these questions about affects and they seek to gather information on an individual's current emotional life. Affect measures are useful for identifying mood changes on a short-term basis. For purposes of comparison, Thailand tracks affect measures more frequently than other countries.[2] With respect to the long-term evaluative experience of life, a similar question is asked but the scope is an individual's entire life. Both affect measures are purely mental concepts of well-being. But they have their correlates that are both mental and non-mental (outside the mind of the subject) factors, and establishing their correlations—and therefore beginning to uncover ways to increase happiness—is the more important part of the inquiry on subjective happiness. Current emotions or feelings are experienced and reported directly. Judgements about current life satisfaction or happiness in life (remembered happiness) as a whole require huge biographical reflection on both the past and the future of one's life course. Often, these two measures are not consistent. However, we should remember that all judgements are summations (or flavours) of our life in totality. They are not mathematical

[1] Variations of this question include: 'Overall, how happy were you yesterday?' (United Kingdom Office for National Statistics); 'Taking all things together, how happy would you say you are?' (European Social Survey); and 'Taking all things together, would you say you are very happy, quite happy, not very happy, or not at all happy?' (World Values Survey).

[2] See the ABAC Poll of Assumption University of Thailand, available at www.abacpoll.au.edu/ (last accessed in March 2016).

aggregations of daily, weekly, and monthly evaluations. Such judgements form the basis of evaluation whenever a survey conducts a biographic evaluation of life as a whole, not only when measuring current happiness on a scale of 0–10.

If scoring a 9 or 10 is considered enjoying an ecstatic state of being, then 6.6 per cent of the global population was ecstatic in 2015 according to the Gallup World Poll. Certainly, a score of zero should be regarded as reflecting a life hardly worth living: 1.7 per cent of the global population recorded this number. If scoring below two were considered unacceptable suffering, then 8.9 per cent of the global population endures such suffering. Notably, this is well below the 21 per cent of the global population who lives on less than $1.25 a day (International Labour Organization 2010: Table A12 as cited in Therborn 2011: 190). The proportion of the global population living on less than $1.25/day roughly matches the share of those who are abjectly unhappy if this is defined as those scoring below three.

From the point of environmental sustainability, the correlation between a high ecological footprint (for example, carbon footprint) and high SWB found in the developed countries is a point of concern. In the future, the path to high SWB cannot be sustained by exerting such a heavy ecological footprint.

The GNH Survey also inquired about the various self-reported causes of happiness through an open-ended question (Figure 3.1). The classification of these self-reported answers in both urban and rural areas shows that financial security, good health, family relationships, housing, and landownership were the top five factors in Bhutan. On the other hand, the self-reported causes of happiness demonstrate that what individuals have already is taken for granted and not reported. These self-reported causes largely appear to be current needs that they lack at the time of the survey and wish for their government to know about it. For example, a good natural environment, which affects SWB, hardly registers as its existence is widespread and therefore taken for granted. Good educational (school) infrastructure, which is also enjoyed widely, is not high on the list either.

Another question that was posed to each of the 7,146 persons in the 2010 GNH Survey in Bhutan was a self-assessment of SWB on a scale of 0–10. The results show that the national average for SWB was 6.06 (SD = 1.6), suggesting a very good level of happiness in Bhutan in spite

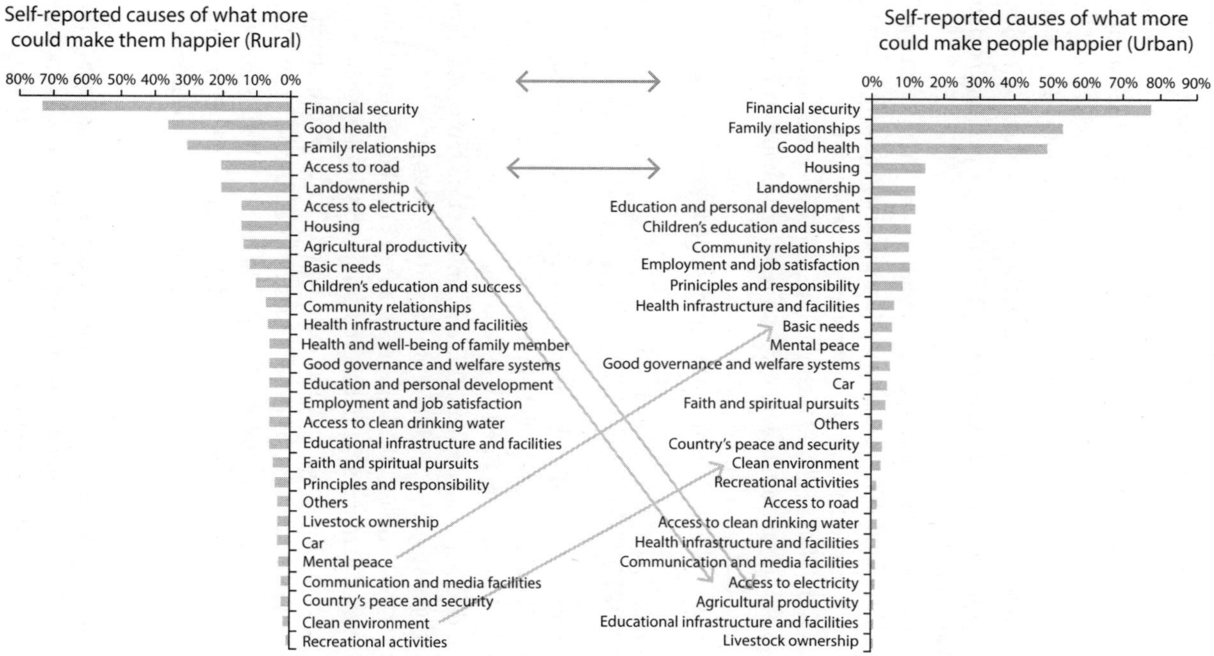

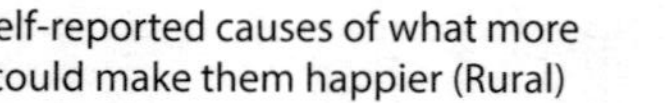

FIGURE 3.1 Self-reported Causes of Happiness—Rural versus Urban Residents

Source: Author's illustration from Gross National Happiness Survey of 2010, available at http://www.grossnationalhappiness.com (last accessed on 1 October 2016).

of having a low per capita income and being classified by the World Bank as among the world's least developed countries.

The percentage distribution of the Bhutanese population on a scale of 0–10 is important as well as the national average. When we group the people into three classes according to the level of their scores, 3.9 per cent of the population scored between 0 and 3, which is a far smaller percentage than the global distribution of this group that might be considered to be desperate. In Bhutan, the bulk of the population, or 78.8 per cent, scored between 4 and 7, while 17.3 per cent scored between 8 and 10.

The 2010 GNH Survey gathered information on variables that can be causally related to SWB. Variables that are positively and significantly related to SWB at the 1 per cent, 5 per cent, or 10 per cent level of significance include: (i) household income (log), (ii) land owned (in acres), (iii) positive emotions (sub-index), (iv) self-reported health, (v) marital status, (vi) meditation, (vii) education level, (viii) frequency of socializing with relatives, and (ix) trust in Bhutanese people in general.[3]

Buddhist Happiness

A second strand views happiness as an inner experience attained (especially) through meditation. Such happiness is an ethical practice for the person meditating and obtained by generating a motivation of compassion and kindness towards others. It is certainly not metaphysical. This view is a secular aspect of Buddhist ethics and psychology.

The 2010 GNH Survey asked questions about both current and long-term emotions. Current and remembered emotions will diverge because memory cannot fully map original experience. To be more specific, memory is a reconstruction of experiences fit into current views. Past emotions are also subjected to revision in light of one's beliefs and self-concepts. Several studies (Fredrickson and Kahneman 1993: 45; Thomas and Deiner 1990: 291) show divergences between actual experiences

[3] This is based on 6,436 observations (after dropping missing values) from the 2010 GNH Survey. Regression analysis using SWB scores as a dependent variable and other plausible variables as independent variables is another method of confirming statistically causes and correlates of SWB. Multivariate regression analysis is useful for finding isolated effects of factors on SWB.

and remembrance or judgement of emotions. We remember the peak and final moments of an experience better than we remember all of it. We also remember more the intensity of emotions rather than their absolute frequency (Deiner and Oishi 2005). Therefore, our memories have regular patterns of distortion.

All of these findings suggest that bad memories need not detain us in a state of low emotions since we fortunately forget painful emotions. However, there is a difference between forgetting painful emotions or feelings and being constantly infused with positive emotions such as kindness and compassion. For happiness, we can and must cultivate positive emotions by changing the pattern of our thoughts since thoughts lead to emotions. This is one of the main insights stressed in Buddhist approaches to happiness and enforced through various types of meditations and trainings.

How happy people feel in the present moment is considered to be a positive affect or emotion. Words such as 'feeling happy now', 'positive emotions', 'positive affects', and 'pleasures' are interchangeable to some extent. Such feelings can change in the course of a day or a week and are, therefore, subject to cycles of fluctuation (Csikszentmihalyi and Hunter 2003).

These fluctuations, however, depend also on the kind of self we harbour; here, the Buddhist notion of happiness makes a mark. Self-centred people, rather than selfless people, are more likely to experience short-term fluctuations between satisfaction and dissatisfaction (Dambrun et al. 2012). A deeply self-centred person is in a double state of confusion. First, he / she is confused about a clear and separated self. Second, he / she is confused about a clear, separate self and separate others. Thus, the boundaries between himself / herself and others also become rigid. Second, he / she mistakenly confuses personal pleasure with happiness. Happiness in a Buddhist sense is somewhat independent of pleasure. Pleasure is circumstantial, but happiness is an inner strength and an inner resource to deal better with circumstances. Furthermore, unhappiness is not suffering, rather it is 'the way in which we experience our suffering' (Ricard 2003: 47).

Buddhism does not distinguish between emotion and thought; it considers them simultaneous and conjoined. There are no separate brain sites for emotion and thought; every site for emotion is also a site for thought (Davidson and Irwin 1999; Ricard 2003). The basic Buddhist message is that unhappiness can be overcome because its cause can be diagnosed and dealt with. Buddhism dichotomizes emotions sharply into destructive and non-destructive ones with regard to others and one's self, while Western psychology simply divides them into negative and positive (Watson, Clark, and Tellegen 1988). Another difference between Buddhism and Western psychology is that in Buddhism destructive emotional states can be changed through various practices so that all individuals can develop traits or dispositions towards happiness, not only those with psychological disorders (Ekman et al. 2005; Wallace 2005). In Western practices, psychoanalysis and cognitive-behaviour therapy alleviate psychopathologies. There are no broad-based practices to shape emotions and traits towards happiness.

The third major difference between Buddhism and Western psychology is that Buddhism is directed towards overcoming craving or 'the desire to acquire objects and situations' (Ekman et al. 2005: 62). This is important in light of escalating addictive behaviours and general patterns of overconsumption that damage the environment (Schor 1999).

The most typical destructive emotions according to Buddhist psychology are the five poisons: (i) desire or craving, (ii) anger or hatred, (iii) pride or ego, (iv) envy or jealousy, and (v) ignorance or delusion. These five poisons can be distilled even further into three toxins: (i) desire, (ii) hatred, and (iii) delusion. These are the true tormentors of human beings. They are states of confusion that obscure the true and fundamental nature of our consciousness. People have to free themselves from these toxins and cultivate their opposites: positive emotions. The anti-venom for hatred is loving kindness. It is stressed in Buddhism that two opposite mental processes cannot take place in one instant of consciousness (Ricard 2003). Therefore, if loving kindness is felt, hatred is not. Therefore, cultivating loving kindness naturally extinguishes hatred. However, the single stroke antidote to both desire and delusion also exists in the Buddhist analysis of the self to reveal its false existence to be an obstruction to happiness. Those who suffer from intense negative emotions are imprisoned by them.

Well-being and Happiness in Gross National Happiness

The third conceptual strand is happiness as defined in GNH, which is a much broader concept of well-being. In the conceptualization of happiness in GNH, a number of objective and subjective conditions are included. Although the list of objective goods differs in the GNH, the thinking behind the states and means specified in GNH is like the objectivist list of central human capabilities given by Nussbaum (2000). GNH is also similar in its broad specification of the areas of concern for well-being (the domains of GNH) that were specified by Stiglitz, Sen, and Fitoussi (2010), though the specific details differ. However, the composition of the GNH is not the same as those things espoused by Martha Nussbaum (2000) or by Stiglitz, Sen, and Fitoussi (2010). Nor does it include, for example, all 24 items of the so-called good life, which are things that people either own or desire to own or experience—including a car, home, TV, swimming pool, or travel abroad, among others—based on a survey taken in the United States (Easterlin 2005).

Each of these three approaches to well-being—SWB, Buddhist happiness, and GNH—has its own emphasis, but they are all different paths of the same journey rather than the same journey to different destinations. There is substantial overlap among all these approaches.[4]

Methodology for Measuring Gross National Happiness and Its Indicators

The GNH Index was devised in 2006 to measure key conditions of well-being that comprise physical and mental health, community vitality, work–life balance, living standards, civic engagement, and ecological integrity. It measures both subjective and objective conditions through periodic national surveys. Subjective elements of GNH are largely based on self-reporting numerous aspects of a survey on respondent's life.

The 2010 GNH Survey comprised a representative national sample covering 7,146 respondents drawn from each of Bhutan's 20 districts. Out of the 33 indicators used in the construction of the GNH Index, 24 are qualitative and 9 are quantitative. The list of conditions or factors

[4] A fourth view on well-being is called preferentialism. It means that an individual's well-being should take into account his/her well-being based on preferences that are completely well informed and rational. Adler and Posner (2008) consider the objectivist list as overlapping with their preferentialism to the extent that the list developed from open-ended questions on personal aspirations provided evidence for preferentialism.

comprising GNH is rather extensive because GNH is a maximal concept, unlike that of poverty, which measures minimum or essential conditions of survival. Setting indicator weights is a crucial component of the measurement design as it affects the index value and the resultant rankings. Equal weights are used when indicators or dimensions are judged normatively almost equal in importance. Within domains, subjective indicators have lighter weights and quantitative ones have heavier weights. Minor changes in the weights do not alter the GNH Index, confirming their robustness. Statistical tools used to confirm the normative weights include principal component analysis, factor analysis, and regression coefficients. However, the weights on the indicators are normative; in fact, weights developed using statistical tools also require judgements in order to design the particular application; they are not value free either.

The nine domains of GNH are equally weighted to reflect the equal importance of each domain for happiness. These domains are: (i) psychological well-being, (ii) time use, (iii) cultural diversity and resilience, (iv) ecological diversity and resilience, (v) community vitality, (vi) good governance, (vii) education, (viii) health, and (ix) living standard. Economic development, which falls under living standard, is given modest weight in the overall framework for GNH as the uses of income and assets are indirectly reflected in other domains. These domains broadly reflect the purposes of governance and values of society. The 33 indicators are on their own useful for the practical purposes of different agencies. The footnotes accompanying the descriptions of various sub-indices are excerpted fully from *An Extensive Analysis of GNH* by Ura et al. (2012). The 33 indicators, along with their weights, are presented in Table 3.1.

Relationships involving a sense of belonging and support within and between households ought to be deep in a community. The GNH Index evaluates the level of giving and receiving of various gifts (for example, social time, labour, and goods). It assesses the cultural continuity of key elements of a community like its dialects and artisan skills, and village celebrations of ritual dramas and masked dances.

The GNH Index has no physical measures of ecological wealth such as biodiversity and local natural resources. The index also does not have chemical measures of pollution and waste. These indicators are tracked imperfectly using perceptions. Still, this placeholder is vitally important. For the happiness of the inhabitants of a place accrues not only from

TABLE 3.1 The 9 Domains and 33 Indicators of Gross National Happiness

Domain	Indicators	Weight (%)
Psychological Well-being	Life satisfaction	33
	Positive emotions	17
	Negative emotions	17
	Spirituality	33
Health	Self-reported health	10
	Healthy days	30
	Disability	30
	Mental health	30
Time Use	Work	50
	Sleep	50
Education	Literacy	30
	Schooling	30
	Knowledge	20
	Value	20
Cultural Diversity and Resilience	*Zorig Chusum* (artistic skills)	30
	Cultural participation	30
	Speak native language	20
	Driglam Namzha (way of harmony)	20
Good Governance	Political participation	40
	Services	40
	Governance performance	10
	Fundamental rights	10
Community Vitality	Donations (time and money)	30
	Safety	30
	Community relationships	20
	Family	20
Ecological Diversity and Resilience	Wildlife damage	40
	Urban issues	40
	Environmental responsibility	10
	Ecological issues	10
Living Standards	Per capita income	33
	Assets	33
	Housing	33

Source: Ura et al. (2012).

its economic benefits, but also from the benefits of the environment. Nature's aesthetic stimuli also matter for happiness. These can be blighted by modernization and urbanization. On the other hand, living in natural surroundings comes at a price to small farmers. They lose a substantial portion of crop output and livestock every year to wildlife ranging from adored tigers to unloved porcupines. The heavy price that Bhutanese farmers pay for conservation, which affects their livelihoods and happiness, is tracked in the GNH Index. It is a difficult policy issue. Killing wild animals outside of a farm boundary is prohibited by law, with the implication that a wild animal may be killed only if it is presently causing harm within a farm's boundary. Hunting is prohibited and farmers do not own guns. Moreover, Buddhism denounces the killing of animals, which is why the raising of poultry and pigs is not widespread.

For each respondent, satisfaction in five life indicators, including mental health and stress levels, is evaluated. Ten self-reported emotions are surveyed to assess the pattern of emotional life and its relationship with other elements of GNH. Because of the correlation between spiritual activities and positive emotions among the Bhutanese population, mental devices that limit the mind's wandering like meditation and meditative prayers are also measured in the GNH Index.

The GNH living standard indicators cover income, land, and quality of housing, as these provide the setting for raising a family. A household's appliances and other technological equipment are also reflected in the living standard indicators.

The GNH Index is designed to be policy relevant. If a certain indicator shows deterioration, it should prompt public discussion and policy corrections. The GNH Index can be decomposed for representative subgroups within the population as a whole. For example, subcomponents of GNH indicators are reported for each of the country's 20 districts by gender, rural–urban area, age, and certain occupational categories. This disaggregation property makes it a useful policy tool.

The GNH Index is calculated using the methodology employed by Alkire and Foster (2011). This includes two threshold levels. The first threshold, sufficiency, is set at a certain level for each variable based on international norms, national standards, and general consensus to arrive at a judgement of what is suitably sufficient for happiness. Table 3.2 gives an example of thresholds for variables within the domain of health. As in a four-point Likert scale, 'very good' is the threshold for self-reported health.

Fixing a threshold level for sufficiency, with respect to a general reference group or some intake limit, is logical. It is reasonable to do so as exceeding a sufficiency threshold does not add to happiness.

TABLE 3.2 Sufficiency Thresholds for Health Domain Indicators

GNH health domain indicators	Response range	Sufficiency threshold	% of people (= respondents above 15 years of age) meeting sufficiency
Self-reported health status	1–5 (very poor to excellent)	Good or excellent	73.8
Healthy days	0–30 (worst to best)	26 days and above	76.5
Disability		No disability or it does not limit their ability to perform daily activities	89.5
Mental health (GHQ)	0–15 (severe distress); 21–36 (normal mental well-being)	Normal mental well-being	86.2

Notes: GHQ = General Health Questionnaire; GNH = Gross National Happiness.
Source: Author's calculations based on data from Gross National Happiness Survey of 2010, available at http://www.grossnationalhappiness.com (last accessed on 1 October 2016).

Those who do not meet the sufficiency threshold for a particular variable are regarded as having an insufficient score in that variable. There are 124 variables when the 33 indicators are unpacked, so the chances of everyone reaching the sufficiency threshold for each of these variables are low. Given that reaching the threshold is important for being happy, the GNH Index increases when the percentage of people reaching the sufficiency threshold in any variable increase.

The second threshold level is set at the level of nine domains. Since variables are grouped into domains, the second threshold is the number of domains with a sufficient score needed for an individual to be happy. At the domain level, the second threshold requires an individual to achieve sufficiency in six out of the nine domains to be considered happy. The second threshold works across the variables. If the variables were equally weighted, a survey respondent would need to achieve sufficiency in more than 83 out of the 124 variables to be happy.[5] The 83 variables can be any of the 124 variables based on the individual's choice; sufficiency in all 124 variables is not needed to be happy. There are no universal requirements at every point in one's life; the required combination of variables may vary depending on personal circumstances at a given point in time.

The analysis of GNH does not dichotomize people as being either happy or unhappy; instead, there is a happiness gradient. Assessing the survey results, the Bhutanese population can be divided into four levels of happiness (the corresponding share of the total population is provided in parenthesis alongside each category): unhappy (10.4 per cent), narrowly happy (47.8 per cent), extensively happy (32.6 per cent), and deeply happy (8.3 per cent). If a person has achieved sufficiency in less than half of the nine domains, she is classified as unhappy. If she has achieved sufficiency in 50–65 per cent of the nine domains, she is classified as narrowly happy. If she has achieved sufficiency in 66–76 per cent of the nine domains, she is classified as extensively happy. Finally, if she has achieved sufficiency in more than 77 per cent of the nine domains, she is classified as deeply happy. By definition, happy people have a balanced life. The meaning of a balanced life has thus been defined technically, while leaving room for personal tastes and circumstances.[6]

Multidimensional Framework: State and Non-official Institutions and Actors

The idea of GNH and its concrete measurements would be of little wider interest if it remained conceptual and not integrated into policy. This section documents how GNH has become a policy tool and introduces the institutional actors and policy levers in Bhutan among the government, private sector, CSOs, and donors. The next section 'Using the Gross National Happiness Policy-screening Tool in Decision-making' sketches how the GNH Index is linked to a policy-screening tool and describes how this tool operates.

[5] More precisely, a person needs to achieve sufficiency in any set of variables whose weighted sum is at least two-thirds of the total.

[6] For a detailed analysis of the GNH Index, see www.grossnationalhappiness.com (last accessed on 1 October 2016).

The Gross National Happiness Commission (GNHC), known as the Planning Commission until 2008, is the coordinating agency for implementation of five-year development plans. Its main function is to combine external and internal resources and arrive at a five-year plan comprising sectoral plans proposed by ministries and autonomous agencies. The renaming of the Commission in 2008 was intended to imbue planning and policymaking in Bhutan with GNH principles. The GNHC does not specialize in GNH research but rather attempts to bring convergence between five-year plans and GNH by incorporating targets of GNH indicators. Theoretically, the five-year plans are supposed to ensure balanced development among the nine domains of GNH. The responsibility of the development of concepts and managerial tools of GNH that are applied by all agencies is vested in the main government research centre, the Centre for Bhutan Studies and GNH Research (CBS). Thus, the CBS works closely with the GNHC and other central agencies. As an autonomous research centre, the CBS conducts all GNH-related empirical research and surveys, and disseminates its finding through publications and conferences. The CBS updates government agencies and the public on its findings.

The GNHC is a board, chaired by the Prime Minister and supported by the GNHC Secretariat. Its membership consists of all 11 secretaries to the government and a few other ex officio members. The Tenth Five Year Plan, 2008–13 was the first such plan to use the GNH Index as an instrument for measuring development. The plan consists of three kinds of programmes that can be differentiated and decomposed financially into two levels: (i) a central level consisting of all 10 government ministries along with other central autonomous agencies, and (ii) local governments. Autonomous agencies include the Royal Civil Service Commission, Royal Monetary Authority, CBS, GNHC, National Environmental Commission, National Commission for Woman and Children, Tourism Council of Bhutan, and Bhutan Information Communication and Media Authority. Local governments consist of the 20 districts, which are further divided into 205 gewogs. Gewogs and districts vary a great deal in size. The district and gewog plans, which constitute 40 per cent of the total budget, reflect increasing degrees of decentralization. The five-year plan budgets, however, exclude investment in hydropower, which alone can rival an entire plan's budget. For example, the budget of the Eleventh Five Year Plan is Nu213 billion, while investment during the plan's period in six hydropower projects is estimated to be Nu182 billion. The financial and physical projections of a five-year plan are calculated on a three-year rolling basis. The budget for a fiscal year is allocated, while the budget estimates and physical plans are projected two years into the future. Computerized quarterly progress reports on physical progress and financial expenditure have to be completed quarterly for funds to be released from the budget department.[7]

For local governments at the district and gewog levels, a simple GNH checklist has been introduced as part of a planning manual to enable the communities to assess their programmes and projects. The GNH checklist is a device to guide village-level agents towards the integrated development envisioned in the GNH framework. The Local Government Act, 2009 established that local governments at the district and gewog levels are to promote the conditions for GNH, similar to the way that the Article 9 of the Constitution prescribes this role for the state as a whole. The GNH checklist helps them do that.

Each of the 20 districts has a district administration. The district government board, known as *Dzongkhag Tshogdu*, is the regulatory and legislative body. The members of the Dzongkhag Tshogdu are the elected heads of a gewog, each of whom is known as a *gup*, and the deputy heads of the gewogs, in addition to elected members of the towns in a district. A district's chief executives, known as *Dzongdag*, and a district's sectoral officials are non-voting observers. The district administration is responsible for carrying out the decisions of the Dzongkhag Tshogdu. As civil servants, the sectoral officials of a district are also accountable to their central ministries and departments with respect to promotions, transfers, and technical responsibilities. This dual accountability is a source of conflicting dynamics (Schroeder 2014).

Gewogs are the lowest layer of local government administration, comprising about 3,000 households each on average. The managing body of a gewog is the *Gewog Tshogdu*. Its head is an elected gup as the chairperson and membership comprises between six and nine other elected members. Civil servants placed in gewog offices are non-voting observers. The Gewog Tshogdu does not have regulatory powers, unlike the Dzongkhag Tshogdu. Like civil servants in a district administration,

[7] The electronic system used in Bhutan, initiated by Ministry of Finance, is known as the Planning and Monitoring System.

officials at the gewog level interface with both the local communities and the hierarchy of civil servants at the district administration and central ministries. Their multiple accountabilities are also sources of pressure that could lead them to deviate from promoting GNH (Schroeder 2014). Schroeder has also noted the lack of analytic and administrative tools in districts and gewogs to guide them towards GNH outcomes.

The outcomes of governance and development are subject to Bhutanese citizens and other internal and external bodies. The government may claim primacy in agency but actual outcomes are not entirely up to it. Among the foremost non-official actors in Bhutan are rural farmers and private sector businesses. The latter are a prominent force in shaping the country's direction. Business people are engaged in retailing, manufacturing, agro-industries, mining, hydroelectric construction, distribution and transporting, tourism, banking, and insurance. Their activities do not fall under GNH to the same extent as official agencies.

Almost half of Bhutan's GDP is produced by the private sector, which includes farmers. Public sector GDP mainly comprises the output of the 20 or so corporations owned partly or wholly under Druk Holding and Investments. Market capitalism in the private sector as well as most public sector enterprises operate under the compulsion of growth, financial viability, and revenue maximization. Standard financial indicators—such as the rate of return on assets, profits, and rate of return on equity, among others—are used by businesses in Bhutan as elsewhere. Large-scale investments—typically exemplified by hydropower and cement plants, banks, and hotels—are decided based on normal cost–benefit analysis. Such decisions are a bit removed from the GNH mode of decision-making. Therefore, in a sense the bottom line remains cash considerations. This is true also of the operation of agencies such as the Ministry of Economic Affairs, which is charged with economic liberalization in terms of free trade and foreign direct investment (FDI). By virtue of their roles, these entities advocate practices that are not ultimately assessed from the point of view of GNH but rather from mainstream economics. It is important to note this internal diversity that allows two very different thought structures to come into play.

This is not to say that there is no notion of corporate social responsibility in Bhutan; there is. However, corporate social responsibility makes no widespread contribution to sustainability anywhere in the world, let alone to collective happiness, as the private sector is probably not directed enough by GNH principles for this to occur. With the new push to make Bhutan friendly for business and FDI (Royal Government of Bhutan 2010), more compromises on GNH-inspired and balanced development may be struck in the future. On the other hand, past and present governments have frequently declared their aim to make the private sector the engine of growth (via GDP expansion), an aim that appears to presume that GNH supports and does not conflict with growth. This is precisely the debatable issue at hand. Whether both aims can be achieved while holding true to GNH is a major challenge that should not be underestimated. One reason why the government is compelled by growth aspirations is that it seeks to generate jobs for the youth. However, cross tabulations show that growth and employment generation are not highly correlated in Bhutan's case due to the peculiarities of its economic growth stemming from the use of foreign labour and construction in the hydropower sector.

The emergence of CSOs in significant numbers is another non-official factor that influences GNH. Each CSO, like each business, has its own priorities that can potentially diverge from GNH principles. Thus, how GNH can contribute to enhancing a new model of business and CSO operations, and how businesses and CSOs can reinforce GNH will be a critical new practice. The Civil Society Organization Act of Bhutan, 2007 nominally requires them to recognize GNH. At present, there is no mandatory requirement for businesses and CSOs to follow project screening using a GNH-filtered lens.

Another formative influence in Bhutan's development is external donors. Almost half of the budget of the government constitutes capital expenditure that is financed from grants and soft loans received from bilateral and multilateral donors and international NGOs. Thus, the government is financially dependent on external aid in implementing its five-year plans. By far the most important source of grant funding for development activities is the Government of India, which contributed an average of 64 per cent of total aid flows during 2002–12 (Royal Government of Bhutan, Ministry of Finance 2014).

Multilateral and bilateral donors generally lend support to Bhutan with regard to the government's GNH priorities. Yet, each donor also has its own mandated interests under which aid is approved and these interests are accommodated to some degree by Bhutan. With a few exceptions, Bhutan follows a national modality for the execution of projects, which means that the Bhutanese government is ultimately responsible for implementing projects. Yet, project designs have to accommodate donor perspectives that may differ to a degree from donor to donor while also having different levels of coherence with GNH.

As mentioned, the task of infusing GNH into ministries and their programmes has been assigned to the GNHC as a coordinating apex body second only to the Cabinet. In operational terms, the GNHC coordinates five-year and annual plans, and supports public policy according to the policy making protocol.[8] With respect to GNH, the GNHC is charged with ensuring that 'GNH principles are mainstreamed into policies, planning, and implementation along with gender, environment, climate disaster, and poverty.'[9] It has become a norm in Bhutan for almost every organization to sign on to a time-bound performance agreement with the current government. The responsibility to mainstream GNH into policies of the government is a part of the agreement between the GNHC and the government.

As the next section describes in more detail, the Royal Government of Bhutan now includes GNH indicators in its five-year national planning, using the GNH policy-screening tool. Every project, programme, or developmental activity can proceed only after obtaining policy clearance based on the GNH policy-screening tool. The current Eleventh Five Year Plan, 2013–18 uses 16 baseline indicators to track changes in ecology, culture, socio-economic development, and good governance, among other areas, primarily by assessing results against data from the 2010 GHN Survey. The plan document states that the 2010 GNH Index composite score of 0.743 will be sustained through the end of the plan in June 2018 (GNHC 2013: 7).

Using the Gross National Happiness Policy-screening Tool in Decision-making

The main objective of the GNH screening tools is to systematically assess impacts of any policy or project on GNH. Two kinds of tools were developed by the CBS: (i) sixteen different GNH project-screening tools for the selection of projects and (ii) a general GNH policy-screening tool

[8] See http://www.gnhc.gov.bt/wp-content/uploads/2011/05/GNH-Policy-Protocol-revised-Feb-20121.pdf (last accessed on 17 October 2016).

[9] See http://www.thebhutanese.bt/performance-agreement-of-six-autonomous-agencies-to-be-reviewed/ (last accessed on 26 January 2015).

for appraising draft policies. The aim of this endeavour is to select GNH-enhancing policies and projects, while rejecting those that adversely affect key determinants of GNH. At present, only the GNH policy-screening tool is applied to assessing and clearing draft policies. The 26 individual criteria of the GNH policy-screening tool are shown in Figure 3.2.

A draft policy is subjected to the GNH policy-screening tools by the proponent agency, usually a ministry, and the GNHC Secretariat as two separate exercises with the results being compared. There are five essential steps involved: (i) prior to screening of a policy, a bilateral session is held between the proponent sector and the GNHC Secretariat on the relevance of certain GNH indicators against the policy in question; (ii) those participating in the screening exercise do so individually; (iii) scorings are discussed and compiled during the screening meeting; (iv) various stakeholders participate in the screening exercise, with a minimum of 15 participants; and (v) the gender focal person of the proponent sector, environmental representatives, and other external key stakeholders are involved in the screening exercise.

1. Equity
2. Economic security
3. Material well-being
4. Engagement in productive activities
5. Decision-making opportunity
6. Corruption
7. Judiciary efficiency
8. Judiciary access
9. Rights
10. Gender equality
11. Information
12. Learning
13. Health
14. Water pollution
15. Air pollution
16. Land degradation
17. Conservation of plant
18. Conservation of animals
19. Social support
20. Family
21. Nature
22. Recreation
23. Culture
24. Values
25. Spiritual pursuits
26. Stress

FIGURE 3.2 Gross National Happiness Policy–Screening Tool Criteria
Note: Each of the 26 screening criteria is to be weighed on a four-point scale ranging from 1 to 4: 1 = negative, 2 = uncertain (lack of knowledge of the effect of the policy), 3 = neutral, and 4 = positive. The final outcome depends of the accumulation of positive scores.
Source: GNHC, Policy and Project Screening Tools, available at http://www.grossnationalhappiness.com/gnh-policy-and-project-screening-tools/ (last accessed on 25 May 2015).

The general aim of policy screening is to provide a systematic appraisal of the potential effects of proposed projects on the GNH of the population based on the expected impacts on key determinants of GNH. It is also to ensure that all relevant dimensions are considered in the project formulation process to support a holistic approach to programmes. In this respect, the criteria for GNH policy screening act as a checklist to acknowledge areas where potential effects are not known or are usually not considered. As some of the criteria are outside the realm of economic issues, the GNH policy-screening tool becomes a vehicle for a number of participants from a variety of backgrounds to work towards a consensus on project impacts. Thus, a heterogeneous group comprising qualified experts and professionals from different occupational backgrounds are expected to assess the policy in question. Vetting of draft policies takes place according to the process detailed in Figure 3.3.

The Cabinet is the final approving authority for new policies after they pass screening. The Cabinet has rejected several policies after screening. Since the introduction of GNH policy screening in 2009, the Cabinet has approved 13 policies, including the (i) National Human Resource Development Policy, 2010; (ii) National Youth Policy, 2010; (iii) Tertiary Education Policy, 2010; (iv) National Health Policy, 2011; (v) National Land Policy, 2011; (vi) National Forest Policy, 2011; (vii) National Irrigation Policy, 2011; (viii) Alternative Renewable Energy Policy, 2012;

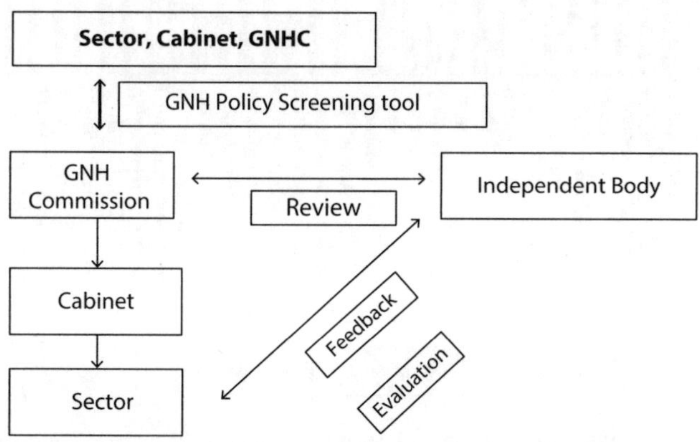

FIGURE 3.3 The Gross National Happiness Policy Screening Process
Source: Author's illustration.

(ix) Renewable Natural Resource Research Policy, 2012; (x) Subsidized Timber and Other Forest Produce Allotment Policy, 2012; (xi) Cottage, Small, and Medium-Sized Industry Policy, 2012; (xii) Food and Nutrition Security Policy, 2012; and (xiii) Eleventh Five Year Plan, 2013–18.

Gross National Happiness Socio-economic Impacts and Policy Outcomes

Findings and Implications of Gross National Happiness Surveys

The discrepancies between men and women in the attainment of sufficiency in each indicator are reported in Figure 3.4. In many cases, women score lower than men.

Only a few of the major findings with relevance for policies are discussed here, beginning with gender-based analysis of the 2010 GNH Survey findings. The enrolment of girls is greater than that of boys at the primary school level. One reason for this may be the enrolment of boys in monasteries. At the tertiary level, however, girls' enrolment

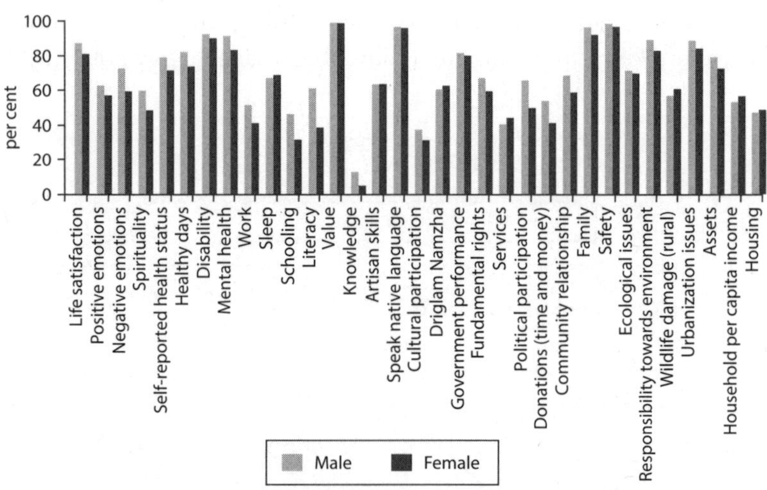

FIGURE 3.4 Percentage of Population Attaining Sufficiency by Indicator and Gender

Source: Centre for Bhutan Studies and GNH Research (2012).

drops below that of boys. In formal sector employment, women form 33 per cent of the total workforce. This percentage holds for both private sector corporations and the civil service. With respect to legal ownership of a household's main asset, land, the official registry shows that women hold about 46 per cent of all land titles.

The inclusion of time use, psychological well-being, and cultural diversity and resilience in GNH offers new possibilities for gender-based analysis in addition to the usual dimensions of education, health employment, and income.

Generally, men are happier than women, except for younger women aged 15–24, in terms of SWB scores. However, women's SWB scores drops considerably after reaching 25 years of age. The domain of psychological well-being—comprising the three indicators of life satisfaction, emotional balance (positive and negative emotions), and spirituality—illustrates some gender differences. In urban areas, the SWB score averaged 6.21 for women compared with 6.48 for men. In rural areas, the SWB scores were 5.81 for women and 6.10 for men. Given a population distribution of 30 per cent in urban areas and 70 per cent in rural areas, there are far more rural women with lower SWB scores than their urban counterparts.

Among general population categories that include never been married, married, divorced, separated, or widowed, severe mental stress is most frequent among those who are separated or widowed. Overall, 11.8 per cent of the general population experience severe mental distress, while 17.4 per cent of those who are separate or widowed experience it (Ritu and Ura forthcoming).

GNH data enable estimations of detailed time use by gender. At a highly aggregated level, hours of work, non-work, and sleep are reported by gender in Figure 3.5. Regardless of location (urban or rural), women work longer hours than men, averaging 8 hours and 21 minutes per day, compared with 7 hours and 31 minutes for men (work comprises productive income generation, household tasks, and community work). In terms of non-work hours, or leisure time, men enjoy approximately 8 hours of leisure per day and women enjoy approximately 7 hours. At the same time, women enjoy slightly more time sleeping than men, likely because they dedicate less time to leisure activities.

Generally, people in rural areas are less happy than urban residents, whether happiness is estimated according to SWB scores or the GNH

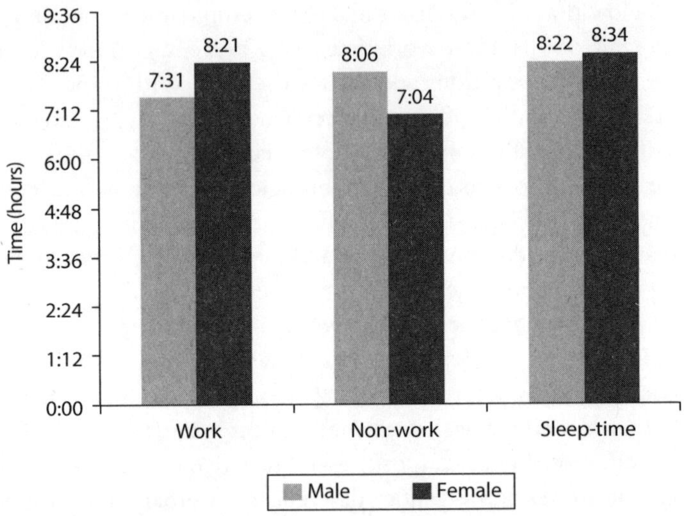

FIGURE 3.5 Average Time for Work, Non-work, and Sleep per Day by Gender
Source: Author's illustration from Gross National Happiness Survey (2010), available at http://www.grossnationalhappiness.com (last accessed on 1 October 2016).

Index. The contribution of domains to happiness also differs by region. Figure 3.6 presents a spider diagram for these domain contributions by region. In rural areas, community vitality, cultural diversity, and good governance contribute more to happiness. In contrast, living standards, education, and health contribute more to happiness in urban areas. Urban people experience insufficiency in terms of governance, time use, and culture, while in rural areas insufficiency is experienced in terms of education and living standards.

To analyse the GNH by dzhongkhag, the districts are classified into three categories of happiness: low, medium, and high. Low levels, which correspond with a GNH Index value of 0.655–0.706, were reported in the districts of Trongsa, Lhuntse, Tashiyangtse, and Samdrup Jongkhar. Medium values of 0.707–0.756 were reported in Samtse, Chhukha, Wangdue Phodrang, Bumthang, Zhemgang, Mongar, Tashigang, and Pemagatshel. Finally, districts in the west—including Haa, Paro, Thimphu, Punakha, and Gasa—and in the south—Dagana, Tsirang, and Sarpang—comprised the category with high levels of happiness with scores of 0.757–0.807.

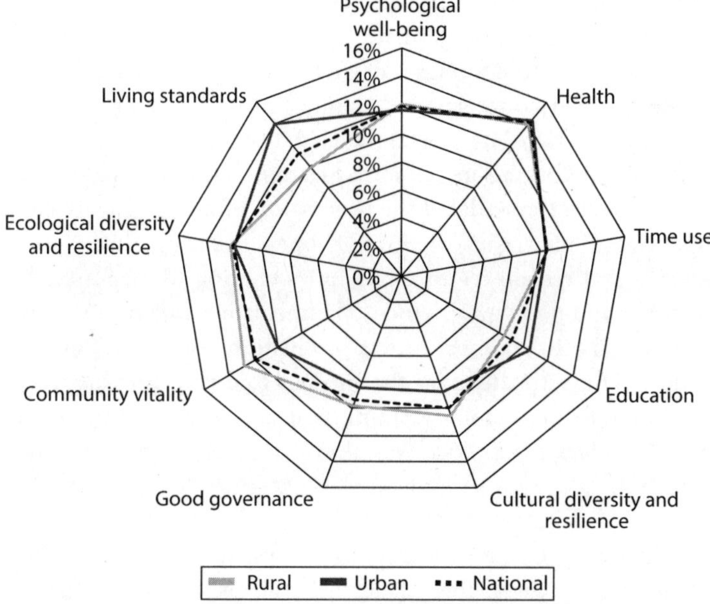

FIGURE 3.6 Contribution to Gross National Happiness Index Domains—Rural versus Urban
Source: Author's illustration from Gross National Happiness Survey (2010), available at http://www.grossnationalhappiness.com (last accessed on 1 October 2016).

Media

Schroeder (2014) provides a systematic assessment of the impact of GNH policies on four distinct fields. He analysed policy implementation and outcomes in four critical areas for GNH assessment: media, tourism, farm–road construction, and human–wildlife conflict. In addition, analysis of the policy outcomes for urban planning in Thimphu carried out by Bajaj (2014) is another informative inquiry into GNH policy outcomes versus policy intentions. Tourism, media, and human–wildlife conflict are discussed here, as they are pervasive influences on the future of GNH-focused development and demonstrate to a certain extent the reality of outcomes versus policy intents and declarations (Schroeder 2014).

Bhutan Broadcasting Service diversified into televised public broadcasting in 1999, providing news and programmes. Private sector broadcasters distribute foreign cable television channels in partnership with their Indian counterparts. At one time, there were 87 foreign channels, which have lately been reduced to about 40 foreign channels. The Bhutan Information, Communications, and Media Act, 2006 (amended in 2012) mandated the promotion of a free, privatized, and competitive media industry through open licencing that would be conducive and responsive to GNH by furthering Bhutanese culture, democracy, and good governance. The media consists of TV stations, newspapers, radio stations, movie production companies, and cable providers. The act states that the media's role is to provide free and fair use of information and communications, and to enhance GNH. Bhutan Broadcasting Service was also given a prescribed role in promoting GNH.

A peculiar development in Bhutan over the last decade has been the proliferation of English-language newspapers, which peaked at 12 at one point. Given low readership, this explosion was probably due to a policy of equal official advertisement placements, mostly of tenders for competitive bidding of procurements and construction that assured a minimum level of revenue to every newspaper. To some degree, the expansion of papers was associated with heightened party politics as competitive, democratic politics began in 2007. The Election Commission of Bhutan allocates a fixed budget for the electoral campaign of each candidate and each party, which is a boon for newspapers every electoral cycle. Collectively, the newspapers became financially unsustainable without advertising revenue from the government and they became professionally unsustainable as untrained journalists ran them. Dependence on advertising revenue from the government opened up possibilities for conflict of interest in the role of media as an unbiased observer. Schroeder (2014) found that the advertising budgets of various government agencies could affect the editorial stance of newspapers vis-à-vis government policies and actions.

The Bhutan Information Communication and Media Authority was created in 2007 and its chief executive officer was recruited through an open and competitive process. Yet, several instances of disagreements between the government and the media have arisen over the interpretation of certain provisions of the act and over whether certain news content was consistent with GNH values. Schroeder (2014: 124) notes that 'overall, the difference of how the regulation of news content has been applied illustrates that various media stakeholders continue to agree on the underlying values of good governance—promoting transparency, accountability, inclusion, and participation—but disagree over how these values are expressed.'

One of the key issues in the media has been the promotion of local content to be sensitive to local culture and GNH values. This is enforced through the Rules on Content, 2010, which shares many common provisions with other countries. In deference to culture, the Rules of Content, 2010 require media programming to be in either English or Dzongkha, the national language, and call for media productions to show the national dress. A newspaper is required to publish both English and Dzongkha editions in order to preserve the national language. However, the sales potential for Dzongkha editions is drastically lower than English editions, and Dzongkha editions (or page insertions) are often printed as expressions of tokenism by newspapers.

The Rules on Content, 2010 do not apply to international television channels, which are avidly watched by a substantial audience in Bhutan, and, therefore, no censorship applies to international channels. In 2012, televisions were owned by 64 per cent of the households in the country (National Statistics Bureau 2012). Television ownership has spread in step with rural electrification programmes; the whole country is close to being electrified, in line with a national goal of electricity for all. The Rules on Content, 2010 have no influence over foreign programmes that may contain elements not allowed in national media productions. Those depictions deemed antithetical to GNH are, therefore, pervasive on television. For example, the Film Review Board of Bhutan may censor objectionable scenes in a local film production on the grounds of GNH, but more objectionable entertainment may be broadcast through international cable channels in Bhutan. The cultural sphere is thus very porous.

Journalists and media types, wary of a government agenda, generally oppose the notion that the media has to promote GNH values. For one thing, what it means to be sensitive to GNH every time a news or programme is produced is unclear and therefore challenged implicitly. The opinions of regulators, journalists, and viewers are not necessarily the same in implementing media policy with regard to GNH. They may have divergent views on different issues. Schroeder (2014: 145) notes that in the implementation of a GNH media policy, 'GNH tools have had little influence ... GNH governance structures and instruments are largely absent in shaping these interactions, yet a common set of values linked to GNH seem to underlie and shape the priorities and practices of all stakeholders.' The overall result is that the media in Bhutan is generally independent and free from government censorship. The 2010 GNH Survey confirmed that 73 per cent of the population thought that the media was either 'quite free' or 'completely free'. Conflicts in the process of media policy are about interpretations rather than control of the freedom of speech. A free media environment in which rules on content cannot be applied to foreign cable channels does not necessarily support Bhutanese culture, though it expands consumer choice. This challenge can be met by making qualitative and quantitative improvements to local programming. A successful example is cinema, where Bhutanese movies have displaced foreign movies in the cinema halls. It must be qualified, however, that cinema halls exist only in some major cities.

Tourism

The first 20 foreign tourists in Bhutan arrived travelling overland through India in 1974. By the end of 2013, the number of international tourists had reached 55,000. The main instrument of tourism policy during the reign of His Majesty Jigme Singye Wangchuck in 1972–2006 was the high tariff and guided tourism. This changed as exceptions to the tariff were made for regional tourists from Bangladesh, India, and the Maldives, whose arrivals now double that of tariff-paying tourists. As the numbers of both tariff-paying and regional non-tariff-paying tourists swell, tourism is a major channel for change in Bhutan. To link GNH to tourism, the Tourism Council of Bhutan, an autonomous agency chaired by the Prime Minster, plays a central role in policymaking.

The guiding principle of Bhutanese tourism is 'high value, low impact', which is a clever adaption of the earlier principle of 'high value, low volume'. To deliver high-value tourism that meets the needs of the government and its guests, environmental and cultural preservation policies that maximize the number of tourists considered to be culturally and ecologically sustainable are needed. In 1999, there were only 33 tour operators working in conjunction with external travel agents. Today, there are over 600 local travel companies. The tourism industry involves both state and non-official actors contributing as decentralized voices in policymaking and implementation. Many CSOs—including the Association of Bhutanese Tour Operators, which represents four companies: the Tourism Development Council, Guide Association of Bhutan, Hotel Association of Bhutan, and Handicraft Association—contribute to the implementation of GNH policies in tourism. In a country that is steeped in subsistence agriculture and with no great history of commercial private entrepreneurship or partnering with foreign entities, the tourism industry is a trailblazer in terms of entrepreneurship. FDI and foreign management are most prominent in the hotel sector.

The tourism industry of Bhutan is an arena where balancing economic growth with cultural and ecological preservation, as required by GNH, can be tested considerably. If—and when—the generation of revenue and economic growth, whether through tourism or any other means, is the overriding goal, growth may be sustained. However, there can be negative externalities from prioritizing such growth over local culture and ecological systems that have their own carrying capacities beyond which they may break down. Where the balance is located and how it can be struck, in terms of quantitative and technical measurements, is an engaging task and a focus of public discussion.

The Royal Government of Bhutan premises its tourism policy on a virtuous GNH circle in the tourism sector. Traditional culture and the environment are promoted through various means for intrinsic reasons and to expand the carrying capacity in a locality as the number of tourists increase. This is expected to fuel economic growth in the tourism-related sectors of transport, hotels, restaurants, and handicrafts, among others.

There was also a subtle change in the government's headline policy in 1999 when the guiding principle of 'high value, low volume' became 'high value, low impact'. The previous government, concerned by the rise of youth unemployment, seemed to have been compelled by the need for more revenue to maximize growth in the tourism sector. However, CSOs and private actors in the tourism sector articulated their priorities, which are perceived as being more consistent with the values underlying GNH. They opposed the recommendations of a 2013 consultant's report by McKinsey, which were backed by the government, to liberalize tariffs in order to attract 250,000 international tourists by 2013 (Schroeder 2014). The CSOs and tour operators fortunately rejected this radical restructuring of tourism. Their opposition was neither about tariff levels nor the number of tourists, but rather about the balance between economic growth, cultural preservation, and environmental integrity. A good balance was maintained in Bhutan by not targeting too many tourists too soon. Yet, there is a potential threat in allowing regional tourists to be exempt from the tariff. The room accorded for regional tourists to travel unaccompanied by a guide and the offering of a visa on arrival could lead to cultural and environmental disruption as this exemption represents a departure from existing tourism policy in Bhutan (Schroeder 2014).

At a broad level, the ecological carrying capacity for tourism is being increased, with more areas devoted to nature parks and biological corridors, which now encompass almost 50 per cent of the country's surface area. Tourism helps raise awareness of eco-friendly technologies and tourist complaints have led to stricter rules regarding garbage and fuel wood use along trekking trails, albeit while also increasing fossil fuel emissions in transportation. Ecotourism initiatives will be a major area of concentration in the future. These green approaches are reinforcing the ecological spirituality of the rural population. In the cosmic consciousness of the Bhutanese people, earth is not just for people; the gods and goddesses of mountains, forests, and water bodies inhabit it permanently.

Wildlife Depredation

Forest conservation is encroaching on agricultural land in Bhutan, a rare kind of advancement. The rising level of forests around homes has led to wildlife predation on crops and livestock. There is no compensation for livestock predation by tigers, leopards, wolves, and Himalayan black bears. Wild boars, deer, monkeys, and porcupines destroy crops. Small farmers' livelihoods are in conflict with wildlife and there is neither compensation nor insurance available for them. The Tiger Conservation Fund, created in 2002, provided compensation for livestock killed by big cats but was discontinued in 2011 when funds ran out. In total, about

Nu6.5 million ($115,000) was paid out in compensation from the fund (Schroeder 2014).

There is no wilful retaliatory killing of wild animals—whether protected or unprotected species—by humans in Bhutan. Ordinary Bhutanese people grudgingly reconcile themselves to the depredation loss, and expect the government to develop effective anti-depredation measures. Farmers who see themselves as victims of conservation regard this problem as a critique of GNH as it privileges urban over rural livelihoods and conservation over farming. It is a very delicate problem for the government. Compensation is too expensive to cover all depredation losses and wildlife killings are not welcome as they may spiral out of control. In some places, electric fencing funded by the government has stemmed wildlife depredation and mitigated crop damage, but the coverage is limited.

The 2010 GNH Survey identified the destruction of crops by wildlife as a major constraint to agricultural production: 72 per cent of rural respondents considered wildlife as a major or moderate constraint to agriculture. Annual average losses for most cereals and potato were estimated to be 20 per cent in a separate survey carried out in 2009 (Ura, Stringer, and Bulte 2009).

Schroeder (2014) suggests that the understanding and interpretations of GNH are varied among different actors across the government and society. Clearly, GNH as a governance framework is not as a cohesive concept across the four policy areas he studied (media, tourism, farm–road construction, and human–wildlife conflict). His case studies show that with respect to media and tourism, GNH policy intentions and outcomes are more or less matched. In both areas, private sector participation is widespread. Though not discussed here, the conclusions of a study of urban planning in Thimphu also indicate deviations between outcomes and plans, which were GNH-oriented (Bajaj 2014). With respect to farming and human–wildlife conflict, complex dynamics have resulted in a far more fragmented and incoherent approach. The conflict between the values of conservation and promotion of rural livelihoods remains unresolved. GNH policy tools and concepts have yet to play a decisive role in their resolution. At a deeper level, the tolerance of the conflict between the policies of conservation and rural livelihoods is rooted in the Buddhist outlook of the people.

GNH Outreach

Over the past 15 years, the pursuit of GNH by the government and the outreach efforts of the CBS have prompted substantial coverage in international and domestic media. Articles have been published on the various aspects of GNH in Bhutan in popular international newspapers and magazines, and discussed on TV programmes worldwide.[10] Theses and journal articles have also been published by foreign and Bhutanese scholars (for example, Bates 2009; Duncan 2008; Frey and Stutzer 2007; Hirata 2006; and Schroeder 2014). Conferences on GNH have been

[10] A web search by Tobias Plaff through LexisNexis database showed that 409 major newspapers carried one or more articles in 2010 that mentioned Bhutan and GNH. The (mostly English) newspapers include: *Bangkok Post*, *Belfast Telegraph*, *Bolivian Express*, *Brisbane News*, *Business Day* (South Africa), *Countryman*, *Daily News* (New York), *Daily Star*, *Daily Telegraph* and *Sunday Telegraph* (Sydney, Australia), *Financial Mail* (South Africa), *Financial Post Investing*, *Global News Wire*, *Herald Sun/Sunday Herald Sun* (Melbourne, Australia), *Het FinancieeleDagblad* (English), *International Herald Tribune*, *Kathmandu Post*, *Kiplinger Publications*, *Korea Herald*, *Korea Times*, *Los Angeles Times*, *Moscow News*, *National Post*, *Newsday*, *New Straits Times* (Malaysia), *Northern Territory News* (Australia), *O Globo* (Brazil), *South China Morning Post*, *Sunday Times* (South Africa), *Sunday Tribune*, *The Advertiser/Sunday Mail* (Adelaide, South Australia), *The Age* (Melbourne, Australia), *The Australian*, *The Business*, *The Business Times Singapore*, *The Canberra Times*, *The Courier Mail/ The Sunday Mail* (Australia), *The Daily Mail* and Mail on Sunday (London), *The Daily Telegraph* (London), *The Daily Yomiuri* (Tokyo), *The Dominion* (Wellington), *The Dominion Post* (Wellington, New Zealand), *The Express*, *The Globe and Mail* (Canada), *The Guardian* (London), *The Herald* (Glasgow), *The Independent* (London), *The Irish Times*, *The Jakarta Post*, *The Japan Times*, *The Jerusalem Post*, *The Jerusalem Report*, *The Kalgoorlie Miner*, *The Mercury/Sunday Tasmanian* (Australia), *The Mirror* (The Daily Mirror and The Sunday Mirror), *The Moscow Times*, *The Nation* (Thailand), *The New York Times*, *The New York Times*—Biographical Materials, *The New York Times*—Government Biographical Materials, *The New Zealand Herald*, *The Observer*, *The Philadelphia Inquirer*, *The Prague Post*, *The Press* (Christchurch, New Zealand), *The Scotsman & Scotland* on Sunday, *The Straits Times* (Singapore), *The Sunday Express*, *The Sunday Telegraph* (London), *The Sydney Morning Herald* (Australia), *The Toronto Star*, *The Toronto Sun*, *The Washington Post*, *The Washington Times*, *The Weekender* (South Africa), *The West Australian*, and *USA Today*.

organized in various parts of the world. The dissemination of GNH concepts to the public and discourse among academics internationally are important parts of global inquiries into this important measure of progress.

Numerous awareness and capacity-strengthening trainings have been given by the CBS over the years. Other trainings have been carried out with schools, college students, government district officials, and civil servants. For instance, in 2011, the CBS undertook trainings on the dissemination of GNH Survey findings to officials in all 20 districts of the country.

The CBS has played a key role in sharing research and disseminating knowledge, including conceptual innovations and methodical approaches, at international and regional conferences, workshops, and meetings. CBS publications are devoted largely to GNH and its related policy issues. The Royal Government of Bhutan has contributed to international forums to promote the inclusion of happiness as a goal. A major activity of the government was the organization of the High-level Meeting on Wellbeing and Happiness at the United Nations General Assembly in April 2012. Furthermore, a report produced by the government, 'Happiness: Towards a New Development Paradigm', was submitted to the United Nations General Assembly in December 2013 (Royal Government of Bhutan 2013).

The influence of GNH in schools and colleges is noticeable through an emphasis in the curriculum on value education and skills development in order to protect the environment and other sentient beings (Ura 2008). GNH education in schools and colleges highlights the importance of a holistic educational approach. A holistic education extends beyond a conventional formal education framework to respond more directly to the task of creating good human beings.

Future Outlook

As of March 2015, the United Nations had shortlisted a collection of potential indicators for the post-2015 development agenda in its Background Information to the Proposed List of Indicators. The GNH Index is one of the six indicators enumerated and proposed by the United Nations Conference on Trade and Development, which proposed the Index of Sustainable Economic Welfare (authored by

Nordhaus and Tobin), Gross National Happiness (Bhutan), Beyond GDP (European Union), Key National Indicators System (United States), Better life Index (Organisation for Economic Co-operation and Development), and Human Development Index (United Nations).

Scientific inquiries have contributed to global awareness about broader concepts of development. Climate change and rising inequality have fuelled the debate about growth-centred development (Picketty 2014; Stiglitz, Sen, and Fitoussi 2010). As Graeber (2011: 382) stated, '... ecologists keep reminding us ... it's impossible to maintain an engine of perpetual growth forever on a finite planet....' The size of an economy (or its level of wealth) cannot be infinite in scope. It must be determined by the capacity of the specific ecology of a country at an objective level within a given time perspective and by what is deemed sufficient at an individual level. This suggests that we cannot avoid coming to terms with the idea of a material sufficiency condition for our happiness and welfare. Beyond a certain level of affluence, research suggests that adding more commodities cannot enhance happiness and welfare, but it will have a negative impact on the environment. As a result, a balance between the economy and ecology is a key consideration of the GNH framework.

Bhutan has been making modest efforts to explore an alternative measure of development that is based on GNH since His Majesty Jigme Singye Wangchuck declared in 1972 that Bhutan should be more aligned with the philosophy of GNH. Research needs to be sustained to deepen interdisciplinary knowledge in the domains of GNH. Under-researched domains—such as time use, psychological well-being, and community vitality—and their role in development are drawing increasing attention from scholarship and government in understanding non-material components of SWB. The concepts and measurement of individual happiness and collective happiness, like the question about the individual versus society, are policy-relevant. Mancall (2004: 33) expressed the view that 'the contradiction between the individual and the collective can be resolved only by means of policies specifically designed according to GNH'.

GNH cannot last long as a movement within a single country, just as a country cannot develop without absorbing positive influences from the international community. GNH is a platform for Bhutan to have a positive influence on the world, not only in theoretical terms but also through concrete practices. For a small country, it has had an outsized, positive influence in fields such as the environment and happiness. The ongoing evolution of GNH in policy and practice extends this influence. The final question is whether GNH as a practical development framework has been effective in Bhutan. Did it alter the path of development in Bhutan? What would Bhutan be like today if it had not embraced GNH?

The answer is clear. GNH has provided a normative orientation for both the state and society to a considerable degree. It has led the state to do things differently by creating new norms of official decision-making and new institutions. Among the outcomes, the balance that Bhutan has struck between modernity and tradition on the one hand, and environment and economic growth on the other, is a prominent achievement that would not have been possible otherwise. GNH's role has been of significant value in guiding public discussions, policies, and laws. A major criterion of success for GNH as a development framework is that Bhutan has remained a reasonably equitable and sustainable society where the proportion of unhappy people is relatively very low given its level of per capita income. GNH is, however, not a blueprint from above to be implemented vertically. The government and Bhutanese society take decisions by assessing viewpoints and opinions as they are expressed in public discussions and findings from GNH Surveys. The aim of these GNH Surveys is to encourage people to discuss and reflect on what brings them happiness, and then make these reflections part of the policy-making process. While there have been many positive changes because of GNH in Bhutan, it has also had an effect on public policy deliberations in other countries. Bhutan has therefore contributed to adding happiness as an important societal objective as part of a shift towards an alternative path of development.

References

Adler, M. and E.A. Posner. 2008. 'Happiness Research and Cost-Benefit Analysis', *The Journal of Legal Studies*, 37(S2): 5263–91.

Alkire, S. and J. Foster. 2011. 'Counting and Multidimensional Poverty Measurement', *Journal of Public Economics*, 95(7): 476–87.

Bajaj, M. 2014. *How Actors Legitimize Deviations from Urban Planning Codes: Evidence from Bhutan*. Thimphu: Centre for Bhutan Studies.

Bates, W. 2009. 'Gross National Happiness', *Asian Pacific Economic Literature,* 23(2): 1–16.

Centre for Bhutan Studies and GNH Research. 2012. *An Extensive Analysis of GNH Index*. Thimphu.

Csikszentmihalyi, M. and J. Hunter. 2003. 'Happiness in Everyday Life: The Uses of Experience Sampling', *Journal of Happiness Studies*, 4(2): 185–99.

Dambrun, M.R., G. Després, E. Drelon, E. Gibelin, M. Gibelin, and O. Michaux. 2012. 'Measuring Happiness: From Fluctuating Happiness to Authentic–Durable Happiness', *Frontiers in Psychology*, 3(16): 1–11.

Davidson, R.J. and W. Irwin. 1999. 'The Functional Neuroanatomy of Emotion and Affective Style', *Trends in Cognitive Science,* 3(1): 11–21.

Deiner, E. and S. Oishi. 2005. 'The Nonobvious Social Psychology of Happiness', *Psychological Inquiry,* 16(4): 162–7.

Duncan, G. 2008. 'Should Happiness Maximization be the Goal of Government?' *Journal of Happiness Studies*, 11(2): 163–78.

Easterlin, R. 2005. 'A Puzzle for Adaptive Theory', *Journal of Economic Behavior and Organization*, 56(4): 513–21.

Ekman, P., R.J. Davidson, M. Ricard, and B.A. Wallace. 2005. 'Buddhist and Psychological Perspectives on Emotions and Well-Being', *American Psychological Society*, 14(2): 59–62.

Fredrickson, B.L. and D. Kahneman. 1993. 'Duration Neglect in Retrospective Evaluations of Affective Episodes', *Journal of Personality and Social Psychology, 65*(1).

Frey, B. and A. Stutzer. 2007. 'Should National Happiness Be Maximized?' IEW Working Paper. Zurich: Center for Research in Economics, Management, and the Arts.

Graeber, D. 2011. *Debt: The First 5000 Years*. New York: Melville House.

Gross National Happiness Commission. 2013. *Eleventh Year Plan*. Available at http://www.gnhc.gov.bt/five-year-plan/ (last accessed on 1 October 2016).

Helliwell, J.F., R. Layard, and J. Sachs (eds). 2013. *World Happiness Report 2013*. New York: Sustainable Development Solutions Network.

Hirata, J. 2006. *Happiness, Ethics, and Economics*. New York: Routledge.

Kundera, M. 1996. *Slowness*. New York: HarperCollins.

Layard, R. 2005. *Happiness–Lessons from a New Science.* New York: Penguin Books.

Mancall, M. 2004. 'Gross National Happiness and Development: An Essay', in K. Gaylay and K. Ura (eds), *Proceedings of the First International Conference on Operationalization of Gross National Happiness*. Centre for Bhutan Studies and GNH Research: Thimphu.

National Statistics Bureau. 2012. *National Accounts Statistics 2012*. Thimphu: Royal Government of Bhutan.

Nussbaum, M. 2000. 'Women's Capabilities and Social Justice', *Journal of Human Development*, 1(2): 221–45.

Oswald, A.J. 2010. 'Emotional Prosperity and the Stiglitz Commission', *British Journal of Industrial Relations*, 48(4): 651–69.

Picketty, T. 2014. *Capital in the Twenty First Century*. Havard: Belknap Press.

Planning Commission. 1999. *Bhutan 2020: A Vision for Peace, Prosperity, and Happiness*. Thimphu: Royal Government of Bhutan.

Ricard, M. 2003. *Happiness–A Guide to Developing Life's Most Important Skill*. London: Atlantic Books.

Ritu, V. and K. Ura. Forthcoming. *Gender Differences in GNH: Power, Equality, and Neutrality in Bhutan*.

Royal Government of Bhutan. 2010. *Economic Development Policy of the Kingdom of Bhutan 2010*. Thimphu.

______. 2013. *Happiness: Towards a New Development Paradigm*, availiable at http://www.newdevelopmentparadigm.bt/2013/12/13/new-development-pardigm-report/ (last accessed on 1 October 2016).

Royal Government of Bhutan, Ministry of Finance. 2014. *National Budget Financial Year 2014–2015*. http://www.mof.gov.bt/wp-content/uploads/2014/07/BR2014-2015ENG.pdf (last accessed on 1 October 2016).

Schor, J. 1999. *The Overspent American: Why We Want What We Don't Need*. New York: HarperCollins.

Schroeder, K. 2014. 'The Politics of Gross National Happiness: Image and Practice in the Implementation of Bhutan's Multidimensional Development Strategy', Doctoral Dissertation.

Stiglitz, J., A. Sen, and J. Fitoussi. 2010. *Mismeasuring Our Lives–Why GDP Doesn't Add Up*. New York: The New Press.

Therborn, G. 2011. *The World*. Cambridge, United Kingdom: Polity Press.

Thomas, D.L. and E. Diener. 1990. 'Memory Accuracy in the Recall of Emotions', *Journal of Personality and Social Psychology*, 59(2).

Ura K. 2008. 'An Approach to the Indicators of GNH', presented at the World Health Organization's Regional Conference on Revitalizing Primary Health Care, 6–8 August, Jakarta.

Ura, K., S. Alkire, K. Wangdi, and Z. Tshoki. 2012. *An Extensive Analysis of GNH*. Thimphu: Centre for Bhutan Studies.

Ura, K., R. Stringer, and E. Bulte. 2009. 'Managing Wildlife Damage to Agriculture in Bhutan: Conflicts, Costs, and Compromise', in L. Lipper, T. Sakuyama, R. Stringer, and D. Zilberman (eds), *Payment for Environmental Services in Agricultural Landscapes: Economic Policies and Poverty Reduction in Developing Countries, Natural Resource Management and Policy*, Volume 31. New York: Springer Press.

Van den Bergh, C.J.M. 2009. 'The GDP Paradox', *Journal of Economic Psychology*, 30: 117–35.

Wallace, B.A. 2005. *Genuine Happiness: Meditation as the Path to Fulfillment*. Hoboken: John Wiley and Sons.

Watson, D., L.A. Clark, and A. Tellegen. 1988. 'Development and Validation of Brief Measures of Positive and Negative Affect: The PANAS Scales', *Journal of Personality and Social Psychology*, 54(6): 1063–70.

4

SABYASACHI MITRA, SARAH CARRINGTON, AND ANTHONY BALUGA

Unlocking Bhutan's Potential

Measuring Potential Output for the Nation

The nature and drivers of sustained medium- and long-term economic growth are central to policymaking in both developed and developing countries. Beginning in the 1950s, notably with Robert Solow and Trevor Swan, neoclassical economists began to analyse theories of why and how economies grow (Harberger 1978). While specific interest in the challenges facing the growth of developing countries reaches back to the 1940s and conceptions of investment coordination failure known as the 'big push' theory of development, more general theories of development economics began with Sir William Arthur Lewis's dual sector growth model published in 1954. This model conceptualized the fundamental dynamics of structural transition from low productivity, agriculture-based economies to higher productivity, and industrialized economies. In the past few decades, analysis in economic growth and development literature has advanced on these foundations, with the objective of deriving policy measures that promote sustainable growth for both developing countries and economies in transition.

For developing countries in particular, and all countries in general, the sustainability and maintenance of growth over time is key for the economic growth to translate into real advances in the standard of living of the population. A core concept that encapsulates the rate of growth that can be sustained by an economy—given its resources, human capital, and technology—is potential output growth. The potential output concept is now widely employed to not only estimate the long-term growth potential of a country given its resources, but also as a key anchor for economic stability. It is defined as measuring an economy's aggregate supply-side capabilities as given by its production structure, available technology, and resources (European Central Bank 2000). In other words, potential output is the maximum output an economy can sustain without overstretching its capacity or pushing up the prices of scarce production resources or generating increased inflation. Thus, the expansion of this potential level of output through investment in capital and technology, and ultimately productivity growth, is necessary for persistent increases in growth rates over time.

The purpose of this chapter is to estimate the potential output of the tiny, landlocked Himalayan Kingdom of Bhutan. Bhutan, an economy of less than 800,000 people living on an average of $2,900 per year (International Monetary Fund 2013), has experienced remarkable growth and dramatic structural change. However, while Bhutan's economic growth over the past three decades has averaged nearly 8 per cent per annum—a remarkable achievement—its growth has simultaneously been highly volatile. The volatility of output in Bhutan derives from the highly non-diversified economy that is dominated by the capital-intensive and low domestic-employment-generating hydropower sector. The agriculture and service sectors remain below their output potential but absorb the majority of the labour force.

Thus, Bhutan's macroeconomic performance hinges on the performance of the hydropower sector and the government's ability to manage and distribute the growth arising from this sector. It is an interesting case in which remarkable rates of growth have been achieved without the traditional transition of a large part of the economy from agricultural to industrial production. Much of the sector's growth has been possible due to external assistance—in particular, Bhutan's close economic and trade links with India, which provide substantial budget support grants and concessional loans to fund investment so that it can benefit from Bhutan's vast hydropower endowment. However, Bhutan's reliance on Indian funding for such a large proportion of its economic activity exposes the economy to risks. Bhutan's choice of a pegged exchange rate, which is fixed at one-to-one with the Indian rupee, and its heavy reliance on imported capital goods and labour to build its hydropower industry make it even more vulnerable to external developments.

This chapter aims to analyse Bhutan's growth performance in terms of potential and actual output growth, and discuss several policies available to pursue augmented potential growth. There are two basic approaches for estimating potential output: (i) statistical filtering and (ii) estimation of structural relationships (Benes et al. 2010; Cerra and Saxena 2000; European Central Bank 2000). The first approach isolates the trend and cyclical components of real output growth. The second method employs a supply-side model production function that relies on structural relationships based on economic theory to construct output; it is essentially a bottom–up approach to the generation of an output series.

We employ a variant of this latter supply-side approach, which uses a growth accounting framework to take into account the dynamics of fundamental drivers of long-term growth. The growth accounting approach allows us to capture the relationship between potential output and its structural determinants—labour, capital, and productivity-related factors, including technical change. It is particularly suitable for our analysis as Bhutan lacks available data to undertake other approaches, which is a commonly experienced constraint in estimating potential output in developing and transition economies. The chosen approach employs a Cobb–Douglas production function to explain the dynamics of growth drivers and uses a Kalman filter to estimate the unobserved variables. The model also incorporates demand-side equations to capture the output gap through inflation dynamics. A key advantage of our approach is that it can be used to forecast potential output as well as the key factors influencing it, including employment, investment, and technological progress. The resulting model is employed to look at the impact of policy measures, some of which have been proposed as the result of a growth diagnostics study on Bhutan (Asian Development Bank 2013b), including increased investment in human capital and economic diversification on the production side of the economy. The trade-off between the quantity of investment and quality of factor inputs in terms of their productivity is also extensively discussed.

From this analysis, we recommend those policies deemed most effective for Bhutan to release its potential output from constraints.

The structure of the chapter is as follows. The section 'Bhutan's Structural Transformation' discusses the structural transformation of Bhutan by qualitatively describing the developments in the real, fiscal, monetary, and external sectors, and by identifying factors that may potentially be hindering Bhutan's growth. The section 'Model, Estimation Technique, and Data' lays out a small, structural macro model and specifies the estimation technique and data used in the chapter's analysis. The section 'Results and Growth Simulations' reports the results of the model's use in projecting potential output growth over the next two decades. A baseline model is first established and subsequently used as a benchmark scenario against which the impacts on forecast output of various potential shocks and policy options can be compared. In the 'Conclusion' the quantitative growth simulations are drawn upon to make policy recommendations and concluding remarks regarding the removal of identified growth impediments.

Bhutan's Structural Transformation

Bhutan's dramatic structural change in recent decades has directly impacted its potential and actual growth rates. This section details the major developments in economic composition from a production and expenditure perspective, documents any transition in government fiscal policy, describes the changes that Bhutan has experienced with respect to its interaction with the external sector, and explains key developments in the monetary and financial sectors of the Bhutanese economy. Throughout this section, the data used to calculate and display the measures are taken from the National Statistics Bureau of Bhutan, the Royal Monetary Authority of Bhutan (RMA), and several annual reports from the Royal Government of Bhutan.

Economic Growth

The phenomenal growth rates experienced by Bhutan over the last three decades are some of the highest seen anywhere in the world over

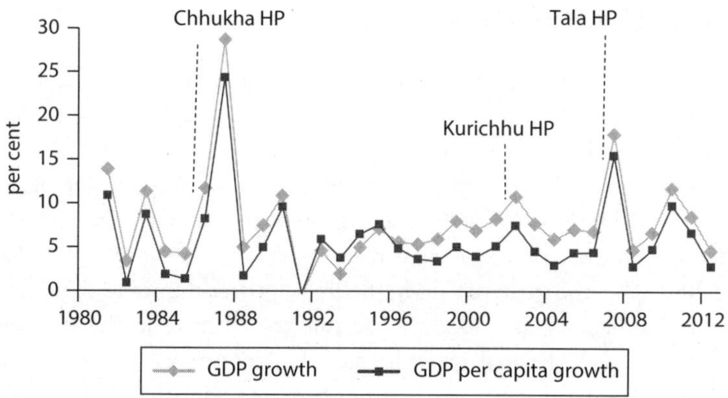

FIGURE 4.1 Annual Gross Domestic Product and Gross Domestic Product Per Capita Growth Rates (%), 1981–2011

Notes: GDP = gross domestic product; HP = hydropower plant.

Sources: Authors' calculations based on data from National Statistics Bureau (2012); RMA, *Annual Report* (various years).

such a long period of time. The average annual growth rate in Bhutan during 1981–2012 was 7.9 per cent on a per capita basis (Figure 4.1).

Figure 4.1 depicts the annual growth rate of gross domestic product (GDP) and GDP per capita during 1981–2012. While average economic growth has been high, it has also been quite volatile over time. This variance is due to the high proportion of economic output pertaining to the hydropower sector and its rapid, albeit lumpy, growth. The observed growth spikes reflect peaks in activity during the construction and commissioning of hydropower projects. The most striking growth spike occurred in 1987 when the Chhukha Hydropower Plant was constructed, propelling Bhutan's growth rate to over 28 per cent that year. The most recent decade was also influenced by a number of large hydropower projects—particularly the operational launch of the Kurichhu and Tala plants. As more plants have come into operation, the proportionate growth spikes caused by new hydropower construction projects have become smaller over time compared with larger overall output, and the average growth rate of the Bhutanese economy has become more stable as a result.

Sectoral Decomposition of Growth

The rapid growth of the Bhutanese economy has been characterized by commensurately rapid structural change. Table 4.1 shows the decomposition of economic growth by sector in 1980–2012 and Figure 4.2 graphically depicts the corresponding annual decomposition. The driving sector of Bhutan's growth performance is clearly the industrial sector. In each of the three sub-periods—1980–90, 1991–2000, and 2001–12—the growth rate in the hydropower-dominated industrial sector significantly exceeded the overall growth rate in the economy, reaching a peak decadal growth rate of 22.6 per cent in the earliest period, and 6.7 per cent and 10.3 per cent per annum in the two subsequent periods respectively. This compares with growth rates of 10.1 per cent, 5 per cent, and 8.4 per cent during the three respective periods for the total economy.

The second highest contributor to growth has been the service sector, which in recent years has comprised mainly tourism and services related to tourism. Growth rates in this sector have been strong and less volatile relative to the industrial sector. The service sector has achieved an average annual growth rate of 8.8 per cent over the review period, and thus its growth rate has exceeded the total economic growth rate. Figure 4.2a shows the increasing contribution of the service sector to overall growth rates. Figure 4.2b shows the gradual, proportionate increase in the relative size of both the industrial and service sectors over time.

With the growth rate in the industrial and service sectors exceeding the economy-wide average, the agriculture sector's contribution to GDP has steadily declined. Growing at an average annual rate of 3.1 per cent in 1980–2012—less than half the economy-wide average over this period—agriculture comprised only 14.5 per cent of the economy in 2012. Yet, agriculture remains the major source of employment, with 62.2 per cent of the labour force employed in what is mainly subsistence agriculture. While agriculture's share of total employment has also seen a decline in recent decades, with a 20 percentage points decline in the last decade alone, the fall in this sector's share of employment has not been commensurate with that of the relative decline in the value of its output. This mismatch between relative contributions to value added and employment has

TABLE 4.1 Decomposition of Economic Growth by Sector, 1980–2012

		Agriculture		Industry		Services	
	GDP Growth Rate	Average Growth Rate	Contribution to GDP Growth	Average Growth Rate	Contribution to GDP Growth	Average Growth Rate	Contribution to GDP Growth
1980–90	10.1	5.6	26.1	22.6	45.4	10.5	26.9
1991–2000	5.0	1.7	9.9	6.7	43.7	6.7	43.3
2001–12	8.4	2.2	5.6	10.3	47.6	9.1	39.4
1980–2012	7.9	3.1	14.7	13.0	46.0	8.8	35.2

Note: GDP = gross domestic product.

Source: Authors' calculations based on data from National Statistics Bureau (2012).

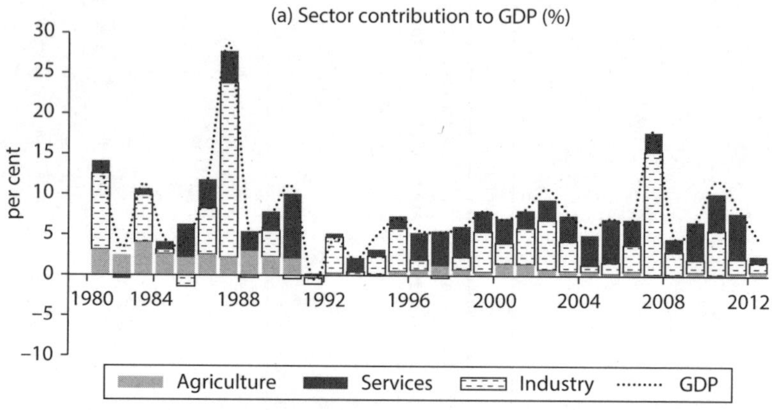

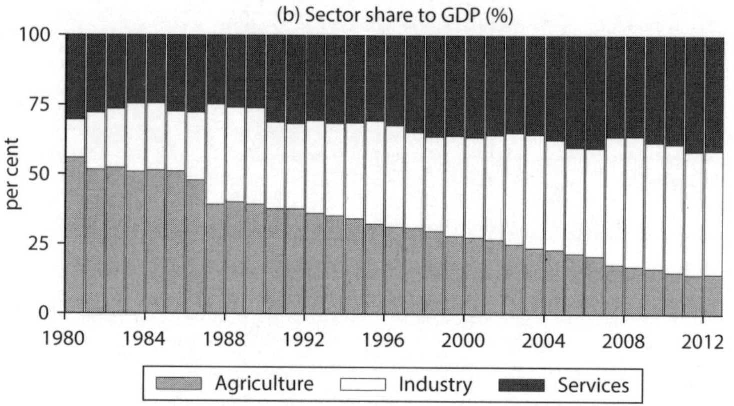

FIGURES 4.2A, 4.2B Sectoral Contribution to Gross Domestic Product, 1980–2012

Note: GDP = gross domestic product.

Sources: Authors' estimates based on data from National Statistics Bureau (2012); RMA, *Annual Report* (various years).

implications for the distribution of income and welfare generated by the long-run growth upswing, and is indicative of the need for future restructuring and upskilling of the labour force to ensure that growth is more evenly distributed. In effect, the hydropower sector's dominance in the Bhutanese economy has implications on the concentration and distribution of economic activities. Even within the industrial sector, existing industries such as construction, cement, chemicals, wood-based products, and metals are highly dependent on and synchronized with the hydropower sector, making much of the industrial activity in Bhutan highly correlated with itself. Thus, the economy is quite vulnerable to any shocks impacting the hydropower sector, which is of course highly dependent on grants and international financing.

Decomposition of Growth by Expenditure

In a similar way to the production side of the economy, the expenditure side has also seen substantial changes over the last three decades (Figure 4.3). The share of the principal driver of GDP growth in the 1980s, household consumption expenditure, approximately halved from 85.1 per cent in 1980 to 43.3 per cent in 2012. From being a consumption-led economy, Bhutan's growth is now largely driven by capital expenditure. Capital accumulation now accounts for more than half (57.9 per cent) of GDP growth, with capital formation reaching average annual growth rates of around 10.7 per cent in 1980–2012, much higher than the GDP growth rate of 7.9 per cent over the same period. At the household level, however, expenditure is still overwhelmingly consumption based. On average, Bhutanese households allocated over 46 per cent of total expenditure in 2001–12 to non-durable goods (for example, food and non-alcoholic beverages; clothing and footwear; and alcoholic beverages, tobacco, and narcotics) and more than 30 per cent to durable goods (for example, housing, water, electricity, gas, household equipment, and home maintenance).

The remarkably large contribution of capital investment to growth is driven by two main factors. The first is the relatively high cost of accumulating hydropower capital in Bhutan. Second, funding for Bhutanese hydropower investment comes from international sources —mainly India—and, thus, investment ratios are not constrained by domestic savings. Such a large proportion of expenditure on capital accumulation—in particular, hydropower investment—over such a long period of time has important implications for the structural balance of the economy in Bhutan. More diversified expenditure patterns and productivity-enhancing investments are needed for increased stability and inclusive economic growth in the future.

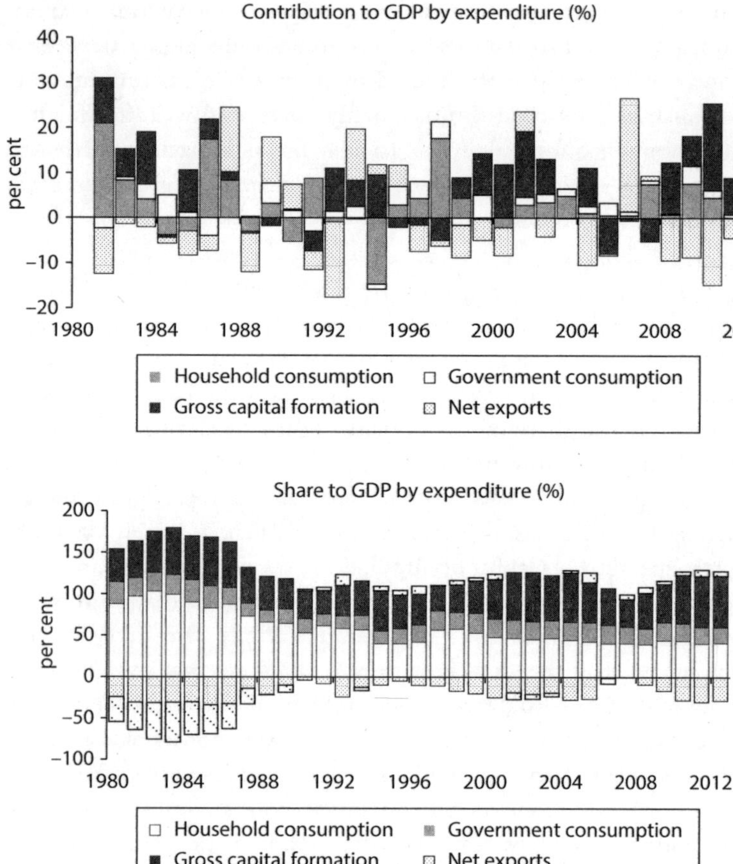

FIGURE 4.3 Composition of Expenditure in Bhutan's Economy, 1980–2012

Note: GDP = gross domestic product.

Sources: Authors' estimates based on data from National Statistics Bureau (2012); and the United Nations Conference on Trade and Development Statistics. Available at: http://unctad.org/en/Pages/Statistics.aspx (last accessed on April 2013).

Fiscal Developments

Decomposition of Government Expenditure

Fiscal policy plays an important role in managing the impact of output fluctuations as well as redistributing the income generated by the hydropower industry. Further, the composition of expenditure has an important influence on the potential output of Bhutan, both at the time of spending and in the future. For example, increased current expenditure relative to capital expenditure can be instrumental in shielding the economy from the impact of an economic downturn, but may come at the expense of increased potential output now or in the future (as expenditure on human capital has a positive impact in potential output, but with a lag). Thus, both the level and the composition of expenditure play an important role in influencing potential output over time.

During the period 1980–2012, the Royal Government of Bhutan varied the level of its expenditure as a proportion of GDP while maintaining relatively equal shares of non-hydropower-related current and capital expenditure to total government expenditure. The peak level of government expenditure relative to GDP occurred in the 1980s, when it reached an average of about 40 per cent of GDP before slightly dipping in the 1990s. In the 2000s, government expenditure picked up again, averaging about 38 per cent of GDP.

Figure 4.4 displays the breakdown of government expenditure by category, including hydropower-related expenditure. In terms of composition, the most recent figures for FY2012 show that proportionate government outlays on general services (for example, roads and housing, among others) nearly halved over the preceding five years, while those on hydropower sector development increased sevenfold. The expenditure of the Royal Government of Bhutan on social services, mainly comprising health and education, slightly declined in terms of proportionate total government expenditure. Transport and communications, and agriculture and mining each diminished slightly in terms of budgetary prominence during the review period.

Government Revenue and Net Borrowing

One of the major benefits of the expansion of the hydropower sector has been the fiscal space it has given the government. From 5.7 per cent of GDP in the 1980s, tax revenue reached 14.8 per cent of GDP in FY2013. As a share of total revenue, tax revenue increased from 32.9 per cent in the 1980s to 71.2 per cent in FY2013. The increasing sales tax revenue from electricity sold to India, royalties from the use of natural resources for hydropower, and corporate taxes from hydropower corporations

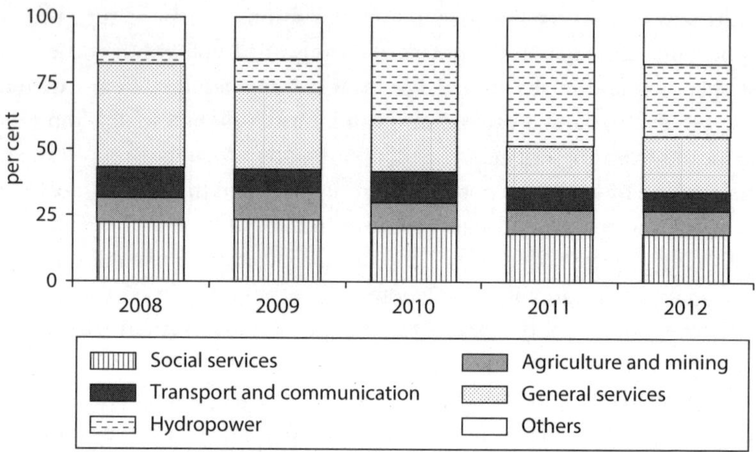

FIGURE 4.4 Composition of Government Expenditure by Sector, FY2008–FY2012

Sources: Authors' estimates based on data from Ministry of Finance (2012); RMA, *Annual Report* (various years).

have been the major drivers of increased government revenues over recent decades as more hydropower plants have come online.

From a very volatile and more sizable fiscal deficit averaging around 5 per cent of GDP in the early 2000s, the government has maintained a more stable debt position of late, resulting in budget balances and even surpluses for most fiscal years since 2006. The stability of the fiscal position has been strongly supported by the growth of grant and donor support in recent years. For the period FY2000–FY2013, grants contributed a sum equal to nearly 37 per cent of total expenditure, or almost 70 per cent of capital expenditure, with the majority of these grants coming from India for hydropower investment. Nevertheless, public debt has increased over time from 60.6 per cent of GDP in FY2002 to 93.7 per cent in FY2013. Further, most of this debt (93.8 per cent) has been sourced externally. Of the outstanding public debt, around 59 per cent is accounted for by the hydropower sector; as the sector develops, this debt should be paid as investments mature. Figure 4.5 details the main sources of revenue and the resulting net budget position FY2000–FY2013.

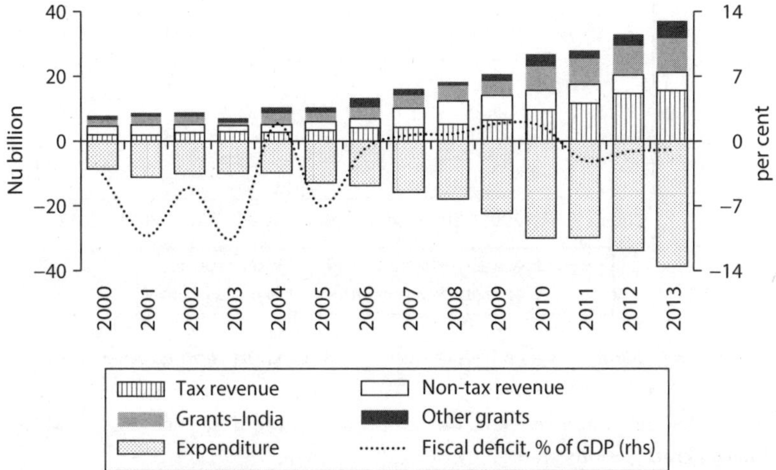

FIGURE 4.5 Composition of Government Revenue and Budget Position, FY2000–FY2013

Notes: GDP = gross domestic product; rhs = right-hand side.

Sources: Authors' estimates based on data from Ministry of Finance (2012); RMA, *Annual Report* (various years).

The Real External Sector

Major Trade Developments

As with the broader Bhutanese economy, the balance of payments (BoP) is also strongly associated with the performance and needs of the hydropower sector. Exports of electricity and imports of capital goods for new hydropower investment are both large components of the current account. Hydropower exports have comprised nearly 35 per cent of total exports on average over the last decade and more than 39 per cent of exports to India, Bhutan's major trading partner, which has received around 80 per cent of Bhutanese exports and provided about 70 per cent of its imports over the same period.[1]

Figure 4.6 displays hydropower exports as a proportion of total exports and of exports to Bhutan's major trading partner, India. As

[1] Bhutan also exports substantial ferro alloys and copper wire to India.

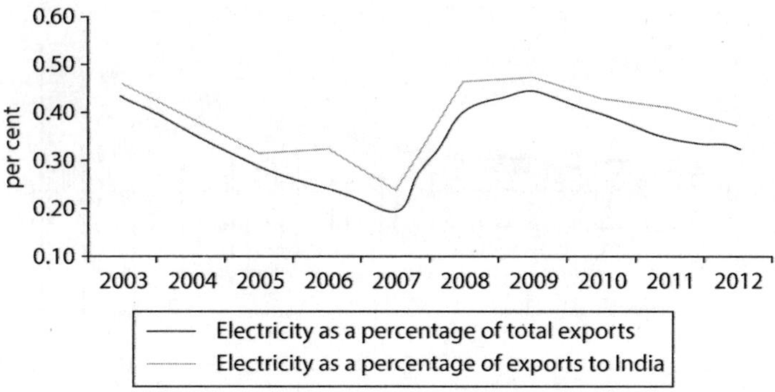

FIGURE 4.6 Electricity as a Proportion of Total Exports and Exports to India, FY2003–FY2012

Sources: Authors' estimates based on data from Ministry of Finance (2012); RMA, *Annual Report* (various years).

expected, both measures move strongly in line with major developments in the hydropower sector. However, with more hydropower plants coming online, the proportional movement in exports over time is less volatile than it was in the earlier phases of hydropower development. This is so because the Bhutanese economy now experiences less volatility in both exports and output.[2] This evolution can be seen in Figure 4.7.

Figure 4.8 displays the (volatile) service trade deficit as a proportion of the total current account deficit that Bhutan has with its trading partners. The volatility of this balance is driven by the variation in the performance of the underlying sectors themselves. However, the major spike in the deficit in this case has more to do with the falling denominator rather than an increase in imports of services. In general, Bhutan has been a net importer of construction and travel services (except in FY2008), a net exporter of transport services (due to Bhutan's ownership of the only flight services licensed to carry passengers to and from Bhutan), and a mixed trader of insurance services.

[2] In the early years of the development of the hydropower sector, export levels would jump as much as 85 per cent in a single year as it did with the commencement of operations at the Chhukha Plant in 1987, which also contributed nearly half of Bhutan's GDP growth in the same year.

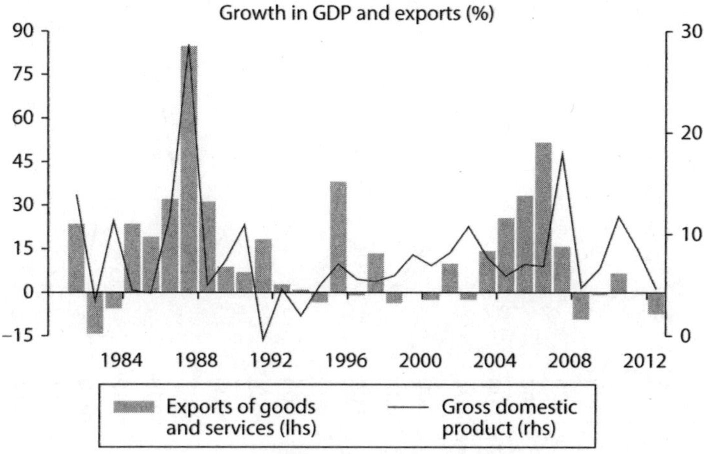

FIGURE 4.7 Evolution of Gross Domestic Product, Exports and Imports, and Trade Market Concentration, FY1981–FY2012

Notes: GDP = gross domestic product; lhs = left-hand side; rhs = right-hand side.

Sources: Authors' Calculations based on data from National Statistics Bureau (2012); RMA, *Annual Report* (various years).

The External Financial Sector

While the financial sector's role is theoretically to facilitate transactions in the real sector, oftentimes the behaviour and composition of financial sector flows can independently impact real sector outcomes.

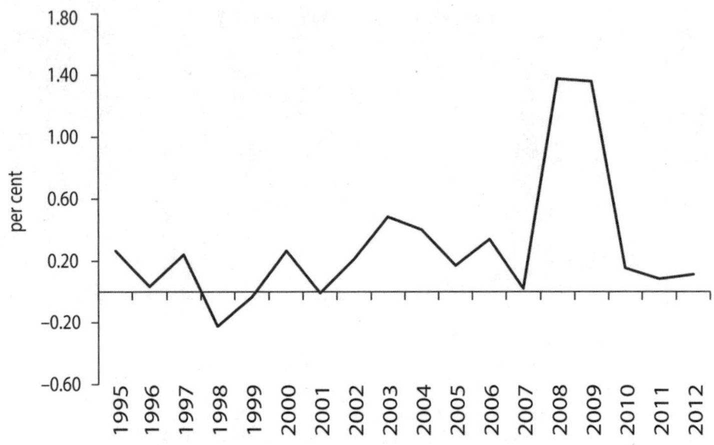

FIGURE 4.8 Service Trade Deficit as a Proportion of Total Current Account Deficit, FY1995–FY2012

Source: Authors' Calculations based on balance of payments data from RMA, *Annual Report* (various years).

By constraining or amplifying real sector behaviour, the financial sector often influences the path of actual output and its long-term path and can even play a part in affecting investment and, in turn, potential output.

Figure 4.9 displays the proportionate composition of Bhutan's capital account in FY1999–FY2012, which refer to dates the breakdown in contributions is available. For much of Bhutan's earlier phase of global integration, Bhutan's heavy reliance on imported goods was largely financed through grants and capital transfers, mainly through India and international development banks and partnerships. However, in line with Bhutan's economic development, the proportion of capital transfers making up total capital inflows declined over time. Comprising about 62 per cent in FY1999, capital transfers fell to under 20 per cent of capital inflows in FY2012. Conversely, investment inflows in the form of capital loans to the government (mainly from India) largely replaced the capital grants that funded Bhutanese investment projects in the past. Portfolio investment flows were the only outgoing category of capital in net terms, and this only occurred once in FY2000. While

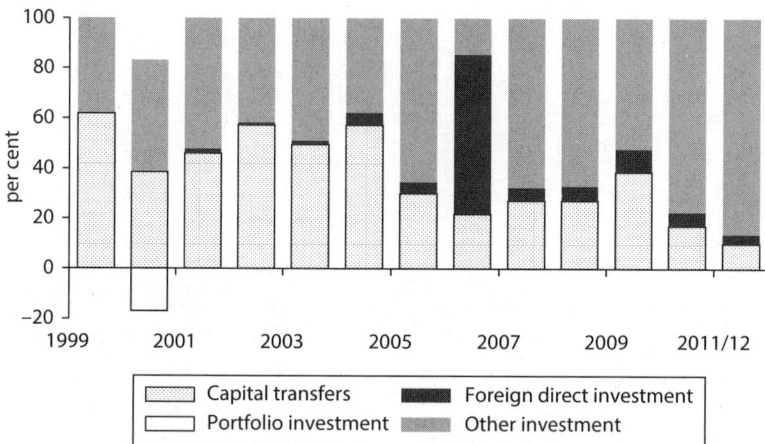

FIGURE 4.9 Composition of the Capital Account, FY1999–FY2012
Sources: Authors' calculations based on balance of payments data from RMA, *Annual Report* (various years).

foreign direct investment is a very small proportion of capital inflows in nearly all years (excepting a one-off large inflow in FY2006), this component has grown steadily over time as a share of total capital inflows. As Bhutan continues on its path of economic development, market-based financing and investment are becoming more prominent in the economy.

Figure 4.10 displays a breakdown of the BoP for Bhutan over the period FY1996–FY2012. As can be seen, the BoP is mostly in surplus as funding—originally in the form of capital transfers, then progressively through outright investment—was sufficient to finance the import bill during the review period. However, the composition of the accounts was quite volatile over the review period due to the aforementioned drivers of external transactions for Bhutan.

Monetary Sector and Reserves

Developments in Bhutan's monetary sector are driven largely by two main factors. First, Bhutan maintains a one-to-one fixed exchange rate peg between the Bhutanese ngultrum and the Indian rupee, the currency of its main trading partner. Second, the banking and financial sectors

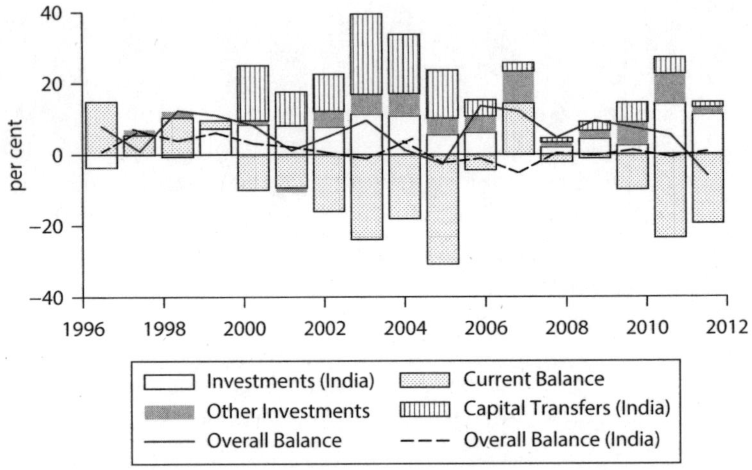

FIGURE 4.10 Capital Flows and Balance of Payments as a Percentage of GDP, FY1996–FY2012

Note: GDP = gross domestic product.

Source: Authors' calculations based on balance of payments data from RMA, *Annual Report* (various years).

in Bhutan are still undeveloped, which has implications for liquidity and credit growth management, and ultimately investment and output.

Foreign Currency Market

Since the ngultrum was first introduced in 1974, its value has been kept at par with the Indian rupee. Due to the increasing integration of Bhutan with the international economy and the remarkable growth in the import-dependent and capital-intensive hydropower sector, the stability of Bhutan's Indian rupee reserve holdings has come under stress in recent years. Capital imports aside, reserve management has been intensified by a confluence of factors operating through the banking system and interacting with growing incomes and demand for credit. The unused funding for hydropower projects and the proceeds from operational plants deposited by the government in the banking system as short-term deposits are of key importance. The funding deposits, alongside deposits from state-owned enterprises required to hold their revenues in demand deposits, have injected substantial liquidity into the banking system in recent years. These factors, in addition to the growing level of deposits from Bhutanese households with increased incomes, have meant that Bhutanese banks have found themselves flooded with liquidity at times. These circumstances provide incentives for banks to leverage their funding positions and extend loans to the growing consumer market, thereby stimulating imports of consumer goods and further exacerbating the net rupee reserve holding position.

Significant imports of capital and consumer goods have caused sizable current account deficits at times. As recently as 2011, the current account deficit widened to about 23.5 per cent of GDP due in large part to considerable import requirements for the development of the Punatsangchhu and Mangdechhu hydropower plants.[3] The widening of the current account deficit in 2011 intensified the rupee shortage (known as the liquidity crisis), which prompted the RMA to sell $400 million of international reserves on two occasions and avail a rupee overdraft loan from India to meet current account requirements. Import controls have also been temporarily implemented since 2011 to constrain the purchase of foreign currency. Thus, the considerable capital inflows funding the hydropower sector's expansion require ongoing supervision and the provision of appropriately composed reserve holdings; the management of system liquidity, particularly with regard to the substantial grant and loan funds; and the regulation and monitoring of banking activity and credit supply.

The Banking Sector and Monetary Policy

As mentioned earlier, the demand for Indian rupees has risen in Bhutan alongside income growth; disposable income expenditure goes largely towards imported consumption goods. However, credit growth in the private sector has amplified these trends, with such credit expanding at an average of 25.5 per cent per year during 2010–13. Much of the credit growth has gone to fund purchases of personal durable consumer goods, which were up more than 6 percentage points between 2009 and 2013 as a proportion of total private sector credit, credit cards,

[3] Rashid (2012) notes in his study of the Bhutanese liquidity crisis that the major trigger for the decline in rupee holdings in the first place is thought to have stemmed from the construction of the Tala hydropower project in 2004–5, which necessitated large capital imports that accounted for up to 70 per cent of the current account deficit.

and transport. In fact, credit to industry, agriculture, tourism, construction, and trade and commerce—mostly domestically anchored activities—has fallen over the same time period. Thus, while the supply of credit was stimulated through the above-mentioned channels, there has also been growing demand for private household credit. In effect, there is evidence of a growing disconnect between the industries driving growth in the economy and the consumer-based household economy. As shown in Figure 4.11, the supply of bank reserves has not kept pace with credit supply. (For a complete description of the liquidity crisis and the banking sector's role, see Rashid 2012.)

The coexistence of a pegged exchange rate and large capital flows alongside a relatively underdeveloped banking system and the absence of a capital market creates a difficult environment in which to manage reserve holdings and their composition. The RMA's attempts to manage the liquidity flows have included introducing a policy interest rate and a base rate for bank lending in September 2012. However, due to the pegged exchange rate, the policy and base rate systems are constrained; any deviation of interest rates from market rates will create a cross-border arbitrage opportunity encouraging capital flows, which will in turn have further impacts on reserve management. Thus, longer-term policy development regarding liquidity management—given the growing linkages between the financial and real sectors—needs to

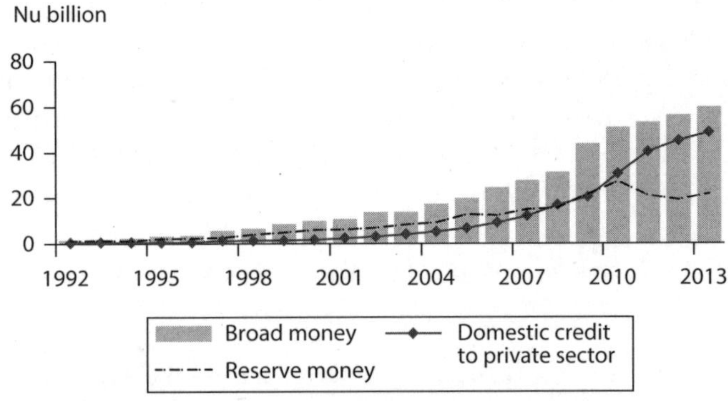

FIGURE 4.11 Growth in Money Supply, Banking Reserves, and Domestic Credit, 1992–2013

Source: Authors' estimates based on data from RMA, *Annual Report* (various years).

give careful attention to the interaction between the tradable sector, the government's use of the banking system, banking incentives, and exchange rate policy.

Model, Estimation Technique, and Data

This section provides a simple framework for estimating and analysing the country's potential output, a useful concept for examining the stability and soundness of Bhutan's structural transition and rapid economic development over the past three decades. We adopt a structural approach to measuring potential output, the method commonly used by the Organisation for Economic Co-operation and Development (Giorno et al. 1995), International Monetary Fund (De Masi 1997), and United States Congressional Budget Office (2001).[4] Its rationale is to obtain potential output from the steady state levels of its structural determinants such as productivity and factor inputs.

The Model

Our approach broadly follows that of Rungcharoenkitkul (2012) in employing a model of potential output that combines both the supply-side production function approach with demand-side equations. The supply-side specification has the advantage of enabling us to capture the dynamics of the different growth drivers of Bhutan's potential output, while the demand-side equations enable us to trace the dynamics of near-term fluctuations around the country's potential output (Figure 4.12). The original model is modified to capture the specific nature of the Bhutanese economy, namely its large reliance on international grants and loans.

Supply-side information is captured by modelling Bhutan's potential GDP, $\overline{Y}_t$, as a Cobb–Douglas production function,

$$\overline{Y}_t = A_t K_t^{\alpha} L_t^{1-\alpha} \qquad (1)$$

where K_t is Bhutan's stock of physical capital, L_t is the country's labour force, and A_t is its productivity level at year t.

[4] It is also the recommended approach by the European Union Economic Policy Committee. See Economic Policy Committee (2001).

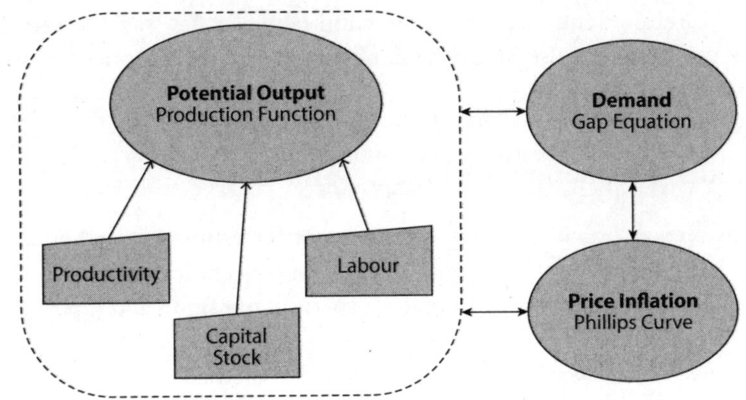

FIGURE 4.12 Estimating Potential Output from a Small Macro Model
Source: Rungcharoenkitkul (2012).

The dynamics of the stock $\overline{Y}_t = A_t K_t^{\alpha} L_t^{1-\alpha}$ of physical capital are described by the capital accumulation equation,

$$K_t = (1-\delta)K_{t-1} + i_t Y_t \tag{2}$$

where δ is the depreciation rate, i_t is the investment-to-GDP ratio (identical to the savings rate plus foreign loans and grants for investment), and Y_t is GDP.

The capital stock is estimated using an augmented Perpetual Inventory Method. In order to apply this method to calculate the current capital stock, there is a need for (i) a time series of investment data, (ii) information on the initial capital stock at the time when the investment time series starts, and (iii) information on the rate of depreciation of the existing capital stock (Berlemann and Wesselhöft 2014). In this chapter, the capital stock is unobserved and is extracted through a filtering mechanism discussed in the succeeding section.

Investment can be financed by either domestic savings or foreign financing. Thus,

$$i_t = s_t + f_t \tag{3}$$

where S_t is the domestic savings-to-GDP ratio, and f_t is the ratio of foreign loans and grants to GDP. S_t and f_t are assumed to be first-order autoregressive processes as follows:

$$\hat{s}_t = \rho_s \hat{s}_{t-1} + \varepsilon_t^s \tag{4}$$

$$\hat{f}_t = \rho_f \hat{f}_{t-1} + \varepsilon_t^f \tag{5}$$

where a hat over the variable indicates the variable's deviation from its steady state, and ε_t^s and ε_t^f are white noise disturbance terms. The dynamic behaviour of the labour force is characterized by

$$\log L_t = l + \log L_{t-1} + \varepsilon_t^L \tag{6}$$

where l is the expected value of the rate of change in the labour supply, and ε_t^L is a white noise process. The productivity variable is a composite of three subcomponents,

$$A_t = AG_t^{bG} AM_t^{bM} AO_t^{bO} \tag{7}$$

where AG_t, AM_t, and AO_t denote the productivity of the agriculture, manufacturing, and other sectors, respectively. We use the dominant hydropower sector as a proxy for the manufacturing sector. These sectoral productivities are assumed to evolve according to the following dynamic equations:

$$\log AG_t = c_G + \log AG_{t-1} + \varepsilon_t^{AG} \tag{8}$$

$$\log AM_t = c_M + \log AM_{t-1} + \varepsilon_t^{AM} \tag{9}$$

$$\log AO_t = c_O + \log AO_{t-1} + \varepsilon_t^{AO} \tag{10}$$

The demand-side information is summarized by two equations. The first equation is the output gap equation, which summarizes how far the current period's actual GDP has deviated from the potential output of the country:

$$gap_t \equiv \log(Y_t / \bar{Y}_t) \tag{11}$$

It is assumed that the output gap is a stationary first-order autoregressive process where both the magnitude of the lagged output gap and the relative deviation of inflation from its target—or equivalently, steady-state value—are used to determine the divergence of the economy from its potential output capacity. The following equation defines this relationship and forms the first of the two equations used to model the demand side of the economy:

$$gap_t = \beta \, gap_{t-1} - \beta_a(\pi_{t-1} - \bar{\pi}) + \varepsilon_t^Y \quad (12)$$

where π_{t-1} is lagged domestic inflation, $\bar{\pi}$ is target inflation, and ε_t^Y is the white noise demand shock. Note the negative effect of the previous period's inflation deviations from target on demand. This is included to capture cost-push effects.[5]

Estimation Technique

Bayesian time series methods have been employed to estimate the system of equations mentioned. The estimation strategy consists of log-linearizing the given equations around the balanced growth path, solving the system by first-order linear approximations; casting them into a state space structure, and given some observed variables employing the Kalman filter to estimate the unobserved state variables and the parameters.

[5] Essentially, the second demand-side equation captures the inflation dynamics via a modified Phillips curve, thus,

$$\pi_t = \gamma \pi_{t-1} + (1-\gamma)[\theta(\text{gap}_t + \bar{\pi}) + (1-\theta)\pi_t^*] + \varepsilon_t^\pi$$

where ε_t^π represents the white noise cost-push shock. This equation specifies that the current rate of inflation is a weighted average of the last year's inflation, and the new developments in the current year relating to Bhutan's output gap and India's inflation, π_t^*. The parameter γ measures the amount of inertia in Bhutan's inflation dynamics, while $(1-\gamma)$ indicates how responsive Bhutan's inflation is to the current year's output gap and India's inflation rates. More specifically, $(1-\gamma)\theta$ captures how sensitive Bhutan's inflation rate is to its own demand pull shocks, while $(1-\gamma)(1-\theta)$ captures how sensitive Bhutan's inflation rate is to the inflation that passes through from India. (Domestic prices in Bhutan closely track those in India, its major trading partner, as the ngultrum is pegged one-to-one with the Indian rupee.) Oil, fuel, and food products, particularly rice and other cereals, are among the top commodities imported from India. The pass through of India's price developments to Bhutan's inflation is high, with about 70 per cent of price shocks passed through within one quarter and full price shocks passed through within four quarters. Thus, a positive shock to India's price causes Bhutan's consumer price to increase and the effect remains statistically significant two periods (or quarters) after the shock.

Essentially, the Kalman filter is used on a system of relevant state equations to produce an estimated series that is optimal given the underlying system and observed information. In other words, the variables of interest generated are consistent with the steady state or full-capacity interpretation of output, which is unobserved but representative of the economy operating in system equilibrium.

In almost all model runs, only loose priors about the parameter values are imposed to allow the data ample room to speak, by setting large prior standard deviations and wide minimum–maximum bounds. The Metropolis–Hastings algorithm is then employed to generate an estimate for the entire distribution of the parameters. Table 4.2 describes prior distributions used in the estimation, as well as the posterior estimates generated by the Bayesian estimation of the model.

Data

The observed variables include real GDP (Y_t), labour force (L_t), investment-to-GDP ratio (i_t), ratio of foreign loans and grants to GDP (f_t), agricultural productivity (AG_t), manufacturing productivity (AM_t), output gap (gap_t), Bhutan's inflation rate (π_t), and India's inflation rate π^*_t). All are annual observations. The full estimation period is 1980–2012. Table 4.3 shows the data definitions and sources for the observed variables.

Results and Growth Simulations

This section undertakes an analysis of potential output growth for Bhutan. It begins by historically outlining the model's estimates of potential growth and then generates a baseline forecast of potential GDP growth from 2013 to 2030. A breakdown of the contributing sectors and factors to growth over the full period is then presented. The baseline forecast and contributions are subsequently used as a benchmark to compare the impacts of various possible policy and shock scenarios on the long-term forecast potential growth path. The subsection 'Scenario 2: Investing in Physical and Human Capital' looks specifically at a positive shock to investment and total productivity that increases human capital and, thus, labour productivity. The subsection 'Scenario 3: Current Government Projections of Investment in Hydropower' looks at the Royal Government of Bhutan's existing hydropower

Table 4.2 Prior Distributions and Posterior Estimates of Parameters

	PRIOR					POSTERIOR*
Model parameters						
	Mode	Lower Bound	Upper Bound	Distribution	Remarks	
α	0.44	0.01	0.9999	logdist.normal(0.44,0.1)	Average share of gross fixed capital formation to gross domestic product	0.37740
δ	0.05	0.01	0.9999	logdist.normal(0.1,0.001)	The depreciation rate allowed for tax purposes in Bhutan for fixed assets such as plant and machinery (Based on the Rules on the Income Tax Act of the Kingdom of Bhutan 2001) World Bank (2007). Economic Growth in South Asia A Growth Accounting Perspective. Chapter 2. South Asia: Growth and Regional Integration.	
I	0.03	0.01	0.999	logdist.normal(0.03,0.1)	Compounded annual growth rate of labour	0.03280
b_o	0.003	0.00001	0.9999	logdist.normal(0.003,0.15)		0.08900
b_g	0.03	0.00001	0.9999	logdist.normal(0.03,0.15)	Average growth rate of labour productivity in agriculture	0.00001
b_m	0.044	0.00001	0.9999	logdist.normal(0.044,0.15)	Average growth rate of labour productivity in manufacturing	0.00180

c_g	0.01	0.01	0.9999	logdist.normal(0.01,0.15)		0.01940
c_m	0.23	0.01	0.9999	logdist.normal(0.23,0.15)	Compounded annual growth rate of cereal yield	0.19180
c_o	0.03	0.01	0.9999	logdist.normal(0.03,0.15)		0.19100
β	0.5	0.01	0.9999	logdist.beta(0.5,0.15)	Beta coefficient of the regression *gap t* = *Betagap t*-1 + *Res*	0.59640
β_a	0.5	0.01	0.9999	logdist.beta(0.5,0.15)		0.34220
γ	0.9	0.01	0.9999	logdist.beta(0.9,0.15)	Gamma coefficient of the regression *pie t* = *gammapie t*-1 + *gap* + Res	0.48360
θ	0.5	0.01	0.9999	logdist.beta(0.5,0.15)		0.38130
π^{-}	0.08	0.01	0.999	logdist.normal(0.08,0.1)	Average inflation rate	0.07370
ρ_s	0.9	0.01	0.999	logdist.beta(0.9,0.15)		0.75130
ρ_f	0.9	0.01	0.999	logdist.beta(0.9,0.15)		0.99990
Standard deviations of transition shocks**						
	Mode	Lower Bound	Upper Bound	Distribution	Remarks	
ε^L	0.01	-0.1	5	logdist.invgamma(0.01,2)		0.03170
ε^{AG}	0.01	-0.1	5	logdist.invgamma(0.01,2)		0.13940
ε^{AM}	0.01	-0.1	5	logdist.invgamma(0.01,2)		0.67090
ε^{AO}	0.01	-0.1	5	logdist.invgamma(0.01,2)		0.14770
ε^{Y}	0.01	-0.1	5	logdist.invgamma(0.01,2)		0.04230
ε^{π}	0.01	-0.1	5	logdist.invgamma(0.01,2)		0.03420

(Cont'd)

TABLE 4.2 (*Cont'd*)

	PRIOR					POSTERIOR*
Model parameters						
	Mode	Lower Bound	Upper Bound	Distribution	Remarks	
$\varepsilon^{\pi\star}$	0.001	-0.1	5	logdist.invgamma(0.01,2)		0.03470
ε^{S}	0.001	-0.1	5	logdist.invgamma(0.01,2)		0.06380
ε^{F}	0.001	-0.1	5	logdist.invgamma(0.01,2)		0.06810

Notes: AG = agriculture productivity; AM = manufacturing productivity; AO = other sector productivity; GDP = gross domestic product invgamma = inverse gamma; logdist = logistic distribution.

* Parameters in model object estimated using posterior maximization.

** Standard deviations adjusted for the common variance factor.

Source: Authors' calculations based on IRIS. The IRIS Toolbox Project, available at http: / / www.iris-toolbox.com (last accessed on April 2013).

TABLE 4.3 Data for Observed Variables and Sources

Variables	Data Description	Period Covered	Sources
Y_t	Real GDP (LCU 2000=100)	1980–2012	WDI
gap_t	HP -filtered cycles, deviation of real GDP to HP-filtered trend	1980–2012	Authors' Calculations
L_t	Total labour force	1990–2010	WDI
i_t	Ratio of gross fixed capital formation to GDP	1980–2012	WDI
f_t	Ratio of foreign loans and grants to GDP	2001–12	Ministry of Finance
AG_t	Cereal yield (kg per hectare)	1980–2011	WDI
AM_t	Electricity production (kWh)	1980–2012	ADBKI
π_t	Inflation, consumer prices (annual %)	1980–2012	WDI, National Statistics Bureau
π_t^*	India wholesale price inflation, WPI (annual %)	1980–2012	WDI

Notes: ADBKI = Asian Development Bank Key Indicators; GDP = gross domestic product; HP = Hodrick–Prescott; kg = kilogram; kWh = kilowatt hour; WDI = World Development Indicators; WPI = wholesale price index.
Sources: ADB (2013a), World Bank (2013).

development agenda as outlined in official projections and the potential output growth that these plans would produce (all else being held constant). The subsection 'Scenario 4: Impact of Increased Government Spending on Education' examines increased government spending on education and its impact on boosting human capital and, ultimately, productivity. Finally, a scenario analysing an improvement in economic diversification is presented. This case specifically looks at an expansion of the tourism-heavy service sector, the sector best positioned to support a relative expansion in the near to mid-term future. Each scenario is compared with the baseline scenario and, where relevant, the other examined scenarios to analyse the relative advantages and opportunity costs of pursuing one particular scenario over another.[6]

[6] See the Appendix for a more detailed explanation of the assumptions and transmission channels through which the interventions have impacted potential and actual GDP growth scenarios.

Scenario 1: Baseline Results

The model is employed to estimate historical potential GDP growth up to 2012, as well as to forecast potential and actual real GDP growth from 2013 to 2030. By having an estimate of Bhutan's potential output, the stability and sustainability of the country's economic growth path can be evaluated in reference to this potential measure. Given the model's construction, the estimation is also able to highlight sectoral growth patterns and the structural features of the economy that have contributed to economic imbalances, which were previously discussed in descriptive terms in the section 'Bhutan's Structural Transformation'.

Figure 4.13 plots the model's estimates of potential GDP against actual GDP growth over the period 1980–2012 and the forecast values of the same over the period 2013–30. The recursive nature of the model generates a process whereby the value of actual and potential output both converge to a steady state of around 6.6 per cent growth per annum. However, these projections are based on steady behaviour with no policy changes or economic shocks taking place. These forecasts are useful as a benchmark and representative of a convergence to a steady state based on the underlying current fundamentals of the economy. However, the actual behaviour of the economy has seen marked variability of both historical real GDP and estimated historical potential GDP. This strong variability has been due to the dominating presence of hydropower in the economy and the lumpy nature of hydropower investment. For example, the large spikes in both the actual and potential output in the mid-1980s were due to the Chhukha Plant, while the substantial increases in the actual and potential output around 2007 were largely due to the Tala Plant. In trend terms, potential output growth has gradually declined from its peak of 8.4 per cent in 2007, with the baseline potential output forecast predicting a declining potential output trend after 2012.

Factor and Sector Contributions to Potential Output and Productivity Growth

Figure 4.14 presents the factor contributions to growth and drivers of Bhutan's economy. On average during the sample period, capital accumulation contributed about 4.2 per cent to potential growth, 1.8 per cent to employment growth, and 1.6 per cent to total factor productivity growth.

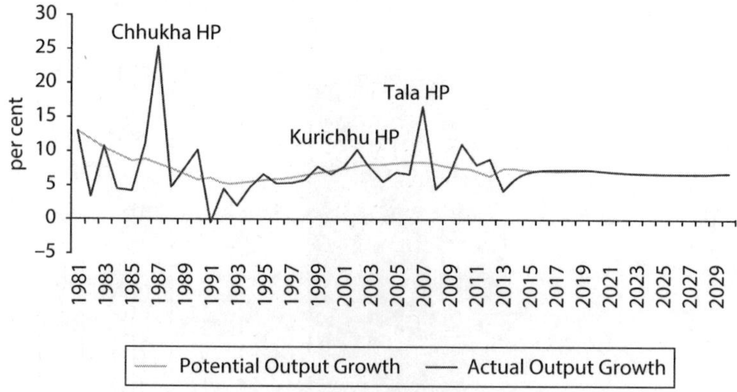

FIGURE 4.13 Baseline Forecasts—Output Growth
Note: HP = hydropower.
Source: Authors' Calculations.

The forecast of potential output is moderate as proportional capital accumulation—mainly investment in hydropower—is expected to slow down.

As Figure 4.14 shows, Bhutan's potential growth has not been driven much by productivity growth. Figure 4.15 shows that in spite of the manufacturing sector's large capital investment and dominant role in the economy its productivity growth has not contributed much to Bhutan's overall productivity growth. Instead, it has been the steadily growing service sector that has led productivity gains in the Bhutanese economy. Of concern is the agriculture sector—the main sector of employment—which remains a drag on total productivity growth.

Scenario 2: Investing in Physical and Human Capital

With the baseline model as a benchmark, it is interesting to investigate the relative impacts of several scenarios on potential output, given the underlying structural relationship of the economy as determined by the model.

Doubling of the Investment Rate

As mentioned in the section 'Bhutan's Structural Transformation', Bhutan's economic growth spikes are nearly entirely attributable to large hydropower investments. However, while physical capital stock has seen dramatic increases over the last decades, the productivity improvements as a result of this investment have been small.

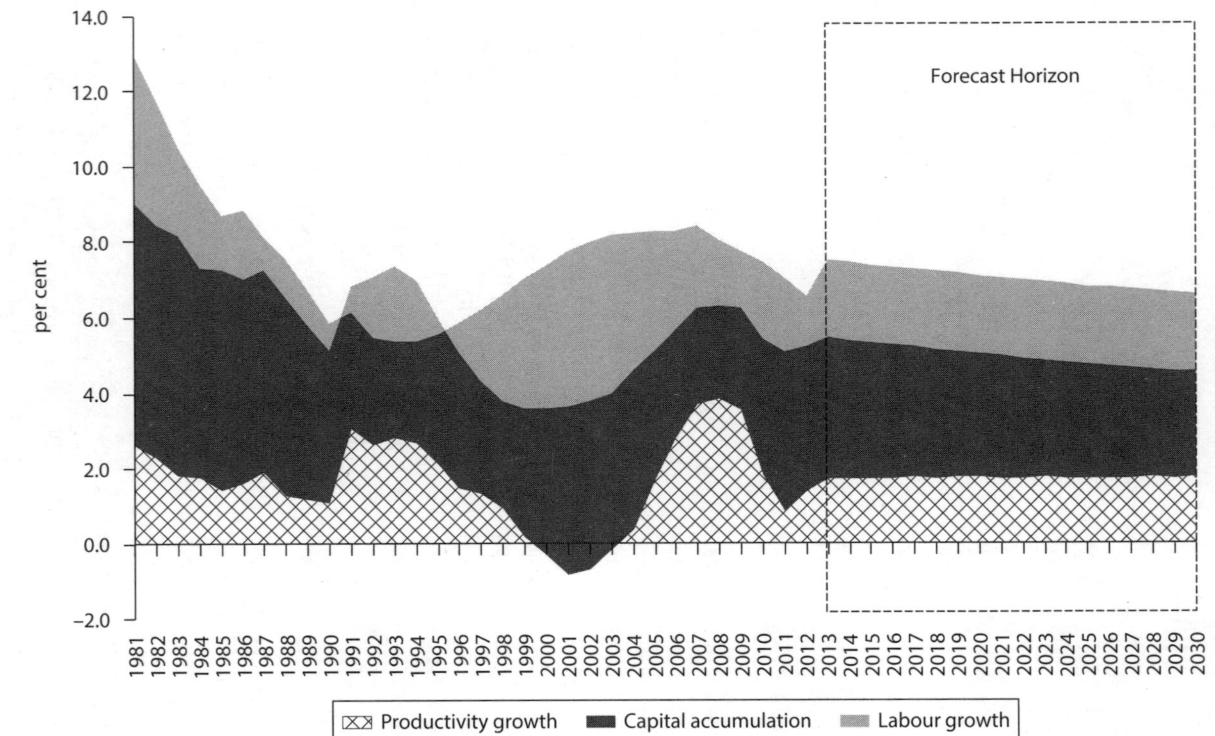

FIGURE 4.14 Contributions to Potential Growth

Source: Authors' Calculations.

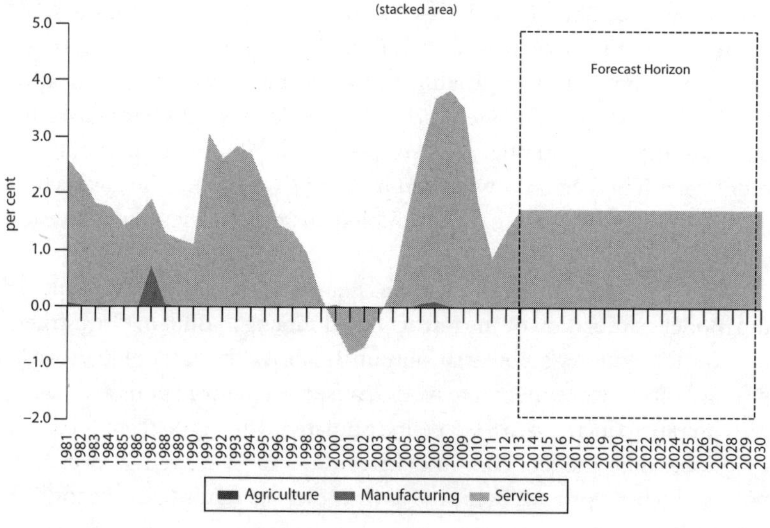

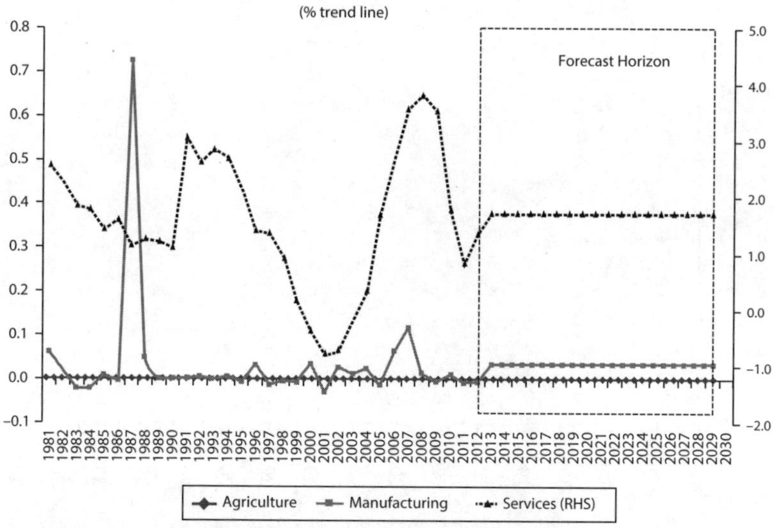

FIGURES 4.15 Contributions to Productivity Growth

Note: rhs = right-hand side.

Source: Authors' Calculations.

In other words, Bhutan has focused strongly on hydropower investment but it now needs to focus on distributing the income generated through such investment into improving human capital, including education and health services. The scenario examined in this subsection asks the question of how potential GDP responds to a doubling of the investment rate. This scenario will then be used to compare the case where productivity growth rates are doubled instead of doubling physical capital accumulation rates.

With this backdrop as motivation, Figure 4.16 presents the results of the model's simulation of the impact of a doubling in Bhutan's investment rate on the country's potential output. It shows that a doubling of the physical capital investment rate would cause the country's potential output growth rate to increase to 8 per cent, compared with 7.4 per cent predicted by the baseline model. The simulated results show a gradual decline in potential output growth over time as the potential output returns towards a steady-state level of potential growth of approximately 6.8 per cent in 2030, compared with 6.6 per cent in the corresponding baseline case. The cumulative nature of the impact of growth rates on output levels means that an increase in investment rates today would have a significant and persisent effect on potential output relative to the baseline scenario.

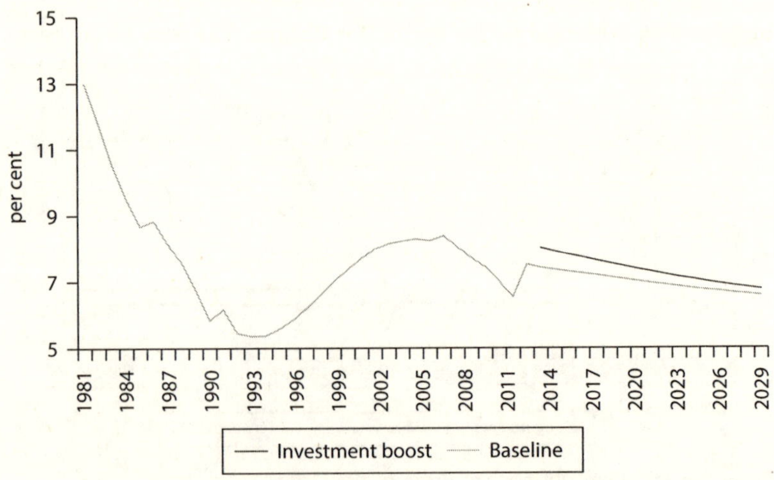

FIGURE 4.16 Baseline versus Investment Boost—Potential Output Growth
Source: Authors' Calculations.

Doubling Productivity Growth

While hydropower investment has been the lifeline of Bhutan's phenomenal growth over the past three decades, the opportunity costs of continuing with this strategy are worth investigating. The next set of simulations shows that potential output can be raised if Bhutan undertakes reforms and policy measures to bridge the gap between productivity and factor accumulation. While doubling productivity growth sounds like a daunting challenge, and as subsection 'Factor and Sector Contributions to Potential Output and Productivity Growth' showed, productivity growth is highly concentrated in the service sector and there is large scope for productivity gains throughout the broader economy. The model results show that in a scenario where Bhutan doubles productivity growth, potential output growth would initially spike to 10.1 per cent, which is a 3 percentage points gain over the baseline scenario. Moreover, the gains from such a scenario are quite persistent, as potential output growth exceeds the baseline scenario by about 1 percentage point even after a decade (Figure 4.17), with steady-state potential growth settling at about 7.4 per cent in 2030. The improvement in the capacity for economic development in Bhutan from such a boost is therefore very significant over time.

Comparing the two scenarios—a doubling of physical capital investment and a doubling of productivity growth—yields some important insights into preferred policy option for Bhutan. For ease of comparison, the potential output growth rates for both scenarios are plotted

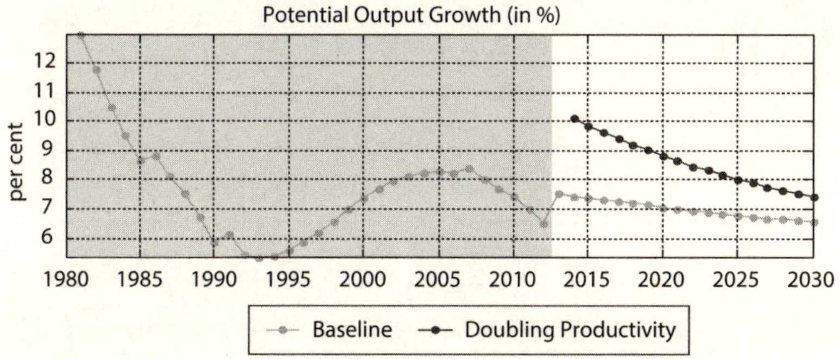

FIGURE 4.17 Baseline versus Doubling Productivity—Potential Output Growth

Source: Authors' Calculations.

against the baseline scenario on the same axes in Figure 4.18. It is seen that enhancing productivity growth not only dramatically improves the baseline scenario, but it is also more beneficial than just the physical capital accumulation-boosting scenario. Indeed, the output differential between the productivity and investment boosting scenarios at 2030 is projected to be 22 per cent; the productivity-enhancing path yields potential output levels that are 22 per cent higher than that of the investment boosting path. This result occurs because of the cumulative nature of the impact of growth rates on the level of economic output over time.

According to these results, Bhutanese policymakers should consider augmenting their current strategy of physical capital stock accumulation—mainly in the hydropower sector—with specific productivity-enhancing measures. Investment in capital that embodies higher technology is one way, with this strategy having the largest impact if it is targeting those sectors where productivity is currently low and that employ the largest amount of people. In Bhutan's case, this sector would be agriculture. The other way to boost productivity over the long term is to heavily invest in human capital. Thus, education and health expenditure should also be prioritized in policies aimed at improving economic output and living standards in the future.

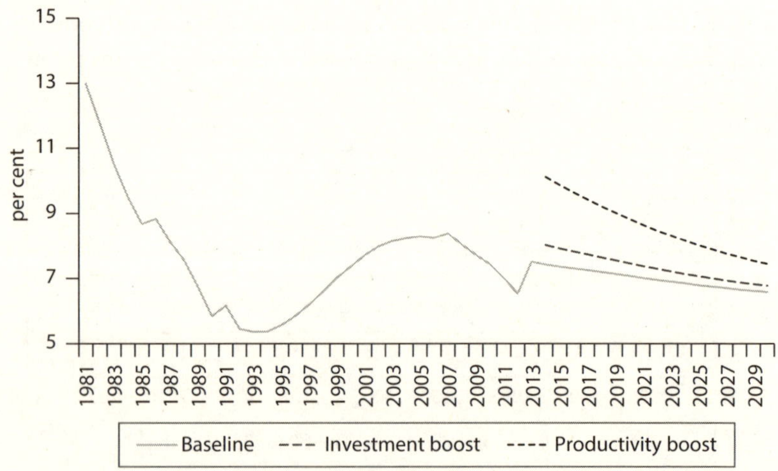

FIGURE 4.18 Potential Output Growth—Investment versus Productivity Boost

Source: Authors' Calculations.

Scenario 3: Current Government Projections of Investment in Hydropower

The government's projections of growth are based largely around the current hydropower investment projections, with aggregate growth expected to be very volatile. Specifically, growth rates are projected to fluctuate between 3.4 per cent and 16.9 per cent in 2013–30. While this translates into high potential output growth—reaching an average growth rate of 7.5 per cent during the forecast period—it also projects actual output that is quite volatile (Figure 4.19). Such volatile growth rates can have severe negative impacts, particularly on the economy's most vulnerable, both directly and through real and financial sector interaction effects that amplify economic fluctuations. (See Loayza et al. 2007 for an overview of the related literature.)

To the extent that the growth path is found to be largely driven by hydropower investment, it is constructive to look at the impact that projected investment in the hydropower sector will have on Bhutan's economy. Thus, this section examines the impact of the government's hydropower development agenda on potential output growth. Completed and projected (pipeline) hydropower plant construction activities are summarized in Table 4.4. Notably, the Royal Government of

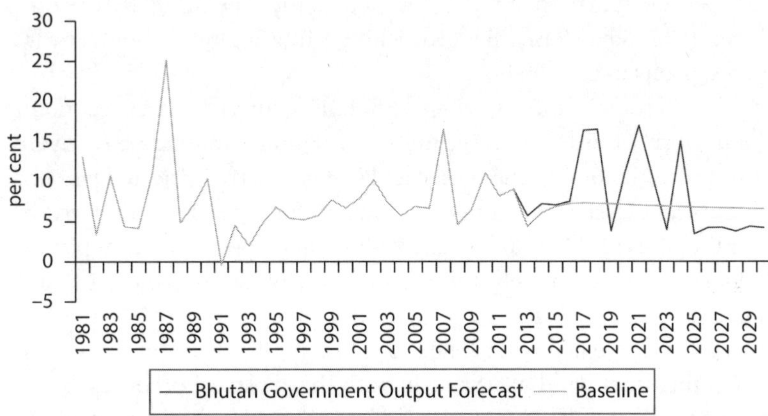

FIGURE 4.19 Baseline versus Government Output Forecast—Actual Output Growth

Source: Authors' Calculations.

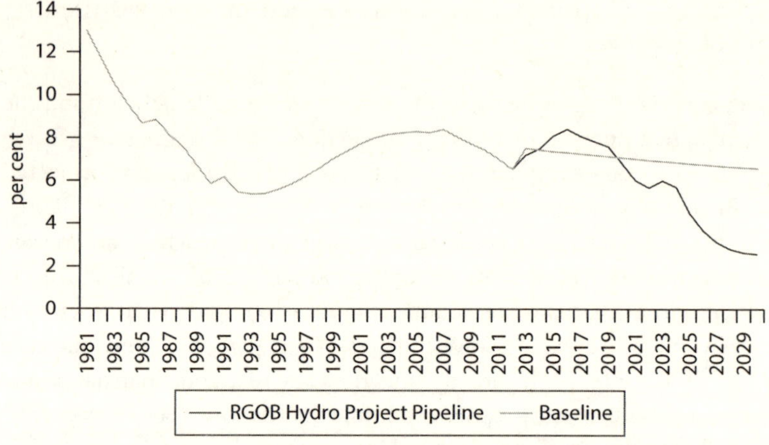

FIGURE 4.20 Baseline versus Pipelined Hydropower Construction—Potential Output Growth

Note: RGOB = Royal Government of Bhutan.

Source: Authors' calculations based on projections from the Government of Bhutan's Macroeconomic Framework Coordination Technical Committee.

Bhutan projects electricity revenue from the hydropower plants to reach about Nu1,718 billion over the period 2013–30. This projection includes electricity from the four currently operating hydropower plants (Chhukha, Basochhu, Kurichhu, and Tala) and the 12 hydropower plants in the pipeline.

The results from feeding Bhutan's current Macroeconomic Framework Coordination Technical Committee projections of hydropower investment into the model and simulating the projected potential output can be seen in Figure 4.20. Impacts for potential output growth over the period 2013–30 are mixed. If all plants come on stream as planned (taking into account only the construction of these plants), Bhutan's potential output is expected to peak at 8.4 per cent in 2016 due to the investment surge before declining to below the baseline forecast in 2020.

On the other hand, factoring in both the construction of the hydropower projects and the associated electricity sales forecasts, potential output growth could sustain an upward momentum of around 7–8 per cent; however, this eventually falls below baseline potential output growth starting in 2026 (Figure 4.21).

TABLE 4.4 Summary of Completed and Projected Hydropower Plants and Projects

	Hydropower Project	Capacity (MW)	Construction Schedule	Development Model	Projected Electricity Production, 2013–30 (in billion units)	Projected Electricity Revenue, 2013–30 (in Nu billion)	Gross value added of hydropower construction, 2013–30 (in Nu billion current prices)
1	Chhukha	336	1974–1978	IG	38.14	80.36	
2	Basochhu	64	1997–2004	IG	5.80	9.41	
3	Kurichhu	60	1995–2001	IG	6.64	10.92	
4	Tala	1020	1997–2006	IG	80.71	151.47	
5	Dagachhu	126	2009–14	PPP (DGPC, NPPF, and TPCL)	8.61	24.40	0.35
6	Punatsangchhu-I	1200	2008–16	IG	70.37	222.14	6.47
7	Punatsangchhu-II	1020	2010–17	IG	54.95	163.99	7.34
8	Mangdechhu	720	2010–17	IG	37.06	94.29	4.36
9	Sankosh Storage	2585	2013–19	IG	61.09	221.08	17.21
10	Kuri-Gongri	3400	2014–22	IG	69.19	280.47	55.14
11	Amochhu Storage	540	2013–19	IG	18.04	71.28	10.54
12	Wangchhu	570	2013–19	JV with Indian PSU	27.32	105.33	n.a.
13	Bunakha Storage	180	2013–19	JV with Indian PSU	18.05	55.90	1.87

(*Cont'd*)

TABLE 4.4 (*Cont'd*)

	Hydropower Project	Capacity (MW)	Construction Schedule	Development Model	Projected Electricity Production, 2013–30 (in billion units)	Projected Electricity Revenue, 2013–30 (in Nu billion)	Gross value added of hydropower construction, 2013–30 (in Nu billion current prices)
14	Kholongchu	600	2013–19	JV with Indian PSU	25.49	59.97	2.2
15	Chamkharchhu-I	770	2013–20	JV with Indian PSU	28.78	127.41	7.26
16	Nikachhu	118	2014–17	DGPC PPP	11.55	39.62	n.a.

Notes: DGPC = Druk Green Power Corporation Limited; IG = intergovernmental development model; JV = joint venture development model; n.a. = not available; MW = megawatt; NPPF = National Pension and Provident Fund; PPP = public–private partnership; PSU = public sector undertaking; TPCL = Tata Power Company Limited.

Sources: Ministry of Finance (2012); RMA (2013).

Scenario 4: Impact of Increased Government Spending on Education[7]

The previous simulations have provided evidence to suggest that productivity-enhancing investment, such as investment in human capital, will provide a large boost to potential output. Improvements in human capital stock not only raise productivity directly but also improve the labour force's skills and improve the productivity of capital in the economy. Both of these advances can have large impacts on the capacity of an economy to produce, innovate, and diversify, as well as to reap benefits from knowledge transfer opportunities that may arrive due to incoming foreign direct investment and trade. A healthy and well-trained labour force is also likely to be more adaptable and flexible to market conditions and better placed to deal with the large macroeconomic fluctuations that Bhutan is prone to experiencing.

Investment in human capital leads to improved education and health services. Although the Royal Government of Bhutan's social expenditure has been increasing over time in absolute terms, it has not kept pace with the economy's expansion. As a percentage of GDP, it has declined in recent years. In particular, the government's current and capital spending on education, as a proportion of GDP, has been showing a declining trend, which has implications on productivity and overall development (Figure 4.22).

[7] A 2013 ADB publication, *Bhutan: Critical Development Constraints*, identified several critical growth constraints facing Bhutan. The publication emphasized that in order to achieve strong, balanced, resilient, and inclusive growth, the relaxation of several critical constraints should be the priority focus of policy interventions. This requires addressing: (i) inadequate and poor quality infrastructure, particularly in transport and connectivity and especially in rural areas; (ii) narrow fiscal space, particularly in the medium- to long-term; (iii) lack of access to finance by micro, small, and medium-sized enterprises; (iv) presence of market failures that limit product diversification and competition; and (v) limited and unequal access to quality education—particularly, secondary, tertiary, and vocational education—and labour market mismatches. Scenarios 5 and 6—increased government spending on education and the promotion of economic diversification in support of tourism sector growth (the second largest and second fastest growing industry in the Bhutanese economy after electricity production), respectively—reflect the broad thrust of the fourth and fifth critical growth constraints identified in the ADB's diagnostic study. While these are only two of the five identified critical constraints, these are the only two scenarios that we can analyse with our model given the data limitations.

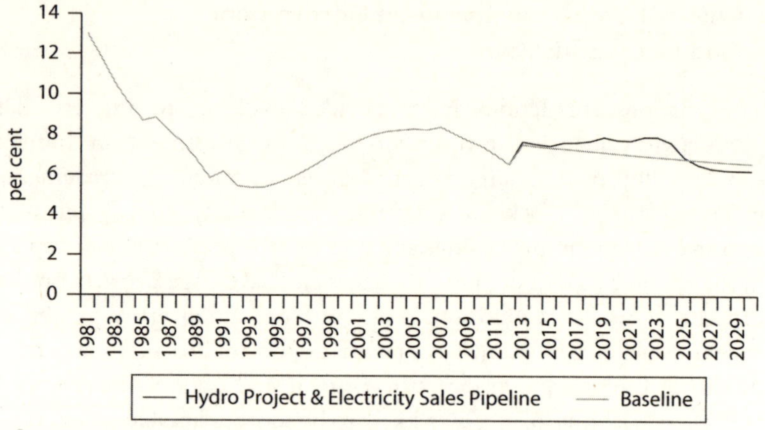

FIGURE 4.21 Baseline versus Pipelined Hydropower Construction and Projected Electricity Sales—Potential Output Growth
Source: Authors' calculations based on projections from the Government of Bhutan's Macroeconomic Framework Coordination Technical Committee.

To understand the impact of declining educational investment in Bhutan, the current projections for future expenditure on education from the government, which show a declining trend, can be fed into the model and the potential output from the simulation can be plotted against the baseline scenario. Our simulations show that relative to the baseline scenario, where there is a maintenance of the past trend of spending on education, dropping educational spending to the government's projected levels will generally reduce potential output. Indeed, the current projection of spending on education is not enough to maintain output growth, as potential output growth dips to 5 per cent in 2014 and declines further in 2017 as potential output remains below the baseline benchmark for most of the remainder of the 2013–30 period (Figure 4.23).[8]

[8] The nature of education is that there is often a lag between expenditure on education and the impacts on output growth, particularly if the expenditure is targeted at improvements across the full education-level spectrum. However, given the small number of observations through which the projections are generated, there is little room to allow for large lag effects in the model. Accordingly, the model's simulations can be read either as increased expenditure on higher level education or a compression of the benefits from a boost to education expenditure that takes place over all educational levels.

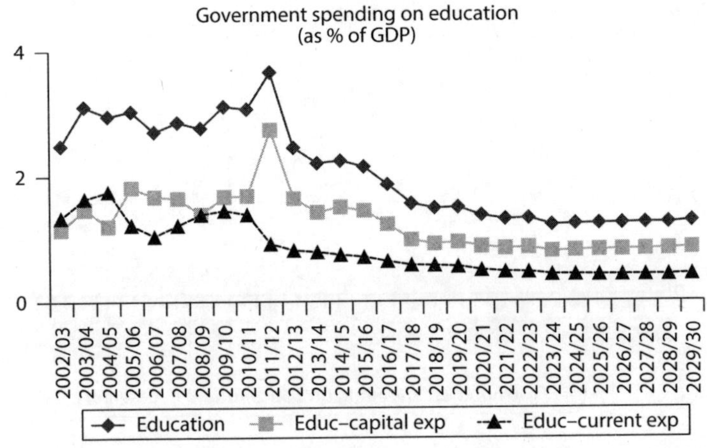

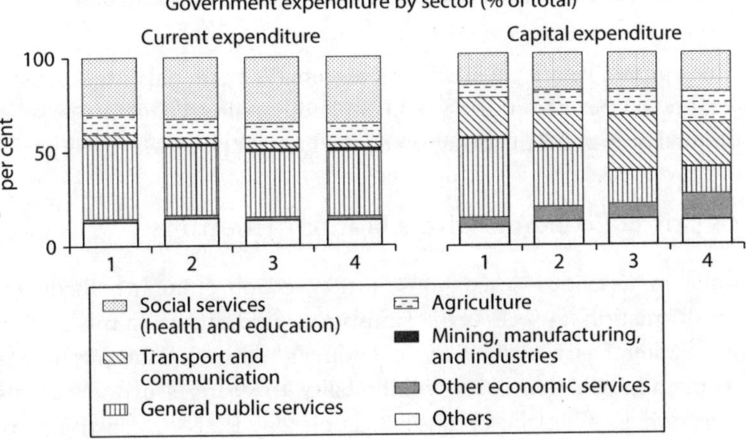

FIGURE 4.22 Government Expenditure
Note: GDP = gross domestic product.
Source: Authors' estimates based on data from Ministry of Finance (2012).

As policymakers might be interested in increasing expenditure on education, we tested a scenario in which government expenditure on education is raised by 10 per cent (Figure 4.24). Feeding this into the model shows that, relative to the case of reduced education expenditure, increased investment in human capital will result in a much more

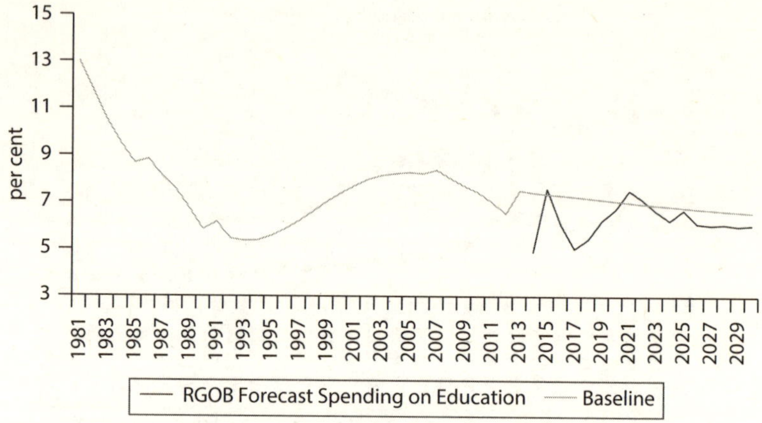

FIGURE 4.23 Baseline versus Forecasted Government Spending on Education—Potential Output Growth

Source: Authors' estimates based on data from Ministry of Finance (2012).

stable output growth path. Under this scenario, potential output growth averages 7.5 per cent during 2013–30 and remains well above baseline potential output for the duration of the forecast period.[9]

Scenario 5: Economic Diversification—Tourism

From the previous discussion in the section 'Bhutan's Structural Transformation' as well as the simulations undertaken in this section, this chapter has identified the economy's narrow economic base as a constraint and source of vulnerability to changes in the external environment. The lack of diversification also leads to constraints on the economy to generate employment for its rapidly expanding and increasingly educated labour force.

[9] Another feature of the model is that it cannot capture the interaction effects of expenditure on education with that of expenditure on higher technology capital. For example, the effect of higher education levels in combination with higher levels of capital investment—particularly in the capital stock embodying technological advances or investment in an undercapitalized sector such as agriculture—could result in a dramatic increase in output. That is, the two investments complement each other and just promoting one without the other does not yield nearly as much of an output boost.

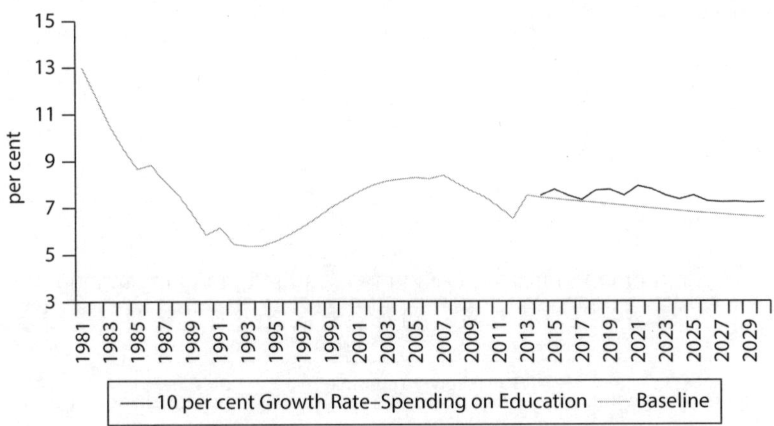

FIGURE 4.24 Baseline versus 10 per cent Growth Rate in Government Education Spending—Potential Output Growth
Source: Authors' estimates based on data from Ministry of Finance (2012).

While the hydropower sector will continue to be the bedrock of the country's economy, the government has recognized the diversification challenge and in the Eleventh Five Year Plan has identified policies to promote self-reliance and accelerate growth. It has tentatively identified a number of sectors for promotion to diversify its production mix, including tourism, agro-processing, non-hydropower-related construction, manufacturing, mining, and small and cottage industries (for example, textiles, arts, and crafts).

Tourism is an industry that has grown strongly in recent decades and is well placed to support expanded growth prospects for Bhutan's economy, especially given the superior productivity growth seen in this sector. Recognizing this, the government has planned to boost spending for the tourism sector. If we feed these projected expenditure increases into the model, the path of potential output growth reveals a modest uptick relative to the baseline scenario. The model projects potential growth will average 7.4 per cent over the next decade with potential growth only falling to or below the baseline projections in the last few years of the 17-year forecast horizon (Figure 4.25).

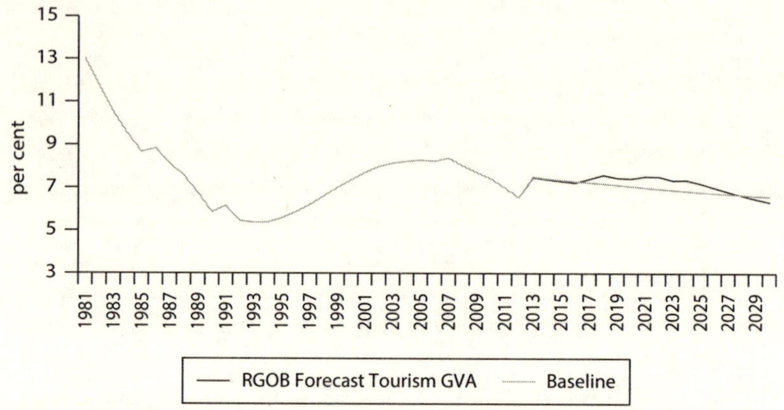

FIGURE 4.25 Baseline versus Forecasted Tourism Gross Value Added—Potential Output Growth

Notes: RGOB = Royal Government of Bhutan; GVA = gross value added.

Source: Authors' estimates based on data from Ministry of Finance (2012).

However, if the government achieves 15 per cent growth in gross value added in the tourism sector, it would generate a higher output growth path—7.8 per cent on average for the period 2013–24—and support the country's diversification efforts (Figure 4.26).

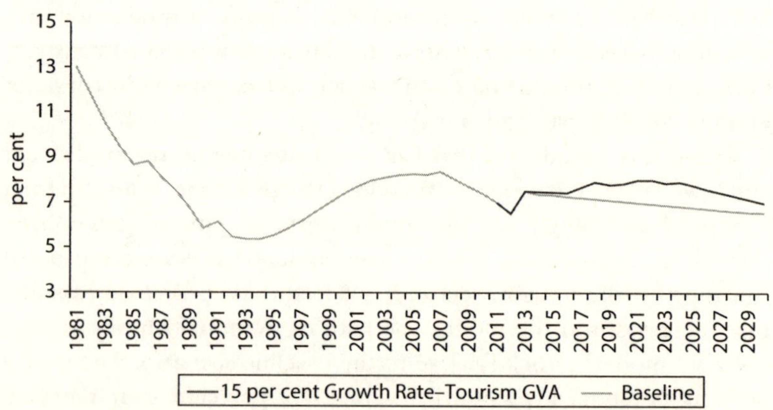

FIGURE 4.26 Baseline versus Diversification via 15 per cent Growth Rate in Tourism Gross Value Added—Potential Output Growth

Note: GVA = gross value added.

Source: Authors' estimates based on data from Ministry of Finance (2012).

***

Bhutan's rapid economic growth over the past three decades has been driven by large investments in the hydropower sector. These investments are lumpy in nature and come with long gestation periods. As a result, the growth pattern has been volatile with output expansion spiking in the years during the construction and installation of a new hydropower plant, and then falling until the next hydropower plant comes on stream. This trend, along with a narrow domestic economic base, makes the economy vulnerable to cyclical swings and external shocks.

Given Bhutan's projections regarding hydropower investment, Bhutan's growth prospects for the next 20 years will likely be underpinned by further development of its ample hydropower resources. Our model simulations show that there will be diminishing marginal returns to capital investment in hydropower unless the revenues generated and some of the new capital investment is directed towards raising future productivity.

The model suggests that this can be achieved by better targeting public expenditure and pursuing economic diversification through the expansion of the tourism sector and identifying new drivers of growth. In particular, the results support increased spending on human capital—education being a key case in point—and putting in place policy measures to enhance productivity in sectors other than hydropower. Spending on higher education today can make a difference even in the near to medium-term, especially if it is vocational in nature and directed towards improving skills that are being used by emerging sectors in the economy.

Clearly, there is a need to improve the quality of the factors of production via investment in education and labour skills, and speed up the diffusion of technology to improve efficiency. As Bhutan's economy climbs up the technology ladder, the shortage of skilled labour will become a more prominent binding growth constraint. Given the lag in human capital investment's impact on the economy, there is a pressing need to speed up investment in human resources now to meet the future needs of the growing economy. At the same time, the government should sustain investment in public infrastructure to lower transaction costs, particularly with regard to transportation. This will also provide a significant boost to productivity, especially for the manufacturing sector.

In terms of implementation priorities, sectors that have greater room to benefit from productivity growth should be identified and promoted upfront. In general, however, Bhutan should aim to move up the value chain of the dominant industry, build upon the comparative advantage of existing industries (through the development of industries such as agribusiness), identify new industries with potential linkages to regional and global value chains, and pursue diversification into other sectors such as tourism. This process of structural change from an agriculture-based society to one that encompasses a broader and more productive production base needs to be a long-term vision for the economy. Putting in place the right policies and priorities in the current period can go a long way to sustaining economic growth and ultimately raising living standards in the small, landlocked Kingdom of Bhutan.

Appendix

Building the Scenarios

Projection Scenario 3

How will the pipelined hydropower constructions and/or projects affect the growth paths of potential and actual output for the period 2013–24?

Hydropower projects are captured in GDP as increases in investments measured by gross fixed capital formation (GFCF).

Model specification for investment:

Investment can be financed either by domestic savings or foreign financing, thus:

$$i_t = s_t + f_t = \tfrac{GFCF}{Y} = \textit{gross savings rate}$$

where *GFCF* refers to gross fixed capital formation and *Y* is actual output (GDP) and *gross savings rate* is the aggregate of s_t domestic savings-to-GDP ratio and f_t is the ratio of foreign loans and grants to GDP.

Therefore, we need to have a projection of $\textit{gross savings rate} = S$, which incorporates the effect of the pipelined hydropower projects.

This study's approach is to compute the share to GFCF of the pipelined hydropower projects (S^{f13-24}_{hconst}) then add this to the projections of the model (the *S* projections from the baseline forecast only captures information in time $t - 1$ and do not capture yet the effect of pipelined hydropower projects):

$$S_{hconst}^{f13-24} = \frac{hconst\ GVA^{ft}}{Y^{ft}} \rightarrow series\ from\ 2013\ to\ 2024$$

$$S^{ft} = S_{hconst}^{ft} + S_{basemodel}^{ft} \rightarrow forecast\ series\ from\ 2013\ to\ 2024$$

Projection Scenario 4

How will the Royal Government of Bhutan's education spending plans affect the growth paths of potential and actual output for the period 2013–24?

The government's education spending plans have significant impact on Bhutan's general level of productivity, A_t. Consequently, productivity gains will result in output growth:

$$A_t = f(RGOB\ educ\ spending_t) \rightarrow GDP_t = f(A_t)$$

Therefore, we need to have a projection of productivity, A_t, which incorporates the information on government's future spending on education. In order to estimate the contribution of education to productivity, A_t, we regress A_t against government spending on education, health, and infrastructure. Then, we make a dynamic forecast of A_t for each education spending series (existing government planned education spending and a 10 per cent hypothetical increase) using the above-established linear relationship.

Projection Scenario 5

How will the projected gross value added in tourism affect the growth paths of potential and actual output for the period 2013–24?

One critical constraint to Bhutan's economic growth is its high dependence on the hydropower sector. The country needs to pursue an economic strategy that will encourage and/or promote a more diversified pool of production sectors. Bhutan's tourism sector is seen as having high potential for contributing to output growth.

This study investigates the impact of the projected tourism value added to future GDP and uses this to simulate the path of potential output:

$$GDP_t = f(Tourism\ GVA_t, Industry\ GVA_t) \rightarrow Potential\ Output$$

To establish this relationship, we regress GDP against three sectoral breakdowns: agriculture, industry, and tourism. Then, we make a dynamic forecast of GDP for each tourism series (existing government projection of tourism gross value added and a 15 per cent hypothetical increase) using the above-established linear relationship.

References

Asian Development Bank (ADB). 2000. *Key Indicators for Asia and the Pacific*. Manila.

———. 2012. *Key Indicators for Asia and the Pacific*. Manila.

———. 2013a. *Key Indicators for Asia and the Pacific*. Manila.

———. 2013b. *Country Diagnostics Studies: Bhutan—Critical Development Constraints*. Manila: ADB/Australian Agency for International Development/Japan International Cooperation Agency.

Benes, J., K. Clinton, R. Garcia-Saltos, M. Johnson, D. Laxton, P. Manchev, and T. Matheson. 2010. 'Estimating Potential Output with a Multivariate Filter', IMF Working Paper. No. 10/285. Washington, DC: International Monetary Fund.

Berlemann, M. and J. Wesselhöft. 2014. 'Estimating Aggregate Capital Stocks Using the Perpetual Inventory Method: New Empirical Evidence for 103 Countries', *Review of Economics*. 65(1): 1–34.

Cerra, V. and S.C. Saxena. 2000. 'Alternative Methods of Estimating Potential Output and the Output Gap: An Application to Sweden', IMF Working Paper No. WP/00/59. Washington, DC: International Monetary Fund.

De Masi, P.R. 1997. 'International Monetary Fund Estimates of Potential Output: Theory and Practice', IMF Working Paper No. WP/97/177. Washington, DC: International Monetary Fund.

Economic Policy Committee. 2001. *Report on Potential Output and the Output Gap*. Brussels.

European Central Bank. 2000. 'Potential Output Growth and Output Gaps: Concepts, Uses, and Estimates', *European Central Bank Monthly Bulletin*, pp. 37–47. Washington, DC: International Monetary Fund.

Giorno C., P. Richardson, D. Roseveare, and P. van den Noord. 1995. 'Estimating Potential Output, Output Gaps, and Structural Budget Balances', OECD Economic Department Working Paper No. 157. Paris: Organisation for Economic Co-operation and Development.

Harberger, A.C. 1978. 'Perspectives on Capital and Technology in Less Developed Countries', in M.J. Artis and A.R. Nobay (eds), *Contemporary Economic Analysis*. London: Croom Helm Ltd.

International Monetary Fund. 2013. *World Economic Outlook Dat*abase. Available at https://www.imf.org/external/pubs/ft/weo/2013/02/weodata/index.aspx (last accessed on April 2013).

IRIS. *The IRIS Toolbox Project*. Available at http://www.iris-toolbox.com (last accessed on April 2013).

Loayza, N.V., R. Rancière, L. Servén, and V. Jaume. 2007. 'Macroeconomic Volatility and Welfare in Developing Countries: An Introduction', *The World Bank Economic Review*, 21(3): 343–57.

National Statistics Bureau. 2004. *National Accounts Statistics 2004*. Thimphu.

———. 2006. *National Accounts Statistics 2000–2006*. Thimphu.

———. 2012. *National Accounts Statistics 2012*. Thimphu.

Rashid, H. 2012. 'Understanding the Causes of the Rupee Shortfall: A Macroeconomic Policy Challenge for Bhutan and the Way Forward'. *United Nations Department of Economic and Social Affairs Report*. New York: United Nations.

Royal Government of Bhutan, Ministry of Finance. 2012. *National Revenue Report 2011–2012*. Thimphu.

———. 2012. *National Revenue Report 2011–2012*. Thimphu.

———. *2013. Annual Report 2012–2013*. Thimphu.

Royal Government of Bhutan, Ministry of Labour and Human Resources. 2006. *Labor Force Survey Report 2006*. Thimphu.

———. 2009. *Labor Force Survey Report 2009*. Thimphu.

———. 2012. *Labor Force Survey Report 2012*. Thimphu.

Royal Monetary Authority of Bhutan (RMA). 2012. *Monetary Policy Statement*. Thimphu.

———. *Annual Report* (various years). Thimphu.

Rungcharoenkitkul, P. 2012. 'Modeling with Limited Data: Estimating Potential Growth in Cambodia', IMF Working Papers No. 12/96. Washington, DC: International Monetary Fund.

United States Congressional Budget Office. 2001. *Congressional Budget Office's Method for Estimating Potential Output: An Update*. Available at http://www.cbo.gov/ftpdocs/30xx/doc3020/PotentialOutput.pdf (last accessed on April 2013).

World Bank. 2013. *World Development Indicators*. Available at http://data.worldbank.org/data-catalog/world-development-indicators/wdi-2013 (last accessed on April 2013).

5

KARMA URA

Bhutan's Rupee Crisis

Macroeconomic Causes and Cures*

This chapter analyses the causes of and cures for the Indian rupee shortage in Bhutan from a macroeconomic point of view. The shortage has persisted since it first erupted in early 2012. In spite of the many quantitative restrictions and controls on access to Indian rupees, the shortage has not fully abated since reaching critical points in 2012 and 2013. Black markets have emerged in towns on both sides of the border with India, where 1 ngultrum, which is officially pegged to the Indian rupee at par, is exchanged for 0.90–0.93 rupee, essentially demonstrating that the ngultrum has depreciated. While there is an ongoing search for more effective fiscal and monetary policies, people have had to reconcile themselves to the rupee shortage as a new feature of the economy.

Neither borrowing large quantities of rupees from India—as has happened in the past—nor an official devaluation of the ngultrum to stem the Indian rupee shortage are attractive options. Hence, Bhutan has to initiate action to avoid these eventualities. A blend of theoretical and empirical understanding of the causes of Indian rupee shortage is key to finding an effective solution. A clear analysis of the problem can lead to understanding the relevant cause-and-effect relationship.

* I would like to acknowledge very helpful comments and guidance I received from Hoe Yun Jeong, senior economist, Asian Development Bank (ADB), in writing this article. Thanks are due also to an anonymous reviewer.

Treating the major causes of the Indian rupee shortage is necessary to end it. With that aim, this chapter looks back at the Indian rupee crisis to draw lessons for the future.

The section 'Salient Features of Bhutan's Economy' of this chapter gives a macroeconomic overview of Bhutan, using the latest data available, to provide a broader understanding of conditions that contributed to the rupee shortage. The Bhutanese economy is small and open, mostly towards India; it is characterized by a fixed exchange regime with very limited capital mobility and downward price rigidity. These fundamental features of the Bhutanese economy should be borne in mind when discussing possible macroeconomic solutions to the rupee shortage. Various aspects of the economy of Bhutan—such as growth, employment, inflation, trade, public finances, external and internal debt service payments, and debt stock—are also reviewed in this section. The Consumer Price Index (CPI) basket is discussed in order to highlight the impact on the current account deficit of a higher inflation rate in Bhutan than in India.

The section 'Economic Relations with India' examines Bhutan's economic relations with India in more detail. The section 'Macroeconomic Causes of the Rupee Shortage' explores the causes of the Indian rupee shortage. The section 'Policy Implications: Lessons Learned and the Way Forward' presents the lessons learned and policy implications. The last section concludes.

Salient Features of Bhutan's Economy[1]

Growth and Sectoral Composition

Since 2008, real economic growth in Bhutan has averaged about 6.4 per cent per year (National Statistics Bureau 2013 and 2014). Gross domestic product (GDP) in constant prices was Nu52.5 billion in 2013. In nominal terms, GDP was about Nu104.3 billion in 2013 (Figure 5.1), leading to GDP per capita of $2,440. In purchasing power parity terms, gross national income per capita was $6,920 in 2013, compared with $5,240 in India and the global average of $14,383 (World Bank n.d.).

[1] The fiscal year (FY) of the Royal Government of Bhutan and its agencies ends on 30 June. Fiscal Year before a calendar year denotes the year in which the fiscal year ends, for example, FY2000 ends on 30 June 2001.

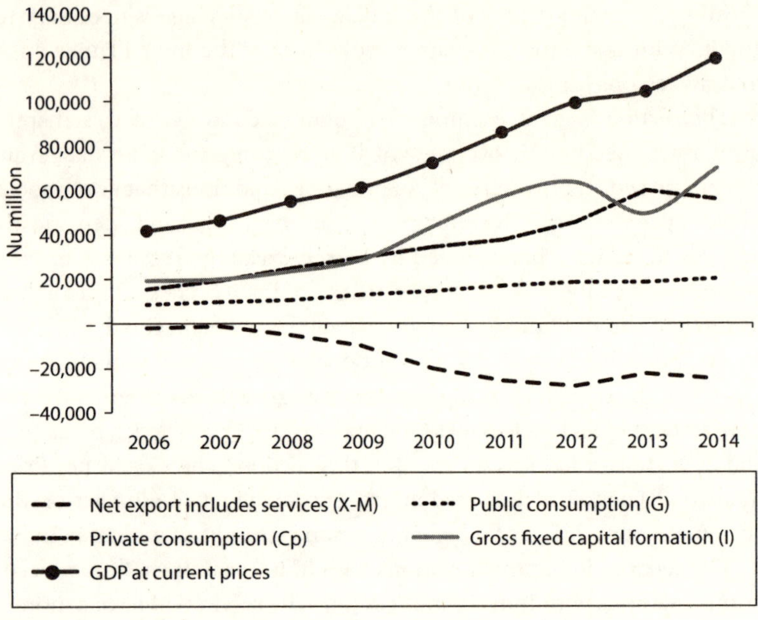

FIGURE 5.1 Gross Domestic Product and Its Determinants
Sources: National Statistics Bureau (2013a), National Statistics Bureau (2012).

The fluctuations in Bhutan's GDP growth rates are mainly caused by investment (gross domestic capital formation), which is erratic (Table 5.1). The fluctuations in investment result mainly from hydropower plant construction and their commissioning. For example, in 2007, the sharp increase in GDP growth was caused by the commissioning of the Tala Hydropower Project. The electricity and construction sectors, which are highly correlated with hydropower plant construction, together comprise about 30 per cent of Bhutan's economy. However, the farming and livestock sectors employ and provide livelihoods for most Bhutanese. Sixty per cent of the employed population works in the agriculture sector, compared with about 22 per cent employed by private firms and the 17 per cent the government directly employs as civil servants in agencies and public corporations (Ministry of Labour and Human Resources 2012). The agriculture sector in Bhutan has low levels of productivity owing to a lack of mechanization and other technological inputs. While nearly

TABLE 5.1 Economic Growth and Gross Domestic Product Aggregates

	2005	2006	2007	2008	2009	2010	2011	2012	2013
GDP Nominal (Nu M)	36,581.1	41,443.5	49,456.6	54,744.3	61,220.6	72,496.6	84,950.0	97,453.0	104,378.1
GDP Constant (Nu M)	28,412.0	30,218.0	36,170.0	37,964.0	40,661.7	45,432.0	49,017.4	51,503.1	52,556.4
Real GDP Growth (%)	8.80	6.90	17.90	4.70	6.70	11.70	8.60	4.60	2.10
GDP Per Capita ($)	1,290	1,387	1,815	1,874	1,852	2,278	2,571	2,533	2,440
Electricity (% of GDP)	10.1	13.1	20.4	21.1	19.3	21.8	13.8	12.4	14.2
Construction (% of GDP)	17.2	14.8	13.7	11.4	12.2	15.1	16.2	16.0	16.9
Agriculture (% of GDP)	22.3	21.4	18.7	18.4	18.2	14.5	16.1	17.0	16.2
Manufacturing (% of GDP)	7.1	7.6	8.2	8.4	8.2	8.7	8.2	9.0	8.5
Services %(GDP)	41.7	40.9	37.3	38.4	39.8	35.4	42.0	38.0	
GDCF (% of GDP)	56.4	45.6	40.0	30.6	35.4	39.6	52.0	67.9	47.3
GDS (% of GDP)	31.7	33.0	37.3	40.2	40.5	40.4	36.4	35.4	25.2

Notes: GDCF = gross domestic capital formation; GDP = gross domestic product; GDS = gross domestic savings; Nu = ngultrum.

Source: National Statistics Bureau. *National Accounts Statistics* (various years).

two-thirds of the workforce is employed in agriculture, the sector accounts for only about 20 per cent of the country's GDP (Royal Government of Bhutan n.d.).

Public Spending

The Government of Bhutan's revenue-to-GDP ratio averaged about 25 per cent in 2009–13 as growth in revenue of 10.3 per cent per year outpaced average GDP growth over the same period by several percentage points. Tax revenue forms about two-thirds of total domestic revenue, while non-tax revenue accounts for the remaining one-third. About 40 per cent of all tax revenue comes from corporate income taxes. The majority of non-tax revenue, which includes profits and dividends, is generated by the electricity sector (National Statistics Bureau 2014).

The ratio of current expenditure to GDP fluctuated between 15 per cent and 22 per cent during 2004–13, with a long-term average of 18 per cent, which is exceptionally high (National Statistics Bureau 2014). Current expenditure is funded from domestic revenue as required by the Constitution. Capital expenditure is financed by development assistance. If revenue grows at about 10 per cent annually compared with current expenditure growth of about 18 per cent, there is bound to be a gap that will have to be closed through a combination of (i) external assistance, (ii) increased revenue from hydropower, and (iii) deficit finance.

Official development assistance, in the form of grants and soft loans, comprised about 34 per cent of total expenditure in fiscal year (FY)2014, down from about 43 per cent in FY2010 (RMA 2014b). External grants have decreased in recent years both as a percentage of official development assistance and in absolute terms. India is Bhutan's biggest development partner, contributing on average about 68 per cent of total grant inflows over the last decade for which data are available (National Statistics Bureau 2013a). Other important donors include the ADB, Austria, Denmark, the European Union, Japan, the Netherlands, Switzerland, the United Nations, and the World Bank.

Foreign capital inflows comprise official development assistance and concessional debt. Foreign direct investment (FDI) inflows have remained relatively small, comprising only about 0.9 per cent of GDP in 2009. The low level of FDI may be related to Bhutan's ranking in the World Bank's *Doing Business 2014*, which was 125 out of 189 countries surveyed (World Bank 2014). For FDI to increase, stringent restrictions on foreign currency capital account transactions will have to be partially lifted. Current account transactions are also controlled in many ways, including ceilings on the amount of foreign exchange that commercial banks can hold, limits on foreign exchange requirements for importers, limits on foreign exchange earnings exporters can retain in a foreign currency, and limits on a foreign currency that business persons and private travellers can take out of the country.

Inflation

Inflation averaged about 7.6 per cent in 2005–14, although a change in the consumer basket in the second quarter of 2013 makes comparisons over this period difficult. In a little more than a decade, the real value of the ngultrum fell by about 55 per cent. While inflation exceeded 12 per cent in 2012, by 2014 it had come back down to about 8 per cent. Part of the reason for this drop was that the CPI weights of food items and non-food items were adjusted in 2013; the global decline in fuel prices in 2014 also contributed. In spite of these factors, inflation remains high in Bhutan. Changes in the cost of material in India increase the prices for imported goods in Bhutan as 57 per cent of the goods in the CPI basket are imported. In response to this, the government assumes a 10 per cent price escalation every year in its budget allocations (Ministry of Finance 2013).

The extent to which rising public expenditure, credit growth, and prices for non-tradable goods leads to inflationary pressure is often not taken adequately into account in fiscal and monetary policies. Inflation targeting remains to be attempted in Bhutan. Fuel, construction materials, and food commodities are the three main imports from India. In 2013, Bhutan imported Nu7.4 billion worth of fuel from India, which accounted for 14 per cent of total imports (Department of Revenue and Customs 2014). Price increases worsened the current account deficit and the overall balance of payments (BoP) situation. Demand for imported goods, in both the public sector and the private sector, does not usually decline amid rising prices.

International Reserves and Debt Stock

Bhutan, like other governments, maintains reserves to meet foreign currency liabilities such as debt repayment, import financing, and unforeseen contingencies. Sizable foreign currency reserves can help mitigate economic contingencies; thus, the financial sense of security any government has depends partly on such reserves.

Since 2007, the Government of Bhutan has been borrowing from both private banks and the Government of India to finance the rupee shortage. The rate of borrowing accelerated in 2012 and 2013. The increase in Indian rupee reserves beginning in FY2013 is a result of this borrowing.

Figure 5.2 shows the gradual accumulation of international reserves—comprising both United States (US) dollars and Indian rupees—leading up to FY2014. Largely due to aid inflows, tourism earnings, and soft loans from multilateral agencies, the level of foreign currency reserves reached the equivalent of $1.2 billion at the end of November 2014 (RMA 2015). Outside of official development assistance, the tourism sector is the main source of US dollar

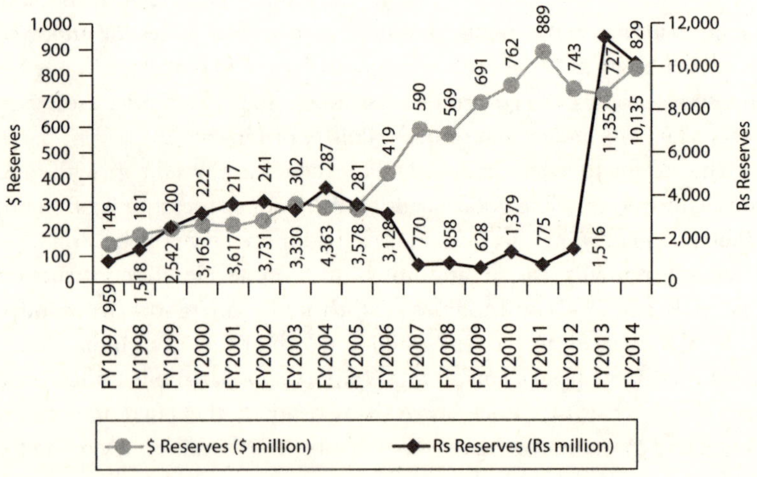

FIGURE 5.2 Convertible Currency and Indian Rupee Reserves
Sources: RMA (2003, 2007, 2013, and 2014b).

earnings. The government charges royalties of $65 per day per tourist. However, as a proportion of total revenue (tax plus non-tax), royalties earned from tourists represented only 4.5 per cent of total revenue in FY2014 (National Revenue Report 2013–14). (Interestingly, the perception exists that tourism is an overwhelming source of revenue for the government.) While the number of tariff-paying tourists increased from 37,481 in 2011 to 44,252 in 2013 (Tourism Council of Bhutan 2013), the total of number of tourists—including Indian tourists who are not subject to the tourism royalty—exceeded 100,000 per year in 2013.

Bhutan's growing debt stock reached Nu106 billion in FY2014, roughly equal to Bhutan's GDP that same year. Since FY2003, the growth rate of total external outstanding debt has averaged 19.5 per cent, indicating an increase in the debt stock of about Nu7 billion every year. With more hydropower plants to be financed by debt, external debt is likely to continue rising (Figure 5.3).

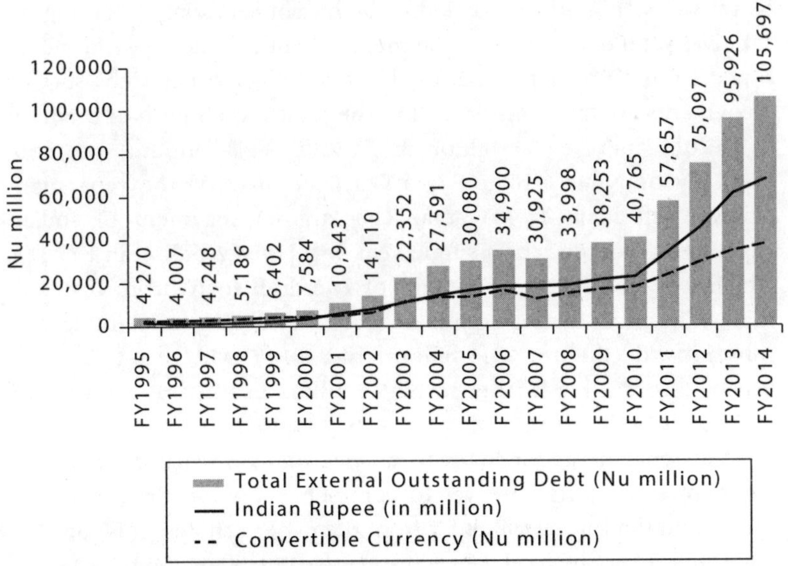

FIGURE 5.3 External Debt Stock
Source: RMA (2003, 2007, and 2013).

Most of the total debt stock consists of Indian rupee debt accumulated by hydropower projects. In FY2014, hydropower project financing comprised 64 per cent of the total debt stock owed to the Government of India. As of March 2014, the shares of Bhutan's convertible currency debt owed to various institutions and governments were as follows: ADB (42 per cent), the World Bank (29 per cent), the Government of Austria (16 per cent), Japan International Cooperation Agency and the Japan Bank for International Cooperation (6.7 per cent), the Government of Denmark (0.9 per cent), and others (0.8 per cent). Debt owed to ADB has comprised an average of 40 per cent of the total convertible currency debt stock over the last two decades and debt to the World Bank has comprised an average of about 27 per cent of the total each year over the same period. In absolute terms, the debt owed to ADB as of March 2014 was $250 million and the debt owed to the World Bank was $182 million.

The amounts of debt service payments have been erratic since FY2011 because of the inclusion of repayment for short-term borrowing, which generally comprises maturities of one year or less. Short-term Indian rupee borrowing from banks in India that has to be repaid within a year has led to high debt servicing costs. Figure 5.4 gives total debt service repayments in both US dollars and Indian rupee from FY2002 to FY2014. If only Indian rupee debt service repayments are taken into account, the total was about Nu8.5 billion in FY2010 and Nu17.5 billion in FY2011. This amount rose substantially to Nu46.1 billion in FY2012 because of the repayment of overdraft loans from India. The largest repayment of Indian rupee debt recorded for a single year was Nu84.2 billion in FY2013, which was fuelled by repayment of overdraft loans from banks in India. The most recent figures on debt service payments indicate a substantial decline to Nu11 billion in FY2014 (RMA 2014). This was expected to decline further to Nu5.1 billion in FY2015 (Ministry of Finance 2014).

Debt repayments for loans to finance the construction of several hydropower projects have yet to commence. Hence, the repayment scenario in the future will differ from the pattern shown in Figure 5.4. As of June 2014, the total debt stock was Nu106 billion (RMA 2013).

In the short term, the debt stock is projected to grow at about 21 per cent annually over the next several years. Sixty-four per cent of the total

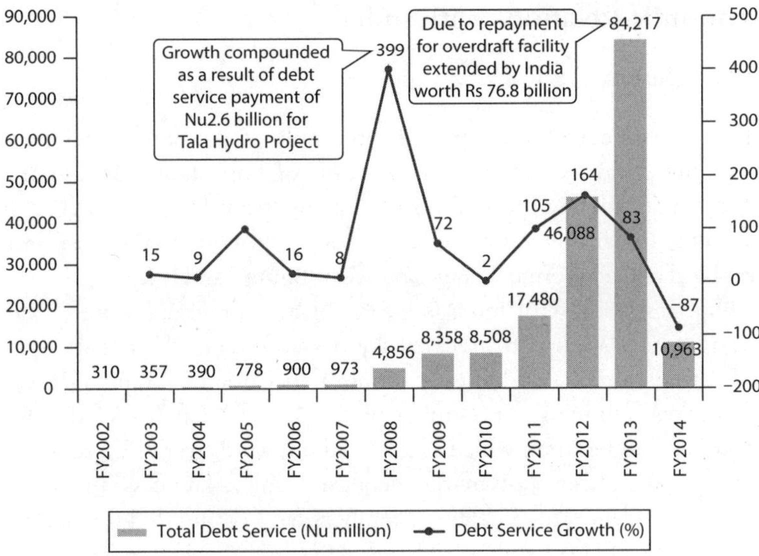

FIGURE 5.4 Total Debt Service Payments
Source: RMA, *Selected Economic Indicators* (various issues).

external debt stock in FY2014 was generated by hydropower project investments, and this component will grow sharply in coming years if hydropower plants are constructed as planned. By FY2020, debt repayment for hydropower projects alone will amount to Nu22 billion and rise steadily over the next 15 years as a consequence of similar projects in the pipeline (Ura 2015).

Seventy per cent of the costs of hydropower projects consist of loans that must be repaid in 12 equal parts over a 12-year repayment period commencing after the project is commissioned. One of the reasons for the swelling of the national debt stock of Bhutan since 2005 is that the modality of financing for hydropower plants changed. Previously, 60 per cent of the costs of a hydropower plant on an average were covered through grants from the Government of India. Currently, about 70 per cent of the costs are covered through loans at a 10 per cent simple interest rate. In addition to hydropower-related debt repayment, the Government of Bhutan also has debt service obligations for loans taken for other purposes.

Economic Relations with India

India–Bhutan Trade

The Government of India provides the bulk of development finance for Bhutan. India is also the main source of imports for Bhutan and the main destination for its exports. The ngultrum has been pegged at par to the Indian rupee since its inception in 1974 due to the close geographical and economic linkages between Bhutan and India.

Bhutan's trade with India is governed by a preferential free trade arrangement. While it includes substantial advantages, there is also very little protection of the domestic economy because of the high degree of openness. Bhutan is a member of the South Asian Association for Regional Cooperation, which as a first step towards transition to a customs union and common market economic union, launched the South Asian Free Trade Area in 2006.[2] Members have committed themselves to phased tariff cuts for an intra-South Asian Free Trade Area trade over a 10-year period concluding in 2016.

In 2013, exports to countries other than India and Bangladesh comprised just 4.4 per cent of total exports, while imports from countries other than India and Bangladesh comprised 17.3 per cent of total imports (Department of Revenue and Customs 2014). In the same year, 91 per cent of Bhutan's total exports went to India and 82.4 per cent of total imports came from India. Bhutan's import-to-GDP ratio stood at about 43 per cent in 2008 and 51 per cent in 2013; in absolute terms, imports more than doubled from Nu23.5 billion in 2008 to Nu53.3 billion in 2013 (Table 5.2).[3]

Primary goods exported to India include hydropower-generated electricity, minerals, and mineral-based commodities. Exports grew sluggishly from Nu22.6 billion in 2008 to Nu31.9 billion in 2013, increasing at a much less rapid pace than imports over the same period. From 2008 to 2013, exports grew at an annual growth rate of only 3.2 per cent, while imports rose sharply at 17 per cent per year on average.

[2] The South Asian Free Trade Area comprises Afghanistan, Bangladesh, Bhutan, India, the Maldives, Nepal, Pakistan, and Sri Lanka.

[3] The major imported items were manufactures representing 32.6 per cent of total imports, agricultural products comprising 12.8 per cent, and petroleum products accounting for 11.8 per cent. Rice accounted for 2.8 per cent of total imports, supplied mainly by India (National Statistics Bureau 2014).

TABLE 5.2 Trade Related Data

in Nu millions

Year	2004	2005	2006	2007	2008	2009	2010	2011	2012	2013
Import	18,625.1	17,024.7	19,012.0	21,745.4	23,495.1	25,650.2	39,084.1	48,697.6	53,093.6	53,273.0
Export	8,270.7	11,386.1	18,771.8	27,859.1	22,590.6	23,992.7	29,324.4	31,486.0	28,420.1	31,853.0
Trade Balance	(10,354.4)	(5,638.6)	(240.2)	6,113.6	(904.5)	(1,657.4)	(9,759.7)	(17,211.7)	(24,673.5)	(21,420.0)
Exports-to-GDP Ratio	0.25	0.31	0.45	0.56	0.42	0.39	0.40	0.37	0.29	0.31
Imports-to-GDP Ratio	0.56	0.47	0.46	0.44	0.43	0.42	0.54	0.57	0.54	0.51
Openness	0.81	0.78	0.91	1.00	0.85	0.81	0.94	0.94	0.84	0.82
Total Trade Value	26,895.8	28,410.8	37,783.8	49,604.5	46,085.8	49,642.9	68,408.5	80,183.6	81,513.7	85,126.0

Notes: 1. GDP = gross domestic product.

2. Openness refers to a ratio of total trade value to GDP. Total trade value is the sum of exports plus imports. Bhutan maintains an extremely large current account deficit with India. In FY2014, the current account deficit with India was about Nu26 billion, while the deficit with all other countries was about Nu2 billion. As a proportion of GDP, the current account deficit with India was about 26 per cent. The overall BoP has remained positive because of capital inflows in the form of grants and loans. Between FY2004 and FY2012, the average annual balance of payments was Nu2.9 billion. This surplus was estimated to be Nu9.2 billion in FY2013.

Sources: RMA, *Selected Economic Indicators* (various issues), National Statistics Bureau (2014).

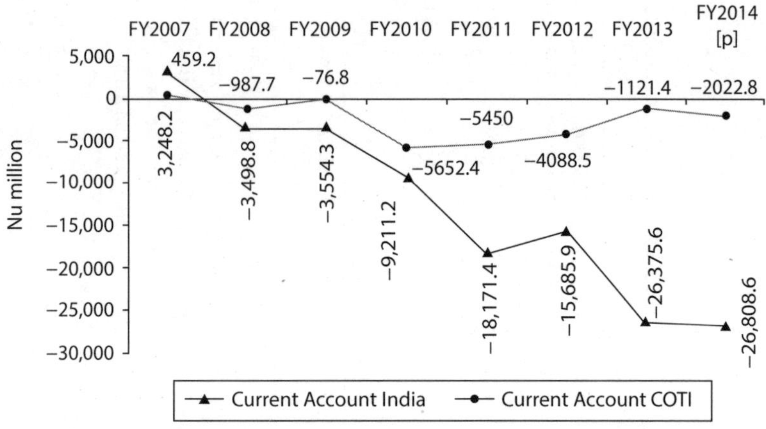

FIGURE 5.5 Current Account Deficits with India and Countries Other Than India (Nu million)

Note: COTI = countries other than India.

Sources: RMA, *Monthly Statistical Bulletin* (various issues); RMA, *Selected Economic Indicators* (various issues).

Indian Rupee Management Prior to the Shortage

Credit Expansion

Monthly data on domestic credit and M2 from July 2011–June 2014 show that domestic credit was almost equal to foreign reserves through December 2011. Afterwards, it exceeded foreign reserves. Domestic credit fell below net foreign assets only at the beginning of 2014, following the introduction of credit controls in 2012. This suggests that the Indian rupee shortage in the financial sector in early 2012 was caused largely by excessive domestic credit that fueled imports. For example, domestic credit in January 2012 was about Nu43.8 billion, while foreign reserves (net foreign assets) were only Nu36.8 billion. Adding together net foreign assets and domestic credit, M2 in January 2012 was Nu55.1 billion.[4] Beginning in January 2012, domestic credit exceeded net foreign

[4] M2 refers to the total amount of currency outside banks, demand deposits, saving deposits, time deposits, and foreign currency deposits held by authorized foreigners (for example, diplomats). M2 constitutes the supply of money.

assets. However, net foreign assets exceeded domestic credit beginning in November 2013 and lasting through October 2014 when the latest data are available. After November 2013, domestic credit fluctuated in a range of Nu50 billion–Nu53 billion, while net foreign assets rose from Nu51.4 billion in November 2013 to Nu62.5 billion in October 2014 (Figure 5.6).

The main lesson from the past is that the January 2011–October 2014 period, in which domestic credit exceeded net foreign assets, coincided with a severe rupee shortage. The growth of domestic credit reached a historically high annual rate of 36.5 per cent in 2011. The excessive growth of credit undoubtedly played a role in the Indian rupee shortage.

Figure 5.7 depicts a situation in which banks have been lending in amounts that exceed deposits, which generally indicates low liquidity. When monthly data are examined, loans given as a percentage of deposits were close to 100 per cent at the beginning of 2012. The loan-to-deposit ratio crossed the 100 per cent threshold in June 2012 when the Indian rupee shortage became evident. For the first time in the financial history of Bhutan, banks had given more loans than

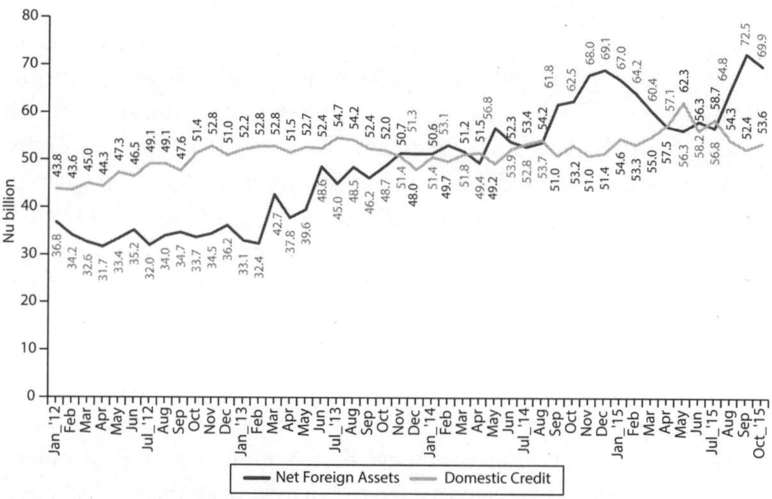

FIGURE **5.6** Net Foreign Assets and Domestic Credit (Nu billion)
Source: RMA (2015).

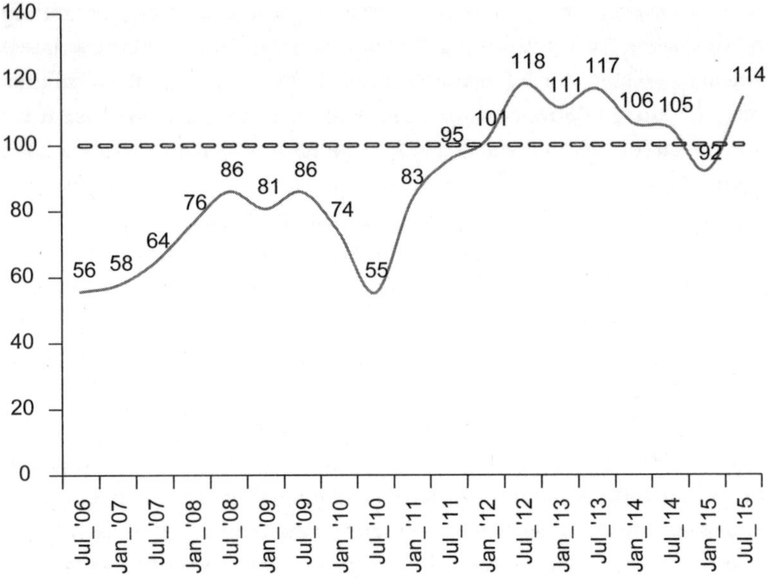

FIGURE 5.7 Biannual Loan–Deposit Ratio, July 2006–July 2015
Source: RMA (2015).

they had deposits to support. The RMA's published data show that in October 2014 the loan-to-deposit ratio was about 98 per cent; that is, for every Nu100 given as loan, there was Nu98 in deposits (RMA 2015). Of course, this loan-to-deposit ratio does not reveal much about the mismatch between loans and deposits. Generally, loans are long-term and deposits are mostly in the form of current (savings) accounts. Nevertheless, Figure 5.7 highlights the mismatch between deposits and credit amid the emergence of rupee shortage. Though it is a simple indicator, the loan-to-deposit ratio suggests that aggressive lending by banks and the consequent borrowing resulted in financial instability.

While seeking profit maximization is a natural function of a private firm, the over-performance of financial institutions can emerge as a problem in the form of an overactive money multiplier, and the consequent Indian rupee shortage that led to borrowing by the RMA at commercial rates of interest from Indian banks to cover current account deficits. Between 2011 and 2012, Bhutan National Bank's profits grew by 37 per cent to Nu697 million, Tashi Bank's profits expanded by 71 per cent to Nu37 million and Druk Punjab National Bank's profits grew by 90 per cent by Nu86 million. Similarly, the Bank of Bhutan (BOB) made a hefty profit of Nu660 million in 2012 and declared a net profit of Nu864 million in 2014 (KuenselOnline 2014). A performance report on the banking sector from the first quarter of 2013 reported that the net profits of the financial sector had increased (RMA 2013). However, the performance of Bhutan's financial institutions should be weighed against the amount of interest payments made by the RMA on Indian rupee borrowing to finance imports. Further research is required to determine whether the amount of taxes and dividends that banks pay to the government may be less than the amount of interest payments made by the RMA on Indian rupee borrowing to finance the BoP.[5]

One of the major reasons for the abnormal rate of credit expansion that coincided with the Indian rupee shortage was the concentration of investments in a few major sectors that drew away more than 10 per cent of all credit. The top five borrowers in 2012 were the country's five largest companies—Tashi, Dungsam Cement Project, Lhaki, Druk Iron & Steel, Royal Thimphu College, and Royal Insurance Corporation of Bhutan—which cumulatively accounted for Nu5.5 billion out of a total of Nu51.3 billion in private lending (Table 5.3).

An official review of the Indian rupee shortage discouraged undertaking big investments within a short span of time. The review cited Tashi Info. Comm., Druk Ferro Alloys, Druk Deothjung Resorts, Bhutan Concast, Drukwang Ferro Alloys, and several other firms as contributing to domestic credit growth and increase in rupee demand. It also highlighted that the construction activities of Dungsam Cement and the Dagachhu Hydropower Project contributed to credit growth as these projects were financed through domestic credit (Royal Government of Bhutan 2012). The spacing of major investments over time, as opposed to crowding them within the same period, would be prudent. Repeating the prior experience would worsen the liquidity situation and exacerbate

[5] Of all the revenue paid to the government in FY2012, the Royal Insurance Corporation of Bhutan contributed Nu137 million, Bhutan National Bank contributed Nu212 million, BOB contributed Nu273 million, and the RMA paid Nu222 million. Government of Bhutan, Department of Revenue and Customs (2014: 21).

Table 5.3 Capital Inflows and Balance of Payments with India and Countries Other than India (Nu million)

	FY2007	FY2008	FY2009	FY2010	FY2011	FY2012	FY2013	FY2014
Capital Inflows	3,730.7	5,171.5	7,736.6	11,788	24,203.1	19,140.9	32,400.9	29,769.5
India	2,891.0	4,374.5	6,575.6	8,378.0	18,555.3	17,093.6	26,201.7	27,066.9
COTI	839.7	797.0	1,161.0	3,410.6	5,647.8	2,047.3	6,199.2	2,702.6
Balance of Payments	**5,421.0**	**688.6**	**6572.6**	**4,410**	**797.5**	**-9,068.4**	**9,212.2**	**4,280.5**

Notes: COTI = countries other than India; FY = fiscal year.

Sources: RMA (2014); RMA, *Monthly Statistical Bulletin* (various issues).

TABLE 5.4 Annual Lending by Domestic Financial Institutions (Nu million)

Financial Institution	FY2009	% of total	FY2010	% of total	FY2011	% of total	FY2012	% of total	FY2013	% of total	FY2014	% of total
Bank of Bhutan Ltd.	8,849.1	37	9,551.4	32	11,821.6	29	17,045	33	18,576.5	33	20,758.5	33
Bhutan National Bank Ltd.	10,051.6	41	11,953.1	40	14,864.2	37	17,324.6	34	18,149.7	32	18,376.2	29
Bhutan Development Bank Ltd.	2,790.5	12	3,277.3	11	4,287.9	11	5,350.8	10	7,644.8	14	1,0236	16
Tashi Bank Ltd.	n.a.		500.7	2	1,952.3	5	2,354.7	5	2,262.9	4	2,189.1	4
Druk Punjab National Bank Ltd.	n.a		824.2	3	2,195.3	5	3,367.6	7	3,693	7	3,715.5	6
Royal Insurance Corporation of Bhutan Ltd.	2,565.8	11	3,668.9	12	5,312.6	13	5,524.8	11	6,088.4	11	7,524.6	12
Bhutan Insurance Ltd.	n.a.		n.a.		211.6	1	337.8	1	363.2	1	386.9	1
Total	24,257		29,775.6		40,645.5		51,305.3		56,778.5		63,186.8	
DC Growth Rate (%)	27.6		22.8		36.5		26.2		10.7		11.3	

Notes: 1. DC = domestic credit, FY = fiscal year, n.a. = not available.

2. Percentage totals may not add up to 100 per cent due to rounding.

Source: RMA (2014).

the Indian rupee shortage. At the same time, due to the advantageous electricity tariff granted to some of these industries compared to the export price of electricity, their operations have the effect of reducing electricity revenue from exports, which they earn in Indian rupee.

New Banks' Contribution to Credit Expansion

In 2010, two new banks opened. The first instance of FDI in the banking sector occurred when India-based Punjab National Bank established Druk Punjab National Bank through a local partnership. The Tashi Group of Companies also opened a bank that same year. The timing of the opening of these banks played a role in the increase in M2 and related credit creation, which further contributed to the Indian rupee shortage in 2012.

To be conclusive about the link between the establishment of two new banks in 2010 and the credit creation boom requires disaggregated data as some existing accounts would have migrated to the new banks and would not count as new loan transactions. Nevertheless, there is sufficient ground to infer that the establishment of two new banks added to the problem of the Indian rupee shortage. They increased both the amount of credit available and the already-high marginal propensity to import. In their first full year of operation in 2011, Tashi Bank and Druk Punjab National Bank together lent Nu4.1 billion out of a total of Nu40.6 billion worth of credit offered by banks that same year (Table 5.4). By 2014, their combined lending had risen to Nu5.9 billion out of total bank lending of Nu63.1 billion. Between 2009 and 2012, domestic credit grew at an average of 28.2 per cent per year, but it grew at only about 11 per cent in 2013 and 2014. Therefore, credit creation likely would have been slightly less if the two new banks had not been established in 2010. From the point of view of timing, the opening of these two banks seems to have aggravated the situation.

Government Borrowing and Credit Growth

Some government officials have claimed that the aggressive lending to and borrowing by the private sector resulted from a lack of opportunity to buy short-term government instruments like bonds or Treasury bills. A closer look at the data disproves this observation.

The government raised a significant amount of credit from the banking sector through Treasury bills, which compounded credit growth in the economy. To maintain its cash flow in FY2013, the government borrowed nearly Nu13 billion, which it repaid in the same fiscal year. This suggests that the government needs to redesign its revenue collection so that its cash flow is less erratic. However, measuring the stock of domestic debt that the government owes local banks because of Treasury bills at the end of year can be misleading. The end-of-the-year position of credit that the government owes the banking sector is smaller because it has redeemed the Treasury bills. However, the total money borrowed by the government every quarter is huge. With a total credit market volume of about Nu53 billion in FY2013, turnover of about Nu13 billion through the sale of Treasury bills can rock the financial system (RMA 2013). In FY2014, the government issued and redeemed a total of Nu6.6 billion of Treasury bills in the same fiscal year. By December 2014, the amount of 90-day Treasury bills being floated was about Nu9 billion. This amount was to be repaid within the same fiscal year ending on 30 June 2015, as well as an additional Nu4.8 billion to be repaid in the following fiscal year, thereby representing an addition to the domestic debt stock (KuenselOnline 2014).

A more analytic appraisal of Treasury bills' impact and a more finely tuned appraisal of the budget deficit is desirable in the future, given the precise knowledge of the limited total deposits available for such purposes. The budget deficit as a percentage of GDP, though used as an indicator around the world, seems to be a blunt and misleading instrument in the case of Bhutan as a large fiscal deficit and 90-day borrowing results in financial crowding out.

Macroeconomic Causes of the Rupee Shortage

The earlier section on Bhutan's economic relations with India showed that the current account deficit worsened sharply between FY2010 and FY2011, doubling from Nu9.2 billion in FY2010 to Nu18.2 billion in FY2011. The deficit stabilized briefly at Nu15.6 billion in FY2012 before climbing to Nu26 billion in FY2013. The doubling of the current account deficit in FY2011 coincided with the tremendous growth of credit (36.5 per cent) in the same year. Thereafter, credit controls on housing construction and vehicle import loans led to a smaller current account deficit.

To address the Indian rupee shortage, the RMA sold $200 million to State Bank of India in December 2011 at the prevailing market rate. In June 2013, the RMA again sold $200 million to be able to keep importing from India and to maintain a minimum level of rupee reserves (*The Bhutanese* 2013). Indian rupee was also borrowed at commercial rates by the government between 2011 and 2013 to finance the current and financial accounts.

Import restrictions and controlled access to the Indian rupee were established in 2012 and 2013, which reduced Indian rupee outflows and stemmed the depletion of the RMA's Indian rupee reserves. Students from Bhutan studying in India were eligible to withdraw up to Rs 10,000 a month. A citizen from Bhutan who wished to travel to India could get up to Rs 30,000 for an air ticket. A licensed businessperson importing goods from India was eligible to withdraw Indian rupees in an amount equivalent to an import invoice that had been verified by customs officials. Those who did not have an import licence were denied access to Indian rupees. Except for trucks, the issuing of licences for imports of automobiles from India was banned until mid-2014. Banks were directed not to give loans for construction since most construction materials had to be imported from India. The bans on vehicle imports and construction loans were partially lifted in 2014 when a new government came to power, but other controlled access measures remain in place.

In 2014, increased annual flows of aid from India commenced as part of Bhutan's Eleventh Five Year Plan (FY2013–FY2018), thereby easing the Indian rupee shortage even though the free exchange of the ngultrum with the Indian rupee that existed before 2012 had not been restored (Gross National Happiness Commission 2013). Had the Indian rupee not been heavily rationed through official measures to restrict imports, the situation would have led to a repeat of the sale of dollar reserves that occurred in 2011 and 2013. The RMA's stock of Indian rupee reserves stood at Rs 8.6 billion in June 2014, which was estimated to be able to finance 27 months of essential imports. The stock of Indian rupee with the RMA has not increased substantially since then; the probability of a crisis recurring is high.

The government's long-term solution is to use hydropower earnings to address the Indian rupee shortage. However, this cannot be the whole solution. Switching consumption to a larger share of domestically produced goods, reducing public expenditure, and expanding domestic production capacity all need to be part of the solution. Labour productivity also needs to be increased to improve competitiveness.

Terms of Trade Deterioration

From a long-term perspective, the Indian rupee crisis has also been driven by a deterioration in the terms of trade. Terms of trade are defined as the ratio of the average price of exports to the average price of imports. An export price index and an import price index are needed to estimate terms of trade improvement or deterioration. Selecting the top 50 import and export items to create these indices can accomplish this, although Bhutan's terms of trade have not been estimated technically.

An example of terms of trade can be given by comparing the growth rate of the import price of diesel from India and the growth rate of the export price of electricity from Bhutan. The import price of a litre of diesel has grown over the years much faster than the export price of a kilowatt-hour of electricity. The electricity export price increased from Rs 1.5 to Rs 2 per kilowatt-hour between 2002 and 2013, resulting in an increase of 33 per cent.[6] For comparison, diesel prices rose 241 per cent between 2001 and 2013.[7] This means that for every litre of fuel imported, Bhutan needs to increase the amount of electricity it exports. Even if the quantity of fuel imported remained constant, the BOP would deteriorate. However, fuel imports are rising significantly every year. The value of diesel and petrol imports from India amounted to nearly Nu5 billion in 2011. In 2013, this figure had risen to Nu7.4 billion, which accounted for 14 per cent of the total value of imports (Department of Revenue

[6] The power tariff is currently Nu2.15 per kilowatt for electricity from the Chhukha Hydropower Plant. The original purchase agreement, signed on 31 August 2002, includes a prevailing rate of Rs 1.5 per kilowatt-hour. The increase of the tariff to Rs 2 per kilowatt-hour came on 1 January 2005, following the King of Bhutan's request to the Prime Minister of India.

[7] The diesel price in Delhi in 2001 was Rs 17 per litre. The diesel price in 2013 in Thimphu was Nu58 per litre. It reached Nu73 per litre in mid-2014 before dropping in late 2014 to Nu58 per litre.

and Customs 2014). In this sense, the rise in revenue from electricity exports discussed previously was roughly enough to cover the increased payments for fuel imports.

Exports are not limited to electricity in the same way that imports are not limited to fuel. Food and beverage imports from India rose from Nu1.8 billion in 2004 to nearly Nu7 billion in 2012. During the same period, food exports increased from Nu675 million to Nu1.2 billion (Department of Revenue and Customs 2014). Thus, the food trade gap has widened sharply over the years.

One structural reason for the Indian rupee shortage is the relatively slow increase in prices for its export commodities. The prices of major export agricultural commodities like apples, oranges, and potatoes rose very slowly in the two decades preceding 2010.[8] For example, the export price of apples to Bangladesh in 1992 was Nu10.7 per kg; in 2010, it was Nu16.6 per kg (Figure 5.8). Therefore, over a 16-year period, the export price of apples rose about 55 per cent. Over the same period, consumer price inflation increased an average of 5.5 per cent per year (World Bank n.d.).

By 2013, the price of apples exported to Bangladesh had risen to Nu39 per kg. Meanwhile, the price of oranges exported to Bangladesh was Nu13.3 per kg in 1992 to Nu14.8 per kg in 2010, reflecting an increase of only 11.3 per cent over nearly two decades. In 2013, the export price for oranges had risen to Nu22 per kg (Figure 5.8). Meanwhile, the export price of potatoes to India was Nu4.1 per kg in 2000 and Nu10.6 per kg in 2010, more than doubling in a decade. However, in some years the export price fell as low as Nu2.0 per kg.[9]

Three lessons emerged from these trends. First, value addition in the agriculture sector is vital if export revenue is to increase. Second, to avoid import of certain commodities, the country should improve the distribution and storage of these commodities. For example, Bhutan exported Nu119.7 million worth of potatoes to India in 2008, but also imported Nu17.7 million worth of potatoes in the same year to meet

[8] For a comprehensive understanding of this crop, see Roder, Nidup, and Chettri (2008) and Ministry of Agriculture and Forests (2007).

[9] These figures are taken from personal communications with the Policy and Planning Division of the Ministry of Agriculture and Forests (13 September 2012, 30 July 2013).

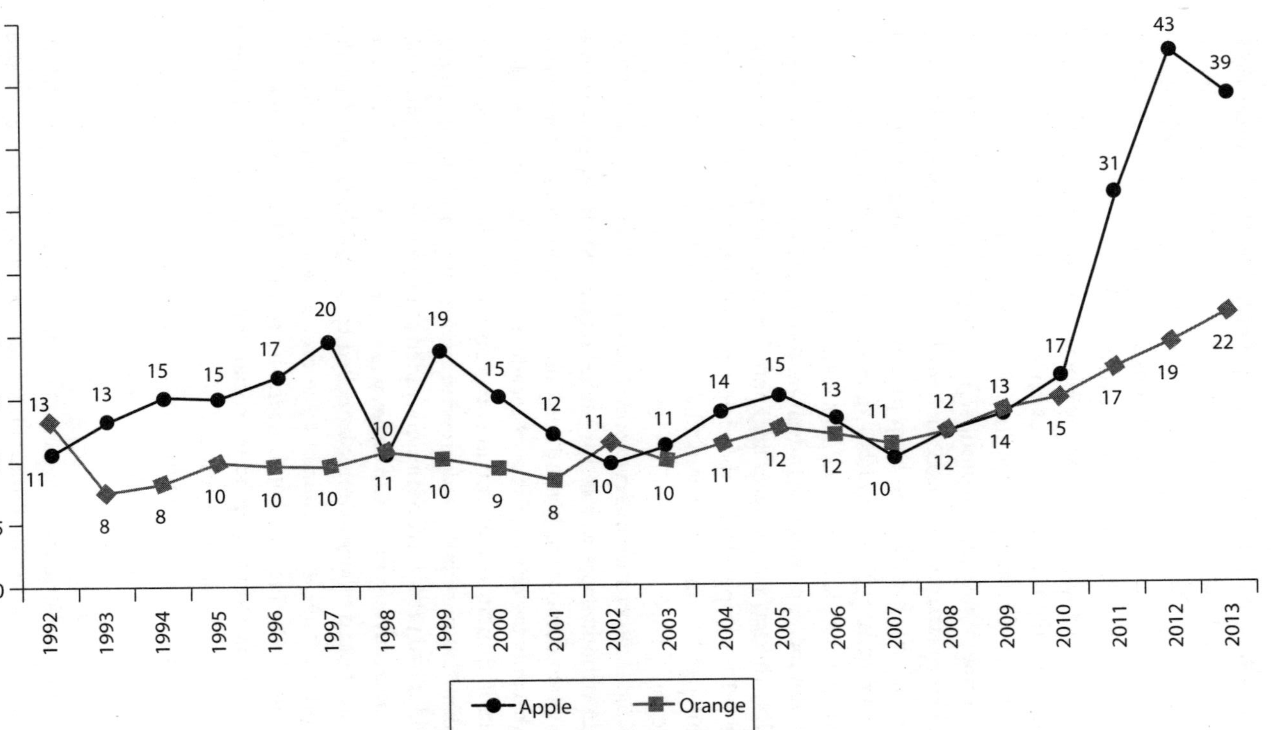

FIGURE 5.8 Annual Export Prices for Apples and Oranges (Nu per kg)
Source: Department of Revenue and Customs (2014)

off-season demand. Similarly, Bhutan exported Nu360.1 million worth of potatoes to India in 2013, while importing Nu56.7 million worth of potatoes from India due to insufficient storage and domestic distribution (Department of Revenue and Customs 2014). This kind of importing should be avoided in order to improve trade balance. Third, and most importantly, demand for these products should be price inelastic—meaning that the price elasticity of an export item should be less than one—for the commodity to improve the current account.

Raw mineral and mineral products comprise the majority of Bhutan's top 10 exports to India (Figure 5.9). Export prices for minerals have also not increased fast enough to keep pace with rising import prices. The pithead price of gypsum, which is one of Bhutan's top 10 exports, was Nu1,000 per metric ton (MT) in 2000 and Nu1,600 per MT in 2011 for a 60 per cent increase over this 11-year period. Coal export prices seem to have done better, with an average annual increase of 10.8 per cent per year over the same period as the export price of coal per MT rose from Nu1,700 per MT in 2000 to Nu4,400 per MT in 2011.[10] As discussed, changes in terms of trade affect the current account, which in turn affects the Indian rupee reserve level.[11]

Unlike the hydropower sector, many sectors of the economy have been rendered uncompetitive by hasty liberalization. Prices of imported goods became lower than those of locally produced substitute goods as a result of Bhutan's economy opening up. In addition, cheaper transport costs also put downward pressure on import prices. For example, vegetables had previously been non-traded goods as imports from India were comparatively more expensive when the road network was limited and isolated villages were compelled to be self-sufficient.[12] Partly as a result of wage–price inflation, the cost of vegetable production in Bhutan gradually increased and vegetables from India became comparatively cheaper after falling costs for haulage and transportation were factored in. By 2014, the capital city of Thimphu and towns in western Bhutan were importing about 20 truckloads of fresh vegetables every day from Falakata, which is close to Phuentsholing, the entry point at

[10] Personal communications with the National Statistics Bureau (1 July 2013).

[11] The impact of terms of trade on the current account and Indian rupee reserves depends on price elasticity of demand for exports and imports.

[12] For more detailed information, please see Chapter 4 in Corden (1981).

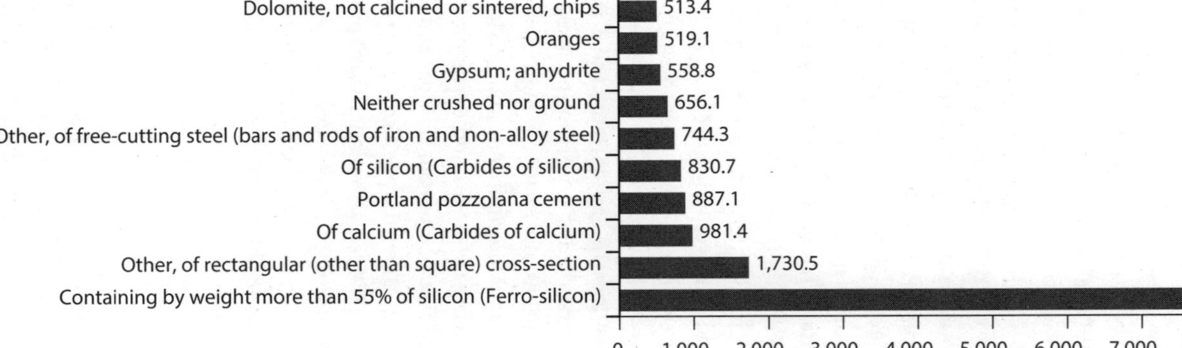

FIGURE 5.9 Top 10 Exports to India in 2013 (Nu million)

Source: Ministry of Finance (2013).

the western border of Bhutan. Thus, vegetables became traded goods in Bhutan.

Cheaper imports create consumer surplus for those who buy imported vegetables, but these imports have to be paid for by selling something in return. To be export competitive, labour productivity has to be high. However, Bhutan's labour productivity is low in all sectors of the economy except in the hotel and hydropower industries. Increased labour productivity can lead to rising export prices, which in turn will improve Bhutan's terms of trade. However, in the agriculture sector, for example, when labour productivity fails to rise, farming becomes uncompetitive and labour will move out of this sector, further depressing production. This effect is already evident in the substantial migration from rural to urban areas in Bhutan, and from other sections of the country to western Bhutan, that is more urbanized and where production is more capital intensive.

The government can intervene to raise labour productivity in sectors like agriculture and services. However, such intervention will not be effective if the government continues to employ people in the public sector at relatively high wages while labour productivity in this sector remains extremely low. In any country, there is a risk that the civil service becomes overstaffed if a portion of it does not generate any efficient output. If wages are relatively high in the public sector, it may attract the most capable employees and gradually make them less innovative, while driving up wages and depriving other sectors of potential employees. The size of the civil services should be decreased gradually by discontinuing irrelevant positions via downsizing and by closing redundant offices. This can also reduce fiscal pressures.

At the same time, downsizing the civil services does not necessarily need to result in increased unemployment. Employment opportunities can be generated outside the public sector, while also increasing the economy's overall production capacity and labour productivity, by using savings from a downsized public sector to create jobs in the private sector, specifically jobs for youths on new hydropower projects.

In trying to address the Indian rupee shortage, it is important to consider the impacts of trade in services as well as trade in goods. Earnings from tourism, which are an invisible export, can help offset Bhutan's current account deficit. However, the per capita difference in gross earnings between regional (primarily Indian) tourists and international tourists must be determined to show if one kind of tourism aggravates the current account deficit while the other helps to reduce it. Gross earnings per regional tourist are estimated to be $476, while gross earnings for an international tourist are estimated to be $5,044. In other words, one additional international tourist can generate about the same gross earnings as 10 regional tourists. Therefore, Bhutan should encourage international tourists and reduce regional tourism, given the concerns for limited cultural and environmental carrying capacity. In 2012, gross earnings from international tourists were $62.8 million, royalties to the government were $16.6 million, and tour operators' net earnings were $44.0 million. Total gross earnings from all tourists were estimated to be $227 million. In 2013, gross earnings from international tourists were estimated to be more than $220 million, including receipts from Drukair, regional tourism, out-of-pocket spending of visitors on shopping, and other tourism-related services and products (Tourism Council of Bhutan 2013).

In 2012, total gross earnings from regional tourists were estimated to be $31.3 million (Figure 5.10). In 2013, the average spending of regional

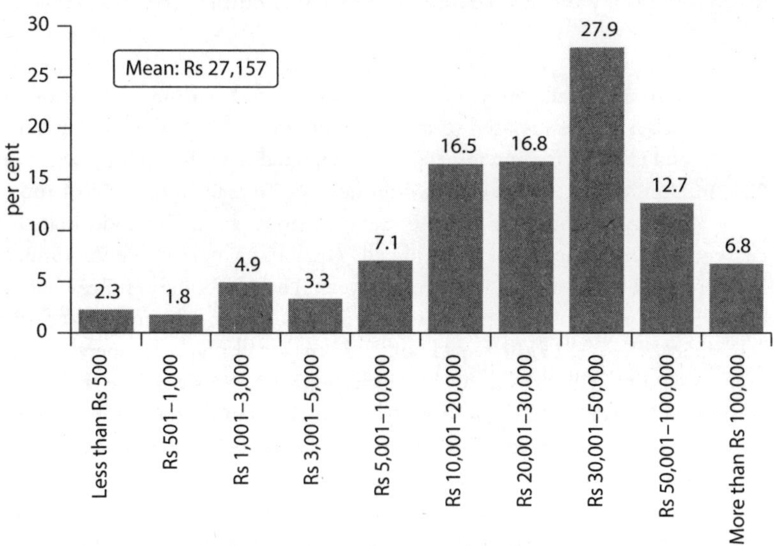

FIGURE 5.10 Spending Patterns of Regional Tourists in 2013
Note: Spending is in Indian rupees and excludes airfare.
Source: Tourism Council of Bhutan (2013).

visitors was down about 20 per cent from the previous year (Tourism Council of Bhutan 2012, 2013). In fact, these estimates may be inflated; therefore, further research is required. As the number of regional tourists increases, more budget hotels will have to be built and construction materials and labour will have to be imported, as well as more fuel and food to support such tourism. Promoting regional tourism is fuel-, car-, and construction-intensive compared to international tourism. Although not a decisive factor, increased imports of cars, fuel, and construction materials from India contribute to the current account's deterioration.

Excessive Monetary Growth

Addressing Bhutan's current account imbalance involves targeting monetary variables more accurately.[13] Targeting monetary variables can be instrumental considering that neither the movement of capital nor interest rates are completely free, while the exchange rate is pegged to the Indian rupee. Thus, deposits do not move out of Bhutanese banks into Indian banks in response to an interest rate rise, or vice versa. Monetary policy is not forfeited under such circumstance; it can still be

[13] For more detail, see Goodhart (1984). Though an old publication, it discusses classic issues related to monetary policy. In Bhutan's case, between FY2012 and FY2014, foreign reserves were depleted with the selling (twice) of $200 million to finance current account deficits. To explain the role of monetary solutions in the Indian rupee crisis, it should be understood that the current account deficit (-CA) is identically equal to changes in the net foreign assets (Δ NFA) held by the RMA in any year. The symbol Δ denotes change between the previous year and the current year. When the current account is in deficit, the rest of the world builds claims on Bhutan as it spends more than its income. Changes in net foreign assets (Δ NFA) should be measured cumulatively over a year, as in the case of the current account, for this relationship to hold. Conventionally, net foreign assets are measured as a stock at a given point in the year instead of measuring change for the whole year like with the current account. It may be noted that $- CA \equiv - \Delta$ net foreign assets. This identity links a current account deficit with changes in the foreign reserves comprising the Indian rupee and the dollar. The monetary sector and the trade sector are intimately linked. Further, Δ NFA + Δ domestic credit $\equiv \Delta$ M2. The preceding identity also can be rearranged as Δ NFA $\equiv \Delta$ M2 - Δ domestic credit.

effective. Monetary policy is ineffective only if complete capital mobility is combined with a fixed exchange rate.

Using monetary policy to sterilize M2 and stabilize the economy can be based on manipulating three broad variables—M2, net foreign assets, and domestic credit—and forecasting their subcomponents up to six months in advance according to certain rules. These forecasts can help influence the policies of agents and financial institutions. Changes in monetary policy that are enforced may introduce distortions. If two variables are well measured beforehand, the third variable can be found residually. Influences on the two variables can also be simultaneously exerted.

Amid a continuously deteriorating current account balance, domestic credit was restricted by the RMA in order to reduce M2. Credit controls were imposed on the two main components of imports: private housing construction material and private vehicle imports. The new government, which came to power in 2013, partially removed the import ban on vehicles and the freeze on private housing construction loans in mid-2014. While the general ban on vehicle imports was lifted, such vehicles were subject to very high import and sales taxes. Depending on engine size, vehicle imports taxes ranged from 50 per cent to 120 per cent.

With credit restrictions in place, M2 rose to Nu56 billion in December 2012 from Nu50 billion in June 2012. By the end of October 2014, M2 had reached Nu70 billion. Figure 5.11 shows the steady expansion of M2 as credit controls kept domestic credit at a fairly stable level. Figure 5.11 also shows that the annual growth of domestic credit slowed from 36.5 per cent in 2011 to 26.2 per cent in 2012, 10.7 per cent in 2013, and 11.2 per cent in 2014. Due to credit controls, the growth of the current account deficit with India was temporarily arrested between 2011 and 2013, before resuming its normal trend.

Operating at a broad level of monetary aggregates alone is, it seems, not sufficient. Understanding empirically the behavioural functions of the subcomponent variables and the transmission mechanism affecting two aggregates (domestic credit and M2) is necessary before proceeding to policy targeting. The task of reducing certain components of M2, particularly its liquid components, needs to be addressed adequately in a way that can be articulated by working on predictive frameworks and behavioural functions. Building such frameworks and functions requires modest research capacity. Considering the information that is available and the size of the economy, it would be possible to

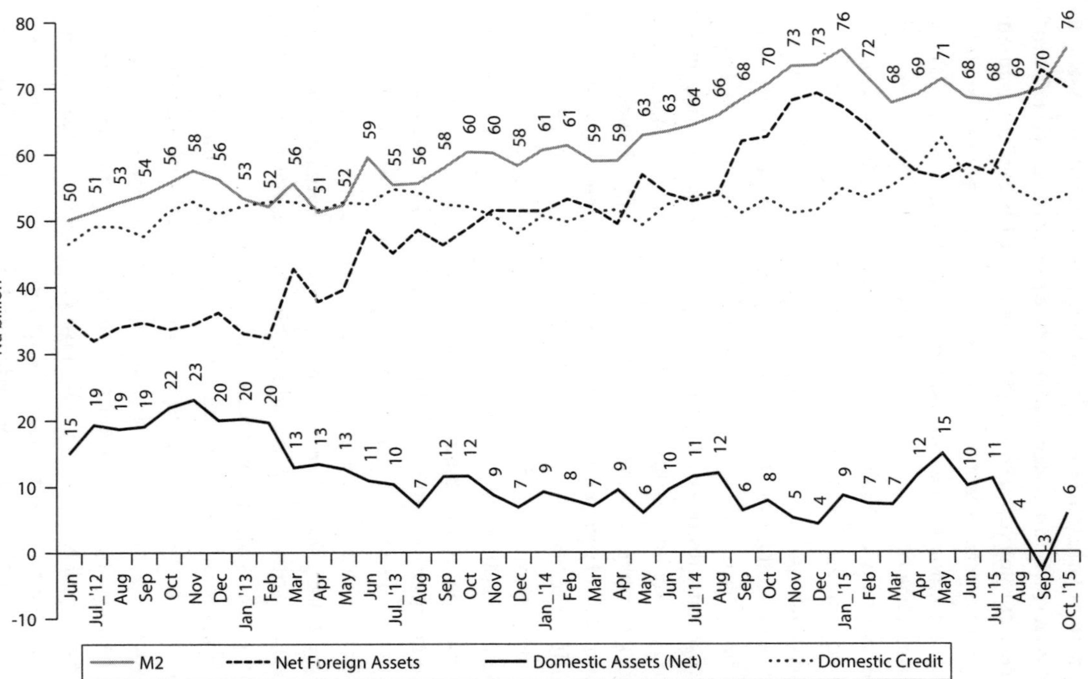

FIGURE 5.11 M2 Money Supply (Broad Money)

Source: RMA (2013, 2014).

build simulation models for the demand and supply of money, as well as inflation functions, while delineating their transmission mechanisms.[14]

Monetary policy alone cannot resolve Bhutan's long-term problems. There are also crucial roles for (i) activities managed by the Gross National Happiness Commission and relevant ministries through fiscal expansion under the Eleventh Five Year Plan, (ii) cash-flow management among the government agencies for which the Ministry of Finance is responsible, (iii) the operations of Druk Holdings Investment and Druk Green Power Corporation, (iv) the export improvement plan of the Ministry of Economic Affairs, and (v) activities of the Bhutan Chamber of Commerce and Industry. If the actions and decisions of these entities are not aligned, it can scupper financial stability. The nature and scope of the Eleventh Five Year Plan is fully implicated in the Indian rupee issue at a deeper level. Its resolution must take into account not only the Eleventh Five Year Plan, including official hydropower investment, but also the business plan of the private sector as represented by the Bhutan Chamber of Commerce and Industry. The effects of bank deposits on hydropower investment and of the Eleventh Five Year Plan on multiplying money have not been adequately taken into account. Nor have the cumulative effects of increasing Treasury bill operations on M2 been fully taken into account.

At the same time, the long-term effects of the five-year plans on the government's financial sustainability need to be re-examined. Revenue growth is not sufficient to cover recurrent expenditures and debt payments. The solution requires detailed examination at the project and sub-sector levels, rather than dealing with broad aggregates of capital versus recurrent allocations. Had these financing issues been analysed adequately in the past, current problems would not have emerged on the scale witnessed.

Such problems will likely intensify without better methods of planning and a deeper understanding of the economy as a whole.

If foreign reserves were to rise, injecting counterbalancing ngultrum into the banking system would increase M2. In addition, M2 will increase when there is an upsurge in official demand deposits resulting from foreign capital inflows. This process is known as round-tripping. To reduce the expanding effect of foreign reserves on M2, one of the

[14] For models that can be adapted to Bhutan, see Sharma (2003).

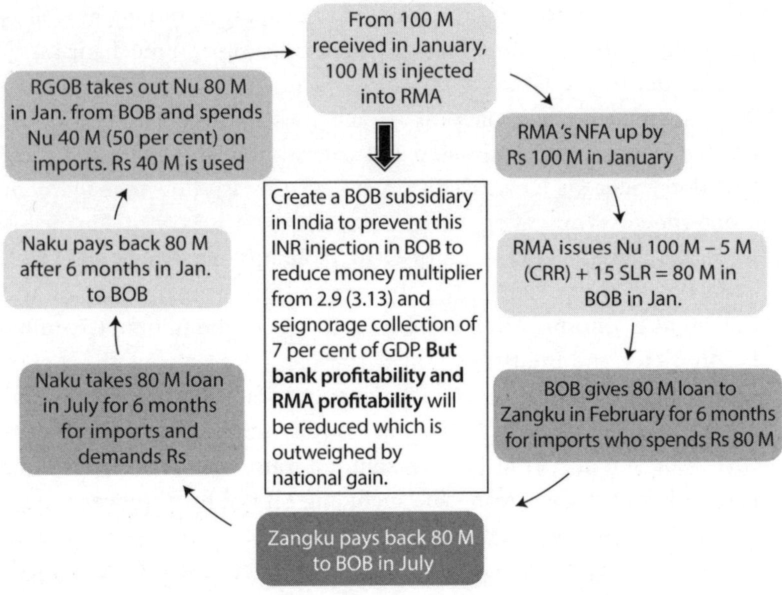

FIGURE 5.12 How the Injection of Rs 100 million Leads to Rs 200 million in Increased Demand within One Year

Notes: BOB = Bank of Bhutan; CRR= cash reserve ratio; RGOB = Royal Government of Bhutan; NFA = net foreign assets; RMA = Royal Monetary Authority of Bhutan; SLR = statutory liquidity ratio.

Source: Author's Illustration.

most feasible options is to keep a certain amount of reserves out of the banking system for a certain period of time (for example, maintaining reserves in a subsidiary branch of BOB in India). This is a variation on the standard measure of stabilization and sterilization, where the measures are usually carried out within the country. However, keeping Indian rupee reserves outside of the Bhutanese banking system for a planned period would be an innovative approach for various other problems. The simple act of establishing a foreign subsidiary of BOB addresses the issue of excessive credit creation, while also meeting transaction and precautionary demand for the Indian rupee. It would restore confidence in the ngultrum. Ideally, there should be subsidiary branches of BOB in Delhi, Jaigoan, Siliguri, Bongaigoan, and Guwahati where Bhutanese traders could settle their transactions in Indian rupee.

If the measure suggested further in the chapter (or its equivalent) is not adopted, then given a money multiplier as high as 2.9 (M2/M0) in Bhutan, the injection of Rs 1 into the banking system can result in credit creation as high as Nu2.9. It is probable that the multiplier is even higher as there might be Indian rupee hoarding and substitution taking place without these transactions being reflected in the official data.

Depending on the marginal propensity to import, the credit creation of Nu2.9 may result in a substantial Indian rupee equivalent requirement as the creditor converts ngultrum holdings into Indian rupee for import purposes. For example, if the marginal propensity to import is 0.63, as the rough estimation shows, an increase in gross national disposable income by Nu1.0 would result in demand for Indian rupee increasing by Nu0.63. In absolute terms, the amount spent on imports will keep rising as GDP expands. However, the estimate of marginal propensity to import is not reliable with the required level of confidence.

Import trade statistics also seem to underestimate actual imports by a substantial margin. Towns along the border with India are growing in size—and now constitute perhaps as much as one-fifth of Bhutan's entire population—as inhabitants are moving to towns in which they can regularly carry out shopping across the border where prices are lower. These types of daily transactions are not officially recorded.

Questions about excessive seigniorage profits and an inflation tax imposed by RMA have been raised by the United Nations Department of Economic and Social Affairs Economist Hamid Rashid.[15] The basic idea of seigniorage is simple. The cost of printing paper currency compared to the face value of currency is almost negligible. Thus, the authority that circulates currency collects seigniorage (or revenue) and excessive issuance of currency relative to the size of economy can result in inflation and undermine the one-to-one peg with the Indian rupee.[16] Rashid has provisionally estimated that such seigniorage in Bhutan was as high as 4.6 per cent of GDP in FY2011. When an inflation tax is included, this figure rises to 7.3 per cent of GDP. According to Rashid, 'this is extremely high by international standards, which typically ranges between 3 per cent and 4 per cent of GDP. Standard

[15] Inflation tax = (tax rate) * (tax base).

[16] Seigniorage = (ΔM) * (1/P), where Δ is change over the previous year, M is money supply, and p is inflation.

economic theory suggests that a small open economy with a pegged exchange rate should not expect to collect a large seigniorage.'[17] The seigniorage issue is relevant because it contributes to the money supply and undermines currency peg, thereby affecting the impacts of monetary policy.

Another important question is why growth in M2, which predominantly comprises domestic credit, accelerated beginning in December 2011. By October 2014, M2 had reached Nu70 billion. Within M2, the amount of currency circulating outside of banks has exceeded Nu5 billion since 2010. This figure was Nu5.5 billion in November 2014, which means that, on average, each of Bhutan's 634,000 nationals held Nu8,564 in cash, or that among Bhutan's 127,000 households each one held an average of Nu42,755 in cash (RMA 2015). The amount of cash held by individual persons and households does not fluctuate much. However, since the distribution of cash is usually skewed, most people in the lower income quintiles would have less cash.

Time deposits comprised about Nu21 billion out of an M2 total of Nu51 billion in April 2013, increasing to nearly Nu40 billion in November 2014. Since 2009, the total amount of time deposits has been less than that of demand deposits, reversing a historical trend. Demand deposit short-term liquidity has seen spectacular growth from Nu2 billion in 1997 to Nu8 billion in 2005, and to Nu25 billion in April 2013. Demand deposits comprised about half of M2 in November 2014. The burgeoning demand deposits of government ministries and Druk Holdings Investment could be responsible for this expansion. The distribution of demand deposit holdings suggests that on average about 10 per cent belongs to government corporations, which at any given time hold about Nu4.5 billion in demand deposits. It is assumed that government offices (as distinct from government corporations) hold about Nu2.5 billion in demand deposits at any given time. About Nu7 billion of demand deposits are held by the public sector, including both government offices and government corporations. The current and capital accounts of the public sector maintained in the form of demand deposits are contributing to M2 growth.

[17] For more details, see H. Rashid (2012), p. 16. I also thank him for his helpful remarks on an earlier version of this chapter.

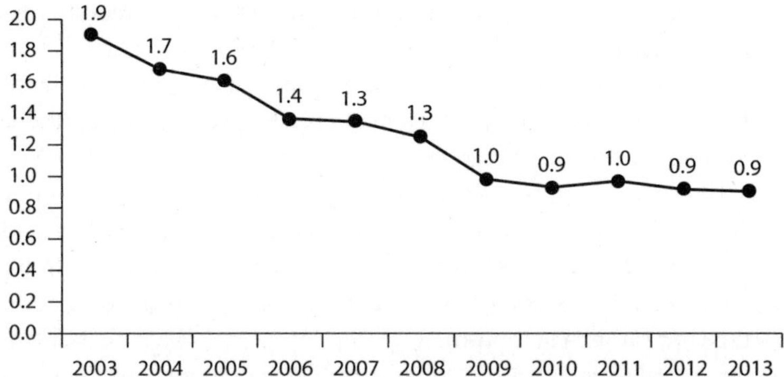

FIGURE 5.13 Income Velocity
Note: Income velocity = gross domestic product at constant prices/M2.
Sources: RMA (2015); RMA, *Selected Economic Indicators* (various issues).

As mentioned previously, the volume of money maintained as time deposits was higher than demand deposits prior to 2009. The shift that took place in 2009 is an important change in the behaviour of the money supply that can be explained by a combination of two factors. The first is the possibility that a higher rate of expected inflation has had a real balance effect; that is, people did not want to hold time deposits because accelerating inflation was undermining their value. Indirect evidence of a real balance effect is the velocity of money (V = PY = real GDP / M2). The velocity of money is influenced by the changing psychology of people about their demand for money.[18] It is inversely related to inflation: it often goes down when inflation goes up as people do not want to hold money. According to the RMA, the velocity of money has slowed from 1.7 in FY2009 to 1.4 in FY2011.[19] However, our estimation shows that income velocity fell even more from 1.9 in 2003 to 1.0 in 2012, reaching its lowest point of 0.9 in 2010 (Figure 5.13).

The second explanatory factor could be that the volume of banks' demand deposits increased due to a rise in public sector revenue and

[18] For an explanation of how the velocity of money declined and frustrated the 2009 stimulus programme of the Obama Administration in the United States, see Chapter 9 of J. Rickards (2011).

[19] RMA. 2012. *Monetary Policy Statement*, June, p. 20.

increasing government expenditure which, importantly, included hydropower investments.

The Indian rupee crisis is attributed by some economists to a change in the composition of foreign currency reserves, represented by Indian rupees and US dollars. Indian rupee reserves as a share of the RMA's total reserves have declined significantly since 2006, the first year in which they comprised a smaller share of reserves than US dollars. This observation that more reserves should be held in the form of Indian rupees instead of US dollars is not a diagnosis of the cause of rupee shortage but rather a symptom.

Figure 5.14 shows that outflows of Indian rupees were greater than the inflows between January 2010 and January 2014. As long as this persists, rupee reserves will decline. How soon before rupee reserves completely run out depends on the initial stock of such reserves and for how many months this stock is able to cover imports. In this respect, US dollar reserves have an advantage as the dollar has been appreciating against the rupee, with further exchange rate gains likely in future.

Bhutan's monetary policy could include efforts to maintain half of all reserves in Indian rupees. But if outflows exceed inflows, changing the composition of foreign reserves in favour of the Indian rupee will

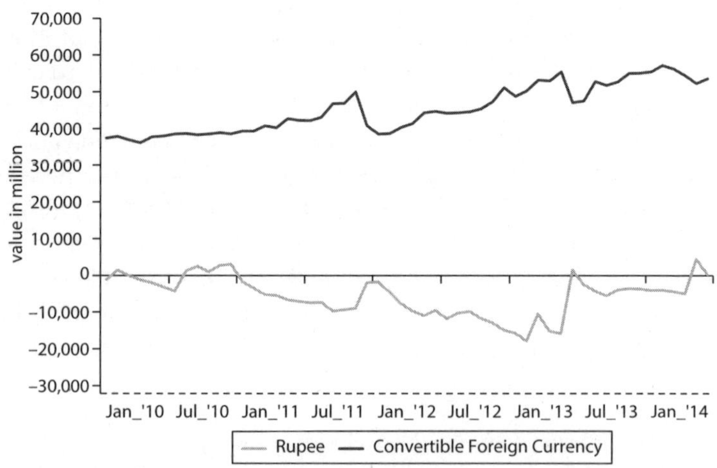

FIGURE 5.14 Monthly Status of Foreign Reserves
Sources: RMA (2013, 2014b).

not resolve the root cause of the problem. Only if the Indian rupee or US dollar reserve inflows are greater than the corresponding outflows can reserves be replenished or expanded.

The monthly record of Indian rupee versus US dollar reserves held by the RMA shows an almost mirror image of one other; when US dollar reserves go up, Indian rupee reserves come down (Figure 5.14). This happens because as US dollars are converted into ngultrum, ngultrum holdings are quickly reconverted into Indian rupee for import purposes. So the round-tripping of dollars into ngultrum and back into Indian rupees seems to take place with very little time lag. The time lag of completing a round trip from ngultrum into Indian rupees in Bhutan seems to be less than a year—and is probably about six months.

Divergence in Inflation

Another fundamental cause of the Indian rupee crisis is the higher inflation rate in Bhutan compared with India. Usually in other countries, stable prices are a goal of monetary policy along with full employment. Full employment is coupled with stable prices because they are inversely related: inflation and full employment have a trade-off. Of course, inflation targeting has proven to be difficult in practice in Bhutan and elsewhere.

Though inflation is a major macroeconomic cause of the Indian rupee shortage, paradoxically, the Indian rupee shortage has also contributed to inflation as the causal relationship can be multidirectional. For example, the Indian rupee shortage led to a rise in food prices in 2012 as the supply of imported foods and vegetables became temporarily restricted due to the scarcity and rationing of the Indian rupee. Nevertheless, this chapter will focus on inflation as a macroeconomic cause of the Indian rupee crisis rather than the Indian rupee crisis as a cause of inflation.

Bhutan's inflation averaged about 9 per cent between 2010 and 2014 on annual rates of 9.2 per cent in 2010, 8.5 per cent in 2011, 9.5 per cent in 2012, 8.5 per cent in 2013, and 8.0 per cent in 2014. The decline in inflation beginning in 2013 was partly due to a change made that year in the weights of the food and non-food components of the CPI. It was also partly due to a drop in fuel prices. For example, in 2014, the price of a litre of petrol in Thimphu dropped from Nu73 at the beginning of the year to Nu59 at the end of the year.

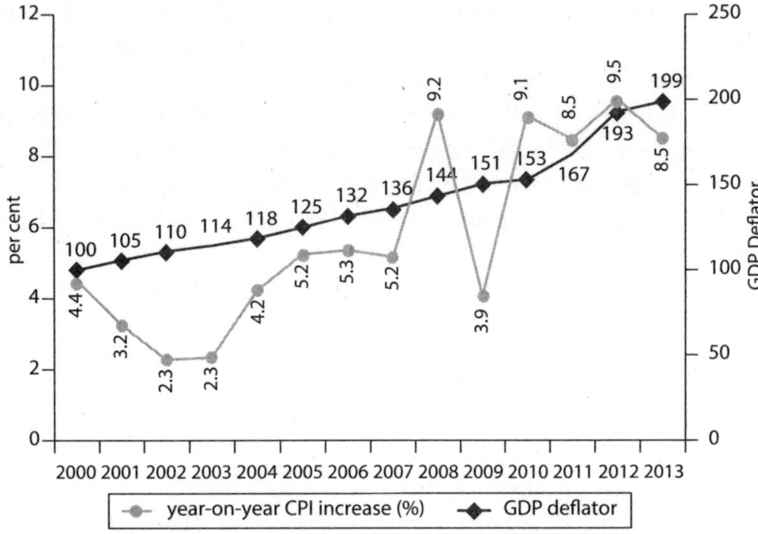

FIGURE 5.15 Percentage Change in the Consumer Price Index and Gross Domestic Product Deflator

Notes: Like the consumer price index (CPI), the gross domestic product (GDP) deflator is a measure of price inflation (deflation) with respect to a specific base year. Similar to the CPI, the GDP deflator of the base year itself is equal to 100. Unlike the CPI, the GDP deflator is not based on a fixed basket of goods and services; the basket for the GDP deflator can change from year to year with people's consumption and investment patterns. However, trends in the GDP deflator will be similar to trends in the CPI. The GDP deflator is calculated by dividing nominal GDP by real GDP, and then multiplying by 100.

Sources: Boundless Economics (2014); RMA, *Selected Economic Indicators* (various issues).

The current method and weights attached to the CPI may underestimate core inflation in Bhutan.[20] This is due to weighted averaging that

[20] The problem with Bhutan's CPI may lie in two areas. First, it has too many items. The basket needs to be pruned to a more sensitive list instead of broadening it to all things bought over a year from exotic drinks and foods to consumer durables. Second, weights should be reallocated among more representative but shorter lists. For example, bananas and chocolates have roughly the same weights of 0.24 per cent and 0.22 per cent, respectively, in the current CPI. Their relative weights do not seem unreasonable. But the weights attached to the cost of tertiary education at 0.39 per cent, the cost of

incorporates 438 items into the CPI (National Statistics Bureau 2012). In contrast, the CPI of the gigantic and diverse economy of India is based on far fewer items.[21]

Bhutan's inflation has resulted in the ngultrum losing 45 per cent of its value since 2000. Given transport and trading costs and taxes, prices for the Indian goods will be higher in Bhutan than in India. However, this should not lead to a sustained divergence in inflation between the two countries as a sustained divergence is primarily caused by either monetary or fiscal expansion, or some combination of both.[22] Such expansion increases demand for traded goods, worsening the current account deficit due to increase in imported goods and imported labour. Bhutan's current account deficit in 2011 was about Nu17.5 billion when total exports and imports are estimated (National Statistics Bureau 2012). Therefore, the current account deficit with India of about Nu12.7 billion comprised the majority of the deficit in 2011 (RMA 2013). This trend held through 2013, the latest year for which reliable data are available.

Increases in Bhutan's demand for imports do not increase the prices of the same goods in India given the size and dynamism of the Indian

---

pre-primary and primary at 0.36 per cent, and the cost of cinemas and theatres at 0.34 per cent, when compared with the weights attached to chocolate and bananas, are debatable. People spend far more on children's primary education than on chocolates; thus, far greater weight should be attached to educational expenditure. The suitability of relative weights can be judged from drinks and meat in the consumer basket. Beer gets a 0.56 per cent weight and fruit juice is given a 0.64 per cent weight. Domestic spirits get a weight of 0.65 per cent, which is perhaps too light given consumption patterns. Drinks seem to fare better in the CPI than meat. Chicken is given a 0.57 per cent weight and pork is given a 0.50 per cent weight, while beef gets a higher 0.98 per cent weight. Potatoes have a weight of 1.04 per cent. Indian inflation, as measured by CPI, should be much lower than that of Bhutan. However, due to the difference in weights and basket size, the inflation rate of Bhutan is implausibly close to that of India, which is deceptive. The Wholesale Price Index of India, which includes about 600 items, is far less relevant for comparison, though the RMA regularly publishes India's Wholesale Price Index for purposes of comparison.

[21] For insight on the Consumer Price Index and Wholesale Price Index (WPI) in India, see Sharma (2013).

[22] For more detail on the nuanced effects of fiscal deficit and crowding out, see S.T. Cook and P.M. Jackson (1979).

economy. However, fiscal and monetary expansion has raised the prices of domestically produced non-traded goods because of the poor supply response.[23] Although not discussed in this chapter, the major fiscal expansion since 2000 is the result of an upward shift in wages and entitlements in public sector employment, as well as the expansion of employment in the public sector.[24] While there is no wage or salary index in Bhutan, the CPI includes rental costs at a weight of 15 per cent.

Higher prices should stimulate higher production of non-traded goods. In an open economy with easy access to sources from India, demand shifts towards imported substitutes of such non-traded goods because of their lower prices. An example are the prices of vegetables produced in the Bhutanese district of Tsirang that rise about 15 per cent every year while the price of the same vegetables produced in the Indian state of Assam increase about 5 per cent a year. Such a divergence in prices contributes to a continuously deteriorating BOP, with respect to vegetable imports in this particular case, and the consequent depletion of Indian rupee reserves. Under the fixed exchange rate between the two countries, this situation cannot go on forever; Bhutan's foreign exchange reserves would eventually be entirely depleted in the absence of any intervention. Of course, Bhutan's Indian rupee reserves will not be entirely depleted as long as grants from the Government of India continue to support Bhutan in one form or another.

[23] The annual growth rate of M2 (broad money) has been high since 2006, reaching 39.7 per cent in 2009 and 16.5 per cent in 2010. Growth decelerated to 4.1 per cent in 2011 and 5.7 per cent in 2012. M2 volume reached Nu43.8 billion in 2009, Nu51.1 billion in 2010, Nu53.2 billion in 2011, and Nu56.2 billion in 2012. Fiscal trends taken at face value are quite deceptive because hydropower and other corporate investments are excluded from budgetary accounts even though their revenue and debt service payments are included in the government budgetary accounts. Even with this proviso applied to fiscal measurement, the total expenditure of the government grew at the following annual rates and reached the following annual totals by year: 29.8 per cent and Nu19.6 billion in 2008, 6.1 per cent and Nu20.8 billion in 2009, 23.7 per cent and Nu25.8 billion in 2010, 14.3 per cent and Nu29.5 billion in 2011, and 28.4 per cent and Nu37.8 billion in 2012.

[24] For an insightful analysis, see Chapter 7 of J.A. Trevithick (1981). He discusses how certain key groups of workers (for example, civil service) will leapfrog others in terms of salaries and as a result the rest will press for higher wages. The process causes spiralling wage–price inflation.

As the GDP of Bhutan increases, so has its propensity to spend on imports. While spending on domestic goods rises in real terms as GDP expands, as a share of GDP spending on domestic goods falls while that on imported goods rises. A small increase in import prices does not exert expenditure-switching effects in favour of domestic goods. The government often considers increasing import taxes as incomes rise so that the price of imports will increase relative to exports. However, a relative increase in import prices from imposing additional taxes can improve the trade balance only if the sum of import-plus-export elasticity exceeds unity. What is known as the Marshall–Lerner condition is most likely not satisfied in Bhutan's economy (Dornbusch 1980). Rising import taxes will have a limited effect on improving the trade balance under such circumstances. Further research with better data should reveal whether this assumption is true or false. In any case, whether an import tax increase improves the trade balance also depends on how the government uses the revenue accrued from increased import taxes. If the government is able to use this revenue to switch its expenditure to domestic goods more than the household sector otherwise would, then the trade balance will improve. Short of this, restricting imports by imposing higher taxes will not sufficiently meet the objective of improving the trade balance, though it will obviously improve revenue for the government.

The divergence in prices for goods produced in India and Bhutan and its effects on Indian rupee reserves in Bhutan have been discussed. Higher wages (wage–price inflation) in Bhutan is another contributing factor to the Indian rupee crisis because it has led to cheaper imported labour for construction, especially in the urban sector. An unskilled labourer from India earns about Nu400 per day, while an unskilled labourer from Bhutan earns a minimum of Nu500 per day. The growth of private housing in urban areas of Bhutan relative to rural areas can be explained by two basic factors. The first is the allocation of credit to the construction sector that occurs mostly in urban areas. The second factor is the ease of importing labour into urban areas relative to rural areas. In fact, there are no clear regulations allowing for the importation of cheaper labour from India for rural housing construction. Since labour costs constitute about 30 per cent of total construction costs, any labour cost differential between rural and urban areas due to imported labour policies will have an impact on investments. In Bhutan, the difficulty of getting permits for cheaper imported labour in rural areas

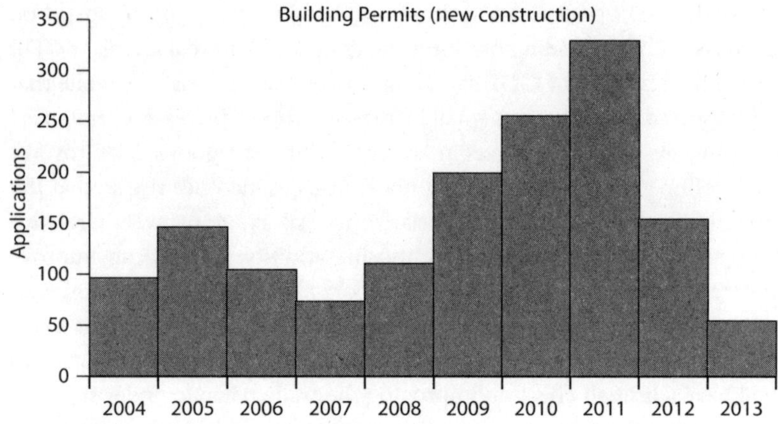

FIGURE 5.16 Increase in Thimphu's Building Permits during the 2009–11 Construction Boom
Source: Thimphu City Corporation.

makes investments in urban construction more viable. This also leads banks to invest more heavily in urban areas.

The major causes of credit growth in Bhutan have been construction booms, inflationary costs of construction material, the resultant trade deficit, and the Indian rupee shortage. This cycle was kicked off in 2005 with the Greater Thimphu Town Declaration that would eventually draw credit into the construction amid a construction boom in Thimphu and western Bhutan. Figure 5.16 shows the abnormal growth in building permits for construction in the capital city in 2009–11, which was prior to the onset of the Indian rupee shortage. Construction loans associated with these permits would have been committed and disbursed in 2012–13 as the Indian rupee shortage became acute.

As of 2014, there were about 60 declared urban sites in Bhutan and their development will require credit (Ministry of Works and Human Settlement 2008). Official credit to the construction sector rose from Nu5.7 billion in 2008 to Nu14.5 billion in December 2012, representing 30 per cent and 27 per cent of total credit in each of these years, respectively (RMA 2013). By the end of June 2014, financial sector investment in building and construction had soared to Nu16.2 billion out of total credit of Nu63.3 billion, or a share of 25 per cent (RMA 2014). Transport and construction loans together constituted 35 per cent of total credit in April 2013. The credit freeze applied to the construction sector that the RMA instituted in 2012 slowed the pace of credit growth before credit for construction was allowed to resume in 2014.

Construction loan totals exclude credit given by the National Pension and Provident Fund, which also provides construction credit. The actual amount could be higher as other credit being used for construction might be disguised. Therefore, it might be better to slow credit growth in the construction sector through administrative measures designed to slow urban development. This would also allow time for the aesthetic, architectural, and functional dimensions of urban planning to be improved. On the other hand, the RMA's credit controls can lead to distortions. The control of vehicle loans temporarily decreased total credit in the transport sector as evidenced in a steady decline from Nu4.8 billion in 2012 to Nu2.4 billion in 2014. The number of registered

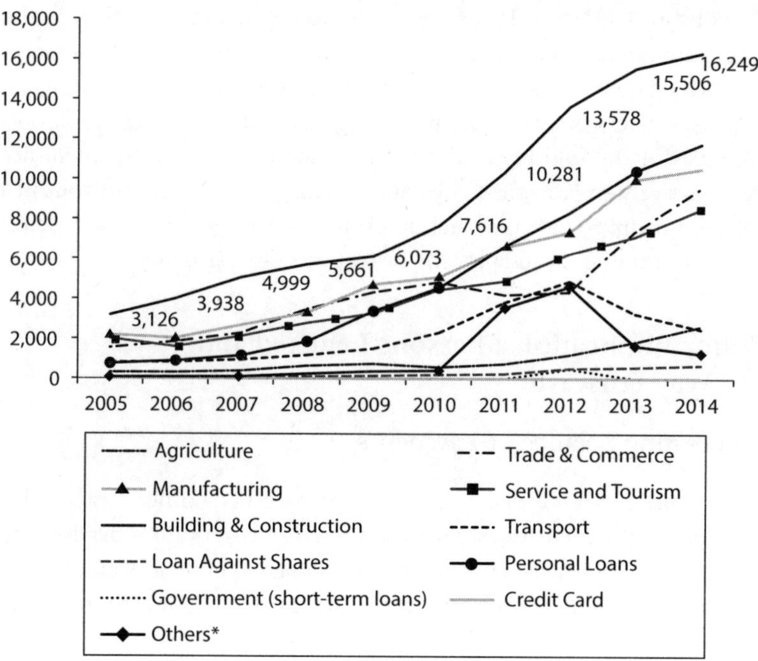

FIGURE 5.17 Financial Sector Investment by Economic Activity (Nu million)
Note: * Others include staff loans, Entrepreneur Development Programme, and Small Business and Artisans Scheme.
Source: RMA (2014b).

vehicles increased from 62,697 in 2011 to 67,449 in 2012, and further to 69,602 in 2014, with nearly two-thirds of all vehicles registered in Thimphu.[25] Disaggregated vehicle data show that the number of light vehicles imported slowed from 4,921 in 2011 to 3,104 in 2012.[26] However, this trend has reversed since the ban on vehicle import licenses was partially lifted in mid-2014.

Foreign workers in Bhutan are mainly engaged in the construction sector. Indian rupee outflows on account of these foreign workers are substantial. In terms of BOP accounting, these outflows are part of the invisible trade that contributes to the current account deficit. In 2011, the equivalent of Nu4.8 billion worth of Indian rupees was paid as remittances due for the wages and salaries of labourers and professionals from India. Therefore, about Nu5 billion worth of Indian rupees in the current account deficit is the result of Bhutanese nationals' unwillingness to work for the same wages as imported Indian workers. However, this is very unlikely to happen in the near future. For Bhutan's citizens, the substitute effect of leisure seems to dominate income effects at the wage rate offered to workers from India. On the other hand, adaptation to working conditions in construction projects could be made attractive to prospective workers through training and better housing conditions. One part of the solution to the current state of underemployment lies in proactively organizing a substantial number of Bhutanese youth to work on hydropower construction projects over the next decade. Their required training should precede hydropower investments.

Policy Implications: Lessons Learned and the Way Forward

Forecasting Balance of Payments

If the outflows of Indian rupees are greater than inflows, and after depleting foreign currency reserves, there are two options available to cope with a deepening current account deficit. The first is an increase in the borrowing of Indian rupees or hard currency to continue

[25] Data on vehicles are available at http://www.rsta.gov.bt/?page_id=81 (last accessed on 28 February 2015).

[26] This information is taken from personal communications with the Road Safety and Transport Authority on 6 August 2013.

financing the current account deficit. However, this will leave future governments and society with a mountain of debt and high debt service payments. Second, the ngultrum could be sharply devalued against the Indian rupee to arrest the deficit from growing any larger. If a one-time devaluation does not eliminate the deficit effectively, a dirty floating exchange rate can be adopted. Devaluation would make imported goods dear and choke import demand to an extent. It would be a painful process before the economy could be restructured. Not only would devaluation cause inflation in Bhutan to spike, it would also immediately increase Indian rupee debt service payments. Bhutan's external debt is mostly in the form of Indian rupees owed to the Government of India. The effect of devaluation on increasing rupee-denominated debt would be extremely serious. Devaluation by 20 per cent, for example, would increase debt service liabilities for both the Indian rupee and dollar-denominated debts by that proportion since more ngultrum per Indian rupee or US dollar would have to be exchanged. As the level of debt service increases, the revenue left for domestic expenditures would decline.

Foreign reserves can be drawn down to pay for the current account deficit when exports cannot cover them. While the government maintains information on its debt service schedule for the next five years, this information is not adequate if we wish to judge the expected level of stress on foreign reserves, for example, over the next 15 years. It is equally important to estimate the future stress on foreign reserves from multiple sources, including the current account deficit.

In general, foreign reserve holdings can change due to a combination of adjustments in the current, capital, and financial accounts.[27] Transactions in the current account comprise trade in goods and services. Foreign aid and hydropower investments affect the capital account. Short-term external borrowing (for example, from the State Bank of India) is under the financial account. The three different accounts should total up to reserve assets. A collation of the three accounts does give a rough estimate, but it does not add up to reserve assets due to statistical discrepancies.

[27] Clarifications on the distinctions between the three accounts and other comments provided by Hamid Rashid through personal communications on 23 July 2013.

The timing of outflows of foreign currency reserves needs to be methodically estimated by taking into account both debt servicing costs and the likely future size of the current account deficit at any given point in time. Only when there are reliable estimates of the two streams of outflows from foreign currency reserves can the level of foreign reserves be reliably estimated. The current state of information maintained by the government should be improved to show the level of outflows in terms of Indian rupees and US dollars over a longer time horizon. Currently, there is no systematic information on current account deficit scenarios over the next five years, although the RMA will be obliged to settle the current account deficit. This deficiency in generating information over a longer period of time compels the government and the RMA to undertake short-term reactions to the problem. They have to borrow hastily to finance current account deficits as evidenced by Indian rupee commercial borrowing in recent years, especially in 2012 and 2013.

The liabilities on international reserves arising from debt service payments over the next few years can be predicted. The horizon for debt service payments needs to be extended more precisely into the next decade and rough estimates are needed for the next two decades. Moreover, the pressure on currency reserves from the current account and financial accounts need to be anticipated with greater salience over the next five years at least. This has implications on international reserves level. Extrapolating from past trends, imports of goods and services from India will place even more demand on Indian rupee reserves in the future. Merchandise imports from India grew at an annual average rate of 17 per cent between 2001 and 2013. Rupee-denominated imports increased from Nu6.9 billion in 2001 to Nu43.6 billion in 2013, which is a spectacular rise that was also the result of structural changes in the economy.[28]

Indian rupee earnings and reserves should be forecast for a much longer period of time for two reasons. First, it is useful to assess the capacity for Indian rupee debt service payments. Second, it is useful to assess the capacity for Indian rupee financing of the current account deficit. Forecasting is difficult yet necessary. It should take into account

[28] See Department of Revenue and Customs (2014) for more details on trade with India.

probabilities of various factors including the likely level of the electricity tariff.[29] Income earned in Indian rupees from electricity exports adjusted for debt service repayment is a key element in export earnings. Changes in the scenarios of future Indian rupee earnings and reserve levels can be updated regularly by feeding information on changing circumstances with a bearing on many vital trends such as fuel and electricity prices, and construction material costs.

In the long term, hydropower investments will earn income in Indian rupees and foreign currency reserves will increase. But there is an overly optimistic view among decision-makers, without realistic quantitative assessment, about the extent of increases. Unfortunately, views that run counter to the rapid attainment of economic self-reliance based on hydropower revenue are too often rejected by decision-makers. By how much and when Indian rupee earnings will increase from hydropower revenue should be quantified with realistic assumptions over a longer time horizon, also taking account of a 250 per cent escalation in costs over the detailed project report with the associated negative consequences for debt servicing. Net Indian rupee earnings from hydropower after deducting the debt service payments must be carefully estimated for fiscal and monetary planning to be more effective. In 2011, Indian rupee earnings from hydropower electricity sales were the equivalent of Nu9.8 billion, while hydropower debt service payments totalled Nu3 billion. By 2014, hydropower export revenue had only increased to Nu10 billion, while petroleum product imports from India, which require payment in Indian rupees, reached the equivalent of Nu8.4 billion (KuenselOnline 2014).

[29] An example of a hazy view of a two-year time horizon is found in the RMA's Monetary Policy Statement from June 2012 (pp. 16–17). It should be substantial and predictive, but is incomplete. The numbers are presented as a percentage of GDP rather than absolute figures, which would be more useful. Furthermore, published GDP statistics comes out with a lag of one year or longer. The public has no access to absolute numbers until then. The estimates of GDP over the next Five-Year Plan period are done by the government's Macroeconomic Coordination Committee of the Ministry of Finance. Unfortunately, the framework is not accessible. For businesses and people to better situate their future plans, GDP data and compositional breakdowns would be very useful.

Arresting Terms of Trade Deterioration

While long-term structural conditions for earning Indian rupees can be improved through increased competitiveness, expenditure in general has to be redirected to domestically produced goods. The import-intensive consumption component of GDP has to be contained. Simultaneously, expenditure switching to domestic goods and expenditure reduction has to occur to bring both internal and external balance. Consumption—both government and private—is growing at a conspicuous rate. It was Nu24.1 billion in 2006, rose to Nu54.6 billion in 2011, and further to Nu78 billion in 2013.[30] Meanwhile, investment dropped to Nu49.3 billion in 2013 from Nu63.6 billion in 2012 (National Statistics Bureau 2014).

To contain the current account deficit, official policy has been to suppress import-oriented private consumption through taxation. However, this is unlikely to be effective even though it is currently the dominant view that shapes decision-making. Private consumption is not growing at a fast pace, unlike government consumption and investment. Changing the size and direction of government consumption and investment will be instrumental in containing current account deficits. Increasing import duties on certain items will reduce the current account deficit substantially if the goods have elastic demand (price elasticity of demand greater than one). It is doubtful whether this is the case with many privately imported consumption goods, such as cars, which are currently subject to high import taxes and therefore generate revenue for the government.[31] Ultimately, it is not import taxes on selective private goods that will make a difference in the current account deficit, but rather how over

[30] However, the estimates from various agencies of the government need major improvement in order to have confidence in them. Statistical discrepancies in the National Statistics Bureau estimates of the consumption component of GDP between 2006 and 2010 are so large that conclusions must be drawn cautiously. For example, in 2007 consumption was estimated to be Nu28.9 billion but statistical discrepancy was Nu1.3 billion.

[31] The motor vehicle tax contributed revenue of Nu177.5 million in FY2012 up from Nu117 million in FY2008, while the green tax imposed will add another Nu3 million annually, assuming that more than 3,000 light vehicles are imported per year.

all government expenditure can be switched to domestic products. Government consumption is significant within Bhutan's economy. Therefore, attention to fiscal policy in terms of expenditure efficiency, expenditure reduction, and expenditure switching to domestically produced goods has to be the focus far more than how to raise taxes to match rising recurrent expenditure. This naturally takes the discussion to fiscal and monetary policies as they relate to the Indian rupee shortage.

Curtailing Monetary Expansion

Monetary and fiscal policies used to address macroeconomic stability, including inflation and the current account deficit, seem ineffective. The cash reserve ratio for banks was raised for a short period to control credit directly and to control the current account deficit indirectly. But this effort was not sustained. The cash reserve ratio fell from 23.1 per cent in 2012 to 18.7 per cent at the end of 2013. It was further brought down to 13.8 per cent in October 2014. The cash reserve ratio cannot be a very effective way to control credit, regardless of the rates, because the RMA permits banks to buy Treasury bills using their cash reserve ratio. Thus, the aims of the cash reserve ratio—to reduce the money supply, control credit and inflation, and contain current account deficit—are undermined.

The issuance of Treasury bills has raised money for the government. Outstanding government debt stood at Nu3.1 billion at the end of FY2011, Nu16.4 billion at the end FY2013, and Nu2.8 billion at the end of FY2014 based on revised figures provided in the national budget report for 2014–15. For the purpose of analysing credit control, money borrowed by the government through Treasury bills and the amount of debt outstanding at the end of the year is not an adequate enough measure. The figures above give the end-of-the-year debt stock of the government. What should also be considered is the cumulative borrowing over the course of a year, including short-term debt that has been repaid. The total turnover of Treasury bills, which is several fold greater than the end-of-the-year debt stock, has an impact on M2 increase and, hence, credit creation. Credit creation correspondingly has an impact on imports from India.

In Bhutan, one major area of investment through bank borrowing is private urban housing construction. For the last 50 years, lending by the banking sector has been mainly channelled towards urban growth. At present, financial institutions supply a negligible amount of credit to rural sector.[32] Rapid urbanization came about due to two fundamental economic factors: easier credit and cheaper imported labour. As shown earlier, the Indian rupee shortage in 2012 was also caused partly by a sudden boom in construction in Thimphu. According to the National Urbanization Strategy, 2005, there are 60 urban sites throughout the country waiting for credit. The proliferation of designated urban sites will stimulate credit demand and the need for imported building materials, which will further strain Indian rupee reserves. Therefore, the National Urbanization Strategy, 2005 needs to be re-examined also from this perspective.

Measures taken in response to the Indian rupee shortage moderated the growth of certain key monetary variables. The control of growth of M2, the measure of broad money, has been fairly effective as it did not expand much in the two years following the imposition of tightening measures.[33] However, this has not translated into control of domestic credit expansion or resulted in a solution to the Indian rupee shortage. A variety of instruments to control domestic credit have been applied yet domestic credit remains on an upward trajectory. Domestic credit was Nu53.4 billion in March 2013 up from Nu45.3 billion in March 2012. The money supply is a product of the money multiplier and high-powered money that includes reserves. Since the money supply as measured by M2, or for that matter M1, has not increased significantly, it is the money multiplier, along with

[32] Credit disbursed to the agriculture sector has usually comprised about 2 per cent of the total, the lowest among all sectors.

[33] It is not clear at this stage as to which measure of money fits the best definition in the context of Bhutan. Supply and demand functions for money have to be modelled to understand their behavioural functions in the context of Bhutan. Simple regression models can be used to estimate the parameters of the relevant independent variables with the objective of leading us to better monetary planning and policy.

the variables that affect it, that has to be targeted more clearly.[34] The money multiplier depends on the behaviour of the public and the banks.[35] Much more quantitative work with a view towards building predictive frameworks and analytic interpretation of the data is needed for policy purposes.

The sterilization of inflows to temper temporary ups and downs in liquidity in the financial system is another measure that should be considered. When the stock of Indian rupees increases in the RMA's reserves due to grants from India and hydropower investment, a counterbalancing amount of ngultrum is injected into the banking system, which increases M2 and domestic credit. To offset this monetary expansion, a certain amount of Indian rupee reserves could be maintained outside Bhutan's banking system for a certain period by opening a subsidiary the BOB in Delhi and in the nearby Indian towns of Siliguri and Bongaigoan. This would reduce M2 and domestic credit creation and make the Indian rupee easily available in BOB subsidiary banks in India for account holders to settle transactions directly.

Exercising control over monetary variables should involve paying close attention on the questions of seigniorage profit, made by issuing currency, and inflation tax. The United Nations Department of Economics and Social Affairs estimated that when seigniorage profit and inflation tax are added together, it comprised 7.3 per cent of GDP in FY2011. Seigniorage revenue should be 3–4 per cent of GDP. Excessive seigniorage revenue is a factor that can contribute to undermining the currency peg.

Containing Fiscal Expansion

In terms of fiscal expansion, the volume of government expenditure is likely to increase on average by about 15 per cent annually based on the long-term trend. At the same time, hydropower investments in the six projects, which are considered off-budget, that have either started construction or are likely to begin construction soon will require

[34] M1 comprises all physical money, such as coins and currency, as well as demand deposits. M1 measures the most liquid components of the money supply, including cash and assets that can quickly be converted into currency.

[35] See Gaudel (2003) for background on the monetary system of Nepal.

significantly increased expenditure. The exact amount invested each year in the hydropower sector will depend on the number of projects that will begin every year. The total expenditure (government expenditure plus hydro-investment in any given year) can be calculated depending on the cost escalation and the staggering of hydropower project construction schedule.[36] Such exercises should further inform decisions on the link between Indian rupee reserve scenarios and total expenditure in the economy.

An increase in expenditure (E) will lead to current account deficit of a magnitude that depends on the absorption capacity of the economy. Absorption capacity is identically equal to E = C + I + G, where C is consumption, I is investment, and G is government consumption. Total spending is usually summed in GDP, though it would be preferable to use gross disposable national income in the case of Bhutan.[37] Rearranging the identity, absorption rate is given by GDP – E = X – M, where X is exports and M is imports of goods and services. As spending rises, spending on domestic goods rises but at a rate far less than GDP growth. This is because part of income is saved but an overwhelming part of it is spent on imports.[38] An expenditure increase will lead to a GDP increase but given the high marginal propensity to import and high money multiplier, it will lead to a current account deficit that will not be fully covered by grants and capital inflows in hydropower investments. If current account deficit and consequent Indian rupee shortage are to be alleviated, expenditure switching to domestic goods has to be pursued vigorously.

One of the main factors for Bhutan's phenomenal fiscal expansion has been the increase in the size of civil service as well as the periodic

[36] Different scenarios give rise to different policy options for debt stock, debt repayment, and revenue streams.

[37] While gross national disposable income is the most appropriate measure of spending for Bhutan (it is 11 per cent–15 per cent higher than GDP because of relatively large transfers to Bhutan), we use GDP in this example.

[38] Bhutan's GDP was Nu85 billion in 2011 when its current account deficit was Nu25 billion. GDP in 2013 rose to Nu104 billion with a current account deficit of about Nu22 billion. Efforts were made to contain its expansions by banning loans for personal vehicles and housing. These restriction were eased in mid-2014.

pay hikes for the civil service and employees of public commercial corporations. The civil service has grown by about 5 per cent annually since the early 2000s. This seems modest on an annual basis but over that period, the size of civil service has more than doubled. The increase in wages and salary and ancillary expenditures has been largely responsible for the fiscal expansion that leads to wage-push inflation. The reduction in the size of the civil service is a current initiative of the government. Control of the wage–price spiral is another initiative that needs to be launched. If not, public sector employment will continue to impose huge costs on society.[39]

Addressing High Inflation

Inflation has had a corrosive effect on living standards. The ngultrum has lost 45 per cent of its value since the early 2000s, yet nominal income has not increased by 45 per cent over the same period. Inflation has a distorting effect on different strata of society and economic sectors because its effects are not equal. It also acts as a disincentive for time deposits and savings. There has been no noticeable growth in the size of time deposits since 2010.

The transmission of inflation from India cannot explain the divergence in core inflation between India and Bhutan. Excessive monetary growth on one hand and huge fiscal expansion on the other have led to an inflationary situation. If the Consumer Price Index were more sensitive, it would show that the current account deficit has grown due to a shift in the demand from non-traded goods to import substitutes, which are cheaper even after taxes, trade, and transport margins.[40]

[39] The pension system will go bankrupt in 2033 under the present system and a substantial injection of public resources will be needed to keep it operational, as reported by the Ministry of Finance in the National Budget presented to Parliament in June 2014.

[40] The CPI is overly extensive in the breadth of goods and services included. The Indian consumer basket, for example, has 260 items while Bhutan's has 438 items. The overall effect of weighted averaging over so many items is that core inflation is most likely underestimated. Bhutan needs to reconsider the basket and weights so that changes in the cost of living can be tracked appropriately for policy purposes.

Factors related to inflation and terms of trade deterioration should be addressed at a more fundamental level through broader economic planning. In support of assessing terms of trade deterioration, there is also a need to compose and launch an export price index and in import price index to assess terms of trade. It can be done quickly for a small economy, perhaps by identifying the top 50 export and import items.

Neither lowering inflation nor improving the terms of trade deterioration is presently considered a major policy objective, nor are addressing the deeper structural causes of Indian rupee shortage. Inflation and a wage spiral will make the economy uncompetitive. Wage–cost inflation has led to higher prices of export goods because the high labour share of value added in any exported good is quite high. Typical export goods from Bhutan consist of agricultural products, raw minerals, mineral-based products, and electricity. All of these export goods, except electricity, contain a high labour share.

The inflationary situation is the main bargaining point for higher wages, especially in the public sector. Any hike in wages in the public sector is essentially being paid for by hydropower revenue. The competitiveness of basic chemical industries like cement manufacturing or steel rolling have been gained by cheaper domestic electricity prices for these industries. Yet the prices of major exports have not been rising fast enough compared to the prices of major imports, leading to a severe deterioration in the terms of trade. As an example, the export price of a unit of electricity has not gone up much in the last decade although the price of fuel has gone up very sharply in the same period. The lessons for what can maximize export earnings is not necessarily to expand output but to pay much greater attention to value maximization. The basic thrust has to be the improvement of labour productivity across the major sectors through the upgrading of skills and technology. Labour productivity can increase as a result of the accumulation of manual experience and technological progress. The application of appropriate technology is vital for increasing labour productivity. Currently, not much attention is being paid to the selection and diffusion of technologies that can enhance labour productivity in agriculture, manufacturing, and construction. There is considerable focus on the adoption of virtual communications technology. More focus ought to be given to machinery and tools that can enhance productivity in the agriculture, small-scale artisan business, and construction sectors. The government's recent establishment of a Business Opportunities and Information Centre that gives loans for rural enterprises is a step in this direction.

★★★

Changes in the capital, current, and financial accounts affect the foreign currency reserves. Better estimations of the likely burden on foreign currency reserves arising from all three accounts over a longer period of time are needed. The current practice has been to estimate debt service payments on the capital account only (usually over the next five years only).

The forecasting of capital inflows during the construction period of a hydropower project and the estimation of construction costs need to be sharpened. The amount of Indian rupees that will flow out to repay the debt contracted for hydropower projects has a critical impact on the Indian rupee reserves and government revenue. It is not only the amount but also the timing of outflows and inflows that matters. Mismatches between outflows and inflows have to be estimated on an annual basis, if not a shorter period.

The current account balance has not improved. How much it will worsen should be forecasted and quantified in order to find ways of improving it. Assessing the size of the current account deficit has become a critical exercise to be undertaken. Macroeconomic difficulties the country faces arise from the high marginal propensity to import (about 0.63 according to our estimate) and the high money multiplier (2.9 according to the RMA estimate).[41] It also arises from a lack of competitiveness due to rising inflation, high costs of production, high capital costs, and a lack of technology.

The Government of Bhutan has been a major borrower from the banking system. Monetary and fiscal policy can usually be managed independently. The distinction depends on whether the fiscal deficit is financed by the sale of Treasury bills to the public or by the sale of

[41] This estimation of marginal propensity to import is not completely reliable as there are data errors in trade statistics, most likely in terms of a substantial underestimation of imports.

Treasury bills to banks via the RMA. It appears that there is not much distinction between monetary and fiscal policy when it comes to financing the fiscal deficit in Bhutan. Banks are the main buyers of Treasury bills and, thus, budget deficits contribute to growth in the money supply and credit creation.[42] In fact, a bank's cash reserve ratio is used to buy Treasury bills. The effect of borrowing through overdrafts and Treasury bills has been substantial. The government needs to lower its impact on the domestic credit market.

A budget deficit financed by borrowing from the banking system leads to an equivalent loss of credit for private investors. Crowding out the private sector is a reality repeatedly attested to by complaints from the Bhutan Chamber of Commerce and Industry about a lack of available credit.

Credit indicators point to tightening liquidity. The credit-to-asset ratio has jumped to 75 per cent and the credit-to-deposit ratio now exceeds 100 per cent. The growth of credit has been matched by aggressive borrowing by several big investors since 2010. A lesson from the recent rupee shortage is that big projects, which depend on large amounts of credit from financial institutions in Bhutan, should not be concentrated within the same time period as this leads to tightened liquidity and a shortage of rupees. Urban expansion, such as the development under way in Thimphu since 2010, led to a jump in lending for construction-related imports and also contributed significantly to Indian rupee shortage. In an economy with a high marginal propensity to import that is extremely open towards India, expanded credit leads to rising imports and an Indian rupee shortage.

[42] The stock of the budget deficit measured at the end of the budget year gives a different picture from the turnover of overdrafts the government took from banks in that budget year. In the FY2013 budget, the deficit was about Nu4 billion. However, the amount borrowed through 90-day Treasury bills from banks and repaid in the same budget year was nearly Nu13 billion, which is a huge amount considering total credit was Nu53 billion during the same year. In FY2015, the government borrowed Nu9 billion through 90-day Treasury bills for cash management purposes. In addition, it was projected that the government would borrow Nu4.8 billion from domestic banks, though this would not be redeemed in the same fiscal year. The combined effect of Treasury bill operations in such large amounts and bank borrowing for longer periods of time has an enormous impact on domestic credit creation.

References

Boundless Economics. 2014. *The GDP Deflator*. Available at https://www.boundless.com (last accessed on 13 February 2015).

Cook, S.T. and P.M. Jackson. 1979. *Current Issues in Fiscal Policy.* Bath: The Pitman Press.

Corden, W. M. 1981. *Inflation Exchange Rates and the World Economy Lectures on the International Monetary Economics*. Oxford: Clarendon Press.

Department of Revenue and Customs. 2014. *Bhutan Trade Statistics 2013*. Thimphu.

———. 2014. *National Revenue Report 2013–14*. Thimphu.

Dornbusch, R. 1980. *Open Economy Macroeconomics*. New York: Basic Books.

Goodhart, C.A.E. 1984. *Monetary Theory and Practice: The UK Experience*. New York: Macmillan Publishers Limited.

Gaudel, Y.S. 2003. *Monetary System of Nepal*. Delhi: Adroit Publishers.

Gross National Happiness Commission. 2013. *11th Five-Year Plan of Bhutan*. Thimphu: Royal Government of Bhutan. http://www.gnhc.gov.bt/wp-content/uploads/2011/04/Eleventh-Five-Year-Plan.pdf (last accessed on 21 May 2014).

KuenselOnline. *Bhutan in 2014*. http://www.kuenselonline.com (last accessed on 28 December 2014).

Ministry of Agriculture and Forests. 2007. *Commodity Chain Analysis: Potato*. Thimphu.

———. 2013. *National Budget for the Financial Year 2013–2014*.Thimphu.

———. 2014. *National Budget for the Financial Year 2014–2015*.Thimphu.

Ministry of Labour and Human Resources. 2012. *National Labour Force Survey 2012*. Thimphu.

Ministry of Works and Human Settlement. 2008. *Bhutan National Urbanization Strategy*. Thimphu.

National Statistics Bureau. 2004. *Poverty Analysis Report 2003*. http://www.nsb.gov.bt/publication/files/pub4kf7409pu.pdf (last accessed on 25 May 2014).

———. 2007. *Poverty Analysis Report 2007*. http://www.nsb.gov.bt/news/news_detail.php?id=98&task=view (last accessed on 16 May 2014).

———. 2012. *National Accounts Statistics 2012*. Thimphu.

———. 2013a. *National Accounts Statistics 2013*. Thimphu.

———. 2013b. *Poverty Analysis Report 2012*.Thimphu.

———. 2013c. *Statistical Year Book of Bhutan 2013*. http://www.nsb.gov.bt/publication/files/pub9ot4338yv.pdf (last accessed on 15 May 2014).

———. 2014. *National Accounts Statistics 2014*. Thimphu.

Rashid, H. 2012. *Understanding the Causes of the Rupee Shortfall: A Macroeconomic Policy Challenge for Bhutan and the Way Forward*. New York: United Nations Department of Economics and Social Affairs.

Rickards, J. 2011. *Currency Wars: The Making of the Next Global Crisis*. London: Macmillan Press.

Road Safety and Transport Authority. Vehicle Statistics. Available at http://www.rsta.gov.bt/?page_id=81 (last accessed on 28 December 2013).

Roder, W., K. Nidup, and G.B. Chettri. 2008. *Potato in Bhutan*. Thimphu: Ministry of Agriculture of Forests.

Royal Government of Bhutan. 2012. *Task Force Report on the Balance of Payments with India and Rupee Shortage*. Thimphu.

———. n.d. *Accelerating Bhutan's Socio-Economic Development*. Available at http://www.gnhc.gov.bt/absd/?page_id=93 (last accessed on 16 December 2015).

———. 2013. *National Budget Financial Year 2013–14*. Thimphu: Ministry of Finance.

———. 2014. *National Budget Financial Year 2014–15*. Thimphu: Ministry of Finance.

Royal Monetary Authority of Bhutan (RMA). 2003. *Selected Economic Indicators*. Thimphu.

———. 2007. *Selected Economic Indicators*. Thimphu.

———. 2012. *Selected Economic Indicators 2012*. Thimphu.

———. 2013. *Annual Report 2011–2012*.Thimphu.

———. 2014a. *Selected Economic Indicators 2013*. Thimphu.

———. 2014b. *Annual Report 2013–2014*.Thimphu.

———. 2015. *Monthly Statistical Bulletin*. January. Thimphu.

Sharma, G.D. 2013. Compilation of Consumer Price Indices and Wholesale Price Index in India. Available at http://www.unescap.org/stat/meet/keyindic/india_cpi_wpi.pdf (last accessed on 4 January 2014).

Sharma, G.Y. 2003. *Monetary System of Nepal*. Delhi: Adroit Publishers.

The Bhutanese. 2013. 'RMA Sells Another $200 m to Meet Rupee Loan Commitments', 29 June.

Tourism Council of Bhutan. 2012. *Bhutan Tourism Monitor 2012*. Thimphu.

———. 2013. *Bhutan Tourism Monitor 2013*. Thimphu.

Trevithick, J.A. 1981. *Inflation a Guide to the Crisis in Economics*. New York: Penguin Books.

Ura, K. 2015. Debt and Vulnerability. Lecture delivered at the Royal Institute of Governance and Strategic Studies. Thimphu. 19 March.

World Bank. 2014. *Doing Business*. Available at http://www.doingbusiness.org/reports/global-reports/doing-business-2014 (last accessed on 4 January 2015).

______. n.d. World Development Indicators. Available at http://data.worldbank.org/data-catalog/world-development-indicators (last accessed on 4 January 2015).

6

HWEE KWAN CHOW

Monetary Policy Framework for the Royal Government of Bhutan

This chapter is aimed at developing forecast models for monetary aggregates in Bhutan. The projections of monetary aggregates generated by the forecast models would serve as inputs to Bhutan's monetary and economic authorities in the annual planning process. Forecast models were constructed in close collaboration with the monetary team in the Royal Monetary Authority of Bhutan (RMA).

To this end, a field study was conducted in Thimphu during 11–13 May 2015 and feedback on the consultancy report was received during a presentation at the Inception and Training Workshop on Economic Surveillance for the Royal Government of Bhutan in Paro on 28 August 2015.

The following topics were discussed with the monetary team at the RMA: (i) the monetary framework adopted by the RMA; (ii) the constraints and risks they face with the current monetary system; and (iii) plans and intentions regarding the system's evolution. In addition, Eviews[1] computer sessions were conducted over two days, during which the monetary team provided inputs on the underlying factors driving the behaviour of the monetary aggregate series. A preliminary

[1] Eviews is a statistical computer package whereby modelling and forecasting can be done through a user-friendly, object-based interface.

analysis of the data was carried out with the team and various potential forecast models were explored. Demonstrations were also held on the use of Eviews to generate predictions from the different forecast models and to evaluate forecast accuracy.

The structure of this chapter is as follows. The next section reviews the current monetary framework and monetary transmission process in Bhutan. The third section 'Data and Patterns in Monetary Aggregates' begins the empirical analysis with a description of the data patterns in the monetary aggregates M1 and M2.[2] These monthly series exhibit an upward trend over the period 2003–14. As in usual practice, we first take the log transformation of each series, which are individually tested for seasonal patterns. The section 'Univariate Time Series Models of Monetary Aggregates' discusses unit root tests and univariate time series models suitable for the series. We find log(M1) has a deterministic trend and log(M2) has a stochastic trend. Apart from adding relevant seasonal dummies to the trend terms, the optimal autoregressive moving average model is chosen for each series.

The univariate time series models forecast the monetary aggregate series using their own past values only. We next explore using information from other related variables to forecast the monetary aggregates. In the case of monetary aggregate M2, we show in the section 'Error Correction Model of Monetary Aggregate M2' that it has a cointegrating relationship with its key disaggregate series, net foreign assets, and domestic credit. Hence, we build an error correction model that includes relevant seasonal dummies as an alternative forecast model for this series. In consideration of the short time span for which data are available, all of the models considered were kept simple and parsimonious.

In the sections 'Forecast Evaluation of Monetary Aggregate M1' and 'Forecast Evaluation of Monetary Aggregate M2', we examine the predictive accuracy of the individual forecast models and a comparison

[2] M1 comprises all physical money, such as coins and currency, as well as demand deposits. M1 measures the most liquid components of the money supply, including cash and assets that can quickly be converted into currency. M2 refers to the total amount of currency outside banks, demand deposits, savings deposits, time deposits, and foreign currency deposits held by authorized foreigners (for example, diplomats), M2 constitutes the supply of money.

is made across the different models. The forecast evaluations in the former section suggest the univariate time series model is suited for the prediction of M1 both one month and one year in the future. In comparison, the forecast evaluations in the latter section suggest that the univariate time series model is only useful for producing one-step ahead predictions of M2. The error correction model has better predictive ability when forecasting M2 multi-steps ahead. The last section concludes with remarks on model updates and a summary table of the recommended forecast models for monetary aggregates.

Review of Monetary Framework and Transmission Process

Bhutan has a fixed exchange rate system with its currency, the ngultrum, pegged at par to the Indian rupee. This serves as a nominal anchor as the country pursues the broader objective of price stability. Apart from instilling confidence in the ngultrum, the currency peg provides domestic firms with a more stable trading environment and enables them to retain their cost-competitiveness. This is important in view of the close trade and financial ties between Bhutan and India. In addition, India is an important development partner providing Bhutan with loans and grants, particularly for the development of hydropower plants.

However, as a consequence of the currency peg, the exchange rate cannot be used as an instrument for macroeconomic adjustments, particularly for offsetting shocks to the economy. In fact, the RMA's ability to pursue independent monetary policy is curtailed since the domestic economy is influenced by economic and monetary conditions in India. For instance, it is likely that the inflation rate in Bhutan is partially determined by inflationary conditions in India. Imported inflation plays an important role in determining inflation in Bhutan. Nonetheless, with reference to the policy dilemma, the use of capital controls on both inflows and outflows, as well as prudential measures, confer Bhutan some degree of monetary autonomy in determining its domestic interest rate.

In the conduct of monetary policy, the RMA uses a variety of monetary policy tools. These include employing direct instruments such as the cash reserve ratio and statutory liquidity ratio to target the reserve base in the banking system, which can ultimately influence the money supply in Bhutan. These instruments are the main policy tools employed to smooth out erratic liquidity conditions caused by structural or long-term factors. Direct measures and administrative interventions are useful, especially when the central bank needs to promptly adjust bank liquidity in the absence of well-developed markets.

The central bank has also made concerted efforts to shift towards the use of market-based monetary policy instruments. In 2012, the RMA introduced a lending facility called the Short-Term Liquidity Adjustment Window (STLAW). Commercial banks can access short-term funds from the RMA through STLAW to meet their short-term outstanding liabilities or for day-to-day operations. In this way, the banking system can react quickly to unanticipated liquidity demands and permit orderly adjustments to reserve shortages. The development of a short-term government securities market will be useful as these securities can serve as collateral. The RMA has been issuing 90-day Treasury bills on an irregular basis when the government needs to raise funds for fiscal purposes. Currently, it is working with the Ministry of Finance in establishing a debt issuance calendar.

Two other market-based measures were introduced in 2012: the policy rate and the base rate. The policy rate is intended to be the primary monetary policy tool. When STLAW was first introduced, the rate charged for using the facility was defined at 100 basis points above the policy rate. The base rate is the lowest interest rate at which it is feasible for financial institutions to lend as this lending rate is computed to reflect their cost of funds. Financial institutions periodically announce their base rates to the public, thereby increasing the transparency of lending rates. This has also resulted in greater competition among banks for deposits as reflected in the movements of bank deposit rates. The intention is for the base rate to serve as a benchmark rate for floating rate loans. In this way, the RMA can signal monetary policy tightening or loosening through the base rate system. Nonetheless, there appears to be interest rate rigidity as domestic interest rates have remained stable over time. A well-functioning interest rate transmission channel, which is necessary for the effective implementation of monetary policy, is in turn predicated on the development of the money market and the interbank market.

Until recently, the RMA had been focusing its efforts on addressing tight domestic liquidity conditions related to the Indian rupee crisis.

The severe shortage of Indian rupees arose from external imbalances and the currency composition of Bhutan's foreign reserves. Despite a rising trend in exports, particularly hydropower exports, large trade deficits emerged over the last couple of years. Even though Bhutan had ample foreign exchange reserves through the receipt of aid inflows and hydropower financing, primarily from India, the bulk of these reserves were in convertible currencies. Consequently, there was a drain on local currency liquidity as rupee reserves were insufficient to meet rupee liquidity needs. In addition to securing alternative financing instruments, temporary loan restrictions were imposed to curb consumption-related demand for Indian rupees. At the same time, the government rationalized its expenditures and introduced new revenue-raising measures. These measures and the use of monetary policy tools eased domestic liquidity and brought relief to the building pressures on rupee reserves. At present, adjustments to the currency composition of Bhutan's reserves are being made.

The RMA continues to take proactive steps in developing its capacity to formulate monetary policy. To this end, the central bank is building a liquidity monitoring framework. This entails determining the key factors driving liquidity developments in the domestic banking system and obtaining timely information on these factors. The Asian Development Bank (ADB) has provided the RMA with a template that can facilitate liquidity monitoring and allow the RMA to make prompt adjustments to undesirable developments in the reserve base of the banking system.

As Bhutan's economy develops, its markets will expand and increase their links to external markets. In this process, direct monetary controls will become less effective and it is therefore important for the RMA to develop indirect controls. In particular, the use of open market operations will give the central bank more flexibility to launch monetary operations at its own initiative in terms of both the timing and volume of operations. One approach is to target a particular interest rate level and allow the amount of reserves to fluctuate. For this approach to work, developed and sensitive markets, particularly the interbank market and short-term securities market, are necessary to transmit the monetary policy impulses. As commercial banks will manage their bank reserves through interbank trading of short-term securities, interest rates will become market-determined. This will help channel changes in the policy rate towards the base rate and onward to other interest rates. The attendant adjustments of deposit and lending rates by financial institutions will have some influence on the level of savings and investment in the domestic economy. In other words, well-developed markets with large and continuous trading volumes and diverse participants can facilitate the effectual working of the interest rate transmission channel, which will in turn increase the effectiveness of monetary policy.

Data and Patterns in Monetary Aggregates

Table 6.1 shows a list of variables provided by the monetary team from the RMA and used in this report. They are Bhutan's monetary aggregates, M1 and M2, and the key components of net foreign assets and domestic credit.

Time Plots of Monetary Aggregate Series

A preliminary data analysis was conducted on each individual variable. We examined the time plots for general patterns in the data series. Figure 6.1 is a time plot of Bhutan's monetary aggregates (M1 and M2). Although monthly data are available from 1997, a major reclassification of all economic sectors could have resulted in a structural break. Hence, we start the sample from 2003. We observe that both M1 and M2 have a general upward trend. Narrow money (M1) was at Nu7,700 in January 2003 and rose to Nu43,300 in December 2014. The corresponding numbers for broad money (M2) were Nu14,600 and Nu73,400, respectively. The summary statistics of the year-on-year growth rates of the

TABLE **6.1** Data Series for Bhutan

Name of Series	Frequency: Period	Comments
Monetary aggregates (M1 and M2)	Monthly: 1997–2014	Structural break before 2003 To analysis from 2003 onwards
Net Foreign Asset	Monthly: 2003–14	
Domestic Credit	Monthly: 2003–14	

Source: Author's Compilation.

TABLE 6.2 Descriptive Statistics of Monetary Aggregate Growth Rates

Summary Statistic	M1 Annual Growth Rate (%)	M2 Annual Growth Rate (%)
Mean	18.66	15.95
Median	16.34	13.93
Maximum	75.54	56.65
Minimum	–23.23	–11.45
Std. Dev.	16.52	12.48

Source: Author's Calculations.

monetary aggregates for the period January 2003–December 2014 are presented in Table 6.2.

We observe from Figure 6.1 an exponential trend in both monetary aggregates. Since we are working with linear models, we take the logarithmic transformation of the series. The time plots of log(M1) and log(M2) are shown in Figure 6.2.

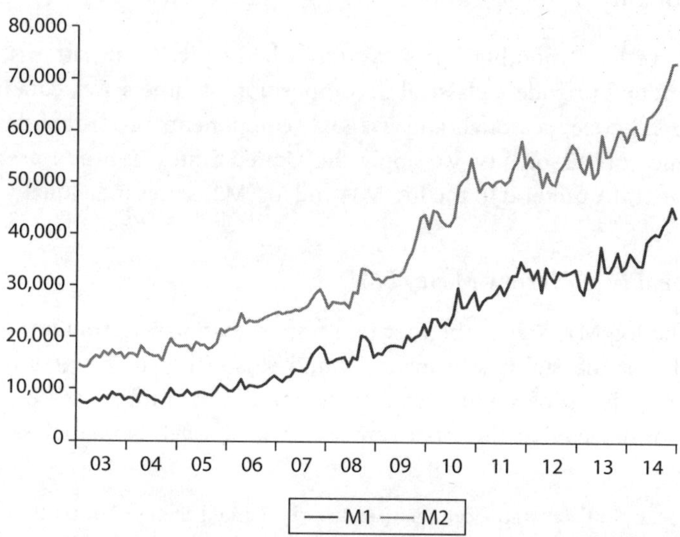

FIGURE 6.1 Monetary Aggregates M1 and M2
Source: Author's Calculations.

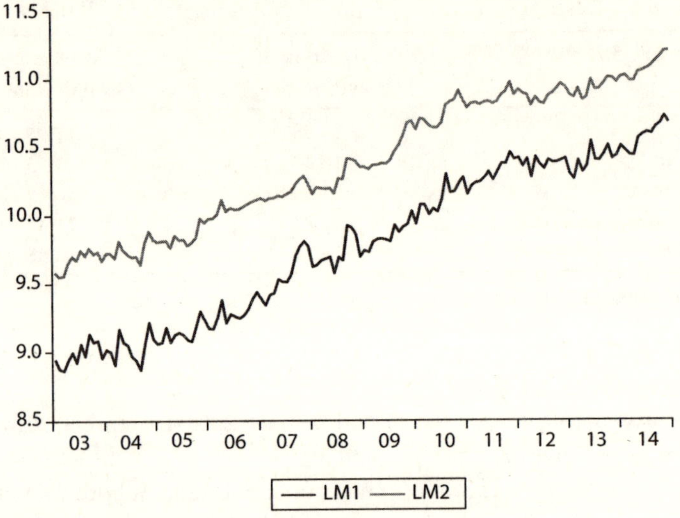

FIGURE 6.2 Log Transformations log(M1) and log(M2)
Source: Author's Calculations.

Seasonality Tests of Monetary Aggregate Series

Since we have monthly series, we test whether seasonal patterns are present and provide a classical decomposition of time series data into the trend-cycle, seasonal, and irregular components. To establish the presence of seasonality, we apply the United States Census Bureau's X-12 ARIMA method to the log(M1) and log(M2) series individually.[3]

Seasonality of Narrow Money LM1

For the log(M1) series, the first two tests shown in Eviews Output 1, which assume stable seasonality, found seasonality to be present at very high levels of significance. At the same time, moving seasonality was not detected at the 5 per cent significance level. Nonetheless, the

[3] Many official statistical agencies use the United States Census Bureau's X-12 seasonal adjustment programme or its variants to remove the seasonal component from data series. For details on this programme, see United States Census Bureau (2006).

Eviews Output 1: Seasonality Tests for log(M1) Series

D 8.A F-tests for seasonality

Test for the presence of seasonality assuming stability.

	Sum of Squares	Degrees of Freedom	Mean Square	F-Value
Between months	0.1205	11	0.01095	3.412**
Residual	0.4237	132	0.00321	
Total	0.5442	143		

**Seasonality present at the 0.1 per cent level.

Non-parametric Test for the Presence of Seasonality Assuming Stability

Kruskal-Wallis Statistic	Degrees of Freedom	Probability Level
38.9192	11	0.005%

Seasonality present at the one per cent level.

Moving Seasonality Test

	Sum of Squares	Degrees of Freedom	Mean Square	F-value
Between Years	0.0251	11	0.002286	1.637
Error	0.1690	121	0.001396	

No evidence of moving seasonality at the five per cent level.

COMBINED TEST FOR THE PRESENCE OF IDENTIFIABLE SEASONALITY

IDENTIFIABLE SEASONALITY PROBABLY NOT PRESENT

*** CONDITIONALLY ACCEPTED *** at the level 1.00

FIGURE **6.3** Eviews Output 1
Source: Author's Calculations.

combined test concluded that identifiable seasonality is probably not present. This is likely due to the large irregular component in the series that masks the seasonal pattern.

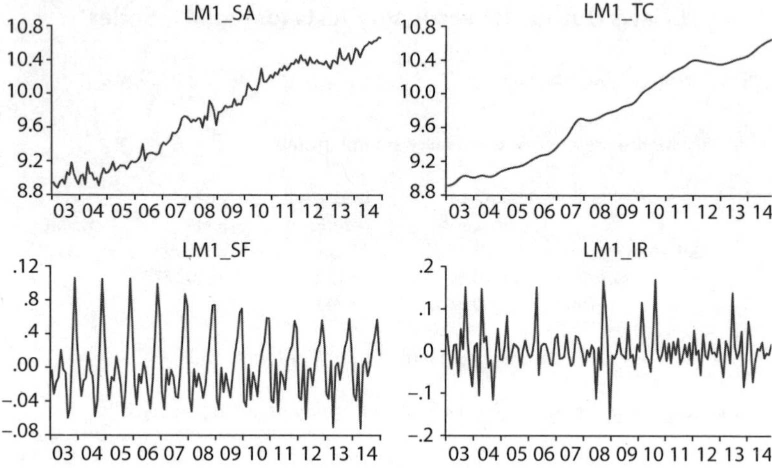

FIGURE 6.4 Components of log(M1) Series
Source: Author's Calculations.

In terms of the quality control statistics, the seasonal adjustment is also conditionally accepted with the overall Q-statistics at one. Figure 6.4 depicts the seasonality adjusted series LM1_SA produced by the procedure along with its trend-cycle (LM1_TC), seasonal factors (LM1_SF), and irregular (LM1_IR) components.

Seasonality of Broad Money log(M2)

In comparison, the results from the seasonality tests on log(M2) clearly show the presence of the seasonal component (Eviews Output 2). Identifiable seasonality is present despite the detection of moving seasonality at the 5 per cent significance level. Further, the seasonal adjustment is clearly accepted with the overall quality control Q-statistic at 0.58. The seasonally adjusted series LM2_SA, trend-cycle (LM2_TC), seasonal factors (LM2_SF), and irregular (LM2_IR) components are graphed in Figure 6.6.

In summary, both narrow and broad money in Bhutan exhibited seasonal patterns in the period 2003–14. Therefore, we have to take into account the seasonal component when we model the monetary

Eviews Output 2: Seasonality Tests for log(M2) Series

D 8.A F-tests for seasonality

Test for the presence of seasonality assuming stability.

	Sum of Squares	Degrees of Freedom	Mean Square	F-Value
Between months	0.1122	11	0.01020	8.491**
Residual	0.1586	132	0.00120	
Total	0.2708	143		

**Seasonality present at the 0.1 per cent level.

Non-parametric Test for the Presence of Seasonality Assuming Stability

Kruskal-Wallis Statistic	Degrees of Freedom	Probability Level
61.2542	11	0.000%

Seasonality present at the one per cent level.

Moving Seasonality Test

	Sum of Squares	Degrees of Freedom	Mean Square	F-value
Between Years	0.0115	11	0.001042	2.027
Error	0.0622	121	0.000514	

Moving seasonality present at the five per cent level.

COMBINED TEST FOR THE PRESENCE OF IDENTIFIABLE SEASONALITY

*** ACCEPTED *** at the level 0.58

FIGURE **6.5** Eviews Output 2
Source: Author's Calculations.

aggregates in the following sections. Otherwise, the models will not be a good representation of the patterns in the two data series and, consequently, will not produce accurate forecasts of the monetary aggregates.

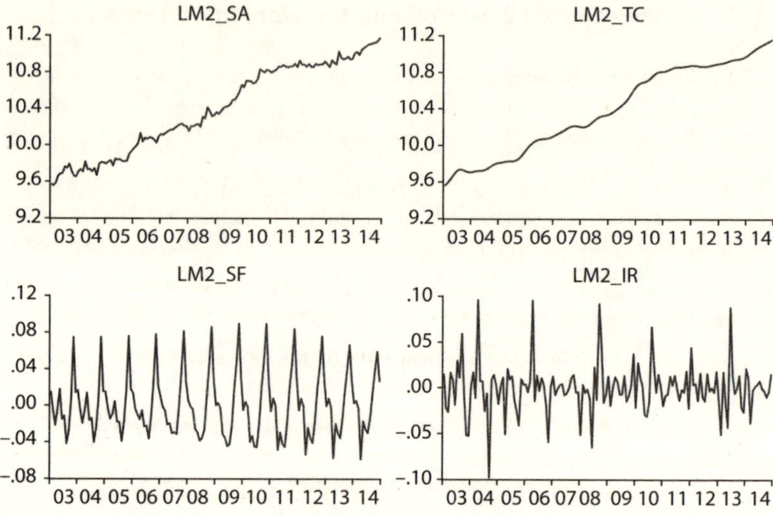

FIGURE **6.6** Components of log(M2) Series
Source: Author's Calculations.

Univariate Time Series Models of Monetary Aggregates

In this section, we model log(M1) and log(M2) using univariate time series methods. In particular, we apply the Box–Jenkins ARMA approach, which comprises three steps.[4] First, we identify potential autoregressive moving average models that can reproduce the short-term patterns in the variables. Second, we fit these models to the data through maximum likelihood estimation. Third, we select the optimal model via assessment of how well they fit the data series. This class of models is commonly used for short-term forecasting of time series variables.

As the ARMA models are only suitable for stationary series, we need to ascertain whether the long-term pattern in the data series is of a deterministic or stochastic nature. This distinction is important as the projections produced from a deterministic trend model behave very differently from the forecasts obtained from stochastic trend models. We perform augmented Dickey–Fuller unit root tests on the log(M1) and log(M2) series to determine whether they have a deterministic or stochastic trend.[5]

[4] For more details, see Diebold (2006: Chapters 8 and 9).

[5] For more details, see Diebold (2006: Chapters 5 and 13).

If the series has a unit root, we first perform differencing to the series to induce stationarity. ARMA models are then identified through the correlogram of the differenced series. Otherwise, if the series is found to not have a unit root, we first detrend the series and the ARMA models are then identified through the correlogram of the detrended series. These models are estimated and residual diagnostics are performed. The best fit model in terms of the lowest Schwarz Information Criterion (SIC) is selected from the group of identified models.

Since the series log(M1) and log(M2) are found to have seasonal components in section titled 'Review of Monetary Framework and Transmission Process', we include seasonal dummies in the ARMA models to account for seasonal patterns in the data. Initially, this includes all 12 seasonal dummies before the insignificant ones are dropped recursively until only the significant seasonal dummies are kept in the model. To distinguish this from other forecast models, we shall call this approach method 1.

Deterministic Trend Model for Narrow Money

When performing the augmented Dickey–Fuller tests, we include a deterministic trend term to take into account the long-term trend pattern in the data series. The unit root test results in Eviews Output 3 (Figure 6.7) and Figure 6.8 suggest that log(M1) is I(0) and has a deterministic trend term.

The detrended series is produced from the residuals of the deterministic trend model. Based on the correlogram of the detrended

Eviews Output 3: Unit Root Tests for log(M1) Series

Null Hypothesis: LM1 has a unit root
Exogenous: Constant, Linear Trend
Lag Length: 0 (Automatic - based on SIC, maxlag=13)

		t-Statistic	Prob.*
Augmented Dickey-Fuller test statistic		–5.170764	0.0002
Test critical values:	1% level	–4.023506	
	5% level	–3.441552	
	10% level	–3.145341	

*MacKinnon (1996) one-sided p-values.

FIGURE **6.7** Eviews Output 3
Source: Author's Calculations and Mackinnon (1996).

Date: 06/11/15 Time : 18:16
Sample: 2003M01 2014M12
Included observations: 144

Autocorrelation	Partial Correlation		AC	PAC	Q-Stat	Prob
		1	0.682	0.682	683.73	0 000
		2	0.558	0.174	114.46	0 000
		3	0.482	0.095	149.10	0 000
		4	0.485	0.174	184.39	0 000
		5	0.453	0.058	215.37	0 000
		6	0.472	0.144	249.29	0 000
		7	0.420	−0.012	276.32	0 000
		8	0.313	−0.140	291.51	0000
		9	0.327	0.111	308.13	0 000
		10	0.290	−0.053	321.32	0 000
		11	0.311	0 079	336.57	0 000
		12	0.295	0.025	350.45	0000
		13	0.233	−0.114	359.14	0 000
		14	0 072	−0 234	359.98	0 000
		15	0.051	−0.020	360.41	0 000
		16	0.045	−0.029	360.74	0.000
		17	0.055	0.032	361.24	0 000
		18	0 010	−0 080	361.25	0 000
		19	−0.066	−0.114	361.99	0 000
		20	−0.126	−0.028	364.68	0 000

FIGURE 6.8 Correlogram of Detrended log(M1)
Source: Author's Calculations.

series, we fit an ARMA(1,1) model since either the AR(1) or MA(1) term alone produces higher SIC values. However, we find that the seasonal dummies are mostly insignificant or weakly significant at the 10 per cent significance level. We drop the insignificant seasonal dummies recursively and eventually are only left with @seas(10). Hence, we fit to log(M1) the ARMA(1,1) model with the seasonal dummy [@seas(10)] and deterministic trend term (@trend), which gives us a lower SIC value for all the models considered. The estimated model and goodness of fit measures are given in Eviews Output 4.

Stochastic Trend Model for Broad Money

By contrast, the unit root test results suggest that log(M2) has a unit root at the 1 per cent significance level. We confirm the non-stationarity of log(M2) by using the Kwiatkowski–Phillips–Schmidt–Shin test, which is another stationarity test. The results in Eviews Output 5 and Figure 6.11 show log(M2) is not stationary at the 1 per cent significance level.

Eviews Output 4: Deterministic Trend Model for log(M1) Series

Dependent Variable: LM1
Method: Least Squares
Date: 05/21/15 Time: 22:43
Sample (adjusted): 2003M02 2014M12
Included observations: 143 after adjustments
Convergence achieved after 9 iterations
MA Backcast: 2003M01

Variable	Coefficient	Std. Error	t-Statistic	Prob.
C	0.971921	0.429989	2.260340	0.0254
@TREND ("2003M01")	0.001466	0.000655	2.236392	0.0269
LM1(-1)	0.890570	0.048780	18.25689	0.0000
@SEAS(10)	0.051931	0.021665	2.397047	0.0179
MA(1)	−0.464172	0.101620	−4.567724	0.0000

R-squared	0.983508	Mean dependent var	9.784279
Adjusted R-squared	0.983030	S.D. dependent var	0.562034
S.E. of regression	0.073215	Akaike info criterion	−2.356489
Sum squared resid	0.739744	Schwarz criterion	−2.252893
Log likelihood	173.4890	Hannan–Quinn criter.	−2.314393
F-statistic	2057.450	Durbin–Watson stat	1.896371
Prob(F-statistic)	0.000000		
Inverted MA Roots	.46		

Correlogram of Residuals

Date: 05/21/15 Time: 22:46
Sample: 2003M01 2014M12
Included obeservations: 143
Q-staistic probabilities adjusted for 1 ARMA term and 1 dynamic regressor

Autocorrelation	Partial Correlation		AC	PAC	Q-Stat	Prob*
		1	0.048	0.048	0.3423	
		2	−0.061	−0.064	0.8908	0.345
		3	−0.098	−0.092	2.3025	0.316
		4	0.018	0.023	2.3490	0.503
		5	−0.033	−0.047	2.5082	0.643
		6	0.123	0.122	4.7978	0.441
		7	0.077	0.066	5.7028	0.457
		8	−0.126	−0.131	8.1549	0.319
		9	0.086	0.140	9.3077	0.317
		10	−0.003	−0.028	9.3089	0.409
		11	0.103	0.106	10.979	0.359
		12	0.139	0.159	14.027	0.231
		13	0.105	0.062	15.790	0.201
		14	−0.171	−0.114	20.482	0.084
		15	−0.078	−0.043	21.467	0.090
		16	0.006	−0.022	21.473	0.122
		17	0.094	−0.088	22.940	0.115
		18	0.089	0.031	24.243	0.113
		19	−0.081	−0.120	25.330	0.116
		20	−0.148	−0.129	29.028	0.066

FIGURE 6.9 Eviews Output 4
Source: Author's Calculations.

Eviews Output 5: Unit Root Tests and Stationarity Test for log(M2) Series

Null Hypothesis: LM2 has a unit root
Exogenous: Constant, Linear Trend
Lag Length: 0 (Automatic - based on SIC, maxlag=13)

		t-Statistic	Prob.*
Augmented Dickey–Fuller test statistic		−3.573564	0.0357
Test critical values:	1% level	−4.023506	
	5% level	−3.441552	
	10% level	−3.145341	

*MacKinnon (1996) one-sided p-values.

Null Hypothesis: D(LM2) has a unit root
Exogenous: Constant
Lag Length: 0 (Automatic - based on SIC, maxlag=13

		t-Statistic	Prob.*
Augmented Dickey–Fuller test statistic		−14.80696	0.0000
Test critical values:	1% level	−3.476805	
	5% level	−2.881830	
	10% level	−2.577668	

*MacKinnon (1996) one-sided p-values.

Null Hypothesis: LM2 is stationary
Exogenous: Constant, Linear Trend
Bandwidth: 9 (Newey-West automatic) using Bartlett kernel

		LM-Stat.
Kwiatkowski-Phillips-Schmidt-Shin test statistic		0.154216
Asymptotic critical values*:	1% level	0.216000
	5% level	0.146000
	10% level	0.119000

*Kwiatkowski–Phillips–Schmidt–Shin (1992, Table 1)

Residual variance (no correction)	0.007265
HAC corrected variance (Bartlett kernel)	0.047083

FIGURE **6.10** Eviews Output 5
Source: Author's Calculations.

We induce stationarity by taking the first difference of the log(M2) series, which is dlog(M2). Applying the same Box–Jenkins procedure to dlog(M2), we find the AR(1) model with seasonal dummies @seas(9), @seas(10), and @seas(11) gives us the lowest SIC value for all the models considered. The estimated model and goodness of fit measures are given in Eviews Output 6.

In summary, over the period 2003–14, Bhutan's narrow money exhibits a straight-line trend superimposed by a cycle. Furthermore, we find seasonal effects for the month of October. In the same period, the patterns in broad money require us to analyse month-on-month growth rates instead. The latter has a short-term cycle and seasonal effects in the months of September, October, and November. The models estimated for the two data series will be used in the sections 'Forecast Evaluation of Monetary Aggregate M1' and 'Forecast Evaluation of Monetary Aggregate M2' to produce predictions of the respective monetary aggregates. As mentioned above, we call this forecast approach method 1.

Date: 05/08/15 Time: 03:44
Sample: 2010M01 2014M12
Included observations: 60

Autocorrelation	Partial Correlation		AC	PAC	Q-Stat	Prob
		1	−0.167	−0.167	1.7649	0.184
		2	−0.153	−0.191	3.3689	0.186
		3	0.175	0.119	5.3671	0.147
		4	−0.053	−0.032	5.5571	0.235
		5	−0.301	−0.290	11.674	0.040
		6	0.009	−0.149	11.680	0.070
		7	0.020	−0.093	11.708	0.111
		8	−0.039	−0.004	11.816	0.160
		9	−0.027	−0.080	11.870	0.221
		10	−0.014	−0.168	11.885	0.293
		11	0.030	−0.033	11.955	0.367
		12	0.209	0.206	15.352	0.223
		13	0.047	0.175	15.526	0.276
		14	0.033	0.122	15.641	0.336
		15	0.047	0.008	15.322	0.394
		16	−0.093	−0.069	16.636	0.410
		17	−0.074	0.066	17.114	0.447
		18	−0.079	0.006	17.668	0.478
		19	−0.033	−0.000	17.768	0.538
		20	−0.091	−0.169	18.541	0.552

FIGURE 6.11 Correlogram of the First Difference of log(M2)
Source: Authors' Calculations.

Eviews Output 6: Stochastic Trend Model for log(M2) Series

Dependent Variable: D_LM2
Method: Least Squares
Date: 05/22/15 Time: 00:40
Sample (adjusted): 2003M03 2014M12
Included observations: 142 after adjustments

Variable	Coefficient	Std. Error	t-Statistic	Prob.
C	0.003211	0.004431	0.724602	0.4699
D_LM2(-1)	-0.276700	0.079141	-3.496301	0.0006
@SEAS(9)	0.039910	0.013893	2.872693	0.0047
@SEAS(10)	0.042936	0.014090	3.047278	0.0028
@SEAS(11)	0.053932	0.014060	3.835819	0.0002
R-squared	0.188335	Mean dependent var		0.011624
Adjusted R-squared	0.164637	S.D. dependent var		0.049734
S.E. of regression	0.045456	Akaike info criterion		-3.309548
Sum squared resid	0.283081	Schwarz criterion		-3.205470
Log likelihood	239.9779	Hannan-Quinn criter.		-3.267255
F-statistic	7.947205	Durbin-Watson stat		1.971661
Prob(F-statistic)	0.000009			

Correlogram of Residuals

Date 05/22/15 Time 00:41
Sample 2003M012014M12
included observations 142
Q-statistic probabilities adjusted for 1 dynamic regressor

Autocorrelation	Partial Correlatiorn		AC	PAC	Q-Stat	Prob*
		1	0.014	0.014	0.0282	0.867
		2	−0.075	−0.076	0.8582	0.651
		3	0.042	0.044	1.1170	0.773
		4	−0.094	−0.102	2.4259	0.658
		5	−0.224	−0.217	9.9041	0.078
		6	−0.010	−0.024	9.9204	0.128
		7	0.039	0.013	10.148	0.180
		8	−0.146	−0.152	13.411	0.098
		9	0.072	0.037	14.217	0.115
		10	−0.005	−0.087	14.220	0.163
		11	0.090	0.112	15.494	0.161
		12	0.046	0.018	15.832	0.199
		13	0.138	0.116	18.846	0.128
		14	−0.031	−0.026	19.000	0.165
		15	0.033	0 078	19.178	0.206
		16	−0.068	−0 065	19.931	0.223
		17	0.010	0.104	19.948	0.277
		18	0.029	0 037	20.091	0.328
		19	−0.062	−0 009	20.734	0.352
		20	−0.129	0 156	23.530	0.264

*Probabilities may not be valid for this equation specification.

FIGURE **6.12** Eviews Output 6

Source: Author's Calculations.

Error Correction Model of Monetary Aggregate M2

The models used to forecast monetary aggregates that have been discussed so far are univariate time series models that do not involve other variables. In the case of broad money, we can perform forecasting by using the information in its key disaggregated components: net foreign assets and domestic credit. Statistical tests have to be performed to determine whether the relationship between log(M2) and its disaggregated variables log(NFA) and log(DC) hold in the short-term and/or in the long-term. If a long-term relationship is detected through the cointegration test, the error correction model will be applied.[6] Otherwise, only growth rates based on short-term relationships will be employed. Again, we take into account the seasonal component in log(M2) by including seasonal dummies in the model. We call this approach method 2.

The forecasts generated from such models require forecasts of the disaggregated variables themselves. Hence, we need to first model log(NFA) and log(DC) individually.

Univariate Time Series Models of Disaggregate Series

As shown in Figure 6.13, log(M2) and log(NFA) follow similar trends up until the onset of the Indian rupee crisis in 2012 when they start to

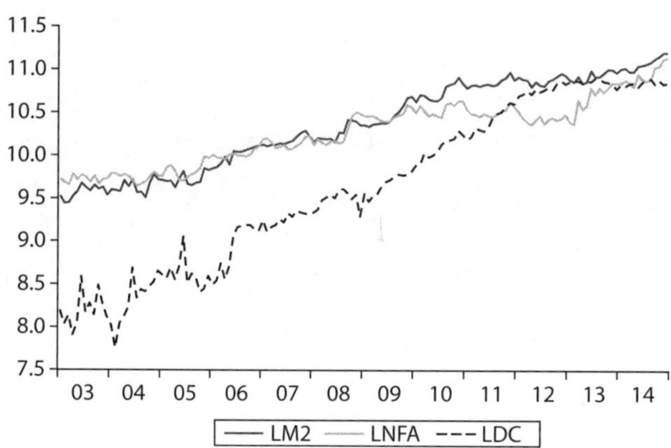

FIGURE 6.13 Log of Monetary Aggregate M2, Net Foreign Asset, and Domestic Credit
Source: Author's Calculations.

[6] For more details, see Stock and Watson (2014: section 16.4).

Eviews Output 7: Seasonality Tests for log(NFA) Series

D 8.A F-tests for seasonality

Test for the presence of seasonality assuming stability.

	Sum of Squares	Degrees of Freedom	Mean Square	F-Value
Between months	0.1782	11	0.01620	7.658**
Residual	0.2793	132	0.00212	
Total	0.4575	143		

**Seasonality present at the 0.1 per cent level.

Non-parametric Test for the Presence of Seasonality Assuming Stability

Kruskal-Wallis Statistic	Degrees of Freedom	Probability Level
57.1506	11	0.000%

Seasonality present at the one per cent level.

Moving Seasonality Test

	Sum of Squares	Degrees of Freedom	Mean Square	F-value
Between Years	0.0130	11	0.001185	1.233
Error	0.1163	121	0.000962	

No evidence of moving seasonality at the five per cent level.

COMBINED TEST FOR THE PRESENCE OF IDENTIFIABLE SEASONALITY

IDENTIFIABLE SEASONALITY PRESENT

FIGURE **6.14** Eviews Output 7
Source: Author's Calculations.

deviate from each other. The log(DC) series exhibits an upward trend and seems to counterbalance log(NFA) beginning in 2012.

Applying the United States Census Bureau's X-12 programme on the disaggregate series reveals that the log(NFA) is seasonal (Eviews Output 7). We see later that the seasonal pattern for the log(NFA) series can be captured by seasonal dummies. In contrast, the log(DC) series does not appear to have an identifiable seasonal component due to the presence of moving seasonality (Eviews Output 8). Hence, the seasonal pattern in the log(DC) series is captured by a seasonal lag term *(t-12)* instead.

We next tested for unit root in the disaggregate series and found the individual series to be integrated of order 1 as is also the case for the log(M2) series (Eviews Outputs 9 and 10).

Eviews Output 8: Seasonality Tests for log(DC) Series

D 8.A F-tests for seasonality

Test for the presence of seasonality assuming stability.

	Sum of Squares	Degrees of Freedom	Mean Square	F-Value
Between months	0.3624	11	0.03295	4.825**
Residual	0.9013	132	0.00683	
Total	1.2637	143		

**Seasonality present at the 0.1 per cent level.

Non-parametric Test for the Presence of Seasonality Assuming Stability

Kruskal-Wallis Statistic	Degrees of Freedom	Probability Level
44.7861	11	0.001%

Seasonality present at the one per cent level.

Moving Seasonality Test

	Sum of Squares	Degrees of Freedom	Mean Square	F-value
Between Years	0.1980	11	0.018001	4.459**
Error	0.4885	121	0.004037	

**Moving seasonality present at the one per cent level.

COMBINED TEST FOR THE PRESENCE OF IDENTIFIABLE SEASONALITY

IDENTIFIABLE SEASONALITY NOT PRESENT

FIGURE **6.15** Eviews Output 8
Source: Author's Calculations.

Eviews Output 9: Unit Root Tests for log(NFA) Series

Null Hypothesis: LNFA has a unit root
Exogenous: Constant, Linear Trend
Lag Length: 0 (Automatic - based on SIC, maxlag=13)

		t-Statistic	Prob.*
Augmented Dickey–Fuller test statistic		−2.915315	0.1609
Test critical values:	1% level	−4.023506	
	5% level	−3.441552	
	10% level	−3.145341	

*MacKinnon (1996) one-sided p-values.

Null Hypothesis: D(LNFA) has a unit root
Exogenous: Constant
Lag Length: 0 (Automatic - based on SIC, maxlag=13)

		t-Statistic	Prob.*
Augmented Dickey–Fuller test statistic		−13.36687	0.0000
Test critical values:	1% level	−3.476805	
	5% level	−2.881830	
	10% level	−2.577668	

*MacKinnon (1996) one-sided p-values.

FIGURE 6.16 Eviews Output 9
Source: Author's Calculations.

Eviews Output 10: Unit Root Tests for log(DC) Series

Null Hypothesis: LDC has a unit root
Exogenous: Constant, Linear Trend
Lag Length: 1 (Automatic - based on SIC, maxlag=13)

		t-Statistic	Prob.*
Augmented Dickey–Fuller test statistic		−3.033790	0.1268
Test critical values:	1% level	−4.023975	
5% level	5% level	−3.441777	
10% level	10% level	−3.145474	

*MacKinnon (1996) one-sided p-values.

Null Hypothesis: D(LDC) has a unit root
Exogenous: Constant
Lag Length: 11 (Automatic - based on SIC, maxlag=13)

		t-Statistic	Prob.*
Augmented Dickey–Fuller test statistic		−4.110318	0.0013
Test critical values:	1% level	−3.480818	
	5% level	−2.883579	
	10% level	−2.578601	

FIGURE 6.17 Eviews Output 10
Source: Author's Calculations.

Eviews Output 11: Pure Time Series Models for dlog(NFA)

Dependent Variable: DLOG(NFA)
Method: Least Squares
Date: 06/17/15 Time: 15:04
Sample (adjusted): 2003M02 2014M12
Included observations: 143 after adjustments
Convergence achieved after 6 iterations
MA Backcast: 2003M01

Variable	Coefficient	Std. Error	t-Statistic	Prob.
C	−0.000589	0.004338	−0.135828	0.8922
@SEAS(9)	0.052309	0.017797	2.939181	0.0039
@SEAS(11)	0.073190	0.017760	4.120965	0.0001
MA(1)	−0.236685	0.083749	−2.826112	0.0054
R-squared	0.155484	Mean dependent var		0.009893
Adjusted R-squared	0.137257	S.D. dependent var		0.062619
S.E. of regression	0.058163	Akaike info criterion		−2.823558
Sum squared resid	0.470230	Schwarz criterion		−2.740681
Log likelihood	205.8844	Hannan–Quinn criter.		−2.789881
F-statistic	8.530444	Durbin–Watson stat		1.972661
Prob(F-statistic)	0.000031			
Inverted MA Roots	.24			

FIGURE **6.18** Eviews Output 11
Source: Author's Calculations.

By repeating the modelling procedure discussed in section 'Seasonality Tests of Monetary Aggregate Series', the univariate time series model estimated for dlog(NFA) is MA(1) with two seasonal dummies @seas(9) and @seas(11) (Eviews Output 11); while that for dlog(DC) has MA(1), MA(3), and AR(12) terms (Eviews Output 12).

Cointegration and Error Correction Model for log(M2) Series

With reference to the time plots in Figure 6.13, it comes as no surprise that we could not identify a cointegrating relationship among the three series when the whole sample period is used. However, a strong cointegrating relationship between log(M2), log(NFA), and log(DC) is detected if we end the sample in December 2011 just before the onset of the Indian rupee crisis (Eviews Output 13).

Since cointegration exists when we discount the rupee crisis period, we build an error correction model for log(M2). With regard to optimal lag lengths, we found that the SIC value is lowest with dlog(M2) at *t-1*, dlog(NFA) at *t*, and dlog(DC) at both *t* and *t-1*. Seasonal dummies

Eviews Output 12: Pure Time Series Models for dlog(DC)

Dependent Variable: DLOG(DC)
Method: Least Squares
Date: 06/17/15 Time: 15:36
Sample (adjusted): 2004M02 2014M12
Included observations: 131 after adjustments
Convergence achieved after 6 iterations
MA Backcast: 2003M11 2004M01

Variable	Coefficient	Std. Error	t-Statistic	Prob.
C	0.013980	0.008256	1.693381	0.0928
DLOG(DC(-12))	0.417969	0.062626	6.674040	0.0000
MA(1)	−0.219270	0.084520	−2.594289	0.0106
MA(3)	0.244832	0.081331	3.010308	0.0031
R-squared	0.364539	Mean dependent var		0.021576
Adjusted R-squared	0.349529	S.D. dependent var		0.113378
S.E. of regression	0.091442	Akaike info criterion		−1.916172
Sum squared resid	1.061921	Schwarz criterion		−1.828380
Log likelihood	129.5093	Hannan–Quinn criter.		−1.880498
F-statistic	24.28502	Durbin–Watson stat		1.956435
Prob(F-statistic)	0.000000			
Inverted MA Roots	.39-.53i	.39+.53i	−.56	

FIGURE 6.19 Eviews Output 12
Source: Author's Calculations.

Eviews Output 13: Cointegration Test for log(M2), log(NFA) and log(DC) Series

Cointegration Test - Engle-Granger
Date: 06/08/15 Time: 16:30
Equation: UNTITLED
Specification: LM2 LNFA LDC C
Cointegrating equation deterministics: C
Null hypothesis: Series are not cointegrated
Automatic lag specification (lag=0 based on Schwarz Info Criterion, maxlag=12)

	Value	Prob.*
Engle-Granger tau-statistic	−5.033121	0.0015
Engle-Granger z-statistic	−41.19763	0.0010

*MacKinnon (1996) p-values.

FIGURE 6.20 Eviews Output 13
Source: Author's Calculations.

Eviews Output 14: Error Correction Model for log(M2)

Dependent Variable: D(LM2)
Method: Least Squares
Date: 06/08/15 Time: 17:17
Sample: 2004M01 2014M12
Included observations: 132

Variable	Coefficient	Std. Error	t-Statistic	Prob.
C	0.042423	0.191318	0.221742	0.8249
LM2(-1)	-0.139303	0.053679	-2.595130	0.0106
LNFA(-1)	0.103867	0.033351	3.114379	0.0023
LDC(-1)	0.034203	0.021938	1.559106	0.1216
D_LM2(-1)	-0.280675	0.071336	-3.934540	0.0001
D_LNFA	0.423422	0.059840	7.075847	0.0000
D_LDC	0.246705	0.033108	7.451426	0.0000
D_LDC(-1)	0.103220	0.035148	2.936740	0.0040
@SEAS(9)	0.030801	0.012721	2.421307	0.0169
@SEAS(10)	0.045537	0.012805	3.556099	0.0005
@SEAS(11)	0.038536	0.013382	2.879757	0.0047

R-squared	0.565135	Mean dependent var	0.012632
Adjusted R-squared	0.529195	S.D. dependent var	0.056258
S.E. of regression	0.038601	Akaike info criterion	-3.591408
Sum squared resid	0.180297	Schwarz criterion	-3.351174
Log likelihood	248.0329	Hannan–Quinn criter.	-3.493788
F-statistic	15.72471	Durbin–Watson stat	1.940150
Prob(F-statistic)	0.000000		

Correlogram of Residuals

Date 06/08/15 Time 17:39
Sample: 2004M01 2014M12
Included observations: 132
Q-statistic probabilities adjusted tor 10 dynamic regressors

Auto–correlation	Partial Correlation		AC	PAC	Q-Stat	Prob*
		1	0.023	0.023	0 0699	0.791
		2	0.011	0.011	0.0864	0.958
		3	−0 054	−0.055	0.4870	0.922
		4	−0.096	−0.094	1.7704	0.778
		5	−0.047	−0.042	2.0783	0.838
		6	0.037	0.039	2.2717	0 893
		7	0.014	0.004	2.2982	0.942
		8	−0.030	−0.046	2.4294	0.965
		9	−0 .054	−0.059	2.8470	0.970
		10	−0.010	−0.002	2.8628	0.984
		11	0.062	0.067	3.4324	0.984
		12	−0.031	−0.047	3.5748	0.990
		13	0.080	0.064	4.5162	0.984
		14	−0 068	−0.068	5.1993	0.983
		15	0.081	0.099	6.1939	0.976
		16	0.037	0.042	6.4055	0.983
		17	0.086	0.081	7.5379	0.975
		18	−0.015	−0.022	7.5735	0.984
		19	−0.072	−0.062	8.3856	0.982
		20	−0 095	−0.063	9.8052	0 972

*Probabilities may not be valid for this equation specification

FIGURE 6.21 Eviews Output 14
Source: Author's Calculations.

@seas(9), @seas(10), and @seas(11) are found to be significant. The estimated model and goodness of fit measures are given in Eviews Output 14.

In summary, over the period 2003–14, broad money in Bhutan was found to have a long-term relationship with its two main components: net foreign assets and domestic credit. Hence, broad money can deviate from this relationship for only a short period of time. Should it deviate from this relationship, it will tend to return to the relationship in future time periods. We will use a model that captures this behaviour to forecast broad money in section titled 'Forecast Evaluation of Monetary Aggregate M2'. This forecast approach is referred to as method 2.

Forecast Evaluation of Monetary Aggregate M1

The predictive ability of the different types of models can be evaluated by performing post-sample predictions. This involves splitting the sample period into an in-sample estimation period and an out-of-sample forecast evaluation period. The univariate time series model selected for log(M1) series is re-estimated using the sample for 2003–13. In this way, we can evaluate the forecast accuracy for 2014. Both static (one-step ahead) forecasts and dynamic (12 steps or 1-year ahead) forecasts are generated from the model. Various measures of forecast accuracy—such as root mean square forecast error, mean absolute error, and mean absolute percentage error—are computed.[7] The smaller the values of these statistics, the more accurate are the forecasts.

Static Forecast Evaluation for log(M1) Series

We first estimate the previously identified ARMA(1,1) model with a deterministic trend term and seasonal dummy (10) to log(M1) series until the end of 2013, and then forecast one-step ahead for January–December 2014. The forecast and its evaluation statistics are given in Figure 6.22.

The static forecasts for log(M1) using method 1 have good forecast evaluation statistics. Hence, the univariate time series model is recommended to produce a one-step ahead forecast of log(M1).

[7] For more details, see Diebold (2006: Chapter 12).

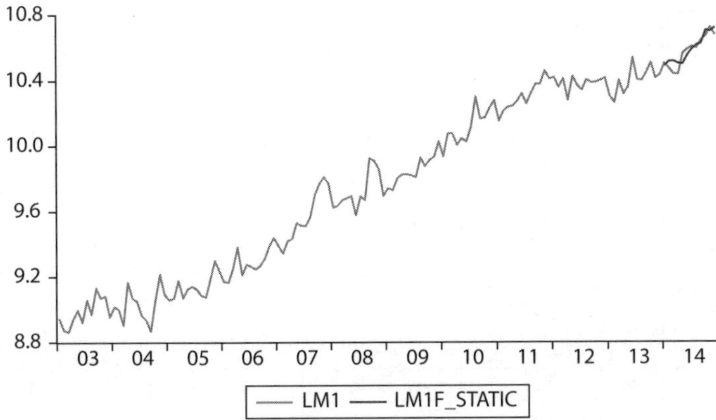

FIGURE **6.22** Static Forecast for log(M1) and Forecast Evaluation Statistics (Method 1)

Root Mean Squared Error	0.044263
Mean Absolute Error	0.039365
Mean Absolute Percentage Error	0.373138

Source: Author's Calculations.

Dynamic Forecast Evaluation for log(M1) Series

We use the same forecast method as in the section 'Univariate Time Series Models of Disaggregate Series' to produce a multi-step ahead forecast for January–December 2014. The multi-step forecast and its evaluation are given in Figure 6.23.

We use the same forecast method as in the section 'Static Forecast Evaluation for log(M1) Series' to produce multi-step ahead forecasts in 2014 month 1–2014 month 12. The multi-step forecasts and their evaluation are given below.

The dynamic forecasts for log(M1) using method 1 have good forecast evaluation statistics. Hence, this method is also recommended for producing dynamic forecasts of log(M1).

In summary, method 1 produces accurate 1-month ahead and 1-year ahead predictions of Bhutan's narrow money and we recommend the use of the model described in section titled 'Deterministic Trend Model for Narrow Money' for forecasting M1.

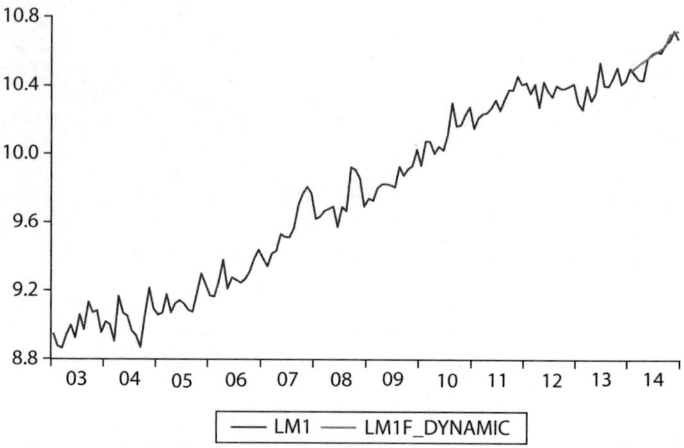

FIGURE **6.23** Dynamic Forecast for log(M1) and Forecast Evaluation Statistics (Method 1)

Root Mean Squared Error	0.046776
Mean Absolute Error	0.032748
Mean Absolute Percentage Error	0.311286

Source: Author's Calculations.

Forecast Evaluation of Monetary Aggregate M2

There are two candidate forecast models for log(M2) series. As in section 'Forecast Evaluation of Monetary Aggregate M1', each model is re-estimated using the sample for 2003–13. Both one-step ahead and multi-steps ahead forecasts are generated from each model for the sample for 2014. Then the accuracy of the predictions is evaluated and compared across the models. We note that the optimal model for short-term predictions is not necessarily the same as that for long-term predictions. Hence, we discuss forecast comparisons for short-term predictions separately from long-term predictions.

Static Forecast Evaluation for log(M2) Series

Method 1: Static Forecasts from Stochastic Trend Model

We first estimate the previously identified AR(1) model with a stochastic trend term and seasonal dummy (9, 10, 11) to log(M2) series until the

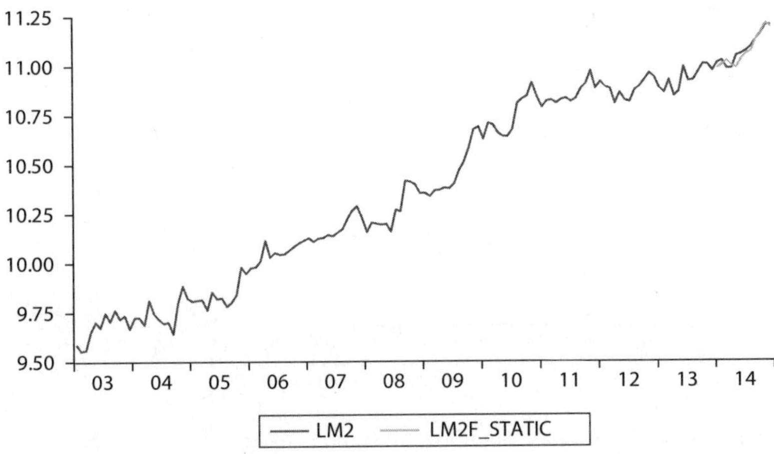

FIGURE **6.24** Static Forecast for log(M2) and Forecast Evaluation Statistics (Method 1)

Root Mean Squared Error	0.026415
Mean Absolute Error	0.020977
Mean Absolute Percentage Error	0.189845

Source: Author's Calculations.

end of 2013 and then forecast one-step ahead for 2014. The forecast and its evaluation statistics are given in Figure 6.24.

The static forecasts for log(M1) using method 1 have good forecast evaluation statistics. Hence, the univariate time series model can be used to produce one-step ahead forecasts of log(M2).

Method 2: Static Forecasts from Error Correction Model

We estimate the previously identified error correction model selected for dlog(M2) through the end of 2013 (Eviews Output 11). One-step ahead forecasts for log(NFA) and log(DC) are first produced from their univariate time series models for 2014 (Eviews Output 9). The one-step forecasts of log(NFA) and log(DC) and their evaluation statistics are shown in Figures 6.25 and 6.26, respectively.

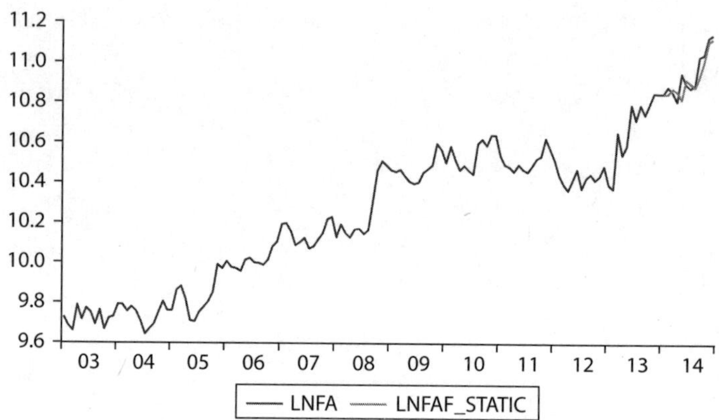

FIGURE **6.25** Static Forecast for log(NFA) and Forecast Evaluation Statistics

Root Mean Squared Error	0.053469
Mean Absolute Error	0.039068
Mean Absolute Percentage Error	0.356548

Source: Author's Calculations.

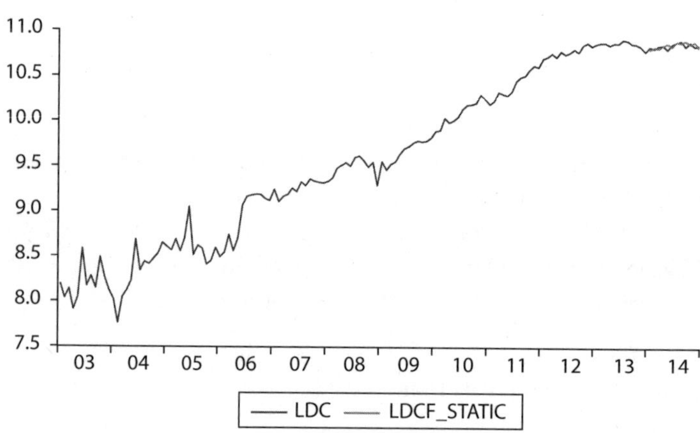

FIGURE **6.26** Static Forecast for log(DC) and Forecast Evaluation Statistics

Root Mean Squared Error	0.034857
Mean Absolute Error	0.028575
Mean Absolute Percentage Error	0.263616

Source: Author's Calculations.

The static forecasts are used to generate a one-step ahead forecast of log(M2) and its evaluation statistics as shown in Figure 6.27.

By comparing Figure 6.27 to Figure 6.24, the static forecasts for log(M2) using method 2 have forecast evaluation statistics that are worse than those of method 1. Hence, method 1 is recommended for one-step ahead forecasts of log(M2).

Dynamic Forecast Evaluation for log(M2) Series

Method 1: Dynamic Forecasts from Stochastic Trend Model

We use the same forecast method as in section 'Method 1: Static Forecasts from Stochastic Trend Model' to produce a multi-step ahead forecast for 2014. The multi-step forecast and its evaluation statistics are shown in Figure 6.28.

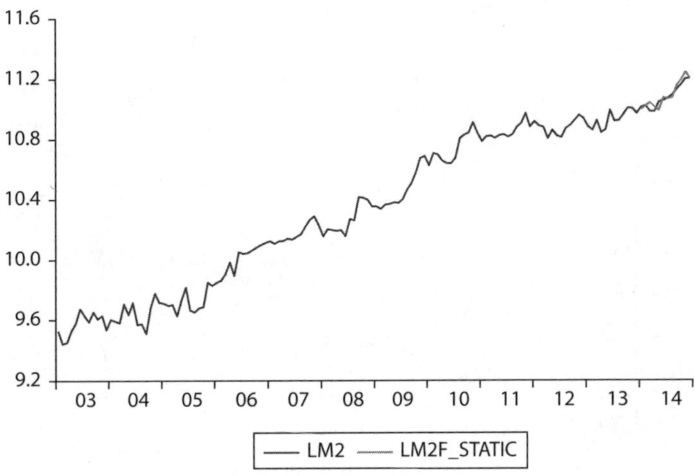

FIGURE 6.27 Static Forecast for log(M2) and Forecast Evaluation Statistics (Method 2)

Root Mean Squared Error	0.031622
Mean Absolute Error	0.025371
Mean Absolute Percentage Error	0.229162

Source: Author's Calculations.

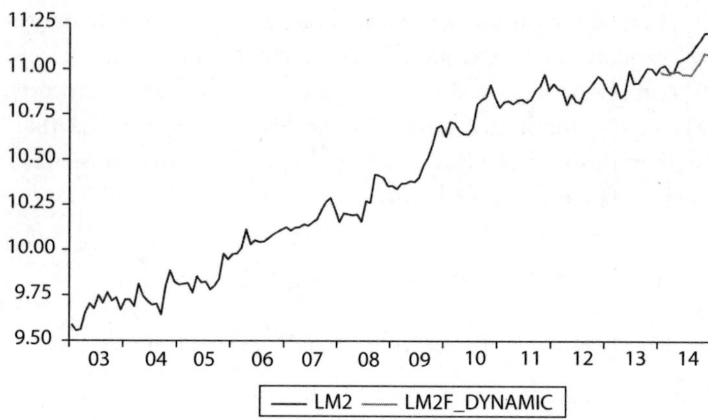

FIGURE **6.28** Dynamic Forecast for log(M1) and Forecast Evaluation Statistics (Method 1)

Root Mean Squared Error	0.089554
Mean Absolute Error	0.077920
Mean Absolute Percentage Error	0.700903

Source: Author's Calculations.

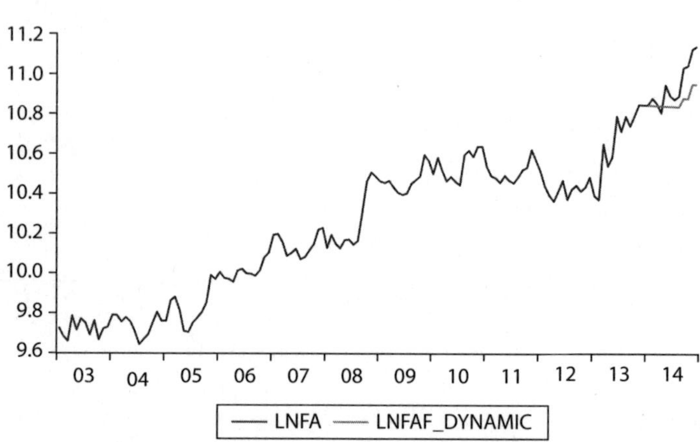

FIGURE **6.29** Dynamic Forecast for log(NFA) and Forecast Evaluation Statistics

Root Mean Squared Error	0.107850
Mean Absolute Error	0.084889
Mean Absolute Percentage Error	0.769871

Source: Author's Calculations.

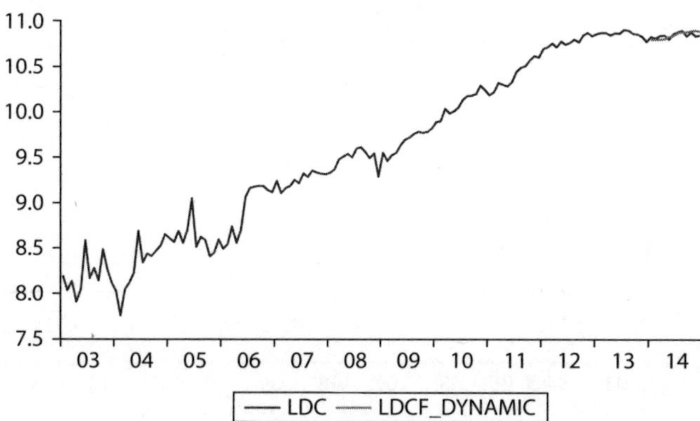

FIGURE **6.30** Dynamic Forecast for log(DC) and Forecast Evaluation Statistics

Root Mean Squared Error	0.034449
Mean Absolute Error	0.030602
Mean Absolute Percentage Error	0.282177

Source: Author's Calculations.

The dynamic forecasts for log(M2) using method 2 have poor forecast evaluation statistics. Hence, method 2 is not suited for long-term forecasting of log(M2).

Method 2: Dynamic Forecasts from Error Correction Model

We use the same forecast method as in section 'Method 2: Static Forecasts from Error Correction Model' to produce multi-step ahead forecasts for 2014, except now we first generate multi-step ahead forecasts for log(NFA) and log(DC). The multi-step forecasts of log(NFA) and log(DC) and their evaluation statistics are shown in Figures 6.29 and 6.30, respectively.

Using these dynamic forecasts, the multi-step forecast of log(M2) and its evaluation statistics are shown in Figure 6.31.

By comparing Figure 6.31 to Figure 6.28, the dynamic forecasts for log(M2) using method 2 substantially improve upon those from method 1. Hence, method 2 is recommended.

In summary, method 1 produces more accurate 1-month ahead predictions of Bhutan's broad money than method 2. The reverse is true for 1-year ahead predictions of broad money. Hence, we recommend

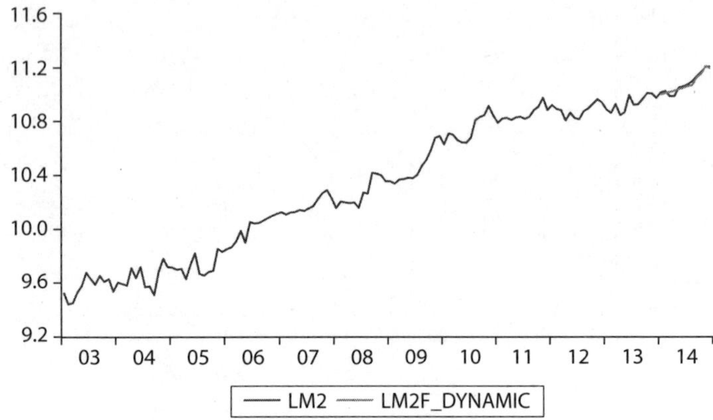

FIGURE **6.31** Dynamic Forecast for log(M2) and Forecast Evaluation Statistics (Method 2)

Root Mean Squared Error	0.020366
Mean Absolute Error	0.017740
Mean Absolute Percentage Error	0.160473

Source: Author's Calculations.

using the model described in the section 'Univariate Time Series Models of Monetary Aggregates' for 1-month ahead forecasting of M2 and the model described in the section 'Error Correction Model of Monetary Aggregate M2' for 1-year ahead forecasting of M2.

* * *

This chapter presents forecast models for monetary aggregates in Bhutan that were developed in collaboration with the monetary team in the RMA. The forecast models generate 1-month ahead (static) as well as 1-year ahead (dynamic) forecasts of the monetary aggregates. These projections are short-term in nature and can serve as inputs to Bhutan's monetary and economic authorities in the annual planning process.

Preliminary analysis over the period 2003–14 shows the monthly monetary aggregates series, log(M1) and log(M2), each has an upward trend as well as identifiable seasonal patterns. Unit root tests results indicate the log(M1) series has a deterministic trend and the log(M2) series has a stochastic trend. Hence, we remove the trend from log(M1) by using the residuals from a deterministic trend model of the series and remove the trend from log(M2) by taking first differences of the series.

We then apply the Box–Jenkins procedure to fit ARMA models to the individual series without trend. In each case, the optimal model is chosen by minimizing the SIC. The log(M1) series is fitted with an ARMA(1,1) with a deterministic trend and an October seasonal dummy. This model produces good static and dynamic forecasts of the log(M1) series. As for log(M2), the optimal model for the differenced series is an AR(1) with seasonal dummies for September, October, and November. While this univariate time series model produces good static forecasts of log(M2), it does not have good predictive ability for dynamic forecasts of log(M2).

An alternative approach is to forecast log(M2) using the forecasts of its key disaggregated components: net foreign assets (NFA) and domestic credit (DC). Cointegration test confirms the presence of a long-term relationship that links log(M2), log(NFA), and log(DC). Hence, we fit an error correction model to log(M2) that minimizes SIC and forecast log(M2) based on the predictions of log(NFA) and log(DC) that are generated from their own univariate time series forecast models. There was substantial improvement in the predictive accuracy of the dynamic forecasts of log(M2) with this approach. The recommended models for forecasting Bhutan's monetary aggregates are summarized in Table 6.3.

These models are chosen based on their goodness of fit and predictive ability using the sample period 2003–14. The proposed models should be re-estimated with the most recent data before they are used to generate forecasts. To reflect changes in the patterns of the monetary aggregate series, periodic re-specification of the models (re-modelling) is also required. We highlight again that these time-series forecasting techniques are more suited for short-term forecasting and the predictions generated are more useful for the annual planning process. Indeed, the same approach can be adopted for short-term projections of other economic variables in Bhutan such as trade variables.

Structural equations that relate the monetary aggregates with other economic variables can be modelled as more data on these

TABLE 6.3 Recommended Forecast Models for Monetary Aggregates

Forecast	Model
M1 (Static)	$\log(M1)_t = \beta_0 + \beta_1 t + \beta_2 \log(M1)_{t-1} + \beta_3 \mathrm{MA}(1) + \beta_4\, seas(10) + \varepsilon$
M1 (Dynamic)	$\log(M1)_t = \beta_0 + \beta_1 t + \beta_2 \log(M1)_{t-1} + \beta_3 \mathrm{MA}(1) + \beta_4\, seas(10) + \varepsilon$
M2 (Static)	$\mathrm{dlog}\,(M2)_t = \beta_0 + \beta_1 \mathrm{dlog} + (M2)_{t-1} + \beta_2 seas(9) + \beta_3 seas(10) + \beta_4 seas(11) + \varepsilon$
M2 (Dynamic)	$\mathrm{dlog}\,(M2)_t = \beta_0 + \beta_1 \log(M2)_{t-1} + \beta_2 \log(NFA)_{t-1} + \beta_2 \log(DC)_{t-1} + \varepsilon$ $\beta_4 \mathrm{dlog}\,(M2)_{t-1} + \beta_5 \mathrm{dlog}\,(NFA)_t + \beta_6 \mathrm{dlog}\,(DC)_t + \beta_7 \mathrm{dlog}\,(DC)_{t-1} + \beta_8 seas(9) + \beta_9 seas(10) + \beta_{10} seas(11) + \varepsilon$
NFA (Static and Dynamic)	$\mathrm{dlog}\,(NFA)_t = \beta_0 + \beta_1 MA(1) + \beta_2 seas(9) + \beta_3 seas(11) + \varepsilon$
DC (Static and Dynamic)	$\mathrm{dlog}\,(DC)_t = \beta_0 + \beta_1 \mathrm{dlog}\,(\mathrm{DC})_{t-12} + \beta_2 MA(1) + \beta_3 MA(3) + \varepsilon$

Notes: DC = domestic credit; NFA = net foreign assets.
Source: Author's Calculations.

variables—in terms of a longer time span as well as higher frequency observations—become available. Such models can generate forecasts of monetary aggregates that factor in changes in related variables (Pagan and Robertson 2004). In addition, they are more suited for producing forecasts over longer time horizons, which are useful for longer-term planning and economic projections.

References

Diebold, F. X. 2006. *Elements of Forecasting* (4th edn). Mason, United States: South-Western Thompson.

Mackinnon, J. 1996. 'Numerical Distribution Functions for Unit Root and Cointegration Test', *Journal of Applied Econometrics*, *11*(6): 601–18.

Pagan, A.R. and J. Robertson. 2004. 'Forecasting for Policy', in M.P. Clements and D.F. Hendry (eds), *A Companion to Economic Forecasting*, pp. 152–78. Oxford: Blackwell Publishing.

Stock, J.H. and M.W. Watson. 2014. *Introduction to Econometrics* (3rd edn). London: Pearson.

United States Census Bureau. 2006. *X12-ARIMA Reference Manual*. Available at https://www.census.gov/ts/x12a/v03/x12adocV03.pdf (last accessed on 5 May 2015).

7

SABYASACHI MITRA, ANTHONY BALUGA,
AND ELBE AGUBA

Bhutan's Consumer Price Inflation and Price Transmission from India

It has been widely observed that price level movements in Bhutan closely follow those in India. The link between the prices of the two countries is supported by the fact that, as a landlocked country, Bhutan's economy is intrinsically tied with India's, which because of geography is its best link for trade with the rest of South Asia. Bilateral cooperation in the area of hydropower development fuels Bhutan's economy and furthers economic relations between the two countries. India not just exports goods and services to Bhutan, but it also finances most of Bhutan's hydropower construction requirements (RMA 2014).

Since 2010, imported goods and services have comprised about 67 per cent of Bhutan's gross domestic product (GDP), the highest level in South Asia next to the Maldives and much higher than the regional and world averages. The share of imports in Bhutan's GDP is comparable to that of similarly landlocked countries, like Namibia or Swaziland. Nearly 80 per cent of Bhutan's imports are from India; the remaining amount is spread out among other Asian countries. In addition to hydropower-related imported materials, Bhutan is highly dependent on food and other consumption imports, with rice among the top five imported commodities.

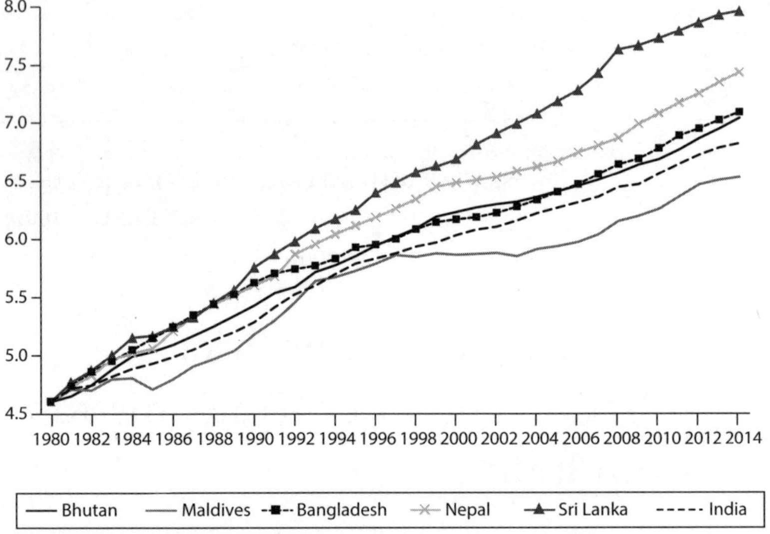

FIGURE 7.1 Average Annual Price Levels in South Asia (log form)
Source: International Monetary Fund (2015).

Because of strong trade and financial relations with India, Bhutan's ngultrum has been pegged one-to-one with India's rupee since its introduction in 1974. One of the outcomes of the peg is that it facilitates the direct transmission of prices from India. Since 1980, annual price movements in India have been subdued compared with most countries in South Asia (Figure 7.1). This has benefited Bhutan, whose annual price levels have broadly followed. Over the three decades preceding 2014, Bhutan's annual inflation averaged nearly 8 per cent, just slightly higher than India's average of 7.2 per cent. This compares favourably with other countries in South Asia, particularly Nepal, Pakistan, and Sri Lanka.

This research attempts to measure the transmission of prices from India as an approach to examining inflationary dynamics in Bhutan, with the analysis based on the purchasing power parity (PPP) framework. Most of the existing literature on PPP is focused on price transmission for individual commodities, mainly staple crops.[1] Related literature using aggregate prices is centred on the role of exchange rates as the channel through

[1] Varela (2012) compiled a summary of literature on this subject.

which external price shocks affect domestic prices, given the floating or market-based exchange rate system in the countries under study. It also focuses on countries that are not highly import dependent. Bhutan makes a very interesting case because of its exceptionally high import dependency vis-à-vis India and its one-to-one pegged exchange rate with its much larger neighbour, both of which reinforce the tendency for price transmission.

No major empirical research has been produced that discusses price transmission dynamics for a case like Bhutan except for a working paper by Ginting (2007), which reviewed price transmission in Nepal, and a short article in the International Monetary Fund's 2014 country report for Bhutan (International Monetary Fund 2014).[2] Ginting (2007) focused on whether long-run price transmission from India flows from headline or core prices. The magnitude to which India's prices affect Nepal's domestic prices was not presented. The International Monetary Fund's 2014 country report for Bhutan confirmed the presence of cointegration with respect to Bhutan and India's consumer price inflation using a vector error correction model. However, no details were provided on either the degree of price transmission in the long-run or short-run dynamics.

This research contributes to the literature by providing empirical evidence on whether the transmission of aggregate prices from India to Bhutan holds in the long run. Based on this result, attempts are made to measure the degree of price transmission. The bounds-testing approach of the autoregressive distributed lag model (Pesaran and Shin 1999; Pesaran, Shin, and Smith 2001) is employed to establish the existence of the long-run equilibrium relationship of prices. An error correction model is used to measure the short-run estimates with respect to the magnitude and speed of price transmission. To disentangle the analysis, we apply this approach and examine the long- and short-run relationships between aggregate prices in India and Bhutan, including the major price disaggregates such as food and non-food prices.

The structure of this chapter is as follows. A broad review of the theoretical background and a brief description of the PPP framework are presented in the section 'Theoretical Background'. The section 'Estimating Cointegration and Price Transmission from India' lays out the econometric methodology and data used in the analysis. The empirical results

[2] Similar to Bhutan, Nepal's currency is also pegged to that of its largest trade partner, India.

of the bounds test, the long- and short-run price elasticities, and the speed of adjustment from the short-run deviation back to the equilibrium are discussed in the section 'Empirical Results'. The linearity result of the real exchange rate, which is necessary for PPP to hold, is also presented. The last section, 'Summary and Policy Implications', provides a summary and the policy implications.

Theoretical Background

The economic framework underpinning the price transmission analysis of this research broadly follows the concept of PPP, or the 'law of one price', in analysing price transmission in a small open economy. A large number of studies on price transmission, including Baltzer (2013), Minot (2011), Ginting (2007), Conforti (2004), and Kenny and McGettigan (1997, 1999), have also used the PPP framework.

Under the PPP framework, for any good *A* in a small open economy, its price will be equivalent with its trading partner when expressed in a common currency:

$$P_{At} = P_{At}^{f} \star ER_t. \tag{1}$$

Expressing this in relative terms and in logarithmic form produces the following equation:

$$P_{At}^{f} - P_{At} + ER_t = RER_t \tag{2}$$

where P_{At}^{f} is the foreign currency price of good A in the trading partner country, P_{At} is the domestic price of good *A*, ER_t is the nominal exchange rate, and RER_t is the real exchange rate. We can assume that what holds for one good may hold for a set of goods that are identical in both countries.

Equations 1 and 2 suggest that changes in the relative prices of goods reflect equivalent movements in the real exchange rate. For PPP to hold, and assuming no transport or tariff costs, it is critical that RER_t is constant over time.

We can expand the framework to distinguish prices between imported and domestically produced goods. The domestic price can be defined as

$$P = \phi P_M + (1-\phi)P_D, \tag{3}$$

where ϕP_M and $(1-\phi)P_D$ are prices in the imported and domestic goods, respectively, and ϕ refers to the share of each component. Correspondingly, we define a similar case for the trading partner: $P^f = \varphi P_M^f + (1-\varphi)P_D^f$.

With PPP, we assume that $P_M = P_M^f$. On the other hand, the price of the domestically produced good is determined by the costs of all production inputs and some fixed operating costs. For import-heavy economies like Bhutan, we can assume that a significant portion of its domestic production inputs are imports. As a price taker—being a small economy—these costs are likely to be influenced by the import price, P_M or P_M^f. Hence, P_D will be a function of the import price of its trading partner and a markup, ξ, to cover the fixed costs as well as profits: $P_D = \left\{P_M^f, \xi\right\}$. Hence, the domestic price can be written as $P = \phi P_M^f + (1-\phi)(P_M^f + \xi)$, or equivalently as

$$P = P_M^f + (1-\phi)\xi. \tag{4}$$

Most studies measuring price transmission implicitly assume constant real exchange rates. Many of these studies tackle the transmission of prices for individual commodities (for example, cereal, rice, and wheat) following the world price hikes in 2008 and 2011. The findings mostly reveal weak, incomplete, or insignificant pass-through of prices from the world economy to domestic economies (Conforti 2004; Dawe 2008; Minot 2011; Robles 2011; and Varela 2012).

There are few studies analysing the transmission of aggregate prices between world and domestic markets. One of the studies by Ginting (2007) on price transmission within the pegged exchange rate system between Nepal and India is a case very similar to Bhutan's. Ginting (2007) examined the relationship between prices in Nepal and India, using both headline and core prices, and found that price transmission exists through core prices. Headline inflation between both countries was shown to have only a weak long-run relationship despite the fact that Nepal's currency is pegged to the Indian rupee and that India is its largest trade partner.

The literature cites various factors that can cause weak transmission of prices, including substantial transport and transaction costs, domestic policy measures, and market structures. Goods reach consumers through layers of production and distribution processes, where various costs (for example, transportation and marketing) are added to the price of the good. A lack of appropriate transport and infrastructure limits the capacity to distribute goods from producers to consumers, which can have a significant effect on the level of prices. Policy measures such as import duties and export tariffs affect the extent to which domestic prices reflect prices in the world market or in the trading partner. Market structure is likewise a contributing factor to price formation. The more competitive the market structure, the greater the tendency for prices to be lower than in a monopolistic type of market structure.

Estimating Cointegration and Price Transmission from India

Consumer Price Data and Trends

Bhutan has been calculating consumer price data semi-annually since 1979. Disaggregated components of the Consumer Price Index (CPI), which comprise 12 major categories, were first made available on a quarterly basis beginning in September 2003.[3] Among the 12 major groups, food is the single largest component, accounting for nearly 40 per cent of the total weight. Non-food components collectively account for about 60 per cent (Table 7.1).

Following the PPP framework presented in equation (2), we use India's CPI for industrial workers to estimate transmission to Bhutan's consumer prices. India's national CPI covering both urban and rural areas is only available from January 2011 (CSO 2015). India has three other CPI series, but those are also segment-specific (that is, price index for agricultural labourers, rural labourers, and urban non-manual employees).

Using the expanded framework in equation (4), India's Wholesale Price Index (WPI) is employed as proxy indicator for import price. Bhutan has an open trade arrangement with India that is facilitated by a

[3] The monthly series of the price disaggregates was produced from January 2013, including new price details that separate imported and domestic goods, along with the revision of methodology and consumption weights that were based on the results of the Bhutan Living Standard Survey 2012. A little over half (52 per cent) of the CPI basket comprises imported goods and the remainder (48 per cent) comprises domestic goods. Correspondingly, more than half of food prices are for imported sources.

TABLE 7.1 Weights of Major Components of the Consumer Price Index[a] in Bhutan and India

Component	Weight (%)			
	Bhutan		India	
	National	Imported[a]	Domestic[b]	CPI[c]
Food	39.91	22.15	17.77	48.47
1. Food and non-alcoholic beverages	36.88			46.20
2. Alcoholic beverages, tobacco, narcotics	3.03			2.27
Non-food	60.09	29.84	30.24	51.53
3. Housing, water, electricity, gas and other fuels	21.70			21.70
4. Transport	11.98			4.41
5. Clothing and footwear	9.20			6.57
6. Health	4.67			4.56
7. Communication	3.03			0.46
8. Recreation and culture	2.35			
9. Furnishing, household equipment, housing maintenance	2.22			
10. Education	1.64			6.18[d]
11. Restaurant and hotels	1.24			
12. Miscellaneous goods and services	2.06			7.65
Total CPI	100.00	51.99	48.01	100.00

Notes: 1. [a] Bhutan's base period is December 2012; for India, it is 2001.
2. [b] Price data available only from January 2013.
3. [c] CPI for India is based on price data from the industrial worker segment of the population. The national CPI covering rural and urban areas is available only from January 2011. CPI = consumer price index.
4. [d] Includes recreation and amusement.
Sources: National Statistics Bureau, Bhutan, available at www.nsb.gov.bt (last accessed on October 2015); Ministry of Statistics and Programme Implementation, India, available at http://mospi.nic.in/Mospi_New/site/home.aspx (last accessed on October 2015).

bilateral free trade agreement (UNCTAD 2011). There are virtually no import tariffs or quotas, and other quantitative restrictions are limited. Hence, most consumer goods are openly sourced from India, which

TABLE 7.2 Weights of Major Components of India's Wholesale Price Index (2004–5 = 100)

Component	Weight (%)
Primary articles	20.12
Food	14.34
Non-food[a]	4.26
Minerals[b]	1.52
Fuel and power[c]	14.91
Manufactured products[d]	64.97
Total WPI	100.00

Notes: 1. WPI = Wholesale Price Index.
2. [a] fibers (raw cotton, jute), oilseeds, sugarcane, flowers, and other non-food primary articles.
3. [b] metallic minerals and crude petroleum.
4. [c] coal; mineral oils (for example, diesel, petrol, and liquefied petroleum gas), and electricity.
5. [d] manufactured food and beverages, textiles, wood, paper, leather products, chemical products, metallic mineral products, basic metal products, and machinery and transport.
Source: Reserve Bank of India, available at https://www.rbi.org.in/home.aspx (last accessed on October 2015).

makes the wholesale price a good proxy indicator for import price or P_M^f. The zero tariff cost supports the PPP assumption and therefore enhances the extent to which prices from India are transmitted to Bhutan. The WPI series comprises primary items (of which food has the single largest share), fuel and power, and manufactured goods (Table 7.2).

As equation (4) invokes the PPP hypothesis that $P_M = P_M^f$, we estimate an import price index for Bhutan using the imported price series data available from January 2013 onwards. We broadly define the index to include import-heavy goods such as food and beverages, transport, clothing, footwear, furnishing, and household equipment.[4]

To disentangle analysis, we use the disaggregated prices to measure price transmission in the food and non-food consumption baskets.[5]

[4] Index is estimated using the Laspeyres index formula with fixed base period weights.

[5] For India, the non-food component of the WPI is estimated by excluding the food-related items such as primary food, manufactured food, and beverages following the weighted arithmetic mean method of the Laspeyres formula.

To look at possible indirect effects, we allow a drift from the framework and measure the price transmission from food to non-food items and from non-food to food items. We also include the Manufactured Products Index (MFG) of India to isolate its impact on Bhutan's prices, given that India is Bhutan's major source of manufactured goods for domestic production inputs. We use quarterly data from the second quarter (Q2) of 2004 through Q2 2015 primarily due to data availability.

Time series plots for Bhutan's CPI and India's WPI are given in Figures 7.2 and 7.3, respectively. For both Bhutan and India, the aggregate price index and the disaggregated food and non-food price indices show steadily rising trends during 2005–15, suggesting that these variables might likely have deterministic trends. Food prices in both Bhutan and India are more volatile, have a higher standard deviation and mean, and grow at a faster rate than non-food prices (see Table 7A.1). Bhutan's CPI moves more closely in line with the non-food price series, given its higher weight. India's CPI moves almost in unison with wholesale food prices, as these prices comprise nearly half of the CPI's weight, which is a higher share than in Bhutan. India's WPI is much more driven by its non-food price component, which accounts for over 70 per cent of the total weight.

As illustrated in the time series plot in Figure 7.4, Bhutan's CPI shows stronger co-movement with India's WPI than India's CPI. India's CPI level has moved upward since 2009 along with the rising trend in its wholesale food prices; since then, Bhutan's CPI has correspondingly been trending lower than India's CPI. This tells us that the difference between India's consumer prices and its wholesale prices are larger than the price difference between Bhutan's CPI and India's WPI for most of the review period (Figure 7.5). Notably, India's WPI began trending downward in 2014, as prices eased for most of the major items, along with the decline in world food and fuel prices (Figure 7A.2). The CPI, however, has consistently remained on an upward trajectory.

Three distinct price hikes are visible in Bhutan CPI's time series data in Q2 2007, Q2 2008, and Q2 2012. The first two increases can be attributed to food price hikes in India, observable in both its CPI and WPI, which are roughly in line with developments in the world market (Lee and Park 2013). The price increase in Bhutan's CPI in Q2 2012 is an isolated case resulting from a domestic liquidity crisis triggered by a shortage of Indian rupees. Rapid credit growth and robust consumption from rising incomes sharply increased demand for imports and, hence, rupees.

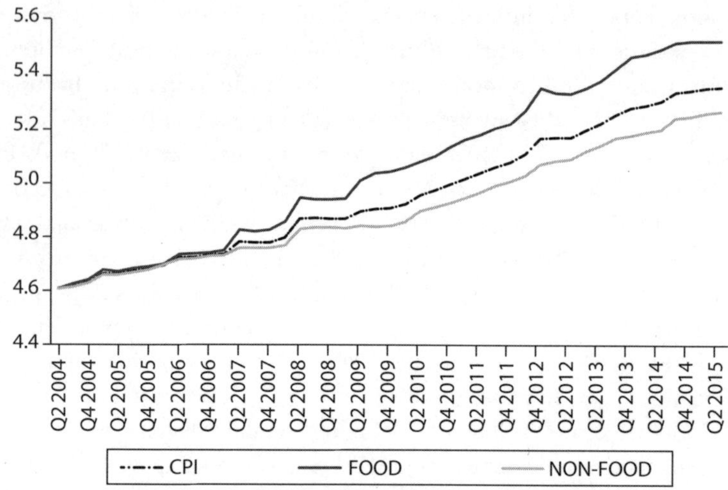

FIGURE 7.2 CPI, Food and Non-food Price Indices[a] in Bhutan
Notes: 1. CPI = Consumer Price Index; Q2 = second quarter; Q4 = fourth quarter.
2. [a] Prices are rebased to the starting date of the series and expressed in log form.
Source: National Statistics Bureau, Bhutan, available at www.nsb.gov.bt (last accessed on October 2015).

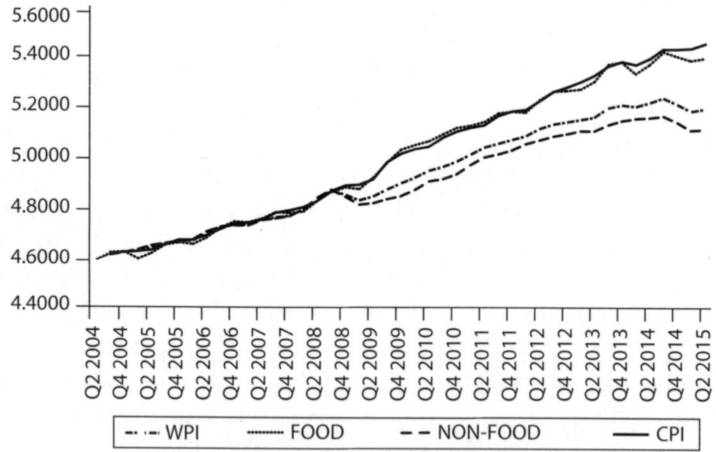

FIGURE 7.3 Aggregate Price, and Food and Non-food Price Indices[a] in India
Notes: 1. CPI = Consumer Price Index; Q2 = second quarter; Q4 = fourth quarter; WPI = Wholesale Price Index.
2. [a] Prices are rebased to the starting date of the series and expressed in log form.
Source: Reserve Bank of India, available at https://www.rbi.org.in/home.aspx (last accessed on October 2015).

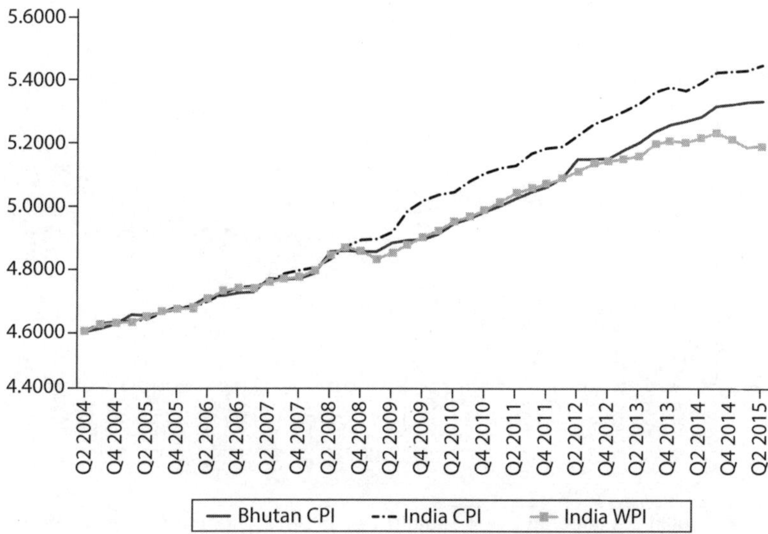

FIGURE 7.4 Aggregate Price Indices in Bhutan and India[a]

Notes: 1. CPI = Consumer Price Index; Q2 = second quarter; Q4 = fourth quarter; WPI = Wholesale Price Index.

2. [a] Prices are rebased to the starting date of the series and expressed in log form.

Sources: National Statistics Bureau, Bhutan, available at, www.nsb.gov.bt; Reserve Bank of India, available at, https://www.rbi.org.in/home.aspx (last accessed on October 2015).

This prompted the Government of Bhutan to introduce rupee rationing and other administrative restrictions, including credit and import bans, that greatly affected Bhutan's commodity supplies and food prices (Asian Development Bank 2013; Ura 2015).

Econometric Methodology

A critical assumption of the PPP framework is that the real exchange rate is constant (linear) over time. However, this might not be the case in practice. Hence, we test for nonlinearity before we employ empirical analysis of the price transmission. This applies to equation (2) involving consumer prices in India and Bhutan, as well as to the PPP assumption of equation (4) that $P_M = P_M^f$. The standard way to measure nonlinearity is through the smooth transition autoregressive model of Terasvirta (1994),

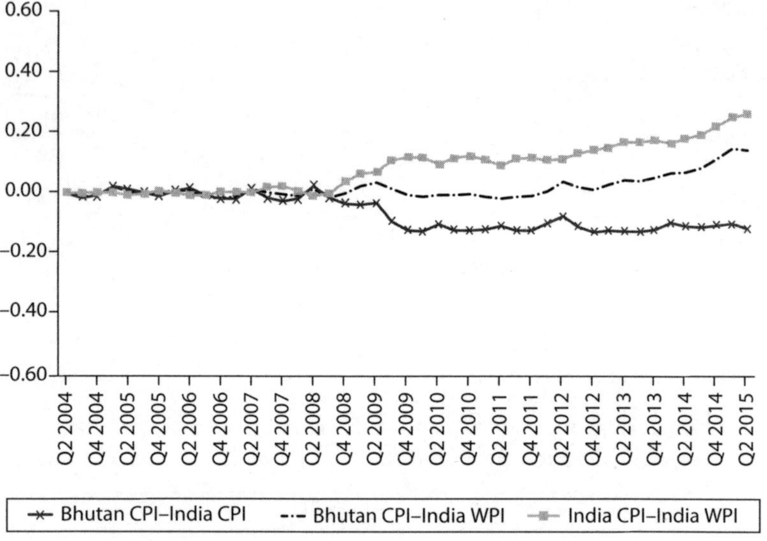

FIGURE 7.5 Differences between Aggregate Prices in Bhutan and India
Notes: 1. CPI = Consumer Price Index; Q2 = second quarter; Q4 = fourth quarter; WPI = Wholesale Price Index.
2. [a] Prices are rebased to the starting date of the series and expressed in log form.
Sources: National Statistics Bureau, Bhutan, available at, www.nsb.gov.bt (last accessed in October 2015); Reserve Bank of India, available at, https://www.rbi.org.in/home.aspx (last accessed in October 2015).

which has the null hypothesis of linearity. We employ this test using the JMulti package of Krätzig (2009), in which the linear hypothesis is checked through an F-test.

To measure the price transmission, we test the variables for the presence of cointegration, or a long-run relationship, and incorporate them in an error correction model. The basic idea of cointegration is that two nonstationary variables are said to be cointegrated, or move together in the long-run, if a linear combination between the two yields a stationary residual (Engle and Granger 1987; Johansen 1988). In other words, using the PPP equation (2), if two price variables, P_{At} and P^f_{At}, have stochastic trends and are integrated of order one, then the two are cointegrated if

$P^f_{At} - \alpha P_{At} = \varepsilon_t$ and ε_t is stationary, where α is the cointegrating parameter, ε_t is the error term.

There are a number of techniques to test for the presence of cointegration or of a long-run relationship between variables. One is the two-step, residual-based cointegration test by Engle and Granger (1987) and a similar approach by Shin (1994). Another is the system-based regression approach of Johansen (1988). For this research, we employ the bounds-testing methodology of the autoregressive distributed lag (ARDL) modelling of Pesaran and Shin (1999) and Pesaran, Shin, and Smith (2001).

The approach of Pesaran, Shin, and Smith (2001) has some advantages over the conventional methods. The use of the ARDL framework allows flexibility in the structure of lags of the regressors, as opposed to the system-based vector autoregression in which the number of lags is fixed for all variables. In addition, and perhaps more importantly, other techniques require that the underlying variables have to be integrated of the same order or integrated of order one or I(1). Many economic price data, however, exhibit deterministic trends. This technique will allow us to use a mixture of trend- or first-difference stationary series. The bounds test is based on standard F-statistics, using two sets of asymptotic critical values provided in Pesaran, Shin, and Smith (2001) to cover possible combinations of the variables into I(1), I(0), or mutually cointegrated.

Empirical analysis is employed using the Eviews package. All price variables were seasonally adjusted using the X-12 method and transformed into logarithmic form. We test for stationarity of the price variables using the Augmented Dickey–Fuller (ADF) test. In some cases, especially with small sample sizes, the ADF test can be unreliable when the root falls close to one or to the nonstationary boundary. We use the Phillips–Perron test and the Kwiatkowski–Phillips–Schmidt–Shin test to confirm the result. A breakpoint unit root test is applied to validate the stationarity process of the variables as well as to determine any significant series break, particularly the effects of the 2012 price hike in Bhutan. It is important that the variables are not I(2) for the application of the bounds test to be valid (Pesaran, Shin, and Smith 2001).

To estimate the price transmission with Bhutan's price series as the dependent variable and India's price series as the regressor, we specify an ARDL model which can be written as

$$logP_{i,t}^{B} = \alpha + \sum_{j=1}^{n} \rho_j logP_{i,t-j}^{B} + \sum_{j=0}^{m} \sigma_j logP_{i,t-j}^{W} + \varepsilon_t \tag{5}$$

where P^B is the Bhutan price series, P^W is the India price series, α is the intercept term, ρ_j and σ_j are the coefficients, ε_t is the error term, and i refers to the specific price index being estimated. Lag specification is based on the Schwarz criterion, which is considered to be a consistent model selector, as it penalizes the log-likelihood value when more lags are added. We check that the residuals of the above specification are serially independent using the Breusch–Godfrey serial correlation test. The model's stability test is conducted by employing the cumulative sum of recursive residuals (CUSUM) and the cumulative sum of squares of recursive residuals (CUSUMsq) (Pesaran, Shin, and Smith 2001).

Without prior knowledge of the relationship between the two underlying variables, we know that if they are cointegrated then there must exist an (unrestricted) error correction form of the ARDL specification, which can be written as

$$\begin{aligned} \Delta logP^B_{i,t} &= \mu_1 + \mu_2 t + \mu_3 D + \lambda_1 logP^B_{i,t-1} + \lambda_2 logP^W_{i,t-1} + \\ &\sum_{j=1}^{n} \phi_j \Delta logP^B_{i,t-j} + \sum_{j=0}^{m} \varphi_j \, \Delta logP^W_{i,t-j} + v_t \end{aligned} \tag{6}$$

where P^B is the Bhutan price series; P^W is the India price series; μ_1, μ_2, and μ_3, are the coefficients of the intercept, trend, and dummy variables, respectively; λ_1, λ_2, ϕ_j, and φ_j, are the coefficients of the regressors; and v_t is the error term. We specify an intercept and time trend, where applicable, in the equation in case some of the variables are trend stationary. We also include a dummy variable to account for the effect of a significant series break in 2012, if applicable. Lag specification is based on the Schwarz criterion.

We perform a bounds test using the above specification and, based on the F-statistic, determine whether a long-run relationship exist between the variables. Using the Pesaran, Shin, and Smith (2001) approach, we test for the absence of a relationship between $logP^B_i$ and $logP^W_i$ through the exclusion of their lagged variables in equation (6). The null and alternative hypotheses for the bounds test, respectively, are written as

$$\begin{aligned} H_0 &= \lambda_1 = 0, \lambda_2 = 0 \\ H_1 &= \lambda_1 \neq 0, \lambda_2 \neq 0 \end{aligned}$$

The computed F-statistics will be tested based on the two sets of asymptotic critical values provided by Pesaran, Shin, and Smith (2001).

Based on this methodology, if the computed F-statistic is outside of the critical value bounds, then we reject the null hypothesis of no cointegration. If the computed F-statistic falls within the lower and upper bound critical values, then the result is inconclusive.

If the variables are cointegrated, we estimate an error correction model. The long-run form is distinguished from the restricted short-run dynamics. The model for each pair of price variables takes the following form in the long run:

$$logP_{i,t}^{B} = \gamma + \beta logP_{i,t}^{W} + \varepsilon_t \quad (7)$$

where β is the long-run elasticity of price transmission. If there is a long-run relationship between the price variables, shocks can result in a disequilibrium in the short-run before the series reverts back to its long-run equilibrium. This speed of adjustment is captured in the error correction term (ECT) calculated from the long-run cointegrating vector:

$$logP_{i,t}^{B} - \gamma - \beta logP_{i,t}^{W} = \varepsilon_t (= ECT) \quad (8)$$

The error correction model is estimated as

$$\begin{aligned} \Delta logP_{i,t}^{B} &= \mu_1 + \mu_2 t + \mu_3 D + \\ &\sum_{j=1}^{n} \delta_j \Delta logP_{i,t-j}^{B} + \sum_{j=0}^{m} \theta_j \Delta logP_{i,t-j}^{W} + \lambda ECT_{t-1} + v_t \end{aligned} \quad (9)$$

where Δ reflects change in price, or $\Delta p_t = p_t - p_{t-1}$. μ, δ, θ and λ are the estimated parameters, where μ_1, μ_2, and μ_3 are the coefficients of the intercept, trend (if applicable), and dummy (if applicable) variables, respectively, δ is the autoregressive term reflecting inflation persistence, θ is the short-run elasticity of Bhutan's price series relative to India's price series, λ is the error correction coefficient that reflects the speed of adjustment, and v_t is the error term. n and m refer to the optimal lag length selected based on the Schwarz criterion.

Empirical Results

Linearity of the Real Exchange Rate

The linearity of the real exchange rate—or equivalently, the relative price index between Bhutan and India's price series since the exchange

TABLE 7.3 Nonlinearity Tests of the Real Exchange Rate

P-values of F-tests
Null hypothesis of linearity

(i) Bhutan CPI/India CPI

Sample range:	[Q2 2005–Q2 2015], T = 41			
lag length	F	F4	F3	F2
1	0.0682	0.4917	0.7480	0.0026
2	0.0651	0.1807	0.7133	0.0136
3	0.0384	0.1164	0.9837	0.0044
4	0.1963	0.5158	0.9817	0.0088
trend	0.3451	0.6330	0.5991	0.0568

Sample range:	[Q2 2005–Q4 2012], T = 31			
lag length	F	F4	F3	F2
1	0.3372	0.7837	0.8200	0.0156
2	0.1510	0.1983	0.7350	0.0477
3	0.1902	0.3096	0.8804	0.0237
4	0.5812	0.7169	0.9919	0.0523
trend	0.0421	0.0645	0.2492	0.1470

(ii) Bhutan TranP/India WPI

Sample range:	[Q2 2005–Q2 2015], T = 41			
lag length	F	F4	F3	F2
1	0.8049	0.8575	0.5168	0.4847
2	0.7033	0.8545	0.1698	0.8666
3	0.3191	0.4571	0.1673	0.4547
4	0.3783	0.1172	0.5998	0.7440
trend	0.2380	0.6921	0.0795	0.2761

Sample range:	[Q2 2005–Q4 2012], T = 31			
lag length	F	F4	F3	F2
1	0.1391	0.0587	0.2403	0.9048
2	0.4726	0.2951	0.7792	0.3043
3	0.5573	0.9960	0.4320	0.0787
4	0.3307	0.2346	0.6436	0.2542
trend	0.2417	0.4530	0.2069	0.1885

Source: Authors' Calculations.

rate is pegged one-to-one—is important for long-run PPP to hold (as discussed in the second section). We test for linearity on two relative price indexes: (i) $\frac{BHU\_CPI}{IN\_CPI}$ for equation (2), and (ii) $\frac{BHU\_T}{WPI}$ for the

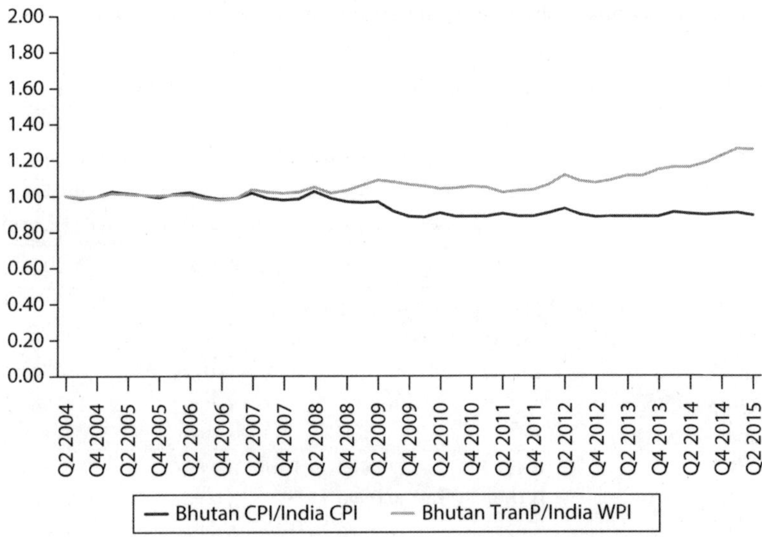

FIGURE 7.6 Relative Price Index
Notes: CPI = Consumer Price Index; Q2 = second quarter; Q4 = fourth quarter.
Source: Authors' Calculations.

PPP assumption in equation (4). The relative price indices presented in Figure 7.6 provide some indications of linearity in both cases.

The results of the smooth transition autoregressive test in Table 7.3 show nonlinearity for (i) for the whole sample, particularly in lags 1–3, but also provide indications of linearity if the sample range is defined up to 2012. For (ii), the results strongly confirm the assumption of linearity across all lags; hence, the PPP hypothesis, $P_M = P_M^f$ is adequate. The P-values of the F-statistic test cannot reject the null hypothesis of linearity whether the sample range is defined up until 2012 or 2015.

Stationarity of the Price Variables

The application of the ADF and Phillips–Perron tests produces mixed results for some of the price variables (Table 7.4). Using the ADF test, all variables are difference stationary or I(1) at the 1 per cent level of significance.[6] In the Phillips–Perron test, the results are similar with

[6] LBHU_TFOOD shows indications of being trend stationary at the 10 per cent level of significance.

TABLE 7.4 Results from the Augmented Dickey–Fuller and Phillips–Perron Unit Root Tests

Series	Augmented Dickey–Fuller				Phillips–Perron	
	Level exogenous: constant, linear trend		First difference exogenous: constant		Level exogenous: constant, linear trend	First difference exogenous: constant
	Prob.	Lag	Prob.	Lag	Prob.	Prob.
Bhutan						
CPI	0.3681	0	0	0	0.3753	0
FOOD	0.0762	1	0	0	0.0932	0
NON-FOOD	0.7559	0	0	0	0.7383	0
India						
WPI	0.8944	2	0.0002	1	0.9916	0.0387
CPI	0.2663	1	0.0006	0	0.292	0.0007
FOOD	0.6591	0	0.0003	0	0.5414	0.0004
NON-FOOD	0.7130	2	0.0003	1	0.9309	0.0423
MANUFACTURING	0.9040	2	0.001	1	0.9432	0.0981

Source: Authors' Calculations.

the exception of the variables LWPI and LIN_NONFOOD, which are first-difference stationary at the 5 per cent level of significance, and LIN_MFG, which is first-difference stationary at the 10 per cent level. Using the Kwiatkowski–Phillips–Schmidt–Shin test, these four variables were found to be trend stationary at the 1 per cent level of significance. The results from the breakpoint unit root test show that the price variables are either trend- or first-difference stationary at the1 per cent level of significance. Although the results are mixed, no price variable is I(2), which is critical for the results of the bounds test to be valid. The differing results further highlight the use of the bounds test as the appropriate approach for cointegration analysis in this case.

Using the breakpoint unit root test in which we specify the intercept break t-statistic to be at the maximum, Q2 2012 is found to be a significant break date at the 1 per cent level of significance, both for the LBHU_CPI and LBHU_TFOOD series. The test for critical values is based on the symptotic one-sided P-values. Hence, we specified a dummy, D_2012, for the equations where the LBHU_CPI and LBHU_TFOOD are the dependent variables.

TABLE 7.5 Results from the ARDL Bounds Test

Null hypothesis: no long-run relationships exist				
Regressor:	India CPI		India WPI	
Sample period:	Q2 2004–Q2 2015	Q2 2004–Q4 2012	Q2 2004–Q2 2015	Q2 2004–Q4 2012
F-statistic value	3.879	2.798	13.015	12.885
Critical Value Bounds				
Significance (per cent)	I0 Bound[a]		I1 Bound[a]	
10.0	4.04		4.78	
5.0	4.94		5.73	
2.5	5.77		6.68	
1.0	6.84		7.84	

Notes: 1. ARDL = autoregressive distributed lag; CPI = Consumer Price Index; Q2 = second quarter; Q4 = fourth quarter; WPI = Wholesale Price Index.
2. [a] For more details on the calculations, see Pesaran, Shin, and Smith (2001).
Source: Authors' Calculations.

Cointegration and Price Transmission Estimates: Aggregate Prices

All ARDL estimations have serially independent errors and were found to be dynamically stable models. The plots of both the CUSUM and CUSUMsq (Figure 7A.3) are within the boundaries, which confirm the stability of the long-run coefficients of the regressors as per Pesaran, Shin, and Smith (2001). The results of the null hypothesis that no long-run relationships exist are presented in Table 7.5. For a check of robustness, we use two sample periods: (i) the base sample period Q2 2004–Q2 2015; and (ii) the shortened sample period Q2 2004–Q4 2012, which is the period just before the two price series diverged considerably.

Based on the empirical results, the LBHU_CPI and LIN_CPI have no stable, long-run relationship. The F-statistic of the bounds test between LBHU_CPI and LIN_CPI falls below the 0.10 lower bound, suggesting the existence of cointegration, but weak at the 10 per cent level of significance only. The result weakens even as the shortened sample is used. This is consistent with the result of the nonlinearity of the relative price index in Table 7.3. The F-statistic of the WPI supports the presence of long-run relationships, which appear to be stable in both sample periods despite the diverging trend observed in their price levels in later years.

TABLE 7.6 Estimation Results of Price Transmission from India to Bhutan

India (source) $p_{i,t}^{W}$	Bhutan (domestic) $p_{i,t}^{B}$	Speed of adjustment, λ	Short-run elasticity, θ_k	Long-run elasticity, β	Persistence δ_j
CPI	CPI[a]	–0.113**	0.265	0.863*	–
	CPI[b]	–0.147**	0.274	0.805*	–
WPI	CPI[a]	–0.155*	0.274*	1.260*	–0.274**
					–0.278**
					–0.288**
	CPI[b]	–0.654*	0.740*	1.012*	–
			–0.473*		

Notes: 1. * = significant at 1 per cent level; ** = significant at 5 per cent level; *** = significant at 10 per cent level.

2. [a] Q2 2004–Q2 2015.

3. [b] Q2 2004–Q4 2012.

Source: Authors' Calculations.

The long- and short-run estimates are presented in Table 7.6. The long-run coefficient for LIN_CPI is about 0.8 for both sample periods, indicating that PPP does not hold. There are weak short-run dynamics and no inflationary persistence. The coefficient of the error term is negative and significant at the 5 per cent level, indicating a very slow speed of adjustment. The weak results for LIN_CPI can be attributed to the nonlinearity of the real exchange rate, which causes distortions in the PPP relationship. The LBHU_CPI and LIN_CPI have differed movement from 2008, when the LIN_CPI series scaled up following the continued rise in India's food prices until November 2013. As food has significant weight in the consumption basket, the food price hike kept the LIN_CPI and its inflation high, forming a trajectory that is higher than the LBHU_CPI as well as LWPI.

The WPI reveals more significant dynamics given the robust results of the cointegration and linearity tests. In the shortened series, where strong co-movement has been observed and the real exchange rate is much more stationary, the elasticity coefficient is 1.0. The short-run elasticity is likewise high, converging strongly with the long-run dynamics. The speed of adjustment is very quick; deviation is restored in about 1.5 quarters.

If we expand the series to include the most recent years for which data are available, the elasticity increases to 1.3, which is expected given how the price levels between the two countries have diverged during this period. This means that over the sample period, when the LWPI grew by 1 per cent, Bhutan's consumer price responded positively, increasing by 1.3 per cent. Price interactions, however will not always traverse across a uniform path. Various transitory shocks can occur arising from external factors that can cause deviations in the flow of production and distribution of goods and result in distortions of the long-run relationship of prices.

When these external shocks occur, the WPI has much weaker impact on Bhutan's inflation. In the short run, the contemporaneity effect of the WPI on the CPI declines considerably, and the adjustment towards the equilibrium level slows down distinctly. The short-run dynamics are driven more by strong inflationary persistence, with current inflation being affected by inflation within the past three quarters. Because of distortions and transitory shocks in the short-run, the lower elasticity coefficient indicates a slow adjustment process to the long-run equilibrium. On average, only about 15 per cent of the deviation from the long-run is restored per quarter when distortions arise in the short run.

The results show that the WPI series provides more insight into Bhutan's inflationary process, and is the more effective indicator of Bhutan's consumer price movements than India's CPI. It has a more significant effect, is more strongly cointegrated with Bhutan's CPI, and has a more stable long-run relationship with the latter despite the deviation in recent years. The results validate the contention that the pegged exchange rate system has helped in anchoring Bhutan's price level movements to those of India, which is supported by the linearity of the real exchange rate.

Bhutan's price elasticity with respect to changes in the WPI is high as its impact on Bhutan's domestic consumer prices occurs through both import and domestic goods, as indicated in the expanded PPP framework in the second section. Long-run elasticity is thus not expected to be, at most, 1.0. The impact of movements in the WPI is captured directly through the costs of imported goods, and indirectly through the costs of imported inputs into domestic production and producer markups.

We disentangle the analysis using the WPI disaggregates in the next subsection.

TABLE 7.7 Results from the ARDL Bounds Test

Null hypothesis: no long-run relationships exist			
	F-statistic value		
	Bhutan CPI	Bhutan FOOD	Bhutan NON-FOOD
India Source			
WPI	13.02***	9.05***	5.41[a]
FOOD	3.22*	4.03*	3.68*
NON-FOOD	13.26***	3.70*	4.73[b]
MANUFACTURING	8.19***	10.71***	3.71*

Notes: 1. ARDL = autoregressive distributed lag.
2. [a] The F-statistic fell inside the lower and upper bound critical values, which makes the result inconclusive. The error correction, however, is significant at the 1 per cent level, which is an alternative way to establish cointegration (Banerjee, Dolado, and Mestre 1998).
3. [b] inconclusive.
4. * = significant at 1 per cent level; ** = significant at 5 per cent level; *** = significant at 10 per cent level.
Source: Authors' Calculations.

Cointegration and Price Transmission Estimates: Disaggregated Prices

We examine the dynamics of price transmission through price disaggregates using the WPI series. We deviate from the framework at this point to account for possible indirect effects and measure the transmission from food-to-non-food and from non-food-to-food prices. The results of the bounds test are presented in Table 7.7. The long- and short-run estimates are presented in Table 7.8.

In the food price basket, there is a long-run relationship in food-to-food price transmission, although it is weak with significance at the 10 per cent level only. Domestic food prices respond positively to changes in India's food prices, although the elasticity of 0.5 is relatively low when compared with the transmission in the overall prices. Bhutan's food is more elastic to changes in the aggregate WPI and the price level of manufactured goods, where the long-run elasticities are high at 1.4 and 1.9, respectively.

The indirect effect from India's non-food prices to Bhutan's food price is likewise positive and significant, with elasticity at 0.5.

TABLE 7.8 Estimation Results of Price Transmission from India to Bhutan

India (source) $p^W_{i,t}$	Bhutan (domestic) $p^B_{i,t}$	Speed of adjustment, λ	Short-run elasticity, θ_k	Long-run elasticity, β	Persistence δ_j
WPI	FOOD	–0.325***	0.557** –0.200 –0.628**	1.438***	–
	NON-FOOD	–0.101***	0.259**	1.060***	–
FOOD	CPI	–0.080***	0.128	0.902***	–
	FOOD	–0.259***	0.290*	0.455**	–
	NON-FOOD	–0.076***	0.070	0.841***	–
NON-FOOD	CPI	–0.148***	0.283***	1.487***	–0.371*** –0.361*** –0.354***
	FOOD	–0.230***	0.356**	0.511**	–
	NON-FOOD	–0.093***	0.240***	1.223***	–
MANUFACTURING	CPI	–0.119***	0.340**	1.759***	–0.250* –0.275** –0.288**
	FOOD	–0.342***	0.604* –0.308 –1.067**	1.949***	–
	NON-FOOD	–0.084***	0.261	1.481***	–

Notes: 1. * = significant at 1 per cent level; ** = significant at 5 per cent level; *** = significant at 10 per cent level.

2. CPI = Consumer Price Index; WPI = Wholesale Price Index.

Source: Authors' Calculations.

This highlights the role of imported inputs in domestic food production and of the market distribution costs of the food supply, both of which thereby affect the formation of Bhutan's food prices. The low elasticity of food-to-food price transmission and much higher elasticity in price transmission from India's manufactured goods suggest a strong impact on Bhutan's domestic and imported food prices.

The cointegration result in the non-food to non-food price basket is not as conclusive, although estimating the error correction model shows a significant error correction term at the 1 per cent level of significance, which is another way to validate cointegration. The weak result could be attributed to the diversity in the price components, as Bhutan's non-food covers prices of both goods and services, while the WPI refers only to tradeable goods. The result is conclusive when the non-food price basket is estimated against the MFG, although the cointegration is significant only at the 10 per cent level. There is a significant and positive indirect effect from India's food prices on Bhutan's non-food prices, with long-run elasticity at 0.8.

In the short-run, only the CPI exhibited a highly significant persistence process, with current inflation significantly affected by inflation in the previous three quarters whether the non-food price index or the MFG is individually used as the regressor. Also, non-food and MFG inflation both showed a strong contemporaneity effect, which measures the short-run impact on Bhutan's inflation, but with no lag effects on CPI inflation.

Bhutan's food and non-food inflation both appear to show no individual dynamics and no autoregressive impact in the short-run. The contemporaneity effect of India's price is the significant indicator, whether the WPI or the non-food price index is used as the regressor. As with the long-run, the coefficients of the contemporaneous variables of WPI and MFG, reflecting their effects on Bhutan's food prices, are higher than those of India's food prices.

In each case of the ECT, its coefficient, λ, is negative and significant at the 1 per cent level, which is important in terms of consistency with the cointegration results. When transitory shocks occur in the short-run, Bhutan's food prices adjust back to their long-run equilibrium faster than non-food prices. This is consistent regardless of which price—WPI, food, non-food, or MFG—is transmitted from India. Between 23 per cent and 34 per cent of the divergence from the long-run equilibrium is restored per quarter; the quickest adjustment occurs with the MFG at 34 per cent per quarter. The speed of adjustment is very slow in Bhutan's non-food prices across all of India's price components. For Bhutan's food and non-food prices, as expected, the adjustment process is slowest when the long-run distortions are stemming from the indirect effects.

Summary and Policy Implications

This chapter examined the dynamics of price transmission from India, Bhutan's major source of imports. The bounds-testing approach of the

ARDL modelling of Pesaran, Shin, and Smith (2001) was employed for the cointegration analysis. This method is known to have the advantage of producing consistent estimates of the long-run coefficient, regardless of whether the regressors are trend or first-difference stationary. The short-run elasticities and the speed of adjustment back to the long-run equilibrium were estimated through an error correction modelling.

The empirical findings affirm the posited observation that a long-run equilibrium relationship exists between India's wholesale prices and Bhutan's consumer prices, with the result significant at the 1 per cent level. Disentangling the price disaggregates show that in the long-run, prices likewise converge in the food basket as well as indirectly between non-food-to-food and food-to-non-food. Prices in the non-food basket however have weak cointegration, arising from dissimilarity in price components and domestic policies, causing prices to deviate to new trajectories. The empirical results affirm four interesting points:

1. Bhutan's large import concentration with India, openly traded through a one-to-one pegged exchange rate with the Indian rupee, has underpinned the extent to which domestic prices has been anchored with India's prices;
2. With the WPI as an import price measure, the results support Bhutan's significant dependence on supply from India, affecting directly through the import prices of goods and indirectly through the costs of the imported inputs to domestic production and distribution of goods;
3. The WPI is the useful price monitoring indicator for Bhutan to anticipate likely domestic price changes and potential sources of inflationary pressures. The use of India's CPI showed strong deviation from the PPP, arising from the nonlinearity of the relative price index, and dissimilarity in price coverage and segment sample, creating trend biases and diverging price patterns;
4. Whether prices fall or rise, prices would be transmitted significantly from India, making Bhutan susceptible to price swings in India. Given the high price elasticities, domestic price increases would be steeper when India's wholesale prices escalate. As India's wholesale prices have been mostly low and stable throughout the years, Bhutan has gained on sustained basis, resulting in lower domestic prices and inflation compared to most countries in the region. The recent shift

to an inflation-targeting policy in India bodes well for more price stability in Bhutan.

Monitoring the dynamics of India's wholesale prices is important in anticipating likely changes in domestic consumer prices, which has great relevance for informed policymaking in Bhutan. High elasticities from indirect price transmission (for example, from non-food to food prices) underscore the need to monitor significant second-round effects and the likely greater impacts on domestic goods, which can cause more deviation from the long-run equilibrium and higher inflation for Bhutan. The strong contemporaneous effect but weak or no lagged effects in the short run suggest that Bhutan's price formation is immediate to the dynamics in the current period. A more frequent tracking mechanism of prices is advisable.

Given the fixed exchange rate system, the exchange rate effectively cannot be used for macroeconomic adjustment; hence, monetary policy actions have to focus on continued monitoring of liquidity and credit conditions to avoid excessive buildup of inflationary pressures. There is greater room for fiscal measures to focus on strengthening Bhutan's trade linkages through investment in infrastructure and the implementation of market-oriented policies aimed at minimizing transport and transaction costs. In either direction that import prices move, it is important for Bhutan to consistently allow market-based price formation processes to occur. Market-based prices reflect opportunity costs, and are therefore good basis for more effective decisions on the production and distribution of goods, which is critical for an efficient distribution of resources on the whole.

Appendix

TABLE 7A.1 Descriptive Statistics for Bhutan and India's Major Price Indices (log form)

	Bhutan Prices				India Prices					
	CPI	Food	Food Non-Beverage	Non-Food	WPI	Food	Fuel	Minerals	Manufacturing	Non-Food
Mean	4.949	5.049	5.045	4.900	4.932	5.082	5.046	5.438	4.845	4.903
Median	4.901	5.033	5.033	4.836	4.907	5.107	4.990	5.428	4.829	4.881
Maximum	5.342	5.514	5.509	5.254	5.243	5.586	5.433	5.981	5.061	5.172
Minimum	4.605	4.605	4.605	4.605	4.605	4.600	4.605	4.605	4.605	4.605
Std. Dev.	0.234	0.299	0.299	0.200	0.208	0.325	0.240	0.440	0.153	0.183

Notes: CPI = Consumer Price Index; WPI = Wholesale Price Index.

Sources: Authors' Calculations; National Statistics Bureau, Bhutan, available at, www.nsb.gov.bt (last accessed on October 2015); Reserve Bank of India, available at https://www.rbi.org.in/home.aspx (last accessed in October 2015).

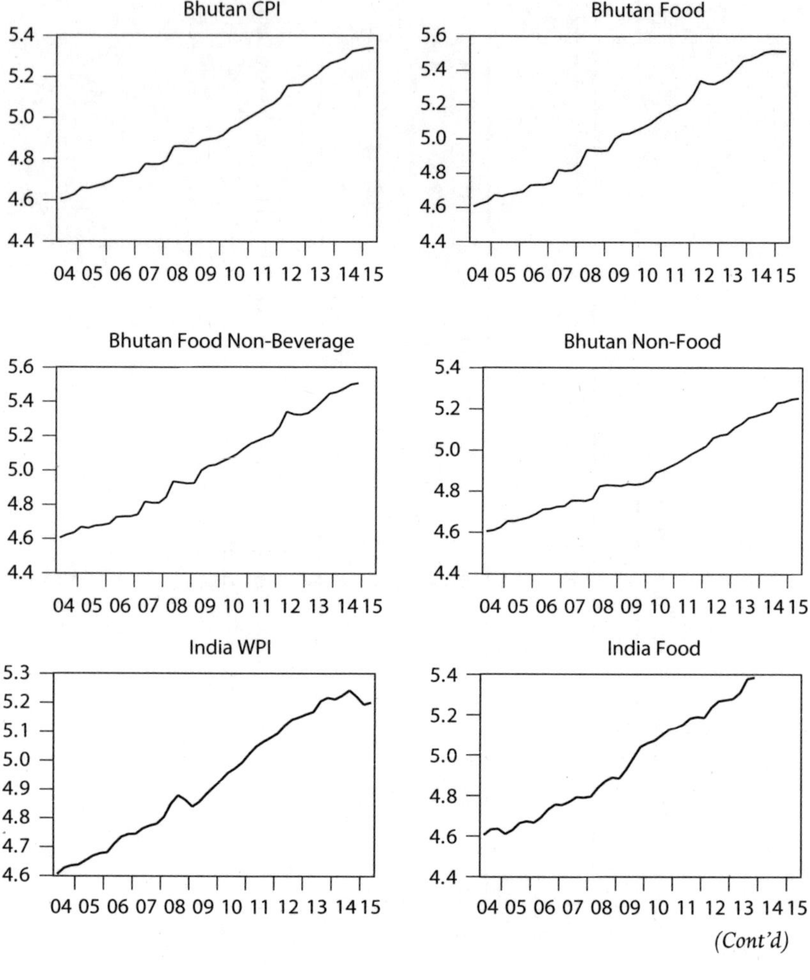

(Cont'd)

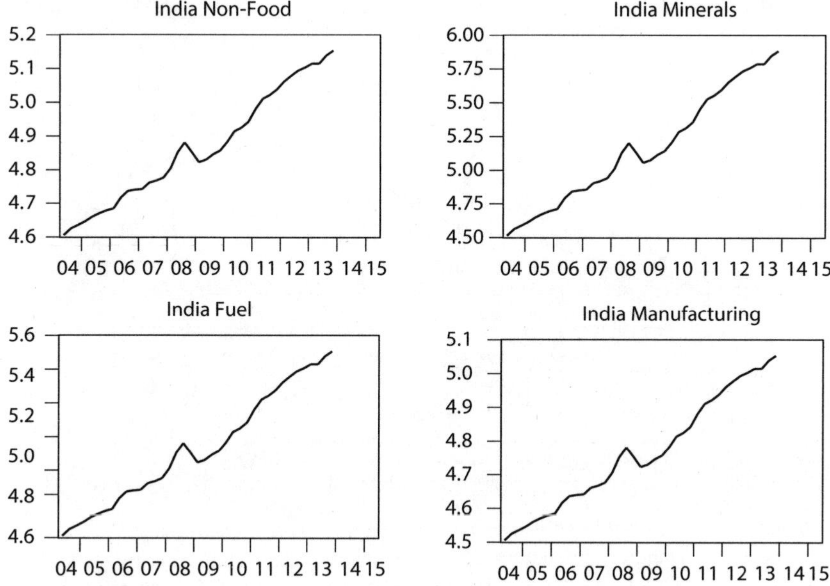

FIGURE 7A.1 Bhutan and India's Price Variables (log form, seasonally adjusted)

Sources: Authors' Calculations; National Statistics Bureau, Bhutan, available at www.nsb.gov.bt (last accessed on October 2015); Reserve Bank of India, available at https://www.rbi.org.in/home.aspx (last accessed on October 2015).

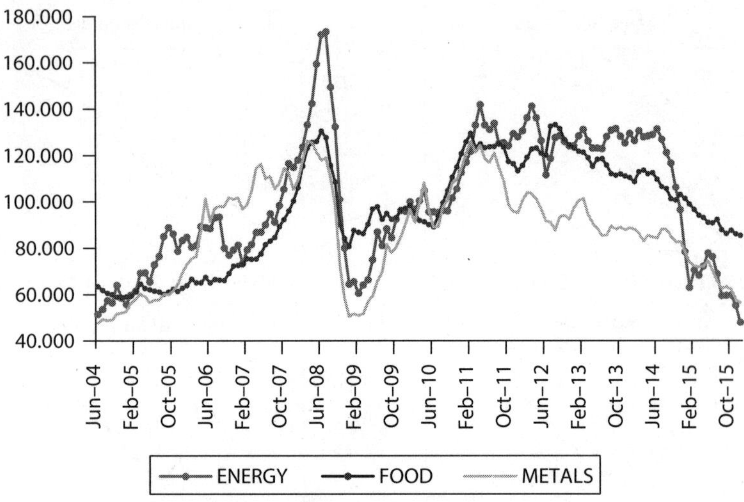

FIGURE 7A.2 World Commodity Prices (2010 = 100)

Note: Monthly indices based on nominal US dollars.

Source: World Bank, Commodity Price Data (Pink Sheet), available at https://knoema.com/WBCPD2015Oct/world-bank-commodity-price-data-pink-sheet-april-2016 (last accessed on April 2016).

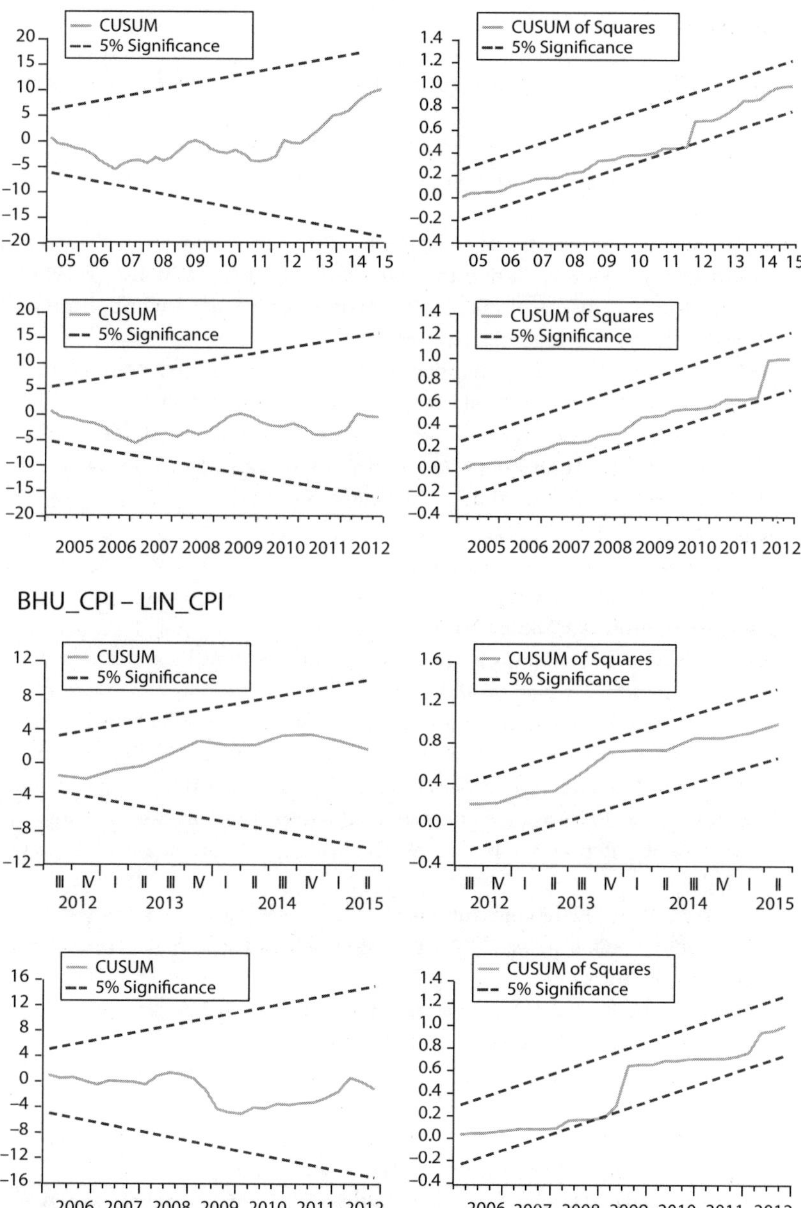

FIGURE 7A.3 CUSUM and CUSUM of Squares Test

Note: CUSUM = cumulative sum of recursive residuals.

Source: Authors' Calculations.

References

Asian Development Bank (ADB). 2013. *Asian Development Outlook: Asia's Energy Challenge*. Manila: ADB.

Banerjee, A., J. Dolado, and R. Mestre. 1998. 'Error-Correction Mechanism Tests for Cointegration in a Single Equation Framework', *Journal of Time Series Analysis*, 19(3): 267–83.

Baltzer, K. 2013. 'International to Domestic Price Transmission in Fourteen Developing Countries during the 2007–08 Food Crisis', WIDER Working Paper No. 2013/031. Helsinki: United Nations University—World Institute for Development Economics Research.

Central Statistics Office. 2015. *Consumer Price Index: Changes in the Revised Series*. India: Ministry of Statistics and Programme Implementation.

Conforti, P. 2004. 'Price Transmission in Selected Agricultural Markets', FAO Commodity and Trade Policy Research Working Paper No. 7. Rome: Food and Agriculture Organization of the United Nations.

Dawe, D. 2008. 'Have Recent Increases in International Cereal Prices Been Transmitted to Domestic Economies? The Experience in Seven Large Asian Countries', ESA Working Paper No. 08–03. Rome: Food and Agriculture Organization of the United Nations.

Engle, R.F. and C.W.J. Granger. 1987. 'Cointegration and Error Correction: Representation, Estimation, and Testing', *Econometrica,* 55(2): 251–76.

Ginting, E. 2007. 'Is Inflation in India an Attractor of Inflation in Nepal?', IMF Working Paper No. 07/269. Washington, DC: International Monetary Fund.

International Monetary Fund. 2014. '2014 Article IV Consultation—Staff Report', Press Release and Statement by the Executive Director for Bhutan. IMF Country Report No. 14/178. Washington, DC: International Monetary Fund.

______. 2015. World Economic Outlook Database. Available at https://www.imf.org/external/pubs/ft/weo/2015/02/weodata/index.aspx (last accessed on 26 October 2015).

Johansen, S. 1988. 'Statistical Analysis of Cointegration Vectors', *Journal of Economic Dynamics and Control,* 12(2–3): 31–254.

Kenny, G. and D. McGettigan. 1997. 'Inflation in Ireland: Theory and Evidence', *Journal of the Statistical and Social Inquiry Society of Ireland,* 27(1997): 157–207.

______. 1999. 'Modeling Traded, Nontraded, and Aggregate Inflation in a Small Open Economy', *The Manchester School,* 5(1999): 60–88.

Krätzig, M. 2009. *JMulti 4: Analyzing Multiple Time Series*, available at www.jmulti.com (last accessed on April 2016).

Lee, H.H. and C.-Y Park. 2013. 'International Transmission of Food Prices and Volatilities: A Panel Analysis', ADB Economics Working Paper Series No. 373. Manila: Asian Development Bank.

National Statistics Bureau. 2008. *Consumer Price Index for the Quarter Ending 31 March 2008*. Thimphu.

______. 2014. *Consumer Price Index for the Quarter Ending 31 March 2014*. Thimphu.

______. 2014. *Monthly Consumer Price Index Bulletin October 2014*. Thimphu.

______. 2015. *Monthly Consumer Price Index Bulletin July 2015*. Thimphu.

Ministry of Finance. 2014. *Bhutan Trade Statistics 2014*. Thimphu.

Minot, N. 2011. 'Transmission of World Food Price Changes to Markets in Sub-Saharan Africa', IFPRI Discussion Paper No. 01059. Washington, DC: International Food Policy Research Institute.

Pesaran, M.H. and Y. Shin. 1999. 'An Autoregressive Distributed Lag Modelling Approach to Cointegration Analysis', in S. Strom (ed.), *Econometrics and Economic Theory in the 20th Century: The Ragnar Frisch Centennial Symposium*, pp. 371–413. Cambridge: Cambridge University Press.

Pesaran, M.H., Y. Shin, and R.J. Smith. 2001. 'Bounds Testing Approaches to the Analysis of Level Relationships', *Journal of Applied Econometrics,* 16(3): 289–326.

Robles, M. 2011. *Price Transmission from International Agricultural Commodity Markets to Domestic Food Prices: Case Studies in Asia and Latin America*. Washington, DC: IFPRI.

Royal Monetary Authority of Bhutan (RMA). 2013. *Annual Report 2012/2013*. Thimphu.

______. 2014. *Annual Report 2013/2014*. Thimphu.

______. 2015. *Monthly Statistical Bulletin August 2015*. Thimphu.

Shin, Yongcheol. 1994. 'A Residual-Based Test of the Null of Cointegration against the Alternative of No Cointegration', *Econometric Theory,* 10(1): 91–115.

Sun, Y. and R. Duttagupta. 2008. 'Price Dynamics in the Eastern Caribbean', IMF Working Paper No. 08/90. Washington, DC: International Monetary Fund.

Terasvirta, T. 1994. 'Specification, Estimation, and Evaluation of Smooth Transition Autoregressive Models', *Journal of the American Statistical Association,* 89(1994): 208–18.

UNCTAD. 2011. *Who is Benefiting from Trade Liberalization in Bhutan? A Gender Perspective*. Geneva: United Nations Conference on Trade and Development.

Ura, K. 2015. 'Bhutan's Indian Rupee Shortage: Macroeconomic Causes and Cures', ADB South Asia Working Paper Series No. 40. Manila: Asian Development Bank.

Varela, G.J. 2012. 'Incomplete, Slow, and Asymmetric Price Transmission in Ten Product Markets of Bolivia', Policy Research Working Paper No. 6291. Washington, DC: World Bank.

8

INKYO CHEONG, TAEHO BARK,
AND HOE YUN JEONG

A Framework of Trade Policy for Bhutan Compatible with the Gross National Happiness

Bhutan's Path of Open Trade

Bhutan is a typical landlocked country and heavily trades with a limited number of neighbouring countries. Because Bhutan has a small domestic market and an unfavourable resource endowment for industrialization, majority of its population lives on primary sectors and trade issues are not national policy priorities. However, Bhutan has increased trade volumes from the 1990s, making trade an indispensable part of its economy. Trade policy is a requisite for all countries. The key issue is how to set up optimal trade policy framework aimed at maximizing economic gains from trade and specialization.

Bhutan is renowned for its gross national happiness (GNH) philosophy, but it faces many social and economic issues. One of these issues is the need to raise Bhutan's living standards. Its economic growth, so far, has been led mainly by hydropower sector development and has not been creating enough jobs, especially for the young. Inequality remains high, even though Bhutan has been successful in reducing poverty. Bhutan thus needs to ensure a more inclusive and job-generating growth.

As a country in the early stages of economic development,[1] Bhutan has been trying to improve its business environment since 2008 in order to attract investments and so improve its people's well-being, although it still lags behind its neighbours in this respect. The country faces many challenges in boosting its economy and attracting foreign direct investments (FDIs) to its target sectors. Easing regulations favours business activities, but it is just one of the factors being considered by investors. Furthermore, investors usually examine the overall competitiveness of the country before investing. Bhutan needs to recognize that its neighbours are also competing for FDIs.

The Government of Bhutan requires new trade policies to meet the threshold score of the GNH index. However, the GNH index includes some factors seemingly unfavourable to an active trade policy. Moreover, although the share of trade reached 80 per cent of gross domestic product (GDP) as of 2013, the involvement of the trade authority in the government is very small (the trade authority belongs to only 1 of 10 departments under the Ministry of Economic Affairs). In most countries, trade policies are administered in the cabinets, such as Ministry of Commerce, Ministry of Trade, or Ministry of Foreign Affairs and Trade. Bhutan is a landlocked country with little economic power, which has resulted in a passive attitude towards international trade.[2]

[1] Bhutan achieved lower-middle-income status in 2006. Using the World Bank Atlas method, middle-income economies for the current 2015 fiscal year are defined as those with a gross national income (GNI) per capita of more than $1,045 but less than $12,746. Lower-middle-income and upper-middle-income economies are separated at a GNI per capita of $4,125. Countries with a GNI of $11,905 or less are defined as developing. (Source: http://data.worldbank.org/about/country-and-lending-groups [last accessed on 4 February 2015]) ADB's *Basic Statistics* (2014b) estimated Bhutan's per capita GNI at $2,420 as of 2012.

[2] Warr (2012: 6) states, '[h]istorically, landlocked countries have generally been pessimistic about the scope for an export-oriented development strategy. They have generally chosen inward-looking development strategies'. Hydropower development is one of Bhutan's top priorities. The Indian government is proud of supporting Bhutan in planning and funding the project that largely exports electricity to India.

Performance of the Macroeconomy and External Sector

Macroeconomy

Although the growth rates in 2012–14 slowed because of a tight monetary policy in 2012, Bhutan's GDP grew by 6.69 per cent on average during the Tenth Five Year Plan (2008–13), achieving commendable socio-economic gains. The domestic economy grew 2.05 per cent in real terms in fiscal year (FY) 2013,[3] and 2.10 per cent in FY2014 (Table 8.1). Total budget spending was moderated in FY2014, but the current account deficit remained elevated (ADB 2014a: 165). It is common for developing countries to have large trade deficits and current account deficits in the early stages of economic development owing to the imports of capital goods. Bhutan's capital formation contributes to the country's production capacity, and the receipt of foreign exchange from newly built facilities plays an important role in managing the macroeconomy.[4]

Bhutan began to record huge trade deficits since 2008, worsening in 2010 and 2011, due to rising imports for building social infrastructure and rising domestic consumption.[5]

While the expansion of the hydropower sector has helped propel Bhutan's economic growth and development, the heavy reliance on the sector has had a deleterious effect on the country's current account deficit. The sector's requirements for imported capital equipment and skilled workforce as well as servicing of its short-term debts have swelled the current account deficit and put pressure on international reserves. Rapid growth in the power sector further spilled over into the other sectors of the economy, creating additional demand for imported goods and services from main trading partner, India.

[3] The fiscal year (FY) of the government ends on 30 June. FY before a calendar year denotes the year in which the fiscal year ends, for example, FY2013 ends on 30 June 2013.

[4] Capital-intensive hydropower development contributed 20.9 per cent on average to Bhutan's GDP growth over 2000–13 (ADB 2014a: 166).

[5] Bhutan's total consumption increased sharply after 1995. The share of final expenditure to GDP was 60 per cent in 1995, growing to 70 per cent in 2000, and to 75 per cent in 2013.

TABLE 8.1 Macroeconomic Performance of Bhutan

Item	FY 2010	FY 2011	FY 2012	FY 2013	FY 2014
GDP ($ billion, current)	1.59	1.82	1.82	1.78	1.70
GDP per capita ($ billion, current)	2.28	2.57	2.53	2.44	2.29
GDP growth (%, in constant prices)	11.73	7.89	5.07	2.05	2.10
Primary	0.85	2.41	2.25	2.94	n.a.
Secondary	12.48	4.06	6.77	3.49	n.a.
Tertiary	15.21	13.89	4.29	0.33	n.a.
Gross domestic capital formation (% of GDP)	62.15	64.43	63.52	40.71	n.a.
Gross domestic savings (% of GDP)	33.42	38.37	43.60	25.24	n.a.
Consumer price index (annual % change)	7.02	8.86	10.92	8.77	8.10
Overall fiscal surplus (deficit) (% of GDP)	1.80	(2.30)	(1.20)	(4.40)	(4.40)
Merchandise trade balance (% of GDP)	(28.70)	(23.10)	(23.40)	(22.60)	(21.50)
Current account balance (% of GDP)	(24.30)	(32.60)	(23.30)	(28.20)	(27.30)
External debt service (% of exports of goods and services)	30.70	51.70	127.10	229.20	26.80
External debt (% of GDP)	66.60	79.50	87.40	98.40	101.30

Notes: n.a.= not available; figures in brackets = negative; GDP = gross domestic product.

Sources: Royal Government of Bhutan (2014a); RMA (2014).

The share of the current account deficit to GDP was as high as 32.6 per cent in 2011, but dropped to 28.2 per cent in 2013 owing to a tightened aggregate demand policy when the country faced a shortage of its Indian rupee reserves in 2012. In order to reduce the trade deficit, the government tightened credit constraints on imports and instituted import restrictions, particularly for large-scale construction projects that required rupee payments.[6] As a result, '[t]he brunt of the downdraft in FY2013 was felt in services. Expansion in transport and communications halved to 5.2% from 10.3%, while growth in retail trade, hotels and restaurants, and other services moderated mainly owing to slower domestic spending, especially on vehicles' (ADB 2014a: 164).

[6] Imports for hydropower development were exempted from the government's import restrictions.

External Sector

Bhutan maintains a close relationship with India, politically and economically, based on the geopolitical environment. Traditionally, India has been Bhutan's most important donor country, both for projects and general-purpose grants. Bhutan's currency is pegged to the Indian rupee, and Indian demand accounts for most of Bhutanese exports. Bhutan trades heavily with India (85 per cent of its total trade), and most of the trade deficit is also with India. The majority of Bhutanese imports of necessities, including food, come from India. Moreover, India is the only country that imports the electricity produced in the valleys along the western province of Bhutan.

With relatively high trade restrictions and no direct access to international ports, Bhutan's trade with the rest of the world is limited. Being a landlocked country and depending on the Indian ports, Bhutan conducts the majority of its cross-border trade with India. Apart from India, Bangladesh and Nepal have traditionally been important trading partners, while recently Northeast Asian countries such as People's Republic of China (PRC), Japan, and the Republic of Korea have also joined as Bhutan's trading partners. Bhutan's trade deficit has been recorded since FY2008, and it peaked in 2011. Facing a rupee crisis in 2012, the country introduced tight fiscal and monetary policies, after which its trade deficit began to decrease.

In 2010, the Bhutanese government issued an all-encompassing economic development policy (Royal Government of Bhutan 2010b) guided by the overarching philosophy of GNH based on the four pillars of sustainable economic development; preservation and promotion of culture and tradition; conservation of environment; and good governance.[7] However, since the document is a unilateral act of the government and therefore lacks an internationally binding mechanism, there is concern that the trade policy stated in it would be modified or reversed

[7] The Economic Development Policy is intended to be the 'apex policy for economic development of the country and shall be the guiding document for all ministries and agencies to stimulate the economy growth and more importantly, to ensure that growth takes place in consonance with the principles of GNH' (Royal Government of Bhutan 2010b: 5).

TABLE 8.2 The Trend in Bhutanese External Performance ($ million)

Item	FY2007	FY2008	FY2009	FY2010	FY2011	FY2012	FY2013	FY2014
Current account	83.90	(111.10)	(76.00)	(318.60)	(521.40)	(393.40)	(500.90)	(463.80)
with India	73.50	(86.60)	(74.40)	(197.50)	(401.10)	(312.00)	(480.80)	(435.90)
Trade balance	78.50	(45.50)	(73.90)	(269.40)	(459.90)	(395.50)	(401.70)	(364.70)
with India	100.70	(0.70)	(12.40)	(125.50)	(334.70)	(254.50)	(313.90)	(286.30)
Exports	573.30	598.70	509.50	524.80	665.80	616.60	545.60	534.60
To India	473.20	538.10	480.00	481.50	562.00	548.00	502.40	486.30
Imports	494.80	644.20	583.30	794.20	1125.70	1012.10	947.30	899.30
From India	372.60	538.80	492.50	607.00	896.70	802.50	816.20	772.60
Services	(29.00)	(65.80)	(42.20)	(71.10)	(94.60)	(94.50)	(61.90)	(87.50)
Credit	60.20	54.70	56.50	68.80	81.80	102.40	123.30	132.10
Debit	89.20	120.40	98.70	139.90	176.30	196.90	185.20	219.60

Note: figures in brackets = negative.

Sources: Royal Government of Bhutan (2010, 2014b); RMA (2014).

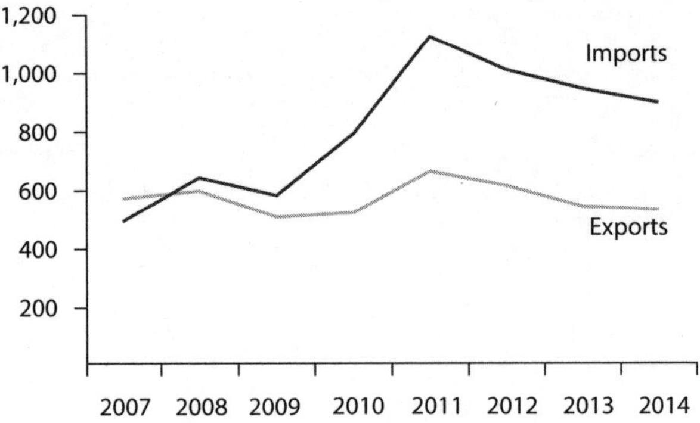

FIGURE 8.1 Trends in Bhutan's Exports and Imports ($ million)
Sources: Royal Government of Bhutan (2010a, 2014b); RMA (2014).

in the future.[8] Therefore, it is not clear whether the government would continue its binding commitments to liberalizing the import regime, including a reduction in most favoured nation tariffs and non-tariff barriers, other than its South Asian Association for Regional Cooperation (SAARC) commitments.[9] As a landlocked country, Bhutan had few trading partners, such as India and Bangladesh, even as recently as the 1990s. However, things are changing as Bhutan is gaining more trading partners. Though India still remains to be an important trading partner, the number of other trading partners has increased to more than 10, beginning 2008. This implicitly indicates that, overall, the country's trade restriction has gradually been eased.

Bhutanese total exports were 29.6 billion ngultrum (Nu) ($0.53 billion) in 2012, down from Nu31.4 billion ($0.64 billion) in 2011, although both years showed an increase from the Nu8.2 billion ($0.18 billion) in 2004. Most trade occurred with geographically adjacent countries, such as India and Bangladesh. In 2012, 98 per cent of Bhutanese exports were sent to India, Bangladesh, and Nepal, and 79 per cent of its total imports were Indian products. As the number of Bhutan's export partners

[8] One of the reasons for joining the World Trade Organization (WTO) is the improvement of binding commitments and transparency on trade policy. Non-WTO members bear international duty of keeping their commitments.

[9] Bhutan has a tariff liberalization plan under a SAARC agreement to gradually reduce peak tariff rates to 5 per cent by end of 2015.

TABLE 8.3 Bhutan's Exports by Year and Destination (Nu million)

	1990	1995	2000	2005	2006	2008	2010	2012	2013
Total	1,221.6	3,350.1	4,615.8	11,386.2	18,771.9	22,590.6	29,324.4	29,618.4	20,625.7
India	1,055.3	3,079.0	4,377.0	9,969.8	14,488.0	21,480.0	26,000.9	27,825.6	17,751.9
	(86.4)	(91.9)	(94.8)	(87.6)	(77.2)	(95.1)	(88.7)	(93.9)	(86.1)
Bangladesh	127.8	201.1	164.8	561.8	470.1	632.4	906.1	1,172.2	1,465.0
	(10.5)	(6.0)	(3.6)	(4.9)	(2.5)	(2.8)	(3.1)	(4.0)	(7.1)
Germany	n.a.	n.a.	n.a.	n.a.	n.a.	2.0	0.4	30.3	298.3
						(0.0)	(0.0)	(0.1)	(1.4)
Hong Kong, China	n.a.	n.a.	0.0	685.9	2,866.0	105.3	2,188.3	79.1	234.7
			(0.0)	(6.0)	(15.3)	(0.5)	(7.5)	(0.3)	(1.1)
Italy	n.a.	n.a.	n.a.	n.a.	n.a.	0.0	15.5	125.0	191.1
						(0.0)	(0.1)	(0.4)	(0.9)
Netherlands	n.a.	n.a.	n.a.	n.a.	n.a.	0.1	0.2	70.1	154.7
						(0.0)	(0.0)	(0.2)	(0.8)
France	n.a.	n.a.	n.a.	n.a.	n.a.	0.4	0.6	0.1	152.1
						(0.0)	(0.0)	(0.0)	(0.7)
Belgium	n.a.	n.a.	n.a.	n.a.	n.a.	11.2	n.a.	n.a.	111.5
						(0.0)			(0.5)
Nepal	n.a.	n.a.	n.a.	n.a.	n.a.	195.8	39.7	107.4	87.1
						(0.9)	(0.1)	(0.4)	(0.4)
Japan	n.a.	n.a.	n.a.	n.a.	n.a.	66.0	132.5	113.7	65.7
						(0.3)	(0.5)	(0.4)	(0.3)
Singapore	n.a.	n.a.	0.9	72.8	585.4	n.a.	n.a.	n.a.	n.a.
			(0.0)	(0.6)	(3.1)				

(*Cont'd*)

TABLE 8.3 (*Cont'd*)

	1990	1995	2000	2005	2006	2008	2010	2012	2013
Thailand	n.a.	n.a.	2.1	32.9	282.4	n.a.	n.a.	n.a.	n.a.
			(0.0)	(0.3)	(1.5)				
Nepal	n.a.	n.a.	28.4	44.8	57.4	n.a.	n.a.	n.a.	n.a.
			(0.6)	(0.4)	(0.3)				
Others	38.5	70.0	42.6	18.1	22.5	97.6	40.4	94.9	113.6
	(3.2)	(2.1)	(0.9)	(0.2)	(0.1)	(0.4)	(0.1)	(0.3)	(0.6)

Notes: 1. n.a. = not available.

2. Figures in parentheses represent an economy's share of Bhutan's total exports in a given year.

3. An entry of '0.0' indicates a marginal value compared to '-' which indicates no value for that particular item.

Sources: RMA (2014, earlier issues of *Annual Report*).

increased to 8–10 economies, the country's export volume jumped in 2004 and 2005. Germany; Hong Kong, China; Italy; Japan; and Nepal became new export destinations, although India and Bangladesh still account for the bulk of the country's exports.

Bhutan's major export items—referring to merchandise goods and excluding services such as electricity and water utilities—are natural resources or semi-processed ones such as ferro-silicon (HS 720221), semi-finished products of iron or non-alloy steel (720712), carbides of calcium (284910), Portland pozzolana cement (252329), and carbides of silicon (284920). The export of ferro-silicon (containing more than 55 per cent of silicon) represented 37 per cent of Bhutan's total exports of goods.

Imports have increased steadily since 1990, and, although the trade deficit was not large, it showed an increasing trend. Imports jumped in 2004, causing the trade deficit to grow beyond Nu10 billion for the first time. The trade deficit then decreased, until the trade balance became a surplus in 2007. However, in 2010, Bhutan's trade deficit began to increase sharply again, growing by 35 per cent in 2012 due

TABLE 8.4 Bhutan's Top 10 Export Goods, 2013 (Nu million, %)

BTC Code	Commodity Description	Value (Nu million)	Share (%)
7202.21.00	Ferro-silicon containing more than 55% of silicon	7,672	37.20
7207.12.00	Semi-finished products of iron or non-alloy steel	1,730	8.39
2849.10.00	Carbides of calcium	981	4.76
2523.29.30	Portland pozzolana cement	887	4.30
2849.20.00	Carbides of silicon	830	4.02
7214.30.00	Bars and rods of iron and non-alloy steel	744	3.61
0908.31.00	Cardamoms (neither crushed nor ground)	656	3.18
2520.10.00	Gypsum; anhydrite	558	2.17
0805.10.00	Dolomite, not calcined or sintered, chips	519	2.52
2518.10.20	Others	513	2.49
		5,531	26.82
Total		20,626	100.00

Note: BTC refers to 'Bhutan Trade Classification'.

Source: Royal Government of Bhutan (2014a).

Table 8.5 Bhutan's Imports by Year and Origin (Nu million)

	1990	1995	2000	2005	2006	2008	2010	2012	2013
Total	1,425	3,642	7,875	17,035	19,012	23,495	39,075	52,674	52,316
India	1,173 (82.3)	2,630 (72.2)	6,231 (79.1)	12,795 (75.1)	13,054 (68.7)	17,340 (73.8)	29,329 (75.1)	41,826 (79.4)	43,666 (83.4)
China, People's Republic of	n.a.	n.a.	1.8 (0.0)	182 (1.1)	282 (1.5)	845 (3.6)	611 (1.6)	1,330 (2.5)	1,089 (2.1)
Thailand	n.a.	n.a.	106 (1.3)	276 (1.6)	258 (1.4)	411 (1.7)	988 (2.5)	741 (1.4)	1,081 (2.1)
Singapore	14 (1.0)	194 (5.3)	251 (3.2)	447 (2.6)	515 (2.7)	965 (4.1)	903 (2.3)	784 (1.5)	970 (1.9)
Sweden	n.a.	n.a.	n.a.	n.a.	n.a.	241 (1.0)	550 (1.4)	609 (1.2)	817 (1.6)
Austria	n.a.	n.a.	n.a.	n.a.	n.a.	25 (0.1)	78 (0.2)	940 (1.8)	696 (1.3)
Germany	23 (1.6)	71 (1.9)	28 (0.4)	200 (1.2)	200 (1.1)	285 (1.2)	362 (0.9)	224 (0.4)	304 (0.6)
Japan	74 (5.2)	412 (11.3)	305 (3.9)	648 (3.8)	396 (2.1)	1,099 (4.7)	845 (2.2)	1,261 (2.4)	296 (0.6)
Switzerland	n.a.	n.a.	n.a.	n.a.	n.a.	131.3 (0.6)	177 (0.5)	393 (0.7)	292 (0.6)
Republic of Korea	n.a.	n.a.	124 (1.6)	248 (1.5)	459 (2.4)	287 (1.2)	2,005 (5.1)	1,659 (3.1)	281 (0.5)
Indonesia	n.a.	n.a.	n.a.	240 (1.4)	1,331 (7.0)	n.a.	n.a.	n.a.	n.a.

Russian Federation	n.a.	n.a.	n.a.	162 (1.0)	875 (4.6)	n.a.	n.a.	n.a.	n.a.
Malaysia	n.a.	n.a.	8 (0.1)	175 (1.0)	352 (1.9)	n.a.	n.a.	n.a.	n.a.
United States	18 (1.3)	13 (0.4)	n.a.	n.a.	n.a.	n.a.	n.a.	n.a.	n.a.
United Kingdom	9 (0.6)	58 (1.6)	n.a.	n.a.	n.a.	n.a.	n.a.	n.a.	n.a.
Others	116 (8.1)	265 (7.3)	749 (9.5)	1,662 (9.8)	1,290 (6.8)	1,868 (8.0)	3,227 (8.3)	2,909 (5.5)	2,824 (5.4)

Notes: 1. n.a. = not available.

2. Figures in parentheses represent an economy's share of Bhutan's total imports in a given year.

3. An entry of '0.0' indicates a marginal value compared to '-' which indicates no value for that particular item.

Sources: RMA (2014, earlier issues of *Annual Report*).

to hydropower development, and exposing the country to a foreign exchange crisis. The bulk of imported goods comes from India. Asian manufacturing powers such as the PRC, Japan, and the Republic of Korea are more recent trade partners, accounting for only 5 per cent of Bhutan's total imports.

Unlike exports, imports are spread evenly to several items. The largest imports are petroleum oils constituting about 11 per cent of the total imports, followed by ferrous metals, DC motors and generators, petrol, brown rice, and hydraulic turbines. Many of the top 10 imports are used for building or maintaining hydropower plants. Bhutan has embarked on a major programme of building 16 hydropower projects to provide electricity for itself and India. As of 2013, four projects were already producing electricity, and work had started on another four. In 2015, a fifth project (Dagachhu) began generating electricity, and work had been planned on five more projects.

Elements and Promotion System of Gross National Happiness

Bhutan's journey with GNH began in the mid-1970s, and initiatives to develop more elaborate and precise metrics to measure GNH have been under way since 2008. GNH is a 'multi-dimensional development

TABLE **8.6** Bhutan's Top 10 Imports, 2013 (Nu million, %)

BTC Code	Commodity Description	Value (Nu million)	Share (%)
2710.19.15	Petroleum oils and oils	5,655	10.66
7203.10.00	Ferrous products	1,888	3.56
8501.33.00	DC motors, DC generators	1,861	3.51
2710.12.10	Motor spirit (petrol)	1,750	3.30
1006.20.10	Husked (brown) rice	1,061	2.00
8410.13.00	Hydraulic turbines and water wheels	1,028	1.94
2701.19.00	Other coal	1,014	1.91
4402.90.00	Wood charcoal	990	1.87
2523.29.30	Portland pozzolana cement	825	1.56
2704.00.10	Coke and semi-coke	753	1.42
	Others	36,220	68.28
Total		53,050	100.00

Note: BTC refers to 'Bhutan Trade Classification'.

Source: Royal Government of Bhutan (2014a).

FIGURE 8.2 The Four Pillars and the Nine Domains of Gross National Happiness
Source: Royal Government of Bhutan (2013).

approach that seeks to achieve a harmonious balance between material well-being and the spiritual, emotional, and cultural needs of Bhutan'.[10]

The GNH Commission ensures that the GNH is properly implemented in plans, policies, and programmes. It is composed of the Prime Minister as the chairperson, the finance minister as the vice chairperson, and the secretaries to the GNH Commission, Cabinet Secretariat, National Environment Commission, and 10 ministries as members.

With several changes to the governance of the GNH, almost all central agencies are now supposed to promote the GNH under the leadership of the Prime Minister. In addition, all new policies should go through evaluation from the viewpoint of the GNH. All relevant dimensions of the GNH are considered in a systematic way while assessing policies and projects. If a policy does not pass the screening test (higher than 66 points across 33 GNH indices are required to pass), the authorities are required to submit a revised policy following the comments and recommendations of the commission.

[10] Gross National Happiness Commission, available at http://www.gnhc.gov.bt (last accessed on 25 December 2014).

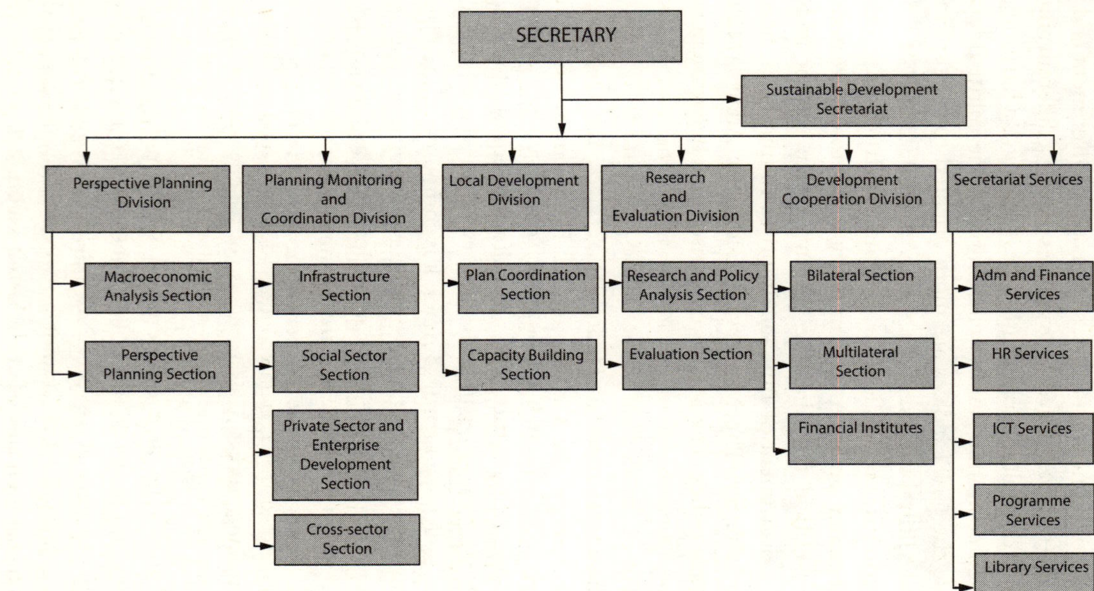

FIGURE 8.3 Structure of the Gross National Happiness Commission

Notes: HR = human resource; ICT = information and communication technology.

Source: GNH Commission, available at http://www.gnhc.gov.bt/organizational-chart/ (last accessed on 3 October 2016).

Trade Policy in the Gross National Happiness System

Trade policy, which falls under Pillar 1 of the GNH, can pass through GNH screening so long as it improves living standards and does not adversely affect noneconomic factors, such as the environment and the national culture. However, active trade policies may be a different animal altogether as it is difficult for trade authorities to achieve a harmonious balance between economic gains (well-being) and the spiritual factor. This is because the GNH indices are more oriented toward spiritual, emotional, and cultural values.[11]

Normally, countries reshuffle their government structure to implement national policy goals. A new ministry tends to be created for dealing with a critical task that the current system cannot address properly. The Government of Bhutan comprises 10 ministries, headed by the Prime Minister. The Ministry of Economic Affairs (MOEA) administers trade policy. The MOEA comprises nine departments and one office: the Department of Trade, the Department of Industry, the Department of Intellectual Property, the Department of Geology and Mines, the Department of Hydromet Services, the Department of Renewable Energy, the Department of Hydropower and Power Systems, the Department of Cottage and Small Industry, and the Office of Consumer Protection. About one-tenth or less of the MOEA is dedicated to international trade policy.

There are very few countries in which trade policy occupies such a small share of the government structure. Many countries have a ministry of commerce or trade (for example, the United States and Singapore),

[11] Ura (2015) noted that certain economic decisions tend to bypass the GNH decision-making process. 'This is true also of the operation of the agencies such as Ministry of Economic Affairs charged with economic liberalization in terms of free trade and FDI. They advocate, by virtue of their role, such practices that are not ultimately assessed from the point of view of GNH but from mainstream economics.' It is important to note this internal diversity that allows two very different thought structures to come into play. The internal debate continues whether GNH supports and does not conflict with growth, noted Ura: '[w]hether both aims can be achieved while holding true to GNH will be a next major challenge that should not be underestimated. One reason why the government is compelled by the growth aspiration is that it seeks to generate jobs for the youth'.

while others have joint ministries for trade and industry (for example, Japan and the Republic of Korea) or for foreign affairs and trade (for example, Australia and Canada). Neighbouring countries such as Nepal, Bangladesh, and Pakistan have ministries of commerce. Designing and defending trade policies require strong professional staff equipped with a background in international economics and the legal aspects of international trading systems, as well as domestic laws and regulations and business information. There are clear limitations to being promoted as an expert on trade policy under the GNH structure. Thus, Bhutanese government officials are not likely to specialize in trade policy, even though the country needs experts in trade theory and practice.

Active trade policy can be one of the most effective tools in improving the GNH. Although Bhutan has limitations in international trade, there is room for joining global supply chains (GSCs) and expanding trade. Active trade policy can be a basis for improving business climate in services, including ecotourism. Bhutan is in transition from a closed country to an open country, and its population is increasing. The country needs to think about how to create quality jobs for its educated young generation. In most countries, youngsters tend to seek modern lifestyle with quality jobs. Active trade policy can create more jobs, which is compatible with the principles of the GNH.

In most cases, ministers tend to act like politicians, making economic decisions based on populist choices so as to be re-elected in the next polls. The ministers of trade in many countries generally make political judgements on sensitive issues. The Bhutanese minister of economic affairs is likely to consider many aspects covered by the ministry when there are conflicts between trade and other policies. Liberalizing trade issues is not a politically popular policy; even the US government sometimes withdraws trade policy agenda during a national election. Rather than earning the ire of the electorate by liberalizing trade policy, politicians tend to choose protective measures, even when a freer trade policy is in the interest of the nation. Thus, many sensitive and important trade policies could be rejected, making binding commitments with regard to an open trade policy unlikely.

Trade policy includes political economic aspects, which tend to become political issues. Active (open) trade policies are not likely to be viable without a combination of a strong will for the policy and political support. This is particularly true among emerging economies, where opposition voices can be much louder than those supporting a policy, even though the logic of the policy is correct and the policy is compatible with national interest. In many cases, the discussion on an active trade policy tends to be biased towards the opposition; hence, there needs to be a balanced treatment of the policy. In the case of Bhutan, this may be more serious. The trade policy capacity should be reviewed and improved, otherwise issues will not be considered properly and the country will become further marginalized in terms of globalization and regional and global economic integration.

The Way Forward

One of the most urgent tasks in Bhutan is to improve general living standards. The authority needs to benchmark successful development strategies in other countries, and to recognize that no country can sustain economic development without an open trade policy in the end. Equally, an appropriate domestic policy needs to be adopted to minimize excessive socio-economic costs from open trade policy.

Most of the augmented capital was allocated to harness hydropower for a decade, which means that productivity growth in the manufacturing sector was limited. The productivity of Bhutanese farmers, who account for 62 per cent of all workers, has not improved, mostly remaining at the subsistence level. Jobs need to be created within the manufacturing sectors for inclusive growth, which will offer employment to rural workers. With the enhancement of an entrepreneurial spirit, the financial infrastructure should be improved so that small- and medium-sized enterprises (SMEs) can have access to credit and financing services.

Trade liberalization is not so simple as to be classified as 'all or nothing', that is, either 'good' or 'bad'. Dynamic processes and the final incidence of a trade policy can be analysed using an in-depth assessment. As a developing country, Bhutan needs a continuous inflow of foreign capital and economic development to enhance the many factors related to human well-being. No substantial FDIs will be feasible without improving the overall business environment in Bhutan. In addition, there needs to be a balanced evaluation of material and spiritual matters. The current trade authority and trade system should be improved and expanded within the government structure. Introducing a separate ministry could be costly, but to make active trade policy viable and to have balanced policy discussions, the country needs a more powerful trade authority. One idea is for the Department of Trade to establish Centre for Trade Policy falling directly under the Prime Minister, which would enable trade policy issues to be discussed with more authority.

Global Supply Chains

Deepening Global Supply Chains

Although the world economy has suffered from serious downturns, including the global financial crisis of 2008, the spread of open economic systems and the increase in international trade have been major sources of global economic growth and welfare improvement. The 2008 crisis severely impacted East Asian economies, but the recovery in East Asia was also faster compared to other regions of the world. East Asian economies' relatively quick recovery from the global financial crisis has largely been attributed to the region's high export capacity and expansionary monetary and fiscal policies.[12]

Open economic systems have progressed with the development of international economic theory since the publication of Adam Smith's *The Wealth of Nations* in 1776. David Ricardo's comparative advantage theory shows that trade liberalization drives the reallocation of production resources and specialization in sectors with a comparative advantage, benefiting all the trading parties. Different factor endowments matter in the Heckscher–Ohlin theorem. A country can collect economic gains by specializing in the production of a product with a relatively rich endowed production factor, which is used intensively in producing that product.[13]

The GNH is consistent with the goal of international trade theory, as both target the maximization of welfare. Appropriate trade policies can promote Bhutan's living standards and facilitate the country's goal of full employment and sustained growth—all of which are also the national goals of Bhutan. The clear benefits of trade were explicitly acknowledged in the *Economic Development Policy* (Royal Government

[12] For example, see Rhee and Posen (2013).

[13] Classical and neoclassical international trade theories were based on inter-industry trade, such as the exporting of automobiles or the importing of food.

of Bhutan 2010b) which, guided by GNH principles, stated thus: 'Trade is an essential part of the economy and has great potential to create employment. The policy on trade shall focus on creating an enabling environment for more robust trade. This will encompass simplifying administrative procedures and deregulating activities wherever feasible. The Royal Government shall facilitate trade between Bhutan and all countries'. Furthermore, international trade leads to other benefits. It can foster deeper economic and financial integration with Bhutan's trading partners; broaden market access and scope for Bhutanese products and services; provide access to up-to-date green technology; facilitate the country's competitiveness with stronger productivity growth; help lift the country from any economic slowdown; help attract foreign investments; create opportunities for innovation through the spread of new ideas; and lower prices and provide greater choice to consumers. Trade agreements, in addition, can provide the enabling framework for good governance and respect for human rights and indigenous culture. In fact, trade agreements with advanced economies such as the European Union, for instance, attach great importance to wider social and environmental issues such as respect for the rule of law, ethical business practices, and the like.

However, open trade policy can also have adverse effects on income distribution and may lead to degradation of the environment, even when national income expands as a whole. That is, trade policy could have its own political and economic pros and cons.

Despite these adverse effects, international trade is inevitable as the Bhutanese economy keeps expanding at its hectic pace, a fact that is clearly understood by Bhutan's government.[14] Here, one of the key aspects to consider is the absolute size of the positive effects versus the negative effects. If the benefits exceed the costs, the remaining task of policymakers should be how to compensate the losers from open trade policy, rather than giving up the opportunity to expand national income and boost the net welfare of citizens due to presence of anticipated

[14] 'The successful implementation of the Economic Development Policy would lead to growth in the trade sector both at the import and export fronts. This will invariably require improvement in domestic laws, rules and regulations that would boost investor confidence' (Royal Government of Bhutan 2010b: 14).

negative effects. The lesson provided by Adam Smith is still effective in modern days, and the importance of trade in improving national welfare is supported when deliberate domestic policy is considered.

The painful transition towards an open trade-oriented economy may be alleviated by direct government policy intervention. Such interventions would necessarily include the institution of safety nets that provide assistance to workers and communities adversely affected by the changes, help train or retrain workers and thus develop a talent pool of technically educated human resources that would attract foreign investments, and support domestic industries to retool and equip for participation in the growing opportunities for ancillarization and subcontracting/outsourcing in international trade.

Although international trade theory is clear about policy direction, it is not easy for developing countries to join the international trade market. There is fierce competition for export markets, and the terms of trade tend to count against emerging economies because of higher value added in advanced technology parts and service-based software embedded in the product. A typical example is the assembly of Apple iPhones in the PRC, highlighting the importance of recognizing the size of value added in trade rather than trade volume. International economic organizations such as the WTO and the Organisation for Economic Co-operation and Development (OECD) began to pay attention to the statistical illusion provided by traditional trade statistics. Concern for value added is consistent with the principle of the GNH, because it drives policymakers to adopt more welfare-improving policies.

The global trade environment has changed substantially since the 1990s, as the information and communication technology (ICT) and the transportation system have developed, along with trade liberalization in the mid-1980s. During the 1990s, cross-national FDIs expanded and multinational companies began to increase the outsourcing of intermediate parts. Production has become increasingly fragmented, and subdivided production stages for inputs and parts are now spread across multiple countries along GSCs.[15] Joining the GSCs became a

[15] According to Stadtler (2005: 5), supply chain management is 'the task of integrating organizational units along a [supply chain] SC and coordinating materials, information and financial flows in order to fulfil (ultimate) customer demands with the aim of improving competitiveness of the SC as a whole'.

basic requirement for a country's industrial development during the time of Baldwin's (2011) 'second unbundling'.[16] Moreover, the stages of production have expanded and fragmented across national boundaries, a phenomenon known as the global production network (GPN). Both the GSC and GPN imply a 'globally organized nexus of interconnected functions and operations' (Henderson et al. 2002). Multinational companies face the task of integrating organizational units for production and distribution, coordinating the flow of materials in each stage, and managing financial flows and the expertise (intellectual property rights) for improving the competitiveness of their products and services.

Developing Economies Joining Global Supply Chains

The world economy has observed fast growing and deepening global value chains in the late 1990s and early 2000s. This provides more opportunities for transition economies to join the international trade, because countries no longer need to build an integrated production facility to execute an entire production. The South–South trade (that is, trade between developing countries) has grown because of fragmented production processes. The distribution of trade is heavily in favour of emerging countries, such as the BRICS countries (Brazil, the Russian Federation, India, the PRC, and South Africa). Many developing economies face serious capacity constraints in taking advantage of new business opportunities. This point has changed the role of international institutions, such as the Asian Development Bank (ADB), Economic and Social Commission for Asia and the Pacific (ESCAP), the World Bank, WTO, and others.

Developing countries have typically pursued two approaches: supporting development and building capacity. In the Doha Development Round, the agenda of development has been a key factor in current multinational trade negotiations led by the WTO. Various international and regional economic institutions and donor countries have supported developing economies, especially in improving the capacity of trade

16 The second unbundling, according to Baldwin, occurred in the post-1985 period when telecommunications became cheap, reliable, and widespread. This made it economical to geographically separate manufacturing stages, which then led to scale economies and the emergence of comparative advantage among countries.

facilitation. 'Aid for Trade' became one of the popular topics in conferences on international trade. Here, one of the main challenges of the developing economies is to establish an open trade system that targets the improvement of international competitiveness. This will enhance the capacity of developing economies to absorb knowledge and utilize international assistance strategically, while allowing them to remain open to international trade and not resorting to unnecessarily protective measures.

Rather than trade policy alone, a joint policy between industrial development and trade consideration is more desirable in the current situation of deepening GSC. This could provide new momentum for developing economies. According to Baldwin (2011: 1), '[r]evolutionary transformations of industry and trade occurred from 1985 to the late-1990s—the regionalisation of supply chains. Before 1985, successful industrialisation meant building a domestic supply chain. Today, industrialisers join supply chains and grow rapidly because offshored production brings elements that took Korea and [Taipei,China] decades to develop domestically'.

Prior to the mid-1980s, low wage rate was one of the primary factors in deciding the location of factory. But during the second unbundling, the competiveness of the overall business environment is considered along with the merits of low wages, since business and transportation costs are critical factors when a part of production stages or tasks are outsourced. While this could be an additional burden for developing countries, it does bring new opportunities. Although, massive production facilities are no longer a prerequisite for a developing country to develop its industry and to join international trade, the country needs to find competitive production stages or tasks and improve the competiveness of its overall business environment.

Many developing countries could join global value chains in numerous sectors, reducing the number of poverty-stricken families, contributing to regional economic development, and improving the living standards in the region and country. The Lao People's Democratic Republic and Nepal, for example, have been successful in this regard.[17]

[17] Recent economic performances of Viet Nam, Mongolia, and Ethiopia are described briefly in Appendix A as examples of developing countries' economic development.

Bhutan's Trade Policy Issues

Trade and Inclusive Growth

Trade can act as a powerful engine for economic growth and development, especially in Asia and the Pacific region.[18] Developing countries have long strived for a development strategy that will sustain high economic growth, create employment opportunities, and eliminate poverty. Developing countries are using trade policy as a tool to attain these development objectives.

It is possible to draw two extreme assessments on Bhutanese trade policy. First, it can be said that the country has open trade policy as its overall effective tariff rate is very low—Bhutan freely trades with India, the dominant trading partner representing over 80 per cent of Bhutan's total imports. Second, it can also be said that Bhutan heavily depends on a single country in trade—this makes Bhutan pay extra social costs to Indian exporters. The challenge is how to diversify the country's trade partners by reducing import tariff and non-tariff barriers.

Trade is considered an important tool in the alleviation of poverty. Trade facilitation can reduce poverty by increasing economic opportunities for everyone. Empirical and qualitative studies make clear that the negative impacts of income inequality can be contained when a government implements trade facilitation measures in a step-by-step manner and provides safety nets (for example, income protection or insurance schemes) to redistribute income during the adjustment process (ESCAP 2013).

It is clear that each policy can have both positive and negative effects, and there is no 'one-size-fits-all' strategy (Higgins and Prowse 2010) as idiosyncratic factors need to be considered. The government's role is critical in creating conditions that ensure that the poor do not suffer from the short-term adjustments that trade facilitation measures might entail. Thus, trade policy can lead to inclusive growth when governments introduce income redistribution and a sophisticated domestic adjustment system. In this regard, De and Raychaudhuri (2013) argue that governments need to provide adequate education and capacity building opportunities.

[18] This section mainly draws on the article by Ratna and Ferracane (2013).

Countries cannot survive without international trade. For its national welfare, Bhutan should promote trade, along with the domestic measures to mitigate any of its adverse effects. It should be a trade policy framework compatible with the principle of the GNH.

Trade Facilitation

The capacity to deliver goods and services in time and at a low cost is crucial to stay competitive in export markets, and it plays a favourable role in encouraging the inflow of FDIs. A reduction of transaction costs for international trade is as important as a reduction of traditional trade restrictions such as tariffs and fees. Since the mid-1990s, an increased awareness of these trade-related, cross-border transactions costs has called for multilateral rule-making, under the heading of 'trade facilitation', by international organizations such as the WTO and World Customs Organization. It has also promoted regional or plurilateral coordination, such as among ADB, Asia-Pacific Economic Cooperation, SAARC, and ESCAP.

The definition of trade facilitation can be as broad as an institutional and physical infrastructure, and is indirectly associated with all the costs incurred in the cross-border movement of goods and services. The WTO (2015) describes trade facilitation as providing faster and more efficient customs procedures through effective cooperation between customs and other authorities on trade facilitation and customs compliance issues. The definition also contains provisions for technical assistance and capacity building.

The primary target of trade facilitation is the reduction or streamlining of the logistics of moving goods through ports and the documentation requirements at a customs post at the border. More precisely, the European Commission defines trade facilitation as the simplification and harmonization of international trade procedures, including import and export procedures. These procedures include 'the activities (practices and formalities) involved in collecting, presenting, communicating and processing the data required for the movement of goods in international trade' (European Commission 2014).

According to the OECD (2013), reducing global trade costs by 1 per cent would increase worldwide income by 0.05 per cent or more

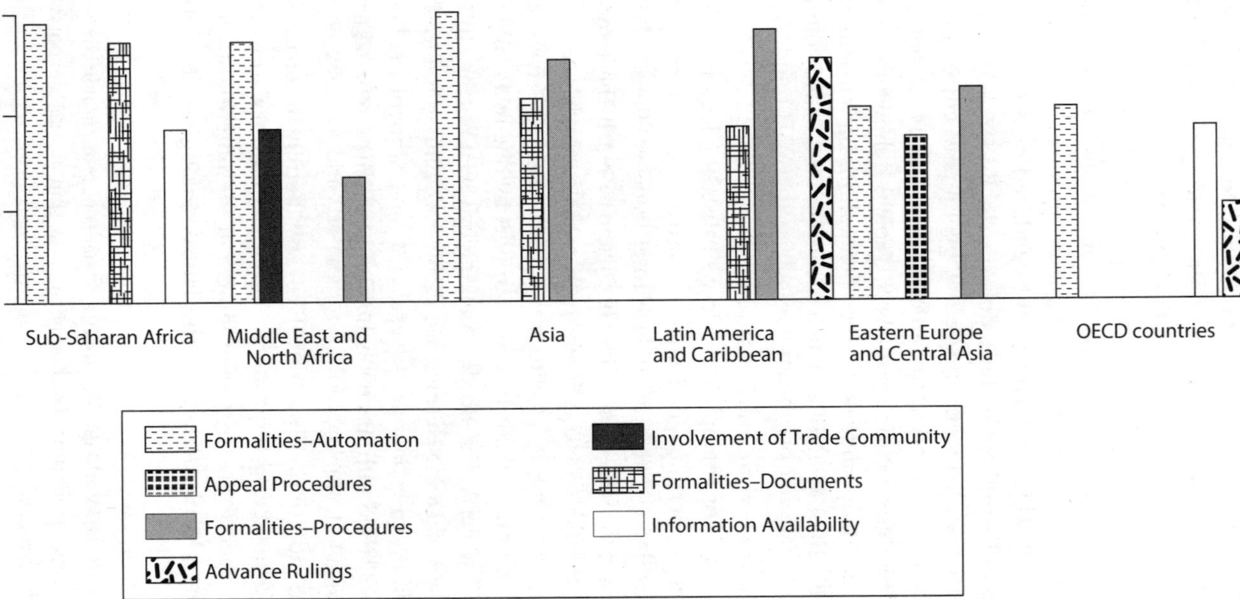

FIGURE 8.4 Potential Cost Reductions in Goods Trade (%)

Source: Organisation for Economic Co-operation and Development (2013).

than $40 billion, 65 per cent of which would accrue to developing countries. The potential cost reduction from comprehensive trade facilitation reform is about 15 per cent for developing countries. For example, customs reforms increased Ethiopian imports and exports by 200 per cent and its tax revenues by over 51 per cent.

Findings from the OECD trade facilitation indicator analysis show a reduction of trade costs for low-income countries of about 10 per cent. More specifically, trade costs can be reduced by 3 per cent by harmonizing and simplifying trade documents, by 2.3 per cent by automating trade and customs processes, by 1.6 per cent by ensuring the availability of trade-related information, and by 1.5 per cent by advanced rulings on customs matters. Table 8.7 shows the status of Bhutan in the major indices of trade facilitation. Bhutan's indices are much worse than Mongolia, which is another landlocked country in Asia.

A country's trade competitiveness also depends on its procedures and infrastructure, for example long delays caused by lengthy procedures in obtaining permits, inadequate infrastructure, and unreliable logistics services would tend to reduce total trade volumes.[19] Small companies in landlocked economies that want to reach the international markets would tend to suffer more from the costly delays.

By reducing the time it takes to import by 1 day to 37 days, and by cutting the number of documents to import by one to 11, Bhutan improved its Trading Across Borders ranking by seven notches to 165 in the latest Ease of Doing Business list (Table 8.8). Bhutan is ahead of two other landlocked economies—Nepal (171) and Mongolia (173). It remains below three South Asian neighbours—Sri Lanka (69), Pakistan (108), and Bangladesh (140).

Bhutan, in addition, does not fare any better in terms of logistics performance, a requisite to develop a country's external trade since it affects the costs of trading and the potential to integrate with the global market. In the latest rankings of Logistics

[19] According to the World Bank (2014a), a 10 per cent reduction in the time it takes to move cargo from the production line to the ship increases exports by 4 per cent, all else being equal.

TABLE 8.7 Bhutan's Status in Trade Facilitation

Index	Examples of Specific Trade Facilitation Measures	Bhutan's Status	Reference (Mongolia)
Transparency	Information on trade regulations through internet	n.a.	Yes
	Advance rulings in tariff classification and customs valuation	No	Yes
	Mechanism to review decisions, right of appeal	n.a.	Yes
	Digital process of trade data	No	Yes
Simplification	Establishment of a 'single window'	No	Yes
	Electronic customs clearance, paperless	No	Some
	Simplification of customs procedures and reduction of documentary requirements	n.a.	Yes
	Simplification of procedures for goods in transit	Yes	
	Pre-arrival examination	n.a.	Some
	Reduction of fees and charges in import or export	n.a.	Some
	Risk management technique, authorized economic operators	No	Yes
Harmonization	Harmonization of customs procedures, documents, and customs valuation methods	n.a.	Yes
	International standards with the WCO and the WTO	n.a.	Yes
	Harmonized tariff classification	Yes	Yes
	Recognition of certification and testing facilities of other countries or international organizations	n.a.	Yes

Notes: n.a. = data not available; WCO = World Customs Organization; WTO = World Trade Organization.

Sources: Created by authors based on interviews conducted in Bhutan and Asia Pacific Institute of Mongolia.

TABLE 8.8 Comparative Rankings in Ease of Doing Business and Trading Across Borders

	Bhutan		Mongolia	Nepal	Bangladesh	Pakistan	Sri Lanka
	Rank	Change					
Ease of doing business(rank)	125	(16)	72	108	173	128	99
Trading across borders(rank)	165	(7)	173	171	140	108	69
Documents to export(number)	9	–	11	11	6	8	7
Time to export(days)	38	–	44	40	28	21	16
Cost to export($per container)	2,230	–	2,745	2,545	1,281	765	560
Documents to import(number)	11	(1)	12	11	9	8	7
Time to import(days)	37	(1)	45	39	34	18	13
Cost to import($per container)	2,330	–	2,950	2,650	1,515	1,005	690

Notes: – = no change; figures in brackets = negative.

Sources: World Bank (2013, 2014a).

TABLE 8.9 Logistics Performance Index, 2014

Economy	Rank	Score	% of highest performer
Bhutan	143	2.29	41.3
Mongolia	135	2.36	43.4
Nepal	105	2.59	50.9
Bangladesh	108	2.56	50.1
Pakistan	72	2.83	58.5
Sri Lanka	89	2.7	54.3

Source: World Bank (2014b).

Performance Index,[20] Bhutan ranked 143rd out of 160 countries, with a low score of 2.29 or 41 per cent of the score of the highest performer. This is the lowest among the landlocked nations, including Mongolia and Nepal, and among neighbouring countries, such as Bangladesh, Sri Lanka, and Pakistan.

The most urgent task for Bhutan is to upgrade its customs clearance system. As an isolated landlocked country, it requires time and large capital to build infrastructure, such as roads, ports, and bridges. While there are many urgent areas in which trade facilitation in the country needs to be enhanced, improving customs clearance has to be done with limited resources and within a short period to break away from the tag of one of the worst regions for trade facilitation as assessed in ESCAP's (2014) *Trade Facilitation in Asia and the Pacific*. Since the primary goal of international trade organizations in supporting developing countries is to improve trade facilitation, Bhutan needs to take advantage of the programmes offered by international institutions and regional economic cooperation organizations.

[20] Logistics Performance Index is the weighted average of the country scores on six key dimensions: (i) efficiency of the clearance process; (ii) quality of trade- and transport-related infrastructure; (iii) ease of arranging competitively priced shipments; (iv) competence and quality of logistics services; (v) ability to track and trace consignments; and (vi) timeliness of shipments. The score cards demonstrate comparative performance ranging from 1 (lowest score) to 5 (highest score).

Incidence of Tariffs in Bhutan

Bhutan relaxed tariffs on imports from India, and has a tariff liberalization plan under the SAARC Agreement that targeted a gradual reduction in peak tariff rates to 5 per cent by end of 2015. This is linked to the fact that Bhutan's trade is heavily dependent on India, and its imports from India are traded without tariffs owing to the bilateral free trade arrangement between the two countries. Logistics costs also play a favourable role for Indian products. This implies that Bhutan may not face a substantial increase in imports after it further liberalizes its trade with countries other than India.

Considering the import dependence on a single country and tariff structure, welfare losses owing to trade diversion may arise. If a country lacks capacity in manufacturing and depends on imports, unilateral liberalization is the best policy, as it eliminates economic losses via trade diversion. For example, Chile adopted flat tariff rates for all goods (6 per cent tariff on all imports) and reduced rates gradually, reducing the economic losses from domestic distortion of resource allocation and improving national welfare.[21] Although, India is expected to remain a dominant exporter to Bhutan, trade liberalization will lead to the diversification of import sources and stable prices of imported goods. In theory, this gain will spread to all consumers, thus improving the welfare (a part of happiness)[22] of Bhutanese people, which outweighs the loss of government revenue.

Bhutanese officials are concerned about the farmers, who account for about 56 per cent of the total employment. Most imported agricultural products from India are tariff free. However, two points need to be noted here. First, logistics costs may be critical for agricultural products in general and more so in Bhutan. This implies that India could enjoy a comparative advantage over other exporting countries. Second, many farmers are living at a subsistence level, and Bhutan needs to improve the productivity of its agriculture sector. Policies that will improve agricultural productivity do not seem to be

[21] Regarding Chile's economic gains from its unilateral liberalization, refer to Fredriksson (1999).

[22] It is understood that happiness contains material and psychological elements. Since welfare is also set by the level of material satisfaction, welfare is a part of happiness.

viable while maintaining the small amount of farmland per farmer. Therefore, new jobs should be created to absorb marginal farmers. The argument that the current trade system should be maintained to help the poorer farmers might sound reasonable, thus gaining political support, but it is not logical from an economic perspective. This is an example of an unbalanced treatment of trade policy that ignores basic economic principles.

World Trade Organization Accession

In principle, economic openness exposes a country to uncertainty and risks. However, this does not necessarily imply that a closed economic system is better. An open trading system is not the goal but a means to improve national welfare. The issue may be the degree of openness. A large economy, which can exercise its market power on world prices, can pursue an optimum liberalization level. For smaller economies, unilateral liberalization is an optimal policy. If a country faces difficulties in reallocating resources across sectors, a gradual approach is desirable, while, at the same time, promoting capacity building to smoothen the structural adjustment. The WTO Agreements have special and differential treatment provisions for developing countries. These special and differential treatment provisions include longer periods for implementing commitments, favourable safeguard measures, support for capacity building, and measures for increasing trading opportunities.

Unnecessary trade barriers need to be removed, while gradually lowering average tariffs. It should be noted that the WTO accession implies setting binding tariff rates and that Bhutan has some buffer between effective rates and binding rates. If tariff concession schedule is well-adopted, Bhutan will not face any serious impact when it joins the WTO. However, the effects of becoming a WTO member will be substantial, and business sectors will have to adapt to the new environment to enhance national competitiveness.

In addition, economic logic should be applied to enhance transparency and predictability. Most developing countries lack transparency and policy certainty, and tend to be exposed to political populism. Although they can upgrade their economic system, they tend to go back to older systems when ruling parties change. As a result, foreign investors, uncertain of the political effects of their FDIs, are reluctant to invest in these countries. This is a more serious issue for small domestic markets. Developing countries need to recognize this drawback and realize that such political uncertainties affect investors' decisions.

The WTO accession involves both the rights and obligations of new members. WTO members can enjoy equal treatment (the most favoured nation principle). Members must abide by the commitments agreed upon during the WTO accession. Regressive changes in laws and rules on trade are not allowed, thus keeping ad hoc populism in check. Some Bhutanese officials fear that WTO accession would impair their national sovereignty. International treaties are voluntary agreements for mutual gain, though some of the national sovereignty would be impaired owing to the binding elements in the agreements. This accession has contributed to improving the business environment, leading to growth in international trade volumes and an improvement in economic welfare. It would not be feasible for small countries to confront large economies bilaterally in trade disputes, but the multilateral trading system provides sound legal institutions to solve such problems. That is, even large economies must follow the guidelines laid down to solve trade disputes.

Economic reform is not easy, but WTO accession provides a chance to review the overall trading infrastructure systemically. Members are not obliged to accept all the WTO rules, and exceptions are allowed, depending on multilateral or bilateral negotiations. The government should review the gains and costs of WTO accession, and evaluate the net gains and compatibility with the GNH, considering the chance for economic reform. In this regard, short-term costs of structural adjustments can be a plausible pretence for rejecting WTO accession. Rather, these costs should be assessed objectively in comparison with the dynamic gains that would be realized over time. Bhutan's political decision pending the negotiations for WTO accession in 2009 should be reconsidered from the viewpoint of national interest. WTO membership symbolizes transparency and predictability owing to the binding effects. The effects of upgrading regulations should be evaluated properly, rather than just pointing out minor problems. Bhutan should not make a one-sided decision, but should focus on what is best for the country.

Exploring Trade and Industry Policy Compatible with Current Gross National Happiness Guidelines

Despite its commendable socio-economic gains, Bhutan urgently needs to broaden its economic base and make its growth more inclusive. Poverty has declined, but inequality has remained high. Bhutan's economic growth has generated limited employment opportunities, since it has been driven mainly by the capital-intensive hydropower sector (ADB 2014a).

Current GNH guidelines permit only Bhutanese business sectors to operate environment-friendly businesses that inflict little environmental damage, if any. Massive production facilities are not feasible because it is a mountainous and landlocked country and the domestic market is small. The GNH guidelines mandate the government to strategically pursue 'high value with a low environmental burden', such as:

1. Ecotourism: Bhutan provides a clean and healthy natural environment with a rich cultural heritage. As of 2015, Bhutan controls the number of foreign tourists by considering the capacity of the tourism infrastructure, such as hotels, but the country can promote special ecotourism zones. This could be expanded for human development, education, health, and so on.
2. Naturally abundant and competitive sectors: Producing and selling quality perfume, herbal medicine, organic food, mountain tea, minerals, and other products. These sectors can operate in line with ecotourism.
3. Research institutes oriented in line with the GNH components such as health, mind control, medicine, food, aging or anti-aging, environment, and others: Illnesses related with urbanization are on growing trend. Bhutan can be a suitable place for researches of health and food which are compatible with the GNH.
4. Processing food and/or medicine rather than exporting raw materials: Bhutan produces valuable herbal medicines, such as *Cordyceps militaris*, which are exported cheaply without processing.
5. Commercializing the image of Bhutan: The international community places a high value on the clean and environmentally friendly image of Bhutan. The country can commercialize this image, as well as related products, to companies and/or international organizations.

For example, the 'Bhutan' brand could be important to automobile companies producing electric or eco-friendly cars.

Although Bhutan is endowed with several unique attractions for international tourists, tourism needs to be industrialized as a service sector. Limited numbers of tourists visit the country at high costs every year. This is according to the government's tourism policy, which is to promote Bhutan as a high-end tourist destination in accordance with the tenets of GNH—that tourism must be environmentally, and ecologically friendly, socially and culturally acceptable and economically viable. However, keeping the principle of the GNH into account, two types of tourism business could be developed: the current tourism business and a special tourism zone (STZ). The STZ can be developed for more commercial tourism in a more convenient location with access to international air transportation. Mass tourism may bring burden to the environment, but a part of the income from tourism can be used for building environment-friendly facilities. The STZ could be effectively kept segregated from the Bhutanese people so that Bhutanese traditional culture and religious customs could remain unaffected.[23] Depending on the evaluation of this project on small-sized STZ, the country may initiate large-scale STZ to create jobs to absorb rising youth unemployment. Step-by-step approach will be desirable, noting the concerns of Bhutanese authorities on the GNH and the current social and economic issues regarding youth unemployment. Appendix B provides a brief discussion of an STZ, the Mount Kumgang International Tourist Region, in the Democratic People's Republic of Korea.

Similarly, a special economic zone can be developed for a few selected sectors such as processing food and medicine. ESCAP (2013: 5) reports 'there are clear economic benefits of EPZs [Export Processing Zones] with regard to poverty reduction', although there are negative impacts too, such as unequal income distribution. Rather than exporting raw materials at low prices, raw materials should be processed inside the country for more value-added businesses. For example, Viet Nam collects

[23] The primary idea is to limit the impact of tourism on the broader population by limiting tourists to the zone, which would feature exclusively designed and constructed tourist attractions and activities. Tours with guides outside the zone would remain available. These would maximize employment opportunities within and outside the zone for the Bhutanese.

as much as 20 times the value added by exporting roasted coffee rather than dry beans.[24] This lesson can be applied to the export of electric power to India. Bhutan needs to find a way to increase its value added using electric power domestically rather than exporting it as a raw material. Ferro-silicon (HS 720221) is also one of Bhutan's primary export goods. A refinery operates on electrical power, and Bhutan has abundant electrical power and rock or soil with rich ferro-silicon. A processing plant will bring more lucrative business to Bhutan.

Some projects require substantial capital at the initial stage. Bhutan needs sophisticated systems to promote and finance public–private projects and reduce business risks. While building four hydropower plants, Bhutan entirely relied on funds from India for the first plant, and from the Government of Austria and ADB for the other plants. Those power plants are government assets with accumulated foreign debt, and have been managed like state-owned enterprises. However, the STZs and special economic zones can be constructed with private investment, in the frame of the public–private project if needed, while reducing national debts.

Although, there are many factors which determine the inflow of FDIs, overall competitiveness of business environment is critical. Trade liberalization level affects national competitiveness, and Bhutan should liberalize its trade further. The provision of specific incentives is another key factor. Bhutan needs to be more aggressive in providing incentives to specific sectors and industries, not just to the general economy.

Most Bhutanese businesses are SMEs. SMEs face difficulties in payments and settlements regarding exports and imports. This is a universal phenomenon, but Bhutanese SMEs could get impacted more severely as even their local banks lack access to international credit facilities. The Bhutanese industries desperately need financial support in mediating export credit and payment settlement, and in taking full charge of arranging a medium- to long-term loan on favourable conditions. A financial institution, such as an export credit agency, was introduced in early days of economic development in other countries. For example, the Republic of Korea adopted its comprehensive export promotion policy in 1965 and established Export-Import Bank of Korea three years later.

[24] Notes reported at the 2014 ARTNet organized by ESCAP in Bangkok, 17 September 2014.

Many developing countries have benchmarked their export credit agencies against Export-Import Bank of Korea, and the bank has assisted many countries in setting up similar financial facilities.

Although Bhutan has a small population it should build its human capacity, targeting strategic sectors. International support from advanced countries will be invaluable in this regard, and Bhutan should improve its capacity to absorb expertise and knowledge. Young businessmen and government officials, with their capacity for absorbing new knowledge and global practices, should be among the first to be trained and educated. It is clear that Bhutan has a limited ability to be competitive internationally in industries that are based on huge production facilities and large-scale logistics. Based on the value of the clean natural environment, secondary values targeting health, leisure, education, and energy should be promoted. While this will maintain the principle of the GNH, the business environment should also improve. To do so, a WTO accession is a minimum requirement, and, based on this, a gradual approach to improving the business environment needs to be pursued.

Bhutan Out of Seclusion

Trade theory, which is based on traditional comparative advantage developed in the nineteenth century, applies to expanding production fragmentation and deepening GSCs. Comparative advantage and specialization are the source of economic gains. Joining a part of GSCs becomes a basic channel to globalization and industrialization for developing economies. This requires trade liberalization and a reduction in excessive regulations, as well as improved international competitiveness.

Although, trade liberalization and economic reforms contribute to economic growth, they also require structural adjustments that lead to socio-economic costs and may widen income inequality. To evaluate the possible consequences of a policy change from macroeconomic and microeconomic perspectives is not an easy task, since the value of the final incidence from a policy change can be viewed differently. In addition, if psychological factors are included as part of policy review guidelines, objective judgement will be more difficult.

This chapter points out that Bhutanese government structure is less oriented to trade policy, and suggests a new organization for promoting active trade policy. Otherwise, trade policy issues will not be regarded as top priority tasks. Also, top policymakers need to understand trade policies in order to have unbiased evaluation of these policies. For this purpose, the government can organize an international advisory council for its trade policy with eminent trade economists from various countries, and have regular meetings for dealing with international trade issues.

Bhutan is not secluded anymore, and it has increased trading with neighbouring countries. Although it is difficult to overcome the weaknesses in trade due to its geographical location, Bhutan should try to adopt the best package of economic policies including reforms and trade liberalization. Its people have been exposed to global economy, and material well-being has become a key part of their daily life. Bhutan needs to expand trade for better living.

Appendixes

Appendix A

Examples of Recent Economic Development in Developing Economies

Viet Nam

The Greater Mekong Subregion is one of the fastest growing economic regions in the world. In particular, Viet Nam has sustained robust economic growth amid the global financial crisis, and is now joining GSCs after several trade and investment reforms. The recent inclusion of Viet Nam into GSCs is mainly attributable to a surge in FDI. During 2000–13, Viet Nam caught up with Thailand, the largest FDI recipient in the region, in terms of FDI (Figure 8A.1).

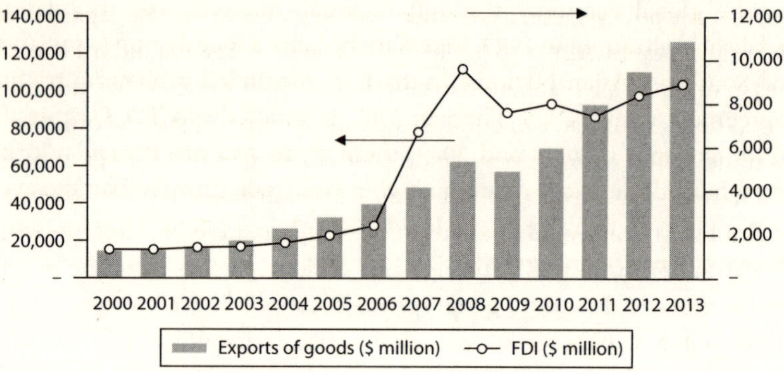

FIGURE 8A.1 Viet Nam's Exports of Goods and Foreign Direct Investments, 2000–13
Source: World Bank (n.d.).

It was Viet Nam's unilateral 'Doi Moi' (renovation) reforms in 1986 that initiated the opening up of the economy to the world. On top of a significant reduction in tariffs, recent key reform measures included the dismantling of quantitative restrictions, initiatives to expose public sector enterprises to greater market discipline, relaxing restrictions on FDI, lifting restrictions on private-sector participation in foreign trade, and setting up business ventures by private entities (Athukorala 2006: 161). The Government of Viet Nam has also actively pursued engaging

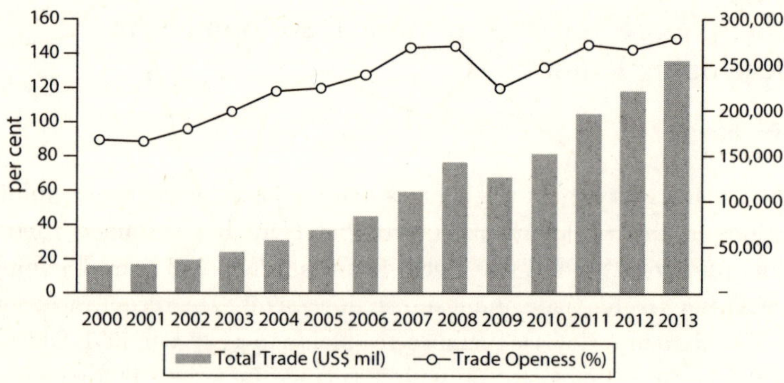

FIGURE 8A.2 Total Trade and Trade Openness of Viet Nam, 2000–13
Source: World Bank (n.d.).

in the global economy through regional, bilateral, and multilateral trade liberalization. In 1995, Viet Nam became a member of Association of Southeast Asian Nations. In 2001, it concluded a bilateral trading agreement with the US. Then, in 2007, it joined the WTO. Despite the trade collapse in 2008 and 2009, these trade and investment reforms have helped Viet Nam maintain higher real trade growth than the average trade growth in East Asia. In addition, trade openness has increased above 100 per cent (Figure 8A.2).

Mongolia

Mongolia, a landlocked country in Northeast Asia, has shown impressive economic performance during 2000–13. The main driver of this rapid economic expansion has been the development of the mining industry. In the past, Mongolia received little attention from foreign investors due to its low level of economic development, small market size, harsh climate, and geographical disadvantage as a landlocked country. Mongolia experienced negative GDP growth in the 1990s, but its economy recovered within a short time, recording an average of about 9 per cent annual GDP growth in the mid-2000s (Figure 8A.3).

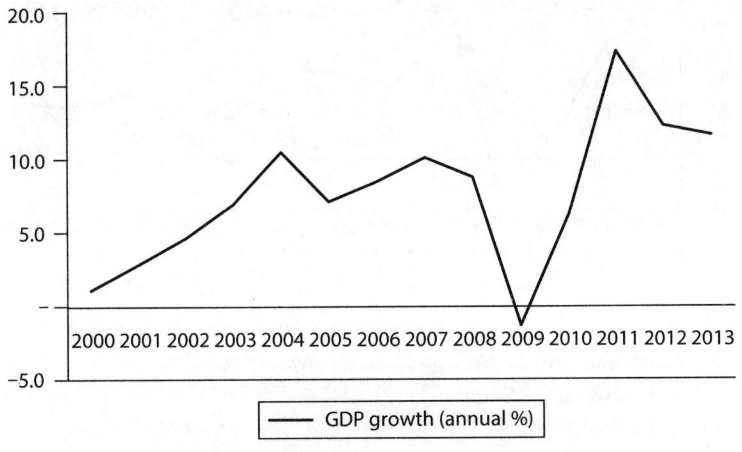

FIGURE 8A.3 Mongolia's Annual Gross Domestic Product Growth, 2000–13 (%)
Source: World Bank (n.d.).

The global financial crisis in late 2008 hit the Mongolian economy hard, but it took only a year for the economy to rebound with the help of a soaring FDI influx into the mining sector, made possible by the Oyu Tolgoi mining contract. The vast majority of the FDI went to the Oyu Tolgoi mine and its sectors, such as mining machinery and equipment (Lee et al. 2012).

Ethiopia

Ethiopia's GDP grew by 12.6 per cent in 2010, becoming the sixth fastest expanding economy in the world. Despite its geographical difficulties as a landlocked country in Sub-Saharan Africa, the economy has experienced strong and broad-based growth during 2004–12, averaging 10.9 per cent per year (Figure 8A.4). During the same period, the regional average was about 5 per cent. Expansion of the services and agriculture sectors accounted for most of this growth, while manufacturing sector performance was relatively modest, according to the World Bank.[25] This growth momentum was expected to continue in 2013 and 2014 (African Economic Outlook 2014).

Ethiopia's economy began to improve when the government embarked on a programme of economic reform, including the

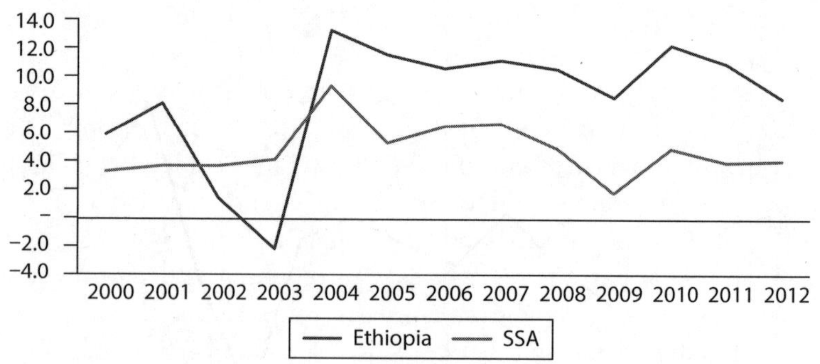

FIGURE 8A.4 Ethiopia's Gross Domestic Product Growth in Comparison with Sub-Saharan Africa's Average Growth, 2000–12 (%)
Note: SSA = Sub-Saharan Africa.
Source: World Bank (n.d.).

[25] Available at http://www.worldbank.org/en/country/ethiopia/overview (last accessed on 4 February 2015).

privatization of state enterprises and the rationalization of government regulation. The Ethiopian government's commitment to economic development has led to its introduction of the 'Growth and Transformation Plan', a national five-year plan to transform the country's economy by developing the agriculture sector and raising the share of industry through expanded investment. Ethiopia aims to achieve a GDP growth of 11–15 per cent per year from 2010 to 2015.

Appendix B

Mount Kumgang International Tourist Region, Democratic People's Republic of Korea

The Mount Kumgang International Tourist Region is a special administrative region of the Democratic People's Republic of Korea. It spreads 40 kilometers (km) from east to west and 60 km from north to south, covering an approximate area of 530 sq. km. Praised by writers and artists, Mount Kumgang (Diamond Mountain) is a national treasure for the Koreans. It is located in the southeast of the country, less than 50 km from the international boundary. The mountain area is famous for its scenic beauty, with waterfalls, springs, lagoons, and Buddhist temples and hermitages.

The Democratic People's Republic of Korea declared the tourist development area as a special autonomous region in 2002. The establishment of the special tourist zone gave an opportunity for tourists, especially from the Republic of Korea, to visit Mount Kumgang. The tourism zone provided revenue for the Democratic People's Republic of Korea through business from tourist arrivals and investments.

Mount Kumgang tourist and development project was signed in October 1998 as part of the inter-Korean economic cooperation that seeks to promote trade and investments, tourism, people to people exchanges and partnership between the North and the South. That year, the honorary chairman of the Hyundai conglomerate, Chung Ju Yung, signed an agreement in Pyongyang with Choe Su Gil, president of the Taesong Bank in the Democratic People's Republic of Korea. The two agreed in principle to jointly develop the area around Mount Kumgang as a tourist site (Chira 1989).

On 5 February 1999, the conglomerate established Hyundai Asan as its subsidiary that specializes in businesses and exchanges with the Democratic People's Republic of Korea. Under the contract signed by the two parties, development rights were granted to Hyundai Asan. The infrastructure development included the construction of a wharf, enhancement of land routes by restoring railroad and road connectivity, building of family reunion centres, and improvement of amenities in the resort area.

In November 1998, the first batch of tourists arrived in the maiden voyage of the 'Hyundai Kumgang' cruise liner; by September 2003, tourists could travel by road after the overland tour to Mt. Kumgang was launched.

Tourism operation in the area created business opportunities and employment (InSung and Lee 2009).[26] Hyundai Asan employed 1,084 people to handle tours as tourist arrivals were estimated to be about 240,000 annually. From late 1998 through 2008, nearly 1.95 million tourists visited the mountain (InSung and Lee 2009). Tourist purchases also contributed to the increase in inter-Korean trade.

To protect and maintain the cultural domain of the Democratic People's Republic of Korea from outside influence and for the safety of the visitors, the government laid out rules. The government allows only organized tour groups coursed through tour partners; it does not permit any independent travels. Tourists must always stay with their group when dining and going around the area. The rules further designate the areas where photographs can be taken and where visitors are restricted. There are also restrictions on what is allowed or prohibited to be carried.

The establishment of the tourist region has contributed to the inter-Korean relations as intended in the inter-Korean economic cooperation. Development in infrastructure and business has also been realized, and the revenues have been a boost to the finances of the Democratic People's Republic of Korea.

[26] The contract signed in 1998 promised Democratic People's Republic of Korea monthly payments of $12 million until February 2005 for a total of $942 million, regardless of the number of tourists. Hyundai further paid $308 million for the development rights and spent $104 million in building the facilities.

References

Asian Development Bank (ADB). 2014a. *Asian Development Outlook 2014: Fiscal Policy for Inclusive Growth*. Manila.

———. 2014b. *Basic Statistics 2014*. Manila.

African Economic Outlook. 2014. Available at http://www.africaneconomicoutlook.org/en/ (last accessed on 4 February 2015).

Athukorala, P.C. 2006. 'Trade Policy Reforms and the Structure of Protection in Vietnam', *The World Economy*, 29(2): 161–87.

Baldwin, R. 2011. 'Trade and Industrialisation after Globalisation's 2nd Unbundling: How Building and Joining a Supply Chain are Different and Why it Matters', NBER Working Paper Series No. 17716. Cambridge, MA: National Bureau of Economic Research.

Chira, S. 1989. 'The Two Koreas Agree to Develop Resort in North', *The New York Times*, 2 February, available at http://www.nytimes.com/1989/02/02/world/the-two-koreas-agree-to-develop-resort-in-north.html (last accessed on 4 February 2015).

De, P. and A. Raychaudhuri. 2013. 'Trade Facilitation and Poverty Reduction in Asia and The Pacific: A Case Study of a South Asian Economic Corridor', in R. Ratnayake, R.S. Ratna, M.F. Ferracane, and Y. Duval (eds), *Impacts of Trade Facilitation Measures on Poverty and Inclusive Growth: Case Studies From Asia*, pp. 153–93. Bangkok: Economic and Social Commission for Asia and the Pacific (ESCAP).

ESCAP. 2013. *Impacts of Trade Facilitation Measures on Poverty and Inclusive Growth: Case Studies from Asia*. Bangkok. Available at http://www.unescap.org/sites/default/files/impacts%20of%20trade%20facilitation.pdf (last accessed on 4 February 2015).

———. 2014. *Trade Facilitation in Asia and the Pacific*. Bangkok.

European Commission. 2014. *Trade Facilitation*. Available at http://ec.europa.eu/taxation_customs/customs/policy_issues/trade_falicitation/index_en.htm (last acessed on 20 December 2014).

Fredriksson, P. 1999. 'Trade, Global Policy, and the Environment: New Evidence and Issues', in P. Fredriksson (ed.), *Trade, Global Policy, and the Environment*, pp. 1–12. Washington, DC: World Bank.

Henderson, J., P. Dicken, M. Hess, N. Coe, and H. W-C. Yeung. 2002. 'Global Production Networks and the Analysis of Economic Development', *Review of International Political Economy*, 9(3): 436–64.

Higgins, K. and S. Prowse. 2010. 'Trade, Growth and Poverty: Making Aid for Trade work for Inclusive Growth and Poverty Reduction', ODI Working Paper No. 313. London: Overseas Development Institute.

InSung, K. and K. Lee. 2009. 'Mt. Kumgang and Inter-Korean Relations', NCNK Issue Brief No. 10, 10 November. Washington, DC. Available at http://www.ncnk.org/resources/briefing-papers/all-briefing-papers/mt.-kumgang-and-inter-korean-relations (last accessed on 4 February 2015).

Lee, J.Y., S.H. Jeh, H-J. Kim, and M. Gantumur. 2012. *Mongolia's Investment Environment and Measures to Expand the Market Entry of Korean Businesses*. Seoul: Korea Institute for Economic Policy.

Mt. Kumgang. n.d. *History of Mt. Kumgang*. Available at http://www.mtkumgang.com/eng/preview/story.jsp

Organisation for Economic Co-operation and Development. 2013. *OECD Trade Facilitation Indicators*. Paris.

Ratna, R.S. and M.F. Ferracane. 2013. 'Trade Facilitation and Poverty Reduction: Literature Review and Framework', in R. Ratnayake, Ratna S.R., M.F. Ferracane, and Y. Duval (eds), *Impacts of Trade Facilitation Measures on Poverty and Inclusive Growth: Case Studies from Asia*, pp. 7–36. Bangkok: ESCAP.

Rhee, C. and A. Posen. 2013. *Responding to Financial Crisis: Lessons from Asia Then, the United States and Europe Now*. Washington, DC: PIIE.

Royal Government of Bhutan. 2010a. *Statistical Yearbook of Bhutan, 2010*. Thimphu: National Statistics Bureau.

———. 2010b. *Economic Development Policy of the Kingdom of Bhutan, 2010*. Thimphu.

———. 2013. *FAQs on GNH*, Gross National Happiness Commission. Available at http://www.gnhc.gov.bt/2013/04/faq-on-gross-national-happiness-gnh/ (last accessed on 3 October 2016).

———. 2014a. *Bhutan Trade Statistics 2013*. Thimphu: Ministry of Finance.

———. 2014b. *National Accounts Statistics 2014*. Thimphu: National Statistics Bureau.

Royal Monetary Authority of Bhutan (RMA). 2014. *Annual Report 2013/14*. Thimphu

Stadtler, H. 2005. 'Supply Chain Management and Advanced Planning—Basics, Overview and Challenges', *European Journal of Operational Research*, 163(3): 575–88.

Ura, K. 2015. 'The Experience of Gross National Happiness as Development Framework', ADB South Asia Working Paper Series No. 42. Manila: Asian Development Bank.

Warr, P. 2012. 'Trade Policy in Landlocked Countries', Paper presented at the World Bank's seminar on Lao PDR: Trade and the Integrated Framework—A Refreshing Workshop, Vientiane, 28 June.

World Bank. 2012. *Mongolia Quarterly Economic Update*. February. Washington, DC.

World Bank. 2013. *Doing Business 2014: Understanding Regulations for Small and Medium-Size Enterprises*. Washington, DC.

———. 2014a. *Doing Business 2015: Going Beyond Efficiency*. Washington, DC.

———. 2014b. *Third Ethiopia Economic Update: Strengthening Export Performance through Improved Competitiveness*. Washington, DC.

———. n.d. *World Development Indicators*. Available at http://data.worldbank.org/data-catalog/world-development-indicators (last accessed on 4 February 2015).

World Trade Organization. 2015. *Trade Facilitation*. Available at http://www.wto.org/english/thewto_e/minist_e/mc9_e/brief_tradfa_e.htm (last accessed on 20 January 2015).

9

HOOI HOOI LEAN AND RUSSELL SMYTH*

Electricity Consumption, Output, and Trade in Bhutan

Hydropower is an important source of economic growth in Bhutan. As one scholar put it: 'The development of a hydropower industry has been recognized as the primary driving force for the economic development for the country' (Dorji 2007: 6). Almost all of Bhutan's electricity is supplied by hydropower schemes and electricity from hydropower represents 12 per cent of gross domestic product (GDP) (Uddin, Taplin, and Yu 2007). Bhutan is also heavily reliant on trade with India, which is its largest trading partner, accounting for 95 per cent of Bhutan's exports and 74 per cent of its imports (Shneiderman and Turin 2012). About 75 per cent of electricity generated in Bhutan is exported to India in accordance with an export tariff bilaterally agreed between the countries (Singh 2013). Electricity exports constitute about 45 per cent of Bhutan's exports to India (Bist 2012). Revenue from the sale of electricity to India provides about 40 per cent of the Royal Government of Bhutan's revenue (Singh 2013). According to Bhutan's Tenth Five Year Plan, 2008–13 the hydropower sector is expected to contribute 50 per cent of GDP and 75 per cent of fiscal revenue by 2020 (Bist 2012).

* We thank Sarah Carrington and anonymous reviewers for helpful suggestions on earlier versions of this chapter.

Beginning with Narayan and Smyth (2009), there is a growing literature that examines the relationship between energy consumption, international trade, and economic growth within an augmented production function framework (see, for example, Lean and Smyth 2010a, 2010b; Sadorsky 2011, 2012; Shahbaz, Khan, and Tahir 2013). The purpose of this chapter is to extend this literature to consider the specific case of Bhutan. We examine the relationship between electricity consumption in Bhutan, international trade between Bhutan and all other countries, and economic growth in Bhutan.

We extend the existing literature on the relationship between energy consumption, international trade, and economic growth in two directions. First, there are no studies that examine the nexus between energy consumption, international trade, and economic growth in which the source of the energy consumption is a renewable energy supply. Existing studies have examined the relationship between renewable energy and economic growth in an augmented production function framework (see, for example, Apergis and Payne 2010a, 2010b, 2011, 2012; Payne and Taylor 2010; Wolde–Rufael and Menyah 2010). We extend these studies to include international trade in the augmented production function.

Second, in existing studies of energy generated from hydropower (or other renewable energy sources), renewable energy typically represents only a very small fraction of a country's total energy supply. Bhutan is an interesting extension to the literature on the relationship between electricity generated by hydropower and economic growth because it is one of the few countries in the world in which hydropower is the main source of electricity.

The Bhutan Context

Bhutan's modernization commenced in the early 1960s with the establishment of basic infrastructure, including power, roads, and telecommunications (Dhakal, Pradhan, Upadhyaya 2009; Uddin, Taplin, and Yu 2007). Since then, Bhutan has forged a middle path to development (Walcott 2011) in which the focus has been on maximizing gross national happiness (GNH) rather than GDP (Brooks 2013; Burns 2011; Walcott 2011; Zurick 2006). The four pillars of GNH are sustainable and equitable social development, environmental conservation, promotion of culture, and good governance. While Bhutan remains one of the least developed countries in the world, with almost one-third of population living below the poverty line, its middle path to development has generated robust economic growth (Dhakal, Pradhan, and Upadhyaya 2009; Uddin, Taplin, and Yu 2007). Since the 1960s, a wage-based exchange economy has developed from a non-monetized traditional economy based almost solely on agriculture (Uddin, Taplin, and Yu 2007). Agriculture as a percentage of GDP has decreased from 33.8 per cent in 1991 to 15.9 per cent in 2011 (World Bank 2013). However, agriculture still accounted for 62 per cent of employment in 2011 (World Bank 2013).

Bhutan has no significant reserves of fossil energy resources (oil, natural gas, or petroleum) except for limited coal reserves in the southwest (Uddin, Taplin, and Yu 2007). Bhutan's energy mix consists primarily of fuel wood and hydropower. Over 99 per cent of its electricity is generated from hydropower, with the remaining share generated from diesel power generating plants (Bist 2012). Bhutan's recent robust economic growth is attributable to the development of its hydropower sector, with hydropower projects such as Chhukha (336 megawatts [MW]), Krichu (60 MW), and Tala (1020 MW) implemented with financial and technical assistance from India. Bhutan has four major river systems—Ammochu, Wangchu, Sankosh, and Mansa—which means it is well endowed to harness hydropower from run-of-the-river plants (Uddin, Taplin, and Yu 2007). Despite the importance of the contribution of electricity from hydropower to economic development in Bhutan, it is estimated that Bhutan currently only taps 5 per cent of its hydropower potential (Singha 2011).

The electricity generated from Chhukha, Krichu, and Tala is exported to India after meeting internal demand. As discussed in the introduction, exports of electricity constitute just under one-half of Bhutan's exports to India. Electricity from hydropower represents not only an important traded good between Bhutan and India, but also figures as a key feature of the Bhutan–India bilateral relationship (Bist 2012).

Existing Literature

Voluminous literature exists on the relationships between energy consumption and economic growth, and between economic growth and trade (see, for example, Ahmad 2001; Giles and Williams 2000; Ozturk

2010; Payne 2010). Studies that examine the relationship between energy consumption, trade, and economic growth using a single augmented production function model are relatively recent (see, for example, Lean and Smyth 2010a, 2010b; Narayan and Smyth 2009; Sadorsky 2011, 2012; Shahbaz, Khan, and Tahir 2013). Overall, the findings from these studies provide mixed support for the export-led and handmaiden hypotheses and competing hypotheses concerning the relationships between energy consumption and economic growth, and between energy consumption and trade.[1]

Several studies exist for South Asian countries that examine the relationship between economic growth and international trade (see, for example, Bahmani–Oskooee and Alse 1993; Chandra 2002, 2003; Dhawan and Biswal 1999; Dodaro 1993; Jimenz and Razmi 2013; Jung and Marshal 1985; Love and Chandra 2004a, 2004b, 2005). The evidence from these studies on the export-led and handmaiden hypotheses, however, is mixed. Moreover, none of these studies consider the specific case of Bhutan.

Similarly, there are a number of studies for South Asian countries that examine the relationship between energy consumption and economic growth (Akhmat and Zaman 2013; Mudakkar et al. 2013; Pradhan 2010; Shahbaz, Zeshan, and Afza 2012; Singha 2011; Wolde–Rufael 2010; Zaman, Khan, and Saleem 2011). Some of these studies have examined the relationship between renewable or alternative energy consumption and economic growth (Akhmat and Zaman 2013; Shahbaz, Zeshan, and Afza 2012; Wolde–Rufael, 2010). A subset of these studies examines the relationship between energy consumption and economic growth in Bhutan (Akhmat and Zaman 2013; Singha 2011). Akhmat and Zaman (2013) found that in Bhutan, there is bidirectional Granger causality between coal and oil consumption on the one hand and economic growth on the other. Singha (2011) found that there is no Granger causality between electricity consumption and economic growth. In a

[1] The export-led hypothesis states that export growth Granger-causes economic growth. The handmaiden hypothesis states that economic growth Granger-causes export growth. These hypotheses are described in more detail later. Gross fixed capital formation serves as a proxy for capital in that changes in investment closely align with changes in the capital stock under the assumption of a constant depreciation rate using the perpetual inventory method (see, for example, Apergis and Payne 2010a, 2010b, 2011, 2012; Liddle 2013; Soytas and Sari 2006a, 2006b, 2007).

related study, Kumar and Rauniyar (2011) found that access to electricity increased income and educational attainment in rural Bhutan.

The only studies, of which we are aware, that examine the relationship between energy consumption, international trade, and economic growth in South Asia are Shahbaz, Lean, and Farooq (2013) and Shakeel, Iqbal, and Majeed (2013). Shahbaz, Lean, and Farooq (2013) examine the relationship between energy consumption, exports, and economic growth in Pakistan. Their findings indicate that energy consumption Granger-causes[2] exports. Shakeel, Iqbal, and Majeed (2013) examine the relationship between energy consumption, trade, and economic growth in five South Asian countries (not including Bhutan) using a panel framework. Their main results were that in the long run there was bidirectional Granger causality between energy and economic growth, and unidirectional Granger causality running from exports to energy. To summarize, there are no studies on the relationship between energy consumption, international trade, and economic growth in Bhutan, and there are no studies that consider electricity as a traded good between countries using an augmented production function approach.

Data, Modelling Strategy, and Hypotheses

Production function

To examine the relationship between electricity consumption, international trade, and economic growth, we use an augmented production function in which output is expressed as a function of capital, labour, electricity consumption, and trade:

$$Y_t = f\ (K_t, L_t, E_t, T_t) \tag{1}$$

In Equation (1), Y_t is aggregate output, K_t is capital stock, L_t is the labour force, E_t is electricity consumption, and T_t is international trade. To measure international trade by following Shahbaz, Khan, and Tahir (2013), we use two measures: total trade = real exports + real imports (Model 1); and trade openness = total trade/GDP (Model 2).

[2] If a variable X1 Granger-causes a variable X2, then past values of X1 should contain information that helps predict X2 above and beyond the information contained in past values of X2 alone.

Data

Table 9.1 presents descriptive statistics for the variables employed in the study. Figures 9.1a–9.1f present the time series of each of the variables in graphic form. Output is measured as real GDP in constant (2000) US dollars, capital is measured as gross capital formation in constant (2000) US dollars, the labour force is measured as total civilian employment, electricity is gross value added of electricity, and international trade is measured as total exports. The use of gross capital formation as a proxy for the capital stock follows Lee (2005), Soytas and Sari (2006a), and Narayan and Smyth (2008) among others. All data are converted to natural logs prior to analysis. The data are annual for the period 1980–2013 from the Asian Development Bank's (ADB) *Key Indicators for Asia and the Pacific, the World Bank's World Development Indicators*, and data from Bhutan's Ministry of Finance.

Econometric Modelling Strategy

The econometric modelling strategy proceeds in four steps consistent with previous studies. First, we ascertain the order of integration of all variables. Second, we test for cointegration to ascertain if there is a long-run relationship between the variables. Third, we derive the long-run and short-run estimates. Finally, we test for Granger causality between electricity consumption, output, and the relevant trade variable.

TABLE 9.1 Descriptive Statistics (In)

Variables	Mean	Std. Dev.	Skewness	Kurtosis	Jarque–Bera
GDP	23.4923	0.6934	0.0098	2.0242	1.3098
Capital	22.6497	0.8504	0.0162	1.9428	1.5384
Labour	12.3083	0.3115	0.4509	1.8255	3.0151
Electricity	20.9340	2.0378	−1.3175	3.3055	9.6748***
Trade	23.1172	0.8697	0.0947	2.0293	1.3449
Openness	−0.3751	0.2035	0.2188	1.9716	1.7175

Notes: 1.*** denotes significance at the 1 per cent level.

2. Std. Dev. = Standard Deviation and GDP = Gross Domestic Product.

Source: Authors' Calculations.

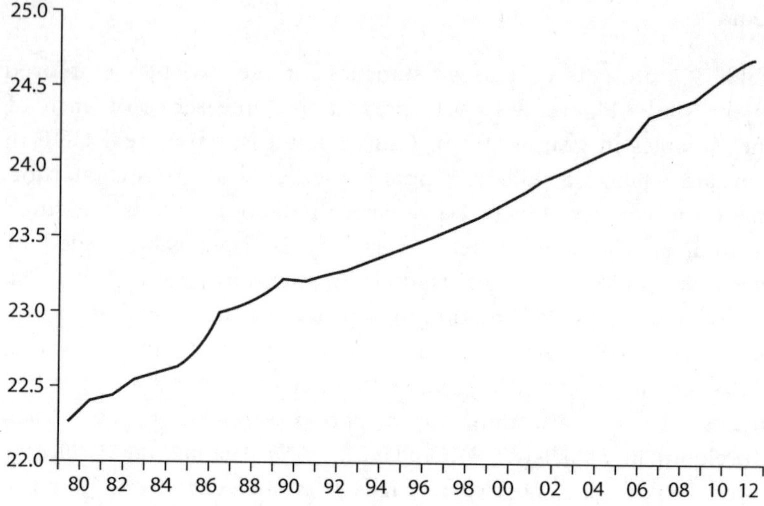

FIGURE 9.1A GDP at Constant (2000) Prices (In)

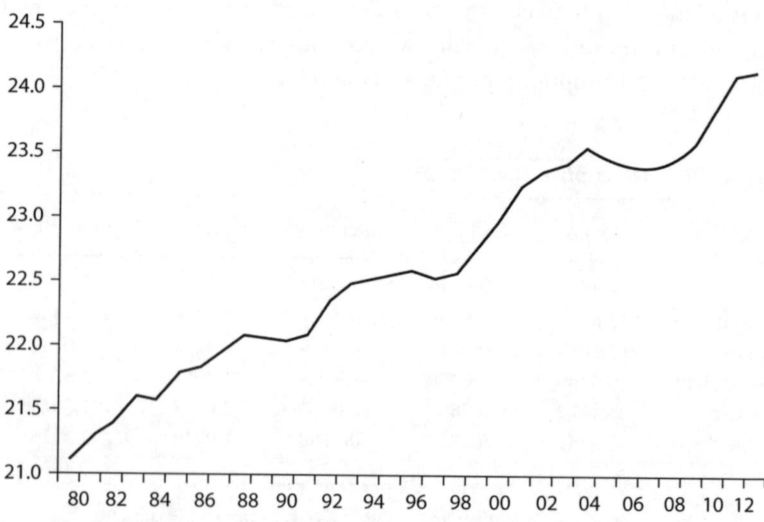

FIGURE 9.1B Gross Fixed Capital Formation, Constant (In)

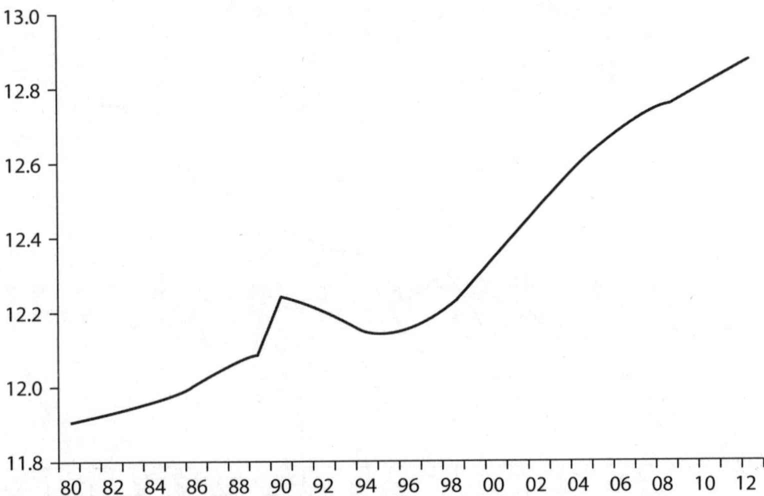

FIGURE 9.1C Labour Force (in thousands) (In)

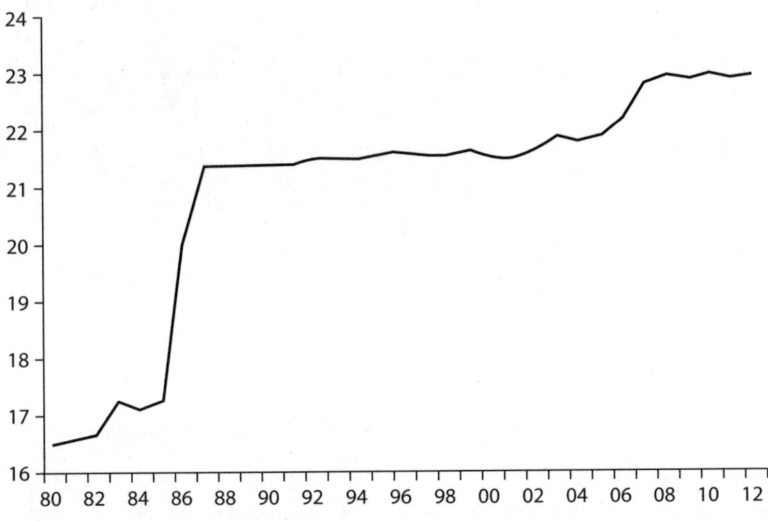

FIGURE 9.1D GVA Electricity and Water, Constant (In)

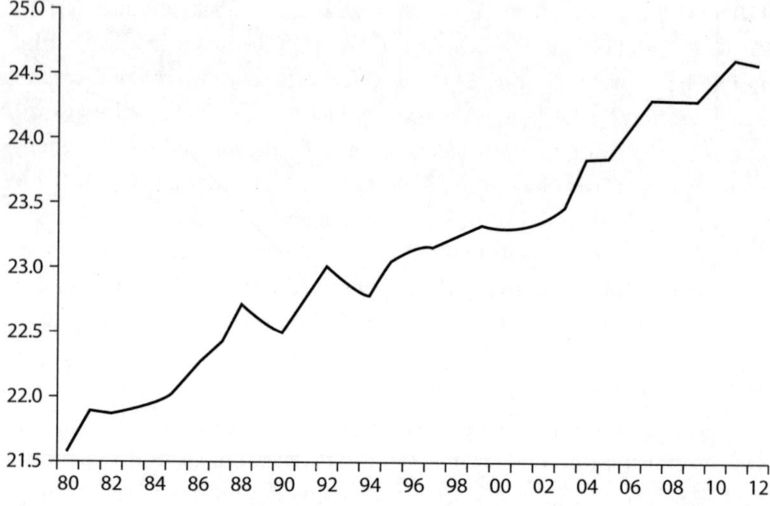

FIGURE 9.1E Trade, Constant (In)

FIGURE 9.1F Openness (In)

Sources: ADB (2014); World Bank (2013); and data provided by the Ministry of Finance.

To test for a unit root we use the Augmented Dickey–Fuller (ADF) unit root test. The null hypothesis for the ADF unit root test is that the variable has a unit root against the alternative of stationarity. We set the maximum number of lags equal to two and use the Akaike Information Criteria to ascertain the optimal lag length. We do not discuss the details of the ADF unit root test here, given that they are well known (see, for example, Maddala and Kim 1998 for a detailed discussion of the ADF test).

To test for cointegration, we use the maximum likelihood test developed by Johansen and Juselius (1990). A maximum likelihood test has the advantage of allowing for (i) all variables to be viewed as endogenous, circumventing the normalization issue; (ii) the presence of more than one cointegrating vector; and (iii) the simultaneous estimation, via maximum likelihood, of the short-run dynamics which increased estimation efficiency. Gonzalo (1994) found that the maximum likelihood test has better asymptotical properties to detect long-run equilibrium than a range of other estimators. Specifically, it performs better than others even when the errors are not normally distributed or when the dynamics are unknown. There are two types of maximum likelihood tests. The first likelihood ratio test, called a trace test, evaluates the null hypothesis of (at most) r cointegrating vectors versus the general null of p cointegrating vectors. The second likelihood ratio test, called the maximum eigenvalue test, evaluates the null hypothesis of r cointegrating vectors against the alternative of $(r+1)$ cointegrating vectors. We use the AIC to determine lag length. Given that we have annual data, for Equation (1) we set the maximum number of lags equal to two. Moreover, because the number of time series observations is short, in Equation (2) we use one lag.

If the likelihood ratio test establishes the existence of a long-run relationship between the variables, we can estimate the long-run parameters. The long-run multivariate models corresponding to Equation (1) are as follows:

$$Y_t = \alpha + \beta_1 K_t + \beta_2 L_t + \beta_3 E_t + \beta_4 T_t + u_t \tag{2}$$

If cointegration exists between the variables, this forms the basis for the specification of the vector error correction model. We are interested in the vector error correction model for the augmented production function, in which GDP is the dependent variable. If there is a long-run relationship between the series, shocks will result in disequilibrium in the short run before the series return to their long-run equilibrium. This is captured in the error-correction term (ECT), calculated from the long-run cointegrating vector. The short-run model corresponding to Equation (1) is as follows:

$$\Delta Y_t = u + \sum_{i=1}^{m} \pi_{1i} \Delta Y_{t-i} + \sum_{i=1}^{m} \pi_{2i} \Delta K_{t-i} + \sum_{i=1}^{m} \pi_{3i} \Delta L_{t-i} + \sum_{i=1}^{m} \pi_{4i} \Delta E_{t-i} + \sum_{i=1}^{m} \pi_{4i} \Delta T_{t-i} + \tau ECT_{t-1} + \upsilon \qquad (3)$$

To test for Granger causality, we use the modified version of Granger causality proposed by Toda and Yamamoto (1995) and Dolado and Lutkepohl (1996) (hereafter, the TYDL approach). The TYDL approach uses a modified Wald test for restrictions on the parameters of the VAR(*k*) model. The test has an asymptotic chi-square distribution with *k* degrees of freedom in the limit when VAR[$k + d_{max}$] is estimated, where d_{max} is the maximal order of integration for the series in the system. Following Dolado and Lutkepohl (1996), we use $d_{max} = 1$ as it performs better than other orders of d_{max}. The optimal lag length, *k*, is selected using the SBC.

Hypotheses Relating to Granger Causality

There are three competing hypotheses concerning the relationship between electricity consumption, international trade, and GDP. The first set of hypotheses concerns the relationship between electricity consumption and GDP. The competing hypotheses are that there is unidirectional Granger causality running from electricity consumption to GDP, unidirectional Granger causality running from GDP to electricity consumption, bidirectional Granger causality between these variables, or no Granger causality in either direction (Mehrara 2007). If there is either unidirectional Granger causality running from GDP to electricity consumption or no Granger causality in either direction, reducing electricity consumption will have little or no adverse effect on aggregate output. On the other hand, if unidirectional Granger causality runs from electricity consumption to GDP, reducing electricity consumption in the market could lead to a fall in income, while increases in electricity consumption contribute to aggregate output. Bidirectional Granger causality between the variables is suggestive of an energy-dependent economy in which there are feedback effects between electricity consumption and aggregate output.

The second set of competing hypotheses concerns the causal relationship between trade (exports) and GDP. The export-led hypothesis states that Granger causality runs from exports to GDP. There are several possible reasons why Granger causality might run from exports to GDP (Ahmad 2001). At its most obvious level, exports increase GDP because exports are a component of GDP in national accounting. At a more subtle level, countries with a high export-to-GDP ratio are more open to outside influences and generate externalities, such as the incentive to innovate. These efficiency gains increase GDP through increasing total factor productivity in the Solow–Swan growth accounting framework (Solow 1956; Swan 1956). One competing hypothesis that Granger causality runs from GDP to exports is captured in variants of handmaiden theories of trade (Kravis 1970) and in the argument that growth mechanisms that are internally generated best explain the growth of exports (Jung and Marshall 1985). Assuming there is growth in total factor productivity due to technological improvements independent of trade, the comparative cost structure of such an economy could evolve in a manner that is consistent with growing exports (Ahmad 2001). Another competing hypothesis is that there is bidirectional Granger causality between the variables.

The third set of competing hypotheses concerns the relationship between trade (exports) and electricity consumption. If Granger causality runs from electricity consumption to trade (exports), or if there is bidirectional Granger causality between the two variables, reducing electricity consumption could impede attempts to expand trade (exports) as an engine of economic growth. However, if there is Granger causality running from trade (exports) to electricity consumption, or no Granger causality running in either direction, it follows that reducing the consumption of electricity can be expected to have no adverse effect on export growth or the growth of trade.

Results

In this section, we present the results for the augmented production function represented in Equation (1) together with the long-run and short-run estimates in Equations (2) and (3). In each case, we present the results for total trade = real exports + real imports (Model 1); and trade openness = total trade/GDP (Model 2).

We begin by testing for a unit root using the ADF unit root test. The results for each of the variables are presented in Table 9.2. Each of the variables is found to be nonstationary in levels but stationary in first differences and, hence, integrated of order one (I(1)). Given the variables are I(1), we proceed to test for cointegration using the maximum likelihood test. The results of both tests, which are presented in Table 9.3, indicate that the variables in each of Model 1 and Model 2 are cointegrated.

The long-run estimates for Equation (2) are presented in Table 9.4. The sign on each of the coefficients is positive and significant at the 1 per cent level. Because the variables are expressed in natural logs, the coefficients can be interpreted as elasticities. A 1 per cent increase in capital results in either a 0.16 per cent increase (Model 1) or a 0.32 per cent increase (Model 2) in output. A 1 per cent increase in labour results in either a 0.25 per cent increase (Model 1) or a 0.52 per cent increase (Model 2) in output. A 1 per cent increase in electricity consumption generates either a 0.03 per cent increase (Model 1) or 0.05 per cent increase (Model 2) in output. A 1 per cent increase in total trade results in a 0.51 per cent increase in output (Model 1). A 1 per cent increase in trade openness results in a 1 per cent increase in output (Model 2).

The findings for the elasticity of electricity consumption with respect to real GDP sit at the lower end of previous studies that have

TABLE 9.2 Augmented Dickey–Fuller Unit Root Test

Variables	Level		First Difference	
	Lag	t-statistic	Lag	t-statistic
GDP	0	–0.1612	0	–5.6381***
Capital	1	–0.3484	0	–4.0754***
Labour	0	0.97405	0	–3.7113***
Electricity	0	–2.1687	0	–3.7839***
Trade	2	–0.1147	1	–6.2799***
Openness	0	–2.1338	1	–6.4741***

Note: *** denotes significance at the 1 per cent level.

Source: Authors' Calculations.

TABLE 9.3 Johansen–Juselius Cointegration Test (Equation 1)

Model 1	Trace Statistic	Max–Eigen Statistic
None	127.8992***	46.4995***
At most 1	81.3997***	35.0750***
At most 2	46.3247***	25.4440**
At most 3	20.8808**	12.1811
At most 4	8.6997*	8.6997*
Model 2	**Trace Statistic**	**Max–Eigen Statistic**
None	127.8992***	46.4995***
At most 1	81.3997***	35.0750***
At most 2	46.3247***	25.4440**
At most 3	20.8808**	12.1811
At most 4	8.6997*	8.6997*

Note: *, **, and *** denote significant at the 10 per cent, 5 per cent, and 1 per cent levels, respectively.
Source: Authors' Calculations.

used aggregate energy consumption as a proxy for energy use (see, for example, Lee 2005; Narayan and Popp 2012; Narayan and Smyth 2008; Sadorsky 2012; Shahbaz, Khan, and Tahir 2013) and studies that have used electricity consumption as the relevant proxy (see, for example, Narayan and Smyth 2009). In terms of studies that have included some form of renewable energy source in the production function, the findings for the elasticity of electricity consumption are smaller than in Apergis and Payne (2010b: 0.20 per cent, 2011: 0.24 per cent, 2012: 0.37 per cent). However, the results are quantitatively similar to Wolde–Rufael's (2010) results for nuclear energy in India (0.04 per cent–0.06 per cent).

TABLE 9.4 Normalized Long-Run Estimation (Equation 2)

Variables	Model 1	Model 2
Capital	0.1559***	0.3156***
Labour	0.2531***	0.5124***
Electricity	0.0269***	0.0545***
Trade	0.5060***	–
Openness	–	1.0244***
Constant	4.6044***	9.3211***

Note: *** denotes significance at the 1 per cent level.
Source: Authors' Calculations.

The findings for the elasticity of capital formation with respect to real GDP (see, for example, Apergis and Payne 2010b, 2011, 2012; Lee 2005; Narayan and Smyth 2008; Shahbaz, Khan, and Tahir 2013) and the elasticity of labour with respect to GDP (see, for example, Apergis and Payne 2010b, 2012; Sadorsky 2012) are similar to previous studies. The findings for the elasticity of total trade and trade openness are generally higher than in previous studies in the energy literature (Sadorsky 2011, 2012; Shahbaz, Khan, and Tahir 2013).

The short-run estimates for Equation (3) are presented in Table 9.5. In each case, the coefficient on the error correction term is negative and statistically significant, which is an alternative way of establishing the existence of cointegration between the variables. Following a shock, the error correction term indicates that the long-run equilibrium is restored at a rate between 29 per cent (Model 2) and 58 per cent (Model 1) within one year. Electricity consumption has a positive effect on output in the short run, which is consistent with the long-run results, although total trade (Model 1) and trade openness (Model 2) have a negative effect on output in the short-run.

TABLE **9.5** Vector Error Correction Model Short-Run Estimation Results (Equation 3)

	Model 1	Model 2
ΔGDP(-1)	0.0497	–0.1330
ΔGDP(-2)	0.1937	0.0752
ΔCapital(-1)	–0.0060	–0.0060
ΔCapital(-2)	0.0466	0.0466
ΔLabour(-1)	0.1405	0.1405
ΔLabour(-2)	0.2877	0.2877
ΔElectricity(-1)	0.0550**	0.0550**
ΔElectricity(-2)	–0.0308	–0.0308
ΔTrade(-1)	–0.1827*	–
ΔTrade (-2)	–0.1185	–
ΔOpenness(-1)	–	–0.1827*
ΔOpenness (-2)	–	–0.1185
ECT(-1)	–0.5826**	–0.2865**

Note: * and ** denote significance at the 10 per cent and 5 per cent levels, respectively.

Source: Authors' Calculations.

The results for the TYDL approach to Granger causality are reported in Table 9.6. In both Model 1 and Model 2, electricity consumption is found to Granger-cause GDP; all other variables are found to be independent. Thus, neither the export-led nor the handmaiden hypothesis is supported and trade is found to have no Granger-causal effect on electricity consumption in Bhutan. The finding that there is unilateral Granger causality in the long-run from electricity consumption to GDP implies that Bhutan is an energy-dependent economy. In countries in which electricity is generated by fossil fuel combustion, the standard conclusion is that policies to curtail electricity consumption to reduce greenhouse gas emissions will restrict economic growth (see, for example, Ozturk 2010; Payne 2010). This is not the case in Bhutan given that almost all electricity is generated through hydropower. Among various types of energy, hydropower has the highest energy payback and lowest greenhouse gas emissions (see, for example, Jia, Punys, and Ma 2012). The result that electricity consumption Granger-causes GDP,

TABLE 9.6 Granger Causality Test ($\chi 2$ Statistics)

Model 1

Variables	GDP	Capital	Labour	Electricity	Trade
GDP	–	0.3534	1.5678	10.2394***	2.8996
Capital	1.0989	–	1.9753	1.5210	0.0870
Labour	0.8416	0.2522	–	0.4666	1.9953
Electricity	2.1735	1.7424	0.4164	–	0.2043
Trade	0.5707	3.3734	0.3092	3.3553	–

Note: *** denotes significance at the 1 per cent level.
Source: Authors' Calculations.

Model 2

Variables	GDP	Capital	Labour	Electricity	Openness
GDP	–	0.3534	1.5678	10.2394***	2.8996
Capital	1.2874	–	1.9753	1.5210	0.0870
Labour	0.5871	0.2522	–	0.4666	1.9953
Electricity	2.2768	1.7424	0.4164	–	0.2043
Openness	1.0081	4.1139	0.2074	1.6511	–

Note: *** denotes significance at the 1 per cent level.
Source: Authors' Calculations.

together with the magnitude of the elasticity of electricity consumption with respect to GDP in the long run, implies that Bhutan should invest more in hydropower infrastructure to further increase real income.

★★★

We have examined the effect of hydroelectricity consumption and trade on economic growth in Bhutan using an augmented production framework. Consistent with the existing literature for other countries, we find that both electricity consumption and trade have a positive effect on economic growth in the long-run. Our main conclusions are that electricity consumption Granger-causes output and that in the long run a 1 per cent increase in electricity consumption produces a 0.03 per cent–0.05 per cent increase in output. The elasticity for electricity consumption is at the low end compared with the results from previous studies for other countries, but is similar to Wolde–Rufael's (2010) results for the elasticity of nuclear energy in India (0.04 per cent–0.06 per cent). The main policy implication is that Bhutan is an energy-dependent economy and that one way to further increase income is to invest in hydropower infrastructure.

The major limitation of the study is the relatively short time series of available data. It would be worthwhile to reconsider the results when a longer time series is available. A second potential limitation is that we use GDP to measure income. Thus, we do not take account of the informal economy. Because of unrecorded economic activities, the size of the informal economy may differ from official GDP data, which suggests a different relationship between energy consumption and output (see, for example, Karanfil 2008). In the case of Bhutan in which the government has set the maximization of gross national happiness as an official goal, it is at least arguable that a broader indicator of well-being should be employed than GDP if the data were available. (See Brooks 2013 for the development of a scale to measure gross national happiness in Bhutan.)

There are at least two avenues for future research in this area with regard to Bhutan. One direction would be to extend the literature on the relationship between energy consumption, international trade, and economic growth by considering the contribution to growth of electricity exports. Traditionally, electricity has been classified as a non-traded good that is produced and consumed within the country of origin.

It is only recently that electricity has been traded between countries (Srinivasan 2013). Bhutan is an interesting case to examine because it not only trades electricity with India, but electricity also represents Bhutan's major export. At this point, there are not enough annual observations of Bhutan's electricity exports to India available to perform a meaningful analysis, but this issue should be revisited in a few years when more time-series observations become available.

A second direction for future research would be to add one or more variables in addition to energy and trade in the augmented production function. The obvious additional variable to include would be tourism. Bhutan has placed a lot of emphasis on developing a high-value, low-volume sustainable tourism industry. Tourism and hydropower are the two main industries supporting Bhutan's economy (Singha 2013). Using an augmented production function that includes energy consumption and tourism on the right-hand side is a recent development in the literature (see Tang and Abosedra 2014). Studying this combination of variables in Bhutan's case, given that both industries figure so prominently in its economy, would be a useful extension of the literature on the energy–output nexus.

References

Ahmad, J. 2001. 'Causality Between Exports and Economic Growth: What do the Econometric Studies Tell Us?' *Pacific Economic Review*, 6(1): 147–67.

Akhmat, G. and K. Zaman. 2013. 'Nuclear Energy Consumption, Commercial Energy Consumption, and Economic Growth in South Asia: Bootstrap Ppanel Causality Test', *Renewable and Sustainable Energy Reviews*, 25: 552–9.

Apergis, N. and J.E. Payne. 2010a. 'Renewable Energy Consumption and Growth in Eurasia', *Energy Economics*, 32(6): 1392–7.

———. 2010b. 'Renewable Energy Consumption and Economic Growth. Evidence from a Panel of OECD Countries', *Energy Policy*, 38(1): 656–60.

———. 2011. 'The Renewable Energy Consumption–Growth Nexus in Central America', *Applied Energy*. 88(1): 343–7.

———. 2012. 'Renewable and Non-renewable Energy Consumption–Growth Nexus: Evidence from a Panel Error Correction Model', *Energy Economics*, 34(3): 733–8.

Asian Development Bank. 2013. *Key Indicators for Asia and the Pacific*. Manila.

Bahmani-Oskooee, M. and J. Alse. 1993. 'Export Growth and Economic Growth: An Application of Cointegration and Error-Correction Modelling', *Journal of Developing Areas*, 27: 535–42.

Bist, M. 2012. 'Bhutan–India Power Cooperation: Benefits beyond Bilateralism', *Strategic Analysis*, 36(5): 787–803.

Brooks, J. 2013. 'Avoiding the Limits to Growth: Gross National Happiness in Bhutan as a Model for Sustainable Development', *Sustainability*, 5(9): 3640–64.

Burns, G. W. 2011. 'Gross National Happiness: A Gift from Bhutan to the World', in R. Biswas-Diener (ed.), *Positive Psychology as Social Change*, pp. 73–87. Berlin: Springer Science + Business Media.

Chandra, R. 2002. 'Export Growth and Economic Growth: An Investigation of Causality in India', *Indian Economic Journal*, 49(3): 64–73.

———. 2003. 'Reinvestigating Export-led Growth in India Using a Multivariate Cointegration Framework', *Journal of Developing Areas*, 37: 73–86.

Dhakal, D., G. Pradhan, and K.P. Upadhyaya. 2009. 'Nepal and Bhutan: Economic Growth in Two Shangri-las', *International Journal of Social Economics*, 36(1/2): 124–37.

Dhawan, U. and B. Biswal. 1999. 'Re-examining the Export-led Growth Hypothesis: A Multivariate Cointegration Analysis for India', *Applied Economics*, 31(4): 525–30.

Dodaro, S. 1993. 'Exports and Growth: A Reconsideration of Causality', *Journal of Developing Areas*, 27(2): 227–44.

Dolado, J.J. and H. Lutkepohl. 1996. 'Making Wald Tests Work for the Cointegrated VAR System', *Econometric Reviews*, 15(4): 369–86.

Dorji, P.K. 2007. 'The Sustainable Management of Micro Hydropower Systems for Rural Electrification: The Case of Bhutan'. MSc Environmental Science thesis, Humboldt State University, California, US.

Giles, J.A. and C.L. Williams. 2000. 'Export-led Growth: A Survey of the Literature and Some Non-causality Results', Part 1, *Journal of International Trade and Economic Development*, 9(3): 261–337.

Gonzalo, J. 1994. 'Five Alternative Methods of Estimating Long-run Equilibrium Relationships', *Journal of Econometrics*, 60(1–2): 203–33.

Jia, J., P. Punys, and J. Ma. 2012. 'Hydropower', in W.Y. Chen, J. Seiner, T. Suzuki, and M. Lackner (eds), *Handbook of Climate Change Mitigation*, pp. 1357–401. Berlin: Springer Science + Business Media.

Jimenez, G.H. and A. Razmi. 2013. 'Can Asia Sustain an Export-led Growth Strategy in the Aftermath of the Global Crisis? Exploring a Neglected Aspect', *Journal of Asian Economics*, 29(December): 45–61.

Johansen, S. and K. Juselius. 1990. 'Maximum Likelihood Estimation and Inference on Cointegration, with Applications to the Demand for Money', *Oxford Bulletin of Economics and Statistics*, 52(2): 169–210.

Jung, S.W. and P.J. Marshall. 1985. 'Exports, Growth, and Causality in Developing Countries', *Journal of Development Economics*, 18(1): 1–12.

Karanfil, F. 2008. 'Energy Consumption and Economic Growth Revisited: Does the Size of the Unrecorded Economy Matter?' *Energy Policy,* 36(8): 3029–35.

Kumar, S. and G. Rauniyar. 2011. 'Is Electrification Welfare Improving? Non-Experimental Evidence from Rural Bhutan', MPRA Working Paper No. 31482.

Kravis, I.B. 1970. 'Trade as a Handmaiden of Growth: Similarities between the Nineteenth and Twentieth Centuries', *Economic Journal,* 80(320): 850–72.

Lean, H.H. and R. Smyth. 2010a. 'Multivariate Granger Causality between Electricity Generation, Exports, Prices, and GDP in Malaysia', *Energy,* 35(9): 3640–8.

———. 2010b. 'On the Dynamics of Aggregate Output, Electricity Consumption and Exports in Malaysia: Evidence from Multivariate Granger Causality Tests', *Applied Energy,* 87(6): 1963–71.

Lee, C.C. 2005. 'Energy Consumption and GDP in Developing Countries: A Cointegrated Panel Analysis', *Energy Economics,* 27(3): 415–27.

Liddle, B. 2013. 'The Importance of Energy Quality in Energy Intensive Manufacturing: Evidence from Panel Cointegration and Panel FMOLS', *Energy Economics,* 34(6): 1810–25.

Love, J. and R. Chandra. 2004a. 'Testing Export-led Growth in India, Pakistan, and Sri Lanka using a Multivariate Framework', *Manchester School,* 72(4): 483–96.

———. 2004b. 'Testing Export-led Growth in Bangladesh in a Multivariate VAR Framework', *Journal of Asian Economics,* 15(6): 1155–68.

———. 2005. 'Testing Export-led Growth in South Asia', *Journal of Economic Studies,* 32(2): 132–45.

Maddala, G.S. and I.M. Kim. 1998. *Unit Roots, Cointegration, and Structural Change.* Cambridge: Cambridge University Press.

Mehrara, M. 2007. 'Energy Consumption and Economic Growth: The Case of Oil Exporting Countries', *Energy Policy,* 35(5): 2939–45.

Mudakkar, S.R., K. Zaman, H. Shakir, M. Arif, I. Naseen, and L. Naz. 2013. 'Determinants of Energy Consumption Function in SAARC Countries: Balancing the Odds', *Renewable and Sustainable Energy Reviews,* 28(December): 566–74.

Narayan, P.K. and S. Popp. 2012. 'The Energy Consumption-real GDP Nexus Revisited: Empirical Evidence from 93 Countries', *Economic Modeling,* 29(2): 303–8.

Narayan, P.K. and R. Smyth. 2008. 'Energy Consumption and Real GDP in G7 Countries: New Evidence from Panel Cointegration with Structural Breaks', *Energy Economics,* 30(5): 2331–41.

———. 2009. 'Multivariate Granger Causality between Electricity Consumption, Exports and GDP: Evidence from a Panel of Middle Eastern Countries', *Energy Policy,* 37(1): 229–36.

Ozturk, I. 2010. 'A Literature Survey on the Energy–Growth Nexus', *Energy Policy*, 38(1): 340–9.

Payne, J.E. 2010. 'A Survey of the Electricity Consumption-growth Literature', *Applied Energy*, 87(3): 723–31.

Payne, J.E. and J.P. Taylor. 2010. 'Nuclear Energy Consumption and Economic Growth in the US: An Empirical Note', *Energy Sources, Part B: Economics, Planning, and Policy*, 5(3): 301–7.

Pradhan, R.P. 2010. 'Energy Consumption-growth Nexus in SSARC Countries Using Cointegration and Error-correction Model', *Modern Applied Science*, 4(1): 74–90.

Sadorsky, P. 2011. 'Trade and Energy Consumption in the Middle East', *Energy Economics*, 33(5): 739–49.

———. 2012. 'Energy Consumption, Output, and Trade in South America', *Energy Economics*, 34(2): 475–88.

Shneiderman, S. and M. Turin. 2012. 'Nepal and Bhutan in 2011: Cautious Optimism', *Asian Survey*, 52(1): 138–46.

Shahbaz, M., S. Khan, and M.I. Tahir. 2013. 'The Dynamic Links Between Energy Consumption, Economic Growth, Financial Development and Trade in China: Fresh Evidence from Multivariate Framework Analysis', *Energy Economics*, 40(1): 8–21.

Shahbaz, M., H.H. Lean, and A. Farooq. 2013. 'Natural Gas Consumption and Economic Growth in Pakistan', *Renewable & Sustainable Energy Reviews*, 18(February): 87–94.

Shahbaz, M., M. Zeshan, and T. Afza. 2012. 'Is Energy Consumption Effective to Spur Economic Growth in Pakistan? New Evidence from Bounds Test to Level Relationships and Granger Causality Tests', *Economic Modelling*, 29(6): 2310–19.

Shakeel, M., M.M. Iqbal, and M.T. Majeed. 2013. 'Energy Consumption, Trade and GDP: A Case Study of South Asian Countries', Working Paper. Islamabad: Quaid-i-Azam University, School of Economics.

Singh, B.K. 2013. 'South Asia Energy Security: Challenges and Opportunities', *Energy Policy*, 63(December): 458–68.

Singha, K. 2011. 'Power Sector and Economic Development in the Himalayan Kingdom of Bhutan: An Observation', *Asia Pacific Journal of Social Science*, 2(1): 29–43.

———. 2013. 'Tourism, Environment and Economic Growth in the Himalayan Kingdom of Bhutan', in S. Nautiyal et al. (eds), *Knowledge Systems of Societies for Adaptation and Mitigation of Impacts of Climate Change*, pp. 651–67. Berlin Heidelberg: Springer-Verlag.

Solow, R.M. 1956. 'A Contribution to the Theory of Economic Growth', *Quarterly Journal of Economics*, 70(1): 65–94.

Soytas, U. and R. Sari. 2006a. 'Energy Consumption and Income in G7 Countries', *Journal of Policy Modeling*, 28(7): 739–50.

———. 2006b. 'Can China Contribute More to the Fight Against Global Warming?' *Journal of Policy Modeling*, 28(8): 837–46.

———. 2007. 'The Relationship between Energy and Production: Evidence from the Turkish Manufacturing Industry', *Energy Economics*, 29(6): 1151–65.

Srinivasan, S. 2013. 'Electricity as a Traded Good', *Energy Policy*, 62(November): 1048–52.

Swan, T.W. 1956. 'Economic Growth and Capital Accumulation', *Economic Record*, 32(2): 334–61.

Tang, C.F. and S. Abosedra. 2014. 'The Impacts of Tourism, Energy Consumption, and Political Instability on Economic Growth in the MENA Countries', *Energy Policy*, 68(May): 458–64.

Toda, H.Y. and T. Yamamoto. 1995. 'Statistical Inference in Vector Autoregressions with Possibly Integrated Process', *Journal of Econometrics*, 66(1–2): 225–50.

Uddin, S.N., R. Taplin, and X. Yu. 2007. 'Energy, Environment and Development in Bhutan', *Renewable and Sustainable Energy Reviews*, 11(9): 2083–103.

Walcott, S.M. 2011. 'One of a Kind: Bhutan and the Modernity Challenge', *National Identities*, 13(3): 253–65.

Wolde–Rufael, Y. 2010. 'Bounds Test Approach to Cointegration and Causality between Nuclear Energy and Economic Growth in India', *Energy Policy*, 38(1): 52–8.

Wolde-Rufael, Y. and K. Menyah. 2010. 'Nuclear Energy Consumption and Economic Growth in Nine Developed Countries', *Energy Economics*, 32(3): 550–6.

World Bank. 2013. *World Development Indicators*. Washington, DC.

Zaman, K., M.M. Khan, and Z. Saleem. 2011. 'Bivariate Cointegration Between Energy Consumption and Development Factors: A Case Study of Pakistan', *International Journal of Green Energy*, 8(8): 820–33.

Zurick, D. 2006. 'Gross National Happiness and Environmental Status in Bhutan', *Geographical Review*, 96(4): 657–81.

10

REBEL A. COLE AND SARAH CARRINGTON

Banking in Bhutan

An Assessment of Financial Sector Development

In this chapter, we provide an overview of Bhutan's financial system and regulatory arrangements, enumerate key issues facing the financial sector, and propose improvements to the supervision of financial institutions in Bhutan. The chapter is based upon information collected during a set of consultative missions in 2014 sponsored by the Asian Development Bank (ADB), where the authors met the senior staff of government regulatory agencies and major financial institutions of Bhutan.

Our findings reveal that, as of 2015, Bhutan's financial system was well-capitalized and highly liquid, but suffered from deteriorating asset quality which adversely affected profitability. Key issues facing the financial sector include excessive concentration of credit risk in housing, personal loans, and loans to the hydropower sector; excessive credit growth; deteriorating asset quality; credit rationing; reliance on collateral rather than cash flow; judicial inefficiency in resolving delinquent loans; and an underdeveloped bond market.

The next section provides an overview of Bhutan and its economy, while the third section provides an overview of the financial system. The fourth section identifies key issues facing the financial sector, whereas the fifth section presents an overview of the regulatory framework. The sixth section discusses improvements to financial supervision. The final section concludes with a set of recommendations for addressing each of the key issues mentioned in the preceding paragraph.

Overview of Bhutan and Its Economy

Bhutan is a lower-middle-income country with a population of about 700,000 that is growing by only about 1 per cent per year. It is located in Asia, in the eastern Himalayan mountains on the northeast border of India and southern border of the People's Republic of China (PRC). Bhutan's land mass spans only about 40,000 square kilometres, more than 70 per cent of which is forestland. By law, this percentage must not fall below 60 per cent. Northern Bhutan is characterized by tall mountain ranges with peaks that exceed 7,000 metres. Central Bhutan is home to valleys with an elevation about 2,000 metres. Southern Bhutan is characterized by low foothills and rivers at an elevation of less than 1,000 metres.

Bhutan has abundant natural resources, including an expanding hydropower industry driven by fast-flowing rivers fed by snowmelt from its mountains. Forests also are a prominent resource, as are mineral deposits such as slate, gypsum, dolomite, copper, graphite, limestone, coal, and tungsten.

While different in terms of level of development and economic characteristics from its neighbours, Bhutan is nevertheless quite dependent on them. Bhutan's currency, the ngultrum, is pegged to the Indian rupee. The peg has engendered confidence in the ngultrum, which in turn has facilitated a trade and development partnership with India. India is Bhutan's largest trading partner, providing about 80 per cent of its imports and receiving about 90 per cent of its exports (RMA 2014a). Hence, stronger economic growth in India bodes well for economic growth in Bhutan. Because of the peg, India's monetary policy is effectively Bhutan's monetary policy, and inflation in Bhutan will closely track inflation in India.

Figure 10.1 shows recent gross domestic product (GDP) growth for Bhutan and neighbouring countries Bangladesh, India, and Nepal from 2005 to 2014. Except for 2007 and 2013, the growth rates of Bhutan and India moved in virtual lockstep during the review period. Bhutan has consistently grown faster than Nepal and (to a lesser extent) Bangladesh. Bhutan was forecast by the World Bank to grow at 7.9 per cent,

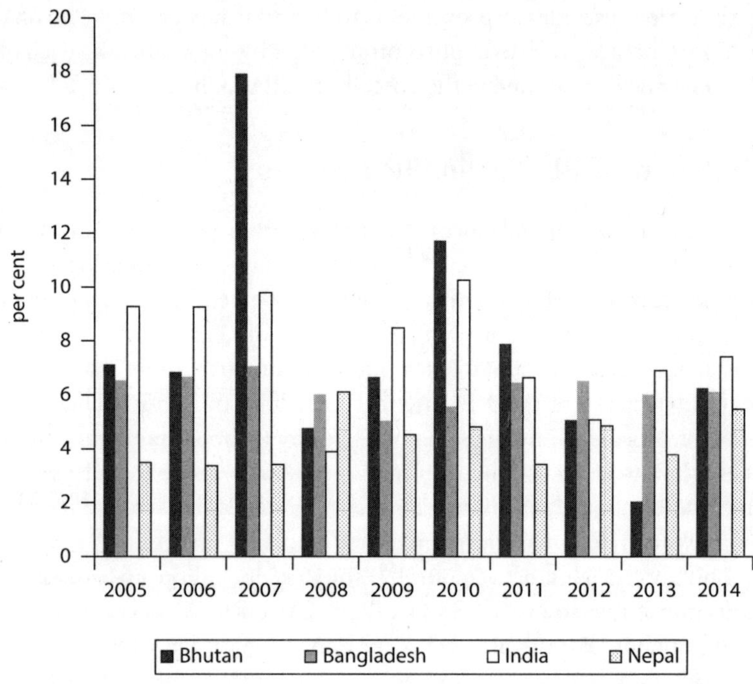

FIGURE **10.1** Growth in Real Gross Domestic Product: Bhutan versus Neighbouring Countries
Source: World Bank, *World Development Indicators* (n.d.).

8.4 per cent, and 7.0 per cent in 2015, 2016, and 2017, respectively, which are slightly faster growth rates than those forecast for India (World Bank 2015).

As shown in Table 10.1, the Government of Bhutan largely depends on development partner grants to fund government expenditures, about two-thirds of which come from India. During fiscal year (FY) 2014, grants accounted for just over one-third of inflows, enabling the government to keep its fiscal deficit at 4.4 per cent of GDP.[1] If development partners reduce funding in coming years, as they are expected to,

[1] The fiscal year (FY) of the government ends on 30 June. FY before a calendar year denotes the year in which the fiscal year ends; that is, FY2014 ends on 30 June 2014.

TABLE 10.1 Government of Bhutan—Revenues and Expenditures (% of GDP)

Account	FY2010	FY2011	FY2012	FY2013	FY2014
Revenues	50.6	38.9	38.4	31.5	31.8
Tax	15.8	16.0	17.3	15.8	14.7
Non-Tax	9.8	8.1	6.7	5.8	6.2
Other Receipts	6.9	0.3	(0.2)	0	0.1
Grants	18.2	14.5	14.7	9.8	10.7
Outlays	48.8	41.2	39.7	35.8	36.2
Current Expenditures	21.1	20.3	19.7	18.6	18.5
Capital Expenditures	27.7	20.8	20.0	17.2	17.7
Fiscal Balance	1.8	(2.3)	(1.2)	(4.4)	(4.4)
GDP (Nu million)	61,221	73,497	84,950	97,453	104,378

Notes: Figures in brackets = negative; FY = fiscal year; GDP = gross domestic product; Nu = ngultrum.
Source: RMA (2014a).

the Royal Government of Bhutan will have to find new revenues to fill this gap, which is why it has been looking to hydropower exports as the solution. Construction is under way or has been completed for a number of hydropower projects already, while others are being planned. Capital expenditures, much of which is allocated for these hydropower projects, account for about half of total public outlays. In keeping with a constitutional requirement, domestic revenues have been sufficient to fund current expenditures.

As shown in Table 10.2, Bhutan runs a considerable trade deficit, primarily with India. Bhutan's external debt as a share of GDP continues to rise, topping 100 per cent in FY 2014 and up from only 80 per cent in FY 2012. About two-thirds of this debt is owed to India, which is helping to fund Bhutan's investments in hydropower.

The ngultrum's peg to the Indian rupee has made it difficult for the monetary authorities of Bhutan to deal with imbalances that have arisen as a result of loose macroeconomic policies and currency flows

TABLE 10.2 Government of Bhutan's Balance of Payments

	FY2011	FY2012	FY2013	FY2014
Trade Balance	(20,835)	(19,881)	(22,038)	(22,427)
with India	(15,160)	(12,795)	(17,219)	(17,607)
Current Account Balance	(23,621)	(19,774)	(27,478)	(28,526)
(% GDP)	(32.6)	(23.3)	(28.2)	(27.3)
with India	(18,172)	(15,686)	(26,375)	(26,809)
(% GDP)	(25.1)	(18.5)	(27.1)	(25.7)
RGOB Loans	11,975	11,435	8,447	8,994
of which: India	7,377	9,878	4,791	6,348
Errors and Omissions	(1,823)	(9,517)	2,279	3,442
Overall Balance	798	(9,068)	9,212	6,069
(% GDP)	1.1	(10.7)	9.5	5.8
External Indicators				
Gross Official Reserves ($ million)	796.2	674.3	916.9	997.9
External Debt (% GDP)	79.5	87.4	98.4	101.3
CC debt (% GDP)	32.5	34.4	35.5	36.2
Rupee Debt (% GDP)	47.0	53.0	62.9	65.0
Debt–ServiceRatio	51.7	127.1	229.2	26.8

Notes: figures in brackets = negative; CC = credit card; FY = fiscal year; GDP = gross domestic product; RGOB: Royal Government of Bhutan.
Source: RMA (2014a).

associated with a series of hydroelectric power projects launched over the past decade. Most of the investments in these projects have required imported material and equipment from India, while much of the funding for these projects came from grants and loans from India. Once in the economy, the extra liquidity led to further volatility in the current account. As the financial sector expanded to accommodate the investment in hydropower, easy credit was extended in other economic sectors as well, especially the consumer and housing sectors. The procyclical nature of bank lending means that the added liquidity stimulated lending, while the borrowed funds were often used to import goods and services, primarily from India. This put pressure on the peg as the government was forced to convert reserves into rupees. The cumulative pressures on rupee reserves risk the peg's sustainability.

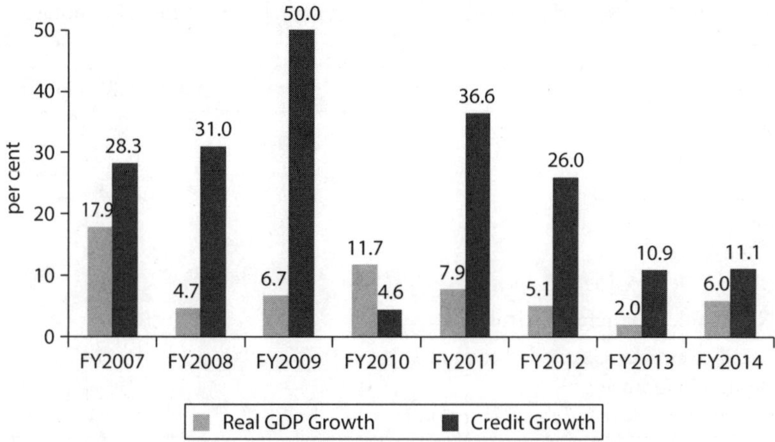

FIGURE **10.2** Growth in Credit and in Real Gross Domestic Product
Notes: FY = fiscal year; GDP = gross domestic product.
Source: RMA (2014a).

This enabled consumption to rise, further exacerbating the currency imbalances shown in Table 10.2, as most consumer goods have to be imported from abroad. New construction primarily uses concrete and steel, which must be imported from abroad, rather than wood, which Bhutan has in abundance. This has exacerbated currency imbalances, which led the Royal Monetary Authority of Bhutan (RMA) to sell 20 per cent of its US dollar reserves in late 2011 before imposing a ban in early 2012 on importing vehicles and construction material, and on loans for vehicles and housing.

As a consequence, credit growth slowed in FY 2012 and FY 2013, and real GDP growth slowed from 7.9 per cent in FY 2011 to 5.1 per cent in FY 2012 and only 2.0 per cent in FY 2013 (Figure 10.2). The ban on housing and vehicle loans was lifted in September 2014 after taxes were raised in a progressive manner on imported vehicles and fuel consumption. In 2013, a newly elected government implemented a stimulus plan that injected the equivalent of 4.0 per cent of GDP into the financial sector with the goal to jumpstart lending to favoured sectors.

Overview of Bhutan's Financial System

The financial sector of Bhutan consists of five commercial banks and three non-bank financial institutions (a pension fund and two insurance

TABLE 10.3 Assets of Banks and Non-bank Financial Institutions in Bhutan, FY2014

Item	Assets (Nu million)
Banks	
Bank of Bhutan	37,423
Bhutan National Bank	21,684
Druk PNB Bank Ltd.	6,064
T-Bank Ltd.	2,650
Bhutan Development Bank	12,718
Non-bank Financial Institutions	
Royal Insurance Corp of Bhutan Ltd.	10,376
Bhutan Insurance Ltd.	544
National Pension and Provident Fund	n.a.

Notes: FY = fiscal year; n.a. = not available; Nu = ngultrum.
Source: RMA (2014a).

companies). Table 10.3 shows each of these financial institutions along with their relative size as measured by total assets. Bank of Bhutan, the largest financial institution in Bhutan, was established as the country's first commercial bank in 1968 through a joint venture of the government and Chartered Bank. It served as the country's central bank until the RMA was established in 1983. The RMA is the primary regulator of financial institutions in addition to its responsibilities of managing the country's monetary policy. In 1972, Bank of Bhutan was reorganized and the State Bank of India (SBI) invested capital in the bank in exchange for a 40 per cent stake in the bank's equity and a share of management responsibilities. In 2002, full management responsibilities were returned to Bhutan and SBI's equity ownership was reduced to 20 per cent. The remaining 80 per cent is owned by the Government of Bhutan through state-owned Druk Holdings and Investments. As of 2014, Bank of Bhutan had 28 branches, 12 extension counters, and more than 60 automated teller machines (ATMs) across Bhutan.

The Royal Insurance Corporation of Bhutan Limited (RICBL) was established in 1975 as the country's sole insurance company, with 40 per cent of its equity owned by the government and 60 per cent owned by the public. RICBL was mandated to offer all types of insurance products and invest the proceeds for its customers. Because of the lack of traditional insurance company assets, RICBL primarily invests in loans, not unlike a commercial bank. As of 2014, RICBL had 26 branches in addition to its main office in Thimphu. In 2000, the government separated the Provident Fund, which was established for employees of the government and public sector companies, from RICBL and established it as the National Pension and Provident Fund (NPPF).

In 1988, the government established the Bhutan Development Finance Corporation Limited (BDFCL) with assistance from ADB to serve the needs of small and medium-sized enterprises in the private sector, especially those in the agriculture sector. BDFCL was subsidized by grants and concessional loans from international multilateral agencies such as ADB. Beginning in 2010, BDFCL began to function as a regular commercial bank and was renamed Bhutan Development Bank Limited. As of 2014, it had more than 30 branches, 5 field offices, and 5 ATMs across the country.

In 1996, the government established the Royal Securities Exchange of Bhutan Limited as the country's first and only stock exchange in an attempt to deepen the financial sector.

Bank of Bhutan held a banking monopoly in the country until the government converted Unit Trust of Bhutan (UTB) into Bhutan National Bank Limited (BNBL) in January 1997. UTB was established in 1980 as a subsidiary of RICBL. From 1992 to 1996, UTB operated as a financial institution promoting savings among the public and channelling funds to productive sectors of the economy. The bank's equity was sold to public investors in 2006, making it the first publicly traded bank in Bhutan. In 2013, the International Finance Corporation invested $29 million in BNBL in exchange for a 20 per cent ownership stake. Public shareholders own 40 per cent of the bank's equity. In 2004, BNBL became the first financial institution to offer ATM services to its customers. As of 2014, the bank operated 11 branches, 13 extension offices, and more than 30 ATMs across the country.

There is no formal system of microfinance in Bhutan, although some informal intermediaries provide limited financial services. Informal intermediaries can be broadly categorized as moneylenders and 'family and friends'.

Recent Major Developments in the Financial Sector

Over the past decade, asset growth in the financial sector has averaged almost 20 per cent per year, with assets rising from only Nu22.4 billion

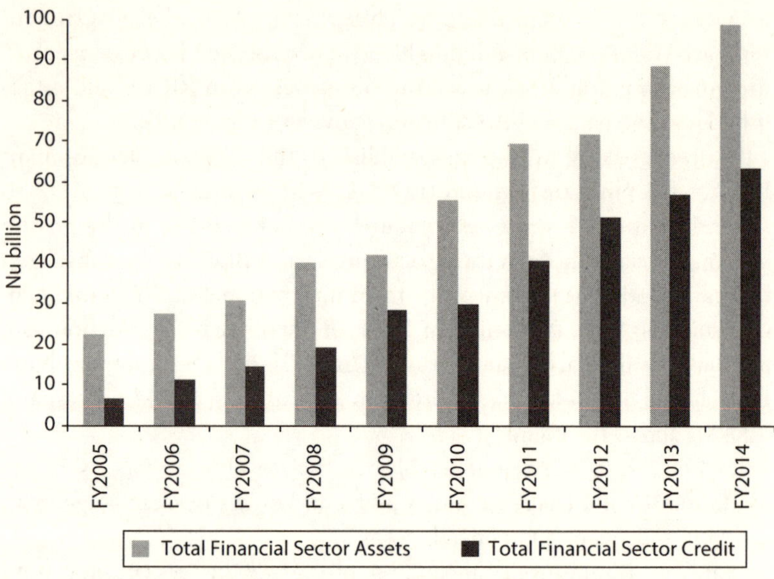

FIGURE 10.3 Financial Sector Assets and Credit in Bhutan
Notes: FY = fiscal year; Nu = ngultrum.
Source: RMA (2014a).

in FY 2005 to Nu98.8 billion in FY 2014 (Figure 10.3). In terms of share of GDP, this represented an increase from 58 per cent to 84 per cent. Much of this growth came directly or indirectly from funding investment in hydropower projects, many of which have come online in the recent years. Consequently, asset growth has largely been driven by loan growth. As of June 2014, the total assets of the financial sector were Nu98.8 billion ($1.62 billion), with banks accounting for about 90 per cent. Total credit was Nu63.2 billion ($1.03 billion). In spite of this growth, the ratio of domestic credit to GDP—a key measure of financial development—remains relatively low, comprising about 60 per cent in FY 2014.

Along with asset and loan growth, came an expanding current account deficit, as much of the goods and services purchased with credit were imported. Steel and concrete for the construction of hydropower plants are imported primarily from India, and much of the labour force working in Bhutan's construction sector is from India and sends remittances back home. Motor vehicles and material for housing construction have traditionally been almost entirely imported from abroad. In December 2011, the RMA was forced to sell $200 million of its international reserves, which are held primarily in US dollars, to meet payment obligations to India. In fact, Indian rupee reserves account for less than 5 per cent of Bhutan's total international reserves.

To combat the shortage of Indian rupees and maintain the currency peg, the RMA introduced a number of administrative measures to contain the demand for Indian rupees. The RMA suspended imports of motor vehicles and construction material in 2012–14 and directed the financial sector to stop making loans in these sectors. This led to a dramatic decline in credit growth that was also reflected in GDP growth.

Since 2009, the financial sector has seen three new banks—Druk PNB Bank Limited, T-Bank Limited, and Bhutan Development Bank Limited—join the ranks of its commercial banks. A new private life insurance company, Bhutan Insurance Limited, has also joined Royal Insurance Corporation of Bhutan Limited in the field of insurance.

Druk PNB Bank Limited was chartered in January 2010 by Punjab National Bank India and several domestic promoters. Punjab National Bank India owns 51 per cent of the new bank, the domestic backers own 19 per cent, and the remaining 30 per cent was sold to the public in an initial public offering. The bank is listed on the Royal Securities Exchange of Bhutan. As of 2014, Druk PNB Bank Limited had 6 branches and 14 ATMs across the country.

T-Bank Limited was chartered in March 2010 by three domestic promoters who each owns a 20 per cent share of the firm's equity. The remaining 40 per cent was sold to the public in an initial public offering in December 2010. The bank is listed on the Royal Securities Exchange of Bhutan. As of 2014, T-Bank Limited had four branches and 10 ATMs.

As mentioned earlier, Bhutan Development Bank Limited was created out of BDFCL.

Bhutan Insurance Limited (BIL) was chartered in July 2009 to deepen Bhutan's insurance sector. As of 2014, its promoters owned 32 per cent of the bank's shares and public investors owned the remaining 68 per cent. BIL is listed on the Royal Securities Exchange of Bhutan and its focus is on non-life insurance products, including personal, commercial, industrial, and liability insurance products. As of 2014, BIL operated 12 branches across the country.

NPPF manages retirement accounts in Bhutan. Before its creation in March 2000, public pensions were managed by RICBL and covered only government workers. NPPF also manages pensions for private sector workers. To facilitate the investment of pension assets, NPPF was licensed by the RMA in 2007 to offer limited financial services, focusing on housing and educational loans. NPPF is also one of the largest real estate developers in Bhutan.

The government allows non-bank financial institutions to engage in retail lending because of the lack of alternative assets with which to fund their liabilities. The supply of government debt is very limited. The Ministry of Finance only began to issue Treasury bills in 2009 as a tool of fiscal management and monetary policy.

The Royal Securities Exchange of Bhutan was established in 1993 with four listed firms. As of 2014, 22 firms traded on the exchange, with a market capitalization of about Nu20 billion, comprising about one-fifth of financial sector assets. The market capitalization doubled between 2010 and 2014, while shareholders numbered more than 62,000 in 2014, up about 50 per cent from 2010.

In the recent years, Bhutan has taken steps to deepen the financial sector by establishing credit and collateral registries. The Credit Information Bureau (CIB) was established within the RMA in 2009 to facilitate monitoring of borrowers to improve access to credit. The Central Registry for Secured Transactions for moveable properties was formally established in July 2014 within the RMA to encourage secured transactions and ease collateral requirements imposed by lenders, thereby improving access to credit. In 2013, the CIB was delinked from the RMA and became an independent institution. Since 2013, the CIB has been used by all of Bhutan's financial institutions and covers all loans except for informal microfinance, covering 97 per cent of individuals and 50 per cent of corporate borrowers. These new entities should help lenders to better identify sound credit so that they can expand lending, especially to small- and medium-sized enterprises.

A system for electronic fund transfers and clearing was put into place in June 2010 to allow the electronic transfer of salaries, dividends, and utility payments. In December 2011, the RMA began operation of the Bhutan Financial Switch, a national card switch system for ATMs and point-of-sale terminals. At the same time, the RMA made available to the public the National Electronic Funds Transfer System to facilitate

TABLE 10.4 Financial Stability Indicators

Item	FY2005	FY2006	FY2007	FY2008	FY2009	FY2010	FY2011	FY2012	FY2013	FY2014
Capital Adequacy—CAR (%)	21.6	22.9	19.9	18.6	17.25	17.09	14.4	19.1	17.9	18.9
Bank CAR					16.47	17.08	14.2	19.1	18.2	20.0
Non-bank CAR					23.64	17.22	16.0	17.9	15.8	14.0
Asset quality—NPL Ratio (%)	12	11.4	12.4	13.3	18.3	10.1	8.6	7.8	9.7	12.0
Bank NPL Ratio					18.4	9.5	7.6	8.2	9.5	12.1
Non-bank NPL Ratio					17.6	15.1	13.9	4.7	11.9	11.4
Earnings—Return on Assets (b.p.)	89	109	59	51	–11	104	56	123	106	11
Bank ROA					–5	92	38	95	70	–4
Non-bank ROA					241	219	238	501	423	67
Liquidity - SLR (%)	21.1	44.6	36.2	29.9	26.2	34.0	17.6	26.7	33.3	37.9
SLR (Bank, %)	21.6	47.5	38.4	32.0	27.9	35.5	18.0	27.5	34.4	38.8
SLR (Non-bank, %)	16.9	18.8	15.5	14.0	10.6	20.9	13.9	19.1	23.8	31.4
Total Financial Sector Assets (Nu billion)	22.4	27.4	30.7	33.51	41.8	55.3	69.6	71.8	88.44	98.81
Bank Assets			27.04	28.64	39.0	50.1	62.7	62.8	79.34	87.14
Non-bank Assets			3.66	4.87	2.9	5.2	6.4	7.2	9.11	11.66
Total Financial Sector Credit (Nu billion)	6.8	11.3	14.5	19.0	28.5	29.8	40.7	51.3	56.9	63.2
Bank Credit				15.6	20.4	27.2	35.1	45.4	50.3	55.3
Non-bank Credit				3.4	8.1	2.6	5.6	5.9	6.5	7.9

(Cont'd)

Table 10.4 (*Cont'd*)

Item	FY2005	FY2006	FY2007	FY2008	FY2009	FY2010	FY2011	FY2012	FY2013	FY2014
FI Capital			3.50	4.00	4.86	6.53	7.6	11.7	14.6	17.5
Bank Capital			2.34	2.67	4.14	5.71	6.4	10.3	12.9	15.0
Non-bank Capital			1.15	1.33	0.72	0.82	1.2	1.44	1.7	2.4
RWA			17.54	21.58	28.17	38.21	52.6	61.9	81.9	92.5
Bank RWA			13.8	16.84	25.14	33.43	45.1	53.8	71.1	75.1
Non-bank RWA			3.64	4.74	3.05	4.76	7.51	8.0	10.8	17.4
NPLs (Nu million)			1.79	2.54	3.99	3.02	3.5	4.0	5.5	7.6
Bank NPLs			0.80	1.48	3.76	2.57	2.68	3.73	4.76	6.7
Non-bank NPLs			0.99	1.06	1.42	0.399	0.78	0.3	0.770	0.900
Earnings—Net Profit	0.2	0.3	0.182	0.172	-0.048	0.574	0.39	0.89	0.937	0.11
Bank					-0.021	0.46	0.241	0.598	0.552	-0.03
Non-bank					0.069	0.114	0.152	0.361	0.385	0.078
NIM							1.46	1.86	1.8	1.7
Quick Assets							10.9	15.7	24.6	30.9
Bank Quick Assets							10.1	14.4	22.8	28.0
Non-bank Quick Assets							0.8	1.3	1.8	2.9
Quick Assets to Total Assets							15.7	21.9	27.8	31.3
Bank Quick Assets to Total Assets							16.1	22.9	28.7	32.1
Non-bank Quick Assets to Total Assets							12.5	18.1	19.8	24.9

FS Cash and Bank Balances							25.4	18.6	28.22	36
Bank Cash and Bank Balances							24.6	17.3	26.46	33.12
Non-bank Cash and Bank Balances							0.8	1.3	1.76	2.88
Asset Growth YoY	n.a.	22%	12%	9%	25%	32%	26%	3%	23%	11.7%
Bank Asset Growth				5.9%	36.2%	28.5%	25.1%	0.2%	26.3%	9.8%
Non-bank Asset Growth				33.1%	-41.3%	81.8%	23.1%	12.5%	26.5%	28.0%
Credit Growth YoY	n.a.	n.a.	28%	31%	50%	5%	37%	26%	11%	11%
Total Deposits (Nu billion)				22.1	27.6	36.4	50.7	47.6	59.3	66.7
Loans to Assets (%)		41.2	47.2	56.7	68.2	53.9	58.5	71.4	64.3	64.0
Loans to Deposits (%)				70.5	74.2	74.6	69.2	95.4	84.9	82.9
Stock market capitalization (Nu billion)	4.3	4.5	5.0	7.4	8.0	10.0	14.4	17.6	19.9	n.a.
Number of shareholders	15,110	16,045	11,782	12,851	17,654	40,774	48,005	48,077	62,687	n.a.

Notes: CAR = capital adequacy ratio; NPL = non-performing loan; Nu = ngultrum; SLR = statutory liquidity ratio ; ROA = Return on Assets; n.a. = not available ; YoY = Year-on-Year.

Sources: RMA (2014a, 2014c).

transfers among individuals and institutions. In 2014, the RMA, in consultation with the Ministry of Finance and the Ministry of Economic Affairs, formulated the Capital Market Master Plan for Bhutan, 2014–24, to reduce reliance upon commercial banks by providing alternative sources of financial intermediation, including microfinance intermediaries, both depository and non-depository. The RMA also established the Financial Stability Unit in 2014 to monitor and assess risks arising from deepening the financial system.

Review of the Health of the Financial Sector

Table 10.4 lists a series of International Monetary Fund (IMF) financial soundness indicators (FSIs) for Bhutan's financial system, including capital adequacy, asset quality, earnings, liquidity, and asset and loan growth rates. Figures 10.4, 10.5, 10.6, and 10.7, respectively, present data graphically for capital adequacy, asset quality, earnings, and liquidity.

In general, the financial system is well-capitalized. As shown in Figure 10.4, the capital adequacy ratio (CAR) for the industry has been well above the 12 per cent regulatory minimum each year since FY 2005. However, the CAR declined from more than 20 per cent in FY 2006 before the Indian rupee crisis to a low of 14.4 per cent in FY 2011 as

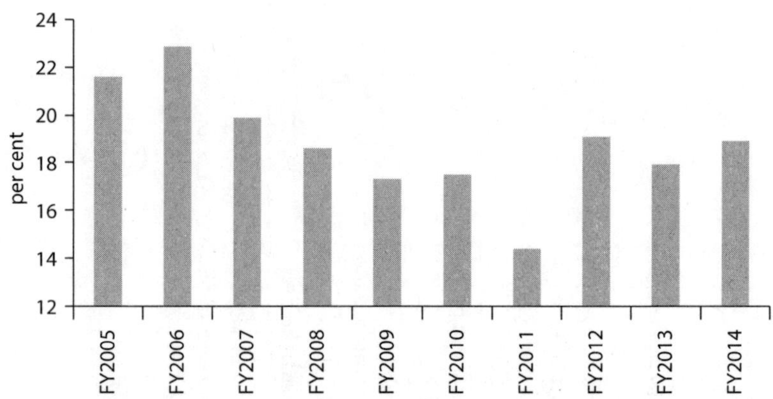

FIGURE **10.4** Financial Sector Capital Adequacy Ratio in Bhutan

Note: FY = fiscal year.

Source: RMA (2014a).

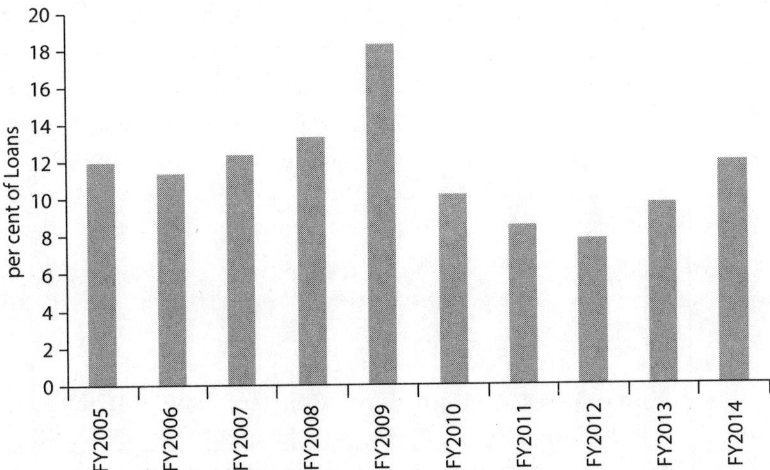

FIGURE **10.5** Financial Sector Asset Quality in Bhutan
Note: FY = fiscal year.
Source: RMA (2014a).

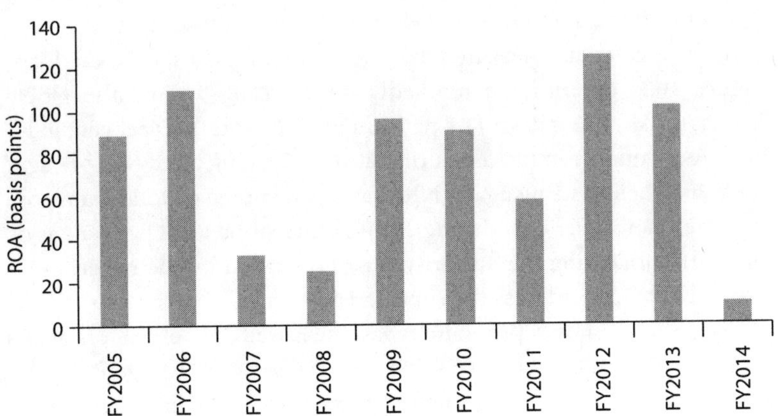

FIGURE **10.6** Financial Sector Profitability in Bhutan
Notes: ROA = return on assets; FY = fiscal year.
Source: RMA (2014a).

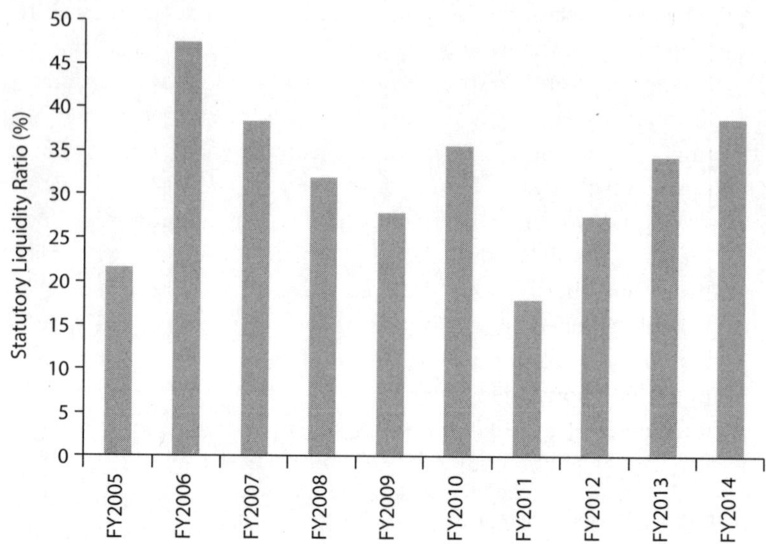

FIGURE **10.7** Financial Sector Liquidity in Bhutan
Note: FY = fiscal year.
Source: RMA (2014a).

non-performing loans (NPLs) surged. In FY 2012, the CAR recovered to 19.1 per cent and it stood at a healthy 18.9 per cent in FY 2014.

Asset quality as measured by the ratio of NPLs to total loans (Figure 10.5) deteriorated markedly during 2007–9 amid the global financial crisis, rising from 11.4 per cent in FY 2006 to 18.3 per cent in FY 2009. Asset quality improved during 2010–12, falling below 8.0 per cent in FY 2012 before rising again. NPLs as a percentage of total loans rose by more than 50 per cent during 2013–14 and stood at 12 per cent as of June 2014, following the austerity measures taken by the government during 2011–13 to address the rupee crisis.

Figure 10.6 shows profitability as measured by return on assets (ROA). In FY 2012 and FY 2013, the financial sector's average ROA was 123 basis points and 106 basis points, respectively. The financial sector's average ROA fell to only 11 basis points in FY 2014 due to a decline in net interest income combined with credit losses at a few banks. Since FY 2009, the profitability of non-bank financial institutions has far exceeded that of banks. This spread exceeded 200 basis points between FY 2009 and FY 2013, before falling to 67 basis points in FY 2014.

The financial sector remains highly liquid given the deposits of the government and state-owned enterprises. Grants received by the government are deposited with commercial banks. Faced with a flood of liquidity, banks were eager to fund new hydropower plants and help consumers finance new housing and consumer goods rather than sit on liquid assets that earned little or no interest. The RMA calculates a statutory liquidity ratio (SLR) for which there is a regulatory minimum of 20 per cent. As shown in Figure 10.7, the SLR exceeded 45 per cent in FY 2006 and then steadily declined to less than 20 per cent in FY 2011 as banks ramped up lending. As credit growth slowed between FY 2012 and FY 2014 following the RMA's imposition of restrictive rules on automobile and housing loans, the SLR rose each year to almost 40 per cent at the end of FY 2014. For non-bank financial institutions, however, liquidity has lagged as compared to banks. Until FY 2013, non-bank financial institutions were below the 20 per cent regulatory minimum in every year except for FY 2010. During FY 2013, non-bank liquidity soared to 31.4 per cent.

For comparison purposes, Table 10.5 presents a subset of core financial soundness indicators from the IMF for Bhutan and other South Asian countries including India, the Maldives, and Sri Lanka. (Indicators are not available for Bangladesh or Nepal.)

Bhutan's banking system is well-capitalized as compared with India's and Sri Lanka's, but trails that of the Maldives's. (However, the 41.1 per cent capital ratio for the Maldives is one of the highest in the world.) Bhutan's banks have lower asset quality than either India's or Sri Lanka's, but asset quality is higher in Bhutan than in the Maldives, which has an extremely high ratio of NPLs to total loans. As measured by ROA, Bhutan's banks are more profitable than India's, are on par with Sri Lanka's, and trail those in the Maldives. (Again, banks in the Maldives tend to be outliers with respect to FSIs.) Table 10.5 also shows that Bhutan's banks are highly liquid compared with banks in India and the Maldives, and are on par with those in Sri Lanka.

Table 10.6 presents common-size balance sheets for the financial sector and, separately, for banks and non-bank financial institutions. In addition to 14 per cent of total assets held as cash and bank balances, banks hold more than one-quarter of their assets as balances with the RMA, which is indicative of excess liquidity in the system. In contrast, non-bank financial institutions do not have any balances with the RMA,

TABLE 10.5 Core Financial Soundness Indicators for Bhutan, India, the Maldives, and Sri Lanka

Core FSIs for Deposit Takers	Bhutan	India	Maldives	Sri Lanka
Regulatory Capital to Risk-Weighted Assets	19.6	12.5	41.1	16.7
Regulatory Tier 1 Capital to Risk-Weighted Assets	15.3	9.6	31.3	14.1
Nonperforming Loans Net of Provisions to Capital	3.8	17.3	8.0	14.3
Nonperforming Loans to Total Gross Loans	6.8	4.3	17.6	4.2
Return on Assets	1.9	0.7	6.5	2.0
Liquid Assets to Total Assets (Liquid Asset Ratio)	27.1	8.5	19.3	32.2

Notes: 1. Financial soundness indicators as of 30 June 2015.
2. FSIs = financial soundness indicators.
Source: International Monetary Fund (2015).

but hold about 21 per cent of assets as cash and bank balances. Banks allocate 54 per cent of their assets to loans and advances, compared with 67 per cent for non-bank financial institutions. Non-bank financial institutions report 9 per cent of their assets as 'other assets', while banks report less than 1 per cent as such assets.

On the liability side, deposits account for 78 per cent of bank assets, while capital and reserves account for 17 per cent. Within deposits, demand deposits comprise about 55 per cent and time deposits about 45 per cent. Within demand deposits, about 40 per cent are current and 60 per cent are savings deposits. Total deposits are split evenly according to the type of customers: retail and corporate. Corporate customers include government- and state-owned enterprises, which account for more than half of corporate deposits. Banks and non-bank financial institutions account for about 40 per cent of corporate deposits. Private companies account for less than 10 per cent of corporate deposits. From FY 2013 to FY 2014, the deposit base of the banking system grew by 12.5 per cent, slightly outpacing growth in total assets. This was due in part to recent initiatives taken by the RMA to make deposits more accessible to a larger proportion of the population.

In contrast, non-bank financial institutions have no deposit liabilities, but as of the end of December 2014 their other current liabilities accounted for 48 per cent of total assets, borrowing for 13 per cent, and capital and reserves for the remaining 21 per cent.

TABLE 10.6 Bank and Non-bank Balance Sheets

Assets (Nu billion)	97.125	12.600	109.724
Account		% of Total Assets	
Assets	Bank	Non-bank	All
Cash and Bank Balances	10.7	21.0	11.9
Balances with Banks in India	1.2	0.3	1.1
Balances with Banks Abroad	2.3	0.0	2.0
Balances with RMA	26.0	0.0	23.1
RMA Bills	3.1	0	2.7
Government Bills and Bonds	0	0	0
Corporate Bonds	1.1	0	0.9
Others	0	0	0
Loans and Advances	53.9	67.1	55.4
Equity Investments	0.3	1.3	0.4
Fixed Assets	0.8	1.4	0.9
Other Assets	0.8	9.0	1.7
Total Assets	100.0	100.0	100.0
Liabilities and Equity			
Deposit Liabilities	77.6	0	68.7
Borrowings	1.1	12.7	2.4
Bonds and Debentures	2.6	0	0
Provisions	2.0	0.1	1.8
Current Other Liabilities	2.7	48.2	7.9
Paid-up Capital	6.3	5.4	6.2
Reserves	10.3	15.7	10.9
Total Liabilities	**100.0**	**100.0**	**100.0**

Notes: 1. Nu = ngultrum; RMA = Royal Monetary Authority of Bhutan.

2. Data as of 31 December 2014.

Source: RMA (2014c).

TABLE 10.7 Bank Loan and Deposit Rates

	FY2005	FY2006	FY2007	FY2008	FY2009	FY2010	FY2011	FY2012	FY2013	FY2014
Deposit Rates by Type of Deposit	Rate of interest (% per annum)									
Savings	4.5	4.5	4.5	4.5–5.0	4.5–5.0	4.5–5.0	4.5–5.0	4.5–5.5	5.0–5.5	5.0–6.0
Fixed deposits										
a) 3 months to less than 1 year	4.5	4.5	4.5	4.5–5.0	4.5–5.0	4.5–5.25	4.5–5.25	5.0–5.5	5.0–5.5	5.0–6.0
b) 1 year to less than 2 years	6.0	6.0	6.0	6.0–6.5	6.0–6.5	6.0–6.5	6.0–6.5	7.0–7.25	7.0–7.5	7.0–7.5
c) 2 years to less than 3 years	6.0–6.5	6.0–6.5	6.0–6.5	7.0	6.0–7.0	6.0–7.0	6.0–7.0	7.5–7.75	7.50–7.75	7.50–7.75
c) More than 3 years	7.0	7.0	7.0	7.0–7.5	7.0–8.0	7.0–8.0	7.0–8.0	8.0–9.0	8.0–8.75	8.0–10.0
Loan Rates by Purpose of Loan	Rate of interest (% per annum)									
1. General Trade	13.75	13.75	13.75	13.75	13.75	13.75	13.0–14.0	13.0–14.0	13.0–14.0	13.0–14.15
2. Export Finance	13.0–14.0	13.0–14.0	13.0–14.0	13.0–14.0	13.0–14.0	13.0–14.0	13.0–14.0	13.0–14.0	13.0–14.0	13.0–14.0
3. Manufacturing Industries	12.0–13.0	12.0–13.0	12.0–13.0	12.0–13.0	12.0–13.0	12.0–13.0	12.0–13.0	12.0–13.0	11.73–13.13	11.73–16.0

4. Service Industries	10.0–13.0	10.0–13.0	10.0–13.0	10.0–13.0	10.0–13.0	10.0–13.0	10.0–13.0	10.0–13.0	11.73–13.13	11.73–16.0
5. Transport	12.0–16.0	12.0–16.0	12.0–16.0	12.0–16.0	12.0–16.0	12.0–16.0	12.0–16.0	10.0–16.0	11.73–16.0	11.73–14.1
6. Agriculture and Livestock	13.0–15.0	13.0–15.0	13.0–15.0	13.0–15.0	10.0–15.0	10.0–15.0	10.0–15.0	10.0–13.0	11.73–13.0	11.73–13.0
7. Housing	10.0–13.0	10.0–13.0	10.0–13.0	10.0–13.0	10.0–13.0	9.75–13.0	9.75–13.0	10.0–13.0	12.73–14.63	12.73–16.0
8. Equity Finance	13.0	13.0	13.0	13.0	13.0	10.0–13.0	10.0–13.0	10.0–13.0	12.0–14.0	11.73–15.0
9. Personal Loans	15.0	15.0	15.0	15.0	15.0–16.0	15.0–16.0	15.0–16.0	15.0–16.0	15.0–16.0	13.0–16.0
10. Loans to Government Employees	12.0	12.0	12.0	12.0	12.0	12.0	12.0	10.0–13.0	12.0–13.13	12.73–14.0

Note: FY = fiscal year.

Source: RMA (2014a).

Table 10.7 presents bank loan and deposit rates between FY 2005 and FY 2012. Banks typically earn large interest spreads of as much as 1,000 basis points, with loan rates in the range of 10.0 per cent–16.0 per cent, compared with deposit rates of only 4.5 per cent–9.0 per cent. This explains the relatively high level of profitability at Bhutan's banks as shown in Table 10.5.

Loan rates are highest for personal loans, agriculture, and transportation, and lowest for housing and service industries. Deposit rates are highest for longer maturities, as would be expected.

Most lending is collateralized and is geographically concentrated in and around the urban areas of Thimphu and Paro.

Key Issues Facing the Financial Sector

Excessive Concentration of Risk

As shown in Figure 10.8, 25 per cent of the financial sector's credit is concentrated in housing. Moreover, this exposure is geographically concentrated as a consequence of excessive building in suburbs of the

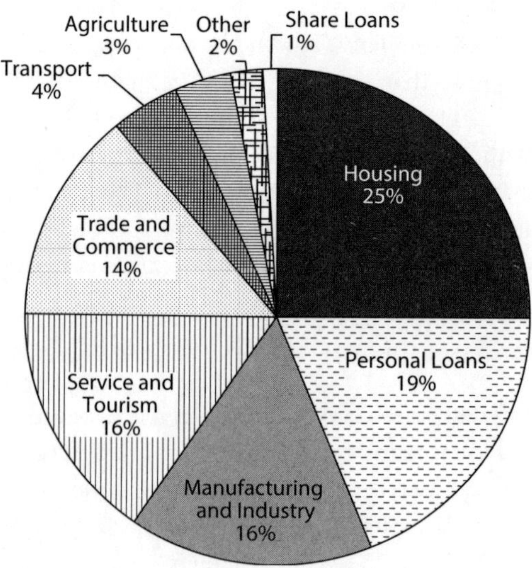

FIGURE 10.8 Sectoral Distribution of Credit in Bhutan, FY2014
Source: RMA (2014a).

major cities of Thimphu and Paro. The authors' discussions with bankers indicate that the majority of newly constructed apartments are for rentals and that rents will not cover the carrying costs associated with financing real estate in these suburbs. This appears to be a housing crisis in waiting.

Following housing, 19 per cent of the financial sector's credit is concentrated in personal loans. The financial sector is also highly exposed to the hydropower industry, which is reflected in the sector's 16 per cent concentration in manufacturing. Should cost overruns emerge on projects, as some government officials worry, this also could develop into a financial sector problem.

Other sectors appear starved for credit. Agriculture accounts for about 16 per cent of GDP but accounts for only about 3 per cent of credit. Transportation contributes about 9 per cent of GDP but comprises only 4 per cent of financial sector credit.

Excessive Credit Growth

Credit as a share of GDP rose from 11 per cent in FY 2002 to 49 per cent in FY 2011. Credit growth has averaged more than 20 per cent per year over the past decade, rising from Nu10 billion in FY 2005 to Nu63 billion in FY 2014. This growth has taken place across the board, although annual growth in personal credit averaged 55 per cent between FY 2008 and FY 2011. As mentioned, in response to a shortage of foreign exchange, the RMA imposed a ban on housing and vehicle loans in March 2012 that lasted through August 2014. This ban slowed growth in personal loans, construction loans, and total loans by one-half. How growth will rebound now that the ban has expired is an open question.

Deteriorating Asset Quality

Asset quality has deteriorated significantly in recent years, with the ratio of NPLs to total loans rising from 7.8 per cent in FY 2012 to 9.7 per cent in FY 2013 and 12.0 per cent in FY 2014. This reflects the slowdown in economic growth as well as the effects of government contracting practices. In Bhutan, the government pays its contractors when a government project is completed rather than during the life of the project. Consequently, contractors must self-finance with overdraft facilities

TABLE 10.8 Credit Growth by Industry (%)

Sector	FY2006	FY2007	FY2008	FY2009	FY2010	FY2011	FY2012	FY2013	FY2014
Agriculture	4	29	71	26	(25)	34	70	36	51
Service and Tourism	45	35	32	19	37	12	26	24	29
Manufacturing	40	33	22	43	8	39	10	30	(2)
Building and Construction	26	27	13	7	25	35	32	12	4
Trade and Commerce	20	24	54	25	13	22	(27)	58	29
Transport	2	14	24	30	52	76	21	(23)	(27)
Personal Loans	16	32	60	81	35	43	28	20	19
Loan against Shares	(28)	38	115	37	36	27	104	7	15
Government (Short-term loans)									
Credit Card							7	10	(7)
Others	(95)	42	109	58	8	163	323	(77)	19
Total	**6**	**28**	**31**	**28**	**23**	**37**	**26**	**11**	**11**

Notes: figures in brackets = negative; FY = fiscal year.

Source: RMA (2014a).

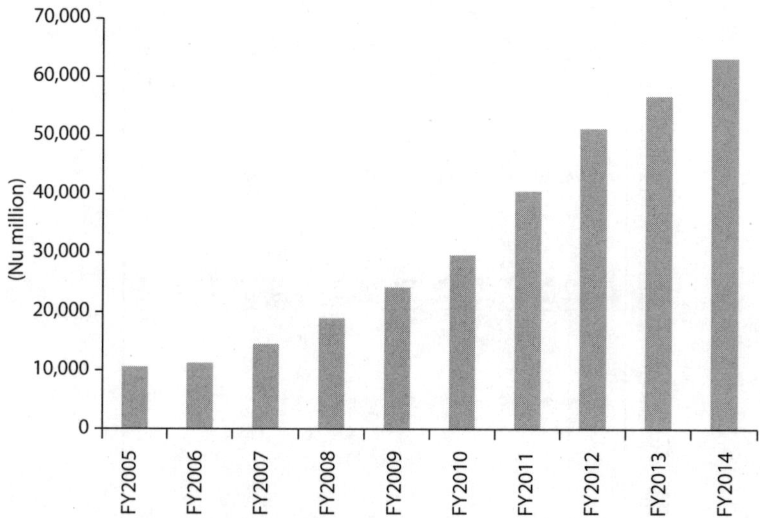

FIGURE **10.9** Total Credit Outstanding
Notes: Nu = ngultrum and FY = fiscal year.
Source: RMA (2014a).

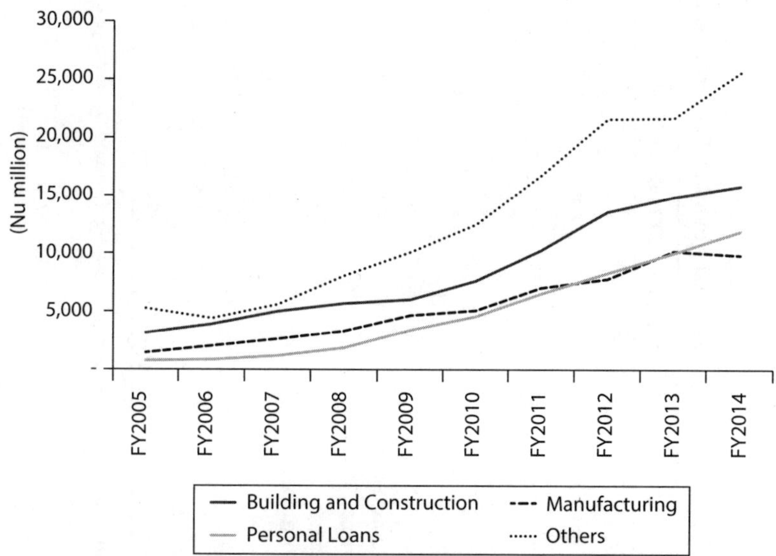

FIGURE **10.10** Outstanding Credit by Industry
Source: RMA (2014a).

Table 10.9 Non-performing Loans by Industry (% of total NPLs)

Sector	FY2006	FY2007	FY2008	FY2009	FY2010	FY2011	FY2012	FY2013	FY2014
Agriculture	6.9	7.0	7.7	4.6	3.6	3.8	4.1	3.8	4.7
Services and Tourism	7.2	8.6	11.5	17.4	14.1	7.4	11.3	8.3	11.1
Manufacturing	12.9	15.3	14.6	24.8	8.1	15.8	13.5	14.6	13.3
Housing	31.9	25.3	21.9	17.2	24.0	12.6	12.5	14.6	17.4
Trade and Commerce	7.3	7.7	7.3	8.6	7.2	18.1	10.8	31.5	29.0
Transport	3.6	4.6	3.9	3.4	5.9	8.7	11.2	12.5	8.3
Personal Loans	8.9	6.0	5.4	7.1	10.1	12.0	12.1	13.5	15.0
Loans against Shares	0.3	0.1	0.3	0.9	0.0	0.2	0.0	0.1	0.6
Government (short-term)	–	–	–	–	–	–	–	–	–
Credit-Card	–	–	–	–	–	0.1	0.1	0.1	0.1
Others	–	0.2	0.3	0.2	0.5	21.3	24.2	0.9	0.6
Overdraft and Working Capital	18.3	25.1	27.2	15.7	26.5	–	–	–	–
Total NPL	**1,291**	**1,792**	**2,526**	**4,438**	**3,019**	**3,460**	**4,014**	**5,756**	**7,601**

Notes: NPL = non-performing loan; Nu = ngultrum; FY = fiscal year.

Source: RMA (2014a)

during the contract period. When government agencies are short of funds, as has been the case in recent years, they do not pay the contractors, who then default on their overdrafts funded by banks.

Table 10.9 shows NPLs by industry. In FY 2014, trade and commerce accounted for the largest portion of NPLs at 29.0 per cent, followed by housing (17.4 per cent), personal loans (15.0 per cent), manufacturing and industry (13.3 per cent), and services and tourism (11.1 per cent). Just two years earlier, trade and commerce accounted for only 10.8 per cent of NPLs, with 'others' being the largest source of NPLs at 24.2 per cent. Housing comprised only 12.5 per cent of total NPLs in FY 2012. Prior to FY 2011, however, overdraft and working capital loans were not categorized by industry, therefore the figures for years before that period are not reliable.

Table 10.10 shows NPL ratios by industry. The NPL ratio in trade and commerce skyrocketed from 10 per cent in FY 2012 to 25 per cent in FY 2014, at the same time the loan volume more than doubled from Nu4.3 billion to Nu8.7 billion. This is strong evidence of poor underwriting by the banks as they competed for customers amid the freeze placed on housing and auto loans. The NPL ratio in transportation ballooned from 9 per cent in FY 2012 to 23 per cent in FY 2014 as loan volume fell from Nu4.9 billion to Nu2.7 billion. The NPL ratio in housing doubled from 4 per cent in FY 2012 to 8 per cent in FY 2014 as volume grew from Nu504 million to Nu1.3 billion. The NPL ratio for personal loans increased from 6 per cent in FY 2012 to 10 per cent in FY 2014 as volume grew from Nu484 million to Nu1.1 billion. The NPL ratio for service and tourism increased from 7 per cent in FY 2012 to 9 per cent in FY 2014, which was a much smaller increase than for overall NPLs, in spite of strong growth in volume from Nu455 million to Nu845 million. Similarly, the NPL ratio for manufacturing and industry increased more slowly than that for overall NPLs, rising from 7 per cent in FY 2012 to 10 per cent in FY 2014 as volume almost doubled from Nu542 million to Nu1.01 billion. Presumably, much of this volume is flowing to the hydropower sector, which is booming and being financed by investors in India and elsewhere.

Market Risks: Foreign Exchange and Interest Rates

As long as the currency peg is in place, currency devaluation is effectively eliminated as a policy instrument for Bhutan. The country's

Table 10.10 Non-performing Loans by Industry (% of total)

Sector	FY2006	FY2007	FY2008	FY2009	FY2010	FY2011	FY2012	FY2013	FY2014
Agriculture	37	41	37	31	22	20	15	14	15
Services and Tourism	6	8	11	24	10	5	7	6	9
Manufacturing	8	10	11	23	5	8	7	8	10
Housing	10	9	10	13	10	4	4	6	8
Trade and Commerce	5	6	5	9	5	11	10	27	25
Transport	6	9	8	10	8	7	9	19	23
Personal Loans	13	9	7	9	7	6	6	8	10
Loans against Shares	10	4	6	28	1	3	0	1	7
Government (short-term)									
Credit Card	–	–	–	–	–	33	71	78	54
Others	–	4	3	2	4	68	21	5	3
Total NPL Ratio	**11.4**	**12.4**	**13.4**	**18.3**	**10.1**	**8.5**	**7.8**	**10.1**	**12.0**

Note: FY = fiscal year.

Source: RMA (2014a).

monetary policy is in large part tied to that of its larger neighbour. The shortage of foreign currency reserves (especially Indian rupee) exacerbates this problem, as does the reliance upon foreign labour and material for construction. In addition, the opportunity cost of holding international reserves as US dollars rather than Indian rupees has been steep, as interest rates in India have been much higher than in the US. The RMA's small holdings of Indian rupee reserves have contributed to the instability of the ngultrum.

Banks make housing loans with 20-year maturities at fixed rates. Given the low-rate environment around the world since 2008, this suggests that considerable interest rate risk is being absorbed by the financial system. Should deposit rates rise, as appears likely given world conditions, banks holding these fixed-rate mortgages will see their margins squeezed.

Availability of Credit: Credit Rationing and Collateral

The World Bank collects information and creates country summary indicators on the availability of credit, ranking Bhutan 71 out of 189 countries (World Bank 2014b). However, a nationally representative World Bank survey of small and medium-sized enterprises found that the percentage of these firms naming access to finance as a constraint to growth more than doubled from 14 per cent to 30 per cent between 2001 and 2009. In the latter year, 22 per cent of firms identified access to credit as their biggest obstacle (World Bank 2014a).

Currently, banks do not price credit; instead, they are forced by the RMA to offer credit at fixed prices and then ration credit based upon loan-to-value ratios. This undoubtedly has restricted the availability of credit to some firms.

In addition, the World Bank survey indicates that only about one-half of commercial firms in Bhutan prepare certified financial statements. This forces banks to rely on collateral rather than cash flow when evaluating prospective borrowers. In combination with the difficulties banks face in seizing collateral, this also restricts the availability of credit. The establishment of the CIB in 2009 and a collateral registry for moveable collateral in 2013 have mitigated this problem to some degree. The government also established the Accounting and Auditing Standards Board of Bhutan with the goal of aligning local accounting standards with International Financial Reporting Standards by 2021. For financial institutions, listed companies, and large public sector companies, an initial 18 Bhutan Accounting Standards took effect in 2014 and likely will be complemented by International Auditing Standards. The government plans to develop a local accounting professional body with training accredited by one or more foreign institutes. Over time, these developments should increase the extent and quality of disclosures by financial institutions and other companies and address risks associated with reliance on foreign standards and practices.

Judicial Efficiency

The World Bank creates summary indicators on the judicial efficiency of countries around the world (World Bank 2014b) by collecting data on the time, cost, and outcomes of insolvency proceedings involving domestic legal entities. It then evaluates the adequacy and integrity of the existing legal framework applicable to liquidation and reorganization. Unfortunately, the information collected by the World Bank covers only proceedings against corporations, not individuals. The World Bank assigns Bhutan a 'no practice' rating because it was unable to find any cases involving judicial reorganization, liquidation, or debt enforcement and/or foreclosure.

The World Bank also collects data on the time, cost, and procedural complexity of resolving a commercial lawsuit. The World Bank reports that in Bhutan it requires 47 procedures spanning 225 days and costing 23 per cent of the value of a claim to enforce a commercial contract, placing Bhutan 74 out of 189 countries ranked (World Bank 2014b). For South Asia, the average is 43 procedures spanning 1,077 days and costing 30 per cent of the value of the claim, so Bhutan is much more efficient than its neighbours with regard to commercial lawsuits.

However, discussions with bankers tell a much different story than the World Bank indicators. Bankers report that banks cannot seize collateral in a timely manner when borrowers default because of an inefficient judicial system that favours the borrowers at the expense of creditors. When borrowers fail to appear at judicial proceedings, the court does not take action; instead, it postpones the case, stretching out the foreclosure process for years. This forces lenders to reduce the availability of credit to all but the most trustworthy borrowers, which undoubtedly has negative effects on economic growth. Bhutan needs judicial reform that will speed up this process. According to lenders, they cannot publish names of delinquent borrowers because borrowers will complain to the Human Rights Commission, which then imposes sanctions on the lender. Another problem mentioned by lenders is the ability of a delinquent borrower to game the credit registry by applying for new credit in the name of his wife, child, or other family member. There is no comprehensive list of related parties to protect lenders.

Another lender mentioned the Removable Property Act, which gives a lender the right to seize collateral underlying a delinquent loan, but requires the lender to get permission from the borrower. Needless to say, such permission is rarely granted. Lenders also complained about the scarcity of judges who understand corporate law. In addition, lenders have to register their complaint as a civil case, which gives the borrower 6 months to respond. Car loans have proved to be problematic as a borrower may sell his/her car to a third party without notifying the lender, after which the buyer might take the car out of the country and sells it to an unknown third party. This makes it virtually impossible for the lender to repossess the vehicle and mitigate the loss on his vehicle loan.

The Government of Bhutan has begun to implement a number of initiatives to improve its Ease of Doing Business indicators with the support of the World Bank under its Fiscal Sustainability and Investment Climate Project (World Bank 2014a). These include registration of collateral, the creation of a property registry, the creation of a business licensing policy, company act amendments, enterprise registration policy, reduced red tape for construction activities, and improved public–private partnership mechanisms. Progress over time in these areas should improve efficiency in the financial sector.

Underdeveloped Treasury Bond and Corporate Bond Markets

While the Government of Bhutan began issuing Treasury bonds in 2009, it still does not maintain an active Treasury Bond market. Instead, it prefers to borrow directly from state-controlled banks. This complicates monetary policy by constraining monetary operations. In conjunction with thinness in the corporate bond market, this practice creates a shortage of high-quality liquid assets. This is especially a problem for insurance companies and pension funds as there is insufficient availability of long-term instruments needed to finance their long-term liabilities. Consequently, insurance companies must fund their long-term liabilities with short-term loans, which puts them in direct competition with commercial banks.

Restrictions on Agriculture

One would expect a country with arable land and water to be self-sufficient in terms of food. However, many in the younger generation no longer want to follow their parents in working the land. Current laws restrict the ability of a farmer to import agricultural workers so domestic farms are unable to meet the agricultural needs of Bhutan. Instead, the country must import much of its food, exacerbating its balance of payments problems. From FY 2012 to FY 2013, Bhutan's food trade deficit increased by 24 per cent from Nu4.2 billion to Nu5.2 billion. During FY 2013, food imports totalled Nu6.3 billion.

Review of Regulatory Arrangements in Bhutan

History of Regulatory Arrangements in Bhutan

The RMA is the primary regulator in Bhutan, responsible for regulating and supervising banks, non-bank financial institutions, the stock market, and pension funds. The RMA was established in 1982 and began operations in 1983, taking over liability for notes and coins previously issued by the Ministry of Finance, as well as taking over liability for unissued notes and coins held by the government. From that point forward, the RMA oversaw the management of Bhutan's foreign exchange reserves. The RMA introduced the cash reserve ratio in 1984 for liquidity management and prudential purposes. With assistance from the IMF, the RMA published its first annual report in 1985. In 1988, the RMA began to serve as the banker to the government by holding the majority of government deposits and providing short-term loans as needed. In 1992, the National Assembly passed the Financial Institutions Act, which provided the RMA with the legal framework to license, regulate, supervise, and inspect financial institutions. In 1993, the RMA established the Royal Securities Exchange of Bhutan to facilitate development of Bhutan's capital market and enable public participation in private companies. The RMA's discount bills were introduced as a monetary policy tool in 1993. (These would later be replaced in 2009 by Royal Government of Bhutan Treasury bills.) In 1996, the RMA introduced reserve repurchases as a second debt instrument; though these were discontinued in 2002. In 1997, the Unit Trust of Bhutan was converted into Bhutan National Bank, a commercial bank. Also in 1997, cheque-clearing facilities were first established to enable commercial banks to settle claims against each other. In 1999, the Moveable and Immoveable Property Act was passed to provide the legal framework for seizing loan collateral. In 2010, the Royal Monetary Authority of Bhutan Act replaced the 1982 act that had established the RMA. The 2010 act converted the RMA into an autonomous central bank with greater powers. Since passage of the act, the RMA has performed all the functions that are typically performed by central banks in other countries.

Current Regulatory Arrangements in Bhutan

The Financial Institutions Act of Bhutan, 1992 has empowered the RMA to promulgate sound banking and financial policies. The implementation of appropriate prudential regulations and guidelines for financial institutions is within the scope of the RMA's regulatory functions. Supervision of financial institutions remains largely compliance-based rather than risk-based.[2]

The Prudential Regulations, 2002 set out micro-prudential regulations for an institutional framework for financial institutions; related party transactions; shares trading; and capital, liquidity, and provisioning requirements designed to preserve the health of individual financial institutions. Issues of licensing, corporate governance, disclosure requirements, and general structural regulations governing banking, insurance, securities businesses, and other financial services are covered in the Financial Services Act, 2011.

Basic prudential regulations established by the Prudential Regulations, 2002 include requirements on capital adequacy and liquidity as well as limits on credit concentration. Capital serves as reserves for financial

[2] The RMA has adopted Basel I, but not Basel II.

institutions and thus, it is necessary for financial institutions to have sufficient capital to withstand unforeseen losses. The RMA sets out a minimum paid-up capital requirement for the licensing of financial institutions. Also, financial institutions are required to maintain a minimum CAR and core CAR. CAR is computed as the ratio of an institution's capital fund to its risk-weighted assets plus risk-weighted off-balance sheet items. The core CAR is the ratio of the institution's total Tier 1 capital to its risk-weighted assets plus risk-weighted off-balance sheet items. Risk weights and definitions of capital are detailed in the Prudential Regulations, 2002.

Aside from maintaining adequate capital, financial institutions must keep a liquidity position to ensure that contractual obligations are met. Minimum requirements for liquidity management are set using the cash reserve ratio and SLR. The RMA also assesses the maturity mismatch for financial institutions using a series of benchmarks for the maximum percentage of the net cumulative mismatch positions as a percentage of total deposit liabilities.

The concentration of credit with a certain borrower, or group of borrowers, exposes financial institutions to risks, since any unfavourable development in the business or the sector to which the borrower belongs can severely affect the position of the financial institution. A credit ceiling limits concentrations to a maximum of 30 per cent of the total capital fund; an additional 10 per cent may be permitted for exposure to the infrastructure sector. There also is a limit on the amount of credit that can be extended to a financial institution's 10 largest borrowers that is equal to 30 per cent of total credit. The credit cap minimizes financial institution exposure and encourages portfolio diversification. More details for the provision are found in the Prudential Regulations, 2002.

A framework for more comprehensive macroprudential regulations was developed by the RMA and announced in 2014.[3] The following seven regulations are included in the framework: (i) leverage ratio; (ii) loan-to-value (LTV) and loan-to-income (LTI) ratios; (iii) debt-to-equity ratio; (iv) restrictions on the distribution of profit; (v) time-varying capital provisioning and margin requirement; (vi) countercyclical capital buffer (CCCB); and (vii) sectoral capital requirement (SCR). The

[3] For more details, see RMA (2014c).

time-varying capital provisioning and margin requirement—CCCB and SCR—are set to be implemented in 2016, while the rest have been effective since 2014.

The leverage ratio serves as a supplementary measure to the CAR. It is meant to ensure that the capital stock of the banking sector is adequate, even if the risk-weighting procedure is not robust. In instances when asset risks are factored and the risk measures are not robust, the CAR might not capture capital inadequacy as it might not be showing deterioration and the leverage ratio can be a supplementary measure since it treats all assets equally. This is to be maintained alongside the CAR to ensure that financial institutions do not keep a disproportionately high level of risky assets and to monitor asset quality. The leverage ratio for Bhutan is calculated as the ratio of Tier 1 capital to total assets. Total assets refer to the sum of on- and off-balance sheet exposures of financial institutions. Financial institutions have to maintain a leverage ratio of at least 3 per cent.

Financial institutions face the risk of default either from falling collateral values or the inadequate repayment capacity of a borrower. The LTV–LTI regulation is meant to mitigate these risks. The LTV ratio addresses the risk arising from falling collateral values as it limits the loan value to a certain percentage of its collateral base. The limit to how much can be extended depends on the type of property being acquired to account for the differential risks attached. Since the ratio is applicable to property loans, the regulation is an indirect method of addressing overexposure in the property sector. The LTI ratio is meant to mitigate default risks arising from repayment capacity and is computed as it compares total monthly obligations on all loans, including the loan being acquired and the total monthly income. The limits on the maximum allowable LTI ratio increase with income.

The regulation on the debt-to-equity ratio for project financing in Bhutan imposes a debt cap on it. It stipulates that debt finances no more than 75 per cent of the total project cost, or equivalently at least 25 per cent of the project cost should be equity financed from the borrower's own resources. Giving the investor a stake in the business not only lowers exposure risk for the financial institution, but encourages more prudent actions for the business owner, which reduces the likelihood of excessive risk-taking that can affect financial positions.

The restriction on the distribution of profits balances both the interests of small deposit holders and shareholders. Limiting profit distribution is for the interest of depositors as it allows financial institutions to build up capital that can protect it against unexpected losses. Profit distribution encourages the participation of investors in the public ownership of banks and to rationalize profit distribution; it is linked to the financial performance of the financial institutions. Moreover, introducing a standard regulation on dividend payments introduces discipline and uniformity to the practice of dividend distribution across the financial sector. For an institution to be qualified to distribute dividends, it must have a CAR of at least 10 per cent in the year it proposes to distribute dividends. The maximum dividend that can be paid out depends on the CAR in the previous two years and the NPL ratio. The two indicators are used together to gauge the performance of the financial institution in those years.

Regulations were introduced to address cyclicality in capital accumulation. Financial institutions hold capital provisions against NPLs to ensure capital adequacy when losses are incurred. Provisioning is generally procyclical such that during good times NPLs are low and thus provisioning requirements are also low. The reverse is true during bad times when high NPLs translate into higher provisioning requirements and the additional burden on capital requirements may result in a decline in credit that further exacerbates dwindling profits. Bhutan's regulation on time-varying capital provisioning helps address this as a capital buffer is built in good times to meet additional capital requirements in down times. Under the provision, institutions are required to keep a 60 per cent provisioning capital ratio. In good times, additional capital is accumulated, as NPL ratios may not be high. In down times, provisioning requirements might be higher but such capital may be drawn from the buffer accumulated during good times and not lead to lower credit.

The CCCB also requires institutions to build up capital in good times to safeguard intermediation activities by ensuring they have adequate capital on hand during the downward phase of the economic cycle. Buffers are built when the gap of the credit-to-GDP ratio is at least 500 basis points from its trend value. The amount of buffer at any given point depends on the size of the gap but shall not exceed 2.5 per cent of risk-weighted assets. When the gap is less than 500 basis points, no additional capital is built up or buffer maintained. When the gap is zero or less, the buffer is released so that capital requirements are still met and lending activities can continue.

A credit boom may be experienced in a specific sector and therefore an SCR may be applicable in this case with capital buffers built up against the risk-weighted assets of a particular sector. It is possible that a credit boom occurs in more than one sector at a time, yet the total size of the buffer shall not exceed 2.5 per cent of the total risk-weighted assets. An SCR may be imposed if a given sector accounts for 15 per cent or more of the economy's total outstanding credit, and the growth of credit to the sector exceeds the overall growth of credit in the economy by 500 basis points or more.

Apart from the macroprudential regulations, the RMA imposes policies on the setting of interest rates and foreign currency holdings. The standard for calculating the minimum rate for lending institutions is included in the Base Rate Operational Guidelines, which became effective in July 2013 (RMA 2013a). Each bank calculates its own base rate on a cost-plus basis, adding the cost to the financial institution for undertaking the lending activity. This includes the cost of deposits, which represents the basic cost of lending plus overhead costs adjusted downward for the interest earned, plus a profit margin, calculated as the ratio of net profit to net worth. The actual lending rate would be calculated as this base rate plus the borrower- or loan-specific costs. The base rate system promotes fair pricing and competition in financial markets and prevents interest rate undercutting. Lending rates are required to be above the floor set by the base rate to prevent excessive credit disbursal and overheating. Monetary policy transmission may also be enhanced through signalling. For example, the base rate declines with a fall in the deposit rate from an expansionary monetary policy stance. Increased transparency in rate setting can improve confidence in the financial system and encourage more participation.

Foreign currency regulation is governed by the Foreign Exchange Regulation, 2013, which repealed and replaced the Foreign Exchange Regulations, 1997 and the Import and Export of Currency Regulations, 2013 (RMA 2013b). Besides being more comprehensive, the current regulation designates the Indian rupee as a foreign currency. Moreover, the current regulation explicitly specifies that all payments and transfers within Bhutan are to be made in ngultrum.

The regulation controls the flow of foreign currency by requiring people importing or exporting foreign currency worth $10,000 or more to declare the value of the same at customs. The same threshold for import–export of the Indian rupee, to and from countries other than Nepal or India, is Rs 10,000. When leaving Bhutan, people other than residents or citizens of Bhutan can take back the balance amount of convertible currency left over from the amount that they brought into the country, while a resident of Bhutan can take out cheques drawn on a foreign currency account maintained with a bank in Bhutan, and banknotes, travellers' cheques, or other instruments denominated in foreign currencies. The regulation also sets forth the acceptable foreign-exchange activities of authorized banks and authorized money changers.

The Credit Rating Agency Regulations, 2014, which define a framework for the development of credit rating agencies in Bhutan, should help in the intermediation activities of financial institutions by providing more borrower information (RMA 2014b). To implement these regulations, the RMA must be aware of any systemic risk building in the economy. This requires macroeconomic monitoring, the regular reporting of risks to financial stability, and stress-testing of the financial sector to possible emergent risks. The Financial Stability Unit within the RMA has been set up to conduct these monitoring activities.

Stress Testing in Bhutan

In 2015, the RMA developed an Excel-based stress-testing template and began periodic stress-testing exercises consisting of single-factor sensitivity tests for credit risk and liquidity risk, with plans to expand to cover interest rate risk, foreign exchange risk, and interbank contagion risk. Two simulations had been conducted through May 2015.

Credit Risk

Three credit shocks were tested:

- X per cent of doubtful loans migrates into loss status;

- All NPLs increase by X percentage points; and
- X per cent of loans in specific economic sectors migrates into non-performing status.

For the first shock, required loan loss reserves are recalculated according to the RMA's provisioning requirements, which are 1 per cent for performing loans, 1.5 per cent for watch, 15 per cent for sub-standard, 50 per cent for doubtful, and 100 per cent for loss. Next, loan loss provisions are transferred from the bank's equity capital to its loan loss reserve account and then the bank's risk-weighted assets and CAR are recalculated to see if it remains above the RMA's regulatory minimum CAR of 10 per cent.

For the second and third shocks, the RMA does not distinguish between the categories of NPLs, so that it makes an undocumented assumption about required provisions, most likely 50 per cent. Otherwise, the calculations are similar to those for the first shock.

Liquidity

For liquidity risk, the RMA simulates two deposit-run shocks: (i) all banks face the same daily percentage rate of deposit withdrawals, and (ii) daily percentage withdrawals vary by the asset size of the bank. For both shocks, the run is assumed to last only five days. Assumed withdrawal rates are higher for demand deposits than time deposits.

Assets are classified into three categories: quick, liquid, and non-liquid. The proportion of each type of asset that can be liquidated each day also is assumed.

For each of the five days, the net cash flow is calculated as new inflows less new outflows. If this difference is positive, then the bank is deemed liquid; if not, the bank is deemed non-liquid and fails the test.

Proposed Improvements to Supervision of Financial Institutions

This section describes proposed measures for the improvement of financial sector stability in Bhutan. Some of these measures are being developed and supported under ADB's Strengthening Economic Management Program II and the technical assistance programmes underpinning it (ADB 2015).

Improvements to Regulation

The RMA should update its capital adequacy framework to account for operational and market risks consistent with the simple or standardized approaches of Basel II and III.

With regard to liquidity management, SLR does not account for asset–liability mismatches. High quality liquid assets are in short supply due to thinness of the corporate and government bond markets. Instead, banks rely on claims against other banks. Currently, the RMA does not collect information on maturity mismatches.

With regard to interest rate risk management, the RMA does not yet collect information on repricing of assets and liabilities, making it difficult if not impossible to assess the exposure of the financial system to interest rate risk.

The RMA should develop policies for crisis management to deal with the possibility of a bank failure. This may involve changes to the Bankruptcy Act, 1999 in order to deal with a financial institution (RMA 1999). The government needs to plan for implementation of a scheme for deposit insurance to support confidence of retail depositors in the event of a crisis of confidence.[4]

There are plans to expand the CIB to include information from microfinance intermediaries, and to develop credit scoring models; to expand the collateral registry to include moveable as well as immovable collateral; and to divest insurance companies of banking business (lending). However, these plans depend upon the deepening of the government bond market, stock exchange, and corporate bond market.

Geography remains a major impediment to access to finance. Both microfinance and technology tied to mobile phones and electronic funds transfer should be targeted to increase access to finance in outlying areas.

Improvements to Judicial Efficiency

The Parliament is encouraged to pass legislation to improve judicial efficiency. It should mandate that the credit bureau develop a comprehen-

[4] The RMA does not consider implementation of deposit insurance to be a pressing issue because of the relatively sound banking indicators and strong regulatory regime, and also because it does not wish to create implicit liabilities for the RMA.

sive list of related parties to protect lenders from delinquent borrowers who seek additional funds in the names of family members or related parties. The Parliament also should amend the Immovable Property Act, 1999 to eliminate the requirement of permission from a borrower to seize collateral.

Eliminating Price Fixing in the Credit Markets

The RMA should take steps to encourage bankers to price credit rather than just to ration credit. In other words, bankers should be allowed to charge borrowers different rates for the same credit product, so long as the rate differentials are based upon the riskiness of the borrower and the loan. This may require passage of some sort of 'safe harbor' regulation protecting bankers from lawsuits by borrowers claiming disparate treatment. Disparate treatment in the form of differential loan rates prices according to the riskiness of the borrower is a normal part of well-functioning credit markets. By allowing bankers to price credit, the RMA will be reducing the incentives of bankers to simply ration credit, thereby increasing the availability of credit to potential borrowers that currently are rationed out of the credit market.

Improving and Expanding Stress Testing

The first credit-risk stress test migrates a portion of doubtful loans into loss status. A logical extension of this test is a formal credit-migration stress test, where a portion of standard loans migrate to substandard, a portion of substandard migrate to doubtful, and a portion of doubtful migrate to loss. This type of test would obviate the need for the second credit-risk stress test, and also could be applied to the sectoral credit-risk stress test. This would allow the RMA to apply its actual provisioning requirements rather than an assumed generic NPL provisioning standard.

The RMA also could apply this sort of stress test to each bank's largest exposures. In this type of test, the assumed shock is a default by the bank's largest (or three to five largest) borrowers.

Given the concentration of exposures in Paro and Thimphu, the RMA should consider incorporating geographic shocks, such as a housing crisis in those metropolitan areas.

Regarding liquidity stress tests, the assumption of a five-day run is inconsistent with the new Basel III liquidity coverage ratio, which seeks to ensure that a bank has sufficient liquidity to meet a 20 calendar day liquidity stress scenario.

As a complement for its existing liquidity stress tests, the RMA should consider a stress test for a large-depositor run. Here, the assumed shock would be the immediate withdrawal of all deposits by the bank's largest (or three to five largest) depositors.

In the longer-run, the RMA should consider more sophisticated cash-flow-based liquidity stress tests that incorporate the actual maturities of the bank's assets and liabilities.

The RMA already plans to implement stress tests for interbank contagion and for market risks, such as foreign exchange risk and interest rate risk. It should proceed with these tests as soon as practicable. The RMA also should begin to develop multifactor sensitivity tests that combine shocks based upon an assumed historical event, such as an earthquake. In the longer run, the RMA should develop dynamic macro-linked stress tests where historical relationships between macroeconomic variables and bank financial drive scenario stress tests. It should be noted that capacity constraints such as the lack of available data have hamstrung the RMA in the development of more comprehensive and advanced stress tests.

Government Payment of Contractors

Requiring government contractors to self-finance work-in-progress transfers credit risk from the government to the private sector, obscuring the underlying sovereign risk. The government should transition away from this practice and begin paying contractors on a monthly or bi-monthly basis. In the interim, the RMA should estimate how much private sector credit is tied to this contracting practice to better quantify sovereign credit risk.

System of Early Warning Indicators

The RMA should formalize a set of early warning and financial soundness indicators. The IMF publishes a standardized set of core and encouraged financial soundness indicators, many of which the RMA provides to the IMF and already reports in its publications.[5] Table 10A.2 shows the IMF's FSIs for Bhutan. Currently, Bhutan reports to the IMF all 12 core FSIs for deposit takers and 8 of the 13 encouraged FSIs for deposit-takers. The FSIs not reported for Bhutan include:

- geographic distribution of loans;
- gross asset positions in financial derivatives;
- gross liability positions in financial derivatives;
- spread between reference lending and deposit rates; and
- spread between highest and lowest interbank rates.

While the lack of information on financial derivatives appears to derive from the absence of such financial instruments in Bhutan, the RMA should be able to provide information on the remaining three FSIs.

When one looks beyond deposit takers, some more troubling omissions appear where key indicators are not available. For example, there are no indicators for the performance of the corporate sector even though the RMA reports that 22 companies trade on the Royal Securities Exchange of Bhutan and the IMF's FSIs indicate that 32 per cent of loans from banks and non-bank financial institutions go to non-financial corporations. As shown in Table 10A.2, there are five encouraged FSIs for the nonfinancial corporate sector:

- non-financial corporate debt to equity;
- non-financial corporate return on equity;
- earnings to interest and principal expenses;
- net foreign exchange exposure to equity; and
- number of bankruptcy proceedings initiated.

The ratios of debt to equity and earnings to interest are important indicators of financial leverage in the non-financial corporate sector. Return on equity is an important indicator of profitability that really should be supplemented with return on assets in order to separate profitability from leverage. Net foreign exchange exposure to equity is an indicator of foreign exchange risk in the non-financial corporate sector. The number of bankruptcy proceedings is an indicator of the financial health of the non-financial corporate sector.

[5] For concepts and definitions, see http://fsi.imf.org/misc/FSI%20Concepts%20and%20Definitions.pdf (last accessed on 30 May 2016).

FSIs for real estate markets also are limited despite the housing sector constituting the largest exposure of Bhutan's financial institutions. Within this sector, the exposure is concentrated in Thimphu and Paro. There are four encouraged FSIs for real estate, two of which are reported by the RMA: the ratio of residential real estate loans to total loans and the ratio of commercial real estate loans to total loans. Missing are the FSIs for residential and commercial real estate prices.

The RMA should consider developing a set of indices of residential real estate prices and rents for Thimphu, Paro, and the rest of the country. Within Thimphu and Paro, there are at least two different submarkets: central and suburban. Discussions with bankers suggest that prices and rents move quite differently in these two sub-markets, with more appreciation in the central submarkets. Consequently, the RMA should attempt to build separate indices for these two sub-markets in each urban area.

Thinness of Treasury-Bond and Corporate-Bond Markets

In spite of issuing Treasury Bonds for the first time in 2009, the government continues to rely on bank financing. This complicates monetary policy and creates a shortage of high-quality assets for financial institutions. Increased and regular issuance of Treasury Bills and Bonds would make monetary policy more effective, provide a benchmark risk-free rate for the financial system, and provide high-quality liquid investments for financial institutions. Similarly, deepening of the corporate bond market also would provide more liquid investments for financial institutions, as well as broadening access to credit for large companies. Credit enhancement by financial institutions might help with new bond issues, but pose added risks to the financial institutions.

The small size of the Bhutan economy and limited investment opportunities in the country create major impediments to a deepening of the corporate bond or equity markets.

Restrictions on Agriculture

Current immigration laws that allow foreign labour in the construction industry but not in the agriculture sector are limiting the ability of Bhutan farmers to produce enough food for Bhutan's population and are contributing to balance of payments problems. Legislation is needed to address this problem by allowing some limited immigration and foreign employment in the agriculture sector.

★ ★ ★

In the recent years, Bhutan has made great strides in enhancing development management for sustainable and inclusive growth. Notable achievements are the deepening of the financial sector and strengthening of the regulatory environment. Yet, much remains to be done. Foremost on the list are legislative reforms to enhance judicial efficiency and the availability of credit, and regulatory reforms to further improve regulation of the financial sector. On the legislative front, reforms are needed to allow bankers to price and ration credit; facilitate payment of government contractors on a timely basis; enhance the ability of creditors to seize collateral; deepen the government bond market; and ease restrictions on agriculture. On the regulatory front, important outstanding tasks include a move from compliance-based to risk-based regulation; the development and implementation of expanded stress tests for financial institutions; and the expansion of early warning indicators to cover the real estate and non-financial corporate sectors.

Appendix

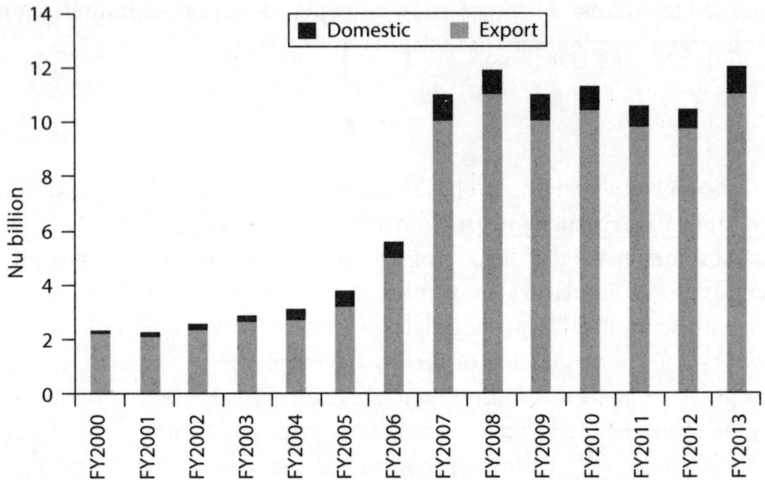

FIGURE 10A.1 Hydropower Sales
Notes: FY = fiscal year; Nu = ngultrum.
Source: RMA (2014a).

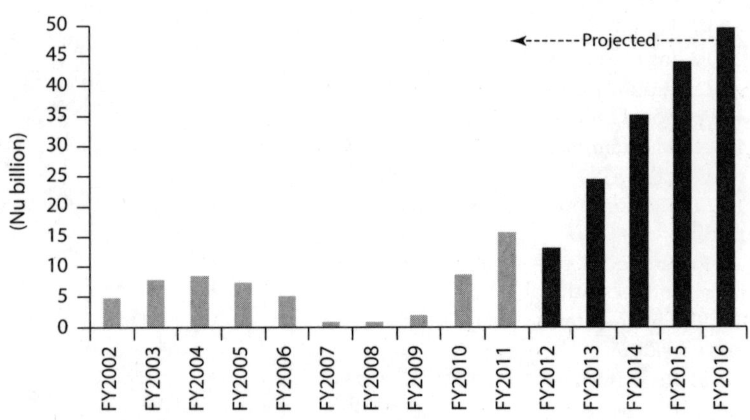

FIGURE 10A.2 Hydropower Expenditures
Notes: FY = fiscal year; Nu = ngultrum.
Source: RMA (2014a).

TABLE 10A.1 Gross Domestic Product Growth by Sector

Sector	FY 2006	FY 2007	FY 2008	FY 2009	FY 2010	FY 2011	FY 2012	FY 2013
I. PRIMARY SECTOR	0.5	0.2	0.1	0.4	0.1	0.3	0.3	0.4
1. Agriculture, livestock, and forestry	0.5	0.2	0.1	0.4	0.1	0.3	0.3	0.4
1.1 Crops	0.1	0.1	0.2	0.2	0.1	0.2	0.2	0.2
1.2 Livestock	0.1	0.2	0	0.1	0.1	0	0.1	0.1
1.3 Forestry and logging	0.3	(0.1)	(0.1)	0.1	(0.1)	0.1	0.1	0.1
II. SECONDARY SECTOR	3.3	15.3	2.8	1.6	5.5	1.8	2.9	1.5
2. Mining and quarrying*	0.3	0.4	0.4	(0.1)	0.2	0.4	0	0.7
3. Manufacturing	0.9	2.0	0.7	0.6	1.8	0.7	0.6	(0.7)
4. Electricity and water	3.6	12.2	3.0	(0.6)	1.2	(1.1)	(0.1)	1.8
5. Construction	(1.6)	(0.7)	(1.3)	1.7	2.4	1.8	2.4	(0.3)
III. TERTIARY SECTOR	3.1	2.5	1.8	4.7	6.1	5.7	1.9	0.1
6. Wholesale and retail trade	0.1	0.2	0	0.3	1.0	1.1	1.1	0.5
7. Hotels and restaurants	0.2	0.1	0.3	(0.1)	0	0.3	0.2	0.2
8. Transport, storage, and communication	0.7	0.7	0.5	0.8	1.0	1.2	0.5	0.3
9. Financing, insurance, and real estate	1.6	0.9	0.5	0.6	0.8	1.9	(0.7)	0.2
9.1 Finance	1.5	0.7	0.4	0.5	0.7	1.8	(0.7)	0.1
9.2 Real estate	0	0.2	0	0.1	0	0.1	0	0.1
9.3 Business services		0	0	0	0	0	0	0
10. Community, social and personal services	0.6	0.4	0.3	3.1	1.7	0.5	(0.8)	(0.6)
10.1 Public administration	(0.2)	0	0.2	1.4	1.0	0.3	(0.4)	(0.3)
10.2 Education and health	0.7	0.4	0.1	1.7	0.7	0.2	(0.4)	(0.3)
11. Private social, personal, and recreational	0.1	0	0	0	0	0	0	0
12. Plus indirect taxes less subsidies	(0.1)	0.1	0.2	0	1.6	0.8	1.6	(0.5)
Total (Real GDP Growth in %)	6.9	17.9	4.7	6.7	11.7	7.9	5.1	2.0

Notes: figures in bracket = negative; FY = fiscal year; GDP = gross domestic product.

Source: RMA (2014a).

TABLE 10A.2 Financial Soundness Indicators for Bhutan

	Core FSIs for Deposit Takers	Bhutan Core FSIs for Deposit Takers 2010–14				
		Q4 2010	Q4 2011	Q4 2012	Q4 2013	Q4 2014
I1	Regulatory Capital to Risk-Weighted Assets	15.9	17.9	18.2	20.4	19.6
I2	Regulatory Tier 1 Capital to Risk-Weighted Assets	13.9	14.7	15.5	17.9	15.3
I3	Non-performing Loans Net of Provisions to Capital	4.8	1.7	4.0	4.1	3.8
I4	Non-performing Loans to Total Gross Loans	5.2	3.9	5.4	7.0	6.8
I5	Sectoral Distribution of Total Loans: Residents	100.0	100.0	100.0	100.0	100.0
	Deposit-takers	1.8	1.1	0.6	0.4	0.2
	Central Bank	n.a.	n.a.	n.a.	n.a.	
	Other Financial Corporations	0.8	1.6	1.4	1.5	1.2
	General Government	n.a.	n.a.	n.a.	n.a.	n.a.
	Non-financial Corporations	1.2	–	2.0	28.2	28.8
	Other Domestic Sectors	96.2	97.3	95.9	69.8	69.8
	Nonresidents	n.a.	n.a.	n.a.	n.a.	n.a.
I6	Return on Assets	n.a.	n.a.	n.a.	n.a.	n.a.
I7	Return on Equity	n.a.	n.a.	n.a.	n.a.	n.a.
I8	Interest Margin to Gross Income	79.6	82.9	142.8	85.2	86.9
I9	Non-interest Expenses to Gross Income	32.8	27.1	46.3	32.7	34.3
I10	Liquid Assets to Total Assets (Liquid Asset Ratio)	33.1	18.6	27.6	19.6	27.1
I11	Liquid Assets to Short-term Liabilities	76.0	41.0	65.2	46.2	61.9
I12	Net Open Position in Foreign Exchange to Capital	n.a.	4.7	7.3	1.8	1.3

	Encouraged FSIs for Deposit Takers					
I13	Capital to Assets	9.3	14.6	17.0	17.5	16.6
I14	Large Exposures to Capital	128.1	100.7	74.1	72.9	70.4
I15	Geographic Distribution of Loans to Total Loans	n.a.	n.a.	n.a.	n.a.	n.a.
I16	Gross Asset Position in Financial Derivatives to Capital	n.a.	n.a.	n.a.	n.a.	n.a.
I17	Gross Liability Position in Financial Derivatives to Capital	n.a.	n.a.	n.a.	n.a.	n.a.
I18	Trading Income to Total Income	1.9	0.9	4.9	5.0	2.2
I19	Personnel Expenses to Non-interest Expenses	56.5	48.7	45.8	46.5	55.0
I20	Spread between Reference Lending and Deposit Rates	n.a.	n.a.	n.a.	n.a.	n.a.
I21	Spread between highest and lowest interbank rate	n.a.	n.a.	n.a.	n.a.	n.a.
I22	Customer Deposits to Total (Non-interbank) Loans	146.4	112.1	117.0	115.5	136.2
I23	Foreign-Currency-Denominated Loans to Total Loans	n.a.	0.9	0.9	0.8	0.7
I24	Foreign-Currency-Denominated Liabilities to Total Liabilities	n.a.	2.4	0.6	0.5	0.4
I25	Net Open Position in Equities to Capital	n.a.	n.a.	n.a.	n.a.	n.a.
	Other Financial Corporations	Q4 2010	Q4 2011	Q4 2012	Q4 2013	Q4 2014
I26	Assets to Total Financial System Assets	n.a.	8.6	8.8	11.1	11.5
I27	Assets to Gross Domestic Product (GDP)	n.a.	10.0	11.4	13.2	11.7
	Non-Financial Corporations Sector					
I28	Total Debt to Equity	n.a.	n.a.	n.a.	n.a.	n.a.
I29	Return on Equity	n.a.	n.a.	n.a.	n.a.	n.a.
I30	Earnings to Interest and Principal Expenses	n.a.	n.a.	n.a.	n.a.	n.a.
I31	Net Foreign Exchange Exposure to Equity	n.a.	n.a.	n.a.	n.a.	n.a.
I32	Number of Bankruptcy Proceedings Initiated	n.a.	n.a.	n.a.	n.a.	n.a.

(Cont'd)

TABLE 10A.2 (*Cont'd*)

	Core FSIs for Deposit Takers	Bhutan Core FSIs for Deposit Takers 2010–14				
		Q4 2010	Q4 2011	Q4 2012	Q4 2013	Q4 2014
	Households	n.a.	n.a.	n.a.	n.a.	n.a.
I33	Household Debt to GDP	n.a.	n.a.	n.a.	n.a.	n.a.
I34	Household Debt Service and Principal Payments to Income	n.a.	n.a.	n.a.	n.a.	n.a.
	Market Liquidity					
I35	Average Bid-Ask Spread in the Securities Market	n.a.	n.a.	n.a.	n.a.	n.a.
I36	Average Daily Turnover Ratio in the Securities Market	n.a.	n.a.	n.a.	n.a.	n.a.
	Real Estate Markets					
I37	Residential Real Estate Prices	n.a.	n.a.	n.a.	n.a.	n.a.
I38	Commercial Real Estate Prices	n.a.	n.a.	n.a.	n.a.	n.a.
I39	Residential Real Estate Loans to Total Loans	23.7	24.9	26.4	26.3	24.9
I40	Commercial Real Estate Loans to Total Loans	n.a.	n.a.	0.2	0.4	0.6

Notes: n.a. = data not available; Q = Quarter; FSIs = financial soundness indicators.

Source: International Monetary Fund (2015).

References

Asian Development Bank (ADB). 2015. *Report and Recommendation of the President to the Board of Directors: Proposed Policy-Based Loan, Grant, and Technical Assistance Grant to the Kingdom of Bhutan: Strengthening Economic Management Program II*. Manila.

International Monetary Fund. 2015. *Financial Soundness Indicators—Concepts and Definitions*, available at http://fsi.imf.org/misc/FSI%20Concepts%20and%20Definitions.pdf (last accessed on 30 May 2016).

Royal Monetary Authority of Bhutan (RMA). 1999. *Bankruptcy Act of the Kingdom of Bhutan*, Thimphu, available at http://www.rma.org.bt/laws_bylawstp2.jsp (last accessed on 30 May 2016).

______. 2013a. *Base Rate Operational Guidelines*, Thimphu, available at http://www.rma.org.bt/laws_bylawstp2.jsp (last accessed on 30 May 2016).

______.2013b. *Foreign Exchange Regulations*, Thimphu, available at http://www.rma.org.bt/laws_bylawstp2.jsp (last accessed on 30 May 2016).

______. 2014a. *Annual Report* (and various years), available at http://www.rma.org.bt/annualreporttp.jsp (last accessed on 30 May 2016).

______2014b. *Credit Rating Agency Regulations*. Thimphu. http://www.rma.org.bt/laws_bylawstp2.jsp (last accessed on 30 May 2016).

______. 2014c. *Macro-Prudential Rules and Regulations*, Thimphu, available at http://www.rma.org.bt/laws_bylawstp2.jsp (last accessed on 30 May 2016).

World Bank. 2014a. *Bhutan–Fiscal Sustainability and Investment Climate Project*, available at http://documents.worldbank.org/curated/en/2014/08/20160277/bhutan-fiscal-sustainability-investment-climate-project (last accessed on 30 May 2016).

______. 2014b. *Doing Business 2015: Going Beyond Efficiency: Bhutan*, available at http://documents.worldbank.org/curated/en/2014/10/20342688/doing-business-2015-going-beyond-efficiency-bhutan (last accessed on 30 May 2016).

______. 2015. Global Economic Prospects, available at https://www.worldbank.org/content/dam/Worldbank/GEP/.../GEP15a_web_full.pdf (last accessed on 30 May 2016).

______. n.d. World Development Indicators. Available at http://data.worldbank.org/data-catalog/world-development-indicators (last accessed on 30 May 2016).

Index

About the Editors and Contributors

Editors

Sabyasachi Mitra is the Deputy Representative at the Asian Development Bank (ADB), European Representative Office. He was formerly the Principal Economist in South Asia Department (SARD), overseeing economic sector research and leading in conceptualizing and implementing ADB's new initiatives on economic and industrial corridors in South Asia. He also initiated and led the work to develop a macroeconomic monitoring and surveillance framework in Bhutan. He has an MPhil in Economics from Jawaharlal Nehru University, New Delhi, India.

Hoe Yun Jeong is a Senior Economist in the Regional Cooperation and Operations Coordination Division of SARD at ADB. Leading the economic sector unit of the division, he has worked on a number of economic corridor development and regional economic integration studies in Asia. Until recently, he was the country team leader for Bhutan. He has a Master's in Business Administration from the University of Washington, United States.

Contributors

Elbe Aguba is a consultant in SARD. She has been involved in a number of research studies on governance, fiscal policy, and economic growth in Asia. She has a Master's in Economics from the University of the Philippines, Philippines.

Anthony Baluga is a consultant in SARD. Prior to joining SARD, he worked as a senior analyst for ADB's Office of Regional Economic Integration, undertaking econometric modelling in the area of financial market integration. He has a Master's in Economics from the Australian National University, Australia.

Taeho Bark is a Professor at Seoul National University in the Republic of Korea. He is a former Minister of Trade for the Government of the Republic of Korea. His areas of expertise are trade policy and negotiation, regional economic integration, and foreign direct investment. He has a PhD in Economics from the University of Wisconsin-Madison, United States.

Sarah Carrington is currently a Lecturer at the Faculdad de Ciencias Economicas y Administrativas, Universidad de Las Américas in Quito, Ecuador. Her areas of research include Bhutan's economic transformation, Bhutan's potential output, and the vulnerability and resilience of small state economies such as Bhutan, the Maldives, and Nepal. She has a PhD in Economics from Monash University, Australia.

Inkyo Cheong is Vice-President of Inha University in the Republic of Korea and a Professor in the Department of Economics at the same university. His research topics include the Republic of Korea's free trade agreement policy, computable general equilibrium models, Republic of Korea–Association of Southeast Asian Nation (ASEAN) trade issues, economic cooperation in the Northeast Asia and East Asia, and tariff and trade policies in ASEAN and Asia-Pacific Economic Cooperation economies. He has a PhD in Economics from Michigan State University, United States.

Hwee Kwan Chow is Professor at Singapore Management University, Singapore. Formerly, she was Lead Economist at the Monetary Authority of Singapore and Vice-President at Overseas Union Bank, Singapore. Her research interests include monetary economics, international finance, and economic forecasting. She has a PhD in Statistics from the London School of Economics and Political Science, UK.

Rebel A. Cole is Kaye Family Endowed Professor of Finance, Florida Atlantic University, Florida, United States. He also is the founder and Chief Executive Officer of Krähenbühl Global Consulting LLC. He has published peer-reviewed articles in top academic journals such as the *Journal of Finance, Journal of Financial Economics*, and *Journal of Financial and Quantitative Analysis*. He has PhD in Business Administration from the University of North Carolina at Chapel Hill, United States.

Joshua E. Greene is a consultant at various international financial institutions, including ADB, and has been a visiting Professor at Singapore Management University, Singapore. His research and writing include a textbook on public finance and papers on fiscal policy, macroeconomics, African debt, and private investment in developing countries. He holds a PhD in Economics and a law degree from the University of Michigan, United States.

Patrick Guillaumont is Professor Emeritus at the University d'Auvergne in France. Prior to this, he was the founder, director, and president of the Centre d'Études et de Recherches sur le Développement International. He has published many books and nearly 200 papers, mainly on development, in a wide set of economic journals. He has a PhD in Economics from Institut d' Études Politiques, Paris, France.

Hooi Hooi Lean is a Professor in the School of Social Sciences (economics programme), Universiti Sains in Malaysia. Her research interests include financial economics, energy economics, and Asia-Pacific and Chinese economies. Lean was the winner of the 2015 National Academic Award from the Ministry of Higher Education, Malaysia. She has published more than 100 scholarly articles in many reputed international journals. She has a PhD in Economics from the National University of Singapore.

Russell Smyth is a Professor in the Department of Economics at the Monash Business School in Australia. He is an Associate Editor of *Energy Economics* and *Economic Modelling* and sits on the editorial boards of several journals, including the *Journal of Empirical Legal Studies*. His research interests include Asian economies, development economics, empirical legal studies, energy economics, and law and economics. He has a PhD in Economics from the University of London, UK.

Karma Ura is President of Center for Bhutan Studies and Gross National Happiness Research (CBS and GNHR). He worked for the Royal Government of Bhutan's Ministry of Planning for 12 years before becoming the Director of the CBS from its founding in 1999 until 2008 when he became its President. He was a member of the Drafting Committee of Bhutan's first Constitution, which was enacted in July 2008. He has an MPhil in Economics from the University of Edinburgh, UK.